Mass Communication in Canada

Compiled and with an introduction by Herbert Pimlott

Third Custom Edition

With material taken from:

Media of Mass Communication in Canada, Fifth Canadian Edition
by John Vivian and Peter J. Maurin

The Contemporary Reader, Eighth Edition
by Gary Goshgarian

*Strategic Writing: Multimedia Writing for Public Relations, Advertising,
Sales and Marketing, and Business Communication*
by Charles Marsh, David W. Guth, and Bonnie Poovey Short

Pop Can: Popular Culture in Canada
edited by Lynne Van Luven and Priscilla L. Walton

Custom Publishing

New York   Boston   San Francisco
London   Toronto   Sydney   Tokyo   Singapore   Madrid
Mexico City   Munich   Paris   Cape Town   Hong Kong   Montreal

Cover Art: Courtesy of brandXpictures

Taken from:

The Media of Mass Communication, Fourth Canadian Edition
by John Vivian and Peter J. Maurin
Copyright © 2006, 2003, 2000, 1997 by Pearson Education
Canada, Inc.
Published by Allyn & Bacon
Toronto, Ontario
Canada

The Contemporary Reader, Eighth Edition
by Gary Goshgarian
Copyright © 2005 by Gary Goshgarian
Published by Longman
A Pearson Education Company
New York, New York 10036

Strategic Writing: Multimedia Writing for Public Relations, Advertising, Sales and Marketing, and Business Communication
by Charles Marsh, David W. Guth, and Bonnie Poovey Short
Copyright © 2005 by Pearson Education, Inc.
Published by Allyn & Bacon
Boston, Massachusetts 02116

Pop Can: Popular Culture in Canada
edited by Lynn Van Luven and Priscilla L. Walton
Copyright © 1999 by Prentice Hall Canada, Inc.

Copyright © 2008, 2007, 2005 by Pearson Custom Publishing
All rights reserved.

Grateful acknowledgement is made to the following sources for permission to reprint material copyrighted or controlled by them:

"Media and Ideology," by Jamie Swift and Jacqueline Davies, reprinted from *Getting Started on Social Analysis in Canada*, Fourth Edition (2003), Between the Lines.

"Blind Spots on Labour, Corporate Power and Social Inequality," by Robert A. Hackett and Richard Gruneau with Donald Gutstein, Timothy A. Gibson, and NewsWatch Canada, reprinted from *The Missing News: Filters and Blind Spots in Canada's Press* (2000), by permission of the Canadian Centre for Policy Alternatives/Garamond Press.

"Laramie or Squamish: What Use is Canadian Culture?" by Tom Wayman, reprinted from *A Country Not Considered: Canada, Culture, Work* (1993), by permission of the House of Anansi Press, Ltd.

Printed in Canada

10 9 8 7 6 5 4 3 2 1

2008560089

MH/MJ

Pearson
Custom Publishing
is a division of

PEARSON

www.pearsonhighered.com

ISBN 10: 0-555-01671-4
ISBN 13: 978-0-555-01671-8

BRIEF CONTENTS

INTRODUCTION

by
Herbert Pimlott

'Life, the University and Communication Studies'

Like all other university students who complete their three- or four- year course of study for the Bachelor of Arts degree in the humanities and social sciences, you will acquire the same skills that are applicable across a range of professions and careers, that are not necessarily related to the particular content of your academic discipline. Students who apply themselves and learn from their mistakes and the feedback from essays and examinations, will develop those sought after skills in thinking, writing, reading critically, assessing information and data, analyzing arguments, presenting ideas, arguing different points-of-view, and learning to use their own initiative. So whether you undertake a degree in Communication Studies or some other subject in the humanities and social sciences, you will acquire the same set of skills. Providing, of course, that you are prepared to engage with the subject material, which means lots of reading and re-reading, writing and re-writing, researching, etc., in order to acquire these skills and successfully complete your degree. Learning is only effective to the degree to which you actively engage in it.

A Bachelor of Arts degree in Communication Studies does not automatically qualify a graduate for a profession in 'communication,' any more than other liberal arts graduates. However, there are areas such as specific content-related issues (e.g. media ownership, ethics, policy), research methods (e.g. content analysis, surveys, questionnaires), and analytical approaches and theoretical frameworks (e.g. semiotics, rhetoric, political economy), that enable Communication Studies graduates to be better prepared to take on board jobs, for example, which involve media relations, monitoring, and/or analysis, without necessarily having to take a college diploma (though employers' preferences will vary in terms of what they want).

There are basically two types of work in the communication industries: administrative, practical, and vocational work, which includes such occupations as photographer, sound engineer, secretary, and lighting technician; and critical, creative, and facilitative work, which includes such professional roles as media relations officer, radio producer, copy editor, and advertising account manager. The communication industries rely primarily upon university liberal arts graduates for most professional roles because these occupations require people who are versatile and know how to adapt to different situations, are able to work under their own initiative, and have the ability to come up with ideas and apply them (i.e. thinking critically, conceptually, 'against the grain'). Your advantage with a Communication Studies degree will be the knowledge and understanding, you have, of the myriad ways in which communication itself works, shaping our views, our knowledge, our culture, our world, ourselves.

'WHAT IS COMMUNICATION STUDIES?'

Some students think Communication Studies refers to the type of remedial courses that one takes in secondary school instead of Grade 11 or 12 English. Others think

Communication Studies is something like 'Business Communications,' or learning how to make videos. The focus in business programs is very different to the approach we take in Communication Studies: there are key differences in the assumptions about knowledge and instrumentality, for example, which usually distinguish the two from each other. Generally, business communications is about learning 'how to market' products, write memos and annual reports, etc. Most courses that teach you how to make a film, use a video camera, or record music are usually run outside the university in colleges or private institutions and may last anywhere from a few months to one or two years. In universities, Communication Studies is primarily an academic subject, where students focus on the different areas of language, media, and culture, although some programs may include 'studio' or 'practical' courses in film-making or radio broadcasting.

While Communication Studies is one of the newest academic disciplines in the university, gradually being established over three decades in the United States, Canada and the United Kingdom, it can actually trace its roots to ancient Greece and Rome, where scholars studied the functions of public discourse in society. By the 20th century, communication came to embrace the studies of interpersonal and small group interaction, human relations in organizations, mass media, popular culture, new technologies, persuasion, publicity and propaganda, and intercultural communication in addition to public discourse, rhetoric and language. Uniting the field is the belief that the role of communication in human experience is basic to comprehending complex situations and problems in the modern world. Communication Studies can thus be defined as essentially the interdisciplinary study of language, media and culture, drawing upon theories, methods and approaches of its own as well as those of other established subject disciplines, such as history, sociology and English, and including such areas as the political economy of symbols and images, ethnographic studies of audiences, and the rhetorical study of cartoons.

THE LANGUAGE OF COMMUNICATION STUDIES

One of the aspects of academic study that most students find the hardest to comprehend at first is the specialized terminology, or what we might less charitably call 'jargon.' Students, who are new to any discipline, will find the language of that discipline, whether it is physics, political science or English, at first strange and baffling; however, without such a specialized vocabulary, scholars and students would find themselves always compelled to work at a fairly basic level: that is, without the 'jargon', you will never be able to work at any level beyond the most common knowledge of a subject (which rather defeats the purpose of 'higher' learning, where university undergraduate students are expected to attain a certain level of expertise and proficiency in the subject matter, approaches and methods of their academic discipline). Clearly, a university education is going to be challenging and provocative in order to produce graduates who will be well-versed in their subject matter and, in their careers, will be able to employ the disciplinary methods, theories and approaches to such subject matter on demand. And, because Communication Studies focuses on aspects of our everyday lives, such as the way men and women speak to each other or television news frames political issues for its viewers, this discipline is quite provocative as it frequently challenges our own assumptions and common-sense understandings of the world.

You will find that the meanings of many of the specialized terms we use in Communication Studies are not necessarily the same as the ones you will find in an ordinary dictionary. It is worthwhile to invest in a specialist dictionary for Communication Studies if you have trouble understanding or remembering some of these terms. Just a few of the words that you will encounter in this book are: 'discourse', 'agenda-setting', 'gate-keeping', 'semiotics', 'rhetoric', 'denotation', 'connotation', and 'ideology'.

ORIGINS OF 'COMMUNICATION'

Raymond Williams, a leading scholar of communications and culture in the U.K., pointed out that the various meanings of the word 'communication' run along a continuum between two 'extremes'. At one end of this continuum, the definition has primarily equated 'communication' with the notion of 'transmission' as a one-way process. So, for example, he points out that 'communication' was used in English from the late 17th century until the early 20th century as a synonym for 'transportation,' because it was during this period that there was a massive extension of canals and roads, and the introduction and expansion of railways throughout England. Thus, 'communication' became the 'abstract general term for these physical facilities': i.e. 'transportation.'

This idea of a one-way process relates also to ideas of 'manipulative communication(s),' something that is widely believed of most 20th century systems of mass communications, such as television, radio, and film. In particular, when we think of the propaganda systems of the Nazis in Germany or in the Soviet Union during the 1930s, we have obvious examples of the one-way process of 'manipulative communications.' However, one-way 'manipulative communication' is not necessarily limited just to totalitarian political systems. For example, those, who assert that video games or television violence cause children to become violent themselves or to engage in other forms of anti-social behaviour, often believe that our media systems are primarily one-way forms of 'manipulative communications.' To the extent that particular media or television programs are influential, such critics may well be correct (or at least partially so).

At the other end of the spectrum of meanings for 'communication,' is 'sharing' or 'a common or mutual process'. This meaning of the word has its origins in the 15th century (1400s) as the verb, 'to make common to many, impart'. Hence, Williams points out, we can see how the term shares meanings with such similar words as 'community', 'communion', and 'communicant.' That is, all of these words share meanings, which at their root are related to this definition of 'communication,' signifying a body or group that shares a common process or holds beliefs and values in common. In the sense of 'imparting' or 'making common to many,' we can see how the term 'communication' has been adopted since the mid-20th century to stand for 'other means of extending or maintaining social contact,' sending messages and imparting values via television, radio, and the press, among other mass media.

This definition of communication relates to the idea of 'participatory communication(s).' In this way, it has the opposite meaning to the one-way, top-down notion of manipulative communication, of which the totalitarian propaganda system mentioned above is exemplary. Those forms of communication, such as community radio or cable access television, for example, that have been established to enable ordinary citizens to speak directly to others in the public sphere, are more in keeping with this second meaning. In particular, this idea 'to make common to many, [to] impart' is what communication ideally should be all about: sharing ideas, perhaps outside the realms of political and economic power, in a non-hierarchical, equitable manner, as we might do in conversations with our friends.

But, it is this notion of sharing and making common to many that is at the heart of the whole ideal of 'democracy': a democracy without a form of sharing, dialogue, and two (or more) ways of exchanging ideas, beliefs, values, information, etc., is not a 'true' democracy. Therefore, you could say that the whole essence of communication is not only what defines us as different from animals, but also what is fundamental to one of the most basic principles of good governance: control by the people. That is, democracy is at its best when communication is a process of sharing and making common.

This is what makes the study of communication 'political' because the very definition of communication reveals different power structures: authoritarian top-down communication, which you find in political dictatorships and most corporate, bureaucratic and institutional structures, versus non-hierarchical, cooperative forms of sharing and exchange, which is integral to truly democratic forms of governance and power-sharing. Thus, the communication process is inherently a political issue: that is, it is almost always about the relations of power in any situation, which is politics in its broadest sense.

COMMUNICATION STUDIES: AN OVERVIEW

'What is communication?' This seemingly simple question is often how the introductory course in Communication Studies begins. At first, it may not seem all that difficult until you start to define communication, and it subsequently becomes difficult to see what might not be considered communication. However, at its most basic, we can think of communication today as one of two simple definitions. One definition is communication as the process of sending a message from one person or group or institution to another, which has an impact on the receiver(s). The second definition of communication is 'as a negotiation and exchange of meaning' within cultures where the interaction between people, messages and 'reality' help to produce particular meanings or understandings of the world (O'Sullivan et al. 1983: 42).

It is important to introduce one of the most enduring models of communication, the Lasswell model, because it is seen as one of the originating points for the eventual emergence of the discipline of Communication Studies as well as providing a good illustration of the first basic definition of communication. Named after Harold Lasswell, who formulated it in 1948, it provides a useful place to start thinking about how communication works:

- who
- says what
- in which channel
- to whom
- with what effect?

I have used the example of teaching university students in a classroom to illustrate how this model of communication can be applied. We would break down the communication process in this model as follows:

- a sender (e.g. professor)
- a channel (or mode) (e.g. speech, whiteboard, website)
- a meaningful message (e.g. lecture)

- a receiver(s) (e.g. students)
- a mutually understood code (e.g. English language)
- a context (e.g. large classroom, many students, university, city, province)
- & usually an effect or response (e.g. taking notes, listening, talking)

However, it should be noted that, communication offers no guarantees that the receiver of the message will understand it perfectly as intended by the sender (a lot of communication is the necessity of repeating and clarifying material, so that everyone understands it—even in conversations between friends!). Misunderstanding or mis-communication, therefore, is as much a part of the process of communication as the accurate and unproblematic reception of messages.

There are a number of ways we try and break down communication in order to better understand its different elements. This includes six basic forms of communication, five uses or functions, and the four spheres of human existence within which communication works.

As a broad overview of communication, we can break it down into six forms.

(1) ORAL COMMUNICATION: the form of communication which distinguishes humans from other animals; includes such things as: interviews between two or more individuals, informal conversations, formal talks and speeches, folklore, oral history and customs, etc.; various paralinguistic features of oral communication (e.g. inflection, tone, accent, stress, intonation);

(2) WRITTEN COMMUNICATION: writing has become one of the most important forms of communication underpinning human societies in the 21st century; includes everything from notes on napkins, personal letters and e-mails, to essays and magazine feature stories, to the texts of advertisements, websites, and books;

(3) NON-VERBAL COMMUNICATION: we often 'read' the 'cues' we get from the way people dress, their hand gestures, body positioning, etc.; important for communicating attitudes, emotions, and roles in society;

(4) GRAPHICAL COMMUNICATION: an important part of understanding the ways in which the symbolic and pictorial modes of graphics work; analyzing how images are put together and the ways in which they work to communicate particular messages;

(5) NUMERICAL COMMUNICATION: understanding the ways in which numerical systems are applied; presentation and interpretation of numerical data; how numerical data can be used to support arguments;

(6) MASS COMMUNICATION: understanding the ways in which new communication technologies, since the introduction of the printing press, enable new means of presenting and integrating oral, written, non-verbal, graphical and/or numerical communication to individuals, groups and masses; includes: newspapers; magazines; books; radio; film; television; internet; world-wide-web; streaming technologies; also means analyzing the uses and impacts of new technologies, their implications for society, the polity and the economy.

Often, when engaging in the analysis of communication or media, we can break it down into different communication elements. For example, if you were to analyze a television news program, you might break it down into four areas: 'oral communication', where you might focus on what the news presenter or anchor is saying, her tone and inflection, accent, etc., including the meaning of the words; 'non-verbal communication', where you might focus on her clothes, body positioning, hand gestures; 'graphical communication', where you highlight the use of images, from the studio set-up and background, use of maps, captions for images that appear in the top right-hand corner of the television screen, etc.; and 'mass communication', where you focus on the technological means by which all these elements are brought into the home and how it actually shapes oral and graphical communication for television. You may also wish to consider that most speech or oral communication on television news is already scripted: that is, it is actually already written, revised, edited and re-written by the news anchor or presenter, other journalists, and/or researchers, and read by the news anchor via a teleprompter.

There are also five uses for communication. The first three are perhaps the most obvious, although it should be noted that rarely does any one form of communication only offer one of these functions. For example, while some economists would contend that advertising just supplies information from producers to consumers, communication scholars will point out that advertising also has a persuasive function and a socialization function, which is why, for example, in magazine advertisements or television commercials, advertising conveys values and beliefs through the associative logic of combining images and words.

(1) information gathering, storage, retrieval and dissemination;
(2) persuasion, propaganda, and publicity;
(3) entertainment;
(4) socialization;
(5) individual attainment.

The last two uses, 'socialization' and 'individual attainment,' are a little less obvious. Communication, and in particular, mass communication, have a socialization function which means that it reinforces norms of behaviour for groups and institutions and helps integrate individuals into groups. For example, television provides not only entertainment and information but it also conveys values and beliefs through the ways in which the problems that arise in the stories it tells are resolved. Television, thus, also acts as a socializing agent by presenting modes of behaviour that are rewarded or punished (e.g. do the criminals get away with their ill-gotten riches?). Individual attainment is less important in thinking about mass communication than the other four functions because it is more about how communication enables individual creative and artistic expression, and personal growth, and contributes to individual interactions in groups.

There are four areas where important issues arise as a result of communication activities and around which the study of communication revolves: ECONOMIC, SOCIAL, POLITICAL, and CULTURAL spheres. Issues in these four spheres of human existence are raised by public debates and framed through such agencies as the mass media, educational institutions, political bodies, agencies of message dissemination (e.g. public relations, advertising, marketing), alternative media, and grassroots social movements. As a result, students of Communication Studies are also expected to be students of politics and economics, culture and society.

WHAT IS 'MASS COMMUNICATION'?

The term 'mass' is often used to refer to audiences 'as a vast, undifferentiated agglomeration of unthinking individuals, likely to behave in a non-rational, if not irrational, manner' (Lorimer and Gasher 2004: 29). That is, as crowds or mobs, who are vulnerable to 'mass psychosis' and the manipulation of demagogues and 'madmen' like

Hitler. This definition and thinking about the majority of our society as a 'mass' reveals a deep-seated fear of ordinary working- and lower middle-class people. As Raymond Williams pointed out, 'there are no masses, only ways of seeing people as masses.' This means that the term reveals more about those who use it to define a group of people than it does about the group it is supposed to define. This definition of 'mass communication' was effectively that of the 'mass distribution of information and entertainment products.' It was also an understanding of communication as a one-way process where 'one message [is] composed and transmitted from one location to many.' Thus, the first definition of mass communication was pejorative.

If we look even closer at the term 'mass communication,' we can also see that the term actually seems to hide the industrial, political and social nature of the organization of mass media institutions. The way our television system is organized, with a public broadcaster, the Canadian Broadcasting Corporation (CBC), and private broadcasting networks, such as CanWest Global and CTV, indicates that it did not 'fall out of the sky' ready-made, but was the result of an ongoing political, economic and cultural struggle between different social formations, interest groups, and powerful political individuals acting in concert or against each other. This struggle between competing groups, interests, and publics evolves and changes over time. At times, the historical context and array of social forces has favoured public broadcasting (that is broadcasters that are not subject to the influence of advertisers and their clients) and at other times it has worked in favour of powerful private corporate interests (i.e. deregulation, privatization).

There are three distinct forms of 'mass communication' today according to Rowland Lorimer and Mike Gasher. There is 'the centralized production and dissemination of mass information and entertainment,' such as the large newspaper chains of Hollinger and Southam, and their links with private broadcasting networks across Canada. Secondly, there is the 'decentralized production and wide accessibility of information and entertainment, primarily by means of public access to the Internet,' which while ensuring that a variety of views can be disseminated, still retains a preponderance of the dominant perspectives of powerful organizations and institutions. And, finally, there is the 'exchange of information that takes place among individuals and groups by means of public access to communication channels,' which can happen via both mainstream and alternative media channels, such as letters to the editor in newspapers, public access cable television discussions, and talk radio call-in shows, among other formats (2004: 30).

Each new wave of communications or media technology has been heralded by its promoters as bringing the previous 'new' wave of media technology to an end: the introduction of radio was supposed to herald the end of the newspaper, film was supposed to supercede radio, and television was supposed to overcome film. However, despite the ever-changing world of communications technologies, older forms continue to exist and are adapted to new or different uses in addition to their earlier uses. Indeed, some scholars are now suggesting that new technologies, like the world-wide-web, have actually enhanced older mass media such as newspapers, radio and television. The introduction of the PC or personal computer in the late 1970s and early 1980s did not lead to the 'paperless office' as originally claimed by its promoters. In fact, it not only contributed to a seemingly never-ending spiral of memos, letters, reports, annuals, etc., but also contributed to a massive expansion of (print) newsletters, magazines and journals.

Ironically, writing, which is one of the oldest forms of communications technologies and cultural practices, is central to the 'knowledge economy.' Writing has become increasingly seen as integral, not only to the general functioning of our whole society in all of its complexity, but also to the functioning of our 'post-industrial' economy. In the U.S. over the last half of the 20th century, over 40 percent of 'new employment growth' has come from knowledge-based companies (Brandt 2005: 166). Writing is, therefore, one of the most important forms of communication in the 21st century world. Writing also underpins much of mass communication itself. (You should also make note, that Communication Studies, like English and history, is a writing-intensive discipline that requires a lot of work in writing, editing and revising one's work to communicate one's ideas as clearly as possible.)

WHY STUDY 'MASS COMMUNICATION'?

Why might the study of 'mass communication' be important? To think about this question, perhaps we should ask: 'Where do we get our ideas?' We live in a society in which almost all aspects of our lives are 'mediated' by various forms of communication technologies and most of what we know about the world comes from various forms of mass communication. Mass communication 'messages' do not just convey 'information' but impart 'values' (e.g. social values, attitudes, behaviours, etc.) and because they do not just convey 'neutral' information but the media should be seen as not only informative but as formative. That is, they shape the way we see the world by framing issues in ways that tend to be favourable to powerful elites and institutions rather than to the majority of the people.

According to a study of students in Ontario carried out for the provincial Ministry of Education, Ontario students by age 18 have spent: some 11,000 hours in school, and 10,500 hours listening to popular music, but 15,000 hours watching television (1989 provincial government data). This study no doubt underestimates the degree of exposure to commercial messages and other forms of media influence because when it was completed in 1989, the daily exposure of people in Canada and the United States to advertisements was already increasing from an average of 1,600 commercial messages per day to an average of 3,500 commercial messages (ads) per day by the mid-1990s. Other studies indicate the degree to which the average person spends considerable time each day watching television: one study points out that on average, adults in North America watch television for nearly one whole day out of every week (not counting sleeping!) (23.4 hours), with the exception of young male adults (16–24 years old), who watch TV the least.

Perhaps the most difficult thing for students to realize is that the various means of mass communication, such as Hollywood blockbuster films like *Star Wars*, or television shows like *The O.C.* are not 'just entertainment'. It is true, if you enjoy them, then they are 'entertaining'. And that is one of five functions of mass communication. There is nothing to stop a TV show, a radio station, or a newspaper, for example, from doing more than one thing to you and the rest of the audience. Indeed, the amount of money that is spent by corporations and governments on advertising in itself is phenomenal. For example, it is estimated that at the end of the 1990s, Canadian companies were spending more than $8 billion on advertising annually (Vivian and Maurin 2006: 185).

Advertising agencies in turn spend a lot of money on different forms of research as well as developing their advertisements precisely to determine the best way to influence audiences to purchase their clients' goods, services, ideas or values. If audiences were easily manipulated by mass media then there would be no need to engage in researching and developing new advertising methods. However, if audiences were not influenced by advertising, then the agencies would go broke and the amount of time, energy and resources put into producing advertisements would not be so great (e.g. a thirty second television advertisement might take two weeks to shoot). (Interestingly, when you talk to people, they always claim that they are not influenced by advertising, but that everybody else is!) Remember, the effectiveness of advertising is to make you think that you chose the product yourself, rather than that they have successfully persuaded you to purchase it.

MASS COMMUNICATIONS: THREE AREAS OF CONCERN

This book highlights three areas of concern in mass communications. It is perhaps easiest to learn about these three areas by asking a series of questions to help focus our thoughts about mass communication. When we approach these questions, we have to specifically keep in mind the context of Canadian politics, economy, culture and society in the early 21st century.

First of all, we want to ask what are the 'impacts and effects' of mass communication:

(a) What is the nature of media influence?
(b) How, and to what extent, do the media influence people?

Secondly, we want to ask a series of questions about the messages or content of mass communication:

(a) Are media images (or representations) a 'reflection' or a 'distortion' of the wider society?
(b) How do mass media shape or 'transform' the message?
(c) Who gets to produce the messages?
(d) Which messages are disseminated by the media?
(e) Which messages are not? (Sometimes, the most revealing aspect of the content of mass media messages is what they do not say or speak about. Silence, it seems, does speak volumes.)

And finally, we have to ask questions about ownership and control:

(a) Who owns the media?
(b) Is control of the media unduly concentrated and/or abused?
(c) What impact(s) does the concentration of the media into fewer and fewer hands have on democracy and our lives?

THE STRUCTURE OF THE BOOK:

This collection of readings is designed for the twelve-week introductory course in mass communication in Canada. The readings are broken into three sections that loosely relate to modes of mass communication (e.g. print, radio, music), critical approaches to issues in mass communication, and practical approaches to academic and media writing, reading critically, and analyzing texts.

Bibliography

Brandt, Deborah (2005) 'Writing for a Living: Literacy and the Knowledge Economy,' *Written Communication*, vol. 22, no. 2 (April), 166-197.

Lorimer, Rowland and Mike Gasher (2004) *Mass Communication in Canada*. Toronto: Oxford University Press. Fifth edition.

O'Sullivan, Tim, John Hartley, Danny Saunders and John Fiske (1983) *Key Concepts in Communication*. London and New York: Routledge.

Vivian, John and Peter J. Maurin (2006) *The Media of Mass Communication*. Toronto: Pearson Education. Fourth edition.

Williams, Raymond (1976) *Keywords*. London: Fontana.

SECTION I

SECTION 1

Chapter One

Economics of Mass Media

NEW MEDIA

Innovation is not new to the mass media. The Beadle Brothers, who introduced dime novels before the Civil War, were the new media of their day, profoundly changing the U.S. book market. Today, innovations outside the mainstream include broad, sometimes fuzzy categories like alternative media, underground media and high-tech media.

ALTERNATIVE MEDIA. Campus and community radio stations in Canada are geared to neighbourhood service with low-power transmitters and have made possible a level of interactivity with their audiences not possible for traditional stations that seek large audiences to draw advertising and pay the bills. These low-power stations, many staffed with volunteers, are alternative voices in the radio universe. There are cur-

rently almost 100 community radio stations in Canada, mostly in Quebec. There are an additional 53 campus stations across Canada. You probably have one on your campus.

UNDERGROUND MEDIA. The generation-defined, anti-establishment press of the 1970s was one form of new media, living on in free-distribution weekly form. The emphasis is heavy on local, live entertainment, usually bar-centred; reformist social and political perspectives; outrageous, often ribald humour; and a high quotient of street vulgarities and sexual innuendo.

HIGH-TECH MEDIA. Technology creates new possibilities. Think what iPods are doing to music stores and radio listenership. Cybercafes are giving way to Wi-Fi. For better or worse, internet bloggers have widened participation in public affairs journalism.

Economics of Mass Media

Study Preview   *With few exceptions, the U.S. mass media are privately owned and must turn profits to stay in business. Except for books, sound recordings and movies, most media income is from advertising, with lesser amounts directly from media consumers. These economic realities are potent shapers of media content.*

ECONOMIC FOUNDATION

The mass media are expensive to set up and operate. The equipment and facilities require a major investment. Meeting the payroll requires a bankroll. Print media must buy paper by the ton. Broadcasters pay gigantic electricity bills to pump their messages through the ether.

To meet their expenses, the mass media sell their product in two ways. Either they derive their income from selling a product directly to mass audiences, as do the movie, record and book industries, or they derive their income from advertisers that place advertisements for mass audiences that the media provide, as do newspapers, magazines, radio and television. Newspapers and magazines are hybrids with both audience and advertising revenue streams. In short, the mass media operate in a capitalistic environment. With few exceptions they are in business to make money.

ADVERTISING REVENUE.   Advertisers pay the mass media for access to potential customers. From print media, advertisers buy space. From broadcasters they buy time.

Book publishers once relied solely on readers for revenue, but that has changed somewhat. Today, book publishers charge for film rights whenever Hollywood turns a book into a movie or a television program. Publishing houses now profit indirectly from the advertising revenue that television networks pull in from broadcasting movies.

Movies too have come to benefit from advertising. Until the 1950s, movies relied entirely on box-office receipts for profits, but moviemakers now calculate what profits they can realize not only from movie-house traffic but also from selling to television and the home video market. High-tech DVDs are replacing VHS tapes, increasing what was already the lion's share of movie producers' income. Today, moviemakers even pick up advertising directly by charging commercial companies to include their products in the scenes they shoot, a technique called product placement.

CIRCULATION REVENUE.   Although some advertising-supported mass media, such as network television, do not charge their audiences, others do. When income is derived from the audience, it's called **circulation** revenue. *Maclean's* may cost $4.95 at the corner store, but little if any of this newsrack charge ends up with Rogers, the parent company. Distribution is costly, and distributors all along the way take their cut. For some publications, however, subscription income makes the difference between profit and loss.

circulation Number of copies of a publication that circulate.

Direct audience payments have emerged in recent years in broadcasting. Cable and satellite subscribers pay a monthly fee. Audience support is the basis of subscription television such as commercial-free TMN or Mpix. Noncommercial broadcasting, including provincial broadcasters such as Saskatchewan's SCN and Ontario's TVO, rely heavily on viewer contributions.

GOVERNMENT SUBSIDIES. While the idea of government support for the mass media might seem to some a waste of public money, both the U.S. and Canadian governments support some form of public broadcasting. In Canada, the **Canadian Broadcasting Corporation (CBC)** is mandated by the government to promote Canadian culture to Canadians. Due to belt tightening since the 1990s, government support for public broadcasting seems to be dropping off, as both Canadian and U.S. government funds for public broadcasting have been cut drastically in the last few years. Despite the cutbacks, the CBC's yearly budget is approximately $1.3 billion or roughly $29 per Canadian.

Canadian Broadcasting Corporation (CBC) Canada's national public television network. Began broadcasting in 1952.

Award-Winning Advertisements. To reach potential customers, advertisers buy space or time in mass media that can deliver audiences. It's the ads themselves, however, that drive home the sales pitch—but first they must get attention. Print ads that did this best in 2003 were "Rebirth" by the ad agency TBWA, Paris, for Sony PlayStation, honoured with the Grand Prix Award at the Cannes international advertising festival; and another by the agency Hopper Galton, for the Discovery Channel documentary *Age of Terror,* winner of the Cannes Golden Lion award.
Courtesy Discovery Networks Europe. Photo by Ernst Fischer.

TERRORISM HAS CHANGED THE WAY WE VIEW THE WORLD

'AGE OF TERROR' Global terrorism in context. The first of four documentaries starts tonight at 9.30.   **DISCOVERY** CHANNEL

ECONOMIC IMPERATIVE

Economics figures into which messages make it to print or to the airwaves. To realize their profit potential, the media that seek large audiences choose to deal with subjects of wide appeal and to present them in ways that attract great numbers of people. A subject interesting only to a small number of people does not make it into *Canadian Living* magazine. CTV drops programs that do not do well in the television ratings. This is a function of economics for those media that depend on advertising revenue to stay in business. The larger the audience, the more advertisers are willing to pay for time and space to pitch their goods and services.

Even media that seek narrow segments of the population need to reach as many people within those segments as possible to attract advertisers. Two Canadian digital channels, Edge TV and WTSN (Women's Television Sports Network), were not able to attract a large enough audience or advertisers. As a result, both stopped broadcasting in 2003.

UPSIDE AND DOWNSIDE

The drive to attract advertising can affect media messages in sinister ways. For example, the television station that overplays the ribbon-cutting ceremony at a new store is usually motivated more by a desire to please an advertiser than by a commitment to reporting news. The economic dependence of the mass media on advertising income gives considerable clout to advertisers, which may threaten to yank advertising out of a publication if a certain negative story appears. Such threats occur, though not frequently.

At a subtler level, lack of advertiser support can work against certain messages. During the 1950s, as racial injustice was emerging as an issue that would rip the nation apart a decade later, U.S. television avoided documentaries on the subject. No advertisers were interested.

DEMASSIFICATION

demassification Media focus on narrower audience segments.

The idea that the mass audience is the largest number of people who can be assembled to hear mass messages is changing. Most media content today is aimed at narrow, albeit often still large, segments. This phenomenon is called **demassification.**

This demassification process, the result of technological breakthroughs and economic pressures, is changing the mass media dramatically. Radio demassified early, in the 1950s, replacing formats designed to reach the largest possible audiences with formats aimed at sectors of audience. Magazines followed in the 1960s and the 1970s, and today most of the 12 000 consumer magazines in the United States cater only to the special interests of carefully targeted groups of readers. Today, with dozens of television program services via cable or satellite in most U.S. households, television also is going through demassification.

The effects of demassification are only beginning to emerge. At first, advertisers welcomed demassification because they could target their pitches to groups of their likeliest customers. The latest trend in demassification has advertisers producing their own media to carry their messages by mail to potential customers who, through computer sorting and other mechanisms, are more precisely targeted than magazines, newspapers, television and radio could ever do. The new **alternative media**, as they are called, include:

alternative media Emerging, narrowly focused advertising vehicles.

- Sponsored websites with games and other lures to attract return visits.
- Direct mail catalogues and flyers to selected addresses.
- Television commercials at the point of purchase, such as screens in grocery store shopping carts.
- Place-based media, such as magazines designed for distribution only in physicians' waiting rooms.
- Telemarketing, in which salespeople make their pitches by telephone to households determined by statistical profiles to be good potential customers.
- Email marketing, sometimes referred to as "spam."

If advertisers continue their shift to these and other alternative media, the revenue base of magazines, newspapers, radio and television will decline. Wholly new ways to structure the finances of these media will be necessary, probably with readers, listeners and viewers picking up the bill directly rather than indirectly by buying advertised products, which is the case today.

Media Conglomeration

Study Preview   *Giant corporations with diverse interests have consolidated the mass media into relatively few hands. One result is that new talent and messengers have a harder time winning media attention.*

MEDIA OWNERSHIP CONSOLIDATION

The trend toward **conglomeration**, sometimes referred to by Canadian writers as "concentration of ownership," involves a process of mergers, acquisitions and buyouts that consolidates the ownership of the media into fewer and fewer companies. The deep pockets of a wealthy corporate parent can see a financially troubled media unit, such as a radio station, through a rough period, but there is a price. In time the corporate parent wants a financial return on its investment, and pressure builds on the station to generate more and more profit. This would not be so bad if the people running the radio station loved radio and had a sense of public service, but the process of conglomeration often doesn't work out that way. Parent corporations tend to replace media people with career-climbing, bottom-line managers whose motivation is looking good to their supervisors in faraway cities who are under serious pressure to increase profits. In radio, for example, management experts, not radio people, end up running the station, and the quality of media content suffers.

conglomeration Combining of companies into larger companies.

The other media trend is **convergence**. This term is used to describe media cross-ownership; some refer to it as "multi-platform media." It refers to the practice of one conglomerate with interests in publishing, broadcasting and the internet. Ted Rogers defined convergence in two different ways: "The computer and the TV set are coming together. You're putting together different media through one instrument. That's technological convergence. And then there's the convergence we might call marketing convergence, where you're packaging together people's needs in a way to make it easier for them. In Rogers's case it may be all the services—telephony, long distance, high speed internet, low speed internet, cable, paging, etc. . . ." It's interesting to note that Rogers made these comments in *Maclean's*—a magazine he owns.

convergence Early 21st-century model of media cross-ownership. Converged companies typically own print, broadcast, and internet holdings.

It's the marketing opportunities that attracted CanWest Global Communications Corp. to purchase Alliance Atlantis, a Canadian production and distribution company. It also owned the specialty channels Showcase, History Television and Food

Media Convergence. The *CSI* franchise is co-produced and distributed by Canada's Alliance Atlantis. The success of the company in producing and distributing winning media content was one reason why it was purchased by CanWest Global in 2007.

Network Canada. When CanWest bought Alliance Atlantis in 2007, the Chief Executive for CanWest, Leonard Asper, explained the rationale for the purchase by saying the merging of the two companies offers new opportunities for cross-promotion of content. According to Asper, "by sharing programming across our multiple platforms, we see opportunities for ratings growth, which we expect will ultimately drive advertising revenue growth. Most importantly, in an increasingly competitive environment, this gives CanWest a great platform for growth in Canada." The merger gave CanWest greater control of the production, distribution and programming aspects of Canadian media content.

CONVERGENCE IN CANADA

How extensive is convergence in Canada? Consider the information on the six media rivals that have established themselves as the major players in Canada, as of 2007:

■ CTVglobemedia is a multimedia company whose major holdings are CTV and *The Globe and Mail*. The company also owns The Comedy Network, CTV Newsnet, and Report on Business Television, and holds a majority interest in TSN. On the digital side, they also have interests in Discovery, Animal Planet, and the NHL Network. In 2006, they purchased CHUM, which included specialty channels MuchMusic, Bravo! and Book TV.

■ CanWest Global is another Canadian media powerhouse with interests in print and television broadcasting. In addition to the Global Television Network, it owns 11 daily newspapers, including the *National Post*. It also owns several conventional and digital specialty channels, including TVtropolis, Deja View, and Lonestar. CanWest Global also has media holdings around the world, such as TV3 in

Ireland and C4 in New Zealand. Online, it owns the Canada.com network, which allows surfers access to all the company's holdings. In 2007, it purchased Alliance Atlantis, pending CRTC approval.

- Quebecor owns TVA (the largest television network in Quebec), Sun Media (the second-largest Canadian newspaper group), and the Canoe.ca website. The company also has interests in 12 publishing houses and Vidéotron, a chain of video rental stores.
- Rogers Media has interests not only in cable TV distribution but also in programming with Sportsnet. In publishing, it owns *Maclean's, Chatelaine,* and *Flare* magazines. Its internet division includes Excite.ca, and Rogers owns radio and television stations in British Columbia, Alberta, Manitoba and Ontario. In addition to all of this, Rogers has a strong presence in wireless communication and owns the Toronto Blue Jays.
- Corus Entertainment's diverse interests include radio stations in western Canada, Ontario and Quebec. Its TV holdings include YTV, Teletoon, and CMT (Country Music Television). Corus is also involved in the production of content through Nelvana, a Canadian production company that produces such kids' fare as *Babar, Franklin* and *Beyblade.*

How significant is convergence? Dwayne Winseck, a journalism professor at Carleton University, says that while convergence and consolidation make sense from a business standpoint, "it is not good for journalism or democracy, where citizens continue to look to the media to reflect, extend and amplify public life."

While technologically possible, the economics of convergence has yet to be worked out. The effects of convergence are only now being felt. Even Matthew Fraser, media columnist for the *National Post,* writes, "convergence, it seems, will take some time to prove itself as a business model." The real impact of convergence for everyone—people working in the media, consumers, and media moguls—won't be felt for years. This opinion was confirmed by Kevin G. Wilson, who wrote in the Montreal *Gazette* that these large converged media companies "have yet to demonstrate that the patchwork of companies they have assembled are capable of generating any beneficial synergies." Even Leonard Asper, speaking after CanWest's purchase of Alliance Atlantis, felt it would be 2010 or 2011 before they would see any of the real effects of the merger.

Converged Media: Links to corporate profiles, annual reports, and detailed information for all of Canada's largest media companies.

www.ctvglobemedia.ca

www.canwestglobal.com

www.corusent.com

www.quebecor.com

www.rogers.com

DUBIOUS EFFECTS OF CONGLOMERATION

Critics such as **Ben Bagdikian** say that conglomeration affects the diversity of messages offered by the mass media. Speaking at the Madison Institute, Bagdikian portrayed conglomeration in bleak terms: "They are trying to buy control or market domination not just in one medium but in all the media. The aim is to control the entire process from an original manuscript or new series to its use in as many forms as possible. A magazine article owned by *the company* becomes a book owned by *the company.* That becomes a television program owned by *the company,* which then becomes a movie owned by *the company.* It is shown in theatres owned by *the company,* and the movie sound track is issued on a record label owned by *the company,* featuring the vocalist on the cover of one of *the company* magazines. It does not take an angel from heaven to tell us that *the company* will be less enthusiastic about outside ideas and production that it does not own, and more and more we will be dealing with closed circuits to control access to most of the public."

Ben Bagdikian Critic of media consolidation.

THE NEW MEDIA MONOPOLY

A COMPLETELY REVISED AND UPDATED EDITION WITH SEVEN NEW CHAPTERS

BEN H. BAGDIKIAN

"NO BOOK ON THE MEDIA HAS PROVED AS INFLUENTIAL TO OUR UNDERSTANDING OF THE DANGERS OF CORPORATE CONSOLIDATION TO DEMOCRACY AND THE MARKETPLACE OF IDEAS AS THE MEDIA MONOPOLY: THIS NEW EDITION BUILDS ON THAT WORK AND SURPASSES IT." —ERIC ALTERMAN, AUTHOR OF WHAT LIBERAL MEDIA?

Media Critic. Ben Bagdikian, called "one of the most considerate voices in journalism today," says that huge media companies are ever more profit-obsessed. Their corporate strategies, he says, often sacrifice high-quality content and public service on the altar of increasing profits. Bagdikian has amassed distressing data on conglomeration in his book *The New Media Monopoly*.

Ben Bagdikian

Nobody begrudges a company making a profit. The difficulty comes when the recycling displaces creative new entries in the mass media marketplace. NBC executive Don Ohlmeyer concedes that a vertically integrated network is disinclined "in even considering projects in which they don't own a financial interest." Independent Hollywood producers, who once competed to produce network shows, are finding themselves out of the loop. The result, says Gary Goldberg, creator of *Spin City* on ABC: "You see this blandness and similarity to the shows. Consumers are the ones who get hurt."

QUALITY. Headquarters push subsidiaries to cut costs to increase profits, a trend that has devastated the quality of writing and editing. Fewer people do more work. At newspapers, for example, a reporter's story once went through several hands—editor, copy editor, headline writer, typesetter, proofreader. At every stage, the story could be improved. In today's streamlined newsrooms, proofreaders have been replaced by spell-check software, which not only introduces its own problems but also lacks the intelligence and judgment of a good proofer. The jobs of the reporter and the typesetter have been consolidated. In many newsrooms, so have the jobs of copy editors and headline writers.

CROSS-PROMOTION. Mega-media companies like NBC Universal are finding more ways to cross-promote their products. NBC tied teaser trailers to its Universal movies before launching its television reality series *The Apprentice* with Donald Trump.

Los Angeles *Times* reporter Tom Rosentiel, writing in the *Columbia Journalism Review,* tells how reporters, pressured to increase productivity, take shortcuts to generate more copy: "Newspapers and newsmagazine interviews today are increasingly conducted over the phone, with reporters assembling stories as much as reporting them, combining elements from electronic transcripts, data bases and television. A growing number of major events, reporters acknowledge, are covered without going to the scene. The stories . . . lack the advantage of serendipity or the authenticity of having been there."

In the book industry, media critic Jacob Weisberg has documented how several major publishers, including Simon & Schuster and Random House, have routinely eliminated important stages in the editing process to rush new titles to print and turn quicker profits. In a revealing article in the *New Republic,* Weisberg lists these results of the accelerated schedules:

- Factual errors, both major and minor, that in earlier times, he says, would have been caught by careful editing.
- Loose, flabby writing from deadline-pressured writers who once could rely on editors to tighten their work. Some books, Weisberg says, are running 100 pages longer than they should.

SAMENESS. You can fly from the East to the West Coast on the same day and read the same Associated Press stories word for word. Newspaper publishers learned long ago that sharing stories via the AP could reduce costs. The resulting economics came at the cost of less diversity in content.

Cultural sociologists fret about the sameness. In recorded music, for example, major record companies often encourage artists to imitate what is already popular. The result is that derivative music squeezes original artists and material out of the marketplace or at least makes it more difficult for these artists to find an audience. Sociologists think that the movement of culture in new directions is slowed by this process.

Barry Diller, who created popular television programs at ABC and later at Fox, says that the problem is the profit-driven trend to recycle existing material for a quick buck. In a speech to magazine executives, Diller pointed out the short-sightedness of recycling: "Taking a movie like *Jurassic Park* and turning it into a video game, that's repackaging. Taking a bestseller and putting it on tape, that's repackaging. Taking magazine articles and slapping them on-line, word for word, that's repackaging." He then likened repackaging to strip mining: "After you've extracted the riches from the surface, there's nothing left."

CORPORATE INSTABILITY. Conglomeration also has introduced instability. Profit-driven corporate parents are quick to sell subsidiaries that fall short of profit expectations even for a short term or just to raise cash. In 2003, AOL Time Warner realized that it had taken on more than it could handle and put Warner Books up for sale. However, bids were too low, and Time Warner reversed its decision. Typically in unstable situations, uncertainty diverts energy and focus from ongoing projects. Some projects are put on hold. There is uncertainty about new projects. Employees, with sudden career jitters, look for jobs elsewhere. None of this serves the media consumer well.

POSITIVE EFFECTS OF CONGLOMERATION

Is convergence good or bad? One industry insider says it's a good thing. Jack Tomik is the past president of CanWest Media Sales. He oversaw sales and marketing for all of CanWest's holdings in Canada. He was also involved in the branding of Global. Unlike critics such as Bagdikian, Tomik sees positive things coming out of convergence and conglomeration. He uses two television stations owned by CanWest to illustrate his point: CH-TV in Victoria and CH-TV in Hamilton are part of the same brand. They share the same logo and the same news intro. But that's where the sameness ends and the quality begins, according to Tomik: "I have a RAM truck. I know there are thousands of them out there, but this one's mine. I have ownership of it. It's the same with a brand. You can have the same look and the same feel, but the station is relevant to that community. It's about how you use a brand and how you service your viewers. It's less about the name and more about what it means to the viewers in that locale. If you're a person who lives on Vancouver Island, you have ownership of the CH brand. It's your local television station. People in Hamilton also have ownership of CH in that market." In 2007, CH-TV was rebranded as E!

There are other examples of the positive effects of convergence or conglomeration. At the end of World War II, the mainline book-publishing business was dominated by family-run publishing houses, all relatively small by today's standards. Although there are still hundreds of small publishers, consolidation has reduced the industry to six giants. Depending on whom you ask, the conglomeration has been a godsend or a disaster. If the effects are looked at positively, the book industry is financially stronger:

■ Parent corporations have infused cash into their new subsidiaries, financing expensive initiatives that were not financially possible before, including multi-million-dollar deals with authors.
■ Because parent corporations often own newspapers, magazines and broadcast companies, book publishers have ready partners for repackaging books in additional media forms.
■ Many of the new parent corporations own book companies abroad, which helps to open up global markets.

In today's business climate, the lure of market dominance and profit, often on a global scale, keeps driving the concentration of media companies into fewer and fewer conglomerates.

CONGLOMERATION CRACKS

Pell-mell conglomeration among media companies might have peaked. Shareholders in Vivendi, the erstwhile French media conglomerate, discovered in 2002 that big isn't always better when, after rapid expansion, the empire verged on collapse. Vivendi sold off Universal to General Electric, which melded the movie studio into its NBC. Vivendi's Houghton Mifflin book-publishing unit was bought by an investor group. Other units went on the auction block too.

Although Vivendi's situation was extreme, it was not alone among troubled media giants that had grown through mergers and acquisitions in the 1980s and 1990s. The union of Time Warner and America Online (AOL) was heralded at the time for the anticipated synergies from which both partners would supposedly derive advantages. But Time Warner ended up trying to sell AOL when it not only underperformed on expectations but also yielded few offsetting benefits. Viacom executives have toyed with spinning off their fast-growth MTV Networks unit, which includes Nickelodeon and the BET network, rather than letting their future be hobbled by CBS and other Viacom entities whose growth has slowed.

Whether the era of giant conglomerates dominating the mass media is fading is not clear. It could be that recent sell-offs are fine-tuning adjustments of their holdings by parent companies, with subsidiaries merely moving from one mega corporate home to another. What is clear is that major media corporations are more cautious about finding acquisitions that are good fits than were Vivendi and Time Warner.

- **Public media.** Financed by citizens and government money to further the public good, like PBS and NPR in the United States and CBC in Canada.
- **Organizational media.** Aimed at serving nongovernment bodies, such as professional groups, tribes, religions and corporations.
- **Individualized media.** Media customized to an individual's needs and interests, as is possible through the web.
- **Political media.** Used by political parties.

MEDIA TIMELINE

Mass Communication Theory

_____	1916	Swiss linguist Ferdinand de Saussure explained that we communicate through signs.
_____	1948	Claude Shannon and Warren Weaver developed a technical model for the study of communication.
_____	1949	Wilbur Schramm defined mass communication as a field of study.
_____	1954	Wilbur Schramm's *The Process and Effect of Mass Communication* was published.
_____	1973	French philosopher Roland Barthes established the role of myth (or connotation) as a vehicle for cultural ideology through mass communication.
_____	1974	The concentric circle model of communication was developed by Ray Hiebert, Donald Ungurait, and Thomas Bohn.

MEDIA TIMELINE

Globalization of Mass Media

_____	1974	Change model was developed by Ray Hiebert, Donald Ungurait, and Thomas Bohn.
_____	1988	Associated Press bought Worldwide Television News.
_____	1993	NBC bought European Super Channel.
_____	1995	Disney bought ABC.
_____	1998	The World Trade Organization adopted the Canadian model of media regulation.

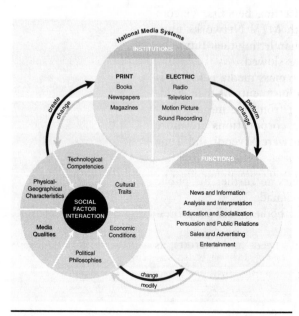

Figure 1.1 Change Model. A 1974 model developed by scholars Ray Hiebert, Donald Ungurait and Thomas Bohn recognizes many factors in media systems.

Thomas Friedman: Official website for this author and *New York Times* columnist.

www.thomaslfriedman.com

Thomas Friedman. This *New York Times* columnist had an epiphany while in India researching a Discovery documentary: Computer software has so empowered individuals that social, business and other infrastructures are in a fundamental transformation.

Mass Media and Nation-States

Study Preview   *The ability of national governments to control media content is diminishing with the technology that is allowing the globalization of the mass media.*

GLOBAL COMMUNICATION

After the 2005 terrorist subway and bus bombings in London, the British news media flooded the streets and airwaves with stories about the suspects. Understandably, coverage was emotional. When the first arrests were made, the front page of the tabloid *Sun* blared: "Got the Bastards." Then the media went silent. British law forbids news coverage once a criminal charge has been filed. The rationale is not to prejudice potential jurors.

Hungry for news about the terrorism investigation and the people arrested, Britons needed to look no further than the internet. The internet's most-used coding structure is called the World Wide Web for a reason. And just down the street, newsstands stocked foreign newspapers and magazines full of ongoing revelations about the suspects. How could British law deal with the influx of information? The logistics would be overwhelming. The volume of internet communication bespeaks the futility of bans.

FRIEDMAN GLOBALIZATION MODEL

Globalization has been explained in a sweeping historical context by analyst Thomas Friedman of *The New York Times*. Friedman sees three great eras over the past 500 years. He casts these in computerese as Globalization 1.0, 2.0 and 3.0.

GLOBALIZATION 1.0. The world shrank as governments projected power beyond their borders from the year 1492 to roughly 1800: "The key agent of change, the dynamic force driving the process of globalization was how much brawn—how much muscle, how much horsepower, wind power, or, later steam power—your country had and how creatively you could deploy it." In this period, Friedman says, the nation-state and commercial activities operating under national flags were supreme.

GLOBALIZATION 2.0. After 1800, multinational companies used declining transportation costs to build global markets, particularly with railroads and steamships. This led industrialists to seek lower labour costs wherever they could be found on the planet because the cost of shipping kept falling and its efficiency kept increasing. In the late 1900s, telecommunication costs dropped dramatically with orbiting satellites, fibre optic cable and the internet. Multinational companies grew exponentially in reshaping human society, displacing some of the earlier power of the nation-states.

GLOBALIZATION 3.0. In the 21st century, a kind of ultimate democratization is occurring. Technology, mostly through computer software, is empowering individuals to chart their own courses in wholly new ways. The new matrix, as Friedman sees it, is a global triad of nation-states, multinational corporations and individuals in dynamic relationships. Individuals, notably, are the new players with access to information that earlier was the province only of governments and corporations.

Global Conglomeration

Study Preview   *Media titan Rupert Murdoch has created the first global content creation and delivery system under a single corporate umbrella, but he's not alone in putting together a global media empire. Still developing are the ways in which global media companies adapt to the internet.*

MULTINATIONAL COMPANIES

The mass media have had international sales for centuries, going back to early book printers. Until the 20th century, however, media companies designed little specifically for export.

Media People

Rupert Murdoch

Rupert Murdoch

People love to hate media mogul Rupert Murdoch. Although his News Corp. is only one of many media companies gobbling up other media outlets, Murdoch's name has become synonymous with media power. Former CBS executive Howard Stringer has called him "the leader of a new Napoleonic era of communications." Now in his late 70s, Murdoch is training his children to take over for him.

Murdoch began by acquiring several British newspapers and then some in the United States. He bought the venerable U.S. book publisher Harper & Row, which he rechristened HarperCollins to fit with his British publishing interests. To qualify to own U.S. television stations, he became a U.S. citizen. That, in the 1980s, allowed him to create Fox as the fourth U.S. television network, which some said couldn't be done, and dovetail it with his recently acquired 20th Century Fox movie and television production studio. He bought the parent company of *TV Guide*. He created the Sky and Star satellite systems in Britain and Asia. Two-thirds of the world's population—3 billion people—watch Star! TV, which shows programming that Murdoch's

company creates or buys. In 2003 he acquired DIRECTV, the major U.S. satellite television delivery service.

The expansion gave Murdoch the components to establish the first global system for content creation and delivery under a single corporate umbrella. This is the Murdochian significance—a grip on distribution that competitors don't have. Critic James Fallows cited how the Murdoch media empire synchronizes production, publicity and support: "They supply the content—Fox movies (*Titanic, The Full Monty, There's Something about Mary*), Fox TV shows (*The Simpsons, Ally McBeal, When Animals Attack*), Fox-controlled sports broadcasts, plus newspapers and books. They sell the content to the public and to advertisers—in newspapers, on the broadcast network, on cable channels. And they operate the physical distribution system through which the content reaches the customers." Murdoch's satellite systems distribute News Corporation content in Europe and Asia.

Critics fret that Murdoch media control too much of the world's media content and note that News Corp. entities have a politically conservative slant. Murdoch calls that balderdash. Using early 2004 data, he once pointed to U.S. talk radio, in which he has no part, and noted how lopsided it is, with 300-plus hours of nationally syndicated conservative talk a week versus five hours of liberal talk. The media, himself included, Murdoch says, merely offer what people want: "Apparently conservative talk is more popular."

FOREIGN BRANCHES. A new awareness of potential markets abroad came in the 1930s, typified by the *Reader's Digest*'s first foray overseas. The magazine, born in the United States in 1922, had obvious international potential. In 1938 publishers DeWitt and Lila Wallace established a British edition. It was largely the same as the U.S. edition, but British editors replaced some articles. Today, the magazine is published in 18 languages. Some editions are extensively edited for distinct audiences.

ACQUISITIONS. Another model for international media companies emerged in the 1980s. Media companies began buying up foreign media companies. Bertelsmann of Germany bought its way into many foreign markets. Acquisitions included the RCA and Arista record labels in the United States, then 14 women's magazines bought from *The New York Times,* then the venerable U.S. book company Random House.

MERGERS. Some media companies have found synergies in merging. A merger of Hachette of France and Filipacchi of Italy created cross-fertilization opportunities that generated more profits from existing products. The new company also exported concepts, such as the French fashion magazine *Elle* being adapted for additional markets, including the United States.

ALLIANCES. Most media companies rely on other companies for foreign distribution of their content. Viacom, for example, sells its television programs to existing networks and stations in other countries. Several magazine publishers have agreements with native companies to produce and distribute foreign editions.

CONTENT-DISTRIBUTION MODEL. Media mogul **Rupert Murdoch,** known mostly for his 20th Century/Fox movie and Fox television empires, has moved media globalization into new directions by combining media content-creation companies and content-distribution companies under a super-corporate umbrella. Murdoch's orbiting satellite companies, including BSkyB, DIRECTV and Star! TV, beam signals directly to consumers, bypassing traditional delivery media. With 20th Century and Fox, he also generates content to supply his delivery system—no middlemen.

THE INTERNET AND GLOBALIZATION

New technologies are opening the way for more companies to seek global audiences directly, with no middlemen, at low cost. E-books, for example, don't require expensive presses to produce. Nor do they need massive warehouses or require expensive shipping. Producers of radio and television programs can use streaming instead of having to negotiate complex deals with networks or individual stations for distribution. In short, the internet can eliminate middlemen.

Easy access to the internet opens opportunities for upstarts to reach global audiences. Whether new companies can establish internet followings that compete with the majors, which also have created presences on the web, isn't clear. With the massiveness of their repertoires, the major players certainly have a leg up.

Effects of Globalization

Study Preview   *Foreign ownership worries some media critics. At stake, as these critics see it, is control of the direction of cultural advancement—something they believe should not be farmed out.*

CULTURAL SUBVERSIVENESS

Experts disagree about the effect of globalization. Some critics, including respected media commentator Ben Bagdikian, fret that "anonymous superpowers" such as Bertelsmann are a potential threat to U.S. cultural autonomy and the free flow of information and ideas. In his book *The New Media Monopoly,* Bagdikian said: "The highest levels of world finance have become intertwined with the highest levels of mass media ownership, with the result of tighter control over the systems on which most of the public depends for its news and information."

Other observers, such as Toni Heinzl and Robert Stevenson at the University of North Carolina, note that many global media companies, including Bertelsmann, have learned to let their local operating companies adapt to local cultures: "Following a global strategy, it is the company's policy to respect the national characteristics and cultural traditions in each of the more than two dozen countries in which it operates. It is impossible to detect even hints of German culture from the product lineup of Bertelsmann's companies abroad. Targeting specific preference of a national public or audience, the company has custom-tailored its products for each country: French culture in France, Spanish culture in Spain, American culture in the United States, and so on." The target is growth.

CORPORATE IDEOLOGY

By and large the agenda of media conglomerates is profits and nothing more. They do not promote ideology. U.S. moviegoers did not see Japanese overtones in Columbia movies or CBS records after the Sony takeover or in MCA products after the Matsushita takeover. At the same time it cannot be ignored that Bertelsmann tried to transplant its successful German geographic magazine *Geo* in the United States in 1979, only to give it up two years and $50 million later when it realized that *National Geographic*'s following was unshakable. In the same vein Murdoch imported British tabloid editors to reshape some of the U.S. newspapers he bought. What can be said with certainty about media globalization is that it is occurring and that observers are divided about its consequences.

Cultural Intrusion

> **Study Preview**   *Some experts claim that the export of U.S. and other Western popular culture is latter-day imperialism motivated by profit and without concern for its effect on other societies. Other experts see charges of cultural imperialism as overblown.*

LATTER-DAY IMPERIALISM

The great concern about media globalization has been about the flow of values not *among* developed countries but *to* developing countries. Critics use the term **cultural imperialism** for this dark side of international communication. Their view is that the media are like the 19th-century European colonial powers, exporting Western values, often uninvited, to other cultures. At stake, these critics say, is the cultural sovereignty of non-Western nations. These critics note the communication flow is one way from the powerful nations to the weak ones. The result, as they see it, is that Western values are imposed in an impossible-to-resist way.

cultural imperialism One culture's dominance of another.

Herbert Schiller Saw Western cultures subsuming others.

Herbert Schiller: Interview with Schiller in *Z Magazine*, from the British Columbia Library Association.
www.vcn.bc.ca/bcla-ip/ governments/schiller.html

Scholar **Herbert Schiller**, who wrote *Mass Communications and American Empire*, argued that the one-way communication flow is especially dangerous because the Western productions, especially movies and television, are so slick that they easily outdraw locally produced programs. As a result, says Schiller, the Western-controlled international mass media pre-empt native culture, a situation he sees as robbery, just like the earlier colonial tapping of natural resources to enrich the home countries.

India is a fascinating recent example of cultural intrusion, if not cultural imperialism. Until 1991 this nation had only one television network, which ran programs that originated in India almost exclusively. Then came Star! TV, Rupert Murdoch's satellite service from Hong Kong, which carried lots of U.S.-originated programming. Writing in *Media Studies Journal*, Shailaja Bajpai, India media critic and editor of an Indian television magazine, offered these observations:

- Many Indians were dressing like the Americans they saw on *Baywatch*.
- While Indian boys once wanted to grow up to be great cricket players, they now wanted to shoot baskets like Yao Ming.

Other anecdotal evidence of U.S. culture rubbing off elsewhere is in South Africa. According to Sebiletso Mokone-Matabane, an executive with the Independent Broadcast Authority there, robbers were shouting "freeze," a word that had no roots in Afrikaans or the indigenous languages, when they stormed into a bank. The robbers had been watching too much U.S. television.

Some media genres translate easily across cultures. Hoping to attract audiences with reality shows, which had been the rage in Europe, Canada and the United States in the early 2000s, Middle Eastern television producers tried a variety of adaptations. Some worked, toned down from their progenitors' risqué edginess. Sex was verboten. Swearing too. No kissing. In *Fear Factor* the female contestants in the swimming stunts wore full-body wet suits. There were no cameras in the showers. The bedrooms in *Big Brother* were off limits to the opposite sex.

U.S. Media Imperialism. Herbert Schiller was one of many media theorists concerned about the influence of American culture on smaller nations.

THE CANADIAN EXPERIENCE WITH CULTURAL INTRUSION

The notion of latter-day imperialism is one of the reasons that the CRTC and the Canadian government have always had some form of content regulations for most Canadian-owned broadcast media. But this fear is not unique to Canada; other countries feel the same way. In fact, many countries look to the CRTC for guidance in how to deal with cultural intrusion. In 1998, the World Trade Organization adopted the so-called "Canadian model of regulation." What this means, according to the CRTC, is that other countries want to "understand how Canada meets public interest goals while encouraging the growth of the private sector."

NON-DOWNWARD MEDIA EXCHANGE

In some ways cultural imperialism is in the eyes of the beholder. Some Latin American countries, for example, scream "cultural imperialism" at the United States but don't object when Mexico exports soap operas to the rest of Latin America, as Brazil and Argentina do. Although they are exercising a form of cultural imperialism, nobody puts the label on them. Media observer Larry Lorenz, who has studied this phenomenon, explains it this way: "What is occurring is simply internationalism brought on by the ever more sophisticated media of mass communication."

The cultural imperialism theory has other doubters among scholars. The doubters note that the theory is a simplistic application of the now-discredited hypodermic needle model of mass communication. Media messages do not have immediate direct effects.

EMERGING GLOBAL MEDIA

Concern about Western cultural imperialism is slowly changing as two related things occur. First, the number of international media players, many in neither Europe nor the United States, is increasing. Second, rather than merely recycling domestic products abroad, U.S.-based media companies are creating new, local-oriented content in the countries where they do business.

For generations, prime-time U.S. television shows have been prime-time fare throughout the world, either with subtitles or dubbed awkwardly into local languages. Today, local media people who have mastered Western production techniques are producing local media content. Although production quality in some countries isn't as slick as for U.S. programs, indigenous programs have their own attractions and are siphoning viewers and advertisers from imported fare. Their programs go over big, attracting viewers and advertisers better than imported programs.

Mideast Reality Show. A Saudi Arabian and a Lebanese contestant sing during a live show of the *Star Academy,* one of the first reality shows to air in the Middle East. Other reality shows, many from Lebanon, are modeled on European and U.S. television and have attracted young viewers.

Media Databank

Movie Power

In ranking the most powerful countries for *Newsweek* magazine in 2003, analyst John Spark used movies as one measure. "Hollywood and Bollywood fantasies of the good life shape the desires of billions," he said in offering these data.

Movie Tickets Sold per Year

India	2.9 billion
United States	1.4 billion
Canada	113 million

Film Investment

United States	$14.7 billion
Japan	1.3 billion
India	192 million
Canada	133 million

You can derive additional meaning from these numbers by re-ranking the nations per capita.

Not only is indigenous local programming taking hold in other countries, especially those with a developing middle class, but also many of these emerging media are exporting their material. Throughout Latin America, for example, people watch soap operas produced by TV Globo in Brazil and Televisa in Mexico. The Belgian broadcast company RTL, which once spent most of its programming dollars on imports like *Dallas* and *Dynasty*, now produces most of its own shows. The French TF-1 and Italian Rai Uno television services have cut back substantially on U.S. programs. The turnaround in Europe has been fueled not only by audience preferences for local material but also by a European Union policy that half of each nation's broadcast programming must originate within the EU.

There is also new competition, much of it well financed. In Europe the television service Canal One has teamed up with Bertelsmann of Germany to create a formidable competitor for the whole European audience. TVB in Hong Kong has its eye on dominating media fare to China, Southeast Asia and the Indian subcontinent. What once were easy pickings for U.S. media companies are now tough markets.

Although more media content is being originated in home countries, some critics say, "Don't be fooled." Shailaja Bajpai says that Indian TV producers clone U.S. television: "The American talk show has inspired Indian imitations. Never have so many Indians revealed so much about their private lives to such a wide audience. Every day a new show is planned. If nothing else, American television has loosened tongues (to say nothing of our morals). Subjects long taboo are receiving a good airing." Those Indian programs may be produced in India, but the concept is hardly Indian.

TRANSNATIONAL CULTURAL ENRICHMENT

Some scholars see transnational cultural flow in more benign terms than Herbert Schiller and his fellow cultural imperialism theorists. George Steiner has noted that European and American culture has been enriched, not corrupted, by the continuing presence of Greek mythology over 2000 years.

Sociologist Michael Tracey makes a similar point in a homey way: "I was born in a working-class neighbourhood called Oldham in the north of England. Before the First World War, Oldham produced most of the world's spun cotton. It is a place of mills and chimneys, and I was born and raised in one of the areas of housing— called St. Mary's—built to serve those mills. I recently heard a record by a local group of folk singers called the Oldham Tinkers, and one track was about Charlie Chaplin. This song was apparently very popular with local children in the years immediately after the First World War. Was that evidence of the cultural influences of Hollywood, a primeval moment of the imperialism of one culture, the subjugation of another? It seems almost boorish to think of it that way. Was the little man not a deep well of pleasure through laughter, a pleasure that was simply universal in appeal? Was it not Chaplin's real genius to strike some common chord, uniting the whole of humanity? Is that not, in fact, the real genius of American popular culture, to bind together, better than anything, common humanity?"

Global Media Players

Associated Press: The news any way you want it—read it, watch it or hear it.
www.ap.org

Reuters: News and financial information.
www.reuters.com

Study Preview   *The first media companies to significantly extend their operations abroad were news agencies such as the Associated Press, Reuters and United Press. Today, companies that produce all kinds of media messages, not just news, are engaged in finding global markets.*

NEWS AGENCIES

Hundreds of agencies cover news around the world and sell their accounts to subscribing media organizations. Most of these are national and regional services. The primary global players are Associated Press, Reuters, Agence France-Presse and Interfax.

ASSOCIATED PRESS. **The Associated Press** is the largest news-gathering organization in the world, disseminating 20 million words and 1000-plus images a day. There are 8500 subscribers in 112 countries. The AP, based in New York, has 142 foreign bureaus in 72 countries. The AP is a nonprofit co-operative organization owned by daily newspapers.

REUTERS. **Reuters** serves 6500 media organizations worldwide, including 290 in the United States and Canada. Altogether, counting subscribers to its financial and business news services, Reuters has 27 000 subscribers worldwide. The service is offered in 11 languages. There are 120 bureaus in 80 countries. U.S. video clients include CNN and NBC.

AGENCE FRANCE-PRESSE. Paris-based **Agence France-Presse** was founded by Charles Havas in 1835. Today AFP is the third-largest global agency. AFP has 2000 people in 150 bureaus worldwide, including 850 full-time journalists. Text, photo, audio and video services are transmitted in Arabic, English, French, German, Spanish and Portuguese to 500 newspapers, 350 radio and 200 television clients and to 99 national news agencies that pass AFP stories on to more media outlets.

INTERFAX. This Moscow-based news agency was founded as Tass in 1925. Today, reconstituted and renamed **Interfax**, the agency supplies reports in Russian, English, German, Spanish and Arabic. At its peak, the agency claimed 5500 media and non-media subscribers, but the disintegration of communism and the shriveling of Russian influence has meant inevitable declines.

VIDEO NEWS SERVICES

The major news networks—ABC, CBS, CNN, CBC, CTV, Fox and NBC—prefer to cover foreign stories with their own crews, but they also subscribe to global video services for stories and pictures that they miss. The largest news video suppliers are, not surprisingly, the world's two largest news services: New York–based Associated Press and London-based Reuters.

SYNDICATES

After Union recruiters swept through Baraboo, Wisconsin, and signed up the local boys for the Civil War, **Ansel Nash Kellogg** lacked the staff to get out his four-page Baraboo *Republic,* so he took to borrowing the inside pages of another newspaper. The practice not only saw Kellogg through a staffing crisis, but also sparked an idea to save costs by supplying inside pages at a fee to other short-handed publishers. By 1865 Kellogg was in Chicago providing ready-to-print material for newspapers nationwide. In journalism history Kellogg is remembered as the father of the newspaper **syndicate**.

In the 1880s **S.S. McClure** had a thriving syndicate, putting out 50 000 words a week in timeless features on fashion, homemaking, manners and literature. McClure

---

Associated Press U.S.-based global news service; largest news-gathering organization in the world.

Reuters British-based global news agency.

Agence France-Presse: Available in several languages.
www.afp.com/english/home

Interfax: Providing more than just the news, including extensive databases.
www.interfax.com

AP Broadcast: Associated Press's broadcast news service.
www.apbroadcast.com

Agence France-Presse Paris-based global news agency.

Interfax Russian news agency.

Ansel Nash Kellogg Founded the first syndicate.

syndicates Provide low-cost, high-quality content to many news outlets.

S.S. McClure Expanded syndicate concept.

and other syndicators charged subscribing newspapers a fraction of what each would have to pay to generate such material with its own staff. Features, poetry, opinion and serialized stories by the period's great literary figures, including Jack London, Rudyard Kipling, George Bernard Shaw, Robert Louis Stevenson and Mark Twain, became standard fare in many newspapers through syndication.

Today, syndicates seek international audiences, spreading expenses among more subscribers and building new revenue. Some syndicate material doesn't travel easily, like sophisticated humour columns and comic strips that reflect the traditions, experiences and values of a particular culture.

Universal Press Syndicate: Comics, Dear Abby, and more.

www.amuniversal.com/ups

Global Media Companies

Study Preview   *National origins of companies in the media business are blurring. Sony of Japan owns Columbia Pictures and many leading U.S. record labels under a subsidiary. Sony also owns a share of Time Warner. Bertelsmann of Germany is a big player in U.S. magazines and books. U.S. companies themselves have foreign stakes.*

U.S.-BASED COMPANIES

Five U.S. media rivals have established themselves as major players in other countries.

Time Warner: Get a feel for this award-winning, global media and entertainment company.

www.timewarner.com/corp

Disney: Check out upcoming movies, play games or plan a vacation to a Disney theme park.

http://disney.go.com

Viacom: Learn more about this diverse, hugely successful entertainment company.

www.viacom.com

NBC Universal: Take a sneak peak at NBC TV programs and movies.

www.nbcuni.com

■ **Time Warner.** Time Warner, operating in 70-plus countries, is the world's largest media company, with a value ranging as high as $183 billion. Its CNN can reach a billion people in 212 countries. HBO Olé attracts legions of subscribers in Latin America. Warner Brothers' movies and TV shows are distributed worldwide. *Time* publishes editions in Europe, Latin America and the South Pacific.

■ **Disney-ABC.** When Walt Disney laboured over his primitive animation for *Steamboat Willie* in 1928, he likely didn't dream that his name would forever be attached to a corporate giant. The huge acquisition of ABC in 1995 provided a domestic outlet for Disney Studio productions, which already had gone global. Theme parks in Tokyo, Hong Kong and Paris have added to Disney's world impact.

■ **Viacom.** Viacom began as a syndication arm of CBS but a change in Federal Communications required it to be spun off. Ironically, Viacom made so much money recycling television shows that it acquired back CBS in 2001. Viacom's wildly profitable MTV can be tuned in at 400 million homes in 164 countries. Viacom's Paramount Pictures has a vault of 50 000 hours of television shows for international marketing.

■ **News Corporation.** Beginning with an inherited newspaper in Adelaide, Australia, Rupert Murdoch built a successful chain, then expanded to Europe where he acquired the prestigious *Times* of London. Moving to the United States, Murdoch nabbed 20th Century Fox studios and created the Fox Television Network whose products are distributed by his BSkyB in Europe and STAR TV in Asia. Adding Murdoch's DIRECTV in 2003, there's scarcely a television set in the world that a News Corporation satellite can't reach.

■ **NBC Universal.** In 2004, General Electric's NBC and Vivendi Universal Entertainment closed a merger that created the fifth-largest media conglomerate, NBC Universal. NBC's television network and cable channels, including Telemundo, joined with Universal's studios and theme parks, and Vivendi's A&M, Geffen, PolyGram and Motown labels. Wall Street figures net assets of the new company at $42 billion.

Non-U.S. Companies

Once U.S. media companies held the commanding lead for overseas markets, but homegrown companies are pumping out more content all the time. Some of these companies have become global players themselves.

Bertelsmann: Media worldwide.

www.bertelsmann.com

Hachette Filipacchi: The U.S. division.

www.hfmus.com/ HachetteUSA/ noflash/index.html

TVB: Hong Kong satellite service.

www.tvb.com

TV Globo: Brazilian media company.

http://tvglobointernacional .globo.com

Televisa: Media giant from Mexico.

www.esmas .com/televisahome

Pearson: Educating and entertaining all ages.

www.pearson.com

Reed Elsevier: Providing information to professionals around the world.

www.reed-elsevier.com

- **Bertelsmann.** The German company Bertelsmann established itself globally as a book and magazine company. It has 200 subsidiaries in 25 countries, many of them operating under the name they had when Bertelsmann acquired them. In the United States these include Random House, Bantam, Dell and Doubleday books. The company's U.S. interests, jointly owned with Sony since 2003, include RCA Records.
- **Hachette Filipacchi.** The French-Italian company Hachette Filipacchi publishes 74 magazines in 10 countries. This includes the 4.5 million circulation *Woman's Day,* which Hachette acquired when it bought the CBS magazine empire in 1988. Another Hachette magazine in the United States is the fashion magazine *Elle*.
- **Televisa.** Throughout Latin America, people watch soap operas, called *telenovelas*. Most of these originate from Televisa, a Mexican media giant.
- **TVB.** Hong Kong-based TVB has started an Asian television-satellite service. This company has plenty to put on the satellite. Its production runs about 6000 hours a year in both Cantonese and Mandarin.
- **TV Globo.** A Brazilian media company, TV Globo, true to its name, has developed a global audience. Its telenovelas air in all the Spanish-speaking and Portuguese-speaking countries and beyond, including China.
- **Pearson.** Once a British newspaper company, Pearson has sold its papers, except the *Financial Times,* to concentrate on book publishing. One subsidiary, Pearson Education, is the largest educational publisher in the United States. Pearson's trade-book imprints include Penguin.
- **Reed Elsevier.** An Anglo-Dutch conglomerate, Reed Elsevier owns the Lexis-Nexis online legal news reference service and publishes more academic journals than any other company. Worldwide, Reed has 36 000 employees. A major revenue source is library subscriptions to its online journals. The California state university library system alone pays $7 million to $8 million a year for Reed journals in an online format.

Distinctive Media Systems

BBC: Listen to the BBC live online.

www.bbc.co.uk

Study Preview   *National systems for operating mass media take many forms. Some are modest variations, like the British and Japanese methods to fund broadcasting. Dictatorships have wholly different infrastructures that determine content.*

Britain

Almost everybody has heard of the BBC, Britain's venerable public service radio and television system. Parliament created the British Broadcasting Corporation in 1927 as a government-funded entity that, despite government support, would have as much programming autonomy as possible. The idea was to avoid private ownership and to give the enterprise the prestige of being associated with the crown. The government appoints a 12-member board of governors, which runs BBC. Although the government has the authority to remove members of the board, it never has. BBC has developed largely independently of the politics of the moment, which has given

Bollywood World: All the latest music, movie and celebrity news out of Bollywood.

www.bollywoodworld.com

it a credibility and stature that are recognized worldwide. The Beeb, as BBC is affectionately known, is financed through an annual licensing fee, about $230, on television receivers.

BBC is known for its global news coverage. It has 250 full-time correspondents, compared to CNN's 113. The Beeb's reputation for first-rate dramatic and entertainment programs is known among English-speaking people everywhere. The great issue today is whether the BBC should leave the government fold. Advocates of privatization argue that BBC could exploit its powerful brand name better if it were privatized. The privatization advocates say that BBC's government ties are keeping it from aggressively pursuing partnerships to make it a global competitor with companies like Time Warner and Rupert Murdoch's News Corporation. But continuing to do business as always, they say, will leave the Beeb in everybody else's dust.

INDIA

Bollywood Nickname for India movie industry.

The world's largest democracy, India has a highly developed movie industry that took root by providing affordable entertainment to mass audiences when the country was largely impoverished. The industry, called **Bollywood**, a contrivance of its historic roots in Bombay and the U.S. movie capital Hollywood, is adapting as India moves rapidly out of its Third World past. Today India is becoming a model for new media applications, like Wi-Fi, as the country brings itself into modern times.

Bollywood. The Indian movie industry, centred in Bombay and sometimes called Bollywood, pumps out an incredible 1200 movies a year. Although India has some internationally recognized moviemakers, most Bollywood productions are formulaic action movies that critics derisively label "curry westerns."

QUESTIONS FOR REVIEW

1. How do media organizations make money to stay in business?
2. Define demassification, convergence and conglomeration. What effects are they having on the mass media?
3. How do gatekeepers and regulators influence media messages? How are they different from each other?
4. What ideology do global media companies export?
5. What is the negative connotation of Herbert Schiller's term "cultural imperialism"?
6. How does media globalization work against indigenous and distinctive media content?
7. Is it a problem when values from dominant cultures subsume those of other cultures?
8. How have global news agencies affected nations they cover for the rest of the world?
9. Where are the major global media companies based?

QUESTIONS FOR CRITICAL THINKING

1. Which is more important to the Canadian mass media: profits or doing social good?
2. Which mass media rely directly on consumer purchases for their economic survival? Advertising provides almost all the revenue for commercial radio and television stations, but indirectly consumer purchases are an important factor. In what way?
3. Do we need the CRTC to regulate broadcasting in the 21st century?
4. What can be expected if global consolidation of mass media companies continues?
5. Assess the view that "cultural imperialism" is a loaded term that misses an enriching aspect of transnational communication.
6. Is human civilization moving toward a monolithic culture?
7. Assess the criticism of some Third World leaders that news agencies like AP and Reuters are lackeys of the government in the country where they're based.
8. Why are the biggest global media companies based mostly in the United States and Europe?

KEEPING UP TO DATE

Scholarly discussion on the communication process can be found in *Communication Yearbook*, published since 1977, and *Mass Communication Review Yearbook*, published since 1986.

The *Journal of Communication* and *The Canadian Journal of Communication* are quarterly scholarly publications.

FOR FURTHER LEARNING

Ken Auletta. *Three Blind Mice: How the TV Networks Lost Their Way* (Random House, 1991).

Ben Bagdikian. *The Media Monopoly*, Fifth edition (Beacon, 1997).

Ben H. Bagdikian. "Special Issue: The Lords of the Global Village." *The Nation* 248 (June 12, 1989): 23, 805–20.

Erik Barnouw and others. *Conglomerates and the Media* (The New Press, 1998).

Roland Barthes. *Mythologies* (Paladin, 1973).

Paul Benedetti and Nancy DeHart. *On McLuhan: Forward Through the Rear View Mirror* (Prentice Hall, 1996).

Arthur Asa Berger. *Media USA: Process and Effect* (Longman, 1988).

"Broadcasters Must Be Canadian: Greenberg." *Broadcaster Magazine Alert* (March 9, 2004).

Andrew Cardozo. "Big Applications and the CRTC." *Broadcast Dialogue* (October 2006): 6.

Benjamin M. Compaine and Douglas Gomery. *Who Owns the Media? Competition and Concentration in the Mass Media Industry*, Third edition (Erlbaum, 2000).

CRTC. *Broadcast Policy Monitoring Report 2006*.

John Fiske. *Introduction to Communication Studies* (Routledge, 1990).

Matthew Fraser. "How Much Con in Convergence?" *National Post* (July 30, 2001).

Matthew Fraser. "Iron Law Brought Us Convergence, Heaven's Gate." *National Post* (June 11, 2001).

Thomas Friedman. *The World Is Flat: A Brief History of the 21st Century* (Farrar, Straus & Giroux, 2005).

Laurel Hyatt. "Letting the Genie out of the Bottle." *Broadcaster Magazine* (March 2001).

Harold Innis. *Empire and Communications* (Oxford Press, 1950).

Daphne Lavers. "deKerckhove." *Broadcast Dialogue* (September 1999).

Robert Lichter, Linda S. Richter and Stanley Rothman. *Watching America: What Television Tells Us about Our Lives* (Prentice Hall, 1991).

Stephen W. Littlejohn. *Theories of Human Communication*, Third edition (Wadsworth, 1989).

Michelle Martin. *Mainstream Models in Mass Communication Research from Communication and Mass Media: Culture, Domination and Opposition* (Prentice Hall Canada, 1997).

Eric McLuhan and Frank Zingrone. *Essential McLuhan* (Anansi, 1995).

Marshall McLuhan. *The Gutenberg Galaxy: The Making of Typographical Man* (University of Toronto Press, 1967).

Marshall McLuhan. *Understanding Media* (Signet, 1964).

Denis McQuail. *Mass Communication Theory* (Sage, 1987).

Denis McQuail and Sven Windahl. *Communication Models for the Study of Mass Communication* (Longman, 1981).

Mark Crispin Miller. "Can Viacom's Reporters Cover Viacom's Interests?" *Columbia Journalism Review* (November–December 1999): 48–50.

Mark Crispin Miller. "Free the Media." *Nation* (June 3, 1996): 9–28.

Glen O'Farrell. "What's to Become of Canadian Media?" *Broadcast Dialogue* (November 2006): 6.

Tara Perkins and Rick Westhead. "CanWest Buying Alliance." *Toronto Star* (January 11, 2007).

Sumner Redstone with Peter Knobler. *A Passion to Win* (Simon & Schuster, 2001).

Grant Robertson. "Biggest Risk in Alliance Deal is Global TV's Performance: Asper." *The Globe and Mail* (January 11, 2007).

Anthony Smith. *The Age of the Behemoths: The Globalization of Mass Media Firms* (Priority Press, 1991).

Susan Sontag. "One Culture and New Sensibility." *Against Interpretation* (Farrar, Straus & Giroux, 1966).

Bohdan Szuchewycz and Jeannette Sloniowski, eds. *Canadian Communications*, Second edition (Prentice Hall Canada, 2001).

Alexis S. Tan. *Mass Communication Theories and Research* (Macmillan, 1986).

James R. Taylor. "The Office of the Future: Weber and Innis Revisited." *Communications in Canadian Society*, Benjamin Singer, ed. (Addison-Wesley, 1983).

Kevin G. Wilson. "The Rise and Fall of Teleglobe." Montreal *Gazette* (May 18, 2002).

Samuel P. Winch. *Mapping the Cultural Space of Journalism: How Journalists Distinguish News from Entertainment* (Praeger, 1998).

Tony Wong. "Redrawing the Media Map." *Toronto Star* (July 13, 2006).

Antonia Zerbisias. "Ready or Not, CRTC Takes on Media Convergence." *Toronto Star* (April 14, 2001).

Wordless Society Ahead?
No, says futurist George Gilder, not even the generation raised on MTV can communicate effectively without words. Visuals can enhance but not replace them, he says.

MEDIA TIMELINE

The Printed Word

1844	George Brown founded *The Globe and Mail*.
1905	*Busy Man's Magazine*, which would eventually be renamed *Maclean's*, was founded by John Baynes Maclean.
1955	Bohemian New York literati founded *The Village Voice*.
1956	O'Leary Commission looked at magazine publishing in Canada.
1967	Jim Michaels founded the Los Angeles–based *Advocate*, the first gay newspaper.
1970	Davey Committee examined Canadian newspapers.
1981	Kent Commission: more investigation of Canadian newspaper ownership.
1996	Magazines went online with Pathfinder and Time Warner. Others followed.
1998	Conrad Black launched the *National Post*.
2001	CanWest Global purchased the *National Post* from Conrad Black.
2001	Bell Globemedia, now known as CTVglobemedia, converged broadcasting and print.

Print

Media in Theory

Wordless Society Ahead? Not Likely

Do newspapers and other word-based print media have a future? In a variation of Canadian Marshall McLuhan's "the medium is the message" theory, media seer **George Gilder** puts his money on word-based media over television, which relies on visuals to tell stories.

Futurist George Gilder says that not even the generation raised on MTV can communicate effectively without words. Visuals can enhance words, but not replace them, he says. As Gilder sees it, people who see the communication of the future as primarily video have missed the fact that video works better than words for only an extremely narrow range of messages: "Video is most effective in conveying shocks and sensations and appealing to prurient interests of large miscellaneous audiences. Images easily excel in blasting through to the glandular substances of the human community; there's nothing like a body naked or bloody or both to arrest the eye." However, human communication goes far beyond shock scenes and sensual appeals, he says, noting that people communicate mostly through words.

The printed product you receive on your doorstep every morning may seem like a technological dinosaur from Johannes Gutenberg's time. The fact, however, is that newspapers are well into the digital age. Reporters dip into digitized data for source material and write stories on computers. Editors edit stories and lay out pages electronically. It is in final production that old technology reigns, with multi-million-dollar presses that consume tons and tons of newsprint and barrels and barrels of ink. In delivery too, with minimum-wage carriers entrusted to get the product to readers, newspapers lag.

That is changing. In the vanguard of changing to electronic production, rather than printing, and to electronic delivery, rather than "carriers and the local newsstand," are newspapers ranging from modest circulation weeklies to major dailies. Some online editions offer only word-for-word versions of what is in the print editions or only selected stories, but some newspapers are repackaging stories to take advantage of opportunities that the internet offers. That includes online videos, podcasts and **blogs**. Still, true to their tradition, the online newspapers remain word-based. Visuals are a useful accoutrement but seldom the heart of the message.

George Gilder Claims wordless society not on the horizon and that words do much to anchor meaning.

blog An amateur website, generally personal in nature, often focused on a narrow subject, such as politics. Short for "web log."

Importance of Newspapers

Study Preview   *Newspapers are the primary mass medium from which people receive news. In most cities no other news source comes close to the local newspaper's range and depth of coverage. This contributes to the popularity and influence of newspapers.*

NEWSPAPER INDUSTRY DIMENSIONS

The newspaper industry dwarfs other news media by almost every measure. More than half of all adult Canadians read a newspaper every day. The data are staggering:

- 100 daily newspapers put out 4.7 million copies a day in Canada. Including weekend editions, 31 million daily newspapers are sold in Canada each week. In the United States there are 1570 daily newspapers.
- Weekly newspapers in Canada publish 12.8 million copies each week; 74 percent of Canadians read their local weekly newspaper.

Sources: The Canadian Newspaper Association's Canadian Daily Newspaper Circulation Data 2007 and Canadian Community Newspapers Association's Snapshot 2007.

Perhaps because television has stolen the glitz and romance that newspapers once had, the significance of newspapers is easy to miss. But the newspaper industry is large by every measure. In an article marveling at an issue of a newspaper as "the daily creation," *The Washington Post*'s Richard Harwood, writing about his own newspaper, said, "Roughly 11 000 people are involved in the production and distribution each day, enough bodies to fill all the billets of an Army light infantry division." Although Harwood stretched to include even the delivery boys and girls in his startling number, his point is valid: newspapers far outdistance other news media in the number of people who gather, edit and disseminate news.

There is no foreign ownership of Canadian newspapers. According to the Income Tax Act, a newspaper is Canadian if the type is set in Canada, it is printed in Canada, and it is published by Canadians.

CONTENT DIVERSITY AND DEPTH

In most communities, newspapers cover more news at greater depth than competing media. A metropolitan daily such as *The Vancouver Province* may carry hundreds of items—more than any British Columbia television or radio station and at greater length. Magazines, for example, offer more depth on selected stories, but the magazines are published relatively infrequently and run relatively few articles.

Newspapers have a rich mix of content—news, advice, comics, opinion, puzzles and data. It's all there to tap into at will. Some people go right for the stock market tables, others to sports or a favourite columnist. Unlike radio and television, you don't have to wait for what you want.

All this does not mean that the newspaper industry is not facing problems from competing media, new technology and ongoing lifestyle shifts. But to date, newspapers have reacted to change with surprising effectiveness. To offset television's inroads, newspapers have put new emphasis on being a visual medium and have shed their drab graphics for colour and aesthetics. To accommodate the work schedule transition in recent decades from factory jobs starting at 7 a.m. to service jobs starting at 9 a.m., newspapers have emphasized morning editions, now that more people have a little extra time in the morning, and phased out afternoon editions, because more people are at work later in the day. Knowing that the days of ink-on-paper technology are limited,

Cool Medium? The Canadian Newspaper Association's 1998 advertising campaign seems to be saying something about the value of reading a newspaper. Referring to the ideas of McLuhan discussed in Chapter 1, are newspapers a "hot" or "cool" medium?

Media Databank

Who Owns What?

The landscape has changed dramatically since the Kent Commission in 1981. Most newspapers in Canada today are owned by one of fourteen different companies, many of them converged, multi-platform media companies. Newspapers are listed in terms of percent share of weekly circulation:

Owner	% Share of Weekly Circulation	Total Number of Papers
CanWest Publications	28%	13
Quebecor/Sun Media/Osprey	26%	37
Torstar	13.9%	4
Power Corporation	9.8%	7
CTVglobemedia	7.1%	1
FP CNLP	3.5%	2
Transcontinental	3.1%	11
Halifax-Herald News	2.2%	1
Brunswick News	2.1%	3
Glacier Canadian Newspapers	1.6%	9

In 2006, there were only four independently owned and operated newspapers in Canada: *L'Acadie Nouvelle* in Caraquet, *Le Devoir* in Montreal, *The Reminder* in Flin Flon, and the *Whitehorse Star*. Their combined circulation represented 0.9 percent of weekly newspaper circulation.

Source: Canadian Newspaper Association, Canadian Daily Newspaper Circulation Data 2007.

electronic delivery Sending news to readers' computer screens.

Canadian Newspaper Association: All the facts that are fit to print about Canadian daily newspapers. **www.cna-acj.ca**

Canadian Community Newspapers Association (CCNA): The national voice for community newspapers in Canada. **www.ccna.ca**

broadsheet A newspaper format with full-size pages; typically six columns wide and 22 or 24 inches long.

the newspaper industry is examining **electronic delivery** methods for the 21st century. For example, in 2006, the *Toronto Star* began publishing an electronic afternoon edition that was delivered right to the subscriber's email inbox.

Some problems are truly daunting, such as the aversion of many young people to newspapers. Also, chain ownership has raised fundamental questions about how well newspapers can do their work and still meet the profit expectations of distant shareholders.

Newspaper Products

Study Preview   *Over years, the size and formats of newspapers grew as printing technologies improved and paper and printing supplies became plentiful. In recent years the size has progressively shrunk as paper costs have risen and tastes have changed.*

BROADSHEETS

The first modern newspapers in the penny press period (see Chapter 8) were pint size. Ben Day's pioneering *New York Sun* of 1833 was the size of a handbill. Canada's first newspaper, *The Halifax Gazette*, founded in 1752, was about half the size of a sheet of foolscap paper. As large, steam-powered presses were introduced and as paper supplies became plentiful, page sizes grew into what came to be called **broadsheets**. Some were so wide that pages had nine two-inch columns per page, although 50-inch paper, folded into 25-inch wide pages, became standard until the 1980s.

Media Databank

Top Newspapers in Canada

Here are the top newspapers in Canada, ranked by weekly circulation, according to the Canadian Newspaper Association. Note the impact of conglomeration and convergence in terms of the ownership groups.

Newspaper	Weekly Circulation	Ownership Group
Toronto Star	3.3 million	Torstar
The Globe and Mail	2 million	CTVglobemedia
Le Journal de Montréal	1.9 million	Quebecor/Sun Media/Osprey
La Presse (Montreal)	1.5 million	Power Corporation
Toronto Sun	1.4 million	Quebecor/Sun Media
National Post	1.2 million	CanWest Publications
The Vancouver Sun	1 million	CanWest Publications
The Gazette (Montreal)	974 000	CanWest Publications
Ottawa Citizen	920 000	CanWest Publications
Winnipeg Free Press	886 000	FP CNLP

Source: Canadian Newspaper Association, Canadian Daily Newspaper Circulation Data 2007.

To save costs, the newspaper industry settled on a trimmer new size, called SAU, short for **standard advertising unit**, in the 1980s. The SAU format made it easier for big advertisers to place ads in multiple papers, all with standardized dimensions. The introduction of SAU precipitated an almost universal change to a six-column format, in contrast with the formerly dominant eight-column format. The saving in newsprint cost was significant. A downside was that there was less room for news and other content.

TABLOIDS

The word **tabloid** has a second-rate connotation from papers featuring eye-catching but tawdry headlines, but newspaper people use the word in a clinical sense for a half-size newspaper that is convenient to hold. Ironically, considering the association of the words *tabloid* and *sensationalism*, none of the papers in the sensationalistic yellow press period (which you will read about in Chapter 8) were tabloids—with the exception of a one-day experiment by New York publisher Joseph Pulitzer on the first day of the 20th century to illustrate the newspaper of the future.

In recent years, with continuing readership declines, especially among young adults, newspaper executives have discovered through surveys that people prefer compact newspapers. The world's leading newspaper designer, **Mario Garcia**, is traversing the country and the globe for comprehensive redesigns. Garcia's team is making two to three broadsheet-to-tabloid conversions a month. Laura Gordon, in charge of a Dallas *Morning News* tabloid variation called *Quick*, makes the point that tabloids are portable in ways that broadsheets aren't: "We call it the Taco Test, the idea that you can have a newspaper open and have a taco at Taco Bell without going into other people's space."

The tabloid format is gaining popularity in Canada. Many Canadian newspapers are changing formats. In 2006, 82 Canadian papers were broadsheets; the other 18 were tabloids. These 18 tabloids accounted for about a quarter of total newspaper circulation in Canada. This trend toward tabloids is expected to continue.

Still, the word *tabloid* carries a stigma. Garcia said in an interview with the trade journal *Editor & Publisher* that one of his newspaper publisher clients wanted a tabloid prototype designed but couldn't handle the word *tabloid*: "He told me, 'You can do a tabloid—but don't call it a tabloid.'" Alternatives include *compact newspaper* and *laptop newspaper*.

NEWSPAPER PRODUCTION

The Industrial Revolution, which began mechanizing manufacturing in the 1600s, reached the newspaper industry in the mid-1800s. Steam-powered presses became the rage. And paper, suddenly manufactured in rolls, not sheets, made press runs of thousands of copies an hour possible. Although the process has been refined, newspaper

standard advertising unit (SAU) A trimmer newspaper broadsheet format with standardized dimensions; introduced in the 1980s.

tabloid A newspaper format with pages half the size of a broadsheet; typically five columns wide and 14 to 18 inches long; *tab* for short; not necessarily sensationalistic despite a connotation the term has acquired.

Mario Garcia Newspaper design expert who champions tabloid formats.

Mario Garcia. On the cutting edge of newspaper design. He has transformed many newspapers from broadsheets to tabloids. He believes that the layout and design of the newspaper, like the content itself, should "tell a story."

Garcia Media: The design firm started by Mario Garcia to help clients develop effective visual tools and communication strategies. www.mariogarcia.com

Q and A with Mario Garcia: Online interview with Garcia from The Poynter Institute. www.poynter.org/content/content_view.asp?id=48680

Le Soleil: This Quebec City newspaper converted to the tabloid format in 2006. www.cyberpresse.ca/section/CPSOLEIL

Smudgy Heritage. The word *tabloid* is correct for any newspaper with half-size pages, but it picked up an unseemly connotation. The **New York** *Daily News*, launched in 1919, dwelled on sensational stories and flashy headlines that shouted for street sales—as with its exclusive, unauthorized photo of Ruth Snyder, the first woman executed in U.S. history. The word *tabloid* was sullied by papers like the *Daily News* that focused on the bizarre and sensational.

New York Daily News
Founded 1919; its focus on the bizarre defined *tabloid* in public thinking as a word for sensationalism.

presses today, more than 150 years later, use the same technology—huge presses at central locations running hour after hour to get each day's issue into distribution. It's all labour intensive. Distribution itself is complex and also labour intensive—getting papers dropped at thousands of individual delivery points by, say, 6:30 a.m.

Digital printing may change all this. Instead of trucks fanning out at predawn from a single giant printing plant with hundreds of thousands of copies of the day's paper, imagine something like photocopiers scattered throughout the paper's circulation area. Each machine spits out only a few hundred copies.

Richard Rinehart, operations executive at the Raleigh, North Carolina, *News & Observer*, sees lots of untapped potential in digital printing beyond the economics. Digital printers at scattered sites, he says, can be programmed to augment their local news with subscriber-chosen add-ons—regional grocery ads included for 617 Maple Street, sports news and comics for 618, financial news and classified ads for 619, and so on.

Newspaper Chain Ownership

Study Preview   *Through the 20th century, newspapers have been incredibly profitable, which, for better or worse, encouraged chain ownership. Today, chains own most North American newspapers.*

TREND TOWARD CHAINS

Reasoning that he could multiply profits by owning multiple newspapers, **William Randolph Hearst** put together a chain of big-city newspapers in the late 1880s. Although Hearst's chain was not the first, his empire became the model in the public's mind for much that was both good and bad about **newspaper chains**. Like other chains, Hearst's expanded into magazines, radio and television. The trend toward chain ownership continues, and today 160 chains own four of every five dailies in the United States. Chain ownership is also coming to dominate weeklies, which had long been a bastion of independent ownership.

Is chain ownership good? The question raised in Hearst's time was whether diverse points of view were as likely to get into print if ownership were concentrated in fewer and fewer hands. While **local autonomy** is consistent with North American journalistic values, a corporate focus on profits raises a dark new question: Are chains so myopic about profits that they forget good journalism? These are the types of questions that were the basis of two royal commissions in Canada.

In 1970, a special Senate committee on the status of the mass media in Canada, headed by Senator Keith Davey, released its report about the state of Canadian newspapers. Part of the rationale for the **Davey Committee** was the growing concern regarding concentration of newspaper ownership in Canada. In its report, the committee noted that "the media is passing into fewer and fewer hands, and that the experts agree that this trend is likely to continue." The commission made many recommendations, including the creation of a press ownership review board, which would monitor ownership changes and proposed mergers. The government's reaction was lukewarm at best, and such a board was never created.

A little more than 10 years later, the situation had not improved. Ownership of Canada's newspapers, particularly in Quebec, had fallen into fewer and fewer hands. The 1981 **Kent Commission** into newspaper ownership in Canada, headed by Tom Kent, came about following an incident that was too convenient to be coincidental. On the same day in August 1980, the *Ottawa Journal*, which had been publishing for 94 years and was owned by the Thomson chain, and *The Winnipeg Tribune*, 90 years old and owned by the Southam chain, closed their doors and ceased publication, leaving Winnipeg and Ottawa as one-newspaper towns. Each city still had a daily newspaper—the *Winnipeg Free Press*, owned by Thomson, and the *Ottawa Citizen*, owned by Southam. Within a week, the Kent Commission was born. Its mandate was to look into the state of newspapers in Canada and to propose a course of action for the government. In a multi-volume report, the Kent Commission made the following recommendations:

- No owner could control more than 5 percent of Canada's total newspaper circulation.
- No owner could own more than five newspapers.
- No owner could own more than one newspaper within a radius of 500 kilometres.
- To stop the trend toward chains, several, including Thomson, would be ordered to "divest" themselves of some of their newspaper holdings.

William Randolph Hearst Chain owner who dictated contents of all his newspapers.

newspaper chain Company that owns several newspapers.

local autonomy Independence from chain headquarters.

Davey Committee 1970 Royal Commission into media ownership.

Kent Commission 1981 Royal Commission into newspaper ownership.

As was the case with the Davey Committee, the Kent Commission's suggestions died before becoming law. In 1984, while the Newspaper Act was being debated in Parliament, an election was held. When Parliament reconvened, the bill died.

Why all the concern about **concentration of ownership** in Canada? After all, in a capitalist society, one should be able to venture into any enterprise one wants to. While the players have changed in the last 25 years, both Davey and Kent leave us with the following points to think about when discussing the effects of concentration of ownership in a democracy:

concentration of ownership
Conglomeration and convergence of media into fewer and fewer hands.

■ News is a product that needs a variety of voices to be produced. Without this variety, newspapers "become more alike, less individual, less distinctive."

■ As newspapers become part of a large corporation, the people who run them likely won't have a background in journalism but will have a background in business or management. Given this scenario, profits become more important than editorial content and the news-gathering and writing process.

■ Too much power in too few hands contradicts the role of the press in a democracy. Concentration of press ownership in Canada may mean power without accountability.

■ While it's true that newspapers face competition from radio and television, it's newspapers that have traditionally been used to record history.

The last word on this issue goes to David Estok of the University of Western Ontario: "The Kent Commission now seems quaint and old-fashioned, resembling a different time and place. But the issues it raised about media ownership, diversity of opinion and political and cultural control of our communications industries are as relevant as ever."

National Dailies

Study Preview   *Although a nation of mostly local newspapers, Canada has two firmly established dailies.*

George Brown Founded *The Globe and Mail.*

Conrad Black Founded the *National Post.*

The Globe and Mail:
Canada's oldest national daily newspaper.
www.theglobeandmail.com

National Post: Browse the latest news or subscribe to the paper's online edition. You can also access CanWest's TV and radio properties through this website.
www.nationalpost.com

THE GLOBE AND MAIL

The Globe and Mail was founded in 1844 in Toronto by Scottish immigrant **George Brown**. Although labeled as politically conservative, Brown was also somewhat of a publishing innovator. He expanded the format of the paper, and *The Globe* began publishing daily in 1853. He also published a weekly edition for readers living outside of Toronto. He was rewarded for his efforts; by 1872, circulation had almost tripled to 45 000. By the end of the 19th century, it had increased to 80 000. *The Globe* merged with the *Mail and Empire* in November 1936.

In 2001, *The Globe and Mail* became part of the multimedia platform owned by Bell Globemedia, now known as CTVglobemedia. It's still a widely read and respected paper, with circulation of about 2 million weekly.

NATIONAL POST

For a relatively new newspaper, the *National Post* has quite a history. In 1998, **Conrad Black** sold his interest in *The Hamilton Spectator*, *The Record* (Kitchener-Waterloo), the *Guelph Daily Mercury*, and the *Cambridge Reporter* to Sun Media for

80 percent of the *Financial Post* and $150 million. Then, on October 27, 1998, Black's Southam entered the national newspaper sweepstakes when it began publishing the *National Post*.

Then, in the summer of 2000, Canadian media history was made when CanWest Global, a broadcast media giant, paid $3.5 billion for a 50 percent interest in the *National Post*, plus 13 Canadian daily newspapers and 136 smaller newspapers. In the fall of 2001, CanWest purchased the remaining 50 percent interest in the *National Post*.

This new paper became a notable presence in the lucrative southern Ontario market. For example, in Toronto, it competes with *The Globe and Mail*, the *Toronto Star*, and the *Toronto Sun*. Although only in existence a few short years, the *National Post* has clearly established itself as an industry leader.

Hometown Newspapers

Study Preview   *Most newspapers in Canada are considered the voice of their hometown area, covering local news and carrying local advertising. Big-city dailies are the most visible hometown newspapers, but medium-sized and small dailies have made significant strides in quality in recent decades and have eroded the metro newspapers' outlying circulation.*

National Post. In 1998, Canada had its first "National" newspaper when Conrad Black launched the *National Post*. In 2000, Black sold 50 percent of the *Post* to CanWest Global. In 2001, he sold the paper outright to CanWest.

METROPOLITAN DAILIES

In every region of the United States there is a newspaper whose name is a household word. These are metropolitan dailies with extensive regional circulation. Vancouver, Montreal and Toronto feature strong metropolitan newspapers. The following is a snapshot of Canada's leading metropolitan daily, the *Toronto Star*.

TORONTO STAR. The *Toronto Star* not only is a metropolitan daily, but also has the largest daily circulation of any newspaper in Canada: over 400 000 copies. The *Star* was founded in 1892 as the Toronto Star and Publishing Company. Its founding fathers were 21 printers who were on strike (or locked out, depending on who you believe). They had worked for the *Toronto News* until a new typesetting process threatened their jobs. Within days of losing their jobs, they borrowed old printing presses and, with each printer assuming the roles of writer, reporter, ad salesperson, and proofreader, the first *Evening Star* was printed on November 3, 1892. The masthead proclaimed "A paper for the people." It's this incident that gave rise to the *Star* being identified as a "liberal" paper for many years.

Today, the *Star* employs more than 4500 people, including almost 400 people in its newsroom. The *Star*'s press centre produces over 3.2 million newspapers per week, and the *Saturday Star* has a circulation of over 600 000. The *Star* is owned by Torstar Corporation. The company also owns the Metroland Media Group, which includes 105 weekly newspapers and a handful of hometown dailies. They also publish Harlequin Romances.

HOMETOWN DAILIES

hometown daily Edited primarily for readers in a defined region.

With their aggressive reporting on national and regional issues, the metro dailies receive more attention than smaller dailies, but most people read **hometown dailies**. By and large, these locally oriented newspapers, most of them chain-owned, have been incredibly profitable while making significant journalistic progress since World War II.

Fifty years ago, people in small towns generally bought both a metropolitan daily and a local newspaper. Hometown dailies were thin, and coverage was hardly comprehensive. Editorial pages tended to offer only a single perspective. Readers had few alternative sources of information. Since then, these smaller dailies have hired better-prepared journalists, acquired new technology and strengthened their local advertising base.

Challenges for Daily Newspapers

Study Preview   *Even with fairly stable circulation figures, daily newspapers face major challenges. Traditional advertising revenue streams are in transition too. New efficiencies are being realized through shared newsrooms and production facilities and other cost-cutting measures. Is the future of newspapers on the internet? Stay tuned.*

CIRCULATION

Except during the Depression of the 1930s, when almost every sector of the economy suffered, newspapers were among the most consistently profitable businesses of the 20th century. Even with circulation down slightly, the industry has continued to be profitable. Most of the major Canadian chains, which own almost every daily, have reported operating profits in the 13 to 15 percent range over the last few years.

Newspaper companies will survive. They are well positioned to dominate the future of news because, in almost every community, they have the largest, most sophisticated staffs for gathering and telling local news. Even with the benefits of convergence within a media company, that resource is unmatched by even the largest television or other news operation.

How can daily newspapers still be making so much money? In part, it's through cost cutting. Technology has facilitated production cost reductions. In many cases, reporting staffs have been trimmed—at the expense of old standards of news coverage. A monopoly on local readers has allowed local newspapers to adjust advertising rates upward without significant merchant resistance. Also, many papers have gone to narrower pages, which reduce paper costs, a significant raw-material expense. Some papers have compounded newsprint savings by printing fewer pages. But there is a significant downside: less room for news.

ADVERTISING

Retail consolidations have hurt newspaper advertising. Major competing department stores and groceries once were a mainstay of revenue for newspapers. Today this is less so. Chains have bought out their competitors, each acquisition eliminating a major local advertiser.

Also, national advertisers don't look much to newspapers anymore. Statistics Canada reports that national advertising accounts for only about a third of a newspaper's ad revenue; the rest are local ads. Magazines and network television deliver larger and more targeted audiences more cost effectively than general-interest hometown newspapers can. The exception has been **free-standing inserts**, the preprinted, usually slick paper advertising circulars that are tucked into newspapers. These FSIs, as they're called, are about all that's left of national advertising for newspapers. FSIs aren't nearly as lucrative as in-the-regular-paper ads. Newspapers have had to keep their FSI rates low, lest these advertisers find distribution less expensive through the postal system.

free-standing inserts (FSIs) Preprinted advertising circulars inserted in newspapers.

MARKETING DATABASES

As a condition for access to their news websites, a growing number of newspapers is requiring visitors to register. Access is free in exchange for personal information that enables the paper to create a single customer database for print subscribers and email subscribers as well as internet visitors for news and classifieds with breakdowns to identify personal interests.

Aside from selling almanacs and occasional other news-related products, newspapers have kept to their primary business: news. This may need to change if advertising revenue for newspapers declines, as expected, with the already occurring emergence of more competing outlets for advertisers to reach potential customers. As media visionary **Barry Diller** sees it, all of the major mass media will go to direct marketing of their own inventories of consumer products to create revenue streams to replace the loss of traditional advertising. Diller's own operations, including the Home Shopping Network on television, as well as his USA Television Network, already are a prototype for other media, including newspapers, to enter the business of retailing products alongside their traditional news and entertainment content.

Barry Diller Television entrepreneur who sees the mass media's financial future shifting to direct sales of products.

INTERNET TRANSITION

Newspapers got into the ground floor of the internet in the 1990s by establishing news sites. Gradually, newspapers have sold online space as an add-on feature to advertisers that already buy space in the paper. Whether these sites will be a significant avenue for newspaper companies in the future is an open question, especially considering that the cost of admission to create a website is low and that lots of other companies, including local television and radio stations, have established competing sites.

Weekly Newspapers

Study Preview   *Many community weekly newspapers, especially in fast-growing suburbs, are thriving.*

Community News. Suburban weeklies are thriving. Readers appreciate the detailed local coverage, and advertisers like the target market and the relatively low cost of ads.

COMMUNITY WEEKLIES

Weekly newspapers are making strong circulation gains, especially in suburban communities, and some have moved into publishing twice a week. In all, over 600 weekly newspapers are published in Canada, with total weekly circulation approaching 12 million, the majority of them tabloids.

To the discomfort of metro dailies, many advertisers are following their customers to the suburban weeklies. Advertisers have found that they can buy space in weeklies for less and reach their likeliest customers. Ralph Ingersoll, whose weeklies give fits to the daily Long Island *Newsday* in New York, explained it this way in an interview with *Forbes*: "If you're an automobile dealer on Long Island, you can pay, say, $14 000 for a tabloid page in *Newsday*, most of which is wasted because the people that get it will never buy a car in your neck of the woods, or you can go into one of the weekender publications and pay a few hundred dollars and reach just the people likely to drive over to your shop."

Some weeklies, particularly those in upscale suburbs, offer sophisticated coverage of community issues. Others feature a homey mix of reports on social events such as who visited whom for Sunday dinner. The success of these weeklies sometimes is called **telephone book journalism** because of the emphasis on names, the somewhat overdrawn theory being that people buy papers to see their names in print. Weeklies have in common that they cover their communities with a detail that metro dailies have neither staff nor space to match. There is no alternative to keeping up with local news.

telephone book journalism Emphasizing readers' names in articles.

RURAL WEEKLIES

Rural weeklies generally have fallen on rough times. Part of their problem is the diminishing significance of agriculture in the national economy and the continuing depopulation of rural North America. In communities that remain retail centres, rural weeklies can maintain a strong advertising base. However, the Main Street of many small towns has declined as improved roads and the construction of major retail stores like Wal-Mart draw customers from miles away. In earlier days those customers patronized hometown retailers, who placed significant advertising in hometown weeklies. Today many of these Main Street retailers, unable to compete with giant discount stores, are out of business.

shopper An advertising paper without news.

SHOPPERS

Free-distribution papers that carry only advertisements have become increasingly important as vehicles for classified advertising. In recent years, **shoppers** have attracted display advertising that earlier would have gone to regular newspapers. Almost all shoppers undercut daily newspapers on advertising rates.

By definition, shoppers are strictly advertising sheets, but beginning in the 1970s some shoppers added editorial content, usually material that came free over the transom, such as publicity items and occasional self-serving columns from legislators. Some shoppers have hired staff members to compile calendars and provide a modicum of news coverage. Most of these papers, however, remain ad sheets with little that is journalistic. Their news-gathering efforts and expenses are minuscule compared with those of a daily newspaper.

The Village Voice: This alternative newsweekly has won numerous awards, including three Pulitzer Prizes. It maintains its no-holds-barred philosophy on which it was founded 50 years ago.
www.villagevoice.com

The Coast: Check out Halifax's weekly alternative newspaper.
www.thecoast.ca

The Georgia Straight: Surf over to Vancouver's weekly newspaper to see how it covers news and entertainment.
www.straight.com

Alternative and Minority Newspapers

Study Preview   *Most newspapers attempt broad coverage for a broad audience, but more specialized newspapers are important in the lives of many people. These include counterculture, ethnic and black newspapers, many of which are expanding and prospering today.*

COUNTERCULTURE NEWSPAPERS

A group of friends in the Greenwich Village neighbourhood of New York, including novelist **Norman Mailer** and **Don Wolf**, decided to start a newspaper. Thus in 1955 was born *The Village Voice*, a free-wheeling weekly that became a prototype for a 1960s phenomenon called the **alternative press** that has continued to thrive.

In its early days, *The Village Voice* was a haven for bohemian writers of diverse competence who volunteered occasional pieces, some lengthy, many rambling. Many articles purported to be investigative examinations of hypocritical people and institutions, but, as *The Voice* veteran Nat Hentoff has noted, nobody ever bothered to check "noisome facts," let alone the "self-righteous author." *The Voice* seemed to scorn traditional, detached, neutral reporting. Despite its flaws, the amateurism gave *The Voice* a charm, and it picked up readership.

The Voice today is more polished and journalistically serious. The characteristics that made it distinctive in its early history, and that were picked up by other **counterculture newspapers**, include:

- Antiestablishment political coverage with a strong antimilitary slant.
- Cultural coverage that emphasizes contrarian music and art and exalts sex and drugs.
- Interpretive coverage focusing more on issues of special concern to alienated young people.
- Extensive entertainment coverage and listings of events.
- A conversational, sometimes crude style that includes four-letter words and gratuitous expletives for their shock value.
- Extensive personal ads for dating and sex liaisons.

ETHNIC NEWSPAPERS

Canada has been officially multicultural since 1971. The Canadian Multiculturalism Act passed in 1988 supports the idea that Canada is pluralist and that all cultures should be encouraged to maintain their heritage and traditions while living in Canada. Given this status as a multicultural country, it's not surprising that Canada is host to scores of ethnic newspapers. The Media Awareness Network says there are more than 250 ethnic newspapers in Canada serving more than 40 cultures. Seven of these ethnic newspapers are dailies.

The first ethnic newspaper in Canada was *Die Welt, und Neuschottländische Correspondenz*, which began publishing in 1788 in Halifax. Research on the ethnic press in Canada and the United States reflects ideological differences between the two countries. In the United States, the model is assimilation; in Canada, it's accommodation. One of the earliest studies on the role of the U.S. ethnic press was done by Robert Park in the early 1920s. He found that most immigrants said they planned to live in the States only temporarily and would return to their native country once they had earned enough money. On the other hand, in their 1990 study of the Portuguese community in Quebec, Alpalhao and Da Rosa found that in some areas of Quebec the existence of an ethnic means of mass communication, as well as other ethnic institutions (social services, churches, etc.), "permit a large percentage of the community to live as if they were still in the milieu of origin."

Black newspapers have been important in Canada since the days of slavery and the underground railroad into Canada. The Centre for the Study of Black Cultures in Canada at York University reports that the earliest black newspapers in Canada were

Norman Mailer Among the founders of *The Village Voice*.

Don Wolf Among the founders of *The Village Voice*.

The Village Voice Model for contemporary alternative press.

alternative press Generally antiestablishment publication for a young alienated audience.

counterculture newspapers Challenge, defy mainstream values.

National Ethnic Press and Media Council of Canada: The voice of ethnic media in Canada.
www.nepmcc.ca

Sing Tao Daily: Canada's largest Chinese newspaper is online.
www.singtao.ca

Pink Triangle Press: Gay, lesbian, bisexual and transgender issues are central to the readers of Pink Triangle Press.
www.xtra.ca

Voice of the Fugitive in 1851 and *The Provincial Freeman* in 1853. Canada's largest ethnic newspaper is *Share*, which is devoted to both local and Caribbean news. *Share*'s publisher, Arnold A. Auguste, says, "*Share*'s focus is on Toronto. It is a community newspaper which covers our community, what we are doing here, in Toronto. *Share* is connected to the community at large." Auguste must be doing something right: *Share* reaches 130 000 readers each week.

Evaluating Newspapers

Study Preview   *Quantitative measures of a newspaper's success include circulation and penetration. How to judge quality? Rankings and awards are indicators, although they are imperfect. You yourself can evaluate whether the newspaper gives adequate resources to coverage.*

CIRCULATION AND PENETRATION

Once upon a time, measuring a newspaper's marketplace success against its competition was simple. The paper with the largest circulation won. Today, though, hardly any cities have competing dailies. Even so, numbers count. Is circulation growing? Declining? Because almost every newspaper reports its circulation to an auditing agency, circulation can be tracked year to year, even quarter to quarter.

penetration Percentage of persons or households that a newspaper reaches in its circulation area.

Even more significant comparative data come from comparing **penetration**. Penetration is the percentage of people or households that get the paper. The Audit Bureau of Circulations (ABC) doesn't collect penetration data, but fairly reliable penetration is easy to calculate: Divide the population by the circulation. Seeking precise penetration data can get tricky. How you measure the circulation area, for example, can make a difference. There are other variables too. Even so, simple math can give you a good indicator of whether a newspaper's acceptance in the marketplace is improving.

QUALITY INDICATORS

While the Canadian Newspaper Association and the Canadian Community Newspapers Association both hold annual awards for excellence in newspaper publishing, there are some quality indicators that you can generically use to evaluate your local paper. These are described below.

news hole Space for news in a newspaper after ads are inserted; also time in a newscast for news after ads.

NEWS HOLE. What percentage of space in the newspaper goes to news? This is called the **news hole**. From a reader's perspective the bigger the news hole, the better. Discount postal rates are available only to newspapers that cap advertising at 70 percent. Many publications push the limit to maximize revenue, sometimes shorting readers on news coverage, commentary and other non-ad content.

CONTENT. Because local coverage is more costly than stories from news agencies, a good measure of quality is whether a newspaper has extensive local coverage or loads up with wire stories. Is local coverage thorough? Is it accurate? Does the newspaper have its own reporter to cover provincial politics? Its own Ottawa bureau?

Media People

Bonnie Fuller

Bonnie Fuller

In charge at American Media publications, Canadian Bonnie Fuller unveiled her remake of the supermarket tabloid *Star* for a 2004 run against celebrity titles *People, Us Weekly* and *InStyle*. For respectability, Fuller threw out the classified advertising and most customer-direct advertising—about half of the magazine's ad pages. She promised advertisers a 116 page publication, compared to the previous 80, and set aside 40 pages for ads, compared to the previous 24. Fuller went cutesy with labels for some features, like "Star Bucks," with celebrities photographed in acts of public consumption; "The Stars Are Out," with celebrities at parties and occasions; and "Doctor to the Stars," with health and beauty tips.

As a magazine editor, Fuller has always had a magic touch. In her six years as editor, she turned *Flare* into the largest fashion magazine in Canada. Then, in New York, she relaunched *YM*, a magazine geared toward young women ages 15 to 24, more than doubling its circulation from 700 000 to more than 1.7 million. In 1994, Fuller joined Hearst Magazines where she launched the French fashion, beauty and lifestyle magazine *Marie Claire* for U.S. readers. Initial circulation of 250 000 rocketed past 500 000. Then Hearst put Fuller in charge of *Cosmopolitan*, which was still riding high on the sex-and-the-single-girl themes of Helen Gurley Brown after more than 30 years—quite an act to follow.

As the new *Cosmo* editor, Fuller used reader focus groups to guide her in making changes and additions. She included articles on AIDS and sexual harassment and, with no holds barred, any issue of concern and relevance to young women, at the same time maintaining the saucy, sexy Helen Gurley Brown tone. In Fuller's first year, *Cosmo* circulation flourished and drew more advertising. Fuller was named 1997 Editor of the Year by the trade journal *Advertising Age*. From 1998 to 2001 she served as editor of *Glamour*.

What next? Fuller took on the editorship of the celebrity magazine *Us Weekly*, which had floundered for years against Time Warner's *People*. Almost instantly, *Us* became a pop culture must-read.

At the risk of being labeled a serial job-hopper, in 2003 Fuller switched to tabloid publisher American Media. At American Media she not only was editing one title but was also editor-in-chief for all the company's magazines. It was a new level of responsibility. Said Fuller: "A chance to do this isn't going to necessarily come up in two years, in three years. It came up now." How could the era's most successful magazine editor stoop as low as American Media's *National Enquirer* and *Star?* Her stock answer in myriad interviews was the same: "Don't fool yourself. Every news outlet is doing tabloid stories."

A hands-on editor, Fuller first tackled American Media's supermarket pulp tabloid *Star*. Coverlines suddenly were less gee-whiz and more upbeat. To reposition *Star*, she had it printed on glossy paper. She shunned old *Star*-type scoops that, while tantalizing, often turned out to be untrue. A successful celebrity magazine, she said, needs credibility.

Would Fuller succeed? The circulation of the *Star* she inherited at first slipped below 1.2 million, but by 2005 it was up to 1.6 million in an increasingly competitive field of celebrity magazines. The question was whether, fully Fullerized, the magazine could top *People* at 3.5 million. Fuller was confident, saying that her target after *Star* would be to rejuvenate American Media's recently acquired *Men's Fitness* and *Muscle and Fitness* and a motley group of other titles, including Latino magazines, *Natural Health, Globe* and perhaps even American Media's flagship *National Enquirer*.

STAFF. What kind of professionals report and edit the newspaper? Seasoned reporters who know the community well? Or beginners? Does the newspaper offer competitive salaries for the best talent? Salary scales are available on newspapers with collective-bargaining agreements.

MANAGEMENT. Does top management have a permanent stake in the community? Or does leadership rotate in and out, with individuals focusing on making a name in order to move up in the corporate structure?

Influence of Magazines

Study Preview   *Today, as through their whole history, the major magazines constitute a mass medium that targets a national audience. At their best, periodicals pack great literature and ideas into formats that, unlike books, almost anybody can afford. Magazines are also a national unifier because they offer manufacturers a nationwide audience for their goods.*

A National Advertising Medium

Advertisers used magazines through the 19th century to build national markets for their products, which was an important factor in transforming North America from an agricultural economy to a modern one. This also contributed to a sense of nationhood. The other mass media could not do that as effectively. Few books carried advertisements, and newspapers, with few exceptions, delivered only local readership to advertisers. Today, advertising is still an important concern to Canadian magazine publishers. The majority of their total revenue is generated by advertisers.

Massive Magazine Audience

People have a tremendous appetite for magazines. There is a Canadian magazine for almost every city and region of the country and for almost any interest. While only 20 percent of magazines available on Canadian newsracks are actually homegrown, Canadians seem to prefer Canadian magazines over American ones because of the Canadian content. Canadian magazines are perceived by readers as being more relevant to the experiences of Canadian readers than are their U.S. counterparts. Here's a snapshot of the Canadian magazine industry from Statistics Canada:

- In 1993, there were 1678 Canadian magazine titles available; by 2003 there were almost 2400.
- Annual total circulation for all Canadian magazines is 778 million or roughly 320 000 sold for each Canadian periodical.
- Advertising revenue is close to a billion dollars a year.

Magazines Canada (Canadian Magazine Publishers Association): Supports and promotes Canadian magazines. Whether you want to subscribe to a Canadian magazine or learn more about the industry, this is an excellent website. **www.cmpa.ca**

Postal Assistance Program (PAP) Discounted magazine mail rates for Canadian magazines.

Canada Magazine Fund (CMF) Support for Canadian magazines through the Department of Canadian Heritage.

Protecting Canadian Magazines

June Callwood calls Canadian magazines "the only ones that will tell you how complex this country is, how interesting, how beautiful, where the troubled places are, they find our rascals and our heroes and they have become the fabric of our ordinary lives. We can look in a magazine and see ourselves." However, content and writing are not the only factors that make Canadian magazines successful. The Canadian government sees magazines as playing a "significant role in the cultural life of Canadians" by reflecting our own distinctive people, places, and lives. For more than a hundred years, the government has helped foster the growth and development of Canadian magazines through many different initiatives. For example, The **Postal Assistance Program (PAP)** helps Canadian magazine publishers offset the cost of distributing their periodicals by mail. This is particularly significant because the majority of Canadian magazines rely heavily on mail subscriptions. It helps about 1200 publications each year. The Department of Canadian Heritage also supports Canadian magazines with marketing, distribution and professional development through the **Canada Magazine Fund (CMF)**.

In 1999, in response to American arguments that **Canada's Bill C-55**, designed to protect the Canadian magazine industry, was unfair under both NAFTA and the WTO, the Canadian government made significant changes to the bill. Now, under the new **Foreign Publishers Advertising Services Act**, U.S. publishers could now begin to accept Canadian advertising and market what have become known as split-run publications. These split runs are American magazines published in Canada with up to 18 percent Canadian advertising. Plus, Canadian advertisers could now deduct the cost of this advertising as a business expense on their income tax forms, something that wasn't allowed prior to 1999. Now, 50 percent of the cost of the ad is tax deductible if the magazine features more than 80 percent foreign content; 100 percent is tax deductible if the magazine has more than 80 percent Canadian content.

Magazines as Media Innovators

Study Preview   *Magazines have led other media with significant innovations in journalism, advertising and circulation. These include investigative reporting, in-depth personality profiles, and photojournalism.*

INVESTIGATIVE REPORTING

Muckraking, usually called "investigative reporting" today, was honed by magazines as a journalistic approach in the first years of the 20th century. Magazines ran lengthy explorations of abusive institutions in the society. It was **Theodore Roosevelt**, the reform president, who coined the term *muckraking*. Roosevelt generally enjoyed investigative journalism, but one day in 1906, when the digging got too close to home, he likened it to the work of a character in a 17th-century novel who focused so much on raking muck that he missed the good news. The president meant the term derisively, but it came to be a badge of honour among journalists.

muckraking Early 20th-century term for investigative reporting.

Theodore Roosevelt Coined the term *muckraking*.

PERSONALITY PROFILES

The in-depth **personality profile** was a magazine invention. In the 1920s, **Harold Ross** of the *New Yorker* began pushing writers to a thoroughness that was new in journalism. They used multiple interviews with a range of sources—talking not only with the subject of the profile but also with just about everyone and anyone who could comment on the subject, including the subject's friends and enemies. Such depth required weeks, sometimes months, of journalistic digging. It's not uncommon now in newspapers, broadcasting or magazines, but before Harold Ross, it didn't exist.

personality profile In-depth, balanced biographical article.

Harold Ross Pioneered the personality profile.

Under **Hugh Hefner**, *Playboy* took the interview in new directions in 1962 with in-depth profiles developed from a highly structured question-and-answer format. This format became widely imitated. *Rolling Stone* uses Q-and-A's regularly, often creating news. In 2003, presidential hopeful Wesley Clark, a retired general, told *Rolling Stone* that a three-star general in the Pentagon had told him that the Iraq invasion was planned only as the beginning of further U.S. invasions in the Middle East and elsewhere, and Clark named the additional target countries. It was a bombshell assertion that made news. Other magazines meanwhile are boiling down the Q-and-A into quick takes. *Time* introduced the "10 Questions" feature in 2002, tightly editing pointed questions and answers to fit on a single page.

Hugh Hefner Adapted the personality profile to Q-and-A.

PHOTOJOURNALISM

Harper's Weekly Pioneered magazine visuals.

Magazines brought visuals to the mass media in a way books never had. *Harper's Weekly* sent artists to draw Civil War battles, leading the way to journalism that went beyond words.

National Geographic Introduced photography in magazines.

The young editor of the *National Geographic*, Gilbert Grosvenor, drew a map proposing a route to the South Pole for an 1899 issue, putting the *Geographic* on the road to being a visually oriented magazine. For subsequent issues, Grosvenor borrowed government plates to reproduce photos, and he encouraged travelers to submit their photographs to the magazine. This was at a time when most magazines scorned photographs. However, Grosvenor was undeterred as an advocate for documentary photography, and membership in the National Geographic Society, a prerequisite for receiving the magazine, swelled. Eventually, the magazine assembled its own staff of photographers and gradually became a model for other publications that discovered they needed to play catch-up.

Aided by technological advances involving smaller, more portable cameras and faster film capable of recording images under extreme conditions, photographers working for the *Geographic* opened a whole new world of documentary coverage to their readers. Following are among *Geographic* accomplishments:

■ A photo of a bare-breasted Filipino woman field worker shocked some *Geographic* readers in 1903, but Grosvenor persisted against Victorian sensitivities to show the peoples of the world as they lived.

■ The first photographs from Tibet, by Russian explorers, appeared in 1905 in an 11-page spread—extraordinary visual coverage for the time that confirmed photography's role in journalism.

■ A 17-page, 8-foot foldout panorama of the Canadian Rockies in 1911 showed that photojournalism need not be limited by format.

National Geographic. The *Geographic* has remained in the vanguard of magazines photographically. For its 100th anniversary in 1988, the cover was the first hologram, a three-dimensional photograph, ever published in a mass-audience magazine. With a circulation of 6.7 million, the *Geographic* is not only among the oldest surviving U.S. magazines but also among the most read.

■ The magazine's 100th anniversary cover in 1988 was the first hologram—a three-dimensional photograph—ever published in a mass-audience magazine. It was a significant production accomplishment.

Life magazine brought U.S. photojournalism to new importance in the 1930s. The oversize pages of the magazine gave new intensity to photographs, and the magazine, a weekly, demonstrated that newsworthy events could be covered consistently by camera. *Life* captured the spirit of the times photographically and demonstrated that the whole range of human experience could be recorded visually. Both real life and *Life* could be shocking. A 1938 *Life* spread on human birth was so shocking for the time that censors succeeded in banning the issue in 33 cities.

Consumer Magazines

consumer magazines Sold on newsracks.

Study Preview   *The most visible category of magazines is general-interest magazines, which are available on newsracks and by subscription. Called consumer magazines, these include publications like* Reader's Digest *that try to offer something for everybody, but mostly they are magazines edited for narrower audiences.*

Seeing the News. Henry Luce's *Life* magazine pioneered photojournalism, beginning with Margaret Bourke-White's haunting shadows of the giant new Fort Peck Dam in Montana for the inaugural issue. When World War II came, *Life* dispatched Bourke-White and other photographers to capture the story, even the horrific details. With people eager for war news, circulation soared.

Rolling Stone: Music news, reviews, photos—if it's key to the scene, *Rolling Stone* has it covered.
www.rollingstone.com

Reader's Digest: Sign up for free newsletters, submit a joke, or preview the current issue of this widely distributed magazine.
www.readersdigest.ca

Time: One of the earliest newsmagazines keeps on ticking.
www.time.com

National Geographic: Website of the National Geographic Society, with articles and the pictures that made the magazine famous.
www.nationalgeographic.com

NEWSMAGAZINES

Although it is often compared to *Time*, *Maclean's*, "Canada's Weekly News Magazine," was founded in 1905 by John Bayne Maclean, almost 20 years before *Time* first appeared. However, the magazine we now know as *Maclean's* was called *Busy Man's Magazine* until 1911. Originally, it was a large-format magazine, about the size of *Life*, but in 1969 it was reduced to a standard size. In content, *Maclean's* is similar to *Time*, with an emphasis on in-depth coverage of national and international stories. Columnists like Peter C. Newman (a former editor of *Maclean's*), Barbara Amiel, and Allan Fotheringham have offered their perspectives to Canadians in the pages of this magazine. *Maclean's* even issues a national edition written in Chinese.

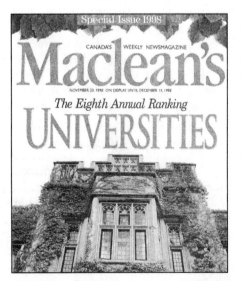

Newsmagazines. Canada's counterpart to *Time* magazine is *Maclean's*. It brings the Canadian journalism tradition of analysis to the newsstands.

Maclean's First Canadian newsmagazine.

Fresh out of Yale in 1923, classmates **Henry Luce** and Briton Hadden begged and borrowed $86 000 from friends and relatives and launched a new kind of magazine: *Time*. The magazine provided summaries of news by categories such as

Henry Luce Founder of *Time* and later *Life*.

Time First American newsmagazine.

Media Databank

Magazine Circulation Leaders: Canada

According to Masthead Online, here are the top Canadian magazines in 2006. Data were compiled by combining advertising revenue and circulation revenue.

Magazine	Total Estimated Revenue (Canadian dollars)
Chatelaine	50 million
Canadian Living	41 million
Reader's Digest	37 million
Maclean's	36 million
Time (Canada)	24 million
Canadian House and Home	22 million
7 Jours	21 million
Flare	17 million
TV Guide	17 million (no longer publishing newsrack edition)
Chatelaine	16 million (French Language Edition)

Source: MastheadOnline.com

Life: Visit the photo archive for a look at over 22 million classic *Life* photos and magazine covers.
www.life.com

American Profile: The regional, weekly supplement with hometown community news.
www.americanprofile.com

national affairs, sports and business. It took four years for *Time* to turn a profit, and some people doubted that the magazine would ever make money, noting that it merely rehashed what daily newspapers had already reported. Readers, however, came to like the handy compilation and the sprightly, often irreverent writing style that set *Time* apart.

While *Time*, *Newsweek* and *U.S. News & World Report* cover a broad range of subjects, specialized newsmagazines focus on narrower subjects. The largest category is those featuring celebrity news, including the gossipy sort. The supermarket tabloid **National Enquirer** focuses on the rich and famous, hyped-up medical research and sensational oddball news and is an incredible commercial success, with 2.1 million in circulation. Time Warner's *People* is at 3.6 million.

National Enquirer Magazine or newspaper?

WOMEN'S MAGAZINES

The first U.S. magazine edited to interest only a portion of the mass audience, but otherwise to be of general interest, was *The Lady's Magazine*, which later became *Godey's Lady's Book*. **Sarah Josepha Hale** helped start the magazine in 1828 to uplift and glorify womanhood. Its advice on fashions, morals, taste, sewing and cooking developed a following, which peaked with a circulation of 150 000 in 1860.

The *Godey's* tradition is maintained today in the competing magazines *Better Homes and Gardens*, *Family Circle*, *Good Housekeeping*, *Ladies' Home Journal*, *Redbook*, *Woman's Day* and the erstwhile *Rosie* (née *McCall's*). While each sister can be distinguished from her siblings, there is a thematic connection: concern for home, family and high-quality living from a traditional woman's perspective.

These traditional women's magazines are sometimes called the **Seven Sisters**. An eighth sister is *Cosmopolitan*, although it may more aptly be called a distant cousin. Under Helen Gurley Brown and later Bonnie Fuller, *Cosmopolitan* has geared itself

Sarah Josepha Hale Founded first women's magazine.

Seven Sisters Leading women's magazines.

to a subcategory of women readers: young, unmarried and working. It's the most successful in a large group of women's magazines seeking narrow groups. Among them are *Elle*, focusing on fashion, and *Essence*, for black women. The teen girl market, dominated by *Seventeen* and *YM*, has become crowded with Little Sister spinoffs *Cosmogirl*, the leading newcomer with 1.1 million circulation in 2004, *ElleGirl* and *Teen Vogue*. In Canada, *Flare*, *Images*, and *Focus on Women* are also geared toward narrow audiences.

MEN'S MAGAZINES

Founded in 1933, *Esquire* was the first classy men's magazine. It was as famous for its pinups as for its literary content, which over the years has included articles from Ernest Hemingway, Hunter S. Thompson and P.J. O'Rourke. Fashion has also been a cornerstone in the *Esquire* content mix.

Hugh Hefner learned about magazines as an *Esquire* staff member, and he applied those lessons when he created **Playboy** in 1953. With its lustier tone, *Playboy* quickly overtook *Esquire* in circulation. At its peak, *Playboy* sold 7 million copies a month. By 2004, however, *Playboy* seemed tired. Circulation was down to 3.2 million. The publisher of copycat *Penthouse* was in bankruptcy. Meanwhile, upstarts like *Maxim* at 2.5 million, *FHM* at 1.1 million and *Stuff* at 676 000 were in an ascendancy despite critics who objected to their raciness. Responding to critics, some retail outlets, notably giant retailer Wal-Mart, ceased stocking some men's titles as well as some women's magazines with provocative covers.

Not all men's magazines dwell on sex. The outdoor life is exalted in *Field & Stream*, whose circulation tops 2 million. Fix-it magazines, led by *Popular Science* and *Popular Mechanics*, have a steady following.

Non-Newsrack Magazines

> **STUDY PREVIEW**   *Many organizations publish magazines for their members. Although these sponsored magazines, including* National Geographic, *resemble consumer magazines, they generally are not available at newsracks. In fact, consumer magazines are far outnumbered by sponsored magazines and by trade journals.*

SPONSORED MAGAZINES

The founders of the National Geographic Society decided in 1888 to put out a magazine to promote the society and build membership. The idea was to entice people to join by bundling a subscription with membership and then to use the dues to finance the society's research and expeditions. Within a few years the *National Geographic* had become a phenomenal success both in generating membership and as a profit centre for the National Geographic Society. Today, more than 100 years old and with U.S. circulation at 6.7 million, the *Geographic* is the most widely recognized **sponsored magazine** in the nation. Other sponsored magazines include *CARP The Magazine*, published by the Canadian Association of Retired Persons for its members.

Demassification. Magazines were the first medium to demassify. *Chatelaine*, a magazine for Canadian homemakers, ranks as one of the best-selling magazines in Canada.

Esquire First classy men's magazine.

Playboy Widely imitated girlie/lifestyle men's magazine.

sponsored magazine Generally non-newsrack magazine, often member-supported.

TRADE JOURNALS

trade journal Keeps members of profession or trade informed.

Every profession or trade has at least one magazine, or **trade journal**, for keeping abreast of what is happening in the field. In entertainment, *Billboard* provides solid journalistic coverage on a broad range of subjects in music: new recording releases, new acts, new technology and new merger deals. *Billboard* is essential reading for people in the music industry. Trade journals covering the Canadian and American mass media include *Marketing* magazine for advertising and marketing, *The Publisher* for the newspaper industry, and *Broadcaster* and *Broadcast Dialogue* for the Canadian radio and television industries. About 4000 trade journals cover a mind-boggling range of businesses and trades. Consider the diversity in these titles: *Rock & Dirt*, *Progressive Grocer*, *Canadian Plastics*, *Hogs Today* and *Hardware Age*.

NEWSLETTERS

Even more focused than trade journals are subscription newsletters, a billion-dollar industry. These newsletters are expensive, generally $600 to $1000 a year, with some as much as $5000. Why do people pay that much? Where else could Chamber of Commerce executives find the information that's in *Downtown Promotion Reporter*? And no other publication duplicates what's in *Food Chemical News*, *Beverage Digest* and *Inside Mortgage Finance*. John Farley, vice-president of the largest newsletter company, Phillips Publishing, contends that newsletters are the purest form of journalism because they carry little or no advertising: "We're answerable to no one but our subscribers." Today, more than 5000 subscription newsletters are published in the United States and Canada. Some newsletters now have subscription websites.

Magazine Demassification

> **STUDY PREVIEW**   *Giant mass-audience magazines, led by* Life, *were major influences in their heyday, but television killed them off by offering larger audiences to advertisers. Today, the magazine industry thrives through demassification, the process of seeking audiences with narrow interests. Critics believe that demassification has changed the role of magazines in society for the worse.*

ASSAULT FROM TELEVISION

The oversize mass-audience magazines do not exist today—at least not as they did in the old days. *Collier's*, having gone bankrupt, published its final issue in 1956. Hemorrhaging money despite a circulation of 4 million, *The Saturday Evening Post* ceased publication in 1969. In 1971 *Look* died. *Life* was not able to capitalize on the fact that it suddenly had less competition, and it went out of business the next year. It had lost $30 million over the previous three years. What had happened to the high-flying, oversize, mass-audience magazines? In a single word: television.

CPM Cost per thousand; a tool to determine the cost effectiveness of different media.

At its peak, *Life* had a circulation of 8.5 million, but in the 1950s the television networks had begun to deliver even bigger audiences to advertisers. The villain for the giant magazines was not merely television's audience size, but **CPM**—advertising jargon for cost per 1000 readers, listeners or viewers (the *M* standing for the Roman numeral for 1000). In 1970 a full-page advertisement in *Life* ran $65 000. For less money an advertiser could have one minute of network television and reach far more potential customers. CPM-conscious advertising agencies could not conscientiously recommend *Life*'s $7.75 CPM when the networks' CPM was $3.60, and advertisers shifted to television.

Calvin and Hobbes

by Bill Watterson

Magazine Demassification. Advertisers favour magazines that are edited to specific audience interests that coincide with the advertisers' products. Fewer and fewer magazines geared to a general audience remain in business today. In Canada, demassified magazines abound from *Going Natural*, a magazine published by the Federation of Canadian Naturists (nudists), and *The Antigonish Review*, for fans of poetry and prose.

A NARROWER FOCUS

With the demise of *Life*, doomsayers predicted that magazines were a dying breed of media. However, advertisers withdrew only from magazines with broad readerships. What they discovered was that although it was less expensive to use television to peddle universally used products such as detergents, grooming aids and packaged foods, television, geared at the time for mass audiences, was too expensive for products appealing to narrow groups. Today, relatively few magazines seek a truly mass audience. These include *Reader's Digest* and the Sunday magazine supplements.

Special-interest magazines, whose content focused on limited subjects and whose advertising rates were lower, fit the bill better than either television or the giant mass-audience magazines for reaching customers with special interests. For manufacturers of $7000 stereo systems, for example, it made sense to advertise in a narrowly focused audiophile magazine such as *Stereo Review*. In the same way, neither mass-audience magazines nor television was a medium of choice for top-of-the-line racing skis, but ski magazines were ideal. For fancy cookware, *Food & Wine* made sense.

CRITICS OF DEMASSIFICATION

Norman Cousins, once editor of the highbrow magazine *The Saturday Review*, criticized demassified magazines for betraying their traditional role of enriching the culture. Cousins said that specialization had diluted the intellectual role of magazines in the society. Advertisers, he said, were shaping magazines' journalistic content for their commercial purposes—in contrast to magazine editors independently deciding content with loftier purposes in mind.

Scholar Dennis Holder put this "unholy alliance" of advertisers and readers this way: "The readers see themselves as members of small, and in some sense, elite groups—joggers, for example, or cat lovers—and they want to be told that they are terribly neat people for being in those groups. Advertisers, of course, want to reinforce the so-called positive self-image too, because joggers who feel good about themselves tend to buy those ridiculous suits and cat lovers who believe lavishing affection on their felines is a sign of warmth and sincerity are the ones who purchase cute little cat sweaters, or are they cat's pajamas." Magazine editors and writers, Holder said, are caught in the symbiotic advertiser–reader alliance and have no choice but to go along.

Norman Cousins and Dennis Holder were right that most consumer magazines today tend to a frothy mix of light, upbeat features, with little that is thoughtful or hard-hitting. There is no question that demassification works against giving readers any kind of global view. However, most readers want to know about other people, particularly celebrities, and about a great many trendy topics. And advertisers want to reach those readers, preferably by steering clear of any controversial magazine coverage that might hurt sales. So profitability for most magazines and their advertisers is locked into providing information their target audiences are interested in rather than serving an indefinable "public interest," which might sometimes be controversial. The emphasis on profits and demassification saddens a number of people who believe that magazines have a higher calling than a cash register. These critics would agree with Cousins, who warned that emphasizing the superficial just because it sells magazines is a betrayal of the social trust that magazine publishers once held. "The purpose of a magazine," he said, "is not to tell you how to fix a leaky faucet, but to tell you what the world is about."

NEW COMPETITION

An ominous sign for magazines is the cable television industry, which is eating into magazine advertising with an array of demassified channels, such as TSN and CBC Newsworld. The demassified cable channels are picking up advertisers that once used magazines almost exclusively to reach narrow slices of the mass audience with a presumed interest in their products and services.

Another drain on magazine revenue is the growth of direct-mail advertising. Using sophisticated analysis of potential customer groups, advertisers can mail brochures, catalogues, flyers and other material, including video pitches, directly to potential customers at their homes or places of business. Every dollar that goes into direct-mail campaigns is a dollar that in an earlier period went into magazines and other traditional advertising media.

INTERNET MAGAZINES

Consumer and trade journals adapted quickly to digital delivery in the late 1990s with internet editions. The Canoe website in Canada offers links to magazines owned by Sun Media, while the Rogers site can connect you to *Maclean's*, *Chatelaine*, and other Rogers-owned publications. Meanwhile, the number of websites offering magazine-type content continues to grow.

Evaluating Magazines

Study Preview   *Circulation and advertising revenue are measures of a magazine's populist success. A new way of evaluating the impact of magazines focuses on the readers themselves.*

READER USAGE MEASURE

A new way of gauging magazine quality, the **Reader Usage Measure**, or **RUM**, was created in 2003 by the magazine industry and Northwestern University media researchers. Thirty-nine statements are put to readers in carefully controlled surveys to ascertain positive and negative reactions. The statements are direct. Answering *Yes* to these statements contributes to a strong RUM score:

Wired: The latest technology news categorized by culture, business and politics.
www.wired.com

The New Republic: You heard it here first. *The New Republic* prides itself on reporting political news before it hits the mainstream.
www.tnr.com

Maxim: Online version of the popular magazine, complete with entertainment, fashion and loads of photos.
www.maximonline.com

Folio: Check out the magazine designed to serve top management in the magazine publishing industry.
www.foliomag.com

Reader Usage Measure (RUM) A tool developed by the magazine industry to score reader experience as a guide for designing magazines conceptually and for editing content.

- I get value for my time and money.
- It makes me smarter.
- I often reflect on it.

Conversely, answering *Yes* to the following statements lowers the RUM score:

- It disappoints me.
- I dislike some of the ads.
- It leaves me feeling bad.

Ellen Oppenheim, a marketing executive with Magazine Publishers of America, said RUM data provide "a quantitative measure of qualitative information" that transcends circulation, ad pages and ad revenue—all of which are advertising-rooted measures. RUM is a reader-rooted measure that points to a magazine's connectedness to its audience.

The first RUM study included 4347 readers of 100 leading magazines, which was a large enough sample to provide demographic breakdowns. Black readers, for example, want magazines about which they can say, "It touched me" and "It grabbed me visually." Generation Y women, who came of age in the 1990s, gravitate to magazines that help them share experiences. Historically, the great magazines have been edited by people with an intuitive sense for their audiences. With RUM there is concrete information to supplement instinctive knowledge about what attracts an audience.

CHAPTER 2 WRAP-UP

Can newspapers and magazines survive? Even if people were to stop buying newspapers and magazines tomorrow, newspaper organizations would survive because they have an asset that competing media lack: the largest, most skilled newsroom staffs in their communities. The presses and the ink-on-newsprint medium for carrying the message may not have a long future, but newspapers' news-gathering capability will endure. The magazine industry once was defined by giant general-interest magazines that offered something for everybody. Advertisers soured on these oversize giants when television offered more potential customers per advertising dollar. Magazines then shifted to more specialized packages. This focused approach worked. Magazines found advertisers who were seeking readers with narrow interests. Now, as other media—particularly television—are demassifying, magazines stand to lose advertisers, which poses new challenges.

QUESTIONS FOR REVIEW

1. How did the mass production of the written word change society?

2. Describe the rise of newspaper chains and the trend toward conglomeration in Canada.

3. Why do most newspapers publish only morning editions now?

4. Why are community newspapers booming?

5. Why have alternative publications experienced increased readership?

6. Are magazines losing their influence as a shaper of the culture? Explain your answer.

7. How have magazines been innovative as a journalistic and a visual medium?

8. How has demassification affected both newspapers and magazines?

QUESTIONS FOR CRITICAL THINKING

1. Did the Davey Committee and Kent Commission leave any legacies from which we can learn?

2. When U.S. magazines came into their own in the 1820s, they represented a mass medium that was distinct from the existing book and newspaper media. How were magazines different?

3. Is demassification good or bad for readers?

4. What will the effect of convergence be on newsroom staff?

5. Discuss the role of these innovators in contributing to magazines as a visual medium: Gilbert Grosvenor and Henry Luce.

6. The late Norman Cousins, a veteran social commentator and magazine editor, worried that trends in the magazine industry were undermining the historic role that magazines have had in enriching the culture. What is your response to Cousins's concerns?

7. There are no laws protecting Canadian newspapers, yet there are many government initiatives in place for magazines. Is this fair?

DEEPENING YOUR MEDIA LITERACY

NEWSPAPERS

Can a newspaper have a personality?
Step 1

Get copies of two different newspapers, daily or weekly.

Dig Deeper
Step 2

Make a list of the following characteristics for each publication:

1. How big is the news hole? An easy way to calculate this is to measure the total number of inches in each column of type, from the top of the page to the bottom, and multiply by the number of columns across the page. Multiply this number by the total number of pages. Then measure the number of inches of non-advertising material and figure the percentage of non-advertising content—that's your news hole.

2. How much of the news is staff-written? How much comes from news services?

3. How diverse is the opinion section?

4. Is the publication chain-owned or independent?

5. What word or phrase describes the overall look of the publication?

6. What kind of news does it carry? Local, sports, entertainment, other?

What Do You Think?
Step 3

Write down a few words or a phrase that describes the personalities of the publications you investigated. Answer these questions: Can you determine the politics of the publisher or editor from reading the newspaper? What text or images led you to this conclusion? Can you determine who the perceived audience of a publication is by reading it? Can you determine what values it expresses? It is said that a truly successful newspaper belongs to the community. Do you think that's true for the newspapers you studied?

MAGAZINES

Should magazines try for universal appeal, or is it better to have a smaller, specialized audience?

Step 1

Make a list of characteristics you think make a trade journal successful. Imagine that you are the publisher of a trade journal. Write down three things you would tell your editor to do to make the magazine successful. Now think about consumer magazines and make the same lists.

Dig Deeper
Step 2

Pick a trade journal and a consumer magazine and make notes on the following characteristics:

1. If you are working with a printed magazine, approximately what percentage of the pages are devoted to advertising? If it is an online magazine, count the number of ads.

2. How many stories are in this issue? How long are they? How many are about controversial subjects?

3. How many photos or illustrations are there?

4. What are the demographics of the audience targeted by the style of the writing, the layout and the advertising? Do there seem to be any ties between advertising and the stories?

5. What else do you see that sets this magazine apart?

What Do You Think?
Step 3

Compare the lists of attributes of a trade journal and a consumer magazine that you made in Step 2. How do they compare to your ideas in Step 1? Does one of the magazines you looked at do a better job than the others of appealing to its audience? If so, why? Does this correlate with how well a magazine reaches its readers? Do you think it is better to choose to serve a bigger audience or a smaller one?

KEEPING UP TO DATE

CARD (Canadian Advertising Rates and Data) is a listing of newspapers and magazines published in Canada. It includes circulation data and current ad rates.

Editor & Publisher is a weekly trade journal for the newspaper industry.

Folio is a trade journal on magazine management. Among major newspapers that track magazine issues in a fairly consistent way are *The New York Times, The Wall Street Journal,* and *USA Today.*

NewsInc. is a monthly trade journal on newspaper management.

Newspaper Research Journal is a quarterly that deals mostly with applied research.

Presstime is published monthly by the Newspaper Association of America.

The Publisher covers community newspapers across Canada.

Many general-interest magazines, such as *Maclean's,* cover print media issues on a regular basis.

FOR FURTHER LEARNING

James Adams. "A Good News, Bad News Issue." *The Globe and Mail* (July 25, 2006).

J. Antonio Alpalhao and Victor Da Rosa. *A Minority in a Changing Society: The Portuguese Communities of Quebec* (University of Ottawa Press, 1980).

Roland Barthes. "The Photographic Message." In *Image-Music-Text* (Fontana, 1973).

James L. Baughman. *Henry R. Luce and the Rise of the American News Media* (Tawyne, 1987).

Bill Bishop. "A Warning from Smithville: Owning Your Own Weekly." *Washington Journalism Review* (May 10, 1988): 4, 25–32.

Leo Bogart. *Preserving the Press: How Daily Newspapers Mobilized to Keep Their Readers* (Columbia University Press, 1991).

Reginald Bragonier, Jr., and David J. Fisher. *The Mechanics of a Magazine* (Hearst, 1984).

Walter M. Brasch. *Forerunners of Revolution: Muckrakers and the American Social Conscience* (University of America Press, 1990).

Robert Brehl. "Conrad Black Takes on Toronto." *The Globe and Mail* (June 13, 1998).

Iain Calder. *The Untold Story: My 20 Years Running the National Enquirer* (Miramax, 2004).

Canada. Royal Commission on Newspapers, 1981.

Canada. Senate Special Committee on the Mass Media, *Report.* 3 vols. (Ottawa, 1970).

J. William Click and Russell N. Baird. *Magazine Editing and Production,* Fifth edition (Wm. C. Brown, 1990).

Ellis Cose. *The Press* (Morrow, 1989).

Jonathan Curiel. "Gay Newspapers." *Editor & Publisher* 224 (August 3, 1991): 32, 14–19.

Gregory Curtis. "The End of the Trail." *Brill's Content* (November 2000): 76–80.

Keith Damsell. "Magazine Numbers Unravelled." *The Globe and Mail* (July 6, 2001).

Francis X. Dealy. *The Power and the Money: Inside* The Wall Street Journal (Birch Lane Press, 1993).

Peter Desbarats. *Guide to the Canadian News Media* (Harcourt, Brace, Jovanovich, 1990).

Edwin Diamond. *Behind the Times: Inside* The New York Times (Villard Books, 1994).

Robert Draper. *Rolling Stone Magazine: The Uncensored History* (Doubleday, 1990).

Elizabeth L. Eisenstein. *The Printing Press as an Agent of Change: Communications and Cultural Transformation in Early-Modern Europe*, 2 vols. (Cambridge University Press, 1980).

Bob Ferguson. "Critics Crank Up Pressure over Black's Newspaper Play." *Toronto Star* (May 23, 1998).

Douglas Fetherling. *The Rise of the Canadian Newspaper* (Oxford University Press, 1990).

Otto Friedrich. *Decline and Fall* (Harper & Row, 1969).

John Geddes. "The Izzy and Leonard Show." *Maclean's* (August 14, 2000).

Douglas H. George. *The Smart Magazines: 50 Years of Literary Revelry and High Jinks at* Vanity Fair, The New Yorker, Life, Esquire *and* The Smart Set (Archon Books, 1991).

The Globe and Mail: 150 Years in Canada (1994).

Dennis Holder, Robert Love, Bill Meyers, and Roger Piantadosi, contributors. "Magazines in the 1980s." *Washington Journalism Review* 3 (November 1981): 3, 28–41.

Ernest C. Hynds. *American Newspapers in the 1980s* (Hastings House, 1980).

M. Thomas Inge, ed. *Handbook of American Popular Culture*, Second edition (Greenwood, 1989).

Amy Janello and Brennon Jones. *The American Magazine* (Harry N. Abrams, 1991).

Sammye Johnson and Patricia Projatel. *Magazine Publishing* (NTC, 2000).

Lauren Kessler. *Against the Grain: The Dissident Press in America* (Sage, 1984).

Wilfred Kesterton. *A History of Journalism in Canada* (McClelland and Stewart, 1967).

Wilfred Kesterton. "The Growth of the Newspaper in Canada, 1981." In *Communications in Canadian Society*, edited by Benjamin Singer (Addison-Wesley, 1983).

Michael Leapman. *Arrogant Aussie: The Rupert Murdoch Story* (Lyle Stuart, 1985).

Kent MacDougall. *The Press: A Critical Look from the Inside* (Dow Jones Books, 1972).

Magazines Canada. *Fast Facts 2006*.

Ted Magder. "Franchising the Candy Store." *Canadian American Public Policy Centre* (April 1998).

Casey Mahood. "Black Daily Marks Sector's Boom." *The Globe and Mail* (April 9, 1998).

Barbara Matusow. "Allen H. Neuharth Today." *Washington Journalism Review* 8 (August 1986): 8, 18–24.

Richmond M. McClure. *To the End of Time: The Seduction and Conquest of a Media Empire* (Simon & Schuster, 1992).

Marshall McLuhan. *The Gutenberg Galaxy* (University of Toronto Press, 1962).

Minister of Supply and Services Canada. *A Question of Balance: Report of the Task Force on the Canadian Magazine Industry* (1994).

Al Neuharth. *Confessions of an S.O.B.* (Doubleday, 1989).

Alan and Barbara Nourie. *American Mass-Market Magazines* (Greenwood, 1990).

D. M. Osborne. "Paying Respects." *Brill's Content* (October 1998): 93–95.

Andrew M. Osler. "From Vincent Massey to Thomas Kent: The Evolution of National Press Policy in Canada, 1981." In *Communications in Canadian Society*, edited by Benjamin Singer (Addison-Wesley, 1983).

Theodore Peterson. *Magazines in the Twentieth Century* (University of Illinois Press, 1964).

Sam G. Riley, eds. *Corporate Magazines in the United States* (Greenwood Press, 1992).

Sam G. Riley and Gary W. Selnow, eds. *Regional Interest Magazines of the United States* (Greenwood Press, 1991).

Katherine Rosman. "The Secret of Her Success." *Brill's Content* (November 1998): 102–111.

Edward E. Scharfe. *Worldly Power: The Making of* The Wall Street Journal (Beaufort, 1986).

William Shawcross. *Murdoch* (Simon & Schuster, 1993).

Ted Curtis Smythe. "Special Interest Magazines: Wave of the Future or Undertow." In *Readings in Mass Communication*, 6th ed., edited by Michael Emery and Smythe (Wm. C. Brown, 1986).

James D. Squires. *Read All About It! The Corporate Takeover of America's Newspapers* (Times Books, 1993).

Jim Strader. "Black on Black." *Washington Journalism Review* 14 (March 1992): 2, 33–36.

W. A. Swanberg. *Luce and His Empire* (Scribners, 1972).

William H. Taft. *American Magazines for the 1980s* (Hastings House, 1982).

John Tebbel. *A History of Book Publishing in the United States*, Vols. 1–3 (R. R. Bowker, 1972–1977).

John Tebbel and Mary Ellen Zuckerman. *The Magazine in America, 1741–1990* (Oxford University Press, 1991).

Hunter S. Thompson. *Fear and Loathing in America: The Brutal Odyssey of an Outlaw Journalism 1968–1976* (Simon & Schuster, 2000).

Times Mirror Center for the People and the Press. *The Age of Indifference* (Times Mirror Company, 1990).

Eric Utne. "Tina's New Yorker." *Columbia Journalism Review* 31 (March/April 1993): 6, 31–37.

Jeannette Walls. *Dish: The Inside Story of World Gossip* (Avon/Spike, 2000).

Jennifer Wells. "Assessing Black's Toronto Plan." *Maclean's* (October 13, 1997).

Anthony Wilson-Smith. "The Scoop on Black." *Maclean's* (March 30, 1998).

Mary Ellen Zuckerman. *History of Popular Women's Magazines in the United States, 1792–1995* (Greenwood, 1999).

Do the Math. Once considered an icon in the Canadian music industry, Sam the Record Man closed the doors on its flagship store in Toronto in 2007. Owners cited competition from music downloading as the primary reason.

Sound Recording

Media in Theory

Analysis of Canadian Content

Since 1971, the Canadian Radio-television and Telecommunications Commission (CRTC) has required that Canadian radio stations play a certain amount of Canadian content (known as **Cancon**) between the hours of 6 a.m. and midnight. While some good Canadian singers and groups emerged in the early 1970s, Canadian music was difficult to find at the time. As a result, some Canadian recordings were seen as inferior to American recordings. In his autobiography, *Taking Care of Business,* Randy Bachman of The Guess Who and Bachman Turner Overdrive said that quite often Canadian radio wouldn't play a Canadian song until it became a "hit" in the United States. That's why the group called itself "The Guess Who": to eliminate any anti-Canadian bias from radio. Hard to believe, but according to Nicholas Jennings in *Before the Goldrush,* when debate began in the late 1960s on the issue of Canadian content on radio, radio stations were against it. Jennings explains that the Canadian Association of Broadcasters claimed that imposing Canadian content regulations on radio would "lower the attractiveness of stations to the listener."

Adding to this negative myth about Canadian music, certain broadcasters played little Canadian content during the day, instead choosing to "bury" it after

10 p.m. on weeknights and early in the morning on weekends, when fewer people listened to the radio. This practice was also reported in 1994, following a two-year study of FM radio stations sponsored by SOCAN (Society of Composers, Authors and Music Publishers of Canada) and CIRPA (Canadian Independent Record Production Association). In its report, the task force found that only 18 percent of music was Canadian during morning drive times, while Canadian music accounted for 26 percent of the music played during the corresponding afternoon period. Nancy Lanthier, in *Music Scene* magazine, has referred to this as the "Cancon Ghetto." Since 1998, English language Canadian radio stations must play 35 percent Cancon equally throughout the day. Stations in Quebec must play 65 percent Cancon.

What Is Canadian about Canadian Content?

Cancon: Short form for Canadian content.

From a semiotic perspective, if music and lyrics (as signs) signify something other than themselves, one might ask, "What does the lyrical and musical content of Cancon say about Canadian culture?"

A statistical analysis of all the songs that reached number one on the CHUM chart for a 13-year period before and a 13-year period after the implementation of Cancon regulations might help answer these questions. CHUM was a Top 40 powerhouse in Toronto from May 1957 to 1986. The survey reveals that 13 Canadian songs reached number one between 1957 and 1969, while between 1970 and 1982 there were 19 number-one Canadian songs. On the surface, this seems to show that the regulations were successful in promoting Canadian talent and the music industry, as six more Canadian songs reached number one. But a closer analysis shows that these songs had few Canadian signifiers in their lyrics.

During the period before the regulations, 1957 to 1969, at least four of the Canadian songs that reached number one were written by Canadians but recorded by Americans. They included "It Doesn't Matter Anymore" by Buddy Holly, "Love Child" by The Supremes, "Aquarius/Let the Sun Shine In" by the Fifth Dimension, and "Sugar, Sugar" by the Archies. From an economic standpoint, these songs undoubtedly helped the Canadian music industry, but their lyrics say little, if anything, about Canada. In essence they are American songs, written for the U.S. market. In addition, two of the number-one Canadian songs were included on American movie soundtracks. For example, "Born to Be Wild" by Steppenwolf was featured in the film *Easy Rider,* while "One Tin Soldier" by The Original Caste was used in the movie *Billy Jack.* The only Canadian song to reach number one that was explicitly about Canada was the novelty song "Clear the Track, Here Comes Shack" by Douglas Rankine & the Secrets. The song was a tribute to Eddie Shack, a hockey player with the Toronto Maple Leafs.

After the Canadian content regulations came into effect in 1970, the number of Canadian number-one singles on the CHUM charts in a 13-year period increased from 13 to 19. However, the same patterns that existed before the Cancon regulations were still evident: American artists continued to record songs written by Canadians. For example, "Puppy Love," recorded by Donny Osmond, and "She's a Lady," sung by Tom Jones, were written by Paul Anka. "Woodstock," about the mythic American music festival, was written by Joni Mitchell and recorded by Crosby, Stills, Nash & Young. Perhaps only two number-one Canadian singles in Canada during this period were openly nationalistic. The first was "American Woman" (which also reached number one in the United States) by The Guess Who. The song's lyrics made clear distinctions between

Canadian and American culture. The other uniquely Canadian number-one single was "Take Off" by Bob and Doug McKenzie (SCTV comics Rick Moranis and Dave Thomas). However, like "Clear the Track, Here Comes Shack," this brand of nationalism was humorous in nature and perhaps reached number one due to its novelty.

Influence of Sound Recordings

Study Preview   *Recorded music has become a pervasive element in our lives. It is everywhere almost all the time. The companies that dominate the music industry, despite revenue leakage to online music-swapping, are a major force in the global music business.*

PERVASIVENESS OF MUSIC

When urban sophisticates in earlier eras wanted music, they arranged to attend a concert. Many middle-class people went to the parlour and sat at the piano. Rural folks had their music too—a fiddle on the front porch in the evening, a harmonica at the campfire. Music was a special event, a social gathering that had to be arranged. To those people, life today would seem like one big party—music everywhere all the time. Yes, we arrange for concerts and major musical events, but we also wake to music, shop to music and drive to music. Many of us work to music and study to music. In fact, the recording industry has products in so many parts of our lives that many people take most of them for granted.

SCOPE OF THE RECORDING INDUSTRY

The recording industry that brings music to mass audiences, both the flashy stuff and everything else, is gigantic. Global sales in 2004 were estimated at $33.6 billion. In 2005, the Ministry of Canadian Heritage reported that music sales were worth $902 million. These totals don't include symbiotic industries like fan magazines, music television and radio. That's worth billions more. Then there are concerts, performers' merchandise, sponsorships and a miscellany of related enterprises.

Even in leaner times, with major losses to online music swapping, recordings from Canadian acts continue to sell well. Canadian artists sold 6.8 million albums in 2001; that rose to 8.5 million by 2004. That's an increase of 25 percent during the heyday of free music downloading.

Recording Industry

Study Preview   *Four major players dominate the global music-recording industry, all with big-name acts. Most of the industry's musical innovations, however, originate with independent recording companies. The indies gave rock 'n' roll its start—rap too.*

MAJORS

The recording industry is concentrated in four major companies known as the Big Four, which have 75 percent of the global market. Each of these companies, in turn, is part of a larger media conglomerate.

Universal Music Group: The largest presence in sales of recorded music.
http://umusic.ca

Sony BMG: Includes music news and links to the many Sony BMG labels.
www.sonybmg.com

EMI Group: Browse EMI's labels and artist sites while listening to music online.
www.emigroup.com

Warner Music Canada: Links to all of Warner's holdings worldwide.
www.warnermusic.ca

Canadian Independent Record Production Association: CIRPA represents the independent sector of the Canadian music and sound recording industry.
www.cirpa.ca

The file-sharing crisis in the early 2000s shook up the industry's corporate landscape. Sony and Bertelsmann merged their music units. Bertelsmann, the German company that is the world's fifth largest media company, runs the combined Sony BMG. Alarmed at declining sales in the new file-swapping era, Time Warner sold its Warner Music in 2004 to Edgar Bronfman Jr. and fellow investors. Bronfman, heir to the Seagram liquor fortune in Canada, earlier had run the Universal movie and recording empire but had sold it to the French media conglomerate Vivendi. Although Vivendi, financially overextended, sold off many holdings to solve its own crisis in 2003, it decided to stay the course with Universal Music. There were no buyers anyway. Times were tough in the industry, and prospects for a recovery were cloudy at best.

INDIES

indies Independently owned record-making companies; not part of Big Four.

For decades a secondary tier of independent recording companies, **indies**, as they were known in industry jargon, struggled against the majors and occasionally produced a hit. When an indy amassed enough successes, it invariably was bought out by a major. The Ministry of Canadian Heritage says that more than 250 independent labels are responsible for roughly 90 percent of Cancon produced here at home. Most of the companies are based in Ontario, but Quebec and British Columbia are also responsible for much of our independent music. Some major Canadian independent labels include Nettwerk, Aquarius, and Quebec's Tacca Musique.

Media Databank

Recording Companies

Four companies dominate the recording industry, although nonmajors, called *indies*, typically claim about 15 percent of U.S. sales—even more globally. This is the global picture, with major acts on the companies' labels:

Universal Music (French) 25.5%

Guns N' Roses (Universal), Jay-Z (Def Jam), Nelly Furtado (Dreamworks), George Strait (MCA Nashville), Snoop Dogg (Geffen), Gwen Stefani (Interscope), The Killers (Island)

Sony BMG (German) 21.5%

Bruce Springsteen (Columbia), Jennifer Lopez (Epic), Santana (Legacy), Travis Tritt (Sony Nashville), Sloan (Yep Rok)

EMI (Anglo-Dutch) 13.1%

Beastie Boys (Capitol), Janet Jackson (Virgin), Tina Turner (Capitol)

Warner Music 11.3%

Doors (Elektra), Rush (Atlantic), Green Day (Reprise), Madonna (Maverick)

Case Study

Streaming: Suicide or Success?

"What if there was a movement to shut down libraries because book publishers and authors were up in arms over the idea that people are reading books for free?" asks Jeff Tweedy, leader of the band Wilco.

Wilco is a success story, and its success came from the internet. Tweedy says that we live in a connected world, and the web is taking the place of radio, MTV and retail stores. The web is where kids are learning about new music.

When the group's label, Warner's Reprise, decided in 2001 that Wilco's fourth album, *Yankee Hotel Foxtrot,* was no good, Wilco got out of its contract by purchasing the album back for $50 000. The band then released the album on its website. That was followed by a sold-out 30-city tour, filled with fans who had found the band on the internet. Then Nonesuch Records, another Warner label, bought the rights to *Yankee Hotel Foxtrot,* reportedly at three times the original price.

Nonesuch wasn't worried that hundreds of thousands of fans had downloaded the band's next release, *A Ghost Is Born,* before the disc came out. Tweedy says when the album started showing up on the internet, the band was contacted by fans who were excited that they had found the album on peer-to-peer (P2P) networks and wanted to give something back in good faith. "We couldn't take the money ourselves, so we pointed them to Doctors Without Borders." The charity ended up receiving about $11 000. And *A Ghost Is Born* picked up two Grammys.

Other bands found similar success when they partnered with the web. Nine Inch Nails and Jupiter Sunrise joined a community website called MySpace.com, which had 240 000 band members and 14 million listener members in mid-2005. The president of MySpace.com describes the experience as being similar to going to a friend's house and hearing music that is new to you. Even music industry reps search sites like MySpace for talent.

Recording artists have many different opinions about using the *internet.* Some see the web as a potential source for hooking new fans, but others think the free downloading is bad for their business. As one DJ says, "I don't work for free, do you?" CD sales in Canada are down. According to the CRIA (The Canadian Recording Industry Association), the 10 best-selling albums in Canada in 1999 sold 5.9 million units. By 2003, the top 10 albums sold only 3.4 million copies. Although many factors may have contributed to this loss—including pricing and competition from DVDs and games, the ever-shrinking playlists on commercial radio, the declining popularity of replacing vinyl with CDs and limited title availability at retail—some artists connect the music industry's troubles to the internet.

Wilco Guitarist Jeff Tweedy. Wilco demonstrated that musicians can succeed without major labels. The band took its album *Yankee Hotel Foxtrot* back after the Warner label Reprise declined to market it aggressively. Wilco posted the album online for free downloading, which spurred sales and led to a profitable tour. Still, there is evidence aplenty that downloading can undermine the economics of the record music industry. The Wilco experience may not be the right business model.

As you will see later in the chapter, Canadian Terry McBride, the CEO of Nettwerk Records, sees peer-to-peer sharing (P2P) as the future. He claims that "kids aren't formatted. They just like music." He agrees with Wilco. The traditional "top-down" method of music popularity, with radio and MuchMusic telling teenagers what's popular, doesn't work anymore. It's word of mouth and sharing of songs that now determines popularity.

Artists who have found success through the internet say that it gives them the power to direct their own futures. Bands can create a buzz in the music world by releasing their work on the web. In 2007, Radiohead released *In Rainbows* online, allowing downloaders to pay whatever they could. Is this a glimpse into the future of music distribution? Time will tell.

What do you think?

1. Will file sharing become a regular part of music promotion?
2. The sound quality of an MP3 is lower than that of the original CD or vinyl record. Do you think that should make a difference in how the record industry views P2P networks?
3. Do you think the Recording Industry Association of America's (RIAA) lawsuits against individual file sharers will slow the streaming of music?

Thomas Edison: Learn more about the inventor who started the march toward today's recording technology.

www.thomasedison.com

Emile Berliner: Learn more about the German-born Canadian inventor who helped Edison.

www.collectionscanada. ca/4/4/m2-3005-e.html

Thomas Edison Built the first audio recorder-playback machine.

Phonograph Trade name for the first recorder-playback machine.

acoustic recording Vibration-sensitive recording technology.

Emile Berliner His machine played discs that could be mass-produced.

Transforming Innovations

Study Preview   *Technology created the recorded music industry, which goes back to Thomas Edison and Emile Berliner. Later innovations reshaped recorded products, mostly through playback discs and digital delivery. Also pivotal in shaping the industry in Canada have been the Cancon regulations.*

SOUND TECHNOLOGY

For years, scientific journals had speculated on ways to reproduce sound, but not until 1877 did anyone build a machine that could do it. That was when U.S. inventor **Thomas Edison** applied for a patent for a talking machine. He used the trade name **Phonograph**, which was taken from Greek words meaning "to write sound."

ACOUSTIC RECORDING. The heart of Edison's invention was a cylinder wrapped in tin foil. The cylinder was rotated as a singer shouted into a large metal funnel. The funnel channeled the voice against a diaphragm, which fluttered to the vibrations. A stylus, which most people called a "needle," was connected to the diaphragm and cut a groove in the foil, the depth of the groove reflecting the vibrations. To listen to a recording, you put the cylinder on a player and set a needle in the groove that had been created in the recording process. Then you placed your ear to a megaphonelike horn and rotated the cylinder. The needle tracked the groove, and the vibrations created by the varying depths of the groove were fed through the horn. This process was called **acoustic recording**.

Edison's system contained a major impediment to commercial success: a recording could not be duplicated. In 1887, Montreal's **Emile Berliner** introduced a breakthrough. Rather than recording on a cylinder covered with flimsy foil, as Edison did, Berliner used a sturdy metal disc. From the metal disc Berliner made a mould and then poured a thermoplastic material into the mould. When the material hardened, Berliner had a near-perfect copy of the original disc—and he could make hundreds of them. Berliner's system, called the Gramophone, led to mass production.

What Edison Wrought. The prolific inventor Thomas Edison devised a machine that took sound waves and etched them into grooves on a foil drum. Although technologically a breakthrough, the sound was primitive. Only the most obvious tones could be picked up. Whatever few tonal subtleties and soft trills were recorded got lost in playback scratchiness. Firm horns and percussions did well.

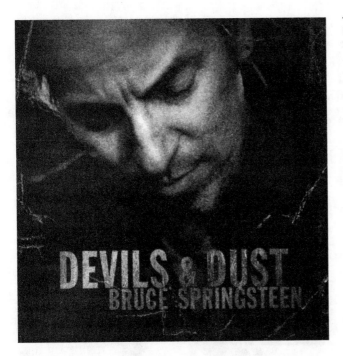

DualDisc. When Bruce Springsteen's 19th album, *Devils & Dust,* was released in 2005, it was on **DualDisc**—a hybrid format with music on one side, like a CD, and video content on the other, like a DVD. Springsteen was the first Top List performer to go with DualDisc, the first major new physical format for recorded music since the compact disc 20 years earlier.

DualDisc Hybrid CD-DVD format introduced in 2005.

Joseph Maxwell Introduced electrical recording in the 1920s.

digital recording Recording and playback system using on-off binary code for sound.

compact disc Digital record format; now dominant.

CD Short for "compact disc."

Elvis Presley: He ain't nothin' but a hound dog. Get all shook up at the official site.
www.elvis.com

Beatles: A multimedia look at the band that started the British Invasion.
www.beatles.com

Rap Dictionary: Decodes the lingo, identifies the artists, and locates the places they talk about.
www.rapdict.org

All Music: An excellent website that covers all genres and artists.
www.allmusic.com

ELECTRICAL RECORDING. In the 1920s the Columbia and Victor record companies introduced records based on an electrical system perfected by **Joseph Maxwell** of Bell Laboratories. Metal funnels were replaced by microphones, which had superior sensitivity. For listening, it was no longer a matter of putting an ear to a mechanical amplifying horn that had only a narrow frequency response. Instead, loudspeakers amplified the sound electromagnetically.

DIGITAL RECORDING. Record-makers developed a technological revolution in 1978: the **digital recording**. No longer were continuous sound waves inscribed physically on a disc. Instead, sound waves were sampled at millisecond intervals, and each sample was logged in computer language as an isolated on-off binary number. When discs were played back, the digits were translated back to the sound at the same millisecond intervals at which they were recorded. The intervals would be replayed so fast that the sound would seem continuous, just as the individual frames in a motion picture become a moving blur that is perceived by the eye as continuous motion.

By 1983 digital recordings were available to consumers in the form of **compact discs**, silvery 4.7-inch platters. The binary numbers were tiny pits on the disc that were read by a laser light in the latest version of the phonograph: the **CD** player. The player itself converted the numbers to sound.

PERFORMER INFLUENCES

The recording industry's main product, pop music, has been shaped by changing public tastes. This has been especially true since the end of World War II.

ROCKABILLY. After World War II, major record labels groomed singers in the sentimental croon-swoon style, typified by Frank Sinatra and Rosemary Clooney in the United States and The Four Lads in Canada. Cavalierly, the majors figured that they could manipulate public tastes to their products. So confident were major labels in their

Elvis Presley. Rock 'n' roll, a new hybrid musical form epitomized by Elvis Presley, took root with independent recording companies. To their peril, major labels tried to ignore the phenomenon, figuring it soon would pass. It didn't. Just when some indies, like Sun, were on the brink of becoming larger players in the recording industry landscape, the majors swept into rock 'n' roll and maintained their dominance in the industry.

strategy that they were blindsided by the sudden grassroots enthusiasm in the 1950s for Elvis Presley, "the white boy who sang coloured," as he was called at the time. In Memphis an independent label, Sun Records, had assembled a lineup consisting of Carl Perkins, Roy Orbison, Johnny Cash and Presley. The music was called **rockabilly**, a linkage of black and hillbilly music.

After months of inroads from rockabilly acts, the major labels scrambled to catch the wave. The major label RCA signed Presley. Other majors absorbed rockabilly indies. In the nick of time the majors saved themselves from the course they had been following and embraced the new genre, which was coming to be called **rock 'n' roll**.

BRITISH INVASION. The U.S. record industry was rocked again in the early 1960s, this time by music from Britain. The Beatles caught the ear of a new generation, not only on radio but also with a series of platinum singles and albums. The **British Invasion** was a new wake-up call for U.S. record-makers. The industry's largely insular concept of itself was no longer viable. International licensing agreements to market music became a new way of doing business and introduced a new view of the global potential for U.S. record-makers. All the major North American record companies were parts of larger media corporations, like RCA and Columbia Broadcasting, and thus had far more financial muscle than their foreign competitors.

RAP. As transforming as rock was, so too, 40 years later, was **rap**. Born in the impoverished Bronx section of New York City, this new style of music had an intense bass line for dancing and rhyming riffs, often attitude-strong and rapid-fire, overlaid on the music. Slowly, rap spread to other black urban areas. Indie-produced *Run-D.M.C.* and *King of Rock* were the first black rap albums to break into the U.S. music mainstream. Major record companies soon were signing up rap acts. Contro-

rockabilly Hybrid of music in the black tradition and hillbilly music; precursor of rock 'n' roll.

rock 'n' roll Genre marked by incessant beat with guitar as the dominant instrument.

British Invasion Popularity in North America of the Beatles and other British acts.

rap Rhythm-heavy music genre usually with rapid-fire, attitude-heavy lyrics.

versial groups Public Enemy and N.W.A., using violence and racism as themes, made rap a public issue in the 1990s, which only fanned die-hard enthusiasm.

GOVERNMENT INFLUENCE ON CANADIAN MUSIC

Historically, the radio and record industries have always been intimately connected. This was the main reason for instituting Canadian content regulations for radio in 1970. But what makes a song "Canadian"? In 1970, **Stan Klees** of *RPM* magazine developed the "Cancon MAPL" to help the industry define Canadian content. To be categorized as Cancon, a song must generally fulfill two of the following four conditions:

Stan Klees Founder of Cancon MAPL.

- **M (music):** The music must be written by a Canadian (citizen or landed immigrant).
- **A (artist):** The music or lyrics must be principally performed by a Canadian artist.
- **P (produced/performed):** The recording must have been either produced in Canada or performed and broadcast live in Canada.
- **L (lyrics):** The lyrics must be written by a Canadian.

Since its introduction in 1970, Canadian content has been a hotly debated topic in Canadian radio circles. Since then, the **CRTC** regulations have required radio stations in Canada to play a certain level of Canadian content. One of the reasons for this policy was to help strengthen the Canadian music industry by encouraging radio to support Canadian singers, songwriters, performers and others involved in the production of Canadian music. Prior to the 1970 regulations, it's estimated that Canadian music made up about 4 percent of all music heard on Canadian radio.

CRTC The Canadian Radio-television and Telecommunications Commission.

While the system seems to favour Canadian artists, it can also discriminate against Canadian singers. A controversy involving Bryan Adams is a good

CRTC: Canada's broadcast regulator.
www.crtc.gc.ca

Media Databank

Best of the Cancon Crop

Since the early days of rock 'n' roll, Canadians have been successful in the United States. According to *Billboard* magazine, here are the top 10 Canadian songs of all time in the United States. Some would argue that the reason these Canadian artists have been able to be successful abroad is due to Cancon regulations here in Canada.

1. "How You Remind Me," Nickelback (2001)
2. "You're Still the One," Shania Twain (1998)
3. "Because You Loved Me," Celine Dion (1996)
4. "Theme from a Summer Place," Percy Faith (1960)
5. "Informer," Snow (1993)
6. "Nobody's Supposed to Be Here," Deborah Cox (1998)
7. "The Power of Love," Celine Dion (1994)
8. "It's All Coming Back to Me Now," Celine Dion (1996)
9. "I Do It for You (Everything I Do)," Bryan Adams (1991)
10. "Have You Ever Really Loved a Woman?" Bryan Adams (1995)

Source: Fred Bronson, "Billboard's Hottest Hot 100 Hits."

example of discrimination against Canadian singers. His song from *Robin Hood: Prince of Thieves*, "I Do It for You (Everything I Do)," and other songs on his album *Waking Up the Neighbours* were not originally considered Canadian content because he co-wrote them with a British songwriter. Due to the controversy that ensued from this classification, the CRTC amended the MAPL formula (the criteria of music, artist, produced/performed, lyrics) to allow for Canadian songwriters who collaborate with foreigners.

Have the Canadian content regulations worked? The regulations had two general objectives: to promote Canadian culture and to help strengthen the Canadian music industry. One could easily argue that the music industry is stronger today than it was in 1970. Canadian music certainly doesn't have the same negative connotation it did in the 1970s and 1980s. A 2005 Decima Research study claims that 93 percent of Canadians consider Canadian music to be as good as or better than music by foreign artists. The study also suggested that over 90 percent of Canadians listen to Canadian music. Cancon is a success.

Social Issues and Music

Study Preview   *Campaigns to ban recorded music are nothing new. In the Roaring Twenties some people saw jazz as morally loose. White racists of the 1950s called Bill Haley's rock "nigger music." War protest songs of the Vietnam period angered many Americans.*

RECORD LABELING

Parents' Music Resource Center Crusaded for labels on "objectionable" music.

In the 1980s, complaints about lyrics narrowed to drugs and sexual promiscuity. In the United States, **Parents' Music Resource Center**, a group led by Tipper Gore and wives of several other influential members of Congress, claimed there were links between explicit rock music and teen suicide, teen pregnancy, abusive parents, broken homes, and other social ills. The group objected to lyrics such as those in Def Leppard's "High and Dry," which extols drug and alcohol use; Mötley Crüe's "Bastard," with its violent overtones; and Cyndi Lauper's "She Bop," which was a thinly veiled song about masturbation.

The Parents' Music Resource Center argued that consumer protection laws should be invoked to require that records with offensive lyrics be labeled as dangerous, similar to cigarette warning labels or the movie industry's rating system. Record companies began labeling potentially offensive records: "Explicit Lyrics—Parental Advisory." In some cases, the companies printed lyrics on album covers as a warning. Online retailers, including iTunes, put a label of "explicit" on songs that might raise the prudish eyebrows.

Artistic Autonomy

Study Preview   *Major labels once dominated the nation's music with expensive talent and recording operations that neither indies nor individual performers could match. Digital recording equipment in the 1980s loosened the majors' artistic control.*

A&R STRUCTURE

The heart of the recording industry once was the powerful **A&R** units, short for **artist and repertoire**, at major labels. In an arrogant tyranny over artists, A&R executives manufactured countless performers. They groomed artists for stardom, chose their music, ordered the arrangements, controlled recording sessions and even chose their wardrobes for public performances.

A&R (artist and repertoire) Units of recording company responsible for talent.

In his book *Solid Gold,* Serge Denisoff quotes a Capitol executive from the 1950s explaining how the A&R system worked: "The company would pick out 12 songs for Peggy Lee and tell her to be at the studio Wednesday at 8, and she'd show up and sing what you told her. And she'd leave three hours later and Capitol'd take her songs and do anything it wanted with them. That was a time when the artist was supposed to shut up and put up with anything the almighty recording company wanted."

The muscle of the major record companies, aiming for mass market sales, contributed to a homogenizing of culture. Coast to coast, everybody was humming the same new tunes from Peggy Lee and other pop singers, who served a robotlike role for A&R managers. The A&R structure was a top-down system for creating pop culture. A relatively small number of powerful A&R executives decided what would be recorded and marketed. It was the opposite of grassroots artistry.

MUSIC DEMASSIFICATION

In the 1980s, sophisticated low-cost recording and mixing equipment gave individual artists and **garage bands** a means to control their art. The million-dollar sound studio, controlled by major labels and their A&R people, became less important. As little as $15 000 could buy digital recorders and 24-channel mixing boards, plus remodeling of the garage, to do what only a major studio could have done a few years earlier. Artists suddenly had an independence that big recording companies were forced to learn to accommodate. Linda Ronstadt, for example, shifted her recording to a home studio in her basement. Some artists, like LL Cool J, went so far as to create their own labels.

garage bands Coined term for upstart performers without a studio contract.

Another result has been greater diversity. A rap fan might never have heard the Dixie Chicks. The music of Barry Manilow is obscure to most young fans of My Chemical Romance. In this sense, recorded music has become less of a unifying element in the whole society. The unification, rather, is in subsets of the mass audience.

TOURING

Big-name performers have found a significant income stream outside of the recording industry by taking their music directly to fans on a new scale. On tour, U2 commands ticket prices from $50 to $170. Prices for the 2005 tours of Paul McCartney and the Rolling Stones were higher. On-tour performances and recorded-music sales fuel each other symbiotically. Also significant, **touring** is controlled not by recording companies but by concert promotion companies. The largest in North America are Clear Channel and the House of Blues. To varying degrees the growth of the touring industry has lessened performers' reliance on the recording industry as their main revenue source. This too has contributed to less recording company control and greater artist autonomy.

touring Live performances in highly promoted road trips; increasingly important revenue source for big-name performers.

Media People

Alan Cross

Alan Cross

Since his days as a political science student, **Alan Cross** has had a passion for music and radio. His first show was on the University of Winnipeg's closed-circuit radio station, CKUW, in 1980. He turned that passion into a radio career that has seen him become somewhat of a music "guru" in Canada.

The radio program "Ongoing History of New Music" has been a staple of the Canadian alternative music scene since its debut in 1993. The show began as a way of educating listeners about the grunge revolution that was happening at the time. According to Cross, "It was obvious that there was a change happening in the world of rock and a new generation was about to take over and displace the hair metal bands that had been around since the 1980s. Our radio station jumped on the new music bandwagon. It was also decided that in order to put this new music into the appropriate context, it was necessary to have a documentary program that would help everybody understand where this music came from, why it's important, where it's going, and where its heritage was."

The music industry has undergone some seismic changes in the last 10 years. "Back in the 1960s, 1970s and 1980s, bands were allowed to develop over time. REM really didn't have a hit until album number six. U2 had to wait until album number three until they had their breakthrough. The major record labels had patience for talent development. Those luxuries don't exist anymore. Although sales of digital downloads continue to climb, they have yet to offset the decline in the sales of physical CDs. Meanwhile, small, nimble independent record companies are able to pounce on trends more quickly—plus they're able to service niche music markets more effectively. In fact, most of the truly groundbreaking new music today is coming from the small independent labels—just like back in the 1950s and 1960s—and is once again becoming more and more prevalent. Small Canadian labels like Sonic Unyon, Arts&Crafts and Maple Music are becoming more important in developing new music."

In regards to Canadian content, Cross also has an interesting point of view: "When the regulations were first introduced more than 35 years ago, Cancon was a necessary cultural and industrial strategy. The country was being completely overrun by international interests. Most record companies were simply branch offices of their American parents and they, naturally, were interested in marketing their American artists. Homegrown performers were squeezed out and not given a chance to develop in any way. It was a vicious circle. You couldn't get on the radio because you weren't good enough, and you couldn't get good enough because you couldn't get on the radio. It was tough, but the imposition of Cancon quotas has been a very successful strategy. It helped create an industry where we actually have vibrant, profitable, and relevant record labels, not to mention some world-class musicians. Canada probably exports more than its fair share of music, given our population."

That being said, Cross feels that since Cancon has made Canadian music successful, we have to ask ourselves, "At what point are the quotas no longer necessary? People will point to the cultural imperialism of the United States and say that the only way to maintain Canadian cultural sovereignty is to maintain or even raise these quotas. They feel the Cancon rules have accomplished their mission and now it's time for Canadian artists to stand on their own. After a few years, the question became 'Should Cancon quotas be raised, lowered or eliminated altogether?' During the CRTC's review of radio in 2006, some groups lobbied for Cancon to be increased from 35% to 40, 45 and even beyond 50% while others argued that with the increasingly popular and borderless world of the Internet, traditional broadcasters shouldn't be hobbled with additional regulation and quotas. When the dust cleared, though, the Commission left levels at 35%. Still, the subject of Cancon levels remains a very politically charged debate amongst broadcasters, record companies, artists, songwriters, music publishers, music collectives, the Heritage Ministry, and the CRTC."

Alan Cross New music historian.

When music industry analysts assess the revenue streams of performers today, they consider three major factors.

RETAIL. The traditional outlet for recorded music, once mostly free-standing record shops, has shifted to giant retailers like Future Shop and Costco. In the post-Napster era, traditional retail sales have slipped.

DOWNLOADING. The new retailing is through download sites like iTunes Music Store and Puretracks. This is a growing revenue source.

TOURING. Concerts are big business for performers who can attract sell-out crowds for their shows, especially the techno-spectaculars.

Streaming Crisis

Study Preview   *Napster and other file-sharing technology that facilitates music swapping seriously eroded music sales and record industry viability.*

FILE SHARING

Shawn Fanning's **Napster** technology ushered in a frenzy of free music-swapping on the internet in 2000. Suddenly, record stores found themselves unable to move inventory. The free fall continued. For the first time in its history the record industry was not in control of new technology—unlike the earlier adjustments, when companies exploited developments to goose sales, such as switches to high fidelity and stereo and the introduction of eight tracks, cassettes and CDs.

The **Recording Industry Association of America (RIAA)**, which represents recorded music companies, went to court against Napster. A federal judge bought the argument that Napster was participating in copyright infringement by facilitating illicit copying of protected intellectual property. Napster was toast. But other file-swapping mechanisms remained, some harder to tackle. Kazaa, for example, kept moving its operations from one offshore site to another, where legal actions were impossible. In a surreal initiative in 2003, RIAA began legal action against individuals who downloaded music without paying. The association's goal was a few hundred highly publicized lawsuits, perhaps some showcase trials, to discourage download piracy. In one respect, the strategy backfired, only engendering hard feelings among music consumers. By 2006, consumers began suing the RIAA.

In Canada, the CRIA (The **Canadian Recording Industry Association**) also went to court. From a legal standpoint, in early 2004, CRIA's hopes of having the law on its side were dealt a severe blow. CRIA was hoping the Supreme Court of Canada would force internet service providers (ISPs) to identify people who shared files using P2P file-sharing programs. The Supreme Court decreed that simply placing files in a shared P2P folder does not constitute copyright infringement.

There's no doubt that file sharing has impacted music sales. Data from the Department of Canadian Heritage claims that one-third of Canadians download music for free. Teenagers, not surprisingly, are the worst offenders with 68 percent of them claiming they prefer to download music for free. For example, in 2005, Gwen Stefani's "Hollaback Girl" was the first song to reach one million (legal) digital downloads in America. In Canada, it was downloaded a mere 20 000 times.

Jeff Rose-Martland, host of VOCM-Radio Labrador, claims that the decline in music sales has little to do with peer-to-peer (P2P) file sharing. Rather, it has to do

iTunes: For a fee, Apple makes music singles available for the iPod and other players. **www.apple.com/ca/itunes**

Puretracks: A Canadian equivalent to iTunes. **www.puretracks.ca**

MySpace.com: The music section of this community website includes featured artists, online prerelease songs and music videos. **www.myspace.com**

Shawn Fanning. The courts found his 1998 Napster music-downloading software violated the copyrights of the music owners. Nonetheless, Napster paved the way for other systems that facilitated free and inexpensive public access to music that transformed the music industry at the start of the 21st century.

Shawn Fanning Inventor of Napster.

Napster First online music-swapping software.

Recording Industry Association of America (RIAA) Trade association of music recording companies.

Canadian Recording Industry Association (CRIA) Canadian trade association of music recording companies.

peer-to-peer sharing (P2P) Music-swapping software without a central server.

with the quality of music today. According to Rose-Martland, "CRIA suggests that sales of all albums are down. Not true. Sales of the currently hyped albums are down. Sales of good-quality standards are up, as downloaders discover *The White Album, Ziggy Stardust,* and *Nevermind.*" In fact, two of the RIAA's top 100 albums of all time are by Canadian artists: Shania Twain's *Come on Over* and Alanis Morissette's *Jagged Little Pill.*

IPOD

iPod Brand name for Apple's handheld digital music device.

Steve Jobs Driving force behind Apple Computer revival, iPod, and iTunes.

iTunes Online music store.

Another favourable development for the industry was already easing the doomsayers' gloomy scenario: the **iPod**. In 2002 the innovator behind Apple Computer, **Steve Jobs**, introduced a handheld music playback device that he called the iPod, which he quickly followed with the online **iTunes** Music Store. From the iTunes site people could sample a song with a single click and then download with another click for 99 cents. In comparison to P2P file sharing, Apple's sound quality was exceptional and virus free. In iTunes' first week, more than 1 million songs were downloaded, juicing a 27 percent spike in Apple stock.

Steve Jobs

A casualty of file sharing might be the record album itself. The introduction of the iPod has given new importance to the single song as an art form and as a commercial product. In 1948, when music was recorded and sold on discs, **Peter Goldmark**, the chief engineer at Columbia Records, had introduced slow-spinning, **long-play** records, LPs for short. An LP could carry 20 to 30 minutes of music per side. Many artists regarded their work not as songs but as coherent bodies of music packaged in albums. In the past, consumers had no choice but to buy the entire album. File sharing and iPods have changed that. Terry McBride, of Canada's Nettwerk Music Group, believes that P2P is the key to the success of the music industry in the future. Just because album sales are down, that doesn't mean people aren't listening to music. Nettwerk found great success using P2P to help them promote Sarah McLachlan's *Wintersong* CD in 2006. They allowed fans to download a vocal track of one of the songs on the album and remix it themselves. McBride says the results were incredible. "There's now hundreds of thousands of Sarah mixes, all over the place, getting played, and it cost us nothing."

Peter Goldmark Inventor of long-play records.

long-play (LP) 33 1/3-rpm microgroove discs that turned the recorded music industry into conceiving of its products as albums.

The Myth of Free Music: Check out the CRIA's website and the myth of free music.

www.cria.ca

Evaluating Recording Companies

Study Preview   *Sales and profits are quantitative measures of a record company's success. How about its artistic success? Qualitative measures are harder to come by. Elitists give high marks to companies that have a commitment to music that breaks new ground artistically.*

POPULIST MEASURES

People vote with their pocketbooks, which means that popularity is an important measure of success for record company products. Measuring success, however, is problematic. Different gauges don't necessarily correlate. A dominant market share, for example, doesn't always translate into profits.

MARKET SHARE. One measure of a record company's success is reflected in market share. In recent years, Universal has led, but rankings can change overnight. A super-selling soundtrack, like *Titanic,* or a runaway hit album, like Coldplay's *X&Y,* can mean a near-instant reshuffling.

SALES. Another measure is the **gold record.** Once a single sells 1 million copies or an album sells 500 000 copies, the RIAA confers a gold-record award. A **platinum record** is awarded for 2 million singles or 1 million albums. In Canada, The Canadian Recording Industry Association (CRIA) awards a **gold seal** for sales of 50 000, a **platinum seal** for sales of 100 000, and a **diamond seal** for recordings that sell 1 million copies in Canada.

PROFIT. Because many conglomerates don't release profit figures for the record company subsidiaries, measuring profitability isn't easy. Aggregate data compiled by the RIAA indicates market share, but numerous variables can render market share an imperfect signal about profitability. One indicator, although usually vague, can be the annual reports to conglomerate shareholders, which sometimes contain hints like "disappointing sales in the music unit."

Another indicator for assessing record company performance is industry insiders who are quoted in the trade journals and in fan magazines like *Rolling Stone.* Another indicator, also reported in the trade journals, is the promotion and firing of record company executives.

QUALITY MEASURES

Media elitists, who argue that the media should lead public taste, not be mere panderers, are not swayed by commercial and popular measures of success. Elitists look to the media, including record companies, to incubate cultural innovation even when it means taking risks. However, most record companies don't take many risks. Have you ever heard pop rock lyrics without the word "baby"? Although there are exceptions galore, redundant and even tiresome themes seem to work in the marketplace. Many people

Billboard: Check out the latest music charts and play music trivia games.
www.billboard.com

Grammy Awards: Learn more about award winners and how the foundation supports the music community.
www.grammy.com

Juno Awards: The Junos have been recognizing the best in Canadian music since 1970.
www.junoawards.ca

gold record Award for sales of 1 million singles, 500 000 albums.

platinum record Award for sales of 2 million singles, 1 million albums.

gold seal Award for sales of 50 000 units in Canada.

platinum seal Award for sales of 100 000 units in Canada.

diamond seal Award for sales of 1 million units in Canada

The "Sopranos Bounce." In the days after the 2007 series finale of HBO's Sopranos, sales of Journey's 1981 song "Don't Stop Believin'" spiked on both iTunes and Amazon.com. This "bounce" effect is usually attributed to the Grammy Awards. The Grammy Bounce is a perennial phenomenon. In 2003 Norah Jones's "Come Away with Me" zoomed to number one within a week. In 2005, sales of Ray Charles's "Genius Loves Company" rose 875 percent in the days after the Grammy tribute to the musical legend.

Nelly Furtado at the Juno Awards. The Junos have signified excellence in the Canadian music industry since 1971.

Grammy Award for excellence in music in the United States.

Juno Award for excellence in music in Canada.

take comfort in familiar lyrics, instrumentation and even performance styles. But this popularity is hardly satisfying to elitist critics who say the media have a responsibility to push the society's cultural explorations to new levels. To these critics, regurgitation, no matter how pleasant, doesn't count for much. In short, a record company that encourages artistic risk-taking will score well among elitists.

Two awards that honour the best in contemporary music are the Grammys and the Junos. The **Grammy** award has been the symbol of music success in the United States since 1957. Winners are determined by members of the National Academy of Recording Arts and Sciences (NARAS) (also known as The Recording Academy). The **Junos** were named after Pierre Juneau, who was head of the CRTC when the Canadian content regulations were implemented. The idea of honouring the Canadian music industry came from Walt Grealis and Stan Klees, who published *RPM,* a music industry trade journal. Like the Grammys, it's a peer award. Members of the CARAS (Canadian Academy of Recording Arts and Sciences) vote on nominees and winners.

CHAPTER 3 WRAP-UP

The impact on the music industry of Shawn Fanning's Napster, which at one point threatened to force a fundamental restructuring, is a reminder that the mass media are technology-driven. But just as digital internet technology bedeviled the recording industry, technology has come to its rescue. The Apple iTunes online store that coordinates the mind-meld between personal computers and iPods has reshaped music retailing. The iPod also has allowed the music-recording industry to survive in its traditional form with a few dominant major companies.

QUESTIONS FOR REVIEW

1. How is the music industry integrated into our daily lives?

2. What are major developments in sound recording from Thomas Edison on?

3. What effects are economic pressures having on the corporate structure of the music-recording industry?

4. How have technological innovations in sound recording affected musical styles?

5. How have innovations in music genres and styles threatened the corporate structure of the recording industry?

6. How has the recording industry answered threats of government control on objectionable lyrics?

7. What has happened to the A&R units at major record companies?

8. How was the recording industry threatened by Napster and other software that facilitates online music-swapping?

9. What are examples of populist measures for evaluating record companies? What are some elitist measures?

10. What are the Juno Awards? Grammy Awards?

QUESTIONS FOR CRITICAL THINKING

1. In recent months, how has new recorded music shaped significant human events? Consider music that is inspiring human actions. This might be war music. It might be music that's flowing from a generation or subculture and giving it an identity. It might be a new love song that has become a standard at weddings.

2. What has been the effect of global conglomeration in the record industry on the music you like?

3. Look into your crystal ball to assess how technological changes in the record business will play out in the future.

4. How has the relationship between artists and recording companies changed since World War II? Why has the change occurred?

5. How are measures of commercial and artistic success different in the recorded music business?

6. Why is airplay important to a recording's becoming a commercial success? Explain the exceptions.

7. What do you see as a solution to the revenue drain created by MP3 technology on the record industry? If there is no solution, what will happen?

8. Discuss the effect of moralists and others who would like to change the content of some recorded music. How do these people go about trying to accomplish their goals? What common threads have there been to their criticism throughout the 20th century?

9. Is Alan Cross right? Given the success of Canadian music in recent years, do we still need Cancon regulations for radio?

DEEPENING YOUR MEDIA LITERACY

Does popular music reflect our personal identity?

Step 1   Write down the lyrics of your favourite song. Conduct a semiotic analysis of this song.

Dig Deeper

Step 2   Consider the following:

1. Why do you like these lyrics and this kind of music?

2. What does your preference in music say about you?

3. What do you think this song's fans have in common?

4. Would your parents like this song? Why or why not?

5. Who would find it objectionable?

What Do You Think?

Step 3   Answer these questions: Does this song or music reflect your life? Does it reflect the lives of its fans? Does it reflect the life of the artist? Do you like this song because you identify with it? Do you think your preference in music reflects your place in society?

KEEPING UP TO DATE

The weekly *Billboard* is the recording industry's leading trade journal.

Consumer magazines that track popular music and report on the record industry include *Canadian Musician, Rolling Stone,* and *Spin.*

Entertainment Weekly and *Maclean's* both have regular sections on music, as do many daily papers, such as *The Globe and Mail* and the *National Post.*

FOR FURTHER LEARNING

Jason Scott Alexander. "Record Labels Got Hip to the Download Culture: Now It's Radio's Turn." *Broadcast Dialogue Magazine* (March 2004).

Paul Audley. *Canada's Cultural Industries* (Lorimer and Company, 1983).

Randy Bachman and John Einarson. *Taking Care of Business* (McArthur and Company, 2000).

Karen Bliss. "25 Years of Canadian Artists." *Canadian Musician* (March/April 2004).

Robert Brehl. "CRTC Causes Static among Radio Bosses." *The Globe and Mail* (June 9, 1998).

Ethan Brown. *Queens Reigns Supreme* (Anchor, 2005).

Iain Chambers. *Urban Rhythms: Pop Music and Popular Culture* (St. Martin's, 1985).

Steve Chapple and Reebee Garofalo. *Rock 'n' Roll Is Here to Pay: The History and Politics of the Music Industry* (Nelson-Hall, 1977).

Stan Cornyn, with Paul Scanlon. *Exploding: The Highs, Hits, Hype, Heroes and Hustler of the Warner Music Group* (Harper, 2002).

R. Serge Denisoff, with William Schurk. *Tarnished Gold: The Record Industry Revisited* (Transaction Books, 1986).

Colin Escort, with Martin Hawkins. *Good Rockin' Tonight: Sun Records and the Birth of Rock 'n' Roll* (St. Martin's, 1991).

Peter Fornatale and Joshua E. Mills. *Radio in the Television Age* (Overlook Press, 1980).

Roland Gelatt. *The Fabulous Phonograph: From Tin Foil to High Fidelity* (J. B. Lippincott, 1955).

Peter Goddard and Phillip Kamin, eds. *Shakin' All Over: The Rock and Roll Years in Canada* (McGraw-Hill Ryerson, 1989).

Hugh Graham. "Rule Changes May See Rebirth of Top 40 Radio." *The Globe and Mail* (July 19, 1997).

Steven Hagar. *Hip Hop: The Illustrated History of Break Dancing, Rap Music, and Graffiti* (St. Martin's Press, 1984).

Ron Hall. *The CHUM Chart Book* (Stardust Publications, 1984).

Dick Hebdige. *Cut 'N' Mix: Culture, Identity and Caribbean Music* (Methuen, 1987).

David N. Howard. *Sonic Alchemy: Visionary Music Producers and Their Maverick Recordings* (Hal Leonard, 2004).

Laurel Hyatt. "Back in the Black." *Broadcaster* (February, 1998).

Nicholas Jennings. *Before the Gold Rush: Flashbacks to the Dawn of the Canadian Sound* (Viking, 1997).

Nicholas Jennings. "Canadian Rock Explodes." *Maclean's* (March 27, 1995).

Jill Jonnes. *Empires of Light: Edison, Tesla, Westinghouse, and the Race to Electrify the World* (Random House, 2003).

Ted Kennedy. *Oh! Canada Cuts* (Canadian Chart Research, 1989).

Nancy Lathier. "The CanCon Ghetto." *Music Scene* (May/June 1989).

Daphne Lavers. "The Canadian Music Industry." *Broadcast Dialogue* (April 2000).

Daphne Lavers. "Canadian Music Week: 2004." *Broadcast Dialogue* (April 2004).

Daphne Lavers. "Canadian Music Week: 2006: That Was Then, This Is Now." *Broadcast Dialogue* (May 2006).

Elianna Lev. "Music Mogul Wants to Change How Music Is Sold." *Canadian Press* (November 30, 2006).

Nanda Lwin. *Canada's Top Hits of the Year, 1975–1996* (Music Data Canada, 1998).

Katherine Macklem. "Turn Up the Music." *Maclean's* (July 30, 2001).

Greil Marcus. *Mystery Train: Images of America in Rock 'n' Roll Music* (Penguin Usapaper Plume, 1997).

Michael McCabe. "CANCON Not the Only Measure of Radio's Contribution." *Broadcaster* (February 1998).

Darryl McDaniels with Bruce Haring. *King of Rock: Respect, Responsibility and My Life with Run-DMC* (St. Martin's, 2001).

Steve McLean. "HMV Analysis Reveals 23% Canadian Sales." *The Record* (May 25, 1998).

Martin Melhuish. *Heart of Gold: 30 Years of Canadian Pop Music* (CBC Enterprises, 1983).

James Miller. *Flowers in the Dustbin: The Rise of Rock 'n' Roll, 1947–1977* (Simon & Schuster, 1999).

Angela Pacienza. "Court Rejects Music Copyright Suit." *Toronto Star* (March 31, 2004).

Mike Roberts. "Finger on the Pulse: MuchMusic Still Strong after 10 Years." *Gazette* (Montreal) (January 22, 1995).

Jeff Rose-Martland. "Takin' Care of Business: Is Suing Your Clientele a Sound Idea?" *Broadcast Dialogue Magazine* (May 2004).

Heather Schoffield and Robert Brehl. "Radio Stations Told to Turn Up the Volume" and "CRTC Opens Radio Markets." *The Globe and Mail* (May 1, 1998).

Barry L. Sherman and Joseph R. Dominick. "Violence and Sex in Music Videos: TV and Rock 'n' Roll." *Journal of Communication* 36 (Winter 1986):1, 79–93.

Stephen Singular. *The Rise and Rise of David Geffen* (Birch Lane, 1997).

Justin Smallbridge. "Think Global: Act Local." *Canadian Business* (June 1996).

Nancy Smith. "Morality in the Media." *Broadcast Dialogue Magazine* (May 2006).

Dick Weissman. *The Music Business: Career Opportunities and Self-Defense* (Crown Publishers, 1979).

Howard Stern. By taking shock jock Howard Stern's show to satellite radio, Sirius aimed to siphon more listeners from traditional stations. In a case study later in this chapter, you will have a chance to discuss the effect Stern has had on radio.

Radio

Media in Theory

What Makes Radio Different?

What makes radio different from other media? **Andrew Crisell**, a cultural theorist, refers to radio as a blind medium: You can't see it with your eyes, like you can television, a movie or a newspaper. You can only see the pictures in your mind. Radio broadcasters use time, not space, as their canvas to communicate their messages. Building on the ideas of Barthes, radio uses four signs to create its imagery: words, sounds, music and silence. As Canada's Radio Marketing Bureau puts it, radio lets you "imagine the possibilities." Even Marshall McLuhan referred to radio as a visual medium.

As discussed earlier, words can be symbolic in that they represent something other than themselves: The phrase *maple leaf* isn't a real maple leaf; it is only a label that our culture attaches to the physical object of a maple leaf. This naming process is entirely arbitrary.

However, words in radio differ from words in print. Why? Because they are spoken. It's not so much what you say, but how you say it. The way in which an announcer or radio performer speaks also communicates meaning. Words end up working on two levels; not only do the words themselves stand for something else, but the way in which they are spoken signifies something as well. For example, an announcer can say "great!" and mean it in two different ways—one positive, one negative.

Sounds or sound effects are indexical signs. The sound of a creaking door is an index of a creaking door. To someone listening to Jerry Howarth broadcast a Blue Jays game, the loud crack of a bat and the cheering of a crowd signify that a home run has been hit. Sounds anchor the meaning or image created by radio; this is important due to the invisible nature of radio. Sounds let us know where we are and what's going on.

The third sign of radio, music, works on several levels. The music you hear on a radio station helps you identify the station. When you hear Paul Brandt or Terri Clark, you know you're listening to a country station; if you hear The New Pornographers or Broken Social Scene, you know the station is not country. Music can also act as a bridge between segments of a radio show, newsmagazine, or play, or it can be used to create a mood in a radio play.

An absence of any of these three signs signifies something in itself. As a sign, silence works to communicate meaning in two ways. First, it can be symbolic. A minute of silence on Remembrance Day symbolizes respect and honour for soldiers who died in war. But silence can also be an index that something's wrong with the broadcast—a power outage, a faulty microphone, or radio transmitter problems can all cause what is known as "dead air."

Influence of Radio

Andrew Crisell Uses the ideas of semiotician Roland Barthes to analyze how radio meaning is created.

Study Preview *Radio has become a ubiquitous mass medium, available everywhere, anytime. As an industry, however, there are troubling signs. Radio's primary programming—music—has become available through other devices, many with no advertising. A key radio audience, the segment aged 12 to 34, has fallen off in recent years.*

UBIQUITY

Radio is everywhere. The signals are carried on the electromagnetic spectrum to almost every nook and cranny. Hardly a place in the world is beyond the reach of radio. At no time in recent Canadian history was this more evident than during the massive east coast blackout in August 2003. At that time, people turned to their portable radios for the latest information. This is a wonderful example of radio doing what it does best. **Howard Christensen,** publisher of *Broadcast Dialogue,* says that that blackout illustrated "just how dependent we can be on local radio stations—and on our ownership of battery powered radios. On August 14 at 4:11 EST, more than 50 million people would have been left in a news dissemination void were it not for this century old, voices in the ether technology. It was radio's community involvement, its caring and, indeed, its sharing. The medium was—gadzooks—rediscovered."

Howard Christenson Publishes *Broadcast Dialogue* magazine.

But why would radio need to be rediscovered, given its ubiquity? Statistics abound about radio's importance. Consider the following data from the CRTC's *Broadcast Policy Monitoring Report 2007*:

■ Canada has 1238 radio stations; 919 of these are English, 286 are French, 33 are Third Language. We are also home to satellite radio.

■ The average Canadian listens to about 18.6 hours of radio each week, while 91 percent of Canadians listen to the radio at some point during the week.

■ Radio is accessible anytime and anywhere; 99 percent of homes have radios and 90 percent of cars do, too.

Radio Marketing Bureau Claims radio is a perfect fit for modern life.

Canada's **Radio Marketing Bureau** sums up the power of radio in its 2007 Foundation Research Study when it says, "Radio is a perfect fit for modern life; it's effortless, easy to listen to during other activities; entertains and informs throughout the day; is compatible with other media and provides a soundtrack for life."

Media Databank

Who's Listening?

Although radio is a ubiquitous medium, listenership is slipping. Here's a look at the changes in radio tuning habits for different age groups between the years of 1999 and 2006 from the CRTC's *Broadcast Policy Monitoring Report 2007*.

Age Group	1999	2006	Difference
12–17	11.3 hours	7.6 hours	–3.7%
18–24	17.3 hours	14.1 hours	–3.2%
25–34	21.3 hours	18.3 hours	–3.0%
35–49	21.6 hours	20.6 hours	–1.0%
50–54	21.6 hours	21.0 hours	–0.6%
55–64	23.2 hours	21.1 hours	–2.1%
65 +	22.7 hours	21.3 hours	–1.4%

Source: CRTC, Broadcast Policy Monitoring Report 2007.

Although radio is important, cracks are developing in the medium's reach. The audience is slipping from the traditional stations to iPods, direct-to-listener satellite services, webcasts and cell phones. Plus, the audience is shifting. Canadians 12 to 34 years old are listening to less radio than in the past. This has serious implications for its future.

Corus Radio: Canada's largest radio chain also has interests in TV. **www.corusent.com**

Standard Radio: Owners of 51 radio stations across Canada, this group was home to the Canadian author of this text for 12 years as an announcer at 610 CKTB in St. Catharines. It was purchased by Astral Media in 2007. **www.standardradio.com**

Rogers Communications: More than cell phones and the Blue Jays. **www.rogers.com**

Astral Media: Not just radio, but TV too. **www.astral.com/ en/radio/**

Radio Marketing Bureau: An excellent resource about the effectiveness of radio and radio advertising in Canada. **www.rmb.ca**

SCOPE OF RADIO INDUSTRY IN CANADA

Of the 1238 radio stations in Canada, more than 700 of them are commercial AM or FM stations. Most of these are owned by large corporations. Corus Entertainment, Standard Broadcasting, Rogers Communications, Astral Media and CHUM Limited are the five largest radio companies in Canada. In total, they combine for over half the radio listening in Canada.

Although radio as a business was 54 percent more profitable in 2006 than it was in 1997, the profits are due less to audience and advertising growth than to the chains' economies of scale and radical cost-cutting. This is an effect of conglomeration within the industry.

Radio Technology

Study Preview   *Human mastery of the electromagnetic spectrum, through which radio is possible, is only a century old. In 1895 an Italian physicist and inventor, Guglielmo Marconi, was the first to transmit a message through the air. Later came Canadian Reginald Fessenden and voice transmissions.*

Electromagnetic Spectrum: The spectrum, illustrated and explained. **http://imagine.gsfc.nasa.-gov/docs/science/know_l1/emspectrum.html**

ELECTROMAGNETIC SPECTRUM

Radio waves are part of the physical universe. They have existed forever, moving through the air and the ether. Like light waves, they are silent—a part of a continuing

electromagnetic spectrum
Energy waves on which radio messages are piggybacked.

Guglielmo Marconi
Produced the first wireless transmission. He is the father of telegraphy.

spectrum of energies: the **electromagnetic spectrum**. As early as 1873, physicists speculated that the electromagnetic spectrum existed, but it was an Italian nobleman, **Guglielmo Marconi,** who made practical application of the physicists' theories while living in Canada.

Young Marconi became obsessed with the possibilities of the electromagnetic spectrum and built equipment that could ring a bell by remote control—no strings, no wires, just turning an electromagnetic charge on and off. In 1895, when he was 21, Marconi used his wireless method to transmit codes for more than a mile on his father's Bologna estate. Then, on December 12, 1901, Marconi stood on Signal Hill, Newfoundland, and received the Morse code signal for the letter "S" from Cornwall, England. Marconi patented his invention in England, and his mother, a well-connected Irish woman, arranged British financing to set up the Marconi Wireless Telegraph Company. Soon oceangoing ships were equipped with Marconi radiotelegraphy equipment to communicate at sea, even when they were beyond the horizon—something never possible before. Marconi made a fortune. Many feel that Marconi is the father of telegraphy, while a Canadian, Reginald Fessenden, is the father of radio.

Reginald Fessenden.
Canadian Reginald Fessenden competed with Marconi in the early days of radio technology.

Lee de Forest Inventor whose projects included the audion tube.

audion tube Made voice transmission possible.

Reginald Fessenden
Canadian who broadcast the first radio program, 1906. Father of radio broadcasting.

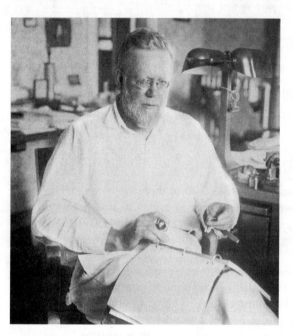

TRANSMITTING VOICES

Breakthroughs came quickly. In 1906 a message was sent across the Atlantic. In 1906 **Lee de Forest,** a promoter who fancied himself an inventor, created what he called the **audion tube** to make voice transmission possible. Some say he stole the underlying technology from Canadian inventor **Reginald Aubrey Fessenden,** who was born in Knowlton, Quebec. Whatever the truth of the matter, it was Fessenden who broadcast the first radio program, also in 1906. From Brant Rock, Massachusetts, where he had a laboratory, Fessenden played the violin, sang the Christmas Carol "O Holy Night" and played an Ediphone recording of Handel's *Largo*. This shocked wireless operators on ships at sea. Instead of the dots and dashes of Morse code, suddenly there was music. Len Arminio, a journalism professor at Ontario's Loyalist College, refers to Fessenden as "broadcasting's overlooked genius." De Forest, however, took the limelight with show-off broadcasts from the Eiffel Tower and other stunts. In 1910 de Forest clearly demonstrated radio's potential as an entertainment medium with a magnificent performance by the tenor Enrico Caruso from the New York Metropolitan Opera House. But it was Fessenden who realized the dream of broadcasting voices through the air.

Who Invented Radio? Numerous theorists conceived of wireless transmission ahead of the Irish-Italian inventor Guglielmo Marconi. A dentist, Mahlon Loomis, detected signals between two mountains in Virginia in 1866 and won a patent for wireless telegraphy in 1872. Scottish mathematician James Maxwell and German physicist Heinrich Hertz did important theorizing. Who, then, invented radio? Admirers of a reclusive but brilliant scientist, Nikola Tesla, have mounted a campaign for him to be recognized as the inventor of radio. Among their evidence is a 1943 U.S. Supreme Court decision recognizing that Tesla transmitted on the electromagnetic spectrum before Marconi.

WHICH CAME FIRST: XWA OR KDKA?

A Pittsburgh engineer, **Frank Conrad,** fiddled with radiotelegraphy in his home garage, playing music as he experimented. People with homemade receivers liked what they heard from Conrad's transmitter, and soon he had a following. When Conrad's Westinghouse bosses learned that he had become a local celebrity, they saw profit in building receivers that consumers could buy at $10 a set and take home to listen to. To encourage sales of the receivers, Westinghouse built a station to provide regular programming of news, sports and music—mostly music. That station, **KDKA** in Pittsburgh, became America's first licensed commercial station in 1920.

Frank Conrad Pioneer whose work led to KDKA.

The licensing of KDKA was important because it demonstrated the United States' commitment to placing radio in the private sector. In Europe, broadcasting was a government monopoly. In Canada, there was, and continues to be, a mix of public and private broadcasting.

KDKA First licensed commercial radio station in the United States.

In 1918, the Montreal-based radio station **XWA** (now 940 News, CINW, owned by Corus), owned by the Marconi Wireless Telegraph Company, was the first station to get a broadcasting licence, under the Radiotelegraph Act of 1913, from the federal government. Its first broadcast took place in May 1920, under Marconi's supervision. XWA was the first station to have regularly scheduled programs, the first of which was a musical program, a Dorothy Lutton concert to the Royal Society of Canada in Montreal. This was the first radio broadcast not only in Canada but also in North America, contrary to what Pittsburgh's KDKA claims. The first broadcast licence for radio was issued to CJCG in Winnipeg in May 1922. This station was on the air for only one year. All in all, 33 radio licences were issued in 1922. Some of those stations are still on the air today, including CKOC in Hamilton and CKCK in Regina.

XWA Canada's first radio station.

FM Radio

Static-free transmission was developed by **Edwin Armstrong**, a Columbia University researcher. In 1939 Armstrong built an experimental station in New Jersey using a new system called **frequency modulation**, FM for short. FM's system, piggybacking sound on airwaves, was different from the older **amplitude modulation**, or AM method. In time, Armstrong developed FM stereo with two soundtracks, one for each ear, duplicating the sensation of hearing a performance live. FM radio wasn't fully used as a medium until the 1950s and 1960s in North America. **CHFI** in Toronto, owned by Rogers, was Canada's first FM station. It began broadcasting in 1961. The CBC developed its network of FM stations in the early 1960s.

New Technologies

In the early 2000s, other technologies were working against the radio industry's traditional infrastructure.

Satellite Radio. Two **satellite radio** operations went on the air in the United States in 2001; by 2005, satellite radio had arrived in Canada. Satellite radio provides digital-quality sound, much of it commercial-free, for a monthly fee ranging between $10 and $13. The companies tried to build an immediate audience by lining up automobile manufacturers to install receivers into new vehicles—about 12 million a year. Both Sirius and XM offered at least a hundred channels—pop, country, news, sports and talk—but also specialized programming like chamber music, Broadway hits, CBC Radio, NHL hockey, Major League Baseball, audio books and gardening tips.

Terrestrial. Listeners to over-the-air or **terrestrial radio** hope their new competitors lose the bet. When the CRTC approved satellite radio, local stations told advertisers that satellite stations wouldn't have radio's traditional local thrust. However, many local stations save money by piping in—usually via satellite—programming from far away sources that serve hundreds of stations simultaneously with the same all-music, all-talk or all-sports content. In reality, many local stations are mere conduits for national programming, although technology allows them to insert local weather forecasts and, of course, advertising. Other than that local factor, some stations' programming could be mistaken for that on Sirius and XM.

iPod. Handheld MP3 players, epitomized by the Apple iPod, siphoned listeners from over-the-air local radio. With these devices and music downloaded from the

Case Study

Howard Stern and Satellite Radio

Howard Stern began his career at Boston University, where he volunteered at the college radio station. His show was cancelled after one broadcast. He had spoofed a game show with contestants confessing their worst sins. It was a precursor of Stern's unorthodoxy: a mix of phone chat, much of it inane; music, a lot of it offbeat; and crude, sophomoric shock-talk. His on-air antics earned him the label "shock jock," a new radio programming genre in the 1980s.

No matter how tasteless, Stern amassed a following. He soon had star status and big bucks—and critics who pushed for federal fines against his on-air vulgarities. At one point, the accumulated unpaid fines totaled $1.7 million. The corporate owner of his flagship New York station had no problem paying the fines from the profits Stern was bringing in.

People kept listening to his bathroom-wall jokes and his topless female studio guests. He even arrived on Canadian airwaves in 1997. During his first Canadian broadcast, he thanked CHOM-FM for "opening up the sewer gate for me to pollute yet another country." During his first few shows, he referred to French Canadians as "peckerheads" and "jack offs." To those Canadians who don't like his approach to morning radio, Stern replied that the show was "just entertainment. Jokes, laughter and whatever's on our minds." By 1998 CHOM-FM had dropped Howard Stern. Q-107 dropped Stern in 2001.

Still the fines kept coming. A $495 000 fine in 2004 brought Stern's career total to $2.5 million. Analysts say the giant Clear Channel chain, which acquired Stern in its buy-up of stations, earned $25 million a year in advertising revenue from Stern's show, which played in 40 cities. That was after $70 million in production costs and Stern's $30 million salary. Clear Channel could afford the fines, but concerned that the government might revoke its stations' licences, the corporate executives became uneasy. In 2004 they tried putting a lid on Stern.

Refusing to be bridled, Stern announced that he wouldn't renew with Clear Channel when his contract expired in 2006. Instead, he would leave so-called terrestrial radio and go to the unregulated airwaves of the fledgling Sirius satellite radio service. With Sirius, Stern's program would go directly to subscribers, bypassing the traditional delivery mechanism through federally licensed local stations that send their signals from land-based towers. His shows, *Howard 100* and *Howard 101,* are also available on satellite radio in Canada.

Typical of his egocentric confidence, Stern declared the death of terrestrial radio with stations licensed to broadcast to local audiences. The future, he said, was in national stations that transmitted directly to individuals, not relaying through local stations. Howard Stern is not alone in seeing problems for the radio industry as everyone had come to know it since the 1920s. Radio has had to withstand the challenges of iPods, the internet and satellite radio.

Depending on who you talk to, Howard Stern represents the best in radio, meeting the interests and needs of a mass audience, or the worst, pandering to the lowest instincts in society and getting rich in the process.

What Do You Think?

1. Would you pay to hear shock jocks like Howard Stern on satellite radio? Why or why not?
2. Is the fact that XM and Sirius merged in 2007 evidence that people simply won't pay for radio, something that has been "free" for almost a century?
3. How does Howard Stern epitomize the crisis in contemporary radio?
4. Is Howard Stern right: is terrestrial radio dead? Does the future of radio lie in national stations that transmit directly to individuals either via satellite radio or the internet?

internet or ripped from their own CDs, people are able to create their own playlists—no inane disc-jockey patter, no commercials, no waiting through less-than-favourite tunes for the good stuff.

PODCASTING. Almost anybody who wanted to create a show could prerecord a batch of favourite music, complete with narration, as an audio file on a personal computer. Then, by adding a hyperlink on a web server, they could let the world download the show for playback on a computer or MP3 player. Whenever the listener links to the server again, a new show from the same source is downloaded automatically. Podcasting has the potential to make everybody a disc jockey. This too cuts into the audience of traditional radio.

WEBCASTING. Most Canadian radio stations stream their signals on the web. In these days of convergence, the web and radio may be perfect partners, says John Harding of the Canadian Radio Marketing Bureau: "As radio content evolves onto the internet, radio will excel in its ability to attract and maintain ears and eyes, that being radio's forte. Radio knows how to hold an audience. The skill sets are transferable from terrestrial radio to internet radio to build and maintain audience loyalty." However, radio does have competition on the web with online music channels such as Canada's Iceberg Radio.

Corporate Radio

Study Preview *A few corporations dominate the Canadian and American radio industries, using mostly programming geared to mass tastes. The approach, however, has earned the disapproving moniker "corporate radio" for its bland sameness. The chains have taken steps to win back listeners who have left for alternative sources of music, news and information.*

corporate radio A disapproving term for programming engineered by radio chains for use in multiple markets.

playlist A list of songs that a radio station plays.

voice tracking A few announcers who prerecord music intros and outros for multiple stations to create a single personality for stations.

Jack An eclectic, somewhat unpredictable musical radio format.

CHAIN OWNERSHIP

In a drive to cut costs to maximize profits, the big radio chains consolidated their new properties in the post-1996 era and centralized not only **playlists** but also disc jockeys. Through a system called **voice tracking**, a handful of announcers can be heard on several radio stations, owned by the same company, in different markets. This robo-programming was efficient. Canadian radio followed suit, many stations voice tracking during evenings, overnights and weekends.

Some stations with robo-programming shifted gears in 2005 with **Jack**, a format developed by Rogers Media of Canada that had a decidedly more eclectic mix of music. Jack playlists typically include 1200 songs. Unlike robo-formulas, few songs get played even once a day in Jack's unlikely patterns, with none of the segues that slide from one tune seamlessly into another. Eight U.S. stations licensed Jack from Rogers in 2005. Others are imitating it. At KSJK in Kansas City, which calls itself 105.1 Jack FM, program director Mike Reilly prides himself on "train wrecks," a collision of unlikely music in sequence: "If you hear MC Hammer go into the Steve Miller Band, I've done my job." It's the kind of programming excitement that people can create on an iPod.

Jack, say critics, is less than it seems. The playlists don't venture beyond what is familiar to listeners. A Jack consultant, Mike Henry, put it this way in an interview in *The Wall Street Journal*: "You're only challenging them on a stylistic level. You're

Media Databank

Top Five Radio Chains by Hours Tuned, 2006

For years the government restricted a radio company to owning no more than two radio stations in any Canadian city. In 1998, the CRTC relaxed ownership limits. Now a company could own up to three radio stations in markets of less than 8 stations; 4 in markets over 8 stations. The only stipulation was that no one company could own more than 2 AM or 2 FM stations in any one city. Here are the biggest radio chains in Canada, by total hours tuned:

Corporation	Total Listening Hours
Corus	87 258 000
Standard	61 653 000
Rogers Communications	46 772 000
Astral	37 681 000
CHUM Limited	34 004 000

Note: In 2007, Astral Media purchased Standard Broadcasting, while CTVglobemedia purchased CHUM Limited.

Source: CRTC, Broadcast Policy Monitoring Report 2007.

not challenging them on a familiar/unfamiliar level." Nirvana grunge may butt up against Village People disco, but both are proven pop.

Canadian media writer and director Doug Thompson argues that Jack, or any of its clones, such as Dave or Bob, isn't really radio, it's a jukebox and "that's not what radio was meant to be. I didn't grow up listening to radio for a bunch of songs played back to back. There is no substitute for a live person talking one on one with a listener." In short, corporate radio needs to look to developing new personalities for radio, not just new formats. Thompson adds that right now, the creative, personality radio DJ is an endangered species.

Some stations set themselves apart with local and distinctive content. These channels tend to be owned by small companies or corporations who are more likely to take a chance on something different. "Radio Newfoundland" features nothing but east coast artists. Country stations in the west continue to serve their largely agricultural listeners well, while CHWO in Oakville calls itself "Prime Time Radio," with an emphasis on older listeners. In Ottawa, Live 88.5 embraced the podcast generation by merging the online music subculture with an alternative music format.

Radio Content

Study Preview   *Radio programming falls mostly into three categories: entertainment, mostly music; news; and talk.*

RADIO ENTERTAINMENT

During the 1920s, radios became an integral part of Canadians' living rooms. These were big radios, some as large as today's home entertainment units. People listened to the radio then in much the same way we watch television today: after supper, with or without the family. A radio was considered a status symbol, and much of the programming reflected this: broadcasts included concerts, political commentary, dramas and comedies. Broadcasts of hockey games, sponsored by General Motors, were the most popular radio programs of the early days of the medium, beginning in 1923. Within 10 years, hockey broadcasts were heard on 20 Canadian radio stations from coast to coast. This sponsorship also marked the beginning of "commercial" radio in Canada.

The comedies, dramas, variety shows and quiz shows that dominated network-provided radio programming in the 1930s and 1940s moved to television in the 1950s. So did the huge audience that radio had cultivated. The radio networks, losing advertisers to television, scaled back what they offered to affiliates. As the number of listeners dropped, local stations switched to more recorded music, which was far cheaper than producing concerts, dramas and comedies. Thus, radio reinvented itself, survived and prospered.

The industry found itself shaken again in the 1970s when the listeners flocked to new FM stations. Because FM technology offered superior sound fidelity, these became the stations of choice for music. AM listenership seemed destined to tank until, in another reinvention, most AM stations converted to nonmusic formats. From roots in 1961 with programming genius Gordon McLendon, who beamed the first 24/7 news into southern California from XTRA across the border in Tijuana, all-news took off as a format in major cities. So did listener call-in shows with colourful hosts.

Media People

Gordon McLendon

Gordon McLendon

A crisis hit the U.S. radio history in the 1950s. As comedies, dramas and quiz shows moved to television, so did the huge audience that radio had cultivated. The radio networks, losing advertisers to television, scaled back what they offered to stations.

As the number of listeners dropped, local stations switched more to recorded music, which was far cheaper than producing programs.

To the rescue came Gordon McLendon, who perfected a new format, the Top 40, which repeated the day's most popular new music in rotation. McLendon developed the format at KLIF in Dallas, Texas, by mixing the music with fast-paced newscasts, disc jockey chatter, lively commercials and promotional jingles and hype. It was catchy, almost hypnotizing—and widely imitated.

With the portable transistor radios that were coming onto the market and a growing number of automobiles outfitted with radios, Top 40 was right for the times. People could tune in and tune out on the go. Most tunes lasted only three minutes or so. It was not programming designed for half-hour blocks. It reshaped radio as a medium that began a recovery in a new incarnation even as some observers were writing the medium's epitaph.

McLendon was no one-shot wonder. He also designed so-called beautiful music as a format at KABL, San Francisco, in 1959; all-news at XTRA, Tijuana, Mexico, aimed at southern California, in 1961; and all-classified ads at KADS, Los Angeles, in 1967. In all of his innovations, McLendon was firm about a strict structure. In Top 40, for example, there were no deviations from music in rotation, news every 20 minutes, naming the station by call letters twice between songs, upbeat jingles and no deadpan commercials. McLendon's classified-ad format bombed, but the others have survived. For better or worse, McLendon is the father of format radio.

RADIO NEWS

Radio news today has diverse forms, some based on the notion of drawing listeners to reports on breaking events as they happen, some more focused on depth and understanding. Mostly, though, radio news is known for being on top of events as they happen.

BREAKING NEWS. Radio news came into its own in World War II, when the networks sent correspondents abroad. Americans, eager for news from Europe, developed the habit of listening to the likes of Edward R. Murrow and other giants of mid-20th-century journalism, including Walter Cronkite. As a medium of instantaneous reporting, radio offered news on breakthrough events even before newspapers could issue special extra editions. The term **breaking news** emerged as something to which radio was uniquely suited.

HEADLINE SERVICE. In the relatively tranquil period after World War II, with people less intent on news, the radio industry recognized that listeners tuned away from lengthy stories. News formats shifted to shorter stories, making radio a **headline service**. Details and depth were left to newspapers. Gordon McLendon's influential rock 'n' roll format in the 1960s epitomized the headline service, generally with 3-minute newscasts dropped every 20 minutes amid 3-minute songs, with no story more than 20 seconds, most only two sentences.

ALL NEWS. As contradictory as it may seem, Gordon McLendon also invented **all-news radio**, also in the 1960s. For the Los Angeles market, McLendon set up a skeletal staff at XTRA across the border in Tijuana to read wire copy nonstop. When XTRA turned profitable, McLendon took over a Chicago station, renamed it WNUS, and converted it to all-news. This was a dramatic departure from the idea of radio as a mass medium with each station trying for the largest possible audience. McLendon's WNUS and later all-news stations sought niche listenerships, finding early profitability in demassification—a narrow part of the larger mosaic of the whole radio market. Today all-news stations are available in almost every Canadian market.

TALK RADIO

Call-in formats were greeted enthusiastically at first because of their potential as forums for discussion of public issues, but there was a downside. Many stations with music-based formats used the advent of news and talk stations to reduce their news programming. In effect, many music stations were saying, "Let those guys do news and talk, and we'll do music." While some might lament the lack of news on all-music stations, in these days of demassification and diversification, people who tune in to a music station are tuning in for music; they don't want much in the way of news and information programming.

Talk radio may offer access to the "commoners," or so it would seem; Paul Rutherford, a communication professor at the University of Toronto, says that talk radio is "providing a voice for people who otherwise wouldn't have one." Today, many Canadians feel a sense of alienation; they believe that politicians simply aren't listening to them. To vent their frustrations, many turn to talk radio. This gives listeners a sense that they are finally being heard. Sometimes politicians listen; sometimes they don't.

Gordon McLendon The Radio Hall of Fame offers a short biography of the creator of format radio. **www.radiohof.org/pioneer/ gordonmclendon.html**

breaking news Reports, often live, on events as they are occurring.

headline service Brief news stories.

all-news radio A niche format that delivers only news and related informational content and commentary.

How is Canadian talk radio different from American talk radio? Many differences exist, according to those who claim that Canadians are "kindler, gentler" talk show participants. Rutherford claims that there are two types of talk show hosts: warriors and father figures. The warrior is clearly American: confrontational and in your face. Male Canadian talk show hosts tend to be father figures and offer more thought-provoking and well-researched fare and content.

Perhaps one of the reasons talk radio is different in Canada is the regional or local nature of talk shows. Compared to the United States, which boasts numerous national talk show hosts, Canadian talk show hosts are generally local or regional. Gary Slaight of Standard Broadcasting says there's only one real issue in the United States, "and that's whether you're left wing or right wing. Whether you're in New York or Seattle, it's the same question. Not in Canada, where we're defined so many ways: English/French, east/west."

Music Radio

Most radio today is based on music programming. Below are terms used to distinguish radio's major music formats for private radio in Canada. Due to demassification, many formats have become fragmented.

Adult Contemporary (A/C). Many advertisers like the A/C format because so many people in the big-spending 25-to-40 age group listen to it. Variations of this format include "soft rock," such as the EZ-Rock brand across Canada.

Top 40. Top 40, also called CHR (short for Contemporary Hits Radio), emphasizes current rock but not as strictly as McLendon insisted. These stations target teenagers. Some variations within this format include Rhythmic Top 40 and Adult Top 40.

Country. Once called country and western, or CW for short, this format goes back to WSM's *Grand Ole Opry* program in Nashville. The music varies significantly from twangy western ballads to what's called "urban country." In Canada, "young country" and "new country" have become two popular music formats. By abandoning Loretta Lynn and George Jones in favour of Shania Twain and Terri Clark, new country radio stations have been able to attract younger listeners.

Album-Oriented Rock (AOR). AOR formats offer songs from the 100 best-selling albums. A casual listener might confuse AOR with Top 40, but album stations go back a couple of years for wider variety. Audiences tend to be aged 18 to 24. This is one of the most diversified formats, with classic rock available on CIRK-FM (Edmonton), mainstream rock on The Goat (Lloydminster), and new music on CFNY (Toronto).

Charles Adler: The only nationally syndicated radio talk show host in Canada, this Winnipegger loves to discuss the issues. www.cjob.com/shows/adler.aspx

Dave Rutherford: This 30-year veteran journalist hosts "The Rutherford Show," which can be heard regionally in Alberta. www.am770chqr.com/station/show_rutherford.cfm

Codi Jeffries, an "80s Chick" Jeffries hosts *That 80s Show* on Majic 100 in Ottawa. The show features everything 1980s from new wave to hair bands. Shows like this are an example of demassified programming in radio. Jeffries is also the music director for Majic 100.

OLDIES. Oldies stations play music that the 45- to 64-year-old demographic grew up with, mostly music of the 1960s and 1970s. It's sometimes called "classic hits."

ETHNIC. More than 9 million Canadians belong to ethnic groups other than First Nations, French or British. These people represent more than 70 different cultures. Given this fact and Canada's official status as a multicultural country, it's not surprising that full-time ethnic radio stations have taken root in many of Canada's urban centres. Toronto has six ethnic stations, Vancouver has three, Montreal has two, and Edmonton, Calgary, Ottawa and Winnipeg each have one. Many other radio stations feature ethnic programming on a part-time basis, during the evenings and on weekends.

CLASSICAL. This format offers the basic repertoire of enduring music since the Baroque era, although some classical stations also play experimental symphonies, operas and contemporary composers. Because highbrow music has a limited following, most classical stations are supported not by advertising but by listener donations, universities and government funding. CBC Radio Two broadcasts classical music on a national basis. CFMX, located in Cobourg, Ontario, has achieved significant ratings in the Toronto area.

RELIGIOUS. Inspirational music is the programming core of religious stations. The music is interspersed with sermons from evangelists who buy time for their programs, seeking both to proselytize and to raise funds to support ministries.

OTHER FORMATS. The CRTC has recently issued licences for some new formats in Canada. These include "smooth jazz" in Calgary and Hamilton, "urban" in Vancouver, Calgary and Toronto, and **AVR** (Aboriginal Voices Radio) across Canada.

A CANADIAN ALTERNATIVE: CBC

As Canada's public broadcaster, CBC Radio brought Canadian programming home to Canadians. Today, CBC Radio is known as either Radio One or Radio Two. Radio One features a mix of information, talk and Canadian music, while Radio Two's programming is more highbrow, with an emphasis on classical music and opera. CBC Radio is commercial-free, funded through taxpayer money. Much of its programming, as mandated by the Broadcasting Act, is regional. More than 85 percent of CBC English Radio is produced at the local level, with much of that broadcast nationally. CBC Radio also spotlights Canadian talent. More than 60 hours of performance programming on both networks focuses on Canadian performers. The listenership for CBC Radio has remained fairly steady in recent years, as 3.5 million Canadians tune in each week to either CBC Radio One or Radio Two.

OTHER ALTERNATIVES: CAMPUS AND COMMUNITY RADIO

Campus and Community radio stations in Canada, geared to neighborhood service with low-power transmitters, have made possible a level of interactivity with their audiences not possible for traditional stations that seek large audiences to draw advertising and pay the bills. These low-power stations, many staffed with volunteers, are alternative voices in the radio universe. Under

Canadian Campus Stations: A link to a listing of all campus stations in Canada.
www.umfm.com/ campus_stations.shtml

National Campus and Community Radio Association: Read about the alternative radio programming available.
www.ncra.ca

Campus Radio. Campus and Community radio stations in Canada allow members of the public access to the airwaves. There are currently almost 100 Community radio stations in Canada, mostly in Quebec. There are an additional 53 campus stations across Canada. You probably have one on your campus.

CRTC conditions of licence, programming on these stations must "differ in style and substance from the services provided by conventional broadcasters." These stations are usually funded through grants, student fees and some advertising. They also support social causes. Every year since 2003, CKUT at McGill University in Montreal has been the host station for something called "The Homelessness Marathon," to raise awareness of the growing problem in Canada. Campus and Community radio stations from across the country simulcast the event, with each station contributing local reports and commentary.

Quality on the Air

Study Preview   *With deregulation, radio programming has become more populist, formulaic and bland. Many stations are devoid of local identity. Even so, some stations set themselves apart with local and distinctive content.*

QUALITY ON THE AIR

Quality is in the beholder's eye—or ear. If wall-to-wall music is a measure of quality, then a lot of superb stations are on the air. Recorded music, though, is a low-overhead format that's so formulaic that stations have a hard time distinguishing themselves from each other. There are, however, other quality measures.

The CRTC states that Canadian radio should reflect a Canadian way of life. The idea was for radio to play the local community back to itself. How well do stations do this? By this standard, a station would get high marks for programming indigenous culture: performances by local musicians, coverage of local news, discussion of local issues and play-by-plays of local athletic events. Radio can have a role in creating a distinctive local culture. Two Ontario radio stations were reprimanded by the CRTC for not serving their local communities. CKDK-FM (The Hawk) in Woodstock and CING-FM (Country 95.3) in Hamilton were licensed to broadcast in their respective communities. However, both stations were targeting larger markets within their radius. Woodstock targeted listeners in London, while Hamilton targeted the Toronto market. They did this with news, weather and traffic reports from those communities rather than their own.

MARKETPLACE VALUES

Audience measures come mostly from the ratings service Bureau of Broadcast Measurement, or BBM for short. Because the surveys are paid for by stations that want numbers to persuade advertisers to buy time, BBM does not release its findings to the public. The results usually surface, however, when station sales reps pass them out to potential advertisers, although the information is often recast to make particular selling points. BBM data are broken down by day parts, like morning drive time, and by audience demographics, like gender and age groupings.

CHAPTER 4 WRAP-UP

While radio will still continue to be a presence in the life of Canadians for many years to come, the medium faces challenging times. Suddenly, at the dawn of the 21st century, new technologies have shaken the structure of the radio industry as listeners opt for cutting-edge alternatives including satellite direct-to-listener radio, iPods, podcasts and webcasts, or online music stations. To stem listener losses, mainstream companies have eased their drive for centralized programming and cost cutting, some trying the new format Jack and copycats.

QUESTIONS FOR REVIEW

1. What is happening to the number of people who listen to traditional radio?

2. How has radio technology evolved since the pioneering work of Guglielmo Marconi and Reginald Fessenden?

3. Who "invented" radio: Tesla, Fessenden or Marconi?

4. How does radio move invisibly through the air on electromagnetic waves?

5. What is the dominant programming of corporate radio? Has it run its course?

6. How has the mix of entertainment and information changed through the course of radio's history?

7. What are measures of excellence in radio?

QUESTIONS FOR CRITICAL THINKING

1. Guglielmo Marconi introduced radio wireless telegraphy, while Fessenden was responsible for the first radio broadcast. What was the difference?

2. Lee de Forest was a technical and programming innovator. Explain the significance of his audion tube.

3. A new way of transmitting radio was developed by Edwin Armstrong in the 1930s, and by the 1980s it had left the original AM broadcast system in economic peril. Discuss Armstrong's invention and how it has reshaped radio.

4. Radio was reshaped by the advent of television in the 1950s. Explain these influences, and be sure to cite radio's transition from literal broadcasting toward demassification. What about the influence of Gordon McLendon? What of the future?

5. Radio listenership seems to be on the decline. Review the Media Databank on listening trends in this chapter. Does the data reflect your own radio listening? That of your parents? Grandparents? What must radio do to stop the slide?

6. Many radio stations have webcams set up in the studio so people can watch announcers/DJs while they perform on air. Given the fact that radio is a "blind medium," is it still radio if you can see the announcers?

DEEPENING YOUR MEDIA LITERACY

What must radio do to survive into the new millennium? Which concept of ownership of the airwaves is more in the public interest?

Step 1   The radio industry in Canada is mostly privately owned. In some countries the airwaves are controlled by the government.

1. Think of the Canadian system, which is more and more controlled by chains and corporations.

2. Consider government-controlled radio such as the BBC, the British broadcasting system that is accountable to Parliament and to household licence payers and that is often cited as one of the world's most independent news sources, and a station in a country that is notorious for censoring media content.

3. Also consider Campus and Community stations.

Dig Deeper

Step 2   Each of these models of airwave ownership has pluses and minuses. Make a list of the pros and cons of privately owned airwaves. Make a second list of the pros and cons of government-owned airwaves. Make a third list of the pros and cons of low-power radio.

What Do You Think?

Step 3   Which model do you think best serves the public interest? Is there some other model, a new one, or a combination of the ones you just analyzed, that would do a better job?

KEEPING UP TO DATE

The trade journals *Broadcaster* and *Broadcast Dialogue* keep abreast of news and issues.

Other news coverage can be found in the *National Post, The Globe and Mail,* and other major daily newspapers.

Scholarly articles can be found in the *Canadian Journal of Communication, Journal of Broadcasting,* *Electronic Media, Journal of Communication,* and *Journalism Quarterly.*

R&R, a weekly trade journal published by Radio & Records, carries charts and playlists that not only reflect what music is getting airtime but also shape what will be getting airtime.

FOR FURTHER LEARNING

Jason Scott Alexander. "Newcap's Latest Arrival is Bringing iPod Listeners Back to Ottawa Radio." *Broadcast Dialogue* (April 2006).

Len Arminio. "Broadcasting's Overlooked Genius." *Broadcast Dialogue* (October 2006).

Erik Barnouw. *A Tower in Babel, A History of Broadcasting in the United States to 1933* (Oxford, 1966).

Erik Barnouw. *The Golden Web, A History of Broadcasting in the United States, 1933–1953* (Oxford, 1968).

Erik Barnouw. *The Image Empire, A History of Broadcasting in the United States, 1953–On* (Oxford, 1970).

John R. Bittner. *Broadcast Law and Regulation* (Prentice Hall, 1982).

Robert Brehl. "CRTC Causes Static among Radio Bosses." *The Globe and Mail* (June 9, 1998).

John Bugailiskis. "Stern's Show Slim on Canadian Content." *Broadcaster* (September 1997).

"CAB Fires Back at Music Industry Radio Content Claims." *Broadcaster Industry News* (April 1996).

Canadian Association of Broadcasters. *A Broadcaster's Guide to Canada's Cultural Mosaic, 1988.*

Gerald Carson. *The Roguish World of Dr. Brinkley* (Holt, Rinehart & Winston, 1960).

CBC Enterprises. *Fifty Years of Radio: A Celebration of CBC Radio 1936–1986.*

Howard Christensen. "Blackout: Radio to the Rescue." *Broadcast Dialogue* (October 2003).

Ray Conlogue. "Radio Shock Jock Strikes a Nerve." *The Globe and Mail* (September 3, 1997).

Andrew Coyne. "Cracking Down on Howard." *St. Catharines Standard* (September 20, 1997).

Andrew Crisell. *Understanding Radio* (Methuen, 1990).

CRTC. *Broadcast Policy Monitoring Report 2007.*

Guy Dixon. "Out of Tune?" *The Globe and Mail* (March 14, 2006).

Thomas Doherty. "Return with Us Now to Those Thrilling Days of Yesteryear: Radio Studies Rise Again." *Chronicle of Higher Education* (May 21, 2004): B12–B13.

Philip Fine. "Radio Stations Ponder Fate of Stern's Show." *The Globe and Mail* (November 22, 1997).

Marc Fisher. "Resurgent Radio." *American Journalism Review* (December 2000): 32–37.

James C. Foust. *Big Voices of the Air: The Battle over Clear Channel Radio* (Iowa State University Press, 2000).

"The Fowler Years: A Chairman Who Marches to His Own Drummer." *Broadcasting* 112 (March 23, 1987): 12, 51–54.

Peter Goddard. "It's Talk, Talk, Talk All over the Radio." *Toronto Star* (October 29, 1995).

Lynne Schafer Gross. *Telecommunications: An Introduction to Radio, Television and Other Electronic Media,* Second edition (Wm. C. Brown, 1986).

John Harding. "Radio—The Momentum Continues." *Broadcast Dialogue* (January 2001).

Susanne Hiller. "That You Bas? After 40 Years on Air, Bas Jamieson's Not Allowed to Retire." *Newfoundlanders Abroad, 2002.*

Laurel Hyatt. "Back in the Black." *Broadcaster* (February 1998).

Laurel Hyatt. "Radio's Recipe for Success." *Broadcaster* (April 1996): 12–15.

Donald Jack. *Sinc, Betty and the Morning Man* (Macmillan, 1977).

Daphne Lavers. "DAB Launch." *Broadcast Dialogue* (August 1999).

Murray B. Levin. *Talk Radio and the American Dream* (D.C. Heath, 1987).

Kirk Makin. "Brrrrring . . . brrrrring: You're on the Air." *The Globe and Mail* (July 16, 1994).

Michael McCabe. "CANCON Not the Only Measure of Radio's Contribution." *Broadcaster* (February 1998).

Doug Saunders. "AM Listeners Tuning Out." *The Globe and Mail* (October 20, 1997).

Heather Schoffield and Robert Brehl. "Radio Stations Told to Turn Up the Volume" and "CRTC Opens Radio Markets." *The Globe and Mail* (May 1, 1998).

Philip M. Seib. *Going Live: Getting the News Right in a Real-Time, Online World* (Rowman & Littlefield, 2000).

Sandy Stewart. *A Pictorial History of Radio in Canada* (Gage, 1975).

Doug Thompson. "Ode to the Disc Jockey." *Broadcast Dialogue* (May 2006).

Kevin G. Wilson. *Deregulating Telecommunications: U.S. and Canadian Telecommunications, 1840–1997* (Rowman & Littlefield, 2000).

Erik Zorn. "The Specialized Signals of Radio News." *Washington Journalism Review* 8 (June 1986): 6, 31–33.

The Sweet Hereafter. Canadian directors, such as Atom Egoyan, have achieved critical success both here and abroad. Sarah Polley, one of the stars of *The Sweet Hereafter,* is now a director. Her film *Away from Her* debuted at the 2006 Toronto Film Festival. Egoyan was the executive producer on the project.

Movies

Media in Theory

American versus Canadian Movies: What's the Difference?

Why are Canadian movies different from American movies? Notice that the question doesn't imply that Canadian movies are "worse" than American movies, although for many Canadians, that seems to be the common belief. For students of communication, the questions really should be: "What makes Canadian movies different from American movies?" and "What do our films say about our culture?"

While funding, marketplace economics, and distribution have certainly all played a role in the development of the Canadian film industry and the "look" of Canadian films, particularly in the early days, there may be other differences as well. **Peter Harcourt,** in his 1976 essay "Introduction," argues that Canadian movie scripts symbolically reflect "our own social uncertainties—both our uncertainty of action as a

MEDIA TIMELINE

Movies

	1826	French scientist Joseph Niépce found chemicals to capture and preserve an image on a light-sensitive metal.
	1888	William Dickson devised a camera to capture sequential motion.
	1891	George Eastman devised flexible celluloid for film that could be run through projectors.
	1895	Auguste and Louis Lumière opened a movie house in Paris.
	1896	The Vitascope was demonstrated in Montreal.
	1906	Canada's first movie theatre, the Ouimetoscope, opened in Montreal.
	1922	Fox used sound in newsreels.
	1927	Warner distributed the first talkie, *The Jazz Singer.*
	1932	Disney issued the first full-colour movie, *Flowers and Trees.*
	1948	Canadian Nat Taylor opened the first multiplex theatre, The Elgin, in Ottawa.
	1970s	Multiscreen movie houses, many in the suburbs, became the norm.
	1999	George Lucas offered a version of *Star Wars Episode I: The Phantom Menace* for digital projection.
	2005	Movie studios agreed to finance a major part of converting theatres for digital movies.
	2007	Cineplex Odeon began converting its Canadian cinemas to digital.

nation and our own present lack of security in dealing with ethnic and cultural problems which, throughout our vast nation, we are trying to define ourselves."

This uncertainty is clearly evident in the films of one of Canada's best-known filmmakers, **Atom Egoyan.** Harcourt, in the journal **Film Quarterly,** described Egoyan's work as "expressing the classic Canadian dilemma as formulated by Northrop Frye . . . Egoyan devises films that register the personal uncertainties of people who are striving to find a place of rest within a culture not their own." **David Cronenberg's** films also feature these themes, and don't always feature the happy endings of Hollywood cinema. According to Cronenberg, both he and

Egoyan "have a horror of the cheap emotional affect of Hollywood movies."

Meanwhile, in Quebec, French-Canadian cinema has developed a strong following in Quebec and around the world. Directors such as **Denys Arcand** are among the best in the world. His works include *The Decline of the American Empire, Jesus of Montreal* and *Les Invasions barbares.* When asked if there were any similarities between French- and English-Canadian movies, Arcand says "there might be something we share in our constant resistance to American genre film." Even the Canadian cult classic film *Ginger Snaps* encourages us to "forget the Hollywood rules."

In her history of Canadian film, *Weird Sex and Snowshoes,* **Katherine Monk** offers a "Canadian checklist" of themes in Canadian movies. These include the following variations of "uncertainty" that Harcourt introduced in 1976: identity issues, being an outsider, empty landscapes, internal demons, personal alienation, language barriers, being on a road to nowhere, questions of faith, survivor guilt and ambiguous endings.

Perhaps our nation's preoccupation with developing a national identity is reflected in the uncertainties of Canadian movies. Many factors are at work here. First, since Canada is officially bilingual and multicultural, how can we have a truly "national cinema" as other countries do? Second, funding has always been an issue for Canadian filmmakers. We simply don't have the economic resources of Hollywood. Finally, finding an audience for Canadian movies has always been a struggle. However, despite all these factors, there have been success stories. Recently, the works of directors Bruce McDonald, Deepa Mehta, Don McKellar and István Szabó have all become successful here at home.

Peter Harcourt Writes that Canadian movies reflect our own uncertainty.

Atom Egoyan Directs movies about personal uncertainty.

David Cronenberg His films are the antithesis to Hollywood endings.

Denys Arcand Award-winning French-Canadian film director.

Katherine Monk Developed a Canadian movie checklist.

Importance of Movies

Study Preview   *The experience of watching a movie uninterrupted in a darkened auditorium has entranced people since the medium's earliest days. It is an all-encompassing experience, which has given movies a special power in shaping cultural values.*

OVERWHELMING EXPERIENCE

Movies have a more intense hold on people, at least while they are watching one, than does any other medium. It is not unusual for a movie reviewer to recommend taking a handkerchief. Never will you hear such advice from a record reviewer and seldom from a book reviewer. Why do movies have such powerful effects? It is not movies themselves. Remember what Canadian Marshall McLuhan said about the medium being the message. Nowhere is this truer than when watching a movie in a darkened theatre. The viewer sits in a darkened auditorium in front of a giant screen, with nothing to interrupt the experience. The rest of the world is excluded. Movies, of course, can be shown outdoors at drive-in theatres and on television, but the experience is strongest in the darkened cocoon of a movie house.

HOLLYWOOD'S CULTURAL INFLUENCE

When Clark Gable took off his shirt in the 1934 movie *It Happened One Night* and revealed that he was not wearing anything underneath, American men in great numbers decided that they too would go without undershirts. Nationwide, undershirt sales plummeted. Whether men prefer wearing underwear is trivial compared with some of the following concerns about how Hollywood portrays U.S. life and its influence:

- Sociologist Norman Denzin says that the treatment of drinking in U.S. movies has contributed to a misleading bittersweet romanticism about alcoholism in the public consciousness.
- Scholars using content analysis have found that exponential increases in movie violence far outpace violence in real life and contribute to perceptions that violence is a growing social problem in modern life.
- Political leaders express concern from time to time that movies corrupt the morals of young people and glamorize deviant behaviour.

Movies are part of our everyday lives in more ways than we realize. Even the way we talk is loaded with movie metaphors. *The New Yorker* magazine noted this while introducing an issue on Hollywood: "Our personal scenarios uncoil in a sequence of flashbacks, voice-overs and cameos. We zoom in, cut to the chase, fade to black."

Because of the perceived influences of movies, some real and some not, it is important to know about the industry that creates them. This is especially true now that television entertainment programming has been largely subsumed by Hollywood and that the book, magazine and sound recording industries are closely tied into it.

Movie Technology

Study Preview   *Motion picture technology is based on the same chemical process as photography. The medium developed in the 1880s and 1890s. By the 1930s, movie houses everywhere were showing "talkies." Today, chemical-free digital shooting and editing are beginning to transform production, distribution and exhibition.*

ADAPTATION FROM PHOTOGRAPHY

The technical heritage of motion pictures is photography. The 1727 discovery that light causes silver nitrate to darken was basic to the development of motion picture technology. So was a human phenomenon called **persistence of vision**. The human eye retains an image for a fraction of a second. If a series of photographs capture something in motion and if those photographs are flipped quickly, the human eye will perceive continuous motion.

All that was needed was the right kind of camera and film to capture about 16 images per second. Those appeared in 1888. **William Dickson** of Thomas Edison's laboratory developed a workable motion picture camera. Dickson and Edison used celluloid film perfected by **George Eastman**, who had just introduced his Kodak camera. By 1891 Edison had begun producing movies.

Edison movies were viewed by looking into a box. In France, the **Lumière brothers**, Auguste and Louis, brought projection to motion pictures. By running the film in front of a specially aimed powerful light bulb, the Lumières projected movie images on a wall. In 1895 they opened an exhibition hall in Paris—the first movie house. Edison recognized the commercial advantage of projection and himself patented the Vitascope projector, which he put on the market in 1896.

The First Talkie: *The Jazz Singer,* with Al Jolson. **www.filmsite.org/ jazz.html**

Early Cinema: An introduction to the first decade of motion pictures. **www.earlycinema.com**

The Silent Film Society of Chicago: A group dedicated to the preservation and presentation of silent films. Provides links to information about silents and places to see them. **www.silentfilmchicago. com**

persistence of vision Retina's capability to retain an image briefly, allowing brain to fill in gaps between successive images.

William Dickson Developed the first movie camera.

George Eastman Devised celluloid film.

Lumière brothers Opened the first movie exhibition hall.

Movies came to Canada in June of 1896 when a private demonstration of the Vitascope was held in Montreal. The report in Montreal's *La Presse* explained what viewers saw and how they reacted to the imagery of a cavalry charge: "You see each and every man in all his glory. There are thousands of them. They are coming right onto the stage. You are going to be crushed—but no, at the crucial moment everything vanishes and you remain gaping. All that was needed to complete the illusion was colour and a phonograph to reproduce sounds. That is soon to come." And it didn't take long to come. Canada's first movie house, the **Ouimetoscope**, opened in Montreal in 1906.

Ouimetoscope Canada's first movie house.

D-Cinema

Digital technology seems destined to replace film that is "pulled through the (chemical) soup" (described in Chapter 1). The pace of the transition is hard to forecast. There remain technical and financial impediments to big-screen digital projection, but the economic advantages of digital are driving a transition. Cameras and editing equipment are handier than massive celluloid filming equipment. Also, shipping the finished product on optical discs is far more efficient than using the back-breaking film canisters that now are carted from movie house to movie house by truck. Even in the projection rooms, reels of film are awkward. Theoretically, the day will arrive when digital movies can be transmitted by satellite to movie-house projectors, even with central projection control.

Industrial Light and Magic: View the movie clips on this luminous site and see what this postproduction visual effects company can do for a movie.
www.ilm.com

DIGITAL TRANSITION. George Lucas, producer of the Star Wars series, pioneered digital work through his Industrial Light and Magic production house. For his 1999 Star Wars instalment, *The Phantom Menace*, Lucas shot several scenes with digital equipment, which facilitated their integration into digitally created special effects scenes. For exhibition, there were two masters: one on film, which is what most moviegoers saw, and one in digital form, which was shown in a few theatres. Thus, *The Phantom Menace* became the first major motion picture to be seen in digital form, albeit only at the few theatres equipped with digital projectors.

Relatively few films have been released in digital form because the conversion of movie houses to show them has been slow. Of 36 485 screens nationwide in 2005, only 92 had digital servers and projectors. From 1999 through 2004, a period with almost 3000 Hollywood releases, only 86 titles were digital.

Champions of **d-cinema**, as the new technology is called, expect a sudden upsurge in digital releases. Only one major director, Steven Spielberg, still edits on celluloid. As well, the studios are keen to cut the cost of making hundreds of celluloid prints that are shipped from theatre to theatre. Hollywood's distribution costs are roughly $630 million a year for the United States and Canada, $1 billion worldwide. Distributing d-cinema via the internet or optical disks could cut costs 90 percent.

d-cinema Digitally filmed, edited, distributed and exhibited movies.

There are purists who prefer traditional over d-cinema technology, but their number is ebbing. Canadian James Cameron, best known for *Titanic*, says he will never shoot on film again. The next stage in three-dimensional (3-D) movies, stereoscopic 3-D, can be done only digitally.

TECHNICAL STANDARDS. The studios seem on the verge of making the plunge. In 2002, Disney, Fox, MGM, Paramount, Sony, Universal and Warner combined forces to develop an industry-wide technical standard for d-cinema. The joint venture, **Digital Cinema Initiatives**, has narrowed the quest to two competing technologies, known as 2K and 4K.

Digital Cinema Initiatives Joint movie studio project to identify an industry standard for d-cinema.

One company, Texas Instruments, has devised a 2K-chip imaging device that displays 2048 pixels across. JVC and Sony are pushing 4K, which displays 4096 pixels on a wider canvas. The early d-cinema films used 4K with the Barco D-Cine DP100 projector, but critics say that 4K is a bandwidth hog that offers a resolution far finer than the human eye can detect—so why bother? For practical purposes, say 2K advocates, the two look equally sharp. Too, it's not just a pixel race. The millisecond rate at which images are updated is more important than the number of pixels to meet the upper limits of human persistence of vision. Cineplex Odeon began converting some of their theatres to d-cinema in 2007 using 2K projectors.

The big remaining issue is the financing of movie-house conversion. At $100 000 a theatre for new equipment, the big exhibition chains, always wary about the consequences of increasing ticket prices, are hesitant to make the investment. In 2005, the studios proposed a $1000 incentive to theatres, called a **virtual print fee**, to offset the cost of the new equipment. The mathematics were promising. Studios would save about $1000 without making and shipping film prints. Theatres, assuming a film runs three weeks, would average about $17 000 a year in new fees, which would pay for the new equipment in six years.

virtual print fee Movie studio payment to theatres for showing a digital-format movie, as an offset for digital projection equipment.

Movie-house chains were cautious, noting that digital projection equipment has a notoriously short life span, about three years compared to decades for older equipment. But exhibitors may have no choice as people become enamoured of digital images on computer screens and the growing trend to digital transmission in television.

Stereoscopic 3-D. Forget those silly, tinted, throw-away glasses required for early-generation 3-D movies. A new technique, possible through digital shooting and which brings the action to the tip of your nose, has caught the fancy of directors, including Canadian-born James Cameron for *Aliens of the Deep* in 2005 and *Battle Angel* in 2007.

James Cameron

Movie Industry Structure

Study Preview   *The movie industry has three major components: production, distribution and exhibition.*

STUDIOS AND PRODUCTION

The flashy corporate names in the movie business are the big studios that are the heart of the **production** component.

production Content-creation component of the movie industry.

studio A company that produces movies, sometimes also involved in distribution.

Paramount Decision The landmark 1948 U.S. Supreme Court anti-monopoly decision which broke the major studios' hold on the U.S. movie industry.

United Artists Upstart artist-directed movie studio, started in 1919.

MAJOR STUDIOS. Some studios are brand names. About 90 percent of the U.S. box office revenue comes from the so-called Big Six: Columbia, Paramount, 20th Century Fox, Universal, Disney and Warner. These companies are called **studios** because each once maintained acres of stage sets—*studios*, if you will. In their heyday, the studios dominated the whole movie industry. Not only did they conceive and nurture movies into existence, but they also controlled the distribution of their products and owned many movie houses. The scope of the studios was trimmed in a landmark 1948 U.S. Supreme Court anti-monopoly decision, the **Paramount Decision** (also known as the Paramount Case or the Hollywood Antitrust Case of 1948), but the studios' high-visibility role in producing Hollywood products continued. For decades, studio publicity machines made idols of scriptwriters, directors and actors and simultaneously promoted themselves with glitz. Even in the uncertain post-1948 period, the studios maintained a reputation for glamour—and with justification. No other country had such a highly developed movie industry.

Hollywood was such a valued homegrown industry that the nation was rattled when Sony, the Japanese electronics company, bought venerable Columbia in 1989. The public generally doesn't have much interest in the owners behind brand names, but there had been modest curiosity a few years earlier when Coca-Cola bought the Columbia studio. It seemed a novel thing for a soda-pop company to do. But now Sony, a company from a distinctly different culture, suddenly had a foothold in the U.S. movie industry. What did it mean? Newsmagazines and pundits had a field day in speculating.

As it turned out, Sony had no alien political, social or ideological agenda. Sony was as profit-driven as corporate parents of the other major studios. There was no magic. Columbia under Sony had as many flops—successes too—as the other studios. Over the next few years, 20th Century Fox became part of Rupert Murdoch's Australian media empire. Universal went into Canadian, then French hands. Now Universal is back in U.S. ownership under General Electric and merged with NBC. One lesson from these transactions is that, whatever the nationality of their headquarters, movie studios are attractive as acquisitions because of either perceived profit potential or synergetic opportunities.

Besides the major studios, all with roots in Hollywood's earliest days, there is United Artists.

UNITED ARTISTS. Concerned that the studios were disproportionately focused on profits and infringing creativity, director D.W. Griffith and box-office darlings Charlie Chaplin, Douglas Fairbanks and Mary Pickford (born Gladys Louise Smith in 1892 in Toronto) created **United Artists** in 1919. With full creative control, they produced movies that scored well among critics and attracted huge audiences. United was among the few insurgent movie companies to make a long-term mark on Hollywood after the giants had established themselves. United Artists' history, how-

Media Databank

Major Movie Studios

In the high-risk movie business, with drastic revenue swings every weekend of new releases, a ranking of the major studios based on revenue is impossible. A single mega-success can catapult one studio to the top instantly, and a series of flops can push a studio toward insolvency. These, though, are the enduring giants of the industry:

	Corporate Parent	Parent Nationality
Columbia	Sony	Japan
Paramount	Viacom	United States
20th Century Fox	News Corporation	Australia
Universal	General Electric	United States
Walt Disney	Disney	United States
Warner Brothers	Time Warner	United States

ever, was rocky. It almost was done in by Michael Cimino's out-of-control spending to make *Heaven's Gate* in 1980. A year later the insurance company that had acquired United Artists, Transamerica, unloaded the studio on MGM. But the amalgamated MGM/UA produced one disaster after another until the early 2000s, when it had money-makers including *Legally Blonde* and *Die Another Day*. Whether MGM/UA can break into the Big Six is an open question.

DREAMWORKS. For 21 years the new kid on the Hollywood block was **DreamWorks**, created by retired record executive David Geffen, former Disney executive Jeff Katzenberg and superdirector Steven Spielberg. It was a dream team of exceptionally able, well-connected and seasoned Hollywood people who, each with a fortune from successful entertainment industry careers, could bankroll major projects. Spielberg's *Saving Private Ryan* in 1998 established an early DreamWorks benchmark for filmic excellence that resonated with audiences. *Gladiator* was 2000's best picture at the Academy Awards. Sixty films later, in 2005, the founding threesome sold DreamWorks to Viacom's Paramount for $1.6 billion. It was yet another incidence of a successful media start-up being absorbed by a larger, more established media company.

DISTRIBUTION

For moviegoers, the least visible part of the movie industry is distribution. The major studios are largely responsible for this task. They schedule the bookings for movie releases at the theatres, perform the marketing activities to promote the release and then supply the actual film to the movie houses for showing the movie. Also, the big studios provide distribution services. Independent producers often contract out the distribution function to the major studios because the cost of building up the network of contacts with the large theatre chains is too steep for small producers.

The major film distributor in Canada is **Alliance Atlantis**. It indirectly owns a majority interest in Motion Picture Distribution LP. In addition to distributing Canadian movies, such as *Trailer Park Boys: The Movie*, it distributes films and DVDs

Sony Pictures: The parent company of the American icon, Columbia Pictures. www.sonypictures.com

Paramount News: About Paramount movies and home videos. You can also link to Paramount's television or entertainment arms. www.paramount.com

Fox Movies: View the trailers for movies in theatres and online, and take a look at what's coming. www.foxmovies.com

Universal Pictures: Learn about current Universal films. You can also hit links to projects still in production, as well as some surprises. www.universalpictures.com

Disney: Links to the corporate side of Disney, including corporate news, attractions, entertainment media magazines, television, interactive features, movies, music and more. http://disney.go.com

Warner: More than just "What's up, Doc?" www2.warnerbros.com

United Artists: See what the company founded by Charlie Chaplin, Douglas Fairbanks and "Canada's Sweetheart" Mary Pickford is up to now. www.unitedartists.com

DreamWorks Upstart movie studio, created in 1994 by David Geffen, Jeff Katzenberg and Steven Spielberg.

Alliance Atlantis Canadian movie distributor.

DreamWorks SKG: Another viable competitor for the Big Six.
www.dreamworks.com/ dreamworks_home.html

Alliance Atlantis: Canada's leading film distributor.
www.allianceatlantis.com

Cineplex: Buy tickets online and skip the line in front of the theatre.
www.cineplex.com

Empire Theatres: See what's playing and buy advance tickets.
www.empiretheatres.com

exhibition What movie houses do.

box office Fanciful term for revenue that a movie earns in exhibition.

Cineplex Entertainment LP Canada's largest theatre chain.

nut Upfront distribution payment to exhibitor.

for New Line Cinema, Dimension Films, Miramax Films, The Weinstein Company and others.

How does Canada fit into the distribution and exhibition plans of Hollywood? We're simply "America Junior." James Adams of *The Globe and Mail* says that "when the U.S. movie industry gathers statistics on how its films are faring at the box office, Canada isn't considered a sovereign nation: It's part of the American domestic market, right alongside Guam, Puerto Rico, the Virgin Islands and various other U.S. unincorporated territories."

EXHIBITION

The motion picture industry once derived all its revenue from **exhibition**—at movie houses, where customers pay to see a movie. The receipts, called the **box office**, are split between the exhibitor and the distributor, and the distributor uses its share to pay the studio for distribution rights. As of 2007, **Cineplex Entertainment LP** was the largest movie exhibitor in Canada, controlling 128 theatres and almost 1300 screens. Movie houses under their corporate umbrella include Cineplex Odeon, Galaxy and Famous Players. Atlantic Canada's Empire Theatres is the second largest movie exhibitor with some 59 theatres with over 400 screens across Canada. Movie theatres aren't just for movies anymore. NHL hockey, WWE events and even the high-brow Metropolitan Opera are now also available at many theatre locations in Canada.

Exhibitors get an upfront payment, called the **nut**, to help cover their costs. After the nut, distributors take the lion's share of box-office revenue, often 90 percent for the first week. Deals vary, but eventually, if a movie runs long enough, the split ends up being 50–50. For movie houses, the concession stand is an important revenue source. Concessions are so profitable that exhibitors sometimes agree to give up their nut entirely for a blockbuster and rely on popcorn and candy to make money. Movie-house markups on confections are typically 60 percent, more on popcorn.

Economics of Movies

Study Preview   *The movie industry is dominated by six companies, all of them subsidiaries of larger companies. Major studios have also found economic advantages in picking up projects from independent producers and capitalizing on auxiliary enterprises. Canadian filmmakers are also eligible for government subsidies.*

STUDIO FINANCING

Just as in D.W. Griffith's time, movies are expensive to make—about $43 million on average. Then there are the big-budget movies. Depending on how the expenses are tallied, the 2005 movie *Chronicles of Narnia: The Lion, the Witch and the Wardrobe* cost more than $200 million to make. Some estimates peg *Titanic* (1997) costs as high as $240 million. Where does the money come from?

major studios Include Warner Brothers, Columbia, Universal, 20th Century Fox, Paramount, Disney, MGM.

MAJOR STUDIOS. Major studios finance many movies with profits from earlier movies. Most movies, however, do not originate with major studios but with independent producers. These producers are autonomous in many ways, but most rely

Media Databank

Big-Budget Movies

Movie Title	Year	Amount Spent ($)
Titanic	1997	240 million
Chronicles of Narnia	2005	200 million
Terminator 3: Rise of the Machines	2003	175 million
Spider-Man	2002	170 million
Matrix Reloaded	2003	170 million
The Hulk	2003	150 million
Pearl Harbor	2001	140 million
Charlie's Angels: Full Throttle	2003	135 million
Bad Boys II	2003	130 million
Harry Potter and the Sorcerer's Stone	2001	120 million
Harry Potter and the Chamber of Secrets	2002	100 million

on major studios for financing. The studios hedge their risks by distributing the movies themselves, a profitable enterprise involving rentals to movie houses and TV, home video sales and merchandise licensing.

The studios, and other financial backers, do more than write cheques. To protect their investments, some get directly involved in film projects. They examine budgets and schedules in considering a loan request. Often, they send representatives to shooting sites to guard against budget overruns.

Major studios that are part of conglomerates can draw on the resources of their corporate parents. In 1952, giant MCA (Music Corporation of America) acquired

D.W. Griffith: Learn more about this early film pioneer from this PBS American Masters website.
www.pbs.org/wnet/ americanmasters/ database/griffith_d.html

Newmarket Films: Film distribution company with only one criterion—quality.
www.newmarketfilms. com

Criterion Collection: Find out about the most important movies of all time, all on DVD.
www.criterionco.com

Media Databank

Global Box-Office Sales

Movie Title	Year	Amount Earned ($)
Titanic	1997	1.8 billion
Harry Potter and the Sorcerer's Stone	2001	980 million
Harry Potter and the Chamber of Secrets	2002	880 million
Spider-Man	2002	820 million
Matrix Reloaded	2003	740 million
Pearl Harbor	2001	450 million
Terminator 3: Rise of the Machines	2003	435 million
Bad Boys II	2003	270 million
Charlie's Angels: Full Throttle	2003	260 million
The Hulk	2003	250 million

the ailing Universal studio and plowed its recording business profits into the studio. Universal turned profitable and MCA became even stronger by having another profitable subsidiary. The Gulf and Western conglomerate later did the same with Paramount. Coca-Cola acquired Columbia in 1982 with a promise to help Columbia through the rough times that had beset the movie company.

In the 1980s several studios acquired new corporate parents, which made it easier to finance movies. The Japanese electronics giant Sony bought Columbia in 1989. At $3.4 billion, it was the biggest Japanese takeover of an American corporation in history. The size of the deal was a sign of the new resources Columbia could tap to make movies. By the early 1990s three of the largest U.S. studios were owned by giant foreign companies with the ability to generate cash from other enterprises to strengthen their new U.S. movie subsidiaries.

INVESTOR GROUPS. Special investment groups sometimes are put together to fund movies for major studios. Less proven producers, or those whose track records are marred by budget overruns and loose production schedules, often seek financing from **risk investors**, who include venture capitalists, tax-shelter organizers and foreign distributors. Risk investors often take a bigger share of revenue in exchange for their bigger risk.

BANKS. To meet front-end production expenses, studios go to banks for loans against their assets, which include their production facilities and warehouses of vintage films awaiting re-release. By bankrolling movies early in Hollywood's history, California-based Bank of America grew into one of the nation's biggest banks.

INDEPENDENT PRODUCERS

Before the U.S. Supreme Court's Paramount Decision in 1948, which broke the major studios' hold on the U.S. movie industry, there was not much opportunity for **independent producers** to get their movies into the distribution and exhibition network. The Big Six controlled almost the entire system. That has changed drastically. Today the big studios scout for independent producers to pick up movies without the development costs.

Mel Gibson's personal take from *The Passion of the Christ* will not be known for years. The money is still coming in. But experts in Hollywood finance wouldn't be surprised if the total exceeded $350 million, perhaps overtaking the record of George Lucas, who spurned the studio system and financed and controlled every aspect, with no studio interference, of his Star Wars movie *The Phantom Menace* in 1999. Both Gibson and Lucas functioned as independent producers. In Gibson's case, he had no choice. He couldn't interest any studio in doing *The Passion of the Christ*.

Gibson is in an elite group of $25 million-a-film actors who have amassed sufficient fortunes from the studios that they can afford to bankroll their own movies. For *Passion*, Gibson paid the $30 million in production costs. He farmed out exhibition to Newmarket Films, which signed up theatres to exhibit the film for a share of the revenue. Capitalizing on controversy about Gibson's portrayal of Jews to increase publicity, Newmarket more than doubled its projection for the initial box office. In the first five days, *Passion* grossed $125 million. Newmarket's projection was $45 million.

Unlike Gibson and Spielberg, many independent producers are unknowns. *The Blair Witch Project*, for example, cost $35 000 in 1998. Within a year it was a commercial smash, with box-office receipts of $141 million. It even spawned a sequel.

risk investors Individuals and companies willing to put capital into ventures shunned by conservative financial institutions.

independent producers Movie production enterprises outside of the major studios.

Studios bankroll projects from independent producers, whose overhead costs are relatively low. This doesn't mean that studio financing is easy to come by, as attested by Spike Lee, the legendary director of black-themed movies, including *Malcolm X*. Even so, Lee has had studio backing for numerous films. Some actors have succeeded in directing and producing on their own, with studio backing, including Clint Eastwood, Tom Hanks and Ron Howard. Then there are independent producers who come from nowhere, it seems, and hit a chord that resonates with the public, like Michael Moore with his bleak 1989 documentary on General Motors, *Roger and Me*, his equally bleak *Bowling for Columbine* in 2002 and his politically charged *Fahrenheit 9/11* in 2004.

The independent producers demonstrate that the major studios have a monopoly on neither originality nor creativity. But as they will tell you, they are outsiders.

GOVERNMENT FUNDING

Financing for Canadian movies can also come from the public sector. Founded in 1967, Telefilm Canada is a crown corporation that provides funding for Canadian filmmakers to help them produce Canadian movies and television programs. According to Telefilm, their "role is to foster the production of films, television programs and cultural products that reflect Canadian society, with its linguistic duality and cultural diversity, and to encourage their dissemination at home and abroad." In 2007, the 40th anniversary of Telefilm, their budget was $390 million.

AFTERMARKETS

When moviemakers plan films today, they build budgets around anticipated revenues that go beyond first runs in movie houses. Unlike the old days, when movies either made it or didn't at the box office, today moviemakers earn more than 5.7 percent of their revenue from pay television services like HBO and TMN after the movie has played itself out in the movie houses. Another 31.4 percent comes from selling videotapes and DVDs.

AUXILIARY ENTERPRISES

Movie studios have found auxiliary revenue sources to wring additional income, besides the box office, from their product. Hollywood has hundreds of lawyers in various specialties, including copyright law, who negotiate deals with other companies to use characters, themes, outtakes and music from movies. Then too there are the television spinoffs, Burger King toys, comic books and school lunch boxes.

MERCHANDISE TIE-INS. Fortunes can be made by licensing other companies to use characters and signature items from a movie. In one of the most successful merchandise tie-ins, 20th Century Fox and George Lucas licensed Ewok dolls, R2D2 posters and even *Star Wars* bedsheets and pillowcases. By 1985, seven years after the movie's release, tie-ins had racked up sales of $2 billion. The licensing fee typically is 10 percent of the retail price of the merchandise. *Batman* tie-ins rang up $500 million in sales in 1989, within six months of the movie's release, and Warner Brothers was earning 20 percent of the retail revenue on some products.

merchandise tie-ins Studio deals to profit from merchandise carrying movie names and logos.

TOYS. For the 1995 film *Batman Forever*, Warner Brothers let the Hasbro toy company dress the Riddler. Hasbro wanted tight pants, not the baggy ones in the script, so the Riddler action toy would look better. The result? The Riddler wore tight pants on screen. A recurrent report from *Pocahontas* animators is that their bosses ordered them to have the raccoon Meeko braid the Indian maiden's hair so that Mattel could market Braided Beauty Pocahontas dolls.

Some moviemakers deny that the cart is ahead of the horse. Disney officials, for example, say that Mattel had no hand in the script for *Pocahontas*; the script came first, the toys second. Whatever the truth, moviemakers have huge financial incentives to do whatever it takes to ensure success. Toymakers pay licensing fees, typically 10 percent of a toy's retail price. Disney earned $16 million, the record, for the 1994 movie *The Lion King*. In 1995, *Batman Forever* paraphernalia generated $13 million, *Pocahontas* $10 million. Power Ranger gear, tied into both the movie and the television series, has totaled $300 million, of which an estimated $30 million went back to Fox—a significant revenue source requiring hardly any studio expense.

Is this kind of commercialism undermining the artistic autonomy that normally is associated with creative enterprises like moviemaking? This is the same elitist–populist issue that is at the heart of the ongoing debate about media content. At one extreme is the pristine elitist preference for creative forces to drive content oblivious to commercial considerations. At the other extreme is the laissez-faire populist belief that nothing is wrong with marketplace forces. Populists say that if a movie's box office suffers because toymakers have had too much sway on script decisions, moviemakers will make future adjustments—and an appropriate balance will result eventually. Some elitists accept that argument but worry nonetheless about the commercial contamination that occurs in the meantime.

Music. Tie-ins are not new. Music, for example, was a revenue source for moviemakers even before talkies. Just about every early movie house had a piano player who kept one eye on the screen and hammered out supportive mood music, and sheet-music publishers bought the rights to print and sell the music to musicians who wanted to perform it on their own. This was no small enterprise. D.W. Griffith's *The Birth of a Nation* of 1915 had an accompanying score for a 70-piece symphony. Today, music has assumed importance beyond supporting the screen drama. It has become a moviemaking profit centre—just count the number of songs in the credits at the end of today's movies.

PropStar: An agency that specializes in placing products and brand names in movies and on TV. www.propstar.com

Product Placement. Moviemakers also have begun building commercial products into story lines in a subtle form of advertising. It was no coincidence that Tom Cruise downed Pepsi in *Top Gun*. Some movie producers work brand names into their movies for a fee. When the alien E.T. was coaxed out of hiding with a handful of candy, it was with Reese's Pieces. The Hershey company, which makes Reese's, paid to have its candy used. Sales soared in the next few months. Producers had first offered the Mars company a chance for the candy to be M&Ms, but Mars executives were squeamish about their candy being associated with anything as ugly as E.T. They did not realize that moviegoers would fall in love with the little alien.

After *E.T.* the product placement business boomed. Miller beer paid to have 21 references in *Bull Durham*. The same movie also included seven references for Budweiser, four for Pepsi, three for Jim Beam and two for Oscar Mayer. A simple shot of a product in the foreground typically goes for $25 000 to $50 000. Some advertisers have paid $350 000 for multiple onscreen plugs.

product placement When a manufacturer pays for its products to be used as props.

Critics claim that **product placements** are sneaky. Some want them banned. Others say the word "advertisement" should be flashed on the screen when the products appear. Movie people, on the other hand, argue that using real products adds credibility. In the old days, directors assiduously avoided implicit endorsements. In a bar scene the players would drink from cans marked "beer"—no brand name. Today, says Marvin Cohen, whose agency matches advertisers and movies, "A can that says 'Beer' isn't going to make it anymore." The unanswered question is how much product-placement deals affect artistic decisions.

Canadian Film Industry

Study Preview   *While Hollywood's focus tends to be on blockbuster movies, the Canadian film industry pursued another direction. The National Film Board of Canada has won innumerable awards for its documentaries and animation. Feature films in Canada have also followed in the documentary tradition.*

Jeannette Sloniowski, in *Canadian Communications: Issues in Contemporary Media and Culture*, sums up the plight of Canadian movies like this: "Canadian Movies: Not Coming to a Cinema near You." Due to economic and distribution issues, Canadian movies account for less than 11 percent of all screen time at movie houses in Canada. Because of this, television is often the only outlet for Canadian films. Canadian channels, both conventional channels like the CBC and specialty, are the primary outlet for Canadian movies to be seen by Canadians. As a result of exposure on television, the Canadian Film and Television Production Association (CFTPA) announced that more than 40 percent of revenue earned by Canadian movies came from pay television.

Canadian movies have always lived in the shadow of American fare. As a result, they have had to struggle to mature and gain acceptance in this country. In his article "American Domination of the Motion Picture Industry," **Garth Jowett** points out that Canada has always been dependent on Hollywood for movies. Jowett writes, "From the outset, Canada because of its geographic situation was considered to be merely one of the many marketing areas designated by the American film industry." Jowett also claims that most Canadians have always preferred Hollywood movies to British or Canadian films. However, this does not mean that filmmaking traditions do not exist in this country.

Garth Jowett Believes Canada has always been dependent on Hollywood movies.

From the earliest days of the medium, movies were shot and produced in Canada. Douglas Fetherling says that the first film shot in Canada was in Manitoba in 1897. Many other short films followed; however, the first Canadian feature film wasn't made until 1913. *Evangeline* was a five-reel film produced by the Canadian Bioscope Company of Halifax. Based on a poem by Longfellow about the flight of the Acadians, it was shot on location in the Annapolis Valley. It featured an American cast and turned a profit. The Canadian Biograph Company was never able to match the success of *Evangeline*. The same was true of other early Canadian filmmakers; it's estimated that only about 70 Canadian feature films were produced during the first half of the 20th century.

American movie mogul D.W. Griffith, whose narrative style was influential in the development of Hollywood movies, visited Toronto in 1925. During that visit, he told Canadian officials that Canada should make Hollywood-type movies to trade with the United States. Almost 15 years later, a British filmmaker disagreed with him and the Canadian film industry went in another direction. That man was John Grierson, and the National Film Board of Canada was born.

The **National Film Board (NFB)** was formed by an act of Parliament in 1939 to "interpret Canada to Canadians." The board's first commissioner was

NFB Canada's award-winning National Film Board.

John Grierson Founder of the NFB.

John Grierson, a British documentary filmmaker. Grierson advocated a strong national film industry. He wanted to make movies that celebrated Canada's geographic and social diversity. In a statement about government film policy, Grierson said that while Canada could never compete with the glamour of Hollywood, it should not abandon the idea of a national film industry. Grierson felt that making short, inexpensive films about Canadians and their experiences could complement more expensive Hollywood fare, while still giving Canadians a cinematic voice. Grierson also believed that films should tackle social issues and that filmmakers should try to produce films that make a difference.

During World War II, the NFB produced several propaganda films in support of the war effort. After the war, Grierson returned to England, but the NFB continued to make successful documentary films. During this time, it became known for a style called **cinéma vérité**, which roughly translated means "truth in cinema." For the NFB, cinéma vérité has meant documentaries by Canadians about Canadians.

cinéma vérité Truth or realism in movies. The basis for the documentary tradition.

The NFB is also known for its animation. The board's animation roots can be traced back to the arrival of **Norman McLaren** in 1941. Although he made 59 films for the NFB, including the propaganda movies *V for Victory* (1941) and *Keep Your Mouth Shut* (1944), animation was McLaren's first love. While his films have won more than 200 international awards, his best-known work is the 1953 Oscar-winning short *Neighbours*. The eight-minute antiwar film is about two neighbours fighting over a flower. The dispute escalates into tribal warfare. The film used live actors, but they were animated with the same techniques used to animate puppets and drawings.

Norman McLaren Canadian innovator in animation.

Telefilm Canada: Government agency dedicated to developing and promoting Canadian film, television, video and multimedia industries. www.telefilm.gc.ca

NFB: The National Film Board of Canada. www.nfb.ca

In 1950, Parliament passed the National Film Act, which changed the NFB's mandate to include producing, promoting and distributing films in the national interest. In the NFB's early days, it would send projectionists from city to city and town to town to show its latest offerings in arenas, community centres, and even fields. These films were also shown in movie houses and eventually on television. NFB films were (and still are) distributed by public libraries, schools, universities and colleges.

Some classic NFB films include *The Corporation* (2003), *A Place Called Chiapas* (1998), *The Champagne Safari* (1996), *Bob's Birthday* (1995), *Manufacturing Consent* (1992), and the controversial *The Boys of St. Vincent* (1992). NFB's women's division, called Studio D, produced 1981's *Not a Love Story* and the controversial *If You Love This Planet* in 1982.

FEATURE FILMS IN CANADA

Despite its success in the documentary and animated areas, Canada, with the exception of Quebec, has left the bulk of dramas and literary adaptations to the

NFB Classic. Richard Condie's Genie Award–winning *The Big Snit* (1985) is just one of many NFB animated shorts to receive plaudits worldwide. The NFB continues to trailblaze in the spirit of Norman McLaren.

Americans. The feature film industry in Canada remained largely dormant until the 1960s. In 1964, two films marked the unofficial start of the feature film industry in Canada: Don Owen's *Nobody Waved Goodbye* and Gilles Groulx's *Le Chat dans le sac*. Both of these films were NFB productions, but they were feature films shot in the documentary tradition that featured regional themes without the glamour of Hollywood movies. The better-known Canadian films from this era include *Goin' down the Road* (1970), *Mon Oncle Antoine* (1971), *Paperback Hero* (1973), *Between Friends* (1973) and the classic *The Apprenticeship of Duddy Kravitz* (1974).

By the late 1970s, government incentives, such as those of the Canadian Film Development Corporation (now known as Telefilm) for producers investing in Canadian feature films, created a glut of product—some good, but mostly bad. It's this time period that gave Canadian movies a bad name. Many people invested money in movies simply as a tax break. The quality of the script, actors and movie were not always factors. *Why Shoot the Teacher?* (1978), *Atlantic City* (1980), *Scanners* (1981), and the largest-grossing Canadian movie of all time, the less than classy *Porky's* (1982), were all produced during this period.

Through the 1990s, Canadian films matured, particularly in English language cinema with movies such as *Margaret's Museum* (1995), *Hard Core Logo* (1996), *The Hanging Garden* (1997) and *Last Night* (1999). This trend continued into the 21st century with such eclectic films as *Ginger Snaps* (2000), *Fubar* (2002), *Men with Brooms* (2002) and *My Big Fat Greek Wedding* (2002).

Issues of ethnicity and multiculturalism continued to be explored in recent Canadian movies. Mina Shum's *Double Happiness* (1994), Davor Marjanovic's *My Father's Angel* (2000), and Deepa Mehta's *Water* (2001) are all excellent examples of Canadian films exploring these themes.

However, despite the increase in the quality of Canadian movies that are being produced, English Canadians don't usually see these films at their local movie theatre. Television, particularly specialty channels, is where most English Canadians watch their national cinema. Brian D. Johnson, the film critic for *Maclean's*, in his article "The Lost Picture Show," says, "welcome to the Byzantine world of English Canadian film financing—a surreal maze of auteur dreams, bureaucratic nightmares and ritualized failure. It's a world where distributors routinely snap up publicly funded movies, flip the TV rights to broadcasters for an easy profit, then dump the films into a few theatres for a token release."

Media Databank

Movie Revenue: Canadian Style

Financially, Canadian films are stronger than ever, but the majority of profits don't come from the box office. On average, only 11 percent of movies shown in Canadian theatres are Canadian, so Canadian film and videomakers must look to other sources of revenue. Data from Statistics Canada illustrates how movies made money in Canada in 2004/2005:

Box office	$446 million
Conventional TV	$404 million
DVD sales	$247 million
Pay television	$135 million

Source: Adapted from Statistics Canada publication "Film, video and audio-visual distribution, 2004/2005," *The Daily*, Catalogue 11-001, August 28, 2006, http://www.statcan.ca/Daily/English/060828/d060828a.htm.

Media Databank

The Best of Canadian Films

Genie Awards Canada's Oscars.

The United States has the Oscars; Canada has the **Genie Awards**, which are awarded annually to the best in Canadian movies by the Academy of Canadian Cinema and Television. Here's a list of recent Genie award winners for best picture in Canada. Any of these films would be a good place to test Harcourt's theory about Canadian movies and the theme of "uncertainty":

1990:	*Jésus de Montréal/Jesus of Montreal*
1991:	*Black Robe*
1992:	*Naked Lunch*
1993:	*Thirty-Two Short Films about Glenn Gould*
1994:	*Exotica*
1995:	*Le Confessional*
1996:	*Lilies*
1997:	*The Sweet Hereafter*
1998:	*The Red Violin*
1999:	*Sunshine*
2000:	*Maelström*
2001:	*Atanarjuat, The Fast Runner*
2002:	*Ararat*
2003:	*Les invasions barbares/The Barbarian Invasions*
2004:	*Les Triplettes de Belleville/The Triplets of Belleville*
2005:	*C.R.A.Z.Y.*
2006:	*Bon Cop, Bad Cop*

Source: www.genieawards.ca. Reprinted with the permission of the Academy of Canadian Cinema & Television.

Canadian Films and Actors: We have a long history of filmmaking in Canada. Find out more at this site. **www.northernstars.ca**

I Dream of Genies: All about the award for Canadian movie excellence. **www.genieawards.ca**

Movie Issues and Trends

Study Preview   *Hollywood's initial response to television was to combat the new medium with technical innovations. Then came movies with edgy content. Today, movies and TV are financially and technologically intertwined. But censorship remains an issue.*

TELEVISION'S CHALLENGE

Movies caught on big early on. There was nothing like them. By the 1920s, opulent theatres had been built, surpassing even the best opera houses in elegant decorations and architectural flourishes. Movies were a unique form of diversion and entertainment. Ticket sales topped $90 million a week in 1946. Then came television.

To buy a television set, many families piggybanked what they had been spending on movies—50 cents for adults, 25 or 35 cents for the kids. Movie attendance plummeted to 46 million by 1955. Was the end of Hollywood at hand?

The movie industry flailed wildly to stem the audience loss. High-budget spectaculars that network television couldn't afford were tried. In 1951 MGM hired 5500 extras for its three-hour *Quo Vadis*. Although such spectaculars drew audiences, the investment was risky. 20th Century Fox almost bankrupted itself by spending an unprecedented $44 million on *Cleopatra* in 1963.

To differentiate itself from television, the movie industry tried technical innovations. Some were immediately forgettable, like Smell-o-Vision. Odours were wafted through movie houses with appropriate scenes to enhance the audience's sensual involvement. Other gimmicks included 3-D, complete with free eyeglasses for the audience, one lens blue, one red. Some movie houses were remodeled with wraparound screens—Cinerama, it was called—to occupy the audience's peripheral vision.

More enduring was the almost total shift to colour. Although colour had been introduced in the 1930s, black and white had remained dominant. In the 1950s colour became the standard—something that early television couldn't match. Also, a less costly alternative to Cinerama, which had required multiple cameras and projectors, was the horizontal CinemaScope screen. The screens, two times wider than they were high, offered more realistic images than the old squarish screens. CinemaScope also differentiated movies from television, which had squarish screens.

CONTENT INNOVATION

Despite the innovations, ticket sales ebbed to 19 million a week. By the 1970s, exhibitors had shuttered many of the grand movie palaces and adjusted to the reality that it was sharing its audience with television. Although only a quarter of its former self, there remained a large audience for movies. At 19 million tickets a week, 52 weeks a year, movies still have a significant financial base.

Hollywood found genres that network television, timid in its infancy, wouldn't touch. There were films on disturbing social issues. MGM released *Blackboard Jungle* in 1955, examining disruptive classroom behaviour in a way that was inconceivable for the television sitcom *Our Miss Brooks*. That same year Warner issued *Rebel Without a Cause,* the James Dean classic about a bad boy from a good family. If television had dared to adapt Tennessee Williams's steamy play *Cat on a Hot Tin Roof,* with its implied homosexuality and marital intimacy, it wouldn't have been recognizable. In 1958 MGM made the movie.

Riding high on an intensive growth period, television executives saw no need to match Hollywood's edginess. Hollywood, meanwhile, continued to test new waters. Columbia and United Artists explored social inequity and injustice, including interracial issues, in a trilogy starring Sidney Poitier: *Guess Who's Coming to Dinner, To Sir with Love* and *In the Heat of the Night.* In *The Wild Bunch* in 1969, director Sam Peckinpah brought new blood-spurting violence to the screen, in slow motion for additional impact. Similar effects in Arthur Penn's 1967 classic *Bonnie and Clyde* left audiences awed in sickened silence. Nevertheless, people kept coming back to movies that showed graphic violence. Sex was taboo on television but not at the movies. It was the theme in *Bob & Carol & Ted & Alice* (1969), *Carnal Knowledge* (1971) and *I Am Curious (Yellow)* (1969). Sex went about as far as it could with the hard-core *Deep Throat* of 1973, which was produced for porno houses but achieved crossover commercial success in regular movie houses.

Documentary Films.net:
Comprehensive source
of information for
documentary viewers
and makers.
**www.documentaryfilms.
net**

Movies came to be made for a younger crowd. By 1985, regular moviegoers fell into a relatively narrow age group: from teenagers through college age. Fifty-nine percent of the tickets were purchased by people between the ages of 12 and 24. Even so, the industry did not produce exclusively for a young audience. Moviemakers recognized that the highest profits came from movies with a crossover audience. These were movies that attracted not only the regular box-office crowd but also infrequent moviegoers. Essential, however, was the youth audience. Without it a movie could not achieve extraordinary success. The immensely profitable *E.T.* was an example. It appealed to the youth audience, to parents who took their small children and to film aficionados who were fascinated by the special effects.

DOCUMENTARIES

documentary A video
examination of a historical
or current event or a natural
or social phenomenon.

Documentaries are nothing new. Canada's NFB has been producing them since 1939. However, the new millennium has seen a dramatic increase in mainstream documentaries coming from the United States. Morgan Spurlock went on a fast-food diet, eating only Big Macs and other McDonald's fare. It wreaked havoc on Spurlock's body, as anybody can see in his movie *Super Size Me*. We learned about the delicate nature of freedom of speech for the Dixie Chicks in 2006's *Shut Up & Sing*. Al Gore's 2006 Oscar winner *An Inconvenient Truth* set the agenda for discussions on global warming. These are among a growing number of point-of-view documentaries that mainstream movie houses have been booking in recent years.

Relatively inexpensive digital filmmaking equipment has driven the new documentaries. Morgan Spurlock could never have persuaded a major studio to provide the budget, several million dollars upfront, for a documentary attacking an American icon like McDonald's. Not even Spurlock's record as an MTV producer would have done it. But with a $3000 digital camera, $5000 in software and an Apple computer, he created his personal statement on fast food. So compelling was *Super Size Me* that 200 theatres showed it, and it grossed $7.5 million in a month. In all Spurlock had spent $65 000 to create the movie.

More typical is $250 000 to plan, shoot and edit a documentary with the production quality of a studio movie—easily within the budgets of small distribution companies and the art-house divisions of major studios. In 2004 Michael Moore's *Fahrenheit 9/11*, which cost $6 million, most of it for archival footage that had to be purchased, grossed $119.2 million. Despite potentially huge profit margins, major studios have been skittish about new-breed documentaries. Miramax, for example, was ready to distribute *Fahrenheit 9/11* when executives at its parent company, Disney, fretting at the movie's anti-Bush and antiwar message, said: "Absolutely not." Disney unloaded the movie, which found its way into theatres through other channels.

MOVIE CENSORSHIP

When things seem wrong in society, people look for a cause. It's easy, although hardly logical, to blame something new for worsening social ills. The mass media, especially when delivering content with new technology, is historically a handy whipping boy. Movies are no exception, not only at their outset but through their history.

MORALITY AS AN ISSUE. It was no wonder in Victorian 1896 that a movie called *Dolorita in the Passion Dance* caused an uproar. There were demands that it be banned—the first but hardly last such call against a movie. In 1907 Chicago passed a law restricting objectionable motion pictures. State legislators across the land were insisting that something be done. To clean up movies, worried moviemakers created in 1922 the **Motion Picture Producers and Distributors of America (MPPDA)**, now known as the Motion Picture Association of America

Michael Moore. His record of activist journalism included a stint at *Mother Jones* magazine, but Michael Moore's reputation for raw-fisted antiestablishment slants was cemented with his *Roger & Me* documentary assault on General Motors. Some thought his unfriendly assessment of the first George W. Bush administration, *Fahrenheit 9/11*, might affect the outcome of the 2004 election. It didn't.

(MPAA). **Will Hays,** a prominent Republican who was an elder in his Presbyterian church, was put in charge. Despite his efforts, movies with titillating titles continued to be produced. A lot of people shuddered at titles such as *Sinners in Silk* and *Red Hot Romance*. Hollywood scandals were no help. Actor William Wallace Reid died from drugs. Fatty Arbuckle was tried for the drunken slaying of a young actress. When the Depression struck, many people linked the nation's economic failure with "moral bankruptcy." Movies were a target.

Under pressure, the movie industry adopted the **Motion Picture Production Code** in 1930 (also known as the Hays Code), which codified the kind of thing that Will Hays had been doing. There was to be no naughty language, nothing sexually suggestive and no bad guys going unpunished.

Church people led intensified efforts to clean up movies. The 1930 code was largely the product of Father **Daniel Lord,** a Roman Catholic priest, and **Martin Quigley,** a Catholic layperson. In 1934, after an apostolic delegate from the Vatican berated movies in an address to a New York church convention, U.S. bishops organized the **Legion of Decency,** which worked closely with the movie industry's code administrators.

The legion, which was endorsed by religious leaders of many faiths, moved on several fronts. Chapters sprouted in major cities. Some chapters boycotted theatres for six weeks if they showed condemned films. Members slapped stickers marked "We Demand Clean Movies" on car bumpers. Many theatre owners responded, vowing to show only approved movies. Meanwhile, the industry itself added teeth to its own code. Any members of the MPPDA who released movies without approval were fined $25 000.

MOVIES AND CHANGING MORES. In the late 1940s the influence of the policing agencies began to wane. The 1948 Supreme Court's Paramount Decision was one factor. It took major studios out of the exhibition business. As a result, many movie houses could rent films from independent producers, many of which never subscribed to the code. A second factor was the movie *The Miracle*, which became a First Amendment issue in 1952. The movie was about a simple woman who was sure Saint Joseph had

Motion Picture Producers and Distributors of America (MPPDA) 1922 Hollywood attempt to establish moral code for movies.

Will Hays Led MPPDA.

Motion Picture Production Code 1930 Hollywood attempt to quiet critical moralists.

Daniel Lord Priest who led a morality crusade against Hollywood.

Martin Quigley Partner of Father Daniel Lord.

Legion of Decency Church listing of acceptable movies.

Media People

Robert Flaherty

Explorer Robert Flaherty, who attended Upper Canada College, took a camera to the Arctic in 1921 to record the life of an Eskimo family. The result was a new kind of movie: the documentary. While other movies of the time were theatrical productions with scripts, sets and actors, Flaherty tried something different: recording reality.

Robert Flaherty

His 57-minute *Nanook of the North* was compelling on its own merits when it started on the movie-house circuit in 1922, but the film received an unexpected macabre boost a few days later when Nanook, the father of the Eskimo family, died of hunger on the ice. News stories of Nanook's death stirred public interest—and also attendance at the movie, which helped to establish the documentary as an important new film genre.

Flaherty's innovative approach took a new twist in the 1930s when propagandists saw reality-based movies as a tool to promote their causes. In Germany the Nazi government produced propaganda films, and other countries followed. **Frank Capra** directed the vigorous five-film series *Why We Fight* for the U.S. War Office in 1942.

After World War II there was a revival of documentaries in Flaherty's style—a neutral recording of natural history. Walt Disney produced a variety of such documentaries, including the popular *Living Desert* in the 1950s.

The CBS television network gained a reputation in the 1950s and 1960s for picking up on the documentary tradition with *Harvest of Shame,* about migrant workers, and *Hunger in America.* In the same period the National Geographic Society established a documentary unit, and

Nanook of the North. The documentary became a film genre with explorer Robert Flaherty's *Nanook of the North* in 1922. This film was an attempt to record reality—no actors, no props. The film was especially potent, not only because it was a new approach and on a fascinating subject but also because, coincidentally, Nanook died of starvation on the ice around the time that the film was released.

French explorer Jacques Cousteau went into the television documentary business.

Such full-length documentaries are now mostly relegated to the CBC in Canada and PBS in the United States. The Documentary Channel is also an excellent outlet for these types of films. The major networks, meanwhile, have shifted most documentaries away from full-length treatments. Typical is CBS's *60 Minutes,* a twice-weekly one-hour program of three minidocumentaries. These new network projects combine reality programming and entertainment in slick packages that attract larger audiences than do traditional documentaries.

Frank Capra Hollywood movie director who produced powerful propaganda movies for U.S. war effort in World War II.

The Miracle case U.S. Supreme Court ruled that the First Amendment protected movies from censorship.

seduced her. Her baby, she believed, was Christ. Critics wanted the movie banned as sacrilege, but in **The Miracle** case, the Supreme Court sided with exhibitors on grounds of free expression. Filmmakers became a bit more venturesome.

At the same time, with mores changing in the wake of World War II, the influence of the Legion of Decency was slipping. In 1953 the legion condemned *The Moon Is Blue*, which had failed to receive code approval for being a bit racy. Despite the legion's condemnation, the movie was a box-office smash. The legion contributed to its own undoing with a series of incomprehensible recommendations. It condemned significant movies such as Ingmar Bergman's *The Silence* and Michelangelo Antonioni's *Blowup* in 1966 while endorsing the likes of *Godzilla vs. the Thing*.

Media Databank

The New Documentaries

This is a sampler of documentaries with a 21st-century point of view that have found their way into the movie-house circuit, with their directors:

Bowling for Columbine (2002) Michael Moore
Tries to relate U.S. gun laws with corporate greed, social dysfunction and political short-sightedness and pandering.

The Corporation (2003) Mark Achbar, Jennifer Abbott and Joel Bakan
Examines how media content and pop culture is controlled by only a few large corporations.

Spellbound (2003) Jeffrey Blitz
Follows eight contenders and their families through regional heats to the three-day national spelling bee final.

Tupac: Resurrection (2003) Lauren Lazin
Tries to explain the life of murdered rapper Tupac Shakur through his own interviews and public appearances.

Control Room (2004) Jehane Noujaim
Demystifies Al Jazeera by eavesdropping on the Arab television network's gatekeepers.

Fahrenheit 9/11 (2004) Michael Moore
Presents the 2003 Iraq war as a non sequitur to the September 11 terrorism attacks.

Super Size Me (2004) Morgan Spurlock
Too many Big Macs make too much you.

March of the Penguins (2005) Luc Jacquet
Traces the courtship of Antarctic penguins on a ritual journey of hundreds of miles.

Shut Up & Sing (2006) Barbara Kopple and Cecilia Peck
Chronicles the freedom-of-speech fallout of lead singer Natalie Maines's comments about the war in Iraq and George Bush.

An Inconvenient Truth (2006) Davis Guggenheim
A look at the causes of, effects of and solutions to global warming. Hosted by Al Gore.

Motion Picture Association of America (MPAA): They rate the movies we all see.
www.mpaa.org

Movie Ratings: A history of how the ratings evolved.
www.mpaa.org/ Ratings_history1.asp

Classification and Rating Administration Board Rates movies on G, PG, PG-13, R, NC-17 scale.

CURRENT MOVIE CODE. Moviemakers sensed the change in public attitudes in the 1950s but realized that audiences still wanted guidance that they could trust on movies. Also, there remained some moralist critics. In 1968 several industry organizations established a new rating system. No movies were banned. Fines were out. Instead, a board representing movie producers, distributors, importers and exhibitors, the **Classification and Rating Administration Board**, placed movies in categories to help parents determine what movies their children should see. Here are the categories, as modified through the years:

- **G:** Suitable for general audiences and all ages.
- **PG:** Parental guidance suggested because some content may be considered unsuitable for preteens.

- **PG-13:** Parental guidance especially suggested for children younger than 13 because of partial nudity, swearing or violence.
- **R:** Restricted for anyone younger than 17 unless accompanied by an adult.
- **NC-17:** No children under age 17 should be admitted.

Whether the rating system is widely used by parents is questionable. One survey found that two out of three parents couldn't name a movie their teenagers had seen in recent weeks.

Media Literacy and Movies

Study Preview   *Populist measures of a movie's success are in box office, aftermarket and merchandise revenue. Critical success is harder to measure. Knowledgeable, sophisticated reviewers are helpful.*

American Film Institute: The quick link feature at this site will get you to AFI's several "100 Years" lists of highlights from the 20th century: 100 movies, 100 heroes and villains, 100 laughs, 100 songs and more.
www.afi.com

The Worst Films of the 20th Century: The Oscars salute great films. The Razzies salute not-so-great films.
www.razzies.com

Variety: Key source of news on the business end of the film industry.
www.variety.com

Internet Movie Database: Comprehensive movie database complete with reviews, movie news, showtimes and message boards.
www.imdb.com

MovieWeb: Movie information and trailers on the web.
www.movieweb.com

The New York Times **Movies:** Movie criticism from the esteemed daily newspaper.
www.nytimes.com/ pages/movies

BOX OFFICE AND GROSSES

Weekends are when Hollywood studio executives bite their fingernails. The success or disappointment of their latest offerings is in the weekend box-office tabulations, the week-to-week tallies of how many customers the latest movies attracted. The numbers, gathered at the turnstile, are accurate in and of themselves. Not much can be inferred from them, though. A great new movie could be hurt if it was opening against strong rivals. Inversely, a weak movie may look better in a single weekend's books than it really should. Also, a single weekend's success is only part of the complex formula for a movie to break even financially. Many strong weeks might be needed to offset the costs of an expensive movie. But a single good weekend could bring a low-budget movie into black ink right away.

An advance indicator of commercial success, though not entirely reliable, is the number of screens nationwide that a movie shows on. Movie houses choose movies according to what they anticipate will be their popularity. Although exhibitors are savvy about what will play well, they make occasional wrong calls.

The least reliable precursor of a movie's success is the predictable marketing hoopla accompanying a release. Actors and directors who make the talk show rounds are enthusiastic. How could they be otherwise with their own careers in the balance? Trailers can be misleading. Some previews draw on scenes that don't even make the final cut.

The best check on a movie's popularity is the long-term box-office record. The all-time leader easily is James Cameron's 1997 *Titanic*. Even with long-term, revenue-based data, look at the criteria on which a ranking is based. Some lists are true box office, the revenue from movie-house showings. Others include aftermarket revenue, like video rentals. Some include merchandise income. Some are domestic, some world-wide. Also, with ticket prices approaching $12 in many cities, currency inflation gives newer movies an edge over classics. Has *Titanic* really been more popular than 1939's *Gone with the Wind*?

MOVIE CRITICISM

Commercial success doesn't always equate with critical success, which is a subjective rating. Some critics applauded *Titanic*. The technical effects, for example, drew rave comments. The praise, however, wasn't universal. Some critics saw the storyline as trite—a bodice-buster cliché that manipulated unsophisticated audiences.

How, then, can a serious media consumer go beyond the box office and the bottom line to assess a movie? Many critics produce immensely helpful reviews and commentary that cut through hype and dazzle to bring a critical, cultivated eye to their reviews. The best reviewers know movies as a medium, including the techniques of the craft. They understand the commercial and artistic dynamics that go into a movie. They know the history of a movie's production, from its seminal moment in a book or whatever the conceptual source.

Where do you find such reviewers? The best sources over the years have included *The New Yorker* magazine and *The New York Times*. Even then, you need to come to know reviewers and their strengths and blind spots. In the end, it is you as a media consumer who makes a critical judgment. This comes from your own increasing sophistication, informed by the dialogue in which the best critics are engaging.

CHAPTER 5 WRAP-UP

Movies passed their 100th birthday in the 1980s as an entertainment medium with an especially strong following among young adults and teenagers. From the beginning, movies were a glamorous medium, but beneath the glitz were dramatic struggles between competing businesspeople whose success depended on catching the public's fancy. The most dramatic period came at mid-century. Fanatic anticommunists in Congress intimidated moviemakers into backing away from cutting-edge explorations of social and political issues, and then a government antitrust action forced the major studios to break up their operations. Meanwhile, television was siphoning people away from the box office. Movie attendance fell from 90 million to 16 million per week. It took a few years, but the movie industry regrouped. More than ever, political activism and social inquiry have become themes in American movies. Moviemakers met the threat from television by becoming a primary supplier of television programming.

QUESTIONS FOR REVIEW

1. Why do movies have such a strong impact on people?
2. What is the role of movie studios in the production and exhibition?
3. What are the major Hollywood studios?
4. What are the advantages of digital technology for the movie industry?
5. How has Hollywood responded to the threat of television?

QUESTIONS FOR CRITICAL THINKING

1. How would you describe the success of these innovations—Cinerama, CinemaScope, 3-D and Smell-o-Vision—in the movie industry's competition against television? What are the prospects for d-cinema?
2. Epic spectaculars marked one period of moviemaking, social causes another, and sex and violence another. Have these genres had lasting effect?
3. What were the contributions of William Dickson, George Eastman and the Lumière brothers to early moviemaking?
4. What is meant by the National Film Board's mandate to "explain Canada to Canadians?"
5. Describe what makes American movies different from Canadian movies.

DEEPENING YOUR MEDIA LITERACY

Are the most popular films the best films?

Step 1   Choose a popular Hollywood movie and either a Canadian, independent or foreign film to compare.

Dig Deeper

Step 2

1. Read several critical reviews of these movies.
2. Look up the box-office receipts of the two movies.
3. Find out how many awards each of these films won.

What Do You Think?

Step 3   Answer these questions:

1. Do critical acclaim, popularity and film awards go hand in hand?
2. Do you think critical acclaim or winning awards is a good way to measure a film's quality? Why or why not?
3. Are box office receipts the best measure of its success? Why or why not?
4. If your movie was Canadian, test Harcourt's idea of uncertainty. Was it evident in the Canadian film you watched? Use Monk's "Canadian checklist" to uncover themes.

KEEPING UP TO DATE

People serious about movies as art will find *American Film* and *Film Comment* valuable sources of information.

Among consumer magazines with significant movie coverage are *Premiere, Entertainment Weekly, Maclean's* and *Rolling Stone.*

Trade journals include *Variety* and *Hollywood Reporter.*

Canadian newspapers that cover movies include the *Toronto Star*, the *National Post, The Globe and Mail.*

FOR FURTHER LEARNING

James Adams. "Our Box Office Not So Boffo." *The Globe and Mail* (February 3, 2007).

Sid Adilman. "Nat Taylor, 98: Canada's First Movie Mogul." *Toronto Star* (March 2, 2004).

Peter Biskind. *Down and Dirty Pictures: Miramax, Sundance and the Rise of Independent Film* (Simon & Schuster, 2004).

Paul Buhle and Dave Wagner. *A Very Dangerous Citizen: Abraham Lincoln Polonsky and the Hollywood Left* (University of California Press, 2001).

Steven DeRosa. *Writing with Hitchcock: The Collaboration of Alfred Hitchcock and John Michael Hayes* (Faber & Faber, 2001).

Bernard F. Dick. *Engulfed: Paramount Pictures and the Birth of Corporate Hollywood* (University Press of Kentucky, 2001).

Harvey Enchin. "Film Industry Has Its Critics." *The Globe and Mail* (September 8, 1997).

Gary Evans. "Canadian Film" in *Mediascapes: New Patterns in Canadian Communication* (Thomson, 2002).

Seth Feldman and Joyce Nelson. *Canadian Film Reader* (Peter Martin and Associates, 1977).

Douglas Fetherling. *Documents in Canadian Film* (Broadview Press, 1988).

Richard E. Foglesong. *Married to the House: Walt Disney World and Orlando* (Yale University Press, 2001).

Louis Giannetti and Jim Leach. *Understanding Movies*, Third Canadian edition (Prentice Hall, 2005).

Dade Hayes and Jonathan Bing. *Open Wide: How Hollywood Box Office Became a National Obsession* (Miramax, 2004).

Nicholas Jarecki. *Breaking In: How 20 Film Directors Got Their Start* (Broadway, 2002).

Brian D. Johnson. "The Lost Picture Show." *Maclean's* (April 17, 2006).

Garth Jowett. "American Domination of the Motion Picture Industry." In *Movies as Mass Communication*, edited by Garth Jowett and James M. Linton (Sage, 1980).

Jim Leach. *Film in Canada* (Oxford University Press, 2006).

Spike Lee, as told to Kaleem Aftab. *Spike Lee: That's My Story and I'm Sticking to It* (Norton, 2005).

Peter Lefcourt and Laura J. Shapiro, editors. *The First Time I Got Paid for It: Writers' Tales from the Hollywood Trenches* (Public Affairs, 2000).

Emmanuel Levy. *Oscar Fever: The History and Politics of the Academy Awards* (Continuum, 2001).

Jon Lewis. *Hollywood v. Hardcore: How the Struggle over Censorship Created the Modern Film Industry* (New York University Press, 2001).

Gayle Macdonald. "The Vast Picture Show." *The Globe and Mail* (January 17, 1998).

Katherine Monk. *Weird Sex and Snowshoes and Other Canadian Film Phenomena* (Raincoast Books, 2001).

David L. Robb. *Operation Hollywood: How the Pentagon Shapes and Censors Movies* (Prometheus, 2004).

Kazi Stastna. "The Golden Age of the Silver Screen." *Montreal Gazette* (January 13, 2006).

Bohdan Szuchewycz and Jeannette Sloniowski. *Canadian Communications: Issues in Contemporary Media and Culture* (Prentice Hall, 2001).

First Telecast. A production still from the CBC's first *Hockey Night in Canada* telecast. The program has been a staple of Canadian television programming for more than 40 years. In 2003, *Hockey Night in Canada* broadcast its first game in HDTV: The Heritage Classic between Montreal and Edmonton.

Television

Media in Theory

Cultural Impact of Television

There's no doubt that television is a big part of our lives. Many of us have two or more television sets and each of us watches about 28 hours of TV per week. We even watch TV on our iPods, laptops and other portable devices.

Scholars and broadcasters may have different views on the potency of television's effect on society, but they all agree that there is some degree of influence. The role of television in riveting attention on serious matters was demonstrated in the fall of 2001 after terrorists launched attacks on the World Trade Center and the Pentagon. For months, people were tuned to CTV Newsnet or CBC Newsworld to hear about the latest developments in the war on terrorism from a Canadian point of view.

Fictional television characters can capture the imagination of the public. Perry Mason did wonders for the reputation of the law profession. Mary Tyler Moore's role as a television news writer showed that women could succeed in male-dominated industries. *The Cosby Show* changed the image of prime-time fatherhood in the 1980s. *Friends* became a ritual on Thursday nights on NBC during the 1990s.

Although television can be effective in creating short-term impressions, there also are long-term effects. A whole generation of children grew up with *Teenage Mutant Ninja Turtles* as part of their generational identity. Later came *Pokémon* and *Beyblade*. The long-term effects exist at both a superficial level, as with *Teenage Mutant Ninja Turtles*, and a serious level. Social critic **Michael Novak** puts the effect of television in broad terms: "Television is a molder of the soul's geography. It builds up incrementally a psychic structure of expectations. It does so in much the same way that school lessons slowly, over the years, tutor the unformed mind and teach it how to think."

What are the lessons to which Novak refers? Scholars **Linda and Robert Lichter** and **Stanley Rothman,** who have surveyed the television creative community, make a case that the creators of television programs are social reformers who build their political ideas into their scripts. The Lichters and Rothman identify the television creative community as largely secular and politically liberal.

Media scholar **George Comstock,** in his book *Television in America,* wrote, "Television has become an unavoidable and unremitting factor in shaping what we are and what we will become." But what of this American influence on English-Canadian culture? Canadian broadcaster **Moses Znaimer** claims that "as transmitter of information and entertainment, television is the acknowledged king. It's also very effective as a reflector of values and teacher of ideals, often in ways you don't notice." If Comstock, Novak, and Znaimer are correct, the need for Canadian television is obvious.

Michael Novak Believes TV is broad shaper of issues.

Linda and Robert Lichter and Stanley Rothman Scholars who claim TV is reformist.

George Comstock Believes TV helps us become who we are.

Moses Znaimer Believes TV reflects values and ideals.

Influence of Television

Study Preview   *Television's huge audiences have made it a medium with not only profound effects on people and on culture but also on other media. Today television is the dominant mass medium for entertainment and news.*

TiVo: Changing the way we watch TV.
www.tivo.com

Bell ExpressVu: Bell offers its version of the TiVo to its digital customers.
www.bell.ca

TELEVISION'S ECONOMIC IMPACT

Although audiences for major networks that provide programming to local affiliate stations have dwindled, the Canadian television industry has continued to grow. Advertising revenue topped $3.2 billion in 2006 percent of the total for all advertising-based media. Newspapers were a distant second at $1.7 billion.

MASS-MEDIA SHAKE-UP

Since television's introduction in the early 1950s, its presence has reshaped the other media. Consider the following.

BOOKS The discretionary time people spend on television today is time that once went to other activities, including reading for diversion and information. To stem the decline in reading, book publishers have responded with more extravagant promotions to draw attention to their products. A major consideration in evaluating fiction manuscripts at publishing houses is their potential as screenplays, many of which end up on television. Also, in deciding which manuscripts to accept, some publishers even consider how well an author will come across in television interviews when the book is published.

NEWSPAPERS Evening television newscasts and 24-hour news channels have been a major factor in the near disappearance of afternoon newspapers. Most have either ceased publication or switched to mornings. Also, hometown newspapers have lost almost all of their national advertisers, primarily to television. Most newspaper redesigns today attempt to be visually stimulating in ways that newspapers never were before television.

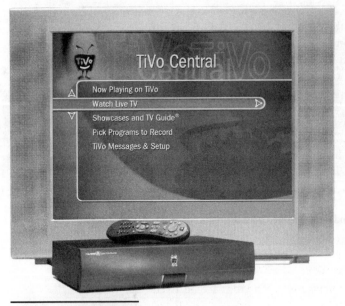

MAGAZINES Television took advertisers from the big mass-circulation magazines such as *Life,* forcing magazine companies to shift to magazines that catered to smaller segments of the mass audience that television could not serve.

RECORDINGS The success of recorded music today hinges in many cases on the airplay that music videos receive on television on MuchMusic.

MOVIES Just as magazines demassified after television took away many of their advertisers, Hollywood demassified after television stole the bulk of its audience. Today, savvy movie-makers plan their projects both for the big screen and for reissuing, to be shown on television via the networks and for home video rental. These aftermarkets, in fact, have come to account for far more revenue to major studios than movie-house exhibition.

Digital Video Recorder. A hot consumer technology introduced in 1999 was DVR, short for "digital video recorder," or PVR, short for "personal video recorder," marketed under names such as TiVo and ReplayTV. DVRs record programs digitally so that people can play back programs when they want to, on their own schedule rather than on the networks' schedule.

RADIO Radio demassified with the arrival of television. The television networks first took radio's most successful programs and moved them to the screen. Having lost its traditional programming strengths, radio then lost both the mass audience and the advertisers it had built up since the 1920s. For survival, individual radio stations shifted almost entirely to recorded music and geared the music to narrower and narrower audience segments.

Technology of Television

Study Preview   *Television is based on electronic technology. In the still-dominant analog technology, light-sensitive cameras scan a scene with incredibly fast sweeps across several hundred horizontally stacked lines. The resulting electronic blips are transmitted to receivers, which re-create the original image by sending electrons across horizontally stacked lines on a screen. Today a shift has begun from analog to digital technology.*

Philo T. Farnsworth: The Farnsworth archives.
http://philotfarnsworth.com

Vladimir Zworykin: Exposition about the work of Zworykin.
www.museum.tv/archives/ etv/Z/htmlZ/zworykinvla/ zworykinvla.htm

Persistence of Vision: Experiments that help in understanding of persistence of vision.
www.exploratorium.edu/ snacks/persistence_of _vision.html

ELECTRONIC SCANNING

In the 1920s an Idaho farm boy, **Philo Farnsworth,** came up with the idea for using a vacuum tube to pick up moving images and then display them electronically on a screen. Farnsworth found financial backers to build a lab, and in 1927 the first live moving image was transmitted. At age 21 Philo Farnsworth had invented television. Farnsworth's tube, which he called the **image dissector,** was an incredible feat, considering that some of the world's great corporate research labs, including RCA's, were trying to accomplish the same thing.

Not wanting to be upstaged, RCA claimed that its **Vladimir Zworykin** had invented a tube, the **iconoscope,** and deserved the credit for television. That would have meant, of course, that RCA would reap a fortune from patent rights. In a patent trial, however, it was learned that both Zworykin and his boss, RCA chief **David Sarnoff,** had visited Farnsworth's lab and had the opportunity to pirate his invention. Zworykin claimed that he had the idea for the iconoscope as early as 1923, but his evidence was not forthcoming. RCA ended up paying Farnsworth a licence fee to use his technology.

In retrospect the technology seems simple. A camera picks up light reflected off a moving subject and converts the light to electrons. The electrons are zapped one at a time across stacked horizontal lines on a screen. The electrons follow each other back and forth so fast that they seem to show the movement picked up by the camera. As with the motion picture, the system freezes movement at fraction-of-a-second intervals and then replays it to create an illusion of movement—the **persistence of vision** phenomenon.

THE EARLY DAYS OF CANADIAN TV

While there were several experimental television broadcasts in Canada through the 1930s and 1940s, Canadians were first exposed to American television signals. The first television broadcast signal received in Canada was in 1947. Engineers at General Electric in Windsor picked up the transmission of WWDT from Detroit. This set the trend for television viewing in the early years of television in Canada. If you lived close enough to the border and had access to a television, you probably watched some American programming.

Television officially arrived in Canada in 1952. As had been the case with the first radio station 30 years earlier, the first television station was in Montreal. **CBFT**, a public station, began broadcasting on September 6, 1952, with **CBLT** Toronto broadcasting two days later. In 1953, stations began broadcasting in Vancouver, Sudbury and Ottawa; by 1954, Winnipeg and Halifax had television stations. At first, programming was a mix of Canadian and American fare. Early Canadian programming also reflected its roots in radio. *Wayne and Shuster* was a staple of Canadian television during the 1960s and 1970s, while *Hockey Night in Canada*, which began on radio in the 1920s, continues to draw a huge audience for the CBC on Saturday nights. A microwave link between Buffalo and Toronto made it possible to carry American programs live. There was no doubt about it: Television was a hit in Canada. A million television sets had been purchased in Canada by 1954. By 1958, the CBC network stretched from Victoria to Halifax. In 1961, CTV began as Canada's first private broadcaster.

Farm Boy Invention. While harvesting an Idaho potato field in 1921, the 13-year-old Philo Farnsworth came up with the idea to transmit moving pictures live on a magnetically deflected electron beam. Crafting his own materials, including hand-blown tubes, Farnsworth completed his first image dissector while barely in his twenties. Later, RCA used the technology for its flamboyant public introduction of television.

DIGITAL TELEVISION FINALLY ARRIVES

In comparison to other countries, federal regulators (FCC in the United States, CRTC in Canada) moved slowly on technology to improve onscreen picture quality. The Europeans have had sharper images since television was introduced, and in the 1980s the Japanese developed high-definition television. Both the European and Japanese systems were refinements of traditional **analog** technology that sends images as pulsing, continuous signals.

Philo Farnsworth Invented technology that uses electrons to transmit moving images live.

image dissector Farnsworth's television vacuum tube.

Vladimir Zworykin RCA engineer who claimed to have invented television.

iconoscope Zworykin's television vacuum tube.

David Sarnoff Head of RCA.

persistence of vision Retina's capability to retain an image briefly, allowing brain to fill in gaps between successive images.

CBFT First Canadian TV channel.

CBLT Second Canadian TV channel.

analog Broadcast transmission that uses a continuous, pulsing signal.

Media People

Don Ferguson

Don Ferguson and the Royal Canadian Air Farce

Canadian content has never been funnier.

For more than a dozen years, Canadians have tuned in to the *Royal Canadian Air Farce* to watch the comedy troupe's take on popular culture and life in Canada. Some of their most memorable characters include Colonel Stacey and his Chicken Cannon, Gilbert Smythe-Bite Me, Melissa the Fast Food Worker, and Jimmy and Seamus from down east.

The *Royal Canadian Air Farce* has been telling Canadian stories and making us laugh at ourselves since 1973. Originally on CBC radio, the *Air Farce* made the transition to television in 1992 and hasn't looked back since. **Don Ferguson** has been with the troupe since its inception. He attributes the success of the *Air Farce* to two reasons: "We have been as funny as anything viewers can get anywhere on TV. The great plus is that it's funny about us."

The fact that the *Air Farce* is "funny about us" is an excellent example of what Barthes refers to as myth in the mass communication process. What the *Air Farce* does is proof that Canadian culture doesn't have to be about beavers, Mounties, and maple syrup. In its simplest form, Canadian culture is simply talking about Canadian people, places, things and ideas. The *Air Farce* has taken aim at our prime ministers, other broadcasters (for example, George Stroumboulopoulos and Don Cherry), and our cultural institutions, such as Tim Hortons and the CBC. For the *Air Farce,* it's simply a way of connecting with its audience and getting viewers thinking about Canada. Ferguson says the *Air Farce* never set out to promote Canadian culture, but it makes a point of *being Canadian* on the show. As a result, it has become part of Canadian culture itself: "We've always felt that we reflect our environment. The sum total of everything we do over the years *becomes* Canadian culture. This becomes part of a Canadian's imaginative life."

Despite competition from American networks and programming, this emphasis on comedy from a Canadian perspective attracts almost 1.3 million Canadian *Air Farce* viewers each week. The reason for big ratings is simple, according to Ferguson: "The one feature that you can't get on American TV is references to our politicians, to hockey, or to our way of life. I think it's extremely important that Canadians see and hear Canadian stories done by the best Canadians possible to help nurture our sense of Canadianness."

Ferguson is a strong believer in government support for Canadian media. He sees the impact television can have as an agent of socialization. "What really amazes me is that the politicians don't really seem to get it. The real danger in not having Canadian stuff on television and being bombarded by American programming is that sooner or later Canadians will wonder why we bother with Ottawa, because it's not important, is it? The really important politicians we have to convince are in Washington. Once people start thinking like that, then the end of Canada is at hand."

Don Ferguson Says Canadians need to see themselves reflected on Canadian TV.

digital Broadcast transmission that sends signals in on-off data bits.

Both the CRTC and FCC spent years in exhaustive evaluations of new possibilities. Digitizing makes for super-sharp screen images—but at a cost. More broadband space was needed per channel, which necessitated a reshuffling of bandwidth and channels. Plus there's the expense to convert to **digital** for broadcasters. By 2005, most channels were broadcasting in HDTV in major cities across Canada. Because the transition from traditional to digital transmission was costly, the CRTC bent to industry pressure to extend the deadline for compliance. Now the deadline is 2009 for all transmission to be digital in the United States; 2011 in Canada.

Television Delivery Systems

Study Preview *The corporate structure of television parallels three waves of technology, beginning with stations licensed by the federal government to serve particular cities.*

Media Databank

Digital Channels: Demassification in Action

Since their introduction in 2001, digital channels have had to compete for subscribers. Here are the top digital channels in Canada, each with a subscriber base of at least one million Canadians, as of August 2005:

Channel	Subscribers
Showcase Action	1 262 000
Animal Planet	1 204 000
Showcase Diva	1 159 000
IFC (Independent Film Channel)	1 111 000
Court TV	1 083 000
Scream	1 070 000

Source: CRTC, Broadcast Policy Monitoring Report 2006.

Animal Planet: Nature programming at its best. **www.animalplanet.ca**

Court TV: Law and order online. **www.courttvcanada.ca**

The Independent Film Channel: For films off the beaten path. **www.ifctv.ca**

Scream: From Boris Karloff to Freddy, Jason, and Michael, they're all here. **www.screamtelevision.com**

Showcase Action: Testosterone television for the Y-chromosome crowd. **www.showcase.ca/action**

Showcase Diva: Chick flicks for the X-chromosome crowd. **www.showcase.ca/diva**

OVER-THE-AIR STATIONS

The engineers and corporate leaders who conceived television really thought in terms of **radio with pictures**. That's not surprising. They were radio people. The television systems they built used towers, just like radio, to send signals via the electromagnetic spectrum to homes, just like radio.

Early American and Canadian television networks thwarted localism and diversity to a great extent by creating popular national programs for local stations. As with radio, this created a two-tier national television system. Stations were local and offered local programs, but the most popular shows came from the national networks. The networks really came into their own, with strong advertising revenue, when **coaxial cable** linked the east and west coasts in 1951. Pioneer broadcast newsman Edward R. Murrow opened his *See It Now* with live pictures from cameras on the Atlantic and Pacific oceans. People marveled at this new technology.

radio with pictures Simplistic definition of TV.

coaxial cable Heavy-duty landline for video signals.

SATELLITE-DIRECT

Stanley Hubbard believed his KSTP-TV in Minnesota, although incredibly profitable, might become a dinosaur. In the age of satellite communication, why should people tune into local stations, which picked up network signals from satellite for local retransmission, when technology had been devised so they could tune in directly to a satellite? Skeptics scoffed, but in 1994 Hubbard joined General Motors to offer a **direct-broadcast satellite** service. People could pick up signals from over the world with home dishes the size of a large pizza.

The biggest global satellite service was put together by media mogul **Rupert Murdoch** with BSkyB in Britain, STAR TV in Asia, SKY Italia in Italy and FOXTEL in Australia. The crown jewel for the Murdoch network, DIRECTV in the United States, was acquired in 2003. Integration of the systems faced government and other hurdles, but Murdoch proceeded to upgrade the systems with shared technology that, among other things, included TiVo-like personal recording devices and the capability of downloading Hollywood movies on demand. Canada's first two direct-broadcast satellite providers, sometimes known as DTH for direct-to-home, were Bell ExpressVu and Star Choice.

Stanley Hubbard Satellite TV pioneer.

direct-broadcast satellite Transmission from orbit to receiver; no TV station or cable system intermediary.

Rupert Murdoch Media mogul who created Fox network.

Over-the-Air Networks

NBC: One of the original Big Three networks.
www.nbc.com

CBS: Another of the original Big Three networks.
www.cbs.com

ABC: The third of the original Big Three networks.
http://abc.go.com

FOX: 20th Century Fox Television.
www.fox.com

CW-TV: The newest American network.
www.CWTV.com

CBC: Links to CBC programs.
www.cbc.ca/television

CTV: Details on all of CTV's shows.
www.ctv.ca

CanWest Global: Official site of Canada's third network.
www.canwestglobal.com

NBC National Broadcast Company. Built from NBC radio network under David Sarnoff. One of the Big Three over-the-air networks.

microwave relays Towers re-angle over-the-air signals to match the earth's curvature.

Pat Weaver Created NBC's *Tonight Show* and *Today.*

General Electric Current NBC owner.

Big Three ABC, CBS, NBC.

CBS Columbia Broadcasting System. Built from CBS radio network under William Paley. One of the Big Three over-the-air networks.

Edward R. Murrow Reporter who criticized Joseph McCarthy.

William Paley Long-time CBS boss.

Study Preview *Three American national television networks, first NBC and CBS, then also ABC, dominated programming to local over-the-air stations until the 1980s, when Fox grew into a formidable competitor. Later, the UPN and WB networks came into existence in the Fox model, but the audience and advertising base were insufficient and the new CW was born. In Canada we have three national networks: CBC, CTV and CanWest Global.*

THE NETWORKS

NBC TELEVISION. The U.S. government licensed the first television stations in 1941, on the eve of U.S. entry into World War II. But when factories converted to war production, no more television sets were manufactured until after peace arrived in 1945. By 1948 the coaxial cables that were necessary to carry television signals had been laid to the Midwest, and **NBC** began feeding programs to affiliates. The coaxial link-up, with some stretches linked by **microwave relays**, connected the east and west coasts in 1951.

NBC innovations included two brainstorms by **Pat Weaver**, an ad executive recruited to the network as a vice-president. In 1951 Weaver created a late-night comedy–variety talk show, precursor to the venerable *Tonight Show.* Weaver also created an early-morning entry, the still-viable *Today.* With those shows, NBC owned the early morning and insomniac audiences for years.

In 1985 **General Electric** bought NBC. During a three-year period, 1982 to 1985, all of the **Big Three** networks (ABC, CBS, NBC) moved out of the hands of the broadcast executives, such as NBC's David Sarnoff, who grew up in the business and nurtured these giant influential entities. As it turned out, the Big Three's heyday was over with new competitive pressures from cable and other quarters. The new owners, with their focus on the bottom line and their cost-cutting instincts, fundamentally changed network television for a new era. General Electric bought the Universal movie studio in 2004 and merged it into a new unit, NBC Universal.

CBS TELEVISION. CBS was outmanoeuvred by NBC in lining up affiliates after World War II, but soon caught up. By 1953 CBS had edged out NBC in audience size by acquiring affiliates and creating popular programs. By 1953 the *I Love Lucy* sitcom series, which eventually included 140 episodes, was a major draw.

CBS established its legacy in television public affairs programming when **Edward R. Murrow**, famous for his live radio reporting from Europe, started *See It Now,* a weekly investigative program. Three years later, when Senator Joseph McCarthy was using his office to smear people as communists when they weren't, it was Murrow on *See It Now* who exposed the senator's dubious tactics. Many scholars credit Murrow with undoing McCarthy and easing the Red Scare that McCarthy was promoting.

The CBS television network was shepherded in its early years by **William Paley**, who had earlier created the CBS radio network. Paley retired in 1982, and Laurence Tisch, a hotel mogul, came into control of CBS. Today, Viacom owns the network.

ABC TELEVISION. ABC established its television network in 1948 but ran a poor third. Things began changing in 1953 when ABC merged with **United Paramount Theaters,** whose properties included several television stations. The new company went into fast production schedules of programs that were aimed at Hollywood-like mass audiences. Live programming, the hallmark of early network television, was not part of ABC's recipe. By 1969 more than 90 percent of the network's programs were on film, tightly edited and with no live gaffes.

ABC's growth was pegged largely to two Disney programs: *Disneyland* in 1954 and *The Mickey Mouse Club* in 1955. Another audience builder was ABC's decision not to carry gavel-to-gavel coverage of the national political conventions. That brought criticism that ABC was abdicating its public responsibility, but by leaving the conventions mostly to CBS and NBC, ABC cleaned up in the ratings with entertainment alternatives. ABC picked up more steam in 1961 with its *Wide World of Sports,* a weekend anthology with appeal that extended beyond sports fans. **Roone Arledge,** the network sports chief, created *Monday Night Football* in 1969. Network television was a three-way race again, and in 1975 ABC was leading by a hair.

CapCities Communications (also known as Capital Cities Communications), a profitable Kansas City–based television station chain, bought ABC in 1985. The network's parent company operated as ABC/CapCities until Disney bought the operation in 1996. Today it is variously called ABC Disney or Disney ABC.

Fox. Conventional wisdom through most of television history was that the dominance of NBC, CBS and ABC precluded a fourth network. The only significant attempt at the fourth network, by television-set manufacturer **Allen DuMont,** fizzled in the mid-1950s. Even though the **DuMont network** transmitted 21 hours of prime-time shows to 160 stations at its peak, the other networks had more affiliates. Also, DuMont stations had smaller local audiences, which made the network less attractive to national advertisers.

Then came **Fox.** In 1986 the Australian media mogul Rupert Murdoch made a strategic decision to become a major media player in the United States. He bought seven non-network stations in major cities and also the 20th Century Fox movie studio. The stations gave Murdoch the nucleus for a fourth over-the-air network, and 20th Century Fox gave him production facilities and a huge movie library. Murdoch recruited **Barry Diller,** whose track record included impressive programming successes at ABC, to head the proposed television network.

When Fox went on the air, the signal went to Murdoch's stations and to other independent stations that weren't affiliated with the Big Three. There were doubts whether Fox would make it, but Diller kept costs low. First there was only a late-night talk show. Then Sunday night shows were added, then Saturday night. There was no costly news operation, just relatively low-cost programming. The programs, however, drew a following. Shows like *Married . . . with Children,* featuring the crude, dysfunctional Bundys, and the cartoon series *The Simpsons* attracted mostly young people in their free-spending years, as did new programs like *Beverly Hills 90210* and *Melrose Place.* The young audience made Fox popular with advertisers.

ABC American Broadcasting Company. Built from ABC radio network. One of the Big Three over-the-air networks.

United Paramount Theaters Strengthened ABC in 1953 merger.

Roone Arledge Created ABC's *Monday Night Football.*

CapCities Communications Owner of ABC before it was purchased by Disney.

Allen DuMont Operated early fourth network.

DuMont network Fourth network, operated 1950–1958.

Prime-Time Leader. CBS surpassed NBC for the prime-time audience in 1953 with comedy and suspense. *I Love Lucy* with husband-wife team Desi Arnaz and Lucille Ball went 140 episodes, which continued decades in reruns and video rentals. *The Twilight Zone* was another CBS draw.

Fox Network launched in 1986.

Barry Diller Created early successful Fox programming.

CW. Seeing the success of Fox, Time Warner launched the WB Television Network in 1995 to create an outlet for its Warner Brothers production unit. A week later Viacom announced it was creating UPN, short for United Paramount Network, for basically the same reasons. Time Warner and Viacom ended up wishing they hadn't. Not only were both networks slow in getting a prime-time schedule running, the audiences just weren't there in the fragmenting media market. Nor were advertisers, at least not in the quantity or with the enthusiasm networks had traditionally commanded.

Not seeing black ink in their future, Viacom and Time Warner folded the UPN and WB into a new broadcast television network, called the **CW network**, for September 2006. The new network, the *C* for *CBS* and the *W* for *Warner*, drew on programming from its predecessors with the target still being the profitable 18–34 age group. Programs included *America's Next Top Model, Veronica Mars, Smallville*, and *Friday Night SmackDown*. The goal was to attract viewers from the four established networks.

CW network Network created in 2006 by merger of the WB and UPN.

CANADIAN NETWORKS

At present, there are three national networks in Canada. Two of them are privately owned, while one, the CBC, is Canada's national public broadcaster.

CBC. The CBC was created by an act of Parliament in 1936 as a radio network. CBC television began in 1952. Today, despite cutbacks in funding, the CBC has developed a loyal following for its programming on several media platforms. CBC television programming outlets include CBC TV in English and French, CBC Newsworld, and Galaxie, a pay audio service available through digital cable and DTH. Over the last few years, some of CBC television's best-known shows include *Hockey Night in Canada, This Hour Has 22 Minutes, Royal Canadian Air Farce*, and *Little Mosque on the Prairie*.

In *Canada's Cultural Industries,* Paul Audley sums up the history of television in Canada well. He writes, "The general pattern from the beginning of television in 1952 until the present has been one of a rapidly expanding private television broadcasting system and an underfinanced public system." Given the changes in the late 20th and early 21st centuries, this still appears to be true. Writing in *Maclean's,* Peter C. Newman argues that Canadians need the CBC to become important again. Says Newman, "With our kids watching 900 hours or more of TV a year—and at least 80 percent of it spreading the gospel of the American way of life—we must maintain a vibrant indigenous alternative." Private broadcasters, such as Global and CTV, would disagree with Newman, claiming that the Canadian identity can be preserved by the private sector.

John Bassett Founded CFTO Toronto, CTV's flagship station.

Spence Caldwell Initiator of the CTV network.

CTV. While the CBC is Canada's public network, CTV was Canada's first privately owned national network. In 1960, the Board of Broadcast Governors or BBG (the forerunner of today's CRTC) held hearings for privately owned television stations. One of the victors was **John Bassett's** CFTO, Channel 9, in Toronto. His background in media included part ownership of both the *Sherbrooke Daily Record* and the *Toronto Telegram;* he founded Baton Broadcasting in 1960 and began broadcasting on CFTO, Channel 9, in Toronto. **Spence Caldwell** wasn't as lucky. His application for a TV channel had been denied, but he didn't let that stop him from becoming a Canadian TV pioneer. He approached several of the new television channels, including Bassett's CFTO, with the idea of forming a network. He eventually was able to convince eight channels to form CTN in 1961 with CFTO as its flagship station. CTN changed its name to CTV in 1962. Today, CTV stations reach more than 99 percent of English Canada with their programming. In addition to airing American programming, CTV stations promote Canadian television with shows such as *Canadian Idol, Robson Arms, Corner Gas* and *W-FIVE*.

GLOBAL. As far back as 1960, Ontario broadcasters **Ken Soble and Al Bruner** had an idea for a Canadian superstation. Although Soble passed away in 1966, Bruner formed Global Communications Limited in 1970. By 1974, CKGN-TV began broadcasting in Ontario. It wasn't a success and lost money from the outset. By 1975 it had been restructured and refinanced. One of its saviours was the late lawyer and journalist **Izzy Asper**. Through a series of buyouts and takeovers that began in the mid-1970s, CanWest Global became Canada's third national network and second private national network in 2000. Its 11 stations in 8 provinces reach more than 94 percent of Canadian viewers. CanWest has interests in both conventional television and specialty channels. Channels under the CanWest banner include TVtropolis, Mystery, and Lonestar. Some of the more notable Canadian productions aired by CanWest are *Blue Murder, Are You Smarter Than a Canadian Fifth Grader?* and *Deal or No Deal Canada*.

Ken Soble and Al Bruner Dreamt of a Canadian superstation.

Izzy Asper Developed Global into Canada's third private TV network.

EDUCATIONAL TV

In addition to commercial broadcasting, North America is also home to many educational broadcasters. With federal funding in 1967, the Public Broadcasting Service began providing programs to noncommercial stations. While PBS has offered some popular programs, such as *Sesame Street,* the biography show *American Masters* and the newsmagazine *Frontline,* commercial stations do not see it as much of a threat. In fact, with its emphasis on informational programming and high-quality drama and arts, PBS relieved public pressure on commercial stations for less profitable highbrow programming. Like PBS in America, noncommercial broadcasting, including provincial broadcasters such as British Columbia's Knowledge Network, Saskatchewan's SCN, and Ontario's TVO, rely heavily on viewer contributions and provincial funding.

NETWORK ADVERTISING

The big television networks have become an enigma. While cable networks and other media choices have nibbled steadily at the audience once commanded by the networks, these major networks still have been able to continue raising their advertising rates. Strange as it seems, advertisers are paying the networks more money than ever to reach fewer viewers.

UPFRONT. Drama prevails every spring when the networks ask big advertisers to commit themselves upfront to spots in the future year's programming. The networks list shows that they plan to continue, as well as a sample of new programs, and announce their asking price per 30-second spot based on audience projections. Then begins jockeying and bidding between the networks and the agencies that represent advertisers. The **upfront**, as the process is called, locks sponsors into specific shows three to five months ahead of the new season, although contracts generally have options that allow an advertiser to bail out.

upfront Advance advertiser commitments to buy network advertising time.

Case Study

French- vs. English-Canadian TV

In 1971, Canadian writer Hugh MacLennan used the term *two solitudes* to describe the differences between French and English Canada. Nowhere is this more evident than in a comparison of what francophones and anglophones watch on television.

The TV viewing experience in Quebec is significantly different from that in English Canada. For example, according to the CRTC's 2007 *Broadcasting Policy Monitoring Report*, while Canadian programming accounts for 48 percent of total viewing in English Canada, it accounts for 66 percent of total viewing in Quebec. In *Building on Success: A Policy Framework for Canadian Television*, the CRTC wonders why Canadian programming is such a success in Quebec, but not in English Canada. The report says: "French-language programming in particular is extremely successful. Canadian programs regularly achieve some of the highest program ratings; in some years, as many as 19 of the 20 highest-rated programs in the Quebec market have been Canadian-produced."

The easy answer, of course, is the language barrier. English-language Canadian shows have to compete with American shows while French-language Canadian shows don't. That's too simple an explanation, according to Patricia Bailey. Writing in the *Winnipeg Free Press*, Bailey argues that the real reason is cultural:

> One fundamental reason for the success of Quebec TV lies in the province's history. Television came on the scene at the right time in this province, and blossomed. Its presence in living-rooms coincided with the start of a major cultural revolution. In the early 1950s, Quebec's artists and intellectuals were frustrated with the repression of both the Duplessis government and the Catholic Church. They needed an outlet, and television provided it. This "revolutionary" class used television as a way to communicate a radical message: Quebec had to change and enter the modern world. Because their vision of a new Quebec was a populist one, their goal from the start was mass appeal. And their preferred tool was drama. At the same time as Quebecers were developing their own unique form of television drama, English-Canadians were being seduced by Ed Sullivan and Jackie Gleason. When the CBC first went to air, thousands of English Canadians had already been setting their aerials to receive signals from the American networks. English CBC decided to focus on news and current affairs rather than drama.

What else accounts for the difference? The CRTC says that the success of French television in Canada is "due in no small part to the well-developed and effective 'star system' in Quebec that showcases Canadian actors and programs." The CRTC is encouraging English-Canadian TV to build a star system of its own. It says "audiences for English-language Canadian entertainment programs are lower than those for either foreign programs or Canadian French-language programs, in part because viewers are unfamiliar with the programs and their stars. In French Canada, a well-developed 'star system' promotes new programs and acting talent

Why are ratings for Canadian shows higher in Quebec than in the rest of the country? *Star Académie*, a reality show, airs on TVA in Quebec.

through all media. In contrast, the pervasive promotion of U.S. television shows and stars through foreign and Canadian media often means that English-speaking audiences are more familiar with programs and stars from Hollywood and New York than those from their own country. Audiences might be more attracted to Canadian entertainment programs if they were better informed through television programs about the Canadian entertainment industry and its performers. Canadian entertainment magazine programs will be considered as priority programs." Shows like Global's *Entertainment Tonight Canada* and the specialty channels Star! and E! attempt to showcase Canadian talent and help foster an English-Canadian star system. Whether this model for promoting Canadian television programming will work remains to be seen.

What Do You Think?

1. Log onto www.bbm.ca and compare the weekly TV ratings for French- and English-speaking Canada. How many of the Top 20 shows in Quebec are Canadian? How many of the Top 20 shows in English Canada are Canadian?
2. What do you feel accounts for any differences in viewing patterns between English and French Canada?
3. How can English-language television in Canada develop a "star system" similar to that in Quebec? Would demassification help?

Law & Order. NBC and CTV found an upscale audience that many advertisers sought with the upscale characters in the long-running prime-time series *Law & Order*. The perps in murders may be seedy, but they're wearing button-down shirts with silk ties. Audiences related.

Eighty percent of a year's commercial time typically gets spoken for in the upfront process. If a show misses its projection, advertisers are given **make-goods**, the industry's term for additional spots to compensate for the financial commitment. If a show turns into a smash hit and exceeds audience forecasts, the price per spot gets jacked higher, or in some cases, if there is no escalation clause, the advertisers end up with a real deal.

make-goods Additional time that networks offer advertisers when ratings fall short of projections.

Until recently, under CRTC regulations, Canadian TV stations could air only 12 minutes of advertising. In 2008, that limit was increased to **15 minutes** per hour to reflect a more American economic model. This was in response to the television industry's call for ways of making more revenue to help offset the cost of transition to digital.

15 minutes CRTC limit on TV advertising per hour.

QUALITY AUDIENCE. The major television networks once based advertising rates entirely on audience size, but by the 2005–2006 prime-time season the concept of "quality audience" had moved to the fore. That translates into "upscale." To attract big-budget advertisers, the networks pitched programs that were expected to draw well-heeled viewers. Their hope was to charge premium rates to advertisers seeking the hard-to-reach high-income audience niche with messages for five-star hotels and luxury automobiles, not home hair-colouring kits and muffler shops. For delivering upscale viewers, networks charge advertisers 5 to 20 percent extra.

What attracts a quality audience? A consensus has emerged that the characters need to be upscale, even the criminals. NBC improved the posture of its venerable *Law & Order* by introducing upper-class perpetrators to whom upscale viewers could relate. Upscale viewers also value high production values, sophisticated dialogue, and less formulaic storylines.

HBO: It's not TV. It's HBO.
www.hbo.com

Rogers: More than just a cable company.
www.rogers.ca

Shaw: Canada's second largest cable company.
www.shaw.ca

Vidéotron: Cable company based in Quebec.
www.videotron.ca

Cable Television

Study Preview   *The cable television industry has grown from independent small-town community antenna systems into a well-heeled, consolidated industry. Today cable is a major threat to the traditional networks and their over-the-air affiliates.*

ROOTS OF CABLE

CATV Short for community antenna television. An early name for cable systems.

In the early 1950s, television networks and their local affiliates reached only major cities. Television signals, like FM radio, do not follow the curvature of the earth, so communities 40 to 50 miles away were pretty much out of range. Rough terrain kept even nearer towns from receiving television. One by one, small-town entrepreneurs hoisted antennas on nearby hilltops to catch television signals from the nearest cities with over-the-air stations. These local cable television systems, called **CATV**, for *community antenna television,* ran a cable down into town and stretched wire on telephone poles to deliver pictures to houses from the hilltop antenna. Everybody was happy. Small towns got big-city television, local entrepreneurs made money, and the networks and their stations gained viewers they couldn't otherwise reach. With this larger, cable-enhanced audience, the networks and stations were able to hike advertising rates.

Interestingly, cable TV arrived in Canada before the first Canadian television station, perhaps reflecting our desire for American programming. An experiment with redistributing U.S. antenna signals in 1952 in London, Ontario, marked the start of cable TV in Canada. Later that year, cable companies were also established in Vancouver and Montreal. The CRTC refers to cable companies as **broadcast distribution undertakings,** or BDUs.

BDU Broadcast distribution undertakings. Technical name for cable companies and satellite providers.

Gerald Levin Offered exclusive HBO programming to cable systems.

HBO Short for Home Box Office. First cable programming via satellite.

pay-per-view Cable companies charge subscribers for each program they watch.

GERALD LEVIN AND HBO

Television entered a new era in 1975 when **Gerald Levin** took over **HBO**, a Time Life subsidiary. HBO had been offering movies and special events, such as championship boxing, to local cable systems, which sold the programs to subscribers willing to pay an extra fee. It was a **pay-per-view** service. Levin wanted to expand HBO to a pay-per-month service with 24-hour programming, mostly movies. If it worked, this would give local cable systems a premium channel from which to derive extra revenue.

For an expanded HBO to succeed, Levin needed to cut the tremendous expense of relaying HBO transmission across the country from microwave tower to microwave tower. Then it occurred to Levin: Why not bypass microwaving and

Media Databank

Canadian Cable and Satellite Operators

Convergence means that cable and satellite companies, known as BDUs (broadcast distribution undertakings) can own cable channels and also provide content for their channels. The following list shows the leading cable and satellite companies in Canada, with their number of subscribers:

Company	Subscribers
Rogers	2 300 000
Shaw	2 200 000
Bell ExpressVu	1 700 000
Vidéotron (Quebecor)	1 500 000
Star Choice	862 000
Cogeco	836 000

Source: CRTC, Broadcast Policy Monitoring Report 2006.

instead send the HBO signal to an orbiting satellite, which could then send it back to earth in one relay to every local cable system in the country? Levin put up $7.5 million to use the Satcom 1 satellite. That allowed him to cut microwave costs while expanding programming and making HBO available to more of the country.

Television Entertainment

Study Preview   *Early national television networks patterned their programs on their successful radio experience, even adapting specific radio programs to the screen. Until* I Love Lucy *in 1951, programs were aired live. Today, most entertainment programming is taped and then polished by editing.*

EARLY PROGRAMMING

In the early days of television, the networks provided their affiliate stations with video versions of popular radio programs, mostly comedy and variety shows. Like the radio programs, the TV programs originated in New York. With videotape still to be invented, almost everything was broadcast live. Early television drama had a live theatrical onstage quality that has been lost with today's multiple taping of scenes and slick postproduction polishing. Comedy shows like Milton Berle's and variety shows like Ed Sullivan's, also live, had a spontaneity that typified early television. Canada had variety shows like *Juliette* and *Don Messer's Jubilee* and comedy with *Wayne and Shuster* during that time period.

Desi Arnaz and Lucille Ball's *I Love Lucy* situation comedy, introduced in 1951, was significant not just because it was such a hit but because it was not transmitted live. Rather, multiple cameras filmed several takes. Film editors then chose the best shots, the best lines and the best facial expressions for the final production. Just as in movie production, sequences could be rearranged in the cutting room. Even comedic pacing and timing could be improved. Final responsibility for what went on the air shifted from actors to editors. Taping also made possible the libraries of programs that are reissued by syndicates for rerunning.

I Love Lucy also marked the start of television's shift to Hollywood. Because Arnaz and Ball, who were married to one another at the time, wanted to continue to live in California, they refused to commute

Lost. ABC and CTV found a prime-time audience for *Lost* with strong cinematic qualities, tight scripting and multi-layered storylines. Plus, fans could also download episodes to their iPods featuring their favourite "losties," including Canadian Evangeline Lilly and her co-star Matthew Fox.

Paley Center for Media: Formerly known as The Museum of Television and Radio, it was renamed in 2007 to honour William Paley's influence on TV. www.paleycenter.org

Theme Songs: TV shows often have catchy theme songs at the beginning. Here is a list of links about those theme songs. www.google.com/Top/Arts/-Television/Theme_Songs

TV Land: A station playing around-the-clock reruns of all your favourite TV shows, including Canadian classics like *King of Kensington* and *Adventures in Rainbow County.* www.tvlandcanada.com

Desi Arnaz and Lucille Ball Introduced taping; led the television industry's move to Hollywood.

to New York to produce the show. Thus, *Lucy* became television's first Los Angeles show. Gradually, most of television's entertainment production went west.

Entertainment programming has gone through phases. Cowboy programs became popular in the 1950s, later supplemented by quiz shows. The cowboy genre was replaced successively by doctor shows, spy shows and cop shows in the 1960s. Through the changes, sitcoms have remained popular, although they have changed with the times, from *Father Knows Best* in the 1950s through *All in the Family* in the 1970s to *Friends* in the 1990s. Reality shows, led by *Survivor* on CBS, began a ride in 2000.

PRODUCING ENTERTAINMENT PROGRAMS

pilot Prototype show for a series.

Until 1995 the networks produced some entertainment programs but relied on independent companies for the majority of their shows. The independent companies create prototype episodes called **pilots** to entice the networks to buy the whole series, usually a season in advance. When a network buys a series, the show's producers work closely with network programming people on details.

syndicators Independent program producers and distributors.

Like the networks, stations buy independently produced entertainment programs. To do this, stations go to distributors, called **syndicators**, which package programs specifically for sale to individual stations, usually for one-time use. Syndicators also sell programs that previously appeared on the networks. Local stations, like the networks, buy old movies from motion picture companies for one-time showing.

CANADIAN PROGRAMMING

Getting Canadians to watch Canadian TV has been a struggle for English-language broadcasters. Although viewership levels have increased, the fact remains that 52 percent of the time, Canadians watch American programming. It's worse for Canadian comedies and dramas; 77 percent of the time, we prefer American programming to homegrown. Meanwhile, in Quebec, the opposite is true: 66 percent of all viewing in Quebec is Canadian. The question for the industry and academics is how to get English Canadians to watch more Canadian programming.

Steve Smith Proud supporter and producer of Canadian TV.

According to Canadian writer, actor and producer of Canadian television programs **Steve Smith** ("Red Green" to many), Canadian television has an important role as a vehicle for Canadian culture. Smith claims that with "Canadians being constantly exposed to and bombarded with American culture, there's a natural tendency to assimilate and, with Canadians, if all they're exposed to is American media, they will become more and more like Americans and less and less like Canadians. We'd be more like North Dakota with more interesting currency. For some people, that doesn't bother them. For me I think that would be a terrible tragedy."

Smith feels very passionately about Canadian television. He says it's unfair to categorize all American TV shows as better than all Canadian shows. "There are some great Canadian shows. If you look at the ratings book, people would be surprised that a lot of Canadian shows outrate a lot of the American shows." Smith says that Canadian sports broadcasts are among the best.

The real problem for English-Canadian TV is "the philosophy behind some of the broadcast outlets in that they really aren't in the business of making Canadian television good or popular. They are really in the business of importing American shows. That bothers me. Canadian broadcasters should be judged on the Canadian shows that they offer to the public, not on how many American shows they run. If Canadian networks lived or died by the success of their Canadian programming, they would find a way to make them great." For many broadcasters in Canada, the production and scheduling of Canadian programming is an afterthought.

It's this last point about Canadian TV becoming an afterthought for Canadian networks that has many upset. As Atallah and Shade argue in *Mediascapes,* the 60 percent Cancon may actually be hurting English-Canadian television. "Content quotas set aside certain hours that *must* be filled with Canadian content. Since that content must be shown, it hardly matters whether it is very popular or very good. Indeed, it may be more rational to satisfy quota requirements as inexpensively as possible."

In 1998, the CRTC's TV Policy hoped to address this issue. The changes offered broadcasters some flexibility in acquiring and scheduling Canadian programs, notably:

- Canadian stations need to schedule **60 percent Canadian content** overall, with at least 50 percent during the "**Peak Viewing Period**" of 7 p.m. until 11 p.m., seven days a week.
- Included in this 50 percent of Canadian content during this time period are "priority programs." These aren't just entertainment programs, such as comedies and dramas, but Canadian-produced entertainment magazines, documentaries, regionally produced programs, dramas and comedies.
- The CRTC also offers a **drama credit** of up to 150 percent for new Canadian dramas. This means that a new, one-hour Canadian drama would count as 90 minutes toward the channel's Cancon requirements for that week.
- The Commission also encouraged English-Canadian broadcasters to learn from the experience and success of French broadcasters, including developing a Canadian "**star system.**"

This policy moved Canadian TV to a more American model of producing television shows. Canadian networks don't have to produce their own Cancon; that's done by independent production houses. Canada has many successful independent television producers, including Alliance Atlantis, Nelvana, S&S Productions Inc. and Salter Street. These companies have an eye for producing television that is not only (as the CRTC requires) "Canadian in content and character" but also exportable to the United States. In other words, quality of the program becomes a factor.

The goal for Canadian networks, according to **Michael McCabe**, former president of the Canadian Association of Broadcasters, is viewing. Says McCabe, "Viewing is what really counts. Not just how many hours we have or how many dollars we spend. These are just proxies for what should be the real goal—more Canadians watching, being informed by and, most importantly, enjoying Canadian television."

60 percent Canadian content Level of Canadian content required by the CRTC.

Peak Viewing Period 7–11 p.m., seven days a week.

drama credit CRTC incentive for production sector and Canadian channels.

star system Helps raise the awareness of Canadian shows and stars.

Michael McCabe Former head of Canadian Association of Broadcasters.

Television News

Study Preview   *The television networks began newscasts with anchors reading stories into cameras, embellished only with occasional newsreel clips. Networks expanded their staffs and programming over the years. Unlike Canadian entertainment programming, Canadian news does well. Given a*

Building on Success: Read more about the CRTC's 1998 TV policy.
www.crtc.gc.ca/Archive/ ENG/Notices1999/ PB99-97.htm

TV News Arrives in Canada: View one of the very first news stories aired on the CBC.
http://archives.cbc.ca/ IDC-1-69-543-2729/ life_society/boyd_gang/

Douglas Edwards Pioneer anchor.

John Cameron Swayze Pioneer anchor.

Fred W. Friendly Partner of Edward R. Murrow; showed power of TV news through *See It Now* and other programs.

Chet Huntley and David Brinkley Headed first 30-minute network newscast.

Walter Cronkite Best-known television news anchor, now retired.

Television News Archive: Research an extensive archive of televised news coverage.
http://tvnews.vanderbilt.edu

magazine programs Investigative news programs, usually with three to four unrelated segments.

choice, 92 percent of Canadians will watch Canadian news and information programming over American news.

TALKING HEADS AND NEWSREELS

The U.S. networks began news programs in 1947, CBS with *Douglas Edwards with the News* and NBC with **John Cameron Swayze's** *Camel News Caravan.* In Canada, news pioneers such as Lloyd Robertson, Knowlton Nash, Peter Desbarats and Harvey Kirck cut their teeth as reporters for this new medium. The evening programs rehashed AP and CP dispatches and ran film clips from movie newsreel companies. The networks eventually built up their own reporting staffs and abandoned the photogenic but predictable newsreel coverage of events like beauty contests and ship launchings. With on-scene reporters, network news focused more on public issues.

Television's potential as a serious news medium was demonstrated in 1951 when producer **Fred W. Friendly** and reporter Edward R. Murrow created *See It Now,* mentioned previously. Television gained new respect when Friendly and Murrow exposed the false, hysterical charges of Senator Joseph McCarthy about communist infiltration of federal agencies. In 1963 the U.S. evening newscasts expanded to 30 minutes with NBC's **Chet Huntley–David Brinkley** team and CBS's **Walter Cronkite** in nightly competition for serious yet interesting accounts of what was happening.

The arrival of television also added an element to Canadian journalism. In *A Guide to Canadian News Media,* Peter Desbarats reports that by the late 1950s, Canadian news programs were becoming in-depth and analytical. René Lévesque's *Point de mire* and Pierre Berton's *Close-Up* were popular newsmagazine-style shows. Probably the best-known newsmagazine in the 1960s was *This Hour Has Seven Days,* hosted by Laurier LaPierre and Patrick Watson. It debuted in the fall of 1964. The program became known for its controversial style and was taken off the air in 1966 after only 50 episodes. *W-5* (now called *W-FIVE*) began broadcasting in 1966 on CTV and is now the longest running newsmagazine in North America. CBC's *Fifth Estate* is also known for hard-hitting, take-no-prisoners journalism. CBC's *The Hour* with George Stroumboulopoulos continues this tradition with a millennial attitude.

CTV aired its first nightly newscast in 1961 with Harvey Kirck as the anchor. Today, people tune in to the trustworthy images of Lloyd Robertson and the *CTV National News,* Peter Mansbridge on CBC's *The National* or Kevin Newman on *Global National.*

SHIFT IN NETWORK NEWS

Some say television news was at its best during the Murrow period. It is a fact that the networks have scaled down their global news-gathering systems since the mid-1980s. New, bottom-line-oriented owners and budget problems forced the changes. Newscasts have suffered most, losing a lot of original coverage from abroad.

Prime-time **magazine programs** like *60 Minutes* and *W-FIVE* once were a sideline of network news divisions. Today, those programs have become so popular with viewers that network news divisions have shifted resources to produce more of them. NBC's *Dateline,* for example, aired four nights a week one season. The proliferation of magazine programs has further reduced the talent and budget for the newscasts that once were the main identity of the network's news. Critics point out that some network magazine projects are of the tabloid mould—flashy but not much substance. Edward R. Murrow set a higher standard.

24-Hour Television News

When Ted Turner launched Cable News Network as an around-the-clock news service in 1980, critics belittled the shoestring operation as "Chicken Noodle News." Gradually, CNN built up its resources and an audience and advertiser base. CNN proved its mettle in the 1991 Persian Gulf War, routinely outdoing the Big Three networks in coverage from the Gulf and being wholly competitive from Washington and other world centres. In 1982, Turner launched Headline News, which offered a quick overview of the latest news, weather and sports. By the late 1990s other players had joined the 24-hour news competition.

Fox News Channel. When Rupert Murdoch decided that CNN needed competition, he hired one-time Richard Nixon confidante Roger Ailes to build **Fox News Channel.** Ailes hired a corps of respected Washington reporters and bright young anchors who trumpeted a "we report, you decide" slogan. However, Ailes's conservative bent rubbed off on the product. Extreme conservative Bill O'Reilly added to the Fox News right-wing image in prime time.

MSNBC. A third all-news cable network, **MSNBC,** was created by a Microsoft–NBC alliance. The network drew on NBC's depth of news-gathering and on-air talent, including Tom Brokaw's successor, Brian Williams.

CBC Newsworld. To offer Canadians a Canadian perspective on the news, *Newsworld* began broadcasting from Halifax, Toronto, Winnipeg and Calgary in 1989. It offers what CBC news has always done well: news with insight and analysis. *Newsworld* is not funded by the government. It relies on advertising revenue and its rather large subscriber base of 10 million viewers.

CTV Newsnet. In 1997, CTV launched an all-news channel. At first, it featured a prerecorded 15-minute "headline news" style of format. Eventually, it developed into a full-service news channel that features *Mike Duffy Live* and *CTV National News*. It boasts 7.5 million subscribers.

Whither Goes Television?

Study Preview   *More than in other traditional mass media, the corporate and social structures that have been built around television are well suited to become the hub of tomorrow's mass communication.*

Time Shifts

The centrepiece of television in people's lives in the evening is already waning, even prime time. With TiVo-like playback devices, people don't need to tune in at 8 p.m. for a favourite sitcom. To be sure, events like the Stanley Cup playoffs, elections and the *American Idol* finale will draw huge prime-time audiences. But the end may be in sight for prime-time scheduling for ongoing network series, the historic foundation of network programming.

60 Minutes: Calling all Andy Rooney fans—watch or read as Andy ponders timely topics.
www.cbsnews.com/ sections/60minutes/ rooney/main3419.shtml

Frontline: Investigative journalism at its finest.
www.pbs.org/wgbh/pages/ frontline

W-FIVE: Interact with Canada's longest running newsmagazine.
www.ctv.ca/wfive

The Hour: News with an attitude.
www.cbc.ca/thehour

Fox News Channel Rupert Murdoch–owned cable news network.

MSNBC Cable news network owned by NBC and Microsoft.

CNN: This is CNN.
www.cnn.com

Fox News: All the latest headlines.
www.foxnews.com

CBC Newsworld: News from a Canadian perspective.
www.cbc.ca/newsworld

BBC News: News network competition from across the pond.
http://news.bbc.co.uk

Media Databank

News Shows

These are the most common types of television nonfiction shows:

Evening Newscasts The major networks have evening newscasts built on reporting the day's main events. These are anchored by seasoned newspeople. Almost all network affiliates carry their flagship local newscast with the network program. Evening newscasts run 30 to 60 minutes.

Sunday Interviews *Meet the Press* on NBC is the longest running show on television. It and similar shows like *Face the Nation* on CBS, *This Week* on ABC and *Question Period* on CTV feature interviews, mostly with government leaders.

Newsmagazines The CBS program *60 Minutes*, which celebrated its 40th anniversary in 2003, comprises several segments on subjects that don't lend themselves to coverage on daily programs. Many segments are investigative. Other newsmagazines include *Dateline* on NBC and *20/20* on ABC, CTV's *W-FIVE* and CBC's *The Fifth Estate*.

Documentaries Sometimes called long-form news, documentaries are lengthy examinations, usually an hour, of a social or political issue. They have been largely displaced in over-the-air network programming by newsmagazines, but they remain a staple at CNN in programs like *CNN Presents*, on PBS with *Frontline* and on CBC Newsworld's *The Passionate Eye*. These shows give producers and correspondents an hour, sometimes longer, to develop an issue.

Morning Shows *Today* on NBC was first a mix of news and softer, but still mostly informational, content. Latter-day morning shows include *Good Morning America* on ABC and *The Early Show* on CBS. CTV's *Canada AM* and *CBC News: Morning* are Canadian versions.

Talk Shows These mostly are independent productions that local stations buy and choose to run at times to build audiences or to fill times during which the networks aren't supplying programming. Some like *Jerry Springer* have been called "trash television," dealing as they do with interpersonal strife of the guests. The two most successful over the years, *Phil Donahue* and *Oprah Winfrey*, cover a broad range of subjects and issues, but rarely breaking news.

Tabloid News Sometimes called *reality shows*, tabloid news programs deal with celebrity news, like the supermarket tabloids, often dwelling on gossipy personal life details. *Entertainment Tonight Canada* and *e-Talk Daily* are among the most widely featured of these programs.

Television News: How to do successful television news. www.tvrundown.com/howto.html

podcasts Downloadable episodes of popular TV shows.

SPACE SHIFTS

People still call television receivers *sets*—but less so. The idea of television as a piece of furniture or even a stationary appliance is giving way as miniaturization, possible with digital technology, makes reception possible on palm-size screens that are so light they can be taken anywhere as easily as, say, a wallet. Television is less a bulky appliance around which people cluster and more a portable device that is often incorporated with other functions like telephone, on-demand music, real-time email communication, web access and personal data storage. Plus, fans can now download **podcasts**, which are often sponsored, of their favourite shows and watch them on their portable devices. What does this technological transformation mean for television as we know it?

ADVERTISING SHIFTS

Once the darling of almost every national brand for marketing, 30-second spots on network television are losing some of their luster. The change reflects partly the declining audience for over-the-air stations served by the traditional networks, partly the continuing network push for higher rates. Also a factor is concern that record-replay devices like TiVo mean more viewers are skipping ads.

WEBISODES. One brand-name advertiser that's shifted away from 30-second spots is American Express. In the mid-1990s, Amex put 80 percent of its advertising budget into network spots. By 2005, however, the amount was down to 35 percent. Where have Amex and other brand-name advertisers diverted their dollars? Some Amex dollars have stayed with the networks through product mention in scripts, which addresses TiVo leakage. But much has gone into web initiatives, concert sponsorships and promotional experiments, such as stocking trendy health clubs with blue-labeled bottled water to hype Amex's blue card. There have been blue popcorn bags at movie houses and Amex-sponsored museum exhibits. Amex has been a leader in **webisodes**, those four-minute mini-movies on the web. Blue card logos were everywhere for an Amex-sponsored concert with Elvis Costello, Stevie Wonder and Counting Crows at the House of Blues in Los Angeles, which was renamed the House of Blue for the event.

PRODUCT PLACEMENT. Mindful that advertisers are scouting for alternative media, television networks have gone to selling paid plugs for products and services in scripts. It's not unlike early radio and 1950s television, when hosts for sponsored programs touted products. For Arthur Godfrey, no tea was as good as Lipton's—and viewers never knew when to expect a plug. This was a leftover from an era when radio advertisers produced their own programs. As the networks took over programs, selling commercial slots to the highest bidder, a purist distinction between creative control of programming content and advertising became a given.

In the 1980s, Hollywood began selling product mentions in movie scripts. The result was a continuing boiling controversy. The controversy now is back in television, with networks—facing the drain of TiVo viewers who watch programs but skip the ads—weaving product names into scripts. CTV's *Corner Gas* was one of the first Canadian shows to include product placement in their Christmas episode entitled "Merry Gasmas." The storyline included mentions of the Sears catalogue. *Rock Star: Supernova* integrated Virgin Mobile phones. Despite protests from some producers, the practice seems destined to stay. As of 2007, the CRTC had no plans to regulate the practice.

Corner Gas Christmas. Don't tell us there's not a lot going on. Besides being a hit with both critics and fans, *Corner Gas* employed product placement of the Sears catalogue during its "Merry Gasmas" episode.

webisodes Mini-movies, generally four minutes long, on the web; usually sponsored and sometimes with the advertiser as part of the storyline.

CHAPTER 6 WRAP-UP

North American television patterned itself after radio. From the beginning, television was a dual national system of locally owned commercial stations and national networks. Companies that were heavily involved in radio were also the television heavyweights. Even television's programming mimicked radio's. The networks—NBC, CBS and ABC in America and CBC, CTV and Global in Canada—were the most powerful shapers of television, leading in entertainment programming and news. Gerald Levin and then Ted Turner led a restructuring when they realized that they could deliver programs to local cable companies via orbiting satellite. Levin's HBO and Turner's WTBS, both movie services, became unique features of cable companies in the 1970s. Now satellite and digital technology is contributing to major changes. Also changing the face of television is conglomeration and the emergence of large, multi-platform media companies.

QUESTIONS FOR REVIEW

1. How does television influence people in the short term and the long term?

2. Describe the development of television technology.

3. What technologies deliver television signals to viewers?

4. How has government regulation shaped programming on Canadian TV?

5. How was radio the role model for early television programming?

6. How do owners of local stations, cable systems and satellite-delivery systems view each other?

7. What are Don Ferguson's views on Canadian television?

8. How is television suited to become the hub medium of tomorrow's mass communication?

QUESTIONS FOR CRITICAL THINKING

1. What did social critic Michael Novak mean when he described television as "a molder of the soul's geography"?

2. How did Philo Farnsworth use electronics to pick up moving images and relay them live to faraway screens? How was his invention different from movie technology?

3. How will the competition for television viewers shake out among satellite delivery systems, cable delivery systems and locally licensed stations?

4. Did the two-tier television system, with locally licensed stations and national networks, make sense when it was put into effect? Does it make sense now? For the future?

5. Affiliate stations of the television networks once shared a monopoly on local television audiences, but their dominance has been chipped away. How can these affiliates adapt? Can they survive in a changing mass media environment?

6. Should product placement be regulated by the CRTC?

7. Television once was a place-based medium. To watch, people gathered at television sets, usually at home in a living room, and scheduled their daily routines around favourite programs. How has technology changed viewing habits? What effects have these changes had on programming?

DEEPENING YOUR MEDIA LITERACY

Is television news on the decline?

Step 1

The big networks have scaled down their global news-gathering systems, creating opportunities for other sources of news. What does this mean for the news-watching public?

DIG DEEPER

Step 2

Interview three or four of your friends about where they like to get their local news, their global news, their breaking news, their sports news, their entertainment news. How much of it is from the traditional television networks, how much from all-news networks, how much from television newsmagazines and how much from talk shows? How much do they get from sources other than television? If another war were declared tomorrow, where would they turn to get the news about it?

What Do You Think?

Step 3

Answer these questions:

1. What can you conclude about the state of television news based on your small sample?

2. Do you see any possible trends for the future of television news? Do they match what the experts predict?

KEEPING UP TO DATE

Playback, Broadcaster, and *Broadcast Dialogue* are broadcasting trade journals. *Television/Radio Age* is another trade journal.

Journal of Broadcasting and Electronic Media and the *Canadian Journal of Communication* are quarterly scholarly journals published by the Broadcast Education Association.

Consumer magazines that deal extensively with television programming include *Entertainment* and *People.*

Newsmagazines that report on television issues more or less regularly include *Newsweek, Maclean's* and *Time.*

Major newspapers with strong television coverage include the *National Post,* the *Toronto Star,* and *The Globe and Mail.*

FOR FURTHER LEARNING

Paul Atallah and Leslie Regan Shade. *Mediascapes: New Patterns in Canadian Communication* (Thomson Nelson, 2002).

Paul Audley. *Canada's Cultural Industries* (Lorimer and Company, 1983).

Patricia Bailey. "Why Canuck TV Sucks—And Quebec Shows Thrive." *Winnipeg Free Press* (July 6, 2003).

Erik Barnouw. *Tube of Plenty: The Evolution of American Television* (Oxford, 1975).

Warren Bennis and Ian Mitroff. *The Unreality Industry* (Carol Publishing, 1989).

Roger Bird. *Documents in Canadian Broadcasting* (Carleton University Press, 1988).

Donald Bogle. *Primetime Blues: African Americans on Network Television* (Straus & Giroux, 2001).

Robert Brehl. "Specialty Channels Change TV Patterns." *The Globe and Mail* (March 21, 1998).

Jennings Bryant and J. Alison Bryant, eds. *Television and the American Family,* Second edition (Erlbaum, 2001).

John Bugailiskis. "TV Finally Gets Interactive." *Broadcaster* (April 2000).

CanWest Global Communications. *2006 Annual Report.*

Mary Lu Carnevale. "Untangling the Debate over Cable Television." *Wall Street Journal* (March 19, 1990): 107, B1, B5, B6.

CBC. *2005–2006 Annual Report.*

Mark Christensen and Cameron Stauth. *The Sweeps* (Morrow, 1984).

CRTC. *Broadcasting Policy Monitoring Report 2007.*

CRTC. "Dramatic Choices: A Report on English Language Drama." 2003.

CRTC. "The New Policy on Canadian Television: More Flexibility, Diversity and Programming Choice."

CTV. *2006 Annual Report.*

Peter Desbarats. *Guide to the Canadian News Media* (Harcourt Brace, 1990).

Ian Edwards. "Specs Enjoy Stellar Growth." *Playback* (March 2004).

Danylo Hawaleshka, "Converging on Your Living Room." *Maclean's* (August 6, 2001).

Helen Holmes and David Tara. *Seeing Ourselves: Media Power and Policy in Canada* (Harcourt Brace, 1996).

Laurel Hyatt. "Canadian Content Key to New Television Policy." *Broadcaster* (July 1999).

Ed Joyce. *Prime Times, Bad Times* (Doubleday, 1988).

J. D. Lasica. *Darknet: Hollywood's War against the Digital Generation* (Wiley, 2005).

John McGrath. "The Smart Road to HDTV in Canada." *Broadcaster* (July 2000).

Joshua Meyrowitz. *No Sense of Place: The Impact of the Electronic Media on Social Behavior* (Oxford, 1985).

Peter C. Newman. "Save the Country by Salvaging the CBC." *Maclean's* (February 19, 1996).

Peter B. Orlik. *Electronic Media Criticism: Applied Perspectives,* Second Edition. (Erlbaum, 2000).

Lucas A. Powe, Jr. *American Broadcasting and the First Amendment* (University of California Press, 1987).

John P. Robinson and Mark R. Levy. *The Main Source* (Sage, 1986).

Reese Schonfeld. *Me and Ted Against the World: The Unauthorized Story of the Founding of CNN* (HarperCollins, 2001).

Roger P. Smith. *The Other Face of Public Television: Censoring the American Dream* (Algora, 2002).

Duncan Stewart. "Video on Demand." *National Post* (September 29, 2003).

Bohdan Szuchewycz and Jeannette Sloniowski. *Canadian Communications: Issues in Contemporary Media and Culture* (Prentice Hall, 2001).

Mary Vipond. *The Mass Media in Canada* (James Lorimer and Company, 1992).

Jennifer Wells. "Izzy's Dream." *Maclean's* (February 19, 1996).

Hank Whittemore. *CNN: The Inside Story* (Little, Brown, 1990).

Chapter Seven

Browser Genius. At 21, Marc Andreessen and a geek buddy created Mosaic, which facilitated web access. Then they trumped themselves by creating Netscape.

The Internet

MEDIA TIMELINE

Internet

_____ **1945**	Vannevar Bush proposed a memex machine for associative links among all human knowledge.
_____ **1962**	Ted Nelson introduced the term *hypertext*.
_____ **1969**	U.S. military created ARPANET to link contractors and researchers.
_____ **1989**	Tim Berners-Lee devised coding that made the web possible.
_____ **1993**	Marc Andreessen created predecessor to Netscape browser.
_____ **1997**	Rob Malda, a college student, created Slashdot, "news for news," one of the first blogs.
_____ **1999**	CRTC decided "not to govern the internet at this time."
_____ **2001**	Dot-com bubble burst.
_____ **2003**	Amazon.com demonstrated a new speed of search engines with "Search Inside a Book."
_____ **2007**	Apple introduced the iPhone.

Media in Theory

Push-Pull Model

Web communication shifts much of the control of the communication through the mass media to the recipient, turning the traditional process of mass communication on its head. Receivers are no longer hobbled to sequential presentation of messages, as on a network television newscast. Receivers can switch almost instantly to dozens, hundreds even, of alternatives through a weblike network that, at least theoretically, can interconnect every recipient and sender on the planet. This is the basic idea behind the **push-pull model.**

The communication revolution requires a new model to understand new ways that the media are working. One new model classifies some media as passive. These are **pull media,** which you steer. Examples are the traditional media, like radio and television, over which you have control to pull in a message. You can turn them on or off. You can pick up a book and put it down. You can go to a movie or not.

Push media, on the other hand, propel messages at you whether invited to or not. A simple, low-tech example is a recorded voice in a grocery store aisle that encourages you to buy a certain brand of cornflakes as you pass by the cereal display. Push media are taking sophisticated forms with the World Wide Web and new technologies that are making the media more pervasive than ever. They're always on.

Some push media you can program include:

- Signing up for an online newsletter on your favourite topic. Ipsos Reid claims that 8 out of 10 Canadians sign up for various internet newsletters.
- Your cell phone that updates the score on a hockey game you can't watch while you're doing something else.
- News and travel updates from Egypt you ask for after booking airline tickets for a vacation to the pyramids.

Other push media intrude gently or are in your face without your doing any programming:

- A heads-up automobile windshield display, like OnStar, that flashes directions to nearby repair shops when sensors detect your engine is overheating.
- Banners across your computer screen that advertise products that your past online purchases indicate you're likely to want.
- Wall screens that push items at you based on assumptions about your interests—like music video samplers for a performing star who is popular on a radio station you listen to.

The editors of *Wired* magazine, describing push media, give this example: You are in your study, answering email from the office when you notice something happening on the walls. Ordinarily, the large expanse in front of you features a montage generated by Sci-Viz (meaning *scientific visualization*)—a global news feed of scientific discoveries, plus classic movie scenes and 30-second comedy routines. You picked this service because it doesn't show you the usual disaster junk, yet the content is very lively, a sort of huge screen saver, which you usually ignore. But just now you notice a scene from your hometown, something about an archaeological find. You ask for the full video. This is always-on, mildly in-your-face networked media.

No model is perfect, which means push media and pull media are extremes that rarely exist in reality. Most media messages are push-pull hybrids. The "media wall" in the *Wired* magazine example intrudes without a specific invitation, but it also leaves it to you to choose what to pull in when you want more detail. Most emerging new media have such hybrid capabilities.

push-pull model Some of the control in the communication process shifts to the receiver.

pull media Messages requested by the receiver.

push media Messages sent to the receiver with or without prior consent.

Influence of the Internet

Study Preview   *The internet has emerged as the eighth major mass medium with a range of content, especially through web coding, that exceeds that of traditional media in many ways.*

NEW MASS MEDIUM

From a dizzying array of new technologies, the internet emerged in the mid-1990s as a powerful new mass medium. What is the internet? It's a jury-rigged network of telephone and cable lines and satellite links that connect computers. Almost anybody on the planet with a computer can tap into the network. A few clicks of a mouse button will bring in vast quantities of information and entertainment that originate all over the world.

Although in some ways the internet resembles a traditional mass medium that sends messages from a central transmission point, it is much more interactive and participatory. Message recipients are able to click almost instantly from one source to another—from ordering online from the Sears catalogue to listening to their favourite music genre from Iceberg Radio to reading their local newspaper online. Users of the internet are also creators of content, from blogs to Wikipedia to Facebook or MySpace. The role of individuals in shaping the internet swayed *Time* magazine to name "You" as their Person of the Year in 2006.

technological convergence Melding of print, electronic and photographic media into digitized form.

TECHNOLOGICAL CONVERGENCE

Today, the traditional primary media are in various stages of transition to digital form. Old distinctions are blurring. This **technological convergence** is fueled by accelerated miniaturization of equipment and the ability to compress data into tiny digital bits for storage and transmission. And all the media companies, whether their products traditionally relied on print, electronic or photographic technology, are involved in the convergence.

As the magazine *The Economist* noted, once-discrete media industries "are being whirled into an extraordinary whole." Anticipating the arrival of phone companies becoming satellite providers and cable companies offering VoIP (voice over internet protocol) phone technology, *USA Today*'s Kevin Maney put it this way in *Quill* magazine: "All the devices people use for communicating and all the kinds of communication have started crashing together into one massive megamedia industry. The result is that telephone lines will soon carry TV shows. Cable TV will carry telephone calls. Desktop computers will be used to watch and edit movies. Cellular phone-computers the size of a notepad will dial into interactive magazines that combine text, sound and video to tell stories."

SCOPE OF THE INTERNET

Every major mass media company has put products on the internet. Thousands of start-up companies are establishing themselves on the ground floor. The technology is so straightforward and access is so inexpensive that millions of individuals have set up their own sites.

How significant is the internet as a mass medium? Statistics Canada estimates that the number of internet users in Canada in 2006 was about 17 million—68 percent of the population, with 81 percent of Canadians using broadband. In only a few years the internet has become a major medium for advertising. In 2006 advertisers spent $519 million for space on the internet.

The significance of the internet is measurable in other ways too. There are people who have given up reading the print edition of newspapers and instead browse through the internet edition. Some of the news sites are updated constantly. Almost every U.S. magazine and newspaper has an **internet site**, from the venerable but tech-savvy *Globe and Mail* to local papers in the hinterlands.

internet site Where an institution establishes its web presence.

NEW TERMINOLOGY

The terms *internet* and *web* are often tossed around loosely, leading to lots of confusion. The fundamental network that carries messages is the internet. It dates to a military communication system created in 1969. The early internet carried mostly text.

The web is a structure of codes that permits the exchange not only of text but also of graphics, video and audio. Web codes are elegantly simple for users, who don't even need to know them to tap into the web's content. The underlying web codes are accepted universally, which makes it possible for anyone with a computer, a modem and an internet connection to tap into anything introduced from anywhere on the global web. The term *web* comes from the spidery links among millions of computers that tap into the system—an ever-changing maze that not even a spider could visualize and that becomes more complex all the time.

The prefix *cyber-* is affixed almost casually to anything involving communication via computer. *Cyberspace* is the intangible place where the communication occurs. *Cyberporn* is sexual naughtiness delivered on-screen. A *cyberpunk* is a kid obsessed with computer protocols and coding.

cyber- Prefix for human connection via computers.

Media Databank

Canadians and the Internet

Ipsos Reid claims that almost 7 in 10 Canadians have internet access at home. What do Canadians do online? Here are some of the reasons that we go online at home, according to Statistics Canada:

Activity	Percentage of Canadians Engaging in Activity from Home
Email	91%
General Browsing	84%
Weather or Road Conditions	67%
Travel Arrangements	63%
News or Sports	62%
Medical or Health Information	58%
Online Banking	58%
Play Games	39%
Chat	38%
Downloading Music (free or paid)	37%

Source: Adapted from Statistics Canada publication "Canadian Internet Use Survey, 2005," The Daily, Catalogue 11-001, August 15, 2006, http://www.statcan.ca/Daily/ English/060815/d060815b.htm.

William Gibson Sci-fi writer who coined the term *cyberspace.*

The term *cyberspace* was introduced by science-fiction novelist **William Gibson** in his book *Neuromancer.* At that point, in 1984, he saw a kind of integration of computers and human beings. Paraphrasing a bit, here is Gibson's definition of *cyberspace:* "A consensual hallucination experienced daily by billions of people in every nation. A graphic representation of data abstracted from the banks of every computer in the human system. Unthinkable complexity. Lines of light ranged in the nonspace of the mind. Clusters and constellations of data." Gibson got it right.

The *Time* 100: William Shockley Profile of William Shockley as part of the *Time* 100 (The Most Important People of the Century). **www.time.com/time/ time100/scientist/ profile/shockley.html**

Internet Technology

Study Preview   *The 1947 invention of the semiconductor led to digitization and compression that became building blocks for technology that made the internet possible. Web coding and the Netscape browser widened access.*

UNDERLYING TECHNOLOGIES

Researchers Walter Brattain, John Bardeen and William Shockley at AT&T's Bell Labs knew they were on to something important for telephone communication in 1947. They had devised glasslike silicon chips—piece of sand, really—that could be used to respond to a negative or positive electrical charge.

semiconductor Silicon chips that are used in digitization.

DIGITIZATION. The tiny chips, called **semiconductors,** functioned very rapidly as on-off switches. With the chips, the human voice could be reduced to a stream of digits—1 for

Semiconductor Inventors. A semiconductor switch can be likened to a tiny triple-decker sandwich. The sandwich, made of silicon, responds to slight variations in electrical current that allow incredibly fast processing of data that have been converted into on-off signals. In addition to speed, the semiconductor ushered in miniaturization of data-processing equipment and storage devices. Since 1947, when Bell Labs engineers devised the semiconductor, it has become possible to store thousands of pages of text on a device as small as a pinhead and to transmit them almost instantly to other devices, like your home computer. The 1956 Nobel Prize went to Bell Labs' Walter Brattain, John Bardeen and William Shockley for inventing the semiconductor.

on, 0 for off—and then transmitted as rapid-fire pulses and reconstructed so fast at the other end that they sounded like the real thing. Digitization dramatically expanded the capacity of telephone systems and revolutionized telephone communication. Brattain, Bardeen and Shockley won a Nobel Prize. Little did they realize, however, that they had laid the groundwork for revolutionizing not just telephonic communication but all human communication.

COMPRESSION. Bell Labs took semiconductors to a new level with **compression** technology in 1965. The on-off digital technology had so compacted messages for transmission that, suddenly, it was possible to break calls into spurts and transmit them simultaneously on a single line, each spurt like a railroad car joining a train on a track and then leaving the train to go to its own destination. People marveled that 51 calls could be carried at the same time on a single wire.

compression Technology that makes a message more compact by deleting nonessential underlying code.

MINIATURIZATION. Semiconductors gradually replaced electrical tubes in broadcast equipment. The idea of a radio as a piece of furniture disappeared with semiconductor-equipped portable radios in the 1950s. But that was only the beginning of miniaturization of all kinds of electrical and mechanical functions. In the emerging field of computers, early models used electrical tubes and were housed in entire buildings. Now the movement is toward central units with footprints of less than four square feet. Laptops are a marvel of miniaturization. The Marquardt Corporation estimates that all the information recorded in the past 10 000 years can be stored in a cube six feet by six feet by six feet.

CREATING THE INTERNET

The internet had its origins in a 1969 U.S. Department of Defense computer network called **ARPANET**, which stood for Advanced Research Projects Agency Network. The Pentagon built the network for military contractors and universities doing military research to exchange information. In 1983 the **National Science Foundation** (NSF), whose mandate is to promote science, took over.

This new National Science Foundation network attracted more and more institutional users, many of which had their own internal networks. For example,

ARPANET Military network that preceded internet.

National Science Foundation Developed current internet to give scholars access to supercomputers.

most universities that joined the NSF network had intracampus computer networks. The NSF network then became a connector for thousands of other networks. As a backbone system that interconnects networks, **internet** was a name that fit.

By 1996 the internet had become clogged with exponential growth in traffic. University network engineers designed a new high-speed backbone to connect research networks. Called **Internet2**, the new backbone was up and running by 1999, carrying data as fast as 2.4 gigabits per second—four times faster than its predecessors. In 2003 it was upgraded to 10 gigabits per second.

One solution, an even faster Internet3, may not be financially possible. An interim possibility is to lease **dark fibre**, the unused fibre optic capacity that commercial telecommunications companies overbuilt in the late 1990s. Already Internet2 is too costly for many colleges. Basic connection and membership fees range from $160 000 to $450 000 a year. Internet3 would cost even more.

WORLD WIDE WEB

The early internet created access to lots of data at speeds that were unprecedented. But it was an uninviting place visually. Text and data were in black-and-white and image-free—something only a researcher could love. Even so, there were possibilities to take the new medium in commercial directions.

INTERNET SERVICE PROVIDERS. A new kind of company, **internet service providers (ISPs)**, went into business in the 1980s to give ordinary folks a portal to the internet and help in navigating the internet's inherent complexity and disorganization. Compuserv was first to provide online service to consumers. These companies charged subscription fees for a combination of services—internet access, email and, most important, a mapping structure to help users get to where they wanted to go among the seemingly infinite number of places to go on the internet.

TIM BERNERS-LEE. A major breakthrough came from English engineer **Tim Berners-Lee**, who in 1991 devised an addressing system that could connect every computer in the world. The name that Berners-Lee came up with for his system sounded audacious, the **World Wide Web**, but it was accurate—a decentralized global network with the potential, theoretically, for everyone at a computer to communicate with everyone else at a computer anywhere on the planet.

Berners-Lee's invention was built on three components:

- **Universal resource locators (URL).** Now known as uniform resource locators, this addressing system was devised by Berners-Lee to give every computer a unique identifier, much like a postal address that enables mail to be delivered to the right place. The identifiers, URLs, allowed computers connected in a network to exchange messages. Being "universal," it was a comprehensive and standardized system that became the foundation for the World Wide Web.
- **Hypertext transfer protocol (HTTP).** This is a protocol that allows computers to connect to read internet files.
- **Hypertext markup language (HTML).** This was a relatively simple computer language that permitted someone creating an internet message to insert so-called hot spots or links that, if clicked, would instantly switch the onscreen image to something else. For example, a research article could include visible indicators, usually the underlining of a term, that when clicked on with a mouse would cause the browser to move to another article on the subject.

internet A network of computer networks.

Internet2 A network consortium owned by research institutions for fast data transfer.

dark fibre Excess telecommunication capacity available for data transfer.

LexisNexis: Subscribe to this online database service or use the à la carte option and pay as you go. **www.lexisnexis.com**

internet service provider (ISP) Company that charges a fee for online service.

The *Time* 100: Tim Berners-Lee Profile of Tim Berners-Lee as part of the *Time* 100 (The Most Important People of the Century). **www.time.com/time/time100/scientist/profile/bernerslee.html**

Canadian ISPs: Looking to change your ISP? Here's a list of 350 Canadian ISPs. **www.canadianisp.com**

Tim Berners-Lee Devised protocols, codes for the World Wide Web.

World Wide Web System that allows global linking of information modules in user-determined sequences.

universal resource locator (URL) Address assigned to a page on the internet. Now known as a uniform resource locator.

Media People

Tim Berners-Lee

Tim Berners-Lee

Single-handedly, Tim Berners-Lee invented the World Wide Web. Then, unlike many entrepreneurs who have used the internet to amass quick fortunes, Berners-Lee devoted his life to refining the web as a medium of communication open to everyone for free.

Berners-Lee, an Oxford engineer, came up with the web concept because he couldn't keep track of all his notes on various computers in various places. It was 1989. Working at CERN, a physics lab in Switzerland, he proposed a system to facilitate scientific research by letting scientists' computers tap into each other. In a way, the software worked like the brain. In fact, Berners-Lee said that the idea was to keep "track of all the random associations one comes across in real life and brains are supposed to be so good at remembering, but sometimes mine wouldn't."

Working with three software engineers, Berners-Lee had a demonstration up and running within three months. As Berners-Lee traveled the globe to introduce the web at scientific conferences, the potential of what he had devised became clear. The web was a system that could connect all information with all other information.

The key was a relatively simple computer language known as HTML, short for hypertext markup language, which, although it has evolved over the years, remains the core of the web. Berners-Lee also developed the addressing system that allows computers to find each other. Every web-connected computer has a unique address, a universal (or uniform) resource locator (URL). For it all to work, Berners-Lee also created a protocol that actually links computers: HTTP, short for hypertext transfer protocol.

In 1992, leading research organizations in the Netherlands, Germany and the United States committed to the web. As enthusiasm grew in the scientific research community, word spread to other quarters. In one eight-month period in 1993, web use multiplied 414 times. Soon "the web" was a household word.

As you would expect, Berners-Lee had offers galore from investors and computer companies to build new ways to derive profits from the web. He said no. Instead, he chose the academic life. At the Massachusetts Institute of Technology he works out of spartan facilities as head of the W3 consortium, which sets the protocol and coding standards that are helping the World Wide Web realize its potential.

It's hard to overrate Berners-Lee's accomplishment. The internet is the information infrastructure that likely will, given time, eclipse other media. Some liken Berners-Lee to Johannes Gutenberg, who 400 years earlier had launched the age of mass communication with the movable type that made mass production of the written word possible.

The Eyeball as a Screen. A Seattle company, Microvision, is hoping to market a device that projects images directly onto the human eyeball. This VRD, short for *virtual retinal display,* is not much more cumbersome to wear than a pair of glasses, and it gives a sharper image than a 70-millimetre IMAX screen. With VRD, people would not need television or computer screens. Microvision says this device can be made for less than $100.

The term **hypertext** was devised by technologist Ted Nelson in his 1962 book *Literary Machines* for a system that would allow people to interrupt themselves while reading through material in the traditional linear way, from beginning to end, and transport themselves nonlinearly to related material. Nelson also called it *nonsequential writing,* but the term *hypertext* stuck.

It was a quarter century later when Berners-Lee devised the HTML coding that made nonsequential reading possible.

BANDWIDTH

An impediment to the web's realizing its potential was the capacity available on traditional telephone systems for transmitting data. Text was no problem, but as graphics joined the mix, this capacity, called **bandwidth**, became packed and transmissions slowed, sometimes to a crawl. Superdetailed photos required several minutes to traverse from point A to point B. The more complex a visual, the more data are needed to make it blossom at the other end. Theoretically, music could be sent on the internet, but it was a bandwidth hog. Video was worse.

A combination of technologies is being used to address the bandwidth issues. Some are eliminating choke points in the pipelines. Others are squeezing more data to consume less space.

FIBRE OPTIC CABLE. While AT&T was building on its off-on digital technology to improve telephone service in the 1960s, **Corning Glass** developed a cable that was capable of carrying light at incredible speeds—theoretically 186 000 miles per second. It was apparent immediately that this new **fibre optic cable** could carry far more digitized messages than could the copper wire used for telephones. The messages were encoded as light pulses rather than as the traditional electrical pulses for transmission.

By the 1980s, new equipment to convert data to light pulses for transmission was in place, and long-distance telephone companies were replacing their copper lines with fibre optics, as were local cable television systems. With fibre optic cable and other improvements, a single line could carry 60 000 telephone calls simultaneously.

MULTIPLEXING. One innovation that expanded bandwidth was **multiplexing**, a process through which a message is broken into bits for transmission through whichever cables have capacity at the moment. Then the bits are reassembled at the delivery point. So instead of a message getting clogged in a pipeline that's already crammed, tiny bits of the message, called packets, find alternative paths through whichever pipeline has room. All of this happens in fractions of a second, with the message ending up at its destination faster.

COMPRESSION. Technology has been devised that screens out nonessential parts of messages so that they need less bandwidth. This is especially important for graphics, video and audio, which are incredibly code-heavy. Coding for blue sky in a photo, for example, need not be repeated for every dot of colour. Even without redundant coding, the sky still appears blue. Unless compressed, audio too is loaded with redundant coding.

Some compression technology further streamlines a message by eliminating details that the human eye or ear will not miss. For example, compression drops sound on a CD that would start dogs howling but that humans cannot hear.

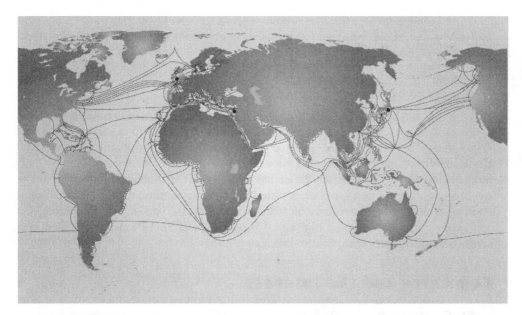

Global Fibre Optics. The Fiber Optic Link Around the Globe, "FLAG" for short, is the longest engineering project in human history—a 17 400-mile communication link of England and Japan. Many of the lines shown are undersea fibre optic routes that are planned or in place. The world is being wired for faster World Wide Web communication.

STREAMING. When a message is massive with coding, such as audio and video, the message can be segmented with the segments stored in a receiving computer's hard drive for replay even before all segments of the message have been received. This is called **streaming**. Most audio and video today is transmitted this way, which means some downloading delay—often only seconds. The more complex the coding, the longer it takes.

streaming Technology that allows playback of a message to begin before all the components have arrived.

Reshaping the Internet

Study Preview   *Wireless internet connections, called Wi-Fi, have added to the portability of the internet. Further untethering from a wired infrastructure is possible through ultrawideband and mesh network technology.*

Looking for Free Wi-Fi? A website that lists free Wi-Fi hot spots not only in Canada, but the United States and Europe. **www.wififreespot.com**

WI-FI

Another development in interactive media is wireless fidelity technology, better known as **Wi-Fi**. It untethers laptops and allows internet access anywhere through radio waves. The coffee chain Starbucks made a splash with Wi-Fi, encouraging people to linger. Hotels and airports were naturals for Wi-Fi. Many Canadian cities from Chilliwack to St. John's have free Wi-Fi "hot spots" in their downtown areas.

One justification for municipal Wi-Fi is to bridge the **digital divide**, the socioeconomic distinction between people that can afford internet access and those that can't.

Wi-Fi Wireless fidelity technology.

digital divide The economic distinction between impoverished groups and societal groups with the means to maintain and improve their economic well-being through computer access.

ULTRAWIDEBAND

Short-range Wi-Fi networks, which become sluggish as more people tap in, may pick up capacity with UWB technology, short for **ultrawideband**, unless opponents prevail. The technology uses existing frequencies, including commercial broadcast channels,

ultrawideband (UWB) Low-power Wi-Fi system that rides on existing frequencies licensed for other uses.

but with such low power that the primary signals seem to be unaffected. The aviation industry is concerned that frequencies used by on-board collision-avoidance systems could be compromised by crowding.

MESH NETWORKS

dynamic routing
Technology that makes every wireless device a vehicle for furthering a message along to its destination, rather than moving in a structured network.

mesh networking The ad hoc network created for each single message to reach its destination; also called *dynamic routing*.

After Wi-Fi, what? The most anticipated next technology is **dynamic routing**, in which every wireless gadget serves also as a receiver and transmitter to every other wireless device within its range. Messages would just keep moving, hop-skipping invisibly from device to device until each reaches its intended destination. There is no formal network; messages go to whatever device has capacity at the moment—or, rather, at the nanosecond. Every wireless device outfitted for dynamic routing would be on call as a stepping stone for however many messages come its way. Engineers say that **mesh networking**, as it is called, using high-speed protocols, will be 15 times faster than currently touted DSL services.

Commerce and the Internet

Study Preview   *The internet has emerged as a commercial medium. Some sites are built around products. Others, in a more traditional vein, are designed to attract an audience with content, such as news. The sites sell access to that audience to advertisers.*

ADVERTISING-FREE ORIGINS

Before the web, the internet was a pristine, commerce-free medium. If somebody put out a message that had even a hint of "filthy lucre," purists by the dozens, even hundreds, deluged the offender with harsh reminders that commerce was not allowed. By and large, this self-policing worked.

When the web was introduced as an advanced internet protocol, its potential for commerce was clear almost right away. The World Wide Web Consortium, which sets standards for web protocols, created the dot-com suffix to identify sites that existed to do business. That decision transformed the internet and our lives.

DOT-COM BUBBLE

By 1996, internet traffic was doubling every three months. On an annual basis that was 800 percent growth. Billions of investment dollars flowed in to finance additional fibre optic infrastructures. The investment frenzy generated more than $1 trillion to wire the world with extraordinary new capacity.

dot-coms Commercial websites, so named because their web address ended with the suffix ".com."

dot-com bubble Frenzied overinvestment in the telephone and internet infrastructure and also internet commerce in late 1990s.

Meanwhile, seeing no end to the exponential growth in **dot-com** companies, investors poured billions of dollars into ventures for exploiting the internet's commercial potential. Much of the investment, it turned out, was reckless. The so-called **dot-com bubble** burst in 2001 and 2002 with bankruptcies and a massive scaling down that caught thousands of internet careers in the downward spiral. Investment portfolios withered with profound implications for pension plans that resulted in many people delaying their retirement.

But there was good news. A vast fibre optic system was in place, with far more capacity than was needed. Nobody was going to dig it up. As telecommunications companies went belly up, banks acquired the assets in bankruptcy sales and then sold the fibre optic networks at 10 cents on the dollar. The new owners operated the networks profitably, having bought them at fire-sale prices. The new owners also installed new transmitter and receiver switches to increase the volume and speed of data moving through the networks.

Thomas Friedman of *The New York Times,* who studied the dot-com phenomenon, described what happened this way: "So as the switches keep improving, the capacity of all of the already installed fibre cables just keeps growing, making it cheaper and easier to transmit voices and data every year. . . . It's as though we laid down a national highway system where people were first allowed to drive 50 mph, then 60 mph, then 70 mph, then 80 mph, then eventually 150 mph on the same highways without any fear of accidents."

INTERNET ADVERTISING

When the bubble burst for so many dot-coms, most remaining sites looked to advertising rather than venture capitalists to sustain them economically. With more than 217 million people with web access in the United States and Canada by 2005, and the number growing, the potential for dot-coms to be advertising-supported was clear. The Interactive Advertising Bureau of Canada claims that many Canadians use the internet as a research tool when making purchases. Also, in 2006, 52 percent of Canadians with internet access had made purchases online. Meanwhile, in its *Broadcast Policy Monitoring Report 2006,* the CRTC claims that internet advertising increased 5090 percent, from $10 million in 1997 to $519 million in 2006.

TRACKING INTERNET TRAFFIC

An impediment to attracting advertisers to the internet was the difficulty of measuring the audience. Advertisers want solid numbers on which to base decisions on placing their ads. Gradually, the Interactive Advertising Bureau and the Advertising Research Foundation developed uniform measurement guidelines. Nielsen, known mostly for surveys on network television audiences, has established monitoring mechanisms.

The most-cited measure of web audiences is the **hit**. Every time someone browsing the web clicks an onscreen icon or onscreen highlighted section, the computer server that offers the web page records a hit. Some companies that operate websites tout hits as a measure of audience, but savvy advertisers know hits are a misleading indicator of audience size. The online edition of *Wired* magazine, *HotWired,* for example, records an average of 100 hits from everybody who taps in. *HotWired*'s 600 000 hits on a heavy day come from a mere 6000 people.

Another measure of web usage is the **visit**, a count of the people who visit a site. But visits too are misleading. At *Playboy* magazine's website, 200 000 visits are scored on a typical day, but that doesn't mean that *Playboy* cyber-ads are seen by 200 000 different people. Many of the same people visit again and again on a given day.

The **clickthrough** has emerged as a measure. When someone clicks a link to an advertising site, the click is registered and a fee is paid to the site from which the ad visitor came, called the gateway site. The gateway site is the internet equivalent of a newspaper, which charges advertisers for space, or a television station, which charges for airtime.

Interactive Advertising Bureau of Canada: Check out Standards and Guidelines to learn how to determine the success of an online ad campaign. **www.iabcanada.com**

Nielsen//NetRatings: A leader in providing information to help clients determine and execute their internet business strategies. **www.netratings.com**

hit Tallied every time someone goes to a web page.

visit Tallied for every person who visits a website.

clickthrough A registered visit to an advertising site from a gateway elsewhere on the internet.

Some electronic publications charge advertisers by the day, others by the month, others by the hit. But because of the vagaries of audience measurements, there is no standard pricing. Knowing that the web cannot mature as an advertising medium until advertisers can be given better audience data, electronic publications have asked several companies, including Nielsen, to devise tracking mechanisms. But no one expects data as accurate as press runs and broadcast ratings any time soon. In the meantime, advertisers are making seat-of-the-pants assessments as to which websites are hot.

Evaluating the Internet

Study Preview   *Traditional gatekeeping processes that filter media content for quality are less present in the internet. Users need to take special care in assessing material they find.*

STRENGTHS OF INTERNET SITES

Webby A major award of excellence for websites.

Several organizations issue awards to excellent internet sites. The most prestigious are the Webby awards, a term contrived from the nickname for the somewhat parallel Emmy awards of television. Many web awards, though, are for design and graphics, not content, although there are many measures of a site's excellence.

CONTENT. The heart of all mass media messages is the value of the content. For this, traditional measures of excellence in communication apply, such as accuracy, clarity and coherence.

NAVIGABILITY. Does the site have internal links so that users can move easily from page to page and among various points on the site? Among the mass media, navigability is a quality unique to the internet.

EXTERNAL LINKS. Does the site connect to related sites on the internet? The most distinctive feature of the internet as a mass medium is interconnectivity with other sites on the global network. Good sites exploit this advantage.

INTUITIVE TO USE. The best sites have navigational aids for moving around a site seamlessly and efficiently. These include road signs of many sorts, including clearly labeled links.

LOADING TIMES. Well-designed sites take advantage of the internet as a visual medium with images. At the same time, pages should load quickly so users don't have to wait and wait and wait for a page to write itself to their screens. This means the site needs a balance. Overdoing images, which require lots of bandwidth, works against rapid downloads. Absence of images makes for dull pages.

ACCURACY

The internet has been called a democratized mass medium because so many people create internet content. Almost anybody can put up a site. A downside of so much input from so many people is that the traditional media gatekeepers (see Chapter 1) aren't necessarily present to ensure accuracy. To be sure, there are many reliable sites with traditional gatekeeping, but the internet is also littered with junk.

To guard against bad information, internet users should pay special heed to the old admonition: Consider the source. Is the organization or person behind a site reliable? If you have confidence in the *National Post* as a newspaper, you can have the same confidence in its website. Another news site, no matter how glitzy and slick, may be nothing more than a person working alone in a dank basement somewhere recasting the news from their perspective. Lobby groups and political parties also publish content on the internet on sites that appear to be neutral. Norman Spector, who was Chief of Staff to Brian Mulroney in the 1980s, says "there's so much concern on the part of the public now as to whether they're getting the straight goods and people are going to the internet, they say, because their confidence in the mainstream media has been shaken. So I think this on the web is problematic."

In research reports, footnotes or endnotes need to be specific on internet sources, including URL addresses. This allows people who read a report to go to the source to make their own assessment—just as traditional footnotes allow a reader to go to the library and check a source.

Even with notations, a report that cites internet sources can be problematic. Unlike a book, which is permanent once it's in print, internet content can be in continuing flux. What's there today can be changed in a minute—or disappear entirely. To address this problem at least in part, notation systems specify that the date and time of the researcher's internet visit be included.

In serious research, you can check whether an online journal is refereed. A mission statement will be on the site with a list of editors and their credentials and a statement about the journal's editorial process. Look to see whether articles are screened through a **peer review** process.

> **peer review** A screening mechanism in which scholarly material is reviewed by leaders in a discipline for its merits, generally with neither the author nor the reviewers knowing each other's identity.

THE INTERNET: GOOD, BAD OR UGLY?

Steve Maich, writing in *Maclean's* magazine in October of 2006, had some issues about the internet. The entire title of his article was "Pornography, Gambling, Lies, Theft and Terrorism: The Internet Sucks (Where Did We Go Wrong?)" His issue wasn't only with the internet itself, but the discourse surrounding it. Maich writes that "right from the beginning, experts competed with one another to see who could come up with the most outrageous superlative to the nascent technology. It was the most important breakthrough since the personal computer, no, since the telephone—or rather the telegraph, or maybe the printing press." Even in 2006 when Google bought out YouTube, creating a "titan of new media," Maich claims the rhetoric hadn't changed.

Maich doesn't believe the internet has lived up to its hype. He says "after 15 years and a trillion dollars of investment, just about everything we've been told about the internet and what the information age would mean has come up short." Instead of Tim Berners-Lee's dream of the internet becoming "an interactive sea of shared knowledge," the internet became a place that "the public at large saw as an invitation to indulge vice on an unimaginable scale."

Despite the issues with the internet, Maich does admit that there's nothing that can be done.

"There's no going back. It is now so deeply entrenched in our culture—in the way we speak and work and create and think—that the only thing to do is try and make it better and hope that maybe we might somehow realize some of the dreams the idealists had when they invented the thing."

> **Steve Maich** *Maclean's* columnist with issues about the impact of the internet and the rhetoric surrounding it.

Public Policy and the Internet

Study Preview *The ability of almost anyone to post content on the internet poses new public policy questions and issues. This whole new media world is illustrated by the free-wheeling nature of blogs. Media issues of privacy, decency and access are posed in newly critical ways.*

BLOGS

In an era when the price of entry to media ownership precludes most mortals, the internet, although young as a mass medium, is already democratizing mass communication. The rules are new. The most powerful member of the U.S. Senate, Trent Lott, never figured that his career would end under pressure created by a pipsqueak citizen in the hinterlands. It happened.

Joshua Marshall, creator of his own website (talkingpointsmemo.com), picked up on a speech by Lott that, depending on your view, was either racist or racially insensitive. Lott uttered his comment at the 100th birthday party of Senator Strom Thurmond, once a strong segregationist.

Mainstream news media missed how Lott's comments could be interpreted. Not Joshua Marshall. In his **blog** (at http://talkingpointsmemo.com) he hammered away at Lott day after day. Other bloggers, also outraged, joined in. Three days later the story hit NBC. Four days later Lott apologized. Two weeks later his Senate colleagues voted him out as majority leader.

As a blogger who made a difference, Joshua Marshall is hardly alone. Best known is Matt Drudge, whose revelations propelled the Bill Clinton–Monica Lewinsky dalliances in the Oval Office into a national scandal. Another blogger, college student Russ Kick, at his computer in Arizona, looked for information on government refusals to release photographs of caskets of fallen U.S. soldiers in Iraq and Afghanistan, which he regarded as documents to which the public, himself included, had legal access. Kick filed a request for the documents under the Freedom of Information Act, then on his website (thememoryhole.org), he posted the photographs of the flag-draped coffins and also of the astronauts who had died in the *Columbia* disaster. The photos became front-page news. At one point Kick's blog was receiving 4 million hits a day—almost twice the circulation of *USA Today*.

Both the beauty and bane of blogs is their free-for-all nature. On the upside, the web gives ordinary citizens access to mass audiences. It can be a loud and effective megaphone that is outside the traditional news media that have resulted from institutionalized practices and traditions.

Joshua Marshall's work on Trent Lott is an example of outside-the-box news reporting. Most bloggers are amateurs at news, and their lack of experience with journalistic traditions has a downside.

blog An amateur website, generally personal in nature, often focused on a narrow subject, such as politics. Short for "web log."

PRIVACY AND THE INTERNET

The genius of Tim Berners-Lee's original web concept was its openness. Information could be shared easily by anyone and everyone. Therein was a problem. During the web's commercialization in the late 1990s, some companies tracked where people ventured on the internet. The tracking was going on silently, hidden in the background, as people coursed their way around the internet. Companies gathering infor-

BlogsCanada: Read what Canadian bloggers have to say about current political issues.
www.blogscanada.ca

mation were selling it to other companies. There was fear that insurance companies, health-care providers, lenders and others had a new secret tool for profiling applicants.

Government agencies began hinting at controls. Late in 1999, Berners-Lee and the web protocol-authoring consortium he runs came up with a new architecture, **P3P**, short for *Platform for Privacy Preferences Project,* to address the problem. With P3P, people could choose the level of privacy they wanted for their web activities. Microsoft, Netscape and other browser operators agreed to screen sites that were not P3P-compliant. In effect, P3P automatically bypassed websites that didn't meet a level of privacy expectations specified by individual web users.

P3P A web protocol that allows users to choose a level of privacy. Short for *Platform for Privacy Preferences Project.*

CYBERPORNOGRAPHY

Moralists, many in elected offices, are trying to eradicate indecency from cyberspace, especially if children have access. How serious is the problem? No one is certain how much **cyberpornography** is out there. Although a lot of internet traffic is to porn sites, Vanderbilt University business professors Donna Hoffman and Thomas Novak estimate that only one-half of 1 percent of the files available on the internet could be described as pornographic. How often kids visit those sites is impossible to measure. Some people would argue that even a single child's exposure to pornography is too much and justifies sanctions.

cyberpornography Indecency delivered by computer.

Still, policing the internet, including websites, presents unique challenges. The nature of the internet is that it is unstructured and unregulated, and the available material is in ongoing flux. The anarchy of the internet is its inherent virtue. The immensity of cyberspace is another problem for would-be regulators. The web system that Tim Berners-Lee and his associates devised has infinite capacity.

Among alternatives to protect children are desktop programs that have come on the market to identify objectionable internet bulletin boards and websites. **SurfWatch**, for example, blocks access to such sites as soon as they are discovered. Bill Duvall of Los Altos, California, who created SurfWatch, hires college students to monitor cyberspace for sexual explicitness and updates SurfWatch regularly. He identifies five to 10 new smut sites a day.

SurfWatch Software that intercepts indecent material.

UNIVERSAL ACCESS

Although internet use is growing dramatically, the fact is that not everybody has access. Those who can afford computers and access fees will benefit tremendously. What about everybody else? This is a profound public policy question, especially in a democracy that prides itself on ensuring equality for every citizen on basic matters like access to information. One line of reasoning is that the government should not have to guarantee **universal access**. This rationale draws on the highway system as an analogy. The government builds the roads, but individuals have to provide the vehicles to drive around on the system.

universal access Giving everyone the means to use the internet.

The counter-argument is that access to information will become so essential to everyone's well-being that we could end up with a stratified society of info-rich and info-poor people. Such a knowledge gap hardly is the democratic ideal.

However, it's not simply a case of access. Limiting individuals' access to the internet also limits their ability to create content for the internet. **Michael Geist**, the Canada Research Chair in Internet and E-Commerce Law at the University of Ottawa, says, "an obvious starting point for connectivity is the role that the federal,

Michael Geist Canadian expert on how new technology is affecting Canadian law.

provincial and municipal governments can play to ensure that all Canadians have access to the high-speed networks that are the price of admission to the participatory Internet."

GLOBAL INEQUITIES

The exchange of information facilitated by the internet boosted North America into unprecedented prosperity going into the 21st century. One measure of efficiency, **diffusion of innovation**, improved dramatically. The time that innovations take to be widely used, which was once 10 years, dropped to 1 year. The Giga Information Group projected that by 2002, businesses would be saving $1.3 trillion because of internet commerce—an incredible 765 percent gain over five years.

A problem, though, is that much of the world isn't well plugged in. All of the Middle East and Africa have only 7.5 million web users in total.

In short, the economic advantages of the internet may be creating new international inequities. If maximum prosperity depends on free trade in a global economy, as many economists argue, then all of the world must be folded fully into the internet.

As the technological breakthroughs leapfrog each other, we will see the traditional media shift increasingly to the internet. Don't expect to wake up one morning, though, and find that the world is paperless and that local television stations have vanished. Just as horses and buggies and the automobile coexisted for 40 years, so will e-books (digital books) and p-books (print books). Television will still be television as we know it today, with many people satisfied with living room sets pretty much as now—although with bigger screens, sharper pictures and movie-house sound quality.

In short, media companies will need to use two redundant modes to maximize their audience. Already we see this with over-the-air radio stations that stream online; magazines and newspapers on paper and on the internet; and recordings available at the record store and also downloadable.

Could the internet lose its diversity? Media mogul Barry Diller, well regarded for his crystal-ball–like view on media trends, sees ownership consolidation ahead for the internet, just like the other media. Citing cable giant Comcast, he said in a *Newsweek* interview: "You can already see at Comcast and others the beginning of efforts to control the home pages that their consumers plug into. It's for one reason: To control a toll bridge or turnstile through which others must pay to go. The inevitable result will be eventual control by media giants of the Internet in terms of independence and strangulation. This is a situation where history is absolutely destined to repeat itself." Most internet users hope Diller is wrong.

THE INTERNET AND THE CRTC

The CRTC was the first broadcast regulator in the world to address the issue of controlling the internet. In 1999, Canada's broadcast regulator announced it would not regulate the internet at that time, as the internet doesn't fall under the authority of Canada's Broadcasting Act. Following are among the reasons they cited for their conclusion:

■ The internet is not, by definition, broadcasting. Its messages are largely communicated using alphanumeric text.

diffusion of innovation
Process through which news, ideas, values and information spread.

- The internet does not replace broadcasting; it simply complements it.
- Web material can be customized by the user, its messages are broadcast for a mass audience in the same way a radio or television broadcast is. The web is a "push" medium.
- There is already a large Canadian presence on the internet.
- The CRTC felt that the Criminal Code of Canada and the use of content-filtering software by users would be the best way to deal with offensive content on the internet.

CHAPTER 7 WRAP-UP

The World Wide Web utilizes the global internet, so computers anywhere can exchange digitized data—including text, visuals and audio. Many media companies are investing heavily in cyberspace, and the expansion of high-capacity fibre optic cable networks will increase capacity tremendously so that audio and moving visuals are on tap live on any computer screen connected to the internet. Two-way communication via the internet already is standard fare. With every passing day, more mass communication is occurring on the internet.

QUESTIONS FOR REVIEW

1. How can the internet be defined as a new and distinctive mass medium?
2. What technological breakthroughs made the internet possible?
3. What are the new directions in which technology is taking the internet?
4. What has been the role of advertising in driving internet development?
5. How is gatekeeping different on the internet than in other major mass media?
6. How is the internet contributing to a melding of the mass media?
7. What public policy questions has the internet raised?

QUESTIONS FOR CRITICAL THINKING

1. What makes books, magazines, newspapers, sound recordings, movies, radio and television different from one another? What will become of these distinctions in coming years?
2. Trace the development of the technology that has made the web possible.
3. What innovations did Tim Berners-Lee introduce that are revolutionizing mass communication?
4. How does hypertext depart from traditional human communication? And does hypertext have a future as a literary form?
5. What obstacles would you have in designing public policy to assure access to the internet for every citizen?
6. Some people say there is no point in trying to regulate the internet. Do you agree? Disagree? Why?
7. Is Steve Maich correct: Does the internet suck? List examples to illustrate your point of view.

DEEPENING YOUR MEDIA LITERACY

Can you trust what you read and see on the internet?

Step 1

Choose two or three different websites that a student might access for information for a paper, such as Google or Wikipedia.

Dig Deeper

Step 2

Write evaluations of the sites you chose based on the following criteria:

1. How is the site funded? What is the intended purpose of the site? And of the information on the site? Is it user-driven or owner/product-driven?

2. Does the site appeal to your emotions? If so, how? What other techniques are used to engage the viewer?

3. All media contain ideological and value messages. What are the messages of the site? Are any of them unintended? Are they positive or negative? Are they obvious or intentionally hidden?

4. Does the site use traditional gatekeepers?

5. Does it use a peer review process?

What Do You Think?

Step 3

Answer these questions: What are the potential drawbacks of using a user-driven site for research? Is the emotional appeal of a site important to a user seeking research information? Are traditional gatekeepers the best way to ensure accuracy on a website? Why or why not? Is how a site is paid for a fair way to measure its trustworthiness? Why or why not? How could the value messages of a site affect its informational worth?

KEEPING UP TO DATE

Industry Standard is the main trade journal of e-commerce.

The magazines *Wired* and *Infoworld* offer coverage of cyberdevelopments, issues and people.

Trade journals *Editor & Publisher, Advertising Age, Playback, Broadcaster* magazine and *Broadcast Dialogue* have excellent ongoing coverage of their fields.

Widely available news media that explore cyberissues include *Time, Maclean's, Toronto Star, National Post* and *The Globe and Mail.*

Don't overlook surfing the web for sites that track internet developments.

FOR FURTHER LEARNING

Alan B. Albarran and David H. Goff, editors. *Understanding the Web: Social, Political and Economic Dimensions of the Internet* (Iowa State University Press, 2000).

Ken Auletta. *World War 3.0* (Random House, 2001).

Tim Berners-Lee, with Mark Fischetti. *Weaving the Web: The Original Design and the Ultimate Destiny of the World Wide Web by Its Inventor* (Harper San Francisco, 1999).

Robert Brehl. "Brave New World." *Toronto Star* (March 30, 1996).

Vannevar Bush. "As We May Think." *Atlantic Monthly* (July 1945).

Bruce Cheadle. "Beware: There's Bad News Behind Internet Headlines." *Hamilton Spectator* (January 15, 2007).

Adam Cohen. "A Wired Village." *Time Digital* (December 2000): 58–62.

"Crime in Cyberspace." *Maclean's* (May 22, 1995): 50–58.

CRTC. *Broadcast Policy Monitoring Report 2006* (CRTC, 2006).

CRTC. "CRTC Won't Regulate the Internet." CRTC (May 19, 1999).

Ben Elgin, with Steve Hamm. "The Last Days of Net Mania." *Business Week* (April 16, 2001): 110–118.

Martha FitzSimons, editor. *Media, Democracy and the Information Highway* (Freedom Forum Media Studies Center, 1993).

Urs E. Gattiker. *The Internet as a Diverse Community: Cultural, Organizational and Political Issues* (Erlbaum, 2001).

Michael Geist. "Time's Choice Could Prove Inspired." *Toronto Star* (January 8, 2007).

George Gilder. *Telecosm: How Infinite Bandwidth Will Revolutionize Our World* (Free Press, 2000).

John Heilemann. *Pride Before the Fall: The Trials of Bill Gates and the End of the Microsoft Era* (Harper-Collins, 2001).

Industry Canada. "An Anti Spam Plan for Canada" (May 2004).

Ipsos Reid Canada. "The Canadian Inter@ctive Reid Report: Fact Guide."

Ipsos Reid Canada. "Digital Divide Remains Wide: Only 6 in 10 Canadians Aged 55 + Have Access to the Internet" (February 15, 2007).

Robert Lucky. *Silicon Dreams* (St. Martin's, 1989).

Steve Maich. "'Pornography, Gambling, Lies, Theft, and Terrorism: The Internet Sucks (Where Did We Go Wrong?" *Maclean's* (October 30, 2006): 44–49.

Kevin Maney. "Will the Techno Tsunami Wash Us Out?" *Quill* (March 1994): 16–18.

Gordon Moore. "Solid State Physicist: William Shockley." *Time* (March 29, 1999): 193–195.

JoAnn Napier. "Online Advertising Rise 96% in a Year." *Ottawa Citizen* (March 20, 2000).

John V. Pavlik. *New Media Technology: Cultural and Commercial Perspectives* (Allyn & Bacon, 1995).

Mark Slouka. *War of the Worlds* (Basic Books, 1996).

Statistics Canada. "Canadian Internet Use Survey." *The Daily* (August 15, 2006).

Statistics Canada. "Internet Service Providers." *The Daily* (December 18, 2006).

Neal Stephenson. "Mother Earth, Motherboard." *Wired* (December 1996): 97–160.

Robert Wright. "The Man Who Invented the Web." *Time* (May 19, 1997): 160–164.

Global National. After spending a few years with ABC, Kevin Newman returned to Canada to anchor *Global National.*

News

MEDIA TIMELINE

Roots of Journalistic Practices

_____ 1690	Benjamin Harris published the first newspaper, *Publick Occurrences,* in Boston.
_____ 1735	Colonial jury exonerated John Peter Zenger of "seditious libel for publishing articles about the governor's incompetence."
_____ 1752	John Bushnell began publishing *The Halifax Gazette,* the first newspaper in Canada.
_____ 1833	Ben Day founded *The New York Sun,* the first penny newspaper.
_____ 1835	Joseph Howe was acquitted of publishing "seditious libel" in the *Novascotian.*
_____ 1844	Samuel Morse devised the telegraph, hastening delivery of faraway news in the United States and Canada.
_____ 1880s	Joseph Pulitzer and William Randolph Hearst's circulation war led to yellow press excesses.
_____ 1917	The Canadian Press was founded.
_____ 1980	CNN introduced 24-hour television news.
_____ 2001	CRTC warned conglomerates to keep newsroom management separate to ensure a diversity of voices in Canadian news.
_____ 2001	A wave of digital cable news channels was unleashed in Canada.

Media in Theory

Gatekeeping

This just in . . . Canadians love news. A 2004 survey conducted by the Canadian Media Research Consortium (CMRC) found that 90 percent of Canadians are "interested" or "somewhat interested" in news and follow it on a daily basis. Although Canadians have a hunger for news, few ask the question: What is news? It's not an easy question to answer in practice or in theory. There is no one single definition of news. In *Canadian Broadcast News: The Basics,* journalism professor **Brian Green** says that news is "the significant, the unusual, that which affects us." However, the definition of what is "significant" is open to personal interpretation. Journalists know they have a high level of responsibility in deciding what to report as news. While most reporters will agree on the newsworthiness of some events and issues, such as a catastrophic storm or a tax proposal, their judgments will result in stories that take different slants and angles. This is the role of a journalist as a **gatekeeper.**

Although individual reporters have independence in determining what to report and how, news work is a team effort. News dispatches and photographs are subject to changes at many points in the communication chain. At these points, called *gates,* gatekeepers delete, trim, embellish and otherwise try to improve messages. You will remember gatekeepers were part of the **concentric circle model** introduced in Chapter 1.

A reporter exercises judgment in deciding what to report and how to report it. Hardly any message, except live reporting, reaches its audience in its original form. Along the path from its originator to the eventual audience, a message is subject to all kinds of deletions, additions and changes of emphasis. With large news organizations, this process may involve dozens of editors and other persons.

The gatekeeping process affects all news. A public relations practitioner who doesn't tell the whole story is a gatekeeper. A reporter who emphasizes one aspect of an event and neglects others is a gatekeeper. Even live, on-scene television coverage involves gatekeeping because it's a gatekeeper who decides where to point the camera, and that's a decision that affects the type of information that reaches viewers.

Gatekeeping can be a creative force. Trimming a news story can add potency. A news producer can enhance a reporter's field report with specific file footage. An editor can call a public relations person for additional detail to illuminate a point in a reporter's story. A newsmagazine's editor can consolidate related stories and add context that makes an important interpretive point.

Most gatekeepers are invisible to the news audience, working behind the scenes and making crucial decisions in near anonymity on how the world will be portrayed in the evening newscast and the next morning's newspaper.

Journalism Traditions

Study Preview   *U.S. journalism has evolved through four distinctive eras: the colonial, partisan, penny press and yellow periods. Each of these periods made distinctive contributions to contemporary news media practices in both the United States and Canada.*

COLONIAL PERIOD

In the American **colonial period**, **Benjamin Harris** published the first newspaper, *Publick Occurrences,* in Boston in 1690. He was in hot water right away. Harris scandalized Puritan sensitivities by alleging that the king of France had dallied with his son's wife. In the colonies, just as in England, a newspaper needed royal consent. The governor had not consented, and Harris was put out of business after one issue.

Even so, Harris's daring was a precursor for emerging press defiance against authority. In 1733 **John Peter Zenger** started a paper in New York in competition with the existing Crown-supported newspaper. Zenger's was backed by merchants and lawyers who disliked the royal governor. From the beginning, the newspaper antagonized the governor with items challenging his competence. Finally, the governor arrested Zenger. The trial made history. Zenger's attorney, **Andrew Hamilton**, argued that there should be no punishment for printing articles that are true. The argument was a dramatic departure from the legal practice of the day, which allowed royal governors to prosecute for articles that might undermine their authority regardless of whether the information in the articles was true. Hamilton's argument prevailed, and Zenger, who had become a hero for standing up to the Crown, was freed.

These traditions from the colonial period remain today:

- The news media, both print and broadcast, relish their independence from government censorship and control.
- The news media, especially newspapers and magazines, actively try to mould government policy and mobilize public sentiment. Today this is done primarily on the editorial page.

Brian Green Canadian journalism professor who defines news as "the significant, the unusual, that which affects us."

gatekeeper Media people who influence messages en route.

concentric circle model Useful radiating model of the mass communication process.

colonial period From the founding of the colonies to the American Revolution.

Benjamin Harris Published *Publick Occurrences.*

Publick Occurrences First colonial newspaper, Boston, 1690.

John Peter Zenger Defied authorities in *New-York Weekly Journal.*

Andrew Hamilton Urged truth as defence for libel.

Zenger Trial. Printer John Peter Zenger, in the dock, won his 1735 trial for criticizing New York's royal governor. The victory fed a colonial exuberance that culminated 46 years later in winning the revolution against British rule.

- Journalists are committed to seeking truth, which was articulated as a social value in Zenger's "truth defence."
- In a capitalistic system the news media are economic entities that sometimes react in their own self-interest when their profit-making ability is threatened.

PARTISAN PERIOD

After the Revolution, newspapers divided along partisan lines. What is called the Federalist period in U.S. history is also referred to as the **partisan period** among newspaper historians. Intense partisanship characterized newspapers of the period, which spanned roughly 50 years to the 1830s.

Initially, the issue was over a constitution. Should the nation have a strong central government or remain a loose coalition of states? James Madison, Alexander Hamilton, Thomas Jefferson, John Jay and other leading thinkers exchanged ideas through articles and essays in newspapers. The *Federalist Papers,* a series of essays printed and reprinted in newspapers throughout the nation, were part of the debate.

After the Constitution was drafted, partisanship intensified, finally culminating lopsidedly when the Federalist party both controlled the Congress and had the party leader, **John Adams,** in the presidency. In firm control and bent on silencing their detractors, the Federalists ramrodded a series of laws through Congress in 1798. One of the things the **Alien and Sedition Acts** prohibited was "false, scandalous, malicious" statements about government. Using these laws, the Federalists made 25 indictments, which culminated in 10 convictions. Among those indicted was **David Brown,** a Revolutionary War veteran who felt strongly about free expression. He put up a sign in Dedham, Massachusetts: "No stamp tax. No sedition. No alien bills. No land tax. Downfall to the tyrants of America. Peace and retirement to the president [the Federalist John Adams]. Long live the vice-president [the anti-Federalist **Thomas Jefferson**] and the minority [the anti-Federalists]. May moral virtues be the basis of civil government." If only criticisms of recent presidents were so mild! But the Federalists were not of a tolerant mind. Brown was fined $400 and sentenced to 18 months in prison.

Here are traditions from the partisan period that continue today:

- Government should keep its hands off the press.
- The news media are a forum for discussion and debate, as newspapers were in the *Federalist Papers* dialogue on what form the Constitution should take.
- The news media should comment vigorously on public issues.
- Government transgressions against the news media will ultimately be met by public rejection of those committing the excesses, which has happened periodically throughout history.

partisan period From the American Revolution at least to the 1830s.

Federalist Papers Essays with diverse views on the form the new nation should take.

John Adams Federalist president.

Alien and Sedition Acts Discouraged criticism of government.

David Brown Punished for criticizing the majority party.

Thomas Jefferson Anti-Federalist president.

Benjamin Day Published *The New York Sun.*

The New York Sun First penny newspaper, 1833.

PENNY PRESS PERIOD

In 1833, when he was 22, the enterprising **Benjamin Day** started a newspaper that changed journalism: *The New York Sun.* At a penny a copy, the *Sun* was within reach of just about everybody. Other papers were expensive, an annual subscription costing

Mass Media Pioneer. When Benjamin Day launched *The New York Sun* in 1833 and sold it for one cent a copy, he ushered in an era of cheap newspapers that common people could afford. Years later his successors pushed circulation past 1 million a week.

Tracing the Story of Journalism: A timeline of journalism in the United States.
www.writesite.org/html/tracing.html

Archiving Early America: Explore the world of early America through the media of the day.
www.earlyamerica.com/earlyamerica

Federalist Papers: The original text of the *Federalist Papers.* View or download the entire plain-text version of all the *Federalist Papers.*
http://memory.loc.gov/ammem/help/constRedir.html

The New York Sun: See the *Sun* today.
www.nysun.com

as much as a full week's wages. Unlike other papers, which were distributed mostly by mail, the *Sun* was hawked every day on the streets. The *Sun*'s content was different too. It avoided the political and economic thrust of the traditional papers, concentrating instead on items of interest to common folk. The writing was simple, straightforward and easy to follow. As a motto for the *Sun,* Day came up with "It Shines for All," his pun fully intended.

Day's *Sun* was an immediate success. Naturally, it was quickly imitated, and the **penny press period** began. Partisan papers that characterized the partisan period continued, but the mainstream of American newspapers came to be in the mould of the *Sun.*

Merchants saw the unprecedented circulation of the **penny papers** as a way to reach great numbers of potential customers. Advertising revenue meant bigger papers, which attracted more readers, which attracted more advertisers. A snowballing momentum began that continues today with more and more advertising being carried by the mass media. A significant result was a shift in newspaper revenues from subscriptions to advertisers. Day, as a matter of fact, did not meet expenses by selling the *Sun* for a penny a copy. He counted on advertisers to pick up a good part of his production cost. In effect, advertisers subsidized readers, just as they do today.

Several social and economic factors, all resulting from the Industrial Revolution, made the penny press possible:

- **Industrialization.** With new steam-powered presses, hundreds of copies an hour could be printed. Earlier presses had been hand-operated.

penny press period One-cent newspapers geared to mass audience and mass advertising.

penny papers Affordable by almost everyone.

InfoPlease: Horace Greeley Encyclopedia information on the famous editor.
www.infoplease.com/ce6/people/A0821713.html

Associated Press: An online look at the first 150 years of the Associated Press wire service.
www.ap.org/pages/about/history/history.html

■ **Urbanization.** Workers flocked to the cities to work in new factories, creating a great pool of potential newspaper readers within delivery range. Until the urbanization of the 1820s and 1830s, the U.S. population had been almost wholly agricultural and scattered across the countryside. Even the most populous cities had been relatively small.

■ **Immigration.** Waves of immigrants arrived from impoverished parts of Europe. Most were eager to learn English and found that penny papers, with their simple style, were good tutors.

■ **Literacy.** As immigrants learned English, they hungered for reading material within their economic means. Also, literacy in general was increasing, which contributed to the rise of mass-circulation newspapers and magazines.

Samuel Morse Invented the telegraph.

lightning news Delivered by telegraph.

inverted pyramid Most important information first.

In 1844, late in the penny press period, **Samuel Morse** invented the telegraph. Within months, the nation was being wired. When the Civil War came in 1861, correspondents used the telegraph to get battle news to eager readers. It was called **lightning news**, delivered electrically and quickly. The Civil War also gave rise to a new convention in writing news, the **inverted pyramid**. Editors instructed their war correspondents to tell the most important information first in case telegraph lines failed—or were snipped by the enemy—as a story was being transmitted. That way, when a story was interrupted, editors would have at least a few usable sentences. The inverted pyramid, it turned out, was popular with readers because it allowed them to learn what was most important at a glance. They did not have to wade through a whole story if they were in a hurry. Also, the inverted pyramid helped editors to fit stories into the limited confines of a page—a story could be cut off at any paragraph and the most important parts remained intact. The inverted pyramid remains a standard expository form for telling event-based stories in newspapers, radio and television.

Associated Press (AP) Co-op for gathering and distributing news.

objective reporting Telling news without bias.

Several New York newspaper publishers, concerned about the escalating expense of sending reporters to gather faraway news, got together in 1848 to share stories. By sending only one reporter to represent all the newspapers, publishers cut costs dramatically. They called their co-operative venture the **Associated Press (AP)**, a predecessor of today's giant global news service. The AP introduced a new tone in news reporting. So that AP stories could be used by member newspapers of different political persuasions, reporters were told to write from a nonpartisan point of view. The result was a fact-oriented kind of news writing often called **objective reporting**. It was widely imitated and is still the dominant reporting style for event-based news stories in the U.S. news media.

There are traditions of today's news media, both print and electronic, that can be traced to the penny press period:

■ Inverted pyramid story structures.

■ Coverage and writing that appeal to a general audience, sometimes by trying to be entertaining or even sensationalistic.

■ A strong orientation to covering events, including the aggressive ferreting out of news.

■ A commitment to social improvement, which included a willingness to crusade against corruption.

■ Being on top of unfolding events and providing information to readers quickly, something made possible by the telegraph but that also came to be valued in local reporting.

■ A detached, neutral perspective in reporting events.

Yellow Period

The quest to sell more copies led to excesses that are illustrated by the Pulitzer-Hearst circulation war in New York in the 1890s, in what came to be known as the **yellow period.**

Joseph Pulitzer, a poor immigrant, made the *St. Louis Post-Dispatch* into a financial success. In 1883 Pulitzer decided to try a bigger city. He bought the *New York World* and applied his St. Louis formula. He emphasized human interest, crusaded for worthy causes and ran lots of promotional hoopla. Pulitzer's *World* also featured solid journalism. His star reporter, **Nellie Bly,** epitomized the two faces of the Pulitzer formula for journalistic success. For one story Bly feigned mental illness, entered an insane asylum and emerged with scandalous tales about how patients were treated. It was enterprising journalism of great significance. Reforms resulted. Later, showing the less serious, show-biz side of Pulitzer's formula, Nellie Bly was sent out to circle the globe in 80 days, like Jules Verne's fictitious Phileas Fogg. Her journalism stunt took 72 days.

In San Francisco, Pulitzer had a young admirer, **William Randolph Hearst.** With his father's Nevada mining fortune and mimicking Pulitzer's New York formula, Hearst made the San Francisco *Examiner* a great success. In 1895 Hearst decided to go to New York and take on the master. He bought the *New York Journal* and vowed to "out-Pulitzer" Pulitzer. The inevitable resulted. To outdo each other, Pulitzer and Hearst launched crazier and crazier stunts. Not even the comic pages escaped the competitive frenzy. Pulitzer ran the *Yellow Kid,* and then Hearst hired the cartoonist away. Pulitzer hired a new one, and both papers ran the yellow character and plastered the city with yellow promotional posters. The circulation war was nicknamed "yellow journalism," and the term came to be a derisive reference to sensational excesses in news coverage.

The yellow excesses reached a feverish peak as Hearst and Pulitzer covered the growing tensions between Spain and the United States. Fueled by hyped stories of atrocities, the tension eventually exploded in war. One story, perhaps apocryphal, epitomizes the no-holds-barred competition between Pulitzer and Hearst. Although Spain had consented to all demands by the United States, Hearst sent the artist **Frederic Remington** to Cuba to cover the situation. Remington cabled back: "Everything is quiet. There is no trouble here. There will be no war. Wish to return." Hearst replied: "Please remain. You furnish the pictures. I'll furnish the war."

The yellow tradition, however, still lives. The New York *Daily News,* founded in 1919 and almost an immediate hit, ushered in a period that some historians characterize as **jazz journalism.** It was just Hearst and Pulitzer updated in tabloid form with an emphasis on photography. Today, newspapers like the commercially successful *National Enquirer* are in the yellow tradition. This tradition is obvious too in tabloid television interview programs like *The Jerry Springer Show,* which pander to public taste for the offbeat, tawdry and sensational.

History of Journalism in Canada

In his *Guide to the Canadian News Media,* **Peter Desbarats** comments that journalism in Canada "has been closer to Main Street USA than to Fleet Street." By this he means that Canadian news traditions followed the U.S. model and not the British model. A comparison of the press periods in Canada and the United States seems to indicate that similar ideals developed, albeit at different times. **Wilfred Kesterton's**

yellow period Late 1800s; marked by sensationalism.

Joseph Pulitzer Emphasized human interest in newspapers; later sensationalized.

Nellie Bly Stunt reporter.

William Randolph Hearst Built circulation with sensationalism.

Joseph Pulitzer

William Randolph Hearst

Frederic Remington Illustrator sent by Hearst to find atrocities in Cuba.

jazz journalism 1920s, similar to yellow journalism.

Peter Desbarats Believes that Canadian journalism traditions are closely related to American traditions.

Wilfred Kesterton Canadian news historian.

Media Databank

Canadian Television News: Demassified

Like other media, news has itself demassified. Sports and entertainment news channels are also included. The number of subscribers indicated is as of August 31, 2005.

Channel	Subscribers
CBC Newsworld	9.7 million
TSN	8.1 million
Rogers Sportsnet	7.6 million
CTV Newsnet	7.5 million
The Score	5.7 million
Business News Network (BNN)	4.8 million
Star! TV	4.4 million
Pulse24 (CP24)	3.0 million

Source: CRTC, Broadcast Policy Monitoring Report 2006.

research on the history and growth of journalism in Canada is regarded as the definitive work in this area. Kesterton observes that Canadian journalists were fueled by ideals similar to those that characterized the partisan and colonial periods in U.S. history. He breaks down journalism in Canada into four periods.

transplant period First period in Canadian journalism, in which newspapers or publishers from Britain and the United States were "transplanted" to Canada.

The R.F. Outcault Society's Yellow Kid Site: Read about the creator of the Yellow Kid, America's first "comic character superstar." www.neponset.com/ yellowkid/index.htm

THE TRANSPLANT PERIOD (1752–1807). Kesterton refers to this press period as the **transplant period** because Canada's first newspapers were literally British or American newspapers or publishers that transplanted, or resettled, in Canada. *The Halifax Gazette,* Canada's first newspaper, was published by John Bushnell, who moved from Boston in 1752. The oldest newspaper in existence, the *Quebec Gazette,* was started by two printers from Philadelphia in 1764. *The Halifax Gazette* appeared every two weeks and had about 70 subscribers, while the *Quebec Gazette* had about 150 subscribers when it began publishing. As conditions improved and immigrants began moving down the St. Lawrence River and into Upper Canada, other newspapers began publishing.

As with their early American counterparts, most of the first papers in Canada were organs for the fledgling governments of British North America. Most of the content of these three- or four-page newsletter-type sheets was government information with a sprinkling of news from "back home." It was felt that for the settlements in the New World to be successful, the government needed this voice to inform and educate settlers. These newspapers were also a primitive advertising tool for early Canadian merchants. The first ads in Canadian newspapers appeared in 1752 when *The Halifax Gazette* printed three ads: for a lawyer, a clerical service and butter. While some ads appeared in these publications, the main source of income for most early newspapers was printing government information. Therefore, the success of newspapers during this time was contingent on government support, both financial and ideological. As a result, most of these papers didn't "rock the boat." In 1766, *The Halifax Gazette* dared to question the government on the new stamp tax. As a result, the government suspended the publication.

THE GROWTH PERIOD (1807–1858). Following the War of 1812, immigration in Canada flourished, particularly in Upper Canada, where the population doubled by the mid-1820s. Combine this population surge with the effects of the Industrial Revolution and you will begin to understand the changing social climate in Canada. People stopped working at home or in the fields and began to work in factories. These factors contributed to the growth of newspapers, and thus to what Kesterton refers to as the **growth period** of Canadian journalism. At the end of the War of 1812, Canada had only a handful of newspapers; by the mid-1820s, that number had risen to almost 300. Canada's first daily newspaper arrived in 1833 with Montreal's *Daily Advertiser.*

As during the penny press period in the United States, growth in immigration and urbanization created markets for Canadian newspapers. As a result, newspapers were less dependent on government revenue for their economic success. This, in turn, created a kind of "partisan" press period in Canada, as newspapers began to take sides along political lines.

The most significant event in this period in Canadian journalism history involved **Joseph Howe.** On New Year's Day, 1835, Howe published "the letter" signed by "the people" in his *Novascotian.* In the letter, he accused the local police and the lieutenant-governor of corruption. In his defence, he asked the jury "to leave an unshackled press as a legacy to your children." Despite the fact that Howe was charged with seditious libel under the criminal code of the day, and the presiding judge instructed the jurors to bring back a verdict of guilty, a jury acquitted him of libel in only 10 minutes. The jury felt that publishing something that is true shouldn't be illegal. As with the earlier American example of Zenger's *New York Journal,* the message to Canadian journalists was clear: Freedom of the press and intellectual freedom were important principles.

THIRD CANADIAN PRESS PERIOD: WESTWARD GROWTH (1858–1900). During the latter half of the 1800s, immigration and migration became two important factors in the growth of Canadian newspapers. As the Canadian population increased, it moved west and north and newspapers soon followed. Kesterton calls this the **westward growth** period of Canadian journalism. The gold rushes in the west made Victoria, British Columbia, a centre for commerce and transportation. In 1858, *The Victoria Gazette and Anglo-American* began publishing. New papers also began publishing in central and eastern Canada: the *Montreal Star* in 1869, the *Toronto Telegram* in 1876, and the *Ottawa Journal* in 1885. By the turn of the century, more than 1200 newspapers served Canada's population, which at that time stood close to 5.5 million.

This period was also a sort of "partisan period" for Canadian journalism. The debate over Confederation, the Riel rebellion, and the completion of the Canadian National Railway were the subjects of many an article. Thomas D'Arcy McGee, George Brown, and Joseph Howe were among the country's most opinionated journalists.

FOURTH CANADIAN PRESS PERIOD: THE TWENTIETH CENTURY ONWARD. In the 1900s, journalism came of age in Canada. Although immigration levels and migration

Early to Print. A snapshot of the Monday, March 23, 1752, edition of *The Halifax Gazette*—Canada's first newspaper.

growth period Second period in Canadian journalism; marked by expansion due to immigration following the War of 1812.

Joseph Howe Advocate of an unshackled press.

westward growth Third period in Canadian journalism: As Canadians moved west, so did the press.

CP The Canadian Press.

Joseph Howe: Read about this Canadian and his fight for freedom of the press. **www.collectionscanada. ca/confederation/ 023001-2350-e.html**

Thomas D'Arcy McGee: One of Canada's most opinionated journalists and a Father of Confederation. **http://www. collectionscanada.ca/ confederation/023001 -2370-e.html**

George Brown: The founder of *The Globe*. **www.collectionscanada. ca/confederation/ 023001-2309-e.html**

The Canadian Press: Home page for the co-operatively owned national news agency. There's also a link for Broadcast News. **www.cp.org**

objectivity A concept in journalism that news should be gathered and told value-free.

patterns were inconsistent due to the world wars and the Great Depression during the first half of the 20th century, improvements in technology helped the newspaper grow to new heights. This technology included better printing presses and better-quality newsprint, which helped improve the form of the newspaper. Improvements in communication and transportation helped distribution. As a result of these changes and the continuing growth of cities, the large metropolitan daily as a business enterprise became the norm for many newspapers.

News agencies arrived in Canada during this period. The Canadian Press (**CP**) was founded in 1917. A statute of Parliament officially made the Canadian Press a corporation in 1923. Today, more than 250 journalists write stories for CP, which supplies news for print and broadcast outlets.

Concepts of News

Study Preview   *The contemporary notion that news media content should be objective is relatively recent. Also, it is a notion not shared in all modern democracies. The word "objectivity" is overused and not very useful. Better is to think of journalism as the process of pursuing truth to tell truth.*

U.S. MODEL

Two phenomena in the mid-1800s, both rooted in the economics of the newspaper industry, introduced the notion of value-free news—or **objectivity**.

ASSOCIATED PRESS. As mentioned earlier in this chapter, several cost-conscious New York newspaper publishers agreed in 1848 to a joint venture to cover distant news. The Associated Press, as they called the venture, saved a lot of money. Inherent in the AP concept was that its stories needed to be nonpartisan to be usable by all of its member newspapers, whose political persuasions spanned the spectrum. The result was an emphasis on fact-driven journalism devoid of even a hint of partisanship. The same is generally true about CP (The Canadian Press) style. In *The Canadian Press Stylebook*, 12th Edition, CP claims that "everything we do must be honest, unbiased and unflinchingly fair."

NEWSPAPER ECONOMICS. A second fundamental shift cemented the AP style, often called an objective style: News became profitable—highly so. The fortune that Benjamin Day made with *The New York Sun* in the mid-1830s was puny compared with the Pulitzer, Hearst and other news empires that came within 50 years. These superpublishers saw their newspapers as money machines as much as political tools. The bottom line gradually and inevitably gained more weight. There was money to be made in presenting news in as neutral a tone as possible. By the early 20th century, when news practices became institutionalized in the first journalism textbooks and in the formation of professional organizations, the notion of a detached, neutral presentation was firmly ensconced. Ethics codes, new at the time, dismissed other approaches as unacceptable and unethical, even though they had been dominant only three generations earlier. The word "objectivity" became a newsroom mantra.

MEDIA CONGLOMERATION. By the late 20th century, the value-free approach to news was more entrenched than ever. Most news organizations had become parts of vast media empires that included government-regulated broadcast outlets. A detached, neutral tone in news content was the least apt to upset political leaders and government agencies from whom the media needed favours—like broadcast licence renewals, broadcast spectrum access, and consent for more mergers and consolidations that reduced competition and could invite scrutiny by government. As a result, the CRTC had to deal with the issue of convergence and editorial control. TVA, CTV, and CanWest Global were asked how they were planning to handle issues of newsroom policy and editorial decision making. Leonard Asper, president and CEO of CanWest Global Communications, had this vision of journalists in a converged media world: "In the future, journalists will wake up, write a story for the web, write a column, take their cameras, cover an event and do a report for TV and file a video clip for the web. What we have really acquired is a quantum leap in the product we offer advertisers and a massive, creative content-generation machine."

Quebec media giant TVA, on the other hand, wanted to keep the broadcast and print newsrooms separate, saying that "information professionals working in the newsrooms of TVA, LCN and LCN affiliates shall at no time transmit, receive, exchange or discuss information by phone, fax, Internet or other technology with information professionals working in the newsroom of Quebecor newspapers."

According to the Broadcasting Act, radio and television stations in Canada must provide varied and comprehensive coverage of significant issues. While the CRTC has no control over what happens in print newsrooms, they do have a say in what goes on in broadcast newsrooms. In its 2001 decisions concerning TVA, Global, and CTV, the CRTC's viewpoint is clear: Keep editorial decisions between multimedia platforms within conglomerates separate. To the CRTC, its favoured approach adds to objectivity and the diversity of voices within the Canadian broadcasting system.

Columbia Journalism Review: Motto: America's premier media monitor. **www.cjr.org**

CAJ: Canadian Association of Journalists' Code of Ethics is described under the "Advocacy – Education – Truth" link. **www.caj.ca**

EUROPEAN MODEL

The notion that news could be conveyed neutrally, devoid of perspective or values, was peculiarly American. In Europe, newspapers traditionally have flaunted their partisanship to attract like-minded readers. The result is flavourful, interesting reporting that flows from a point of view—and, say its defenders, is more truthful than the U.S. model. Leonard Doyle, foreign editor at *The Independent* in London, claims the European model encourages journalists to tell about events as they see them, rather than through the eyes of government officialdom, which can have its own agendas. The U.S. model, by contrast, tends merely to chronicle claims as provided by supposedly credible albeit partisan sources. There is too little attention in the U.S. model, say critics, to sorting through the claims with journalistic analysis.

In a forum sponsored by *Columbia Journalism Review,* Doyle offered striking examples of failures of the U.S. model. One was during the 2002 Afghan war. CNN quoted Pentagon authorities who said that B-52 bombers had dropped dozens of precision-targeted bombs in the Tora Bora area in an attempt to flush out terrorist mastermind Osama bin Laden. That, in itself, was accurate, but CNN missed what the Pentagon had not released: that the bombs had killed 115 people in the village of Kama Ado. The British press, less inclined to merely echo official views, told about the Kama Ado carnage—the whole story.

Doyle says that U.S. journalists' quest for "objectivity" has led to the tying of every fact to a source that can be named. This is a kind of timidity that Doyle says leaves journalists vulnerable to being duped: "The loudest demands for objectivity are made by groups or lobbies who want to ensure that they get equal time." The loudest and most persistent groups make the news. The U.S. approach, as Doyle sees it, is largely clerical and lacks the probing that would serve the audience better by coming closer to truth.

British journalists gloat that their U.S. counterparts uncritically reported the repeated but erroneous claim of President George W. Bush, in pushing for war, that Iraq possessed weapons of mass destruction. The redundancy of the message over many months fueled the early U.S. public support for the war, even though it turned out that no such weapons existed. To U.S. journalists, Doyle says: "Ask why the God of Objectivity so failed you in your hour of need." The British government had advanced the same claims about weapons of mass destruction, but many British newspapers, openly unfriendly to the government, kept casting doubt on the claim, which tempered British public enthusiasm for the Iraq war. Europeans argue that their model, which places an emphasis on judgment and analysis, yields reporting that comes nearer to truth.

Evolving News Models

How did the British and North American press end up so different? The newspaper industry in Britain, and the rest of Europe too, never consolidated on the scale of U.S. or Canadian newspapers. Historically, European papers have found profits by pandering to the political preferences of segments in the mass audience. In contrast, U.S. newspaper ownership consolidated to the point that the United States is a nation of mostly one-paper towns. Now media conglomerates have their feet also in broadcast news. The financial might of conglomerates, far greater than that of any European news organization, perpetuates itself more easily with blander news coverage. The thrust is to tell news as safely as possible, which means to seek to avoid alienating anybody—readers, advertisers and, increasingly, government.

Europeans will argue that their newspapers, characterized by reporting that reflects values, are not only livelier but also more effective. Thirty million Brits, out of a population of 58 million, read a morning newspaper—a far higher percentage than in the United States. Too, everyone agrees that British and other European audiences are better informed about public issues and more engaged.

Defining Objectivity

In North American journalism, the concept of objectivity is often extolled, but journalists back off the term when pressed. Considering that all human beings, journalists included, have personal values

The Independent: Online version of the British daily. **www.independent.co.uk**

Financial Times: You can get the headlines and introductions, but need to subscribe for most full-text articles. **http://news.ft.com/home/us**

BBC News: Round-the-clock news from around the world. **http://news.bbc.co.uk**

Michael Getler. The fact orientation (or, some say, obsession) of U.S. news has a defender in Michael Getler of *The Washington Post.* Getler says the perspective-oriented British model, dominant in much of the world, gets in the way of telling news and leaves readers suspicious about whether they're getting good information.

that influence all that they do, objectivity, being value-free, is an impossible ideal. Only someone who is totally amoral can be objective. That means that journalists can do nothing more than work at appearing to be free of any values, which requires playing word games to conceal their values. That, say critics, is a fraud perpetrated on the news audience. It also works against journalists' asking tough questions that might hint at personal values. This all suggests that the word "objective" and the concept of objectivity are so problematic that they have limited usefulness.

A more useful concept, one on which North Americans and Europeans can agree, is that journalists do their best work when they pursue news with the goal of telling truth. What is truth? **Truth** is a broad and accurate understanding, which the Europeans note is far more important than the factual detail about which American journalism obsesses. With truth as the goal, journalists can be honest about the personal values they bring to their work. When the goal is to find truth, values become secondary. In fact, journalists with different values can all have the same goal: truth.

truth A broad and accurate understanding.

Both North American and European models of news are fact-driven and committed to accuracy. The Europeans argue, however, that facts yield truth only when sorted through and subjected to analysis. *Truth,* a word for broad understanding, does not result automatically from an array of facts or quotes from shouting partisans. In short, the Europeans caution, don't confuse facts and factual accuracy with *truth,* which is broader and more important.

Journalists' Personal Values and Biases

Study Preview   *As gatekeepers, journalists make important decisions on which events, phenomena and issues are reported and which are not. The personal values that journalists bring to their work and that therefore determine which stories are told—and also how they are told—generally coincide with mainstream values.*

The journalistic ideal, an unbiased seeking of truth and an unvarnished telling of it, dictates that the work be done without partisanship. Yet, as human beings, journalists have personal values that influence all that they do, including their work. Because the news judgment decisions that journalists make are so important to an informed citizenry, we need to know what makes these people tick.

When asked whether biases exist in journalism, **David Rooney**, author of *Reporting and Writing for Canadian Journalists* and a teacher at Calgary's Mount Royal College, says, "Of course they do. No one gets through life without acquiring political attitudes and prejudices and journalists are no different in that regard. But, for the most part, conscientious reporters keep their biases out of their copy. They leave it to fellow journalists—the columnists and editorial writers—to openly advocate particular policies or ideologies."

David Rooney Believes that bias in journalism is inevitable.

A sociologist who studied stories in the American news media for 20 years, **Herbert Gans** concluded that journalists have a typical North American value system. Gans identified primary values, all in the North American mainstream, that journalists use in making news judgments:

Herbert Gans Concluded that journalists have mainstream values.

- *Ethnocentrism.* Ethnocentrism means journalists see things through their culture's eyes, which affects news coverage.
- *Commitment to democracy and capitalism.* Coverage of other governmental forms dwells on corruption, conflict, protest and bureaucratic malfunction. Gans also

ethnocentrism Seeing things on the basis of personal experience, values.

found that when they report corruption and misbehaviour in business, journalists treat these events as aberrations.

■ *Small-town pastoralism.* Like most of their fellow citizens, journalists romanticize rural life. Given similar stories from metropolitan Vancouver and tiny Estevan, Saskatchewan, editors usually opt for the small town. This helps explain the success of Wayne Rostad's long-running *On the Road Again* series on CBC.

■ *Individualism tempered by moderation.* Gans found that journalists love stories about rugged individuals who overcome adversity and defeat powerful forces. This is a value that contributes to a negative coverage of technology as something to be feared because it can stifle individuality.

■ *Social order.* Journalists cover disorder—earthquakes, catastrophes, protest marches, the disintegrating nuclear family and transgressions of laws and mores. This coverage, noted Gans, is concerned not with glamorizing disorder but with finding ways to restore order.

In the final analysis, news is the result of journalists' scanning their environment and making decisions, first on whether to cover certain events and then on how to cover them. The decisions are made against a backdrop of countless variables, many of them changing during the reporting, writing and editing processes.

Variables Affecting News

Study Preview   *The variables that determine what is reported include things beyond a journalist's control, such as how much space or time is available to tell stories. Also, a story that might receive top billing on a slow news day might not even appear on a day when an overwhelming number of major stories are breaking.*

NEWS HOLE

news hole Space for news in a newspaper after ads are inserted; also time in a newscast for news after ads.

A variable affecting what ends up being reported as news is called the **news hole**. In newspapers the news hole is the space left after the advertising department has placed in the paper all the ads it has sold. The volume of advertising determines the number of total pages, and generally, the bigger the issue, the more room for news. Newspaper editors can squeeze more stories into a fat Wednesday issue than a thin Monday issue.

In broadcasting, the news hole tends to be more consistent. A 30-minute television newscast may have room for only 22 minutes of news, but the format doesn't vary. When the advertising department doesn't sell all the seven minutes available for advertising, it usually is public-service announcements, promotional messages and program notes—not news—that pick up the slack.

NEWS FLOW AND NEWS STAFFING

flow Variation from day to day in significance of events worth covering.

Besides the news hole, the **flow** varies from day to day. A story that might be played prominently on a slow news day can be passed over entirely in the competition for space on a heavy news day.

On one of the heaviest news days of all time—June 4, 1989—death claimed Iran's Ayatollah Khomeini, a central figure in U.S. foreign policy; Chinese young people and the government were locked in a showdown in Tiananmen Square; the

Polish people were voting to reject their one-party communist political system; and a revolt was under way in the Soviet republic of Uzbekistan. That was a heavy news day, and the flow of major nation-rattling events pre-empted many stories that otherwise would have been considered news, like the grand opening that weekend of the SkyDome (now the Rogers Centre) in Toronto.

Staffing affects news coverage, for example, whether reporters are in the right place at the right time. A newsworthy event in Nigeria will receive short shrift on television if the network correspondents for Africa are occupied with a natural disaster in next-door Cameroon. A radio station's city government coverage will slip when the city hall reporter is on vacation or if the station can't afford a regular reporter at city hall.

staffing Available staff resources to cover news.

PERCEPTIONS ABOUT AUDIENCE

How a news organization perceives its audience affects news coverage. The *National Enquirer* lavishes attention on unproven cancer cures that *The Globe and Mail* treats briefly if at all. Canada's BNN (Business News Network) sees its purpose as news for viewers who have special interests in finance, the economy and business.

AVAILABILITY OF MATERIAL

The availability of photographs and video is also a factor in what ends up being news. Television is often faulted for overplaying visually titillating stories, such as fires, and underplaying or ignoring more significant stories that are not photogenic. The media are partial to stories with strong accompanying visuals, as shown with images of the Red River flooding in Manitoba, guns and gangs violence in Toronto, and the pomp and ceremony of the funeral of former prime minister Pierre Trudeau.

COMPETITION

One trigger of adrenaline for journalists is landing a scoop and, conversely, being scooped. Journalism is a competitive business, and the drive to outdo other news organizations keeps news publications and newscasts fresh with new material.

Competition has an unglamorous side. Journalists constantly monitor each other to identify events that they missed and that they need to catch up on to be competitive. This catch-up aspect of the news business contributes to similarities in coverage, which scholar Leon Sigal calls the **consensible nature of news**. It also is called "pack" or "herd" journalism.

consensible nature of news News organization second-guessing competition in deciding coverage.

Influences on News

Study Preview   *The subtlety of most attempts outside the newsroom to control news coverage makes them difficult to count. Even one is too many. External influence undermines journalists as honest brokers of news and information.*

ADVERTISER INFLUENCE

Special interests sometimes try to squelch stories or insist on self-serving angles. Usually, these attempts are made quietly, even tacitly, among executives—country-club decision making. Sometimes the pressure is exerted on media advertising people, who quietly exert influence on the newsroom.

When a Wyoming grocery store was concerned over a warning from a state agency that Bon Vivant vichyssoise was possibly tainted with botulism, the advertising manager at the *Laramie Boomerang,* the only newspaper in town, kept the story out of the paper. A Laramie radio station that aired the story lost the grocery store's advertising.

To their credit, most news organizations place allegiance to their audiences ahead of pleasing advertisers, as Terry Berger, president of an advertising agency representing the Brazilian airline Varig, found out from the *Condé Nast Traveler,* a travel magazine. After an article on air pollution in Rio de Janeiro, Berger wrote this to the magazine: "Is your editorial policy then to see how quickly you can alienate present and potential advertisers and at the same time convince your readers to stick closer to home? I really think that if you continue with this kind of editorial information, you are doing both your readers and your advertisers a disservice. For this kind of information, people read *The New York Times.* I therefore find it necessary to remove the *Condé Nast Traveler* from Varig's media schedule." Unintimidated, the magazine's editor, Harold Evans, did not recant. Not only did Evans print the letter, but he followed with this comment: "Mrs. Berger is, of course, entitled to use her judgment about where she advertises Brazil's national airline. I write not about that narrow commercial issue, but about her assertion that it is a disservice to readers and advertisers for us to print true but unattractive facts when they are relevant. This goes to the heart of the editorial policy of this magazine. . . . We rejoice in the enrichments of travel, but our aim is to give readers the fullest information, frankly and fairly, so they can make their own judgments."

David Rooney explains the strained relationship between advertiser and journalist like this: "Once an advertiser understands that news stories are about placing people, events, and comments in a broadly understood context and not about taking one side or another in a dispute, the less likely it is that he or she will feel abandoned or beleaguered by the local media."

Condé Nast Traveler: Find out what kind of news the audience of this magazine gets.

www.concierge.com/ cntraveler

CORPORATE POLICY

No matter how committed journalists may be to truth seeking and truth telling, the people in charge have the final word on matters big and small. It is owners, publishers, general managers and their immediate lieutenants who are in charge. Their corporate responsibilities dictate that they are business executives before all else, even if once they were journalists. Executives sometimes make self-serving decisions on coverage that gall the journalists who work for them, but that is how chains of command work.

Lowell Bergman, former executive producer at *60 Minutes,* recalls his days at CBS: "You could not do a story about a supplier or major advertiser. You could try to do it, but you were taking a lot of risks getting close to the limit." At both ABC and CBS, Bergman said, he was told that the networks would not initiate a critical story about the business practices and histories of National Football League team owners. The networks, of course, stood to derive handsome revenue from airing NFL games if they were awarded contracts for play-by-play coverage.

Admonitions not to go near certain stories are not in written policy, although they are real. ABC newspeople got an unusual overt reminder when Michael Eisner, then chair of Disney, which owns ABC, said in an interview on the NPR program *Fresh Air,* "I would prefer ABC not to cover Disney. I think it's inappropriate." Eisner went on to say that *ABC News* knew of his preference.

In fairness it must be said that media owners generally are sensitive to their truth-seeking and truth-telling journalistic responsibilities and assiduously avoid calling the shots on news coverage. Those who answer to a call other than journalistic soundness are within their court-recognized First Amendment rights, which allow media people to exercise their freedom responsibly as well as irresponsibly. Journalists who are bothered by wrong-headed news decisions have three choices: persuade wayward owners of the error of their ways, comply with directives, or quit and go to work for a more respectable journalistic organization.

SOURCE PRESSURE

Journalists sometimes feel external pressure directly. At the courthouse, valuable sources turn cold after a story appears that they don't like. A tearful husband begs an editor not to use his wife's name in a story that points to her as a bank embezzler. A bottle of Canadian Club arrives at Christmas from a sports publicist who says she appreciates the excellent coverage over the past year. Most journalists will tell you that their commitment to truth overrides external assaults on their autonomy. Even so, external pressures exist.

The relationship between journalists and publicists can be troublesome. In general, the relationship works well. Publicists want news coverage for their clients and therefore provide information and help reporters to line up interviews. Some publicists, however, are more committed to advancing their clients' interests than to advancing truth, and they work to manipulate journalists into providing coverage that unduly glorifies their clients.

Staging events is a publicity tactic to gain news coverage that a cause would not otherwise attract. Some staged events are obvious hucksterism, such as flagpole-sitting stunts by celebrity disc jockeys. Covering such events is usually part of the softer side of news and, in the spirit of fun and games and diversion, is relatively harmless.

Of more serious concern are staged events about which publicists create a mirage of significance to suck journalists and the public into giving more attention than the event deserves. For example, consider the following:

- The false impression created when hundreds of federal workers are released from work for an hour to see an incumbent's campaign speech outside a government office building.
- The contrived photo opportunity at which people, props and lighting are carefully, even meticulously, arranged to create an image on television.
- Stunts that bring attention to a new product and give it an undeserved boost in the marketplace.

Staged events distort a balanced journalistic portrayal of the world. Worse, they divert attention from truly significant events.

You Be the Producer: This game from CNN shows you that news producing is not a job for the decision-impaired.
www.cnn.com/EVENTS/ 1996/anniversary/how. things.work/producer. game

Canadians and the News Media: Read all about Canadians and the love . . . and perception . . . of news online.
www.cmrcccrm.ca/ english/reportcard2004/ 01.html

Case Study

Diversity: Women Are Still Missing as News Sources

Women make up slightly more than half of the population, but you would never know it if your news comes from television, the internet or newspapers.

Women are particularly absent in coverage of politics, the military, and foreign policy, according to a study released in 2005 by the Project for Excellence in Journalism, a Washington-based think tank affiliated with the Columbia University Graduate School of Journalism. Women are most likely to be included in feature stories about children, celebrities and homemaking.

The study examined nearly 17 000 news reports by 45 different news outlets during 20 randomly selected days over 9 months in 2004. Three-quarters of all stories studied contained at least one male source. Just one-third contained a female source. The sourcing gap widened as the number of sources in a story increased. Reporters were more than three times as likely to cite two or more men within a news story as to cite at least two women. "Finding a male as the best first source does not apparently lead a journalist to look for a female as the second or third source," the report said. The worst offenders were cable television and PBS, and newspapers gave women the most exposure.

The dismal trend of using few women as sources in news stories hasn't changed much since it was first studied in 1989. A series of studies beginning that year found that women were mentioned less than 25 percent of the time on the front pages of newspapers, and those who were mentioned were often of a lower socioeconomic status than male sources. A 2000 study of news coverage of the military found that civilian experts and politicians commenting on military stories almost never are women. Research by Canadians Gertrude Robinson and Armande Saint Jean for the International Federation of Journalists echoes the findings of these studies. Their 2001 investigation found that only 28 percent of print journalists and 37 percent of broadcast journalists are female.

The London-based Media Diversity Institute says that women are further discriminated against when they are members of minority ethnic communities: "When individuals are mentioned in stories less than 3 percent of them are women, which is three and half times less than men at 35 percent. The majority of women appear in roles that comply with the dominant patriarchal pattern—women are mostly victims and witnesses of events."

Authority Figure. A United Nations representative, unusual in being a woman, addresses a refugee crisis in Jordan. Study after study of media coverage find women represented much less in the news than in their growing presence in political, research and academic leadership.

What Do You Think?

1. Should women be quoted as authorities in stories about the military? Why or why not?
2. Does the media's lack of female sources in news stories reflect and/or reinforce existing cultural beliefs and values? If so, how?
3. Could the media, as agenda-setters, change the way women are regarded in society?

Are you up to the challenge? See how well you can diversify a newsroom by playing the interactive game at www.maynardije. org/resources/game.

Media Databank

Where Do Canadians Go for News and How Do They Define Trust?

Here is a summary of findings of the *Report Card on Canadian News Media,* according to a 2004 Canadian Media Research Consortium telephone survey of 3012 Canadians. The research was conducted by researchers from the University of British Columbia Graduate School of Journalism, The York/Ryerson Joint Graduate Program in Communication and Culture, and the Communications Program at Laval University.

Media used for news and information:

TV	67%
Newspapers	42%
Radio	57%
Internet	33%

The survey also found that the most important factors influencing the perception of trust included:

Accuracy	33%
Impartiality	32%
Credibility	16%
Ownership	15%

Source: Canadian Media Research Consortium, Report Card on Canadian News Media, 2004.

Journalism Trends

Study Preview   *The explosion of 24/7 news on television and the internet is transforming news gathering and redefining news practices and audience expectations. Traditional avenues for news, sometimes called mainstream media, were shaken in the 2004 political campaign by individuals, mostly without journalistic training, generally operating alone, who created hundreds of blog sites. Bloggers offer an interconnected web of fascinating reading. Sometimes they score scoops.*

CNN: Largest global staff in television reporting.
www.cnn.com

CTV Newsnet: Online news, 24/7.
www.ctvnewsnet.com

CBC Newsworld: News 24/7 from the Canadian Broadcasting Corporation.
www.newsworld.ca

NONSTOP COVERAGE

Reporters for news agencies were a breed apart through most of the 20th century. In contrast to most newspaper reporters, who had one deadline a day, agency reporters sent dispatches to hundreds of news organizations, each with its own deadlines. Agency reporters literally had a deadline every minute.

The advent of all-news radio and then all the demassified 24/7 news channels expanded **nonstop coverage** beyond the news agencies. This is no better illustrated than on Parliament Hill where reporters race from an event or interview to a camera for a live stand-up report, often ad-libbing from notes scribbled on the run, and then, adrenaline surging, run back to sources for a new angle or event. This is event-based reporting, which emphasizes timely reports but which has a downside. Going on air a dozen times a day, perhaps more when the news flow is heavy or especially

nonstop coverage News reporting geared to ever-present deadlines, as 24/7 formats.

significant, stand-up reporters have scant time to think through implications and context. Theirs is a race to cover events more than to provide understanding. This too was a classic criticism of the news agencies.

In short, nonstop coverage, whatever the advantage of keeping people on top of breaking events, has shortcomings. The pressure for new angles tends to elevate the trivial. Also, context and understanding are sacrificed.

LIVE NEWS

Over the past 150 years, the news media have evolved standard and accepted practices. These practices, taught in journalism schools and institutionalized in codes of ethics, guide reporters and editors in preparing their summaries and wrap-ups. In general, the traditional practices worked well when newspapers were the dominant news medium, and they worked well in broadcasting too—until the advent of highly portable, lightweight equipment that enabled broadcasters to carry news events live, bypassing the traditional editing process.

Investigative Reporters and Editors: Provides educational services to reporters, editors and others interested in investigative journalism. **www.ire.org**

With television cameras focused on the towers of the World Trade Center as they turned into infernos in the 2001 terrorist attack, trapped people began jumping from windows hundreds of feet above ground. The plunges were desperate and fatal, and audiences viewing the scene live were shocked and horrified. Neither the video nor still photographs were included in some later newscasts or newspapers.

UNEDITED BLOGS

blog An amateur website, generally personal in nature, often focused on a narrow subject, such as politics. Short for "web log."

When the *Columbia Journalism Review* created a website for commentary on reporting of the 2004 presidential campaign, the magazine went out of its way to distance the new site from the thousands of web log sites, called **blogs**, on which amateurs post whatever is on their minds. No, said *CJR*, its website (http://campaigndesk.org) would be held to the highest journalistic standards. Their concern was that a lot of irresponsible content gets posted on the web by people without any journalistic training or sense of journalistic standards. The web has made it possible for anyone to create a blog that is as easily accessible as are sites from news organizations that consciously seek to go about journalism right.

Greg Oliver Wrestling journalist.

No gnashing of teeth, however, will make blogs go away—and their impact is substantial. Blog rumours, gossip and speculation, even when untrue, gain such currency that the mainstream media cannot ignore them. It's become a cliché, drawn from the tail-wags-dog metaphor, that blogs can wag the media.

Bob Woodward Bernstein's colleague in the Watergate revelations.

EXPLORATORY NEWS

Carl Bernstein *Washington Post* reporter who dug up Watergate.

Watergate Reporting of the Nixon administration scandal.

investigative reporting Enterprise reporting that reveals new information, often startling; most often these are stories that official sources would rather not have told.

Although in-depth reporting has deep roots, the thrust of U.S. journalism until the 1960s was a chronicling of events: meetings, speeches, crimes, deaths and catastrophes. That changed dramatically in 1972. Two persistent *Washington Post* reporters, **Bob Woodward** and **Carl Bernstein**, not only covered a break-in at the Democratic national headquarters, at a building called the Watergate, but also linked the crime to the White House of Republican President Richard Nixon. The morality questions inherent in the reporting forced Nixon to resign. Twenty-five aides went to jail. The **Watergate** scandal created an enthusiasm for **investigative reporting** and in-depth approaches to news that went far beyond mere chronicling, which is relatively easy to do and, alas, relatively superficial.

Media People

Greg Oliver

Quebecor Media's Canoe is an excellent example of the recent emergence of online journalism. Canoe is a web portal for all kinds of online news and information. The "Sports" link from www.canoe.ca will take you to SLAM! Sports, which in turn will take you to the place **Greg Oliver** has called home since 1996: the SLAM! Wrestling page.

Oliver's been writing about pro wrestling since 1985 when, as a high-school student, he created *The Canadian Wrestling Report,* a monthly newsletter that he published and marketed out of his basement for five years. Then, after graduating from Toronto's Ryerson University, Oliver went to work for the *Toronto Sun.* He has also written three books for ECW Press: *The Pro Wrestling Hall of Fame: The Canadians, The Pro Wrestling Hall of Fame: The Tag Teams* and *The Pro Wrestling Hall of Fame: The Heels.*

But is this legitimate journalism? Greg Oliver thinks so. "SLAM! Wrestling is proof that pro wrestling journalism doesn't need to be an oxymoron. We're legitimate journalists. We just happen to write about wrestling. Wrestlers are fascinating people with fascinating tales. Isn't that what journalism is all about? Journalism is about telling stories. Sure, it's a worked sport, but how is it any different than an actor trying to get his or her break or the young baseball player trying to break into the majors? It's human interest in the end, and that's what any good story should be. We're not rumour mongers. Our strength is talking to people and telling their stories."

Oliver will always remember the biggest story he broke: "Nothing has ever compared to the night Owen Hart died. I called the *Calgary Sun* within seconds to get the ball rolling. I penned a column that night on my own personal experiences with Owen, then led the site to its biggest numbers ever—the only time wrestling was ever the top sport on the SLAM! Sports site, dislodging the perennial number one: hockey."

Greg Oliver (left)

Writing for SLAM! Wrestling has offered Oliver the chance to apply his love of wrestling in many different ways. He's not only a writer, but also an editor and mentor to other aspiring wrestling journalists. "I'm the guy assigning stories, shepherding new writers, offering editing advice, or setting up interviews for other people. I enjoy that as much as I do writing. But every now and then I get a real urge to write."

Oliver's advice to would-be wrestling writers? "Wrestling journalism is about more than your opinion. It takes real skill to interview somebody and to check your sources and facts and create some good writing. You need to be able to develop suggestions and ideas for stories."

Is SLAM! Wrestling true journalism? While many critics and mainstream journalists may not appreciate it, fans certainly do. SLAM! Wrestling gets approximately 50 000 page views a day.

SOFT NEWS

In contrast to hard investigative reporting came a simultaneous trend toward **soft news**. This included consumer-help stories, lifestyle tips, entertainment news and off-beat gee-whiz items often of a sensational sort. The celebrity-oriented *National Enquirer,* whose circulation skyrocketed in the 1960s, was the progenitor of the trend. Time Life launched *People* magazine. The staid *New York Times* created *Us.* Newspaper research found that readers liked soft stuff. Soon many dailies added

soft news Geared to satisfying audience's information wants, not needs.

"People" columns. The television show *Entertainment Tonight Canada* focuses on glamour and glitz, usually as a follow-up to the evening news on many Global stations.

War Zones: Combat Reporting

Study Preview   *The need in a democracy for people to be informed doesn't square easily with military necessity in time of war. The United States has tried a wide range of policies for war coverage. The latest—embedded reporters in the 2003 Iraq war—generally worked well from the military, media and public perspectives. All the historic media–government arrangements for war coverage, however, raise the looming question of how global media serving international audiences can be faithful both to truth and to competing national causes.*

War Stories: An interactive exhibition from the Newseum.
www.newseum.org/ warstories

South Asian Journalists Association: Tips on War Reporting.
www.saja.org/ tipsreportingwar.html

War is a danger zone for journalists. The Committee to Protect Journalists, which tracks reporters in peril, tallied 54 reporters killed doing their work in 2004—23 in Iraq alone—compared to 13 in 2003. In addition, 22 journalists were kidnapped in Iraq.

EARLY LESSONS

The struggle to find ways for journalists to report from the battlefield without getting in the way or jeopardizing operations is not recent.

In World War II, correspondents wore uniforms with the rank of captain and usually had a driver and a Jeep. The reporters generated lots of field coverage, but the reporting, reflecting the highly patriotic spirit of the times, as evidenced by the reporters' actually wearing military uniforms, was hardly dispassionate and sometimes propagandist.

VIETNAM REPORTING

rice-roots reporting
Uncensored field reporting from the Vietnam War.

Reporters had great freedom in reporting the Vietnam War in the 1960s and 1970s. Almost at will, reporters could link up with South Vietnamese or U.S. units and go on patrols. The result, dubbed **rice-roots reporting**, included lots of negative stories on what was, in fact, an unsuccessful military campaign that was unpopular among many troops and a growing majority at home. For the first time the reporting was filmed for television, with gruesome footage being pumped by the networks into living rooms across the nation on the evening news, deepening opposition to the war.

Commanders didn't like negative reports, which some blamed for losing the public's support for the war. In the end, demoralized, the United States withdrew in defeat—the first war the nation had lost in its history. For the next wars, relatively quick incursions, the Pentagon had new rules. In 1983, when the United States took over the Caribbean nation of Grenada, a naval blockade kept reporters out. The war, secretly planned, surprised the news media. Scrambling to get on top of the story but barred from the action, enterprising reporters hired small boats to run the blockade but were intercepted.

POOL SYSTEM

Major newspapers, the networks and news agencies protested loudly at being excluded. Acknowledging that the policy had ridden roughshod over the democratic principles on which the nation was founded, with an informed electorate essential for the system to work, the Pentagon agreed to sit down with news media leaders to devise new ground rules. The result was a **pool system**, in which a corps of reporters would be on call on a rotating basis to be shuttled to combat areas on short notice for the next quick war.

In 1989, when U.S. forces invaded Panama to capture dictator Manuel Noriega on drug charges, the Pentagon activated the pool system and took reporters along. Top military commanders, however, still smarting from their Vietnam experience and blaming the news media, carefully controlled the reporters and their access to information. Army drivers took reporters only to secure areas. For a while reporters were locked in a windowless building and had only information the Army fed them. When the military had accomplished its mission, news organizations again protested. Plainly, the Pentagon had failed again to find a system that met both military necessity and democratic principles.

pool system Reporters chosen on a rotating basis to cover an event to which access is limited.

EMBEDDED REPORTERS

The 2003 Iraq war was covered by journalists like no other. The U.S. government, after flip-flopping on rules for war correspondents for 50 years, seemed to recognize the futility of trying to manipulate information in the digital age. Months before the invasion, the Pentagon chief for media relations, Victoria Clarke, invited news organizations to send reporters to special combat mini-courses to get up to speed—and also into physical shape—to go to war with combat units. These reporters would be

CNN-Equipped Humvee. The news network CNN dispatched 250 reporters, producers and photographers to cover the 2003 Iraq war. Equipment included a fleet of Humvees for journalists embedded with combat units to transmit live via satellite to Atlanta and New York for, in some cases, real-time coverage.

embeds A 2003 Iraq war term for reporters accompanying, or embedded with, U.S. military combat units.

embedded in the units to cover combat for the duration of hostilities. The reporters, called **embeds**, would need to supply their own equipment, including vehicles, but would be free to tell the story of the war as they saw it. Commanders were told to let the cameras roll whenever the journalists wanted.

Ground rules were few. Among them was not to disclose unit positions, lest the enemy be tipped to locations. Also, the Pentagon warned that it might need to black out reports for "operational security, success of the mission, and the safety of the people involved."

News organizations sent hundreds of reporters to Pentagon boot camps. Time Warner set aside $30 million to cover the war and dispatched Eason Jordan, CNN's chief news executive, to the Middle East to buy a fleet of Humvees to haul crews and their equipment, including satellite uplink dishes, into combat.

How well did the embedded reporter system work?

The Pentagon was pleased. Yes, the embeds showed the ugliness of war, as well as gaffes. But the invasion went well for the United States and its allies, and the Pentagon concluded that the coverage, perceived by the public as honest and independent, contributed to public enthusiasm for the war during the initial combat phase. The news media were pleased, too, remembering that only 10 years earlier, in the Kuwait war, reporters were kept away from combat and had access only to information fed to them at headquarters briefings.

Critics said the embeds were too limited in their perspective, lacking an overview, and that, losing objectivity, they picked up the gung-ho spirit of the units they were assigned to. The criticism, however, missed the fact that reporters were in regular contact with editors and producers in their home newsrooms, as well as in field newsrooms, who fed them information from other sources. Also, reports from the embeds were integrated into newscasts and stories that presented the broad picture.

Could the embedded system work better? Walter Cronkite, whose war reporting experience went back to World War II, noted that embeds, almost all with frontline units, missed details in the haste of moving forward. He suggested that reporters be assigned to follow up to verify information and ask questions that frontline embeds didn't have time to pursue.

Whatever the critics say, embedded journalism in times of war is likely here to stay. While CBC News did not allow its journalists to embed, Tony Burman, editor-in-chief of CBC News, said, "The introduction of technology, the video phone, the satellite phone, the incredible ease to satellite feeds, pictures, sound reports and obviously the whole embedding experience, the whole notion that you can, in fact, get live pictures from the front, is quite unprecedented." The president of CTV News, Robert G. Hurst, says that in the future, we may see battles live on TV and journalists embedded on both sides of a conflict. Bill Schiller, formerly the foreign editor for the *Toronto Star,* says that would not be in the best interests of journalism. He says that embedded journalists do no more than serve the interests of the status quo—in the case of the 2003 Iraq war, the Pentagon: "Editorial independence is everything. It's fundamental to what we do, no matter how good the pictures are."

CHAPTER 8 WRAP-UP

Journalism is an art, not a science. Judgments, rather than formulas, determine which events and issues are reported and how—and no two journalists approach any story exactly the same way. This leaves the whole process of gathering and telling news subject to second-guessing and criticism. Journalists ask themselves all the time whether there are ways to do a better job. All journalists can do is try to find truth and to relate it accurately. Even then, the complexity of modern news-gathering—which involves many people, each with an opportunity to change or even kill a story—includes dozens of points at which inaccuracy and imprecision can creep into a story that started out well.

QUESTIONS FOR REVIEW

1. What contemporary news practices are rooted in the various press periods in U.S. and Canadian history?
2. What is the core difference between the U.S. and European concepts of news?
3. What variables beyond journalists' control affect news?
4. What pressures from outside the media affect news reporting?
5. What responsibilities do journalists have as gatekeepers?
6. Is there a contradiction between the two contemporary journalistic trends of exploratory reporting and soft news?
7. How has convergence affected journalism in Canada?

QUESTIONS FOR CRITICAL THINKING

1. The 19-year-old son of the premier of a troubled Central American country in which the CIA has deep involvement died, perhaps of a drug overdose, aboard a Northwest Airlines plane en route from Tokyo to Singapore. On the plane was a young female country-western singer, his frequent companion in recent weeks. The plane was a Boeing 747 manufactured in Washington state. Northwest's corporate headquarters is in Minnesota. The death occurred at 4 a.m. Eastern time. Consider the six elements of news—proximity, prominence, timeliness, consequence, currency and drama—and discuss how this event might be reported on morning television newscasts in Miami, Minneapolis, Nashville, Seattle and the District of Columbia. How about in Managua? Singapore? Tokyo? Rome? Istanbul? Johannesburg? What if the victim were an ordinary college student? What if the death occurred a week ago?
2. Explain news judgment.
3. How do the news hole and news flow affect what is reported in the news media?
4. *Time* and *Maclean's* carry cover stories on the same subject one week. Does this indicate that executives of the magazine have conspired, or is it more likely to be caused by what Leon Sigal calls *the consensible nature of news*?
5. How does the nature of news provide ammunition to conservatives to criticize the news media as leftist promoters of change?
6. Discuss whether the news media reflect mainstream North American values. Do you see evidence in your news media of an underlying belief

that democracy, capitalism, rural small-town life, individualism and moderation are virtues?

7. Do you feel that the mass media revel in disorder? Consider Herbert Gans's view that the media cover disorder from the perspective of identifying ways to restore order.

8. If a college president calls a news conference and makes a major announcement, who are the gatekeepers who determine how the announcement is covered in the campus newspaper?

DEEPENING YOUR MEDIA LITERACY

How important is freedom of the press to you?

Step 1   Write down your definition of freedom of the press.

Dig Deeper

Step 2   Imagine that you are a blogger covering Parliament Hill and you have uncovered a scandal. Compare how you would cover it with freedom of the press and how that would change without freedom of the press.

What Do You think?

Step 3   Answer these questions:

1. If you exercise freedom of the press irresponsibly, should your right be revoked?

2. How important is editorial independence to freedom of the press?

3. Do you think freedom of the press and the Canadian *Charter of Rights and Freedoms* are important to you and your life as a Canadian? Are they more important to a student, to a parent, to a businessperson, to a journalist, to a politician, to a religious person, to a person who belongs to a minority?

4. How would your life change without freedom of the press?

KEEPING UP TO DATE

Among publications that keep current on journalistic issues are *Columbia Journalism Review, Quill, American Journalism Review,* and *Editor & Publisher.*

Bridging the gap between scholarly and professional work is *Newspaper Research Journal.*

FOR FURTHER LEARNING

Angus Reid Group. *Canadians and the News Media* (Canadian Corporate News, 1998).

Jim Bawden. "Taking Care of Business." *Starweek Magazine* (May 17, 1997).

L. Brent Bozell III and Brent H. Baker, editors. *And That's the Way It Isn't: A Reference Guide to Media Bias* (Media Research Center, 1990).

Ben Bradlee. *A Good Life: Newspapering and Other Stories* (Simon & Schuster, 1996).

"Brits vs. Yanks: Who Does Journalism Right?" *Columbia Journalism Review* (May/June 2004): 44–49.

Canada. *Kent Commission on Newspapers, Canadian News Services,* Volume 6 (Ottawa: Supply and Services, 1981).

Canada. *Kent Commission on Newspapers, The Journalists,* Volume 2 (Ottawa: Supply and Services, 1981).

Canadian Media Research Consortium. *Report Card on Canadian News Media* (CMRC, 2004). Available online at http://www.cmrcccrm.ca/english/reportcard2004/01.html.

Robert Cribb. "Iraqi War Reshaped Reporting." *Toronto Star* (April 16, 2003).

James L. Crouthamel. *Bennett's New York Herald and the Rise of the Popular Press* (Syracuse University Press, 1989).

Daniel J. Czitrom. *Media and the American Mind: From Morse to McLuhan* (University of North Carolina Press, 1982).

Peter Desbarats. *Guide to the Canadian News Media* (Harcourt Brace, 1990).

Hazel Dicken-Garcia. *Journalistic Standards in the Nineteenth Century* (University of Wisconsin Press, 1989).

Rosie DiManno. "Too Many Critics Shooting the Messenger in Iraq." *Toronto Star* (March 26, 2004).

Edwin and Michael Emery. *The Press and America,* Fourth edition (Prentice Hall, 1984).

Kathleen L. Endress. "Help-Wanted Finale: *Editor & Publisher* Frames Civil Rights Issue." *Journalism and Mass Communication Quarterly* (Spring 2004): 7–21.

Mark Fishman. *Manufacturing the News* (University of Texas Press, 1980).

Thomas L. Friedman. *From Beirut to Jerusalem* (Farrar, Straus & Giroux, 1989).

Herbert J. Gans. *Deciding What's News: A Study of* CBS Evening News, NBC Nightly News, Newsweek *and* Time (Pantheon, 1979).

Brian Green. *Canadian Broadcast News: The Basics* (Harcourt Canada, 2001).

Jane T. Harrigan. *Read All About It! A Day in the Life of a Metropolitan Newspaper* (Globe Pequot Press, 1987).

Michael Higgins. "Vigilant, Honest Media Imperative in a War." *The Record,* Kitchener-Waterloo (March 25, 2003).

Norman E. Isaacs. *Untended Gates: The Mismanaged Press* (Columbia University Press, 1986).

Ryszard Kapuscinski. *The Soccer War* (Alfred A. Knopf, 1991).

H.G. Kariel and L.A. Rosenvall. *Places in the News: A Study of News Flows* (Carleton University Press, 1995).

Wilfred Kesterton. *A History of Journalism in Canada* (McClelland and Stewart, 1967).

Anne Kingston. "Pamela Wallin's Wild Kingdom." *Saturday Night* (June 1997).

Brooke Kroeger. *Nellie Bly: Daredevil, Reporter, Feminist* (Random House, 1994).

Molly Moore. *A Woman at War: Storming Kuwait with the U.S. Marines* (Scribner's, 1993).

Michael Parenti. *Inventing Reality: The Politics of the Mass Media* (St. Martin's, 1988).

Nancy Roberts. *The Press and America: An Interpretive History of the Mass Media,* Eighth edition (Allyn & Bacon, 1997).

David F. Rooney. *Reporting and Writing for Canadian Journalists* (Prentice Hall, 2001).

Karenna Gore Schiff. *Lighting the Way: Nine Women Who Changed Modern America* (Miramax, 2006).

Michael Schudson. *Discovering the News: A Social History of American Newspapers* (Basic Books, 1978).

Pamela J. Shoemaker with Elizabeth Kay Mayfield. *Building a Theory of News Content: A Synthesis of Current Approaches.* Journalism Monographs, No. 103 (June 1987.

David Walkis, editor. *Killed: Great Journalism Too Hot to Print* (Nation, 2004).

David H. Weaver and G. Cleveland Wilhoit. *The American Journalist: A Portrait of U.S. News People and Their Work,* 2nd edition (Indiana University Press, 1991).

Anthony Wilson-Smith. "Wall to Wall News." *Maclean's* (March 2, 1998).

Bob Woodward and Carl Bernstein. *All the President's Men* (Simon & Schuster, 1974).

Antonia Zerbisias. "The News about TV News." *Toronto Star* (July 20, 1997).

Public Relations

Media in Theory

Public Relations as "Sleaze"?

Public relations operates in the realm of what Canadian Joyce Nelson calls the "legitimacy gap" in her book *The Sultans of Sleaze: Public Relations and the Media.* The term *legitimacy gap* was coined by business professor Prakash Sethi to describe the difference between a corporate image and the corporate reality. Nelson applies Jungian psychology to the term in her analysis of public relations. She argues that a corporation has two sides: a persona and a shadow. The persona is its corporate image, the positive image that is promoted via **advertising**; the shadow is its dark side, which is not usually seen in the news media and certainly not in advertising. According to Nelson, the shadow may include "the ways in which [the corporation's] activities infringe upon our health and safety, our environment, [and contribute] to our oppression or to that of others, despite what all their persona-

related activity would like us to believe." When something happens that threatens the persona and reveals the shadow of a corporation, public relations professionals are called to fix the problem.

Nelson provides an interesting example. In a two-week period during the summer of 1981, Ontario Hydro was involved in two environmental accidents. First, it dumped heavy water containing 3500 curies of radiation into the Ottawa River. The event received front-page coverage in *The Globe and Mail* and was reported on television news. A week later, almost 4000 gallons (18 000 litres) of radioactive water were accidentally spilled at Ontario Hydro's Bruce nuclear power plant. More than twice as much tritium—about 8000 curies—was released in the accident. These incidents created a problem for Ontario Hydro. The nuclear power industry's persona centres on concern for public safety and the environment. But Nelson argues that these spills raised questions about the safety of nuclear power, thus revealing Hydro's shadow.

The second incident received less coverage in both *The Globe and Mail* and the *Toronto Star.* One of the reasons for this may have been "information overload"; perhaps the news media were simply tired of writing about problems at nuclear power plants. According to Nelson, another reason the second accident received less negative coverage had to do with the well-crafted press release that ended up as a news story in the *Toronto Star.* Consider the lead of the news story: "Armed with mops, pails and pumps, an Ontario Hydro crew has recovered 3400 gallons of radioactive heavy water at the Bruce

Nuclear Power Plant." This passage succeeds in diverting attention from the accident by focusing instead on the cleanup. Any suspicions the reader may have about the corporation's shadow are discarded. The story goes on to outline the cost of the cleanup in detail, which underlines Hydro's commitment to protecting the environment, whatever the cost, and thus reinforces its corporate image, or persona. The story makes no mention of damage to the surrounding area.

The Canadian Public Relations Society would agree—and disagree—with Nelson's ideas. In the article "Truth Pays Dividends with Public," **Jean Valin** argues that up to 50 percent of the public will not believe most media messages due to a lack of trust of the media. However, Valin discounts Nelson's idea that public relations is "smoke and mirrors." She says that, in the end, "organizations will always be well served by telling the truth. It takes a long time to build your credibility and an even longer time to rebuild it . . . this provides all the more reason to practice good public relations and avoid the pitfalls of manipulation and disinformation—honesty pays."

Importance of Public Relations

Study Preview *Public relations is a persuasive communication tool that people can use to motivate other people and institutions to help them achieve their goals.*

Defining Public Relations

Edward Bernays, the public relations pioneer, lamented how loosely the term **public relations** is used. To illustrate his concern, Bernays told about a young woman who approached him for career advice. He asked her what she did for a living. "I'm in public relations," she said. He pressed her for details, and she explained that she handed out circulars in Harvard Square. Bernays was dismayed at how casually people regard the work of public relations. The Canadian Public Relations Society says that public relations is "the management function which evaluates public attitudes, identifies the policies of an individual or organization with the public interest, and plans and executes a program of action to earn public understanding and acceptance." An Ipsos Reid poll, released in 2000, claimed that 96 percent of Canadian CEOs felt that good public relations is essential for businesses today.

Four steps are necessary for public relations to accomplish its goals:

Joyce Nelson Says public relations has two sides: the shadow and the persona.

advertising Unlike public relations, advertising seeks to sell a product or service.

Jean Valin Believes organizations are served best when they tell the truth.

public relations A management tool to establish beneficial relationships.

IDENTIFY EXISTING RELATIONSHIPS. In modern society, institutions have many relationships. A college, for example, has relationships with its students, its faculty, its staff, its alumni, its benefactors, the neighbourhood, the community, the legislature, other colleges, accreditors of its programs, perhaps unions. The list could go on and on. Each of these constituencies is called a public—hence the term *public relations*.

EVALUATE THE RELATIONSHIPS. Through research, the public relations practitioner studies these relationships to determine how well they are working. This evaluation is an ongoing process. A college may have excellent relations with the legislature one year and win major appropriations, but after a scandal related to the president's budget the next year, legislators may be downright unfriendly.

Paul Garrett Devised the notion of enlightened self-interest.

DESIGN POLICIES TO IMPROVE THE RELATIONSHIPS. The job of public relations people is to recommend policies to top management to make these relationships work better, not only for the organization but also for the partners in each relationship. **Paul Garrett,** a pioneer in corporate relations, found that General Motors (GM) was seen in unfriendly terms during the Great Depression, which put the giant auto maker at risk with many publics, including its own employees. GM, he advised, needed new policies to seem neighbourly—rather than as a far-removed, impersonal, monolithic industrial giant.

enlightened self-interest Mutually beneficial public relations.

IMPLEMENT THE POLICIES. Garrett used the term **enlightened self-interest** for his series of policies intended to downsize GM in the eyes of many of the company's publics. Garrett set up municipal programs in towns with GM plants and grants for schools and scholarships for employees' children. General Motors benefited from a revised image, and in the spirit of enlightened self-interest, so did GM employees, their children and their communities.

Public relations is not a mass medium itself, but PR often uses the media as tools to accomplish its goals. To announce GM's initiatives to change its image in the 1930s, Paul Garrett issued news releases that he hoped newspapers, magazines and radio stations would pick up. The number of people in most of the publics with which public relations practitioners need to communicate is so large that it can be reached only through the mass media. The influence of public relations on the news media is extensive. Half of the news in many newspapers originates with formal statements or news releases from organizations that want something in the paper. It is the same with radio and television.

PUBLIC RELATIONS IN A DEMOCRACY

Misconceptions about public relations include the idea that it is a one-way street for institutions and individuals to communicate to the public. Actually, the good practice of public relations seeks two-way communication between and among all the people and institutions concerned with an issue.

Public Relations Society of America Professional public relations association.

A task force established by the **Public Relations Society of America** (PRSA) to explore the stature and role of the profession concluded that public relations has the potential to improve the functioning of democracy by encouraging the exchange of information and ideas on public issues. The task force made these points:

■ Public relations is a means for the public to have its desires and interests felt by the institutions in our society. It interprets and speaks for the public to organizations that otherwise might be unresponsive, and it speaks for those organizations to the public.

- Public relations is a means to achieve mutual adjustments between institutions and groups, establishing smoother relationships that benefit the public.
- Public relations is a safety valve for freedom. By providing means of working out accommodations, it makes arbitrary action or coercion less likely.
- Public relations is an essential element in the communication system that enables individuals to be informed on many aspects of subjects that affect their lives.
- Public relations people can help to activate the social conscience of the organizations for which they work.

Origins of Public Relations

Study Preview   *Many big companies found themselves in disfavour in the late 1800s for ignoring the public good to make profits. Feeling misunderstood, some moguls of industry turned to Ivy Lee, the founder of modern public relations, for counsel on gaining public support.*

MOGULS IN TROUBLE

Nobody would be tempted to think of **William Henry Vanderbilt** as being very good at public relations. In 1882 it was Vanderbilt, president of the New York Central Railroad, who said, "The public be damned," when asked about the effect of changing train schedules. Vanderbilt's utterance so infuriated people that it became a banner in the populist crusade against robber barons and tycoons in the late 1800s. Under populist pressure, state governments set up agencies to regulate railroads. Then the federal government established the Interstate Commerce Commission to control freight and passenger rates. Government began insisting on safety standards. Labour unions formed in the industries with the worst working conditions, safety records and pay. Journalists added pressure with muckraking exposés on excesses in the railroad, coal and oil trusts; on meat-packing industry frauds; and on patent medicines.

The leaders of industry were slow to recognize the effect of populist objections on their practices. They were comfortable with **social Darwinism**, an adaptation of **Charles Darwin**'s survival-of-the-fittest theory. In fact, they thought themselves forward-thinking in applying Darwin's theory to business and social issues. It had been only a few decades earlier, in 1859, that Darwin had laid out his biological theory in *On the Origin of Species by Means of Natural Selection*. To cushion the harshness of social Darwinism, many tycoons espoused paternalism toward those whose "fitness" had not brought them fortune and power. No matter how carefully put, paternalism seemed arrogant to the "less fit."

George Baer, a railroad president, epitomized both social Darwinism and paternalism in commenting on a labour strike: "The rights and interests of the laboring man will be protected and cared for not by labor agitators but by the Christian men to whom God in His infinite wisdom has given the control of the property interests of the country." Baer was quoted widely, further fueling sentiment against big business. Baer may have been sincere, but his position was read as a cover for excessive business practices by barons who assumed superiority to everyone else.

Meanwhile, social Darwinism came under attack as circuitous reasoning: Economic success accomplished by abusive practices could be used to justify further abusive practices, which would lead to further success. Social Darwinism was a dog-eat-dog outlook that hardly jibed with democratic ideals, especially not as described

William Henry Vanderbilt
Embodied the bad corporate images of the 1880s, 1890s with "The public be damned."

social Darwinism
Application of Darwin's survival-of-the-fittest theory to society.

Charles Darwin Devised survival-of-the-fittest theory.

George Baer Epitomized offensive corporate paternalism in the 1890s.

Ivy Lee

Ivy Lee Laid out fundamentals of public relations.

in the preamble to the U.S. Constitution, which sought to "promote the general welfare, and secure the blessings of liberty" for everyone—not for only the chosen "fittest." Into these tensions at the turn of the century came public relations pioneer Ivy Lee.

THE IDEAS OF IVY LEE

Coal mine operators, like railroad magnates, were held in the public's contempt at the start of the 20th century. Obsessed with profits, caring little about public sentiment or even the well-being of their employees, mine operators were vulnerable in the new populist wave. Mine workers organized, and 150 000 in Pennsylvania went out on strike in 1902, shutting down the anthracite industry and disrupting coal-dependent industries, including the railroads. The mine operators snubbed reporters, which probably contributed to a pro-union slant in many news stories and worsened the operators' public image. Not until six months into the strike, when President Theodore Roosevelt threatened to take over the mines with Army troops, did the operators settle.

Shaken finally by Roosevelt's threat and recognizing Roosevelt's responsiveness to public opinion, the mine operators began reconsidering how they went about their business. In 1906, with another strike looming, one operator heard about Ivy Lee, a young publicist in New York who had new ideas about winning public support. He was hired. In a turnabout in press relations, Lee issued a news release that announced: "The anthracite coal operators, realizing the general public interest in conditions in the mining regions, have arranged to supply the press with all possible information." Then followed a series of releases with information attributed to the mine operators by name—the same people who earlier had preferred anonymity and refused all interview requests. There were no more secret strike-strategy meetings. When operators planned a meeting, reporters covering the impending strike were informed. Although reporters were not admitted into the meetings, summaries of the proceedings were given to them immediately afterward. This relative openness eased long-standing hostility toward the operators, and a strike was averted.

Lee's success with the mine operators began a career that rewrote the rules on how corporations deal with their various publics. The following are among his accomplishments.

CONVERTING INDUSTRY TOWARD OPENNESS. Railroads had notoriously secretive policies, not only about their business practices but even about accidents. When the Pennsylvania Railroad sought Ivy Lee's counsel, he advised against suppressing news—especially on things that inevitably would leak out anyway. When a train jumped the rails near Gap, Pennsylvania, Lee arranged for a special car to take reporters to the scene and even take pictures. The Pennsylvania line was applauded in the press for the openness, and coverage of the railroad, which had been negative for years, began changing. A "bad press" continued plaguing other railroads that persisted in their secretive tradition.

TURNING NEGATIVE NEWS INTO POSITIVE NEWS. When the U.S. Senate proposed investigating International Harvester for monopolistic practices, Lee advised the giant farm implement manufacturer against reflexive obstructionism and silence. A statement went out announcing that the company, confident in its business practices, not only welcomed but also would facilitate an investigation. Then began a campaign

Ludlow Massacre. Colorado militiamen, called in to augment company guards, opened fire during a 1914 mine labour dispute and killed women and children. Overnight, John D. Rockefeller Jr. became the object of public hatred. It was a Rockefeller company that owned the mine, and even in New York, where Rockefeller lived, there were rallies demanding his head. Public relations pioneer Ivy Lee advised Rockefeller to tour the Ludlow area as soon as tempers cooled to show his sincere concern and to begin work on a labour contract to meet the concerns of miners. Rockefeller ended up a popular character in the Colorado mining camps.

Burson-Marsteller: With 24/7 crisis contacts posted on its site, this company works around the clock to protect the reputation of its clients. **www.burson-marsteller. com**

Weber Shandwick: Check out the company named 2005 Agency of the Year by *PRWeek.* Weber Shandwick maintains the largest PR network in the world, in terms of number of employees and geographical coverage. **www.webershandwick. com**

Fleishman-Hillard: With practice groups ranging from grassroots marketing to homeland security to youth marketing, this international communications firm serves a wide range of clients. **www.fleishman.com**

that pointed out International Harvester's beneficence toward its employees. The campaign also emphasized other upbeat information about the company.

PUTTING CORPORATE EXECUTIVES ON DISPLAY. In 1914, when workers at a Colorado mine went on strike, company guards fired machine guns and killed several men. More battling followed, during which 2 women and 11 children were killed. It was called the Ludlow Massacre, and **John D. Rockefeller Jr.**, the chief mine owner, was pilloried for what had happened. Rockefeller was an easy target. Like his father, widely despised for the earlier Standard Oil monopolistic practices, John Jr. tried to keep himself out of the spotlight, but suddenly mobs were protesting at his mansion in New York and calling out, "Shoot him down like a dog." Rockefeller asked Ivy Lee what he should do. Lee began whipping up articles about Rockefeller's human side, his family and his generosity. Then, on Lee's advice, Rockefeller announced that he would visit Colorado to see conditions himself. He spent two weeks talking with miners at work and in their homes and meeting their families. It was a news story that reporters could not resist, and it unveiled Rockefeller as a human being, not a far-removed, callous captain of industry. A myth-shattering episode occurred one evening when Rockefeller, after a brief address to miners and their wives, suggested that the floor be cleared for a dance. Before it was all over, John D. Rockefeller Jr. had danced with almost every miner's wife, and the news stories about the evening did a great deal to mitigate antagonism and distrust toward Rockefeller.

AVOIDING PUFFERY AND FLUFF. Ivy Lee came on the scene at a time when many organizations were making extravagant claims about themselves and their products. Circus promoter **P.T. Barnum** made this kind of **puffery** a fine art in the late 1800s, and he had many imitators. It was an age of puffed-up advertising claims and fluffy rhetoric. Lee noted, however, that people soon saw through hyperbolic boasts and lost faith in those who made them. In launching his public relations

John D. Rockefeller Jr. Ivy Lee client who had been the target of public hatred.

P.T. Barnum Known for exaggerated promotion.

puffery Inflated claims.

Edelman: Visit the site of the only independent global PR firm. Check out the "6 a.m." blog and get a feel for this free-thinking company. **www.edelman.com**

OmnicomGroup: This strategic holding company for firms specializing in marketing, advertising, communications and media boasts over 5000 clients worldwide. **www.omnicomgroup.com**

Hill & Knowlton: Check out the posted case studies (with real client names) and get a feel for the work this company performs. **www.hillandknowlton. com**

Ogilvy: From expert views to case studies to the pressroom, this site gives a thorough look into Ogilvy Public Relations Worldwide. **www.ogilvypr.com**

agency in 1906, Lee vowed to be accurate in everything he said and to provide whatever verification anyone requested. This became part of the creed of good practice in public relations, and it remains so today.

Public Relations Services

Study Preview   *Public relations deals with publicity and promotion, but it also involves less visible activities. These include lobbying, fundraising and crisis management. Public relations is distinct from advertising.*

HOW PUBLIC RELATIONS IS ORGANIZED

No two institutions are organized in precisely the same way. At General Motors, 200 people work in public relations. In smaller organizations, PR may be one of several hats worn by a single person. Except in the smallest operations, the public relations department usually has three functional areas of responsibility:

EXTERNAL RELATIONS. External public relations involves communication with groups and people outside the organization, including customers, dealers, suppliers and community leaders. The external relations unit is usually responsible for encouraging employees to participate in civic activities. Other responsibilities include arranging promotional activities like exhibits, trade shows, conferences and tours.

Public relations people also lobby government agencies and legislators on behalf of their organization, keep the organization abreast of government regulations and legislation, and coordinate relations with political candidates. This may include fundraising for candidates and coordinating political action committees.

In hospitals and nonprofit organizations, a public relations function may include recruiting and scheduling volunteer workers.

INTERNAL RELATIONS. Internal public relations involves developing optimal relations with employees, managers, unions, shareholders and other internal groups. In-house newsletters, magazines and brochures are important media for communicating with organizations' internal audiences.

MEDIA RELATIONS. Communication with large groups of people outside an organization is practicable only through the mass media. An organization's coordinator of **media relations** responds to news media queries, arranges news conferences and issues news releases. These coordinators coach executives for news interviews and sometimes serve as their organization's spokesperson.

PUBLIC RELATIONS AGENCIES

Even though many organizations have their own public relations staff, they may go to **public relations agencies** for help on specific projects or problems. In the United States today, hundreds of companies specialize in public relations counsel and related services.

The biggest agencies offer a full range of services on a global scale. Hill & Knowlton has offices in Cleveland, its original home; Toronto; Dallas; Frankfurt; Geneva; London; Los Angeles; New York, now its headquarters; Paris; Rome; Seattle; and Washington, D.C. The agency will take on projects anywhere in the world, either on its own or by working with local agencies.

external public relations Gearing messages to outside organizations, constituencies, individuals.

internal public relations Gearing messages to inside groups, constituencies, individuals.

media relations Using mass media to convey messages.

public relations agencies Companies that provide public relations services.

Besides full-service agencies, there are specialized public relations companies, which focus on a narrow range of services. For example, clipping services cut out and provide newspaper and magazine articles and radio and television items of interest to clients. Among specialized agencies are those that focus exclusively on political campaigns. Others coach corporate executives for news interviews. Others coordinate trade shows.

Some agencies bill clients only for services rendered. Others charge clients just to be on call. Agency expenses for specific projects are billed in addition. Staff time usually is charged at an hourly rate that covers the agency's overhead and allows a profit margin. Other expenses are usually billed with a 15 to 17 percent markup.

ACTIVITIES BEYOND PUBLICITY

Full-service public relations agencies provide a wide range of services built on two of the cornerstones of the business: **publicity** and **promotion**. These agencies are ready to conduct media campaigns to rally support for a cause, create an image or turn a problem into an asset. Publicity and promotion, however, are only the most visible services offered by public relations agencies. Others include the following.

publicity Brings public attention to something.

promotion Promoting a cause, idea.

LOBBYING. Every province has hundreds of public relations practitioners whose specialty is representing their clients to legislative bodies and government agencies. In one sense, **lobbyists** are expediters. They know local traditions and customs, and they know who is in a position to affect policy. Lobbyists advise their clients, which include trade associations, corporations, public interest groups and regulated utilities and industries, on how to achieve their goals by working with legislators and government regulators. Many lobbyists call themselves "government relations specialists."

lobbyists Influence public policy, usually legislation or regulations.

POLITICAL COMMUNICATION. Every provincial capital has political consultants whose work is mostly advising candidates for public office in **political communication**. Services include campaign management, survey research, publicity, media relations and

political communication Advising candidates, groups on public policy issues, usually in elections.

Media Databank

Top Public Relations Firms in Canada

The following are the largest public relations firms in Canada, according to a survey conducted by *Marketing Magazine*. The list was compiled based on companies that provided financial information.

Company	Gross Revenues, 2003 (in Canadian Dollars)
Thornley Fallis Group	$3.2 million
Torchia Communications	$2.8 million
Allard Johnson Communications	$2.5 million
Marketing Communication Group	$1.5 million
PALM Publicite Marketing	$359 000

Source: Marketing Magazine, June 21, 2004. Reprinted with permission.

image consulting. Political consultants also work on elections, referendums, recalls and other public policy issues.

image consulting Coaching individuals for media contacts.

IMAGE CONSULTING. Image consulting has been a growing specialized branch of public relations since the 1970s. Jacqueline Thompson, author of *Directory of Personal Image Consultants,* listed 53 entries in 1981 and has been adding up to 157 new entries a year since then. About these consultants, said Thompson: "They will lower the pitch of your voice, remove your accent, correct your 'body language,' modify your unacceptable behavior, eliminate your negative self-perception, select your wardrobe, restyle your hair, and teach you how to speak off the cuff or read a speech without putting your audience to sleep."

FINANCIAL PUBLIC RELATIONS. Financial public relations dates to the 1920s and 1930s, when the U.S. Securities and Exchange Commission cracked down on abuses in the financial industry. Regulations on promoting sales of securities are complex. It is the job of people in financial PR to know not only the principles of public relations but also the complex regulations governing the promotion of securities in corporate mergers, acquisitions, new issues and stock splits.

FUNDRAISING. Some public relations people specialize in fundraising and membership drives. Many colleges, for example, have their own staffs to perform these functions. Others look to fundraising firms to manage capital drives. Such an agency employs a variety of techniques, from mass mailings to telephone soliciting, and charges a percentage of the amount raised.

contingency planning Developing programs in advance of an unscheduled but anticipated event.

crisis management Helping a client through an emergency.

CONTINGENCY PLANNING. Many organizations rely on public relations people to design programs to address problems that can be expected to occur, known as **contingency planning.** Airlines, for example, need detailed plans for handling inevitable plane crashes—situations requiring quick, appropriate responses under tremendous pressure. When a crisis occurs, an organization can turn to public relations people for advice on dealing with it. Some agencies specialize in **crisis management,** which involves picking up the pieces either when a contingency plan fails or when there was no plan to deal with a crisis.

POLLING. Public-opinion sampling is essential in many public relations projects. Full-service agencies can either conduct surveys themselves or contract with companies that specialize in surveying.

EVENTS COORDINATION. Many public relations people are involved in coordinating a broad range of events, including product announcements, news conferences and convention planning. Some in-house public relations departments and agencies have their own artistic and audiovisual production talent to produce brochures, tapes and other promotional materials. Other agencies contract for these services.

PUBLIC RELATIONS AND ADVERTISING

Both public relations and advertising involve persuasion through the mass media, but most of the similarities end there.

MANAGEMENT FUNCTION. Public relations people help to shape an organization's policy. This is a management activity, ideally with the organization's chief public relations person offering counsel to other key policymakers at the vice-presidential level.

Advertising, in contrast, is not a management function. The work of advertising is much narrower. It focuses on developing persuasive messages, mostly to sell products or services, after all the management decisions have been made.

MEASURING SUCCESS. Public relations "sells" points of view and images. These are intangibles and therefore are hard to measure. In advertising, success is measurable with tangibles, such as sales, that can be calculated from the bottom line.

CONTROL OF MESSAGES. When an organization decides that it needs a persuasive campaign, there is a choice between public relations and advertising. One advantage of advertising is that the organization controls the message. By buying space or time in the mass media, an organization has the final say on the content of its advertising messages. In public relations, by contrast, an organization tries to influence the media to tell its story a certain way, but the message that actually goes out is up to the media. For example, a news reporter may lean heavily on a public relations person for information about an organization, but the reporter also may gather information from other sources. In the end, it is the reporter who writes the story. The upside of this is that the message, coming from a journalist, has a credibility with the mass audience that advertisements don't. Advertisements are patently self-serving. The downside of leaving it to the media to create the messages that reach the audience is surrendering control over the messages that go to the public.

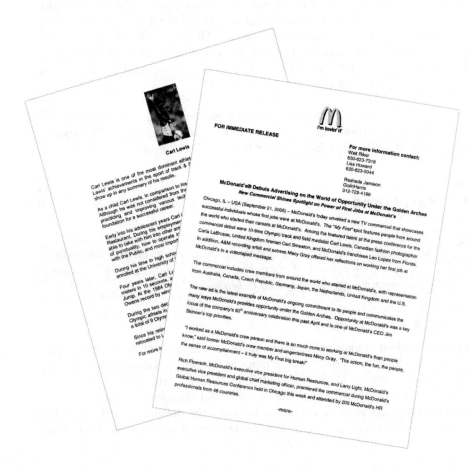

News Release. The workhorse of media relations is the news release, issued to newspapers, broadcast stations and other media to stir reporter interest in covering an event or developing a story or in hope of getting a point of view included in news stories. Studies have found that as many as 90 percent of news stories rely to some extent on information in news releases. Some releases even are reported verbatim, particularly in small-market, low-budget newsrooms.

INTEGRATED MARKETING

For many persuasive campaigns, organizations use both public relations and advertising. Increasingly, public relations and advertising people find themselves working together. This is especially true in corporations that have adopted **integrated marketing communication (IMC)**, which attempts to coordinate advertising as a marketing tool with promotion and publicity of the sort that public relations experts can provide. Several major advertising agencies, aware of their clients' shift to integrated marketing, have acquired or established public relations subsidiaries to provide a wider range of services under their roof.

integrated marketing communication
Comprehensive program that links public relations, advertising.

It is this overlap that has prompted some advertising agencies to move more into public relations. The WWP Group of London, a global advertising agency, has acquired both Hill & Knowlton, the third-largest public relations company in the United States, and the Ogilvy PR Worldwide, the ninth largest. The Young & Rubicam advertising agency has three public relations subsidiaries: Burson-Marsteller, the largest; Cohn & Wolf, the 13th largest; and Creswell, Munsell, Fultz & Zirbel, the 50th largest. These are giant enterprises that reflect the conglomeration and globalization of both advertising and public relations.

To describe IMC, media critic James Ledbetter suggests thinking of the old Charlie the Tuna ads, in which a cartoon fish made you chuckle and identify with the product—and established a brand name. That's not good enough for IMC. "By contrast," Ledbetter says, "IMC encourages tuna buyers to think about all aspects of the product. If polls find that consumers are worried about dolphins caught in tuna nets, then you might stick a big 'Dolphin Safe' label on the tins and set up a website featuring interviews with tuna fishermen." The new wave of IMC, according to one of its primary texts, is "respectful, not patronizing; dialogue-seeking, not monologuic; responsive, not formula-driven. It speaks to the highest point of common interest—not the lowest common denominator."

institutional advertising
Paid space and time to promote an institution's image, position.

Public relations and advertising crossovers are hardly new. One area of traditional overlap is **institutional advertising**, which involves producing ads to promote an image rather than a product. The fuzzy, feel-good ads of agricultural conglomerate Archer Daniels Midland, which pepper Sunday morning network television, are typical.

Media Relations

Study Preview   *Public relations people generally favour candor in working with the news media. Even so, some organizations opt to stonewall journalistic inquiries. An emerging school of thought in public relations is to challenge negative news coverage aggressively and publicly.*

OPEN MEDIA RELATIONS

The common wisdom among public relations people today is to be open and candid with the mass media. It is a principle that dates to Ivy Lee, and case studies abound to confirm its effectiveness. A classic case study on this point is the Tylenol crisis.

Johnson & Johnson had spent many years and millions of dollars to inspire public confidence in its painkiller Tylenol. By 1982 the product was the leader in a crowded field of headache remedies with 36 percent of the market. Then disaster

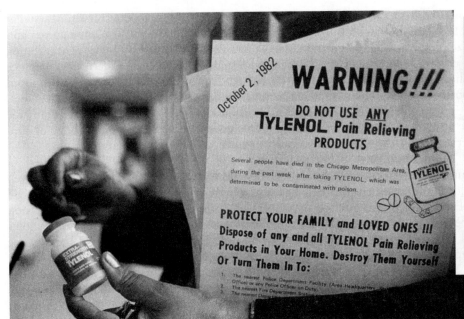

James Burke

Product-Tampering Crisis. When cyanide-laced Tylenol capsules killed seven people in Chicago, the manufacturer, Johnson & Johnson, responded quickly. Company President James Burke immediately pulled the product off retailers' shelves and ordered company publicists to set up a press centre to answer news media inquiries as fully as possible. Burke's action and candor helped to restore the public's shaken confidence in Tylenol, and the product resumed its significant market share after the crisis ended. It turned out that it probably was somebody outside Johnson & Johnson's production and distributing system who had contaminated the capsules rather than a manufacturing lapse.

struck. Seven people in Chicago died after taking Tylenol capsules laced with cyanide. James Burke, president of Johnson & Johnson, and Lawrence Foster, vice-president for public relations, moved quickly. Within hours, Johnson & Johnson had accomplished the following:

- Halted the manufacture and distribution of Tylenol.
- Removed Tylenol products from retailers' shelves.
- Launched a massive advertising campaign requesting people to exchange Tylenol capsules for a safe replacement.
- Summoned 50 public relations employees from Johnson & Johnson and its subsidiary companies to staff a press centre to answer media and consumer questions forthrightly.
- Ordered an internal company investigation of the Tylenol manufacturing and distribution process.
- Promised full co-operation with government investigators.
- Ordered the development of tamper-proof packaging for the reintroduction of Tylenol products after the contamination problem was resolved.

Investigators determined within days that an urban terrorist had poisoned the capsules. Although the news media exonerated Johnson & Johnson of negligence, the company nonetheless had a tremendous problem: how to restore public confidence in Tylenol. Many former Tylenol users were reluctant to take a chance, and the Tylenol share of the analgesic market dropped to 6 percent.

To address the problem, Johnson & Johnson called in the Burson-Marsteller public relations agency. Burson-Marsteller recommended a media campaign to capitalize on the high marks the news media had given the company for openness during the crisis. Mailgrams went out inviting journalists to a 30-city video teleconference to hear James Burke announce the reintroduction of the product. Six hundred reporters turned out, and Johnson & Johnson officials took their questions live.

media kit A packet provided to news reporters to tell the story in an advantageous way.

To stir even wider attention, 7500 **media kits** had been sent to newsrooms the day before the teleconference. The kits included a news release and a bevy of supporting materials: photographs, charts and background information.

The resulting news coverage was extensive. On average, newspapers carried 32 column inches of copy on the announcement. Network television and radio as well as local stations also afforded heavy coverage. Meanwhile, Johnson & Johnson executives, who had attended a workshop on how to make favourable television appearances, made themselves available as guests on the network morning shows and talk shows. At the same time, Johnson & Johnson distributed 80 million free coupons to encourage people to buy Tylenol again.

Sarah Evans of the Canadian Public Relations Society says that "this is the classic example in public relations annals of how to deal with a situation. You take immediate action, you worry about people first, you provide as much information as you can as fast as you've got it. Did Johnson & Johnson stock suffer? No. Did Tylenol suffer? No."

PROACTIVE MEDIA RELATIONS

Although public relations campaigns cannot control what the media say, public relations people can help to shape how news media report issues by taking the initiative. In the Tylenol crisis, for example, Johnson & Johnson reacted quickly and decisively and took control of disseminating information, which, coupled with full disclosure, headed off false rumours that could have caused further damage. This is a good example of **proactive media relations**.

proactive media relations Taking initiative to release information.

PROACTIVE CRISIS RESPONSES. A principle in crisis management is to seize leadership on the story. This involves anticipating what journalists will want to know and providing it to them before they even have time to formulate their questions. Ivy Lee did this time and again, and Johnson & Johnson did it in 1982.

For successful crisis management, public relations people need strong ongoing relationships with an organization's top officials. Otherwise, when a crisis strikes, they likely will have difficulty rounding up the kind of breaking information they need to deal effectively with the news media. During the 1991 Persian Gulf War, Pentagon spokesperson **Pete Williams** received high marks as a public relations person for shaping news coverage of the conflict. Williams did this by tapping his close working relationships with Secretary of Defense Dick Cheney and the Joint Chiefs of Staff for information favourable to the war effort. At regular news briefings, sometimes several a day, Williams provided so much grist for the journalistic mill that reporters were overwhelmed at putting it together for stories, which reduced the time available for them to go after stories on their own. The war was reported largely as the Pentagon wanted.

Pete Williams Tilted news coverage by overwhelming the media with information during the Persian Gulf War.

ONGOING MEDIA RELATIONSHIPS. Good media relations cannot be forged in the fire of a crisis. Organizations that survive a crisis generally have a history of solid media relations. Their public relations staff people know reporters, editors and news directors on a first-name basis. They avoid hyping news releases on routine matters, and they work hard at earning the trust of journalists.

Many public relations people, in fact, are seasoned journalists themselves, and they understand how journalists go about their work. It is their journalistic background that made them attractive candidates for their PR jobs. Pete Williams, for example, was a television news reporter before making a midcareer shift to join Dick Cheney's staff in Washington when Cheney was first elected to Congress from Wyoming.

SOUND OPERATING PRINCIPLES. An underlying strength that helped to see Johnson & Johnson through the Tylenol crisis was the company's credo. The credo was a written vow that Johnson & Johnson's first responsibility was to "those who use our products and services." The credo, which had been promoted in-house for years, said, "Every time a business hires, builds, sells or buys, it is acting *for the people* as well as *for itself,* and it must be prepared to accept full responsibility." With such a sound operating principle, Johnson & Johnson's crisis response was, in some respects, almost reflexive. Going silent, for example, would have run counter to the principles that Johnson & Johnson people had accepted as part of their corporate culture for years.

AMBIVALENCE IN MEDIA RELATIONS

Despite the advantages of open media relations, there are companies that choose not to embrace that approach.

Some corporations take a middle ground, currying media coverage selectively. This is an example of **ambivalent media relations**. Giant IBM, which receives 30 000 media queries a year, frets that news coverage would underscore its sheer size and invite federal antitrust scrutiny. IBM has long turned away journalists' questions on many issues, including the company's long-term planning. The corporation's PR chief, Seth McCormick, explicitly spurned Ivy Lee's maxim that corporate executives should be "on display." In an interview, McCormick told *Fortune:* "We control what is said about the company through the sparsity of heads for the outside world to talk to. We like it that way."

ambivalent media relations
Mix of proactive, reactive and inactive media contacts.

Public relations never figured much in Sam Walton's thinking as he built the world's largest retail chain, Wal-Mart. To Walton, PR was a frill. It didn't fit his keep-costs-minimal concept. Even after Walton died, his legacy lingered. By 2005 his company had only a 17-member public relations staff—minuscule in business. How minuscule? Wal-Mart sales exceeded $285 billion, yet the company had but one public relations staffer per $216 billion in earnings. Put another way, the company had one public relations person per 76 000 employees.

Realizing that inattentiveness to image would no longer work, Wal-Mart had begun to dabble in traditional public relations techniques in 2004 by sending its chief executive out for a few broadcast interviews. The company also invested in feel-good, paid television messages depicting happy employees and suppliers. In 2005 the company invited reporters to its spartan corporate headquarters in Bentonville, Arkansas, for the first time.

This was all new for Wal-Mart. At the media open house in Bentonville, a Wal-Mart senior executive mounted a stage seeming to expect reporters to jump to their feet in cheering enthusiasm, as adoring Wal-Mart employees always do. Discombobulated

Herb Schmertz

by the news reporters' cool, journalistically detached demeanour, the executive blew a basketball joke that was intended as an icebreaker. Realizing that the joke had bombed, he started to elaborate on how he thought it was funny. Finally a reporter shouted, "Blah, blah, blah."

Not only was the executive unprepared for the meeting, he was clueless about how journalists approach their work. These are fundamental errors in public relations that must be anticipated and resolved before executives put themselves on display. A major component of public relations is to be on the same wavelength as the news media.

Rescuing the executive from disaster, somebody shouted out an on-the-spot lesson about news reporters: "They don't applaud. They don't play basketball." The executive laughed, acknowledging a lesson learned the hard way. Everyone else laughed too, easing the tension of the first moments of what Wal-Mart had hoped would be a grand excursion into open public relations.

ADVERSARIAL PUBLIC RELATIONS

Public relations took on aggressive, even feisty tactics when Mobil Oil decided in the 1970s not to take media criticism lightly any more. **Herb Schmertz**, vice-president for Mobil's public affairs, charted a new course by:

- Filing formal complaints with news organizations when coverage was unfair in the company's view.

- Taking Mobil's case directly to the general public with paid advertising, called **advertorials**—a splicing of the words "advertising" and "editorial"—that explained the company's views.
- Sending corporate representatives on media tours to spread Mobil's side to as many constituencies as possible.

Schmertz's energetic counterattacks, an example of **adversarial public relations**, were a departure from conventional wisdom in public relations, which was to let criticism go unanswered or, at most, to complain privately to executives of news organizations that negative coverage is unwarranted. The conventional wisdom was that a public response would only bring more attention to the negative coverage.

adversarial public relations
Attacking critics openly.

In abandoning passivity, Mobil was adapting what sports fans call the Red Auerbach technique. Auerbach, the legendary coach of the Boston Celtics, was known for criticizing referees. He realized he would never get a ref to change a call, but he believed that refs would be less inclined to make questionable calls against the Celtics in the future if they knew that Auerbach would jump all over them. Mobil President Rawleigh Warner Jr. explained the new Mobil policy this way: "People know that if they take a swipe at us, we will fight back."

Schmertz employed the full range of PR tools in 1974 when ABC aired a television documentary that raised critical questions about the U.S. oil industry. Mobil objected first to ABC and then fired off a formal complaint to the National News Council, a volunteer media watchdog group. Mobil claimed 32 inaccuracies and instances of unfairness and requested that the council investigate. Mobil also issued an unusually lengthy news release, quoting from the documentary and offering point-by-point rebuttals.

Advertorials were part of Mobil's initiatives. Under Schmertz, as much as $6 million a year went into newspaper and magazine ads explaining the company's position. Mobil also began producing its own television programs on energy issues and providing them free to stations. The programs had a journalistic tone, and many stations ran them as if they were actual documentaries rather than part of Mobil's media campaign.

The jury is still out on whether Schmertz's aggressive sparring is good policy. Most organizations continue to follow the traditional thinking that taking on the media only generates more attention on the original bad news. On the other hand, Schmertz's approach has been tried by some major corporations. Bechtel, Illinois Power and Kaiser Aluminum all have called for independent investigations of stories that reflected badly on them.

Another adversarial approach, though not recommended by most public relations people, is for an offended organization to sever relations with the source of unfavourable news—an **information boycott**. In 1954, in a spectacular pout, General Motors cut off contact with *Wall Street Journal* reporters and withdrew advertising from the newspaper. This approach carries great risks:

information boycott
Severing ties with news media.

- By going silent, an organization loses avenues for conveying its message to mass audiences.
- An organization that yanks advertising to punish detractors is perceived negatively for coercively wielding its economic might.
- An organization that quits advertising in an effective advertising medium will lose sales.

A boycott differs from Schmertz's adversarial approach in an important respect. Schmertz responded to negative news by contributing to the exchange of information and ideas, which is positive in a democratic society. An information boycott, on the other hand, restricts the flow of information. Today, GM's policy has returned to the conventional wisdom of not arguing with anyone who buys paper by the ton and ink by the barrel—with the exception of its suit against NBC for faking the explosion of a GMC truck.

Professionalization

Study Preview   *Public relations has a tarnished image that stems from short-sighted promotion and whitewashing techniques of the late 1800s. Although some dubious practices continue, PR leaders are working to improve standards.*

A TARNISHED IMAGE

whitewashing Covering up.

Unsavoury elements in the heritage of public relations remain a heavy burden. P.T. Barnum, whose name became synonymous with hype, attracted crowds to his stunts and shows in the late 1800s with extravagant promises. Sad to say, some promoters still use Barnum's tactics. The claims for snake oils and elixirs from Barnum's era live on in commercials for pain relievers and cold remedies. The early response of tycoons to muckraking attacks, before Ivy Lee came along, was **whitewashing**—covering up the abuses but not correcting them. It is no wonder that the term *PR* is sometimes used derisively. To say something is "all PR" means that it lacks substance. Of people whose apparent positive qualities are a mere façade, it may be said that they have "good PR."

Although journalists rely heavily on public relations people for information, many journalists look at PR practitioners with suspicion. Not uncommon among seasoned journalists are utterances such as "I've never met a PR person I couldn't distrust." Such cynicism flows partly from the journalists' self-image as unfettered truth-seekers whose only obligation is serving their audience's needs. PR people, on the other hand, are seen as obligated to their employers, whose interests do not always dovetail with the public good. Behind their backs, PR people are called "flaks," a takeoff on the World War II slang for anti-aircraft fire intended to stop enemy bombers. PR **flacks**, as journalists use the term, interfere with journalistic truth-seeking by putting forth slanted, self-serving information that is not necessarily the whole story.

flacks Derisive word for public relations people.

The journalism–PR tension is exacerbated by a common newsroom view that PR people try to get free news-hole space for their messages rather than buying airtime and column inches. This view might seem strange, considering that 50 to 90 percent of all news stories either originate with, or contain information supplied by, PR people. It is also strange considering that many PR people are former news reporters and editors. No matter how uncomfortable PR people and journalists are as bedfellows, they are bedfellows nonetheless.

public information One alternative word for public relations; others are public affairs, corporate communication.

Some public relations people have tried to leapfrog the negative baggage attached to the term *PR* by abandoning it. The U.S. military shucked *PR* and tried **public information**, but it found itself still dogged by the same distrust that surrounded "public relations." The military then tried *public affairs,* but that was no solution either. Many organizations have tried *communication* as a way around the problem. Common labels today include the military's current *public affairs* offices and businesses' *corporate communication* departments.

STANDARDS AND CERTIFICATION

Canadian Public Relations Society Professional public relations association.

In 1948, two public relations groups, one in Montreal and the other in Toronto, merged. By 1953, they became the **Canadian Public Relations Society** (CPRS); in 1957, they became recognized as a national society. Today, CPRS has 16 member

Media People

Edward Bernays

Edward Bernays

Integrity was important to public relations pioneer Edward Bernays. When he was asked by agents of fascist dictators Francisco Franco and Adolf Hitler to improve their images in the United States, he said no. "I wouldn't do for money what I wouldn't do without money," Bernays said.

After graduation from college in 1912, Edward Bernays tried press agentry. He was good at it, landing free publicity for whoever would hire him. Soon his bosses included famous tenor Enrico Caruso and actor Otis Skinner. Bernays felt, however, that his success was tainted by the disdain in which press agents were held in general. He also saw far greater potential for affecting public opinion than his fellow press agents did. From Bernays's discomfort and vision was born the concept of modern public relations. His 1923 book *Crystallizing Public Opinion* outlined a new craft he called public relations.

Bernays saw good public relations as counsel to clients. He called the public relations practitioner a "special pleader." The concept was modeled partly on the long-established lawyer–client relationship in which the lawyer, or counsellor, suggests courses of action.

Because of his seminal role in defining what public relations is, Bernays sometimes is called the "Father of PR," although some people say the honour should be shared with Ivy Lee.

No matter, there is no question of Bernays's ongoing contributions. He taught the first course in public relations in 1923 at New York University. Bernays encouraged firm methodology in public relations, a notion that was captured in the title of a book he edited in 1955: *The Engineering of Consent.* He long advocated the professionalization of the field, which laid the groundwork for the accreditation of the sort the Public Relations Society of America has developed.

Throughout his career, Bernays stressed that public relations people need a strong sense of responsibility. In one reflective essay, he wrote, "Public relations practiced as a profession is an art applied to a science in which the public interest and not pecuniary motivation is the primary consideration. The engineering of consent in this sense assumes a constructive social role. Regrettably, public relations, like other professions, can be abused and used for anti-social purposes. I have tried to make the profession socially responsible as well as economically viable."

Bernays became the Grand Old Man of public relations, still attending PRSA and other professional meetings past his 100th birthday. He died in 1993 at age 102.

---

societies in major cities across Canada. The association adopted the following code of professional standards. Although CPRS is a Canadian association, its codes clearly reflect lessons learned in both the United States and Canada.

Canadian Public Relations Society Code of Professional Standards

Members of the Canadian Public Relations Society feel strongly about standards within the profession and abide by the following codes of ethics:

- A member shall practice public relations according to the highest professional standards.
- A member shall deal fairly and honestly with the communications media and the public.
- A member shall practice the highest standards of honesty, accuracy, integrity and truth, and shall not knowingly disseminate false or misleading information.
- A member shall deal fairly with past or present employers/clients, with fellow practitioners, and with members of other professions.

The Canadian Public Relations Society Canada's only professional public relations society, representing more than 1500 PR practitioners across the country.
www.cprs.ca

International Association of Business Communicators IABC is a not-for-profit international network for communications professionals.
www.iabc.com

- A member shall be prepared to disclose the name of their employer or client for whom public communications are made and refrain from associating themselves with anyone that would not respect such policy.
- A member shall protect the confidences of present, former and prospective employers/clients.
- A member shall not represent conflicting or competing interests without the express consent of those concerned, given after a full disclosure of the facts.
- A member shall not guarantee specified results beyond the member's capacity to achieve.
- Members shall personally accept no fees, commissions, gifts or any other considerations for professional services from anyone except employers or clients for whom the services were specifically performed.

(Reprinted by permission of the CPRS.)

APR Indicates CPRS accreditation.

In a further professionalization step, the CPRS established a certification process. Those who meet the criteria and pass exams are allowed to place **APR**, which stands for *accredited public relations professional,* after their names. Canadian public relations professionals can apply for accreditation only after they've worked in the business for at least five years. Exams are held once a year.

CHAPTER 9 WRAP-UP

When Ivy Lee hung up a shingle in New York for a new publicity agency in 1906, he wanted to distance himself from the huckstering that marked most publicity at the time. To do that, Lee promised to deal only in legitimate news about the agency's clients and no fluff. He invited journalists to pursue more information about the agency's clients. He also vowed to be honest and accurate. Those principles remain the bulwark of good public relations practice today.

QUESTIONS FOR REVIEW

1. What is public relations? How is public relations connected to the mass media?
2. Why did big business become interested in the techniques and principles of public relations beginning in the late 1800s?
3. How is public relations a management tool?
4. What is the range of activities in which public relations people are involved?
5. What kind of relationship do most people strive to have with the mass media?
6. Why does public relations have a bad image? What are public relations professionals doing about it?

QUESTIONS FOR CRITICAL THINKING

1. When Ivy Lee accepted the Pennsylvania Railroad as a client in 1906, he saw the job as "interpreting the Pennsylvania Railroad to the public and interpreting the public to the Pennsylvania Railroad."

2. How are public relations practitioners trying to overcome the complaints from journalists that they are flacks interfering with an unfettered pursuit of truth?

3. Defend or rebuke Canadian Joyce Nelson's idea that public relations creates a persona for a corporation in an attempt to hide its shadow.

4. How do public relations agencies turn profits?

5. When does an institution with its own in-house public relations operation need to hire a PR agency?

6. Explain the concept of enlightened self-interest.

7. How did the concept of social Darwinism contribute to the emergence of modern public relations?

8. Showman P.T. Barnum epitomized 19th-century press agentry with extravagant claims, such as promoting the midget Tom Thumb as a Civil War general. To attract crowds to a tour by an unknown European soprano, Jenny Lind, Barnum labeled her "the Swedish Nightingale." Would such promotional methods work today? Keep in mind that Barnum, explaining his methods, once said, "There's a sucker born every minute."

DEEPENING YOUR MEDIA LITERACY

Do press releases serve the public?

Step 1

Get a copy of a newspaper that you can mark up.

Dig Deeper

Step 2

Mark all the stories that you think came from press releases, in whole or in part. Choose one of them—it can be on any subject, for example, an upcoming concert or event, an award ceremony or an announcement from a local business.

What Do You Think?

Step 3

Answer these questions in relation to the press release you chose:

1. How does this story benefit the public? Which public? Who else does it benefit?

2. Is this story, or the part of it that came from a press release, socially responsible?

3. Is the press release proactive?

If all the press releases were taken out of the newspaper, how much news would you miss?

KEEPING UP TO DATE

PRWeek is the industry trade journal.

The trade journal *O'Dwyer's PR Services* tracks the industry on a monthly basis.

Other sources of ongoing information are *Public Relations Journal, Public Relations Quarterly* and *Public Relations Review.*

FOR FURTHER LEARNING

Scott M. Cutlip, Allen H. Center, and Glen M. Broom. *Effective Public Relations,* 6th edition (Prentice Hall, 1985).

Stewart Ewen. *PR! A Social History of Spin* (Basic Books, 1996).

Rene A. Henry. *Marketing Public Relations* (Iowa State University Press, 2000).

Ray Eldon Hiebert. *Courtier to the Crowd: The Story of Ivy Lee and the Development of Public Relations* (Iowa State University Press, 1966).

Robert Jackall and Janice M. Hirota. *Image Makers: Advertising, Public Relations and the Ethos of Advocacy* (University of Chicago Press, 2000).

Bruce Livesey. "PR Wars: How the PR Industry Flacks for Big Business." *Canadian Dimension* (November–December 1996).

George S. McGovern and Leonard F. Guttridge. *The Great Coalfield War* (Houghton Mifflin, 1972).

Kevin McManus. "Video Coaches." *Forbes* 129 (June 7, 1982).

Lael M. Moynihan. "Horrendous PR Crises: What They Did When the Unthinkable Happened." *Media History Digest* 8 (Spring–Summer 1988): 1, 19–25.

Joyce Nelson. *The Sultans of Sleaze: Public Relations and the Media* (Between the Lines, 1989).

Barbara Pollock. "A Profession for Tomorrow." Canadian Public Relations Society. Available online at www.cprs.ca/cprsprof_tom.html (July 9, 1998).

"The Rankings." *Marketing Magazine* (June 21, 2004).

Sally J. Ray. *Strategic Communication in Crisis Management: Lessons from the Airline Industry* (Quorum, 1999).

Herbert Schmertz and William Novak. *Good-bye to the Low Profile: The Art of Creative Confrontation* (Little, Brown, 1986).

Michael S. Sweeney. *Secrets of Victory: The Office of Censorship and the American Press and Radio in World War II* (University of North Carolina Press, 2001).

Ray Truchansky. "In Today's Business World, Good PR is Priceless." *Edmonton Journal* (April 7, 2001).

Larry Tye. *The Father of Spin: Edward L. Bernays and the Birth of Public Relations* (Crown, 1998).

Jean Valin. "Truth Pays Dividends with Public." Canadian Public Relations Society. Available online at www.cprs.ca/cprstruth.htm (July 9, 1998).

Perry Dean Young. *God's Bullies: Power Politics and Religious Tyranny* (Henry Holt, 1982).

Sex in the Clams? Author Wilson Bryan Key is convinced that Madison Avenue hides sex in advertisements to attract attention and sell products. To demonstrate his point, he outlines the human figures that he saw in an orgy in a photograph of clam strips on a restaurant menu. Most advertising people dismiss his claims. It's a good example of what communication theorists call connotation.

Advertising

MEDIA TIMELINE

Development of Advertising

1468	William Caxton promoted a book with the first printed advertisement.
1704	Joseph Campbell included advertisements in *The Boston News-Letter*.
1833	Benjamin Day created *The New York Sun* as a combination news and advertising vehicle.
1869	F. Wayland Ayer opened the first advertising agency, in Philadelphia.
1890s	Brand names emerged as an advertising technique.
1899	Anson McKim opened the first Canadian advertising agency.
1950s	David Ogilvy devised brand imaging technique.
1950s	Jack Trout devised positioning technique.
1957	James Vicary claimed success for subliminal advertising.
1960s	Rosser Reeves devised unique selling proposition technique.
1963	Canadian Code of Advertising Standards was established.
1980s	Conglomeration hit the advertising world through mergers and acquisitions.
2003	Store brands emerged as a major challenge to brand names.
2004	Thirty-second spot during the Super Bowl cost US$2.5 million.

Subliminal Advertising

Jim Vicary claimed in 1957 that he had studied the effect of inserting into movies messages such as "Drink Coca-Cola" and "Eat popcorn." The messages, although flashed too fast to be recognized by the human eye, still registered in the brain and, said Vicary, prompted moviegoers to rush to the snack bar. In experiments at a New Jersey movie house, he said, Coke sales increased 18 percent and popcorn sales almost 60 percent. Vicary's report stirred great interest, and also alarm, but researchers who tried to replicate his study found no evidence to support his claim.

Despite Vicary's dubious claims, psychologists have identified a phenomenon they call **subception**, in which certain behaviour sometimes seems to be triggered by messages perceived subliminally. Whether the effect works outside of laboratory experiments and whether the effect is strong enough to prod a consumer to buy something is uncertain. Nevertheless, there remains a widespread belief among the general population that **subliminal advertising** works, and fortunes are being made by people who peddle various devices and systems with extravagant claims that they can control human behaviour. Among these are the "hidden" messages in stores' sound systems that say shoplifting is not nice.

Jim Vicary Made dubious subliminal advertising claims.

subception Receiving subconscious messages that trigger behaviour.

subliminal advertising Ads that cannot be consciously perceived.

Wilson Bryan Key believes he sees subliminal advertising widely used.

This idea that advertising is loaded with hidden messages has been taken to extremes by **Wilson Bryan Key**, who spins out books alleging that plugs are hidden in all kinds of places for devil worship, homosexuality, and a variety of libertine activities. He has accused Nabisco of baking the word *sex* into Ritz crackers. At Howard Johnson restaurants, he has charged, placemat pictures of plates heaped with clams portray orgies and bestiality. Though widely read, Key offers no evidence beyond his own observations and interpretations. In advertising circles, his views are dismissed as amusing but wacky. The views of Nabisco and Howard Johnson are less charitable.

In 1990, Wilson Bryan Key's views suffered a serious setback. He was a primary witness in a highly publicized Nevada trial on whether the Judas Priest heavy metal album *Stained Glass* had triggered the suicide of an 18-year-old and the attempted sui-cide of his 20-year-old friend. The families said that the pair had obsessed about a Judas Priest album that dealt with suicide and that one song was sub-liminally embedded with the words "Do it" over and over. The families' attorneys hired Key as an expert witness to help make their point. From Key's per-spective, the case did not go well. Millions of televi-sion viewers who followed the trial strained to make out the supposed words "Do it," but even when iso-lated from the rest of the music, they were almost impossible to decipher. It turned out the sounds were neither lyrics nor even vocals but rather instrumental effects. Members of Judas Priest testified that they had not equated the sound to any words at all and had inserted it for artistic effect, hardly to encourage suicide. The jury sided with Judas Priest, and Key left town with his wobbly ideas about subliminal messages having taken a serious blow under a jury's scrutiny.

David Ogilvy, founder of the Ogilvy & Mather agency, once made fun of claims like Key's, pointing out the absurdity of "millions of suggestible con-sumers getting up from their armchairs and rushing like zombies through the traffic on their way to buy the product at the nearest store." The danger of "Vote Bolshevik" being flashed during the *NBC Nightly News* is remote, and whether it would have any effect is questionable.

Subliminal Advertising: A discussion of subliminal advertising, complete with visual examples.
www.poleshift.org/sublim

The Advertising Archives: Reference source for all those who are interested in art, social history and every product that has been advertised in the last 150 years.
www.advertisingarchives .co.uk

John W. Hartman Center for Sales, Advertising & Marketing History: Offers several collections of images of early ads.
http://library.duke.edu/ specialcollections/hartman/

Importance of Advertising

Study Preview   *Advertising is vital in a consumer economy. Without it, people would have a hard time even knowing what products and services were available. Advertising also is the financial basis of important contemporary mass media.*

CONSUMER ECONOMIES

The essential role of advertising in a modern consumer economy is obvious if you think about how people decide what to buy. If a shoe manufacturer were unable to tout the virtues of its footwear by advertising in the mass media, people would have a hard time learning about the product, let alone knowing whether it is what they want.

In *Canadian Advertising in Action,* Keith Tuckwell estimates that Canadian companies spend more than $8 billion a year on advertising. General Motors of Canada alone spends about $130 million on advertising each year. When produc-tion of goods and services is up, so is advertising spending. When production fal-ters, as it did in the early 1990s, many manufacturers, distributors and retailers reduce their advertising expenditures.

ADVERTISING AND PROSPERITY

Advertising's phenomenal continuing growth has been a product of a plentiful society. In a poor society with a shortage of goods, people line up for necessities like food and clothing. Advertising has no role and serves no purpose when survival is the question. With prosperity, however, people have not only discretionary income but also a choice of ways to spend it. Advertising is the vehicle that provides information and rationales to help them decide how to enjoy their prosperity.

Besides being a product of economic prosperity, advertising contributes to prosperity. By dangling desirable commodities and services before mass audiences, advertising can inspire people to greater individual productivity so that they can have more income to buy the things that are advertised.

Advertising also can introduce efficiency into the economy by allowing comparison shopping without in-person inspections of all the alternatives. Efficiencies also can result when advertising alerts consumers to superior and less costly products and services, which displace outdated, outmoded and inefficient offerings.

On the other hand, Canadian economist **John Kenneth Galbraith**, in his classic book *The Affluent Society,* argued that advertising did more than just satisfy our *needs*. It actually created *wants*. By creating wants, those in power could sell products that made people live beyond their means and buy more than they needed. Andrew Potter, writing in *Maclean's,* refutes Galbraith's ideas. Potter claims each of us has free will (or at least self-restraint) and isn't easily duped by every ad campaign we see. "That is not to say that advertising isn't harmless, but that it's more like seduction than brainwashing. Just as you can't seduce someone who is not interested in sex, you can't sell teeth whitener to someone who is not concerned about their appearance."

John Kenneth Galbraith
Advertising isn't about needs, it's about wants.

ADVERTISING AND DEMOCRACY

Advertising first took off as a modern phenomenon in the United States and Canada more than elsewhere, which has given rise to a theory that advertising and democracy are connected. This theory notes that North Americans, early in their history as a democracy, were required by their political system to hold individual opinions. They looked for information so that they could evaluate their leaders and vote on public policy. This emphasis on individuality and reason paved the way for advertising: Just as Americans looked to the mass media for information on political matters, they also came to look to the media for information on buying decisions.

Advertising has another important role in democratic societies in generating most of the operating revenue for newspapers, magazines, television and radio. Without advertising, many of the media on which people rely for information, for entertainment and for the exchange of ideas on public issues would not exist as we know them.

Origins of Advertising

Study Preview *Advertising is the product of great forces that have shaped modern society, beginning with Gutenberg's movable type, which made mass-produced messages possible.*

STEPCHILD OF TECHNOLOGY

Advertising is not a mass medium, but it relies on media to carry its messages. **Johannes Gutenberg**'s movable type, which permitted mass production of the printed word, made mass-produced advertising possible. First came flyers. Then advertisements in newspapers and magazines were introduced. In the 1800s, when technology created high-speed presses that could produce enough copies for larger audiences, advertisers used them to expand markets. With the introduction of radio, advertisers learned how to use electronic communication. Then came television and the internet.

Flyers were the first form of printed advertising. The British printer **William Caxton** issued the first printed advertisement in 1468 to promote one of his books. In America, publisher **John Campbell** of *The Boston News-Letter* ran the first advertisement in 1704, a notice from somebody wanting to sell an estate on Long Island. Colonial newspapers listed cargo arriving from Europe and invited readers to come, look and buy.

INDUSTRIAL REVOLUTION

The genius of **Benjamin Day**'s *New York Sun,* in 1833 the first penny newspaper (see Chapter 8), was that it recognized and exploited so many changes spawned by the Industrial Revolution. Steam-powered presses made large press runs possible. Factories drew great numbers of people to jobs within geographically small areas to which newspapers could be distributed quickly. The jobs also drew immigrants who were eager to learn—from newspapers as well as other sources—about their adopted country. Industrialization, coupled with the labour union movement, created unprecedented wealth, with labourers gaining a share of the new prosperity. A consumer economy was emerging, although it was primitive by today's standards.

A key to the success of Day's *Sun* was that, at a penny a copy, it was affordable for almost everyone. Of course, Day's production expenses exceeded a penny a copy. Just as the commercial media do today, Day looked to advertisers to pick up the slack. As Day wrote in his first issue, "The object of this paper is to lay before the public, at a price within the means of everyone, all the news of the day, and at the same time afford an advantageous medium for advertising." Day and imitator penny press publishers sought larger and larger circulations, knowing that merchants would see the value in buying space to reach so much purchasing power.

National advertising took root in the 1840s as railroads, another creation of the Industrial Revolution, spawned new networks for mass distribution of manufactured goods. National brands developed, and their producers looked to magazines, also delivered by rail, to promote sales. By 1869 the rail network linked the Atlantic and Pacific coasts.

PIONEER AGENCIES

By 1869 most merchants recognized the value of advertising, but they grumbled about the time it took away from their other work. In that grumbling, a young Philadelphia man sensed opportunity. **F. Wayland Ayer**, aged 20, speculated that merchants, and even national manufacturers, would welcome a service company to help them create advertisements and place them in publications. Ayer feared, however, that his idea might not be taken seriously by potential clients because of his youth and inexperience. So when Ayer opened a shop, he borrowed his father's name, N.W. Ayer, for the shingle. The Ayer agency not only created ads but also offered the array of services that agencies still offer clients today:

- Counsel on selling products and services.
- Design services, that is, actually creating advertisements and campaigns.
- Expertise on placing advertisements in advantageous media.

In 1872, Toronto newspapers began selling advertising space to clients outside their geographic area when the *Toronto Mail* sent a young man to Montreal to sell advertising space. **Anson McKim** saw this as a great opportunity and he began to act as a broker for other publications in south-central Ontario. By 1889, McKim opened Canada's first ad agency in Montreal, A. McKim and Company. McKim also published the first directory of media in Canada, *The Canadian Newspaper Directory*, in 1892.

Anson McKim Founded the first ad agency in Canada.

Advertising Agencies

Study Preview   *Central in modern advertising are the agencies that create and place ads on behalf of their clients. These agencies are generally funded by the media in which they place ads. In effect, this makes agency services free to advertisers.*

AGENCY STRUCTURE

Full-service advertising agencies conduct market research for their clients, design and produce advertisements and choose the media in which the advertisement will run. The 500 leading U.S. agencies employ 120 000 people worldwide. The responsibilities of people who work at advertising agencies fall into these broad categories:

CREATIVITY. This category includes copywriters, graphics experts and layout people. These creative people generally report to **creative directors**, art directors and copy supervisors.

creative director Key person in ad campaigns.

LIAISON. Most of these people are **account executives**, who work with clients. Account executives are responsible for understanding clients' needs, communicating those needs to the creative staff and going back to clients with the creative staff's ideas.

account executives Agency reps to clients.

BUYING. Agency employees called **media buyers** determine the most effective media in which to place ads, and then place them.

media buyers Decide where to place ads.

RESEARCH. Agency research staffs generate information on target consumer groups, data that can guide the creative and media staffs.

Many agencies also employ technicians and producers who turn ideas into camera-ready proofs, colour plates, videotape, audio clips and web-based ads, although a lot of production work is contracted to specialty companies. Besides full-service agencies there are creative boutiques, which specialize in preparing messages; media buying houses, which recommend strategy on placing ads; and other narrowly focused agencies.

Media Databank

Advertising Agencies

These are the largest worldwide advertising organizations, all operating numerous subsidiaries, ranked by worldwide revenue:

	Headquarters	Worldwide Revenues ($)
Omnicom	New York	7.5 billion
Interpublic	New York	6.2 billion
WPP	London	5.8 billion
Publicis	Paris	2.7 billion
Dentsu	Tokyo	2.1 billion

Here are the largest marketing communication service agencies in Canada, according to a survey done by *Marketing* magazine. These are "full-service" companies that not only provide traditional advertising services but also offer direct and digital marketing, market research, and media planning and buying.

Firm	Headquarters	Gross Revenues*
Cossette Communication Group	Quebec City	$143 403 000
MDC Partners	Toronto	$61 635 000
Maritz Canada	Mississauga	$51 882 000
Carlson Marketing Group Canada	Toronto	$48 011 000
Nurun	Montreal	$33 200 000

* All figures are in Canadian dollars and represent domestic business.

Source: Marketing, June 19, 2006.

AGENCY COMPENSATION

Advertising agencies once earned their money in a standard way—15 percent of the client advertiser's total outlay for space or time. On huge accounts, like Procter & Gamble, agencies made killings.

commission contract An advertising agency earns an agreed-upon percentage of what the advertising client spends for time and space, traditionally 15 percent.

COMMISSIONS. The 15 percent **commission contract** system broke down in the 1990s when businesses scrambled to cut costs to become more competitive. Today, according to a guesstimate by the trade journal *Advertising Age,* only 10 to 12 percent of agency contracts use a standard percentage. Agency compensation generally is negotiated. Big advertisers, like P&G, are thought to be paying 13 percent on average, but different agencies handle the company's brands, each in a separate contract. For competitive reasons, all parties tend to be secretive about actual terms.

performance contract An advertising agency earns expenses and an agreed-upon markup for the advertising client, plus bonuses for exceeding minimal expectations.

PERFORMANCE. Commission contracts have been replaced largely with **performance contracts.** The advertiser pays an agency's costs plus a negotiated profit. In addition, if a campaign works spectacularly, agencies land bonuses.

equity contract An advertising agency is compensated with shares of stock in an advertising client.

EQUITY. In the 1990s dot-com boom, a performance contract variation was to pay agencies with shares in the company. **Equity contracts** are chancy for agencies because an advertiser's success hinges on many variables, not just the advertising, but the return for an agency with a soaring client can be stratospheric.

ADVERTISER'S ROLE IN ADVERTISING

Most companies, although they hire agencies for advertising services, have their own advertising expertise among the in-house people who develop marketing strategies. These companies look to ad agencies to develop the advertising campaigns that will help them meet their marketing goals. For some companies the **advertising director** is the liaison between the company's marketing strategists and the ad agency's tacticians. Large companies with many products have in-house **brand managers** for this liaison. Although it is not the usual pattern, some companies have in-house advertising departments and rely hardly at all on agencies.

advertising director
Coordinates marketing and advertising.

brand manager
Coordinates marketing and advertising for a specific brand.

Placing Advertisements

Study Preview   *The placement of advertisements is a sophisticated business. Not only do different media have inherent advantages and disadvantages in reaching potential customers, but so do individual publications and broadcast outlets.*

MEDIA PLANS

Agencies create **media plans** to ensure that advertisements reach the right target audience. Developing a media plan is no small task. Consider the number of media outlets available: daily or weekly newspapers, magazines, radio stations and television stations. Other possibilities include direct mail, banners on websites, billboards, blimps, skywriting and even printing the company's name on T-shirts.

Media buyers use formulas, some very complex, to decide which media are best for reaching potential customers. Most of these formulas begin with a factor called **CPM**, short for cost per thousand readers, listeners or viewers. If airtime for a radio advertisement costs 7.2 cents per thousand listeners, it's probably a better deal than a magazine with a 7.3-cent CPM, assuming that both reach the same audience. CPM by itself is just a starting point in choosing media. Other variables that media buyers consider include whether a message will work in a particular medium. For example, radio wouldn't work for a product that lends itself to a visual pitch and sight gags.

Media buyers have numerous sources of data to help them decide where advertisements can be placed for the best results. The **Audit Bureau of Circulations**, created by the newspaper industry in 1914, provides reliable information based on independent audits of the circulation of most newspapers. Survey organizations like Nielsen Media Research and BBM conduct surveys on television and radio audiences. *Canadian Advertising Rates and Data* (CARD) publishes volumes of information on media audiences, circulations and advertising rates.

Global Marketing. Knowing the following that Houston Rockets star Yao Ming has in his China homeland, the distributor for the Chinese beer Yanjing paid $6 million for Chinese-language billboards at the Rockets' arena.

media plan Lays out where ads are placed.

CPM Cost per thousand; a tool to determine the cost effectiveness of different media.

Audit Bureau of Circulations
Verifies circulation claims.

MEDIA CHOICES

Here are the pluses and minuses of major media as advertising vehicles.

NEWSPAPERS. The hot relationship that media theorist Marshall McLuhan described between newspapers and their readers attracts advertisers. Newspaper readers are predisposed to consider information in advertisements seriously. Studies show that

shelf life How long a periodical remains in use.

pass-along circulation All the people who see a periodical.

people, when ready to buy, look more to newspapers than to other media. Because newspapers are tangible, readers can refer back to advertisements just by picking up the paper a second time, which is not possible with ephemeral media like television and radio. Coupons are possible in newspapers. Newspaper readers tend to be older, better educated and higher earning than television and radio audiences. Space for newspaper ads usually can be reserved as late as 48 hours ahead, and 11th-hour changes are possible. Newspapers account for 20 percent of all advertising revenue spent in Canada.

However, newspapers are becoming less valuable for reaching young adults. To the consternation of newspaper publishers, there has been an alarming drop in readership among these people in recent years, and it appears that, unlike their parents, young adults are not picking up the newspaper habit as they mature.

Another drawback to newspapers is printing on newsprint, a relatively cheap paper that absorbs ink like a slow blotter. The result is that ads do not look as good as they do in slick magazines. Slick, stand-alone inserts offset the newsprint drawback somewhat, but many readers pull the inserts out and discard them as soon as they open the paper.

MAGAZINES. As another print medium, magazines have many of the advantages of newspapers plus longer **shelf life**, an advertising term for the amount of time that an advertisement remains available to readers. Magazines remain in the home for weeks, sometimes months, which offers greater exposure to advertisements. People share magazines, which gives them high **pass-along circulation**. Magazines are more prestigious, with slick paper and splashier graphics. With precise colour separations and enameled papers, magazine advertisements can be beautiful in ways that newspaper advertisements cannot. Magazines, specializing as they do, offer more narrowly defined audiences than do newspapers. Twelve percent of all advertising revenue is spent on magazines.

Media Databank

Advertising Spending by Medium

According to the CRTC, this is how the 2005 advertising pie was divided among Canadian media. Notice how each medium has experienced significant growth in revenue since 1997, particularly the internet:

Medium	Advertising Revenues	% Change from 1997 to 2005
Television	$3.01 billion	43
Daily newspapers	$1.8 billion	15
Radio	$1.3 billion	54
Magazines	$1.03 billion	59
Weekly newspapers	$883 million	39
Internet	$519 million	5090
Billboards	$404 million	84

Source: CRTC, Broadcast Policy Monitoring Report 2006.

On the downside, magazines require reservations for advertising space up to three months in advance. Opportunities for last-minute changes are limited, often impossible.

RADIO. Radio stations with narrow formats offer easily identified target audiences. Time can be bought on short notice, with changes possible almost until airtime. Comparatively inexpensive, radio lends itself to repeated play of advertisements to drive home a message introduced in more expensive media like television. Radio lends itself to jingles that can contribute to a lasting image.

However, radio offers no opportunity for a visual display, although the images that listeners create in their minds from audio suggestions can be more potent than those set out visually on television. Radio is a mobile medium that people carry with them. The extensive availability of radio is offset, however, by the fact that people tune in and out. Another negative is that many listeners are inattentive. Also, there is no shelf life. Still, radio accounts for 14 percent of all advertising in Canada.

TELEVISION. As a moving and visual medium, television can offer unmatched impact, and the rapid growth of both network and local television advertising, far outpacing other media, indicates its effectiveness in reaching a diverse mass audience. It's the king of all media with 34 percent of the advertising pie.

Drawbacks include the fact that production costs can be high. So are rates. The expense of television time has forced advertisers to go to shorter and shorter advertisements. A result is **ad clutter**, a phenomenon in which advertisements compete against each other and reduce the impact of all of them. Placing advertisements on television is a problem because demand outstrips the supply of slots, especially during prime hours. Slots for some hours are locked up months, even whole seasons, in advance. Because of the audience's diversity and size, targeting potential customers with any precision is difficult with television—with the exception of emerging narrowly focused cable services.

ONLINE SERVICES. One advantage of **online advertising** is that readers can click to deeper and deeper levels of information about advertised products. A lot more information can be packed into a layered online message than within the space and time confines of a print or broadcast ad. High-resolution colour is standard, and the technology is available for moving pictures and audio.

Advertisers are not abandoning traditional media, but they are experimenting with online possibilities. For mail-order products, orders can be placed over the internet right from the ad. For some groups of potential customers, online advertising has major advantages. To reach college students, almost all of whom have computer access, online advertising makes sense.

GOOGLE ADS. The internet search engine Google, capitalizing on its superfast hunt technology, has elbowed into the traditional placement service provided by advertising agencies. Google arranges for advertising space on thousands of websites, many of them narrowly focused, like blogs, and places ads for its clients on the sites. Every blog visitor who clicks a **sponsored link** placed by Google will go to a fuller advertisement. Google charges the advertiser a **clickthrough fee**. Google pays the site for every clickthrough. Google matches sites and advertisers, so a search for new Cadillacs doesn't display ads for muffler shops.

Google also places what it calls "advertiser links" on search screens. *The New York Times,* for example, has a licence to use Google technology for readers who enter search terms for searches on the *Times* site. The licence allows Google to display ads of

Radio Marketing Bureau: Log on and listen to award-winning radio commercials from Canada. **www.rmb.ca**

Extra Awards: Canada's best print ads are here. **www.prixextraawards.com**

Cassie Awards: The Cassies (Canadian Advertising Success Stories) are awarded for the best Canadian advertising campaigns. **www.cassies.ca**

Interactive Advertising Bureau of Canada: The IAB's mission is to help online and interactive companies increase their revenues. **www.iabcanada.com**

ad clutter So many competing ads that all lose impact.

online advertising Provide messages to computers.

sponsored link Onscreen hot spot to move to an online advertisement.

clickthrough fee A charge to advertisers when an online link to their ads is activated; also a fee paid to websites that host the links.

likely interest whenever a *Times* site reader conducts an internal site search. A search for *Times* coverage of news about Jamaica, for example, will produce links to *Times* stories on Jamaica as well as to advertisements for Caribbean travel elsewhere on the internet. If a *Times* reader clicks on an ad link, Google pays the *Times* a clickthrough fee—from the revenue the advertiser paid to Google to place its ads.

Google has quickly become a major player in internet advertising. Of an estimated $10 billion spent by advertisers for online messages in 2004, Google had $1.9 billion. Nobody was earning more advertising revenue from the internet.

Pitching Messages

Study Preview *When the age of mass production and mass markets arrived, common wisdom in advertising favoured aiming at the largest possible audience of potential customers. These are called lowest-common-denominator approaches, and such advertisements tend to be heavy-handed so that no one can possibly miss the point. Narrower pitches, aimed at segments of the mass audience, permit more deftness, subtlety and imagination.*

IMPORTANCE OF BRANDS

A challenge for advertising people is the modern-day reality that mass-produced products intended for large markets are essentially alike: Toothpaste is toothpaste is toothpaste. When a product is virtually identical to the competition, how can one toothpaste maker move more tubes?

BRAND NAMES. By trial and error, tactics were devised in the late 1800s to set similar products apart. One tactic, promoting a product as a **brand** name, aims to make a product a household word. When it is successful, a brand name becomes almost the generic identifier, like Coke for cola and Kleenex for facial tissue.

Techniques of successful brand-name advertising came together in the 1890s for an English product, Pears' soap. A key element in the campaign was multimedia saturation. Advertisements for Pears' were everywhere—in newspapers and magazines and on posters, vacant walls, fences, buses and lampposts. Redundancy hammered home the brand name. "Good morning. Have you used Pears' today?" became a good-natured greeting among Britons that was still being repeated 50 years later. Each repetition reinforced the brand name.

BRAND IMAGE. David Ogilvy, who headed the Ogilvy & Mather agency, developed the **brand image** in the 1950s. Ogilvy's advice: "Give your product a first-class ticket through life."

Explaining the importance of image, Ogilvy once said: "Take whisky. Why do some people choose Jack Daniel's, while others choose Grand Dad or Taylor? Have they tried all three and compared the taste? Don't make me laugh. The reality is that these three brands have different images which appeal to different kinds of people. It isn't the whisky they choose, it's the image. The brand image is 90 percent of what the distiller has to sell. Give people a taste of Old Crow, and tell them it's Old Crow. Then give them another taste of Old Crow, but tell them it's Jack Daniel's. Ask them which they prefer. They'll think the two drinks are quite different. They are tasting images."

Media Databank

Best Brands in Canada

According to Interbrand and *Report on Business Magazine,* the following were the top-ranking brands by brand value in 2006:

RBC Financial Group

TD Canada Trust

Petro Canada

Bell

Shoppers Drug Mart

Tim Hortons

Source: www.interbrand.ca, Best Canadian Brands 2006, July 2006.

Using Ogilvy's assumptions, do Canadians taste coffee or image? Consider this: Many Canadians don't go for coffee any more. For some, the brand "Tim Hortons" has become synonymous with coffee. They go to "Hortons" or to "Timmy's." It's no wonder that in Interbrand's list of the Best Canadian Brands of 2006, Tim Hortons was among the top brands. Why is Tim Hortons successful? Interbrand claims that Canadians view Tim Hortons as their "fourth place, after home, work and the hockey/curling rink." Meanwhile, John Gray, writing in *Canadian Business,* says, "The brand has become a part of Canadian culture. That happened by design and not by accident. The company measures just about everything it does against its list of brand characteristics: unpretentious, friendly, dependable, caring—characteristics you might use to describe an ideal Canadian."

LOWEST COMMON DENOMINATOR

Early brand-name campaigns were geared to the largest possible audience, sometimes called an LCD, or **lowest-common-denominator,** approach. The term *LCD* is adapted from mathematics. To reach an audience that includes members with IQs of 100, the pitch cannot exceed their level of understanding, even if some people in the audience have IQs of 150. The opportunity for deft touches and even cleverness is limited by the fact they might be lost on some potential customers.

LCD advertising is best epitomized in contemporary advertising by USP, short for **unique selling proposition,** a term coined by **Rosser Reeves** of the giant Ted Bates agency in the 1960s. Reeves's prescription was simple: Create a benefit of the product, even if from thin air, and then tout the benefit authoritatively and repeatedly as if the competition doesn't have it. One early USP campaign boasted that Schlitz beer bottles were "washed with live steam." The claim sounded good—who would want to drink from dirty bottles? However, the fact was that every brewery used steam to clean reusable bottles before filling them again. Furthermore, what is "live steam"? Although the implication of a competitive edge was hollow, it was done dramatically and pounded home with emphasis, and it sold beer. Just as hollow as a competitive advantage was the USP claim for Colgate toothpaste: "Cleans Your Breath While It Cleans Your Teeth."

lowest-common-denominator Messages for broadest audience possible.

unique selling proposition (USP) Emphasizing a single feature.

Rosser Reeves Devised unique selling proposition.

Perhaps to compensate for a lack of substance, many USP ads are heavy-handed. A unique selling proposition need be neither hollow nor insulting, however. **Leo Burnett**, founder of the agency bearing his name, refined the USP concept by insisting that the unique point be real. For Maytag, Burnett took the company's slight advantage in reliability and dramatized it with the lonely Maytag repairman.

Market Segments

Rather than pitching to the lowest common denominator, advertising executive **Jack Trout** developed the idea of **positioning**. Trout worked to establish product identities that appealed not to the whole audience but to a specific audience. The cowboy image for Marlboro cigarettes, for example, established a macho attraction beginning in 1958. Later, something similar was done with Virginia Slims, aimed at women.

Positioning helps to distinguish products from all the LCD clamour and noise. Advocates of positioning note that there are more and more advertisements and that they are becoming noisier and noisier. Ad clutter, as discussed earlier in this chapter, drowns out individual advertisements. With positioning, the appeal is focused and caters to audience segments, and it need not be done in such broad strokes. Campaigns based on positioning have included Johnson & Johnson's baby oil and baby shampoo, which were positioned as adult products by advertisements featuring athletes; and Alka-Seltzer, once a hangover and headache remedy, which was positioned as an upscale product for stress relief among health-conscious, success-driven people.

Redundancy Techniques

As we learned in Chapter 1, a redundant message is one that's easy to decode. Advertising people learned the importance of **redundancy** early on. To be effective, an advertising message must be repeated, perhaps thousands of times. Redundancy is expensive, however. To increase effectiveness at less cost, advertisers use several techniques:

- **Barrages.** Scheduling advertisements in intensive bursts called **flights** or **waves.**
- **Bunching.** Promoting a product in a limited period, such as running advertisements for school supplies in late August and September.
- **Trailing.** Running condensed versions of advertisements after the original has been introduced, as auto makers do when they introduce new models with multipage magazine spreads, following with single-page placements.
- **Multimedia trailing.** Using less expensive media to reinforce expensive advertisements. Relatively cheap drive-time radio in major markets is a favourite follow-through to expensive television advertisements created for major events like the Super Bowl.

Marshall McLuhan, the media theorist prominent in the 1960s, is still quoted as saying that advertising is important after the sale to confirm for purchasers that they made a wise choice. McLuhan's observation has not been lost on advertisers that seek repeat customers.

Under-the-Radar Advertising

Inundated with advertisements, 6000 a week on network television, double since 1983, many people tune out. Some do it literally with their remotes. Ad people are concerned that traditional modes are losing effectiveness. People are overwhelmed. Consider, for example, that a major grocery store carries 30 000 items, each with

---

Leo Burnett Unique selling proposition doesn't need to be insulting.

Jack Trout Devised positioning.

positioning Targeting ads for specific consumer groups.

redundancy Repetition of media messages.

barrages Intensive repetition of ads.

flights Intensive repetition of ads.

waves Intensive repetition of ads.

bunching Short-term ad campaign.

trailing Running shorter, smaller ads after campaign is introduced.

Prop Star: An agency that specializes in placing products and brand names in movies and on TV.
www.propstar.com

packaging that screams "buy me."
More commercial messages are put
there than a human being can handle.
The problem is ad clutter. Advertisers
are trying to address the clutter in
numerous ways, including stealth ads,
new-site ads and alternative media.
Although not hidden or subliminal,
stealth ads are subtle—even covert.
You might not know you're being
pitched unless you're attentive, really
attentive.

STEALTH ADS. So neatly can **stealth ads**
fit into the landscape that people may
not recognize they're being pitched.
Consider the Bamboo lingerie company,
which stenciled messages on a Manhattan sidewalk: "From here it looks like
you could use some new underwear."
Sports arenas like Rexall Place in
Edmonton work their way into sports-
casts and everyday dialogue, subtly reinforcing product identity. In 2007, movie
theatres began being sponsored when
the Paramount Theatre in Toronto was
renamed the Scotiabank Theatre.

Viral Advertising. Automakers have experimented with what's called "viral
advertising"—producing compelling action stories on the web that viewers will want
to pass on, viruslike, to friends. Embedded in storylines, like Ford's "Evil Twin" for its
SportKa in Europe, are product messages. BMW estimates that 55.1 million
people have seen its "For Hire" series. Honda couldn't be more pleased with its "Cog"
mini-story. A Honda executive said: "I have never seen a commercial that bolted
around the world like 'Cog' in two weeks."

PRODUCT PLACEMENT. In the 1980s, advertisers began wriggling brand-name products into movie scripts, creating an additional although minor revenue stream for
moviemakers. The practice, **product placement**, stirred criticism about artistic
integrity, but it gained momentum. Fees zoomed upward. For the 2005 release of
The Green Hornet, Miramax was seeking an automaker willing to pay at least $35
million for its products to be written into the script, topping the $15 million that
Ford paid for its 2003 Thunderbird, Jaguar and Aston Martin lines to be in the
James Bond movie *Die Another Day.*

Later, placing products into television scenes gained importance with the advent
of **TiVo** and DVRs that allow people to record shows and replay them commercial-
free at their convenience. Their growing popularity worried the television industry,
whose business model was dependent on revenue from advertisers to which it guaranteed an audience for ads. With TiVo and DVRs, audiences no longer were trapped
into watching commercials. Was the 30-second spot commercial doomed? The television and advertising industries struck product placement deals that went beyond
anything seen before. For a fee, products are being built into scripts not only as
props but also for both implicit and explicit endorsement.

INFOMERCIALS. Less subtle is the **infomercial**, a program-length television commercial
dolled up to look like either a newscast, a live-audience participation show or a
chatty talk show. With the proliferation of 24-hour television service and of cable
channels, airtime is so cheap at certain hours that advertisers of even offbeat products
can afford it.

stealth ads
Advertisements, often
subtle, in nontraditional,
unexpected places.

product placement Writing
a brand-name product into
a television or movie script.

TiVo A television recording
and playback device that
allows viewers to edit out
commercials. Also called a
digital video recorder (DVR)
or personal video recorder
(PVR).

infomercial Program-length
broadcast commercial.

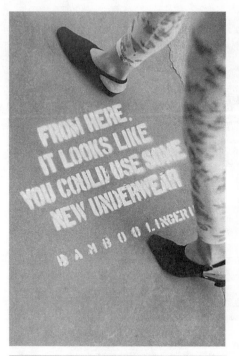

Omnipresent Ads. Bamboo Lingerie's stenciled sidewalk messages may have been unsettling to some folks, but they sold underwear. Like many advertisers worried that their messages are lost in ad-crammed traditional media, Bamboo has struck out for nontraditional territory to be noticed. Regina Kelley, director of strategic planning for the Saatchi & Saatchi agency in New York, said: "Any space you can take in visually, anything you can hear, in the future will be branded."

'zine Magazine whose entire content—articles and ads—pitches a single product or product line.

store brands Products sold with a store brand, often manufactured by the retailer. Also called *house brands* and *private labels*.

'ZINE. A print media variation is the **'zine**, a magazine published by a manufacturer to plug a single line of products with varying degrees of subtlety. 'Zine publishers, including such stalwarts as IBM and Sony, have even been so brazen as to sell these wall-to-wall advertising vehicles at newsstands. In 1996, if you bought a splashy new magazine called *Colors*, you paid $4.50 for it. Once inside, you probably would realize it was a thinly veiled ad for Benetton casual clothes. *Guess Journal* may look like a magazine, but guess who puts it out as a 'zine? It's the makers of the Guess fashion brand.

An under-the-radar advertisement tries "to morph into the very entertainment it sponsors," wrote Mary Kuntz, Joseph Weber and Heidi Dawley in *Business Week*. The goal, they said, is "to create messages so entertaining, so compelling—and maybe so disguised— that rapt audiences will swallow them whole, oblivious to the sales component."

POST-BRAND-NAME ERA

Perhaps prematurely, perhaps not, obituaries are being written for brand names—and brand-name advertising. Retailers are pushing **store brands**, on which they typically score 10 percent higher profits. Every time somebody buys Wal-Mart's Ol' Roy dog chow, Purina and other brand-name manufacturers lose a sale. Wal-Mart spends virtually nothing other than packaging costs for in-store displays to advertise Ol' Roy, which has knocked off Purina as top-seller. The store-brand assault has struck at a whole range of venerable brand names: Kellogg's, Kraft, Procter & Gamble and Unilever. Forrester Research, which tracks consumer trends, said in a 2002 report: "Wal-Mart will become the new P&G." In Canada, popular store brands include President's Choice (Loblaws), Master Choice (A&P) and Compliments (Sobeys).

Before the mega-retailers, brand names gave products an edge—with network television and national magazines carrying the messages. In those days the major networks—ABC, CBS and NBC—delivered messages to millions of consumers with greater effect than could small retailers. Not only are small retailers disappearing, but also the networks can't deliver what they used to. Television systems with 500 channels and the highly diverse web have divided and subdivided the audience into fragments. In a 2003 newsletter to clients, the ad agency Doremus noted, despairingly, that "it's almost impossible to get your name in enough channels to build substantial awareness." Willard Bishop Consulting came to a similar conclusion from a study on network television, noting that three commercials could reach 80 percent of one target audience, 18- to 49-year-old women, in 1995. That penetration level required 97 ads in 2000. In an analysis of the phenomenon, *Fortune* magazine writer Michael Boyle said the big superstores are displacing brand-name advertising as the new direct connection to consumers. The new mass channel, he said, is the superstore.

Air Canada Centre. New site ads, like corporate sponsorship of sports arenas such as the Air Canada Centre in Toronto, offer a new revenue stream for owners but may also add to the problem of "ad clutter."

Media People

Dave Nichol. Canadian who was a store brand pioneer.

Dave Nichol

Dave Nichol didn't invent store brands, but he was the wizard of the phenomenon that is rewriting the rules of consumer marketing. When he was an executive at the Canadian grocery chain Loblaws, he introduced knock-off products under the brand No Name in 1978. Nichol's emphasis was quality on par with that of brand names at lower cost. After all, he had no advertising expenses, which can add 25 cents to the cost of a tube of toothpaste.

Nichol then created a coffee blend, President's Choice, modeled on the coffee in a top Toronto restaurant. Then came Decadent cookies, with 39 percent chocolate chips, compared to 19 percent in Chips Ahoy. When Kellogg's proclaimed two scoops of raisins in its bran flakes, Nichol's Loblaws brand put in four scoops.

Nichol, with a law degree from Harvard, regards himself as a food connoisseur and has his own vineyard. His contribution to marketing consumer products has been packaging higher quality into products than is in brand-name products and selling them for less. He also expanded the Loblaws store brands by selling them to U.S. chains. President's Choice coffee picked up a quick following—without advertising—in 15 chains in 36 states.

In 1990, Wal-Mart founder Sam Walton hired Nichol to devise a store brand plan for Wal-Mart. A year later, Sam's Choice, modeled on Loblaws' President's Choice, was on Wal-Mart shelves. Next came a value brand of Wal-Mart coffee, Great Value. Then came vitamins, batteries, toilet paper, and even tuna. By 2000, 40 percent of Wal-Mart's sales were store brands, and that share is growing.

Advertising Regulation

Product Placement. A financial linchpin for the CBS adventure series *Survivor* was integrating identifiable brand-name products into the storylines for a price. Advertisers have gravitated to product placement to counter viewership that's lost to fast-growing use of DVRs.

caveat emptor Buyer beware.

caveat venditor Seller beware.

Edward Bok Set media standards for ads.

Competition Act Federal regulator of advertising in Canada.

ASC Advertising Standards Canada, the self-regulatory body for advertising.

Study Preview   *The "buyer beware" underpinning of much of 19th-century advertising has given way to "seller beware." Today, advertising is regulated on many fronts: by the media that carry advertisements, by the advertising industry itself and by government agencies.*

MEDIA GATEKEEPING

A dramatic reversal in thinking about advertising has occurred in the 20th century. The earlier *caveat emptor* ("let the buyer beware") mindset tolerated extravagant claims. Anybody who believed that the same elixir could cure dandruff, halitosis and cancer deserved to be conned, or so went the thinking. Over the years, owing partly to the growing consumer movement, the thinking changed to *caveat venditor* ("let the seller beware"), placing the onus on the advertiser to avoid misleading claims and to demonstrate the truth of claims.

In advertising's early days, newspapers and magazines skirted the ethics question posed by false advertisements by saying that their pages were open to all advertisers. Under growing pressure, publications sometimes criticized dubious advertisements editorially, but most did not ban them. **Edward Bok**, who made *Ladies' Home Journal* a runaway success in the 1890s, crusaded against dishonest advertising. In one exposé on Lydia E. Pinkham's remedies for "female maladies," Bok reported that Lydia, to whom women readers were invited in advertisements to write for advice, had been dead for 22 years. Yet the advertisements continued.

ADVERTISING REGULATION AND SELF-REGULATION

The advertising industry in Canada must adhere to a variety of laws and regulations, most notably the **Competition Act**. This is a federal statute that covers many different aspects of advertising in Canada. According to the Act, any representation (flyer, brochure, in-store display, newspaper ad, or material on the internet, radio or television) that offers a product or service for sale must adhere to specific guidelines. Some specific aspects covered by the act include false and misleading advertising, bait-and-switch advertising, selling at a higher than advertised price and testimonials. Fines levied under the Competition Act can be steep.

The advertising industry itself has numerous organizations that try, through ethics codes and moral suasion, to eradicate falsity and deception. Besides the explicit purposes of these self-policing mechanisms, their existence can be cited by advertising people to argue that their industry is able to deal with misdeeds itself with a minimum of government regulation. Advertising Standards Canada (ASC) is the self-regulatory body that oversees advertising in Canada. The ASC administers many industry codes. The Canadian Code of Advertising Standards, which has been in place since 1963 but most recently updated in 2005, includes 14 clauses with an emphasis on the following themes:

- Clear and accurate information on the price, availability, and performance of goods or services.
- No deceptive price claims.
- Warranties and guarantees must be fully explained.
- Products cannot be shown encouraging use that may be dangerous.
- Children's advertising should not exploit their naïveté, nor should it harm them physically, morally or emotionally.
- If the good or service is prohibited to minors, for instance tobacco or alcohol, its advertising cannot appeal to underage people.
- Advertising cannot exploit violence, gender or sexuality. It should always be in good taste.

Advertising Standards Canada: Industry self-regulatory body. **www.adstandards.ca**

Competition Act: Federal watchdog for advertising. Search the site for hefty fines paid by advertisers. **www.competitionbureau .gc.ca/internet/index .cfm?itemID= 1863&lg=e**

Problems and Issues

Study Preview   *People are exposed to such a blur of ads that advertisers worry that their messages are being lost in the clutter. Some advertising people see more creativity as the answer so that people will want to see and read ads, but there is evidence that creativity can work against an ad's effectiveness.*

ADVERTISING CLUTTER

Leo Bogart of the Newspaper Advertising Bureau noted that the number of advertising messages doubled through the 1960s and 1970s and, except for the recession at the start of the 1990s, the trend continues. This proliferation of advertising creates a problem: too many ads. The problem has been exacerbated by the shortening of ads from 60 seconds in the early days of television to today's widely used 15-second format. At one time the CRTC limited the amount of TV commercials a station could air to 12 minutes. In 2008, that limit was raised to 15 minutes. While this may make it easier for TV stations to make money, it will only contribute to ad clutter.

Ad clutter is less of an issue in the print media. Many people buy magazines and newspapers to look at ads as part of the comparative shopping process. Even so, some advertisers, concerned that their ads are overlooked in massive editions, such as a 7-pound metro Sunday newspaper or a 700-page bridal magazine, are looking to alternative means to reach potential customers in a less cluttered environment.

The clutter that marks much of commercial television and radio today may be alleviated as the media fragment further. Not only will demassification create more specialized outlets, such as narrowly focused cable television services, but there will be new media. The result will be advertising aimed at narrower audiences.

Advertisers are reviewing whether creativity is as effective an approach as hard sell. **Harry McMahan** studied **Clio Awards** for creativity in advertising and discovered that 36 agencies that produced 81 winners of the prestigious awards for advertisements had either lost the winning account or gone out of business.

Predicted advertising commentator E.B. Weiss: "Extravagant license for creative people will be curtailed." The future may hold more heavy-handed pitches, perhaps with over-the-counter regimens not only promising fast-fast-fast relief but also spelling it out in all caps and boldface with exclamation marks: **F-A-S-T! F-A-S-T!! F-A-S-T!!!**

Clio Awards: Each year the advertising industry presents the Clio Awards, showcasing the most creative television commercials worldwide. **www.clioawards.com**

Adcritic.com: Extensive collection of TV commercials in QuickTime format. **http://creativity-online.com**

Adbusters: "A global network of artists, activists, writers, pranksters, students, educators and entrepreneurs who criticize advertising and consumption." **http://adbusters.org**

False Advertising: A gallery of advertising parody. **http://parody.organique.com**

Harry McMahan Dubious about ad creativity.

Clio Award Award for advertising creativity.

ADVERTISING EFFECTIVENESS

Gerald Tellis Dubious about TV ads.

Long-held assumptions about the effectiveness of advertising itself are being questioned. **Gerald Tellis**, a University of Iowa researcher, put together a sophisticated statistical model that found that people are relatively unmoved by television advertisements in making brand choices, especially on mundane everyday products like toilet paper and laundry detergents. Tellis's conclusions began with consumer purchasing studies in Eau Claire, Wisconsin. Not surprisingly, considering its self-interest, the advertising industry has challenged the Tellis studies.

MEASURING CREATIVITY

Consumer-products giant Procter & Gamble has adopted a computerized tool to measure the creativity of advertising agencies competing for its accounts. By quantifying creativity, the company hopes to identify agencies that can bring new ideas and imagination to promoting P&G products.

Former P&G executives who formed Cincinnati Consulting Consortium devised the system. Although the system is cloaked in secrecy, it's known that the system assigns points for prizes that agencies win for creativity contests. Awards are weighed according to their prestige. Plugged in, too, are other numbers, including the number of awards for advertising per every dollar that's spent.

Procter & Gamble began applying the tool in 2005 not only to advertising agencies already holding P&G accounts but also to competing agencies. Agencies can expect new pressure to show external confirmation for their creativity.

Nice Smile. Actress Nicollette Sheridan, known most recently as a serial divorcee who kept the neighbourhood buzzing on television's *Desperate Housewives,* opens an old-fashioned photo booth to promote Crest Whitestrips at a Central Park skating rink in New York. The promotional stunt for the Procter & Gamble Crest product was typical of a new wave of alternatives to traditional media for advertising.

CHAPTER 10 WRAP-UP

The role of advertising in North American mass media cannot be overstated. In one sense, advertisers subsidize readers, viewers and listeners who pay only a fraction of the cost of producing publications and broadcasts. The bulk of the cost is paid by advertisers, who are willing to do so to make their pitches to potential customers who, coincidentally, are media consumers.

Besides underwriting the mass media, advertising is vital for a prosperous, growing consumer economy. It triggers demand for goods and services, and it enables people to make wise choices by providing information on competing products. The result is efficiency in the marketplace, which frees more capital for expansion. This all speaks to an intimate interrelationship involving advertising in a democratic and capitalistic society.

QUESTIONS FOR REVIEW

1. Why is advertising essential in a capitalistic society?
2. Trace the development of advertising since the time of Johannes Gutenberg.
3. What is the role of advertising agencies?
4. Why do some advertisements appear in some media and not others?
5. What are the major tactics used in advertising? Who devised each one?
6. How do advertising people use psychology and research to shape their messages?
7. What are the advantages and the problems of the globalization of the advertising industry?
8. Does advertising still follow the dictum "let the buyer beware"?
9. What are some problems and unanswered issues in advertising?

QUESTIONS FOR CRITICAL THINKING

1. How does the development of modern advertising relate to Johannes Gutenberg's technological innovation? To the Industrial Revolution? To long-distance mass transportation? To mass marketing?
2. Why does advertising flourish more in democratic than in autocratic societies? In a capitalistic more than in a controlled economy? In a prosperous society?
3. What were the contributions to advertising of F. Wayland Ayer, Anson McKim, Rosser Reeves, Jack Trout, Wilson Bryan Key and David Ogilvy?
4. What are the responsibilities of advertising account executives, copywriters, media buyers, researchers, brand managers, ad reps and brokers?
5. What are the advantages of the commission system for advertising agency revenue? Of the fee system? The disadvantages of both?
6. Describe these advertising tactics: brand-name promotion, unique selling proposition, lowest-common-denominator approach, positioning and redundancy.
7. How is ad clutter a problem? What can be done about it?
8. How has Advertising Standards Canada improved the image of companies that advertise, agencies that create advertisements and media that carry advertisements? Give examples.

DEEPENING YOUR MEDIA LITERACY

How does advertising affect the consumer?
Step 1

Find a newspaper or magazine with a lot of ads.

Dig Deeper
Step 2

Make a list of the persuasion techniques used in advertising. Find ads in your publication that best exhibit each technique.

What Do You Think?
Step 3

Answer these questions:

1. Which ad do you like best? Why?
2. Which ad do you like least? Why?
3. Which ad do you think is most persuasive? Why?
4. Are any of the ads unfair? In what way?

KEEPING UP TO DATE

Weekly trade journals are *Marketing* magazine, *Advertising Age* and *AdWeek*.

Scholarly publications include *Journal of Marketing Research* and *Journal of Advertising*. *The Globe and Mail* regularly reports on the industry.

The *Journal of Consumer Psychology* includes analysis, reviews, reports and other scholarship on the role of advertising in consumer psychology.

FOR FURTHER LEARNING

Mary Billard. "Heavy Metal Goes on Trial." *Rolling Stone* 582–583 double issue (July 12–26, 1990): 83–88, 132.

Competition Bureau. "Law and Litigation: About the Acts." Available online at www.competitionbureau.gc.ca.

CRTC. *Broadcast Policy Monitoring Report, 2006.*

Bruce DeMara. "Now Playing: Corporate Sponsorship." *Toronto Star* (January 24, 2007).

Stephen Fox. *The Mirror Makers: A History of American Advertising and Its Creators* (Morrow, 1984).

John Kenneth Galbraith. *The Affluent Society* (Mariner Books, 1998).

Interbrand. *Interbrand's Best Canadian Brands, 2006.* Available at www.interbrand.ca.

Wilson Bryan Key. *Subliminal Seduction: Ad Media's Manipulation of a Not So Innocent America* (New American Library, 1972).

Otto Kleppner, Thomas Russell, and Glenn Verrill. *Advertising Procedure*, 8th edition (Prentice Hall, 1990).

Bob Levenson. *Bill Bernbach's Book: A History of the Advertising That Changed the History of Advertising* (Random House, 1987).

Jay Conrad Levinson and Charles Rubin. *Guerrilla Advertising* (Mariner Books, 1998).

Nancy Millman. *Emperors of Adland: Inside the Advertising Revolution* (Warner Books, 1988).

David Ogilvy. *Confessions of an Advertising Man* (Atheneum, 1963).

David Ogilvy. *Ogilvy on Advertising* (Vintage, 1985).

Andrew Potter. "Galbraith's Theory of Advertising Had Us All Fooled." *Maclean's* (May 15, 2006).

Anthony Pratkanis and Elliot Aronson. *Age of Propaganda: The Everyday Use and Abuse of Persuasion* (W. H. Freeman, 1992).

Brenda Pritchard and Susan Vogt. *Advertising and Marketing Law in Canada,* Second Edition (Butterworth's, 2006).

Ronald H. Rotenberg. *Advertising: A Canadian Perspective* (Allyn and Bacon, 1986)

Paul Rutherford. *The New Icons? The Art of Television Advertising* (University of Toronto Press, 1994).

Michael Schudson. *Advertising: The Uneasy Persuasion: Its Dubious Impact on American Society* (Basic Books, 1984).

Alan Shanoff. *Advertising and Law* (Hallion Press, 1995).

Keith J. Tuckwell. *Canadian Advertising in Action* (Prentice Hall, 2000).

Robbin Lee Zeff and Brad Aronson. *Advertising on the Internet,* Second edition (John Wiley, 1999).

John Perry Barlow. He doubts the traditional notion that creativity is dependent on the financial incentive created by copyright law. New technology, Barlow says, is rendering copyright concepts archaic—a fascinating but contentious view.

Mass Media Law and Ethics

MEDIA IN THEORY

Digital Technology and Media Law

As former lyricist for the Grateful Dead **John Perry Barlow** envisions the future, giant media companies will shrivel. The internet makes it possible for people to acquire mass messages, like pop music, directly from artists.

Such direct transactions between artists and consumers undermine the profitable role that media companies have been playing in the dissemination of messages.

To make his point, Barlow, cofounder of the Electronic Frontier Foundation, points to Napster file-sharing technology that burst onto the scene in 1999. Until the courts stopped the practice in 2001, music fans used Napster to bypass media companies and traditional record-sales channels. Record companies were cut out. What's happened with records, Barlow says, inevitably will happen with other kinds of mass messages.

Chapter Eleven

MEDIA TIMELINE

Landmarks in Canadian Media Law and Ethics

_____	**1923**	First code of ethics was adopted as the Canons of Journalism of the American Society of Newspaper Editors.
_____	**1926**	Canadian Association of Broadcasters was formed.
_____	**1928**	Canada's first royal commission into broadcasting began looking at the role radio plays in the daily lives of Canadians.
_____	**1932**	Canadian Radio Broadcasting Act was passed.
_____	**1936**	CBC was formed; it was Canada's first public broadcaster and its first broadcast regulator.
_____	**1957**	Fowler Report was released, and the Board of Broadcast Governors (BBG) was formed to regulate broadcasters in Canada. It also introduced the idea of Canadian content for television.
_____	**1982**	*Canadian Charter of Rights and Freedoms* was passed into law, guaranteeing media freedom.
_____	**1990s**	CRTC began the slow process of deregulating radio and television.
_____	**1990**	SOCAN was formed in Canada.
_____	**1990**	Canadian Broadcast Standards Council (CBSC) was formed by the Canadian Association of Broadcasters.
_____	**1992**	Butler ruling on pornography.
_____	**2004**	For the first time in history, the CRTC revoked the licence of a radio station: CHOI in Quebec

No wonder media executives were watching closely when the record industry went to court to shut Napster down and later to sue individual downloaders. The issue was copyright law, which guarantees that people who create intellectual property, like music, hold the right to benefit financially from their work. According to conventional wisdom, the financial incentive inspires creative people to keep producing and thus enriches society.

Until the internet, creative people almost always turned over the ownership of their work to media companies because those companies owned the only means to disseminate messages to mass audiences. In exchange, media companies gave a percentage of their revenue to the creative people.

In court against Napster, the record companies argued that composers, lyricists and performers were in danger of losing their share of the revenue generated by the record companies. Without that financial incentive, according to these anti-Napster forces, creativity would suffer, perhaps dry up.

To that, Barlow said balderdash. He argues that creative people hardly need copyright protection, either legal or ethical, to do their thing. Rhetorically, he asks, how about Shakespeare? Da Vinci? Homer? His point is that creativity is inherent in human nature and occurs independently of financial incentives. Further, Barlow says, technology makes it possible for the first time in modern history for creative people to reach mass audiences on their own. In short, as he sees it, the underlying premise for copyright is an archaic relic from the pre-internet era. Equally archaic, he says, is the need for creative people to rely on media companies to disseminate their creative work and, in return, take a lion's share of the revenue. In short, Napster and similar technologies undermine the entire financial foundation on which media companies have been built.

In this chapter you will explore copyright to help you assess the merits of Barlow's argument, as well as that of the media companies. You also will learn about other aspects of mass media law and ethics.

John Perry Barlow Believes copyright laws are archaic.

The *Canadian Charter of Rights and Freedoms*

Study Preview   *Since 1982, the* Canadian Charter of Rights and Freedoms *bars the government from limiting freedom of expression, including expression in the mass media, or so it seems. There are limits to freedoms.*

Canadian Charter of Rights and Freedoms Basis for all laws, including media laws, in Canada.

The *Canadian Charter of Rights and Freedoms* is the basis for both media law and ethics codes. Interestingly, in the United States, "freedom of the press" has been a First Amendment Right since 1791. While the phrase "freedom of the press" was included in Canada's Bill of Rights in 1961, it only covered federal statutes and still wasn't a protected constitutional right. Officially, the media in Canada have only held these press freedoms since Queen Elizabeth II signed the Constitution Act on April 17, 1982. In his *Pocket Guide to Media Law,* Stuart Robertson states that three specific parts of the Charter affect the Canadian media:

Electronic Frontier Foundation: Defending freedom in a digital world. **www.eff.org**

Canadian Charter of Rights and Freedoms: Everything you want and more regarding your rights under Canadian law. **http://laws.justice.gc.ca/ en/charter/index.html**

- *Section 1.* The Charter "guarantees the rights and freedoms set out in it subject only to such reasonable limits prescribed by law as can be demonstrably justified in a free and democratic society."
- *Section 2.* All Canadians have "freedom of thought, belief, opinion and expression, including freedom of the press and other media of communication."
- *Section 52(1).* "The Constitution of Canada is the supreme law of Canada, and any law that is inconsistent with the provisions of the Constitution is, to the extent of the inconsistency, of no force or effect."

Robertson goes on to argue that the Charter has affected the media in at least two ways. First, it has granted all Canadians the same basic rights and freedoms. Second, it protects everyone, including those who work in the media, from unfair limitations on expression.

However, although freedom of the media is listed in the Charter, it isn't guaranteed. That is made explicit in Section 1 of the Charter. The rights in the Charter are guaranteed only "to such reasonable limits prescribed by law as can be demonstrably justified in a free and democratic society." In simpler terms, this means that while there is media freedom, the media must also take responsibility for their actions and there may be times when the media's right to free speech may be limited.

PUBLICATION BANS

For many years, the courts tended to put an individual's right to a fair trial above the rights of the media. Although the media are granted freedom of speech under the Charter, **publication bans** were often issued limiting what could be reported by the media. That changed in 1994 when the Supreme Court of Canada issued its **Dagenais ruling**. It all began with the CBC scheduled to air the NFB's movie *The Boys of St. Vincent* about atrocities at a Maritime orphanage. The movie was based on actual events at the Mount Cashel orphanage in Newfoundland and the movie was set to air nationally during the actual trial. Lawyers for the defence argued that the movie might affect their right to a fair trial. The judge agreed and, based on legal precedence, ordered the CBC not to show the movie. The CBC appealed the ban and, in a landmark ruling, the Supreme Court of Canada quashed the publication ban. Dean Jobb, writing in *Media Law for Canadian Journalists,* explains Chief Justice Lamer's rationale for the outcome: "the Charter entrenches the right of accused persons to a fair trial . . . the publication ban imposed on *The Boys of St. Vincent* however had a profound impact on the right of the film director to express himself, the CBC's interest in broadcasting the film, the public's interest in viewing it and society's interest in having an important issue—child abuse—publicly exposed and debated." Since Dagenais, judges need to weigh the individual's right to a fair trial against the media's freedom of speech before making a decision to issue a publication ban.

    There are times when the judge has no choice but to issue a publication ban. For example, under Canada's new **Youth Criminal Justice Act**, it is illegal to print or broadcast the name(s) of anyone under 18 who has been charged with or convicted of a crime, unless that person received an adult sentence. It also prohibits the naming of parents or siblings of those who have been charged, underage witnesses, or victims of crimes unless parental consent is given.

publication bans Limitations on media freedom of speech.

Dagenais ruling Rights need to be balanced.

Youth Criminal Justice Act Prohibits reporting on trials involving minors.

PORNOGRAPHY VERSUS OBSCENITY

One other limit on freedom of the press deals with obscenity. Why are sexually explicit movies available on Viewer's Choice Canada or on Showcase? The reason is that there is a difference between pornography and obscenity in Canada, based on the **Butler ruling** of 1992. Obscenity can be controlled by the government, but pornography cannot.

Butler ruling Supreme Court ruling that defined legal differences between obscenity and pornography.

Defamation

Study Preview   *When the mass media carry disparaging descriptions and comments, they risk being sued for defamation, which is a serious matter. Not only are reputations at stake when defamation occurs, but also losing a suit can be so costly that it can put a publication or broadcast organization out of business.*

defamation False comments that harm a reputation.

libel A written defamation.

slander A spoken defamation.

THE CONCEPT OF DEFAMATION

A civil limitation on media freedom of speech is the issue of defamation. If someone punched you in the face for no good reason, knocking out several teeth, breaking your nose and causing permanent disfigurement, most courts would rule that your attacker should pay your medical bills. If your disfigurement or psychological upset causes you to lose your job, to be ridiculed or shunned by friends and family or perhaps to retreat from social interaction, the court would probably order your attacker to pay additional amounts. Like fists, words can cause damage. Freedom of speech and the press is not a licence to say absolutely anything about anybody.

Defamation is sometimes referred to as **libel** or **slander**. Canadian lawyer Michael G. Crawford, who has worked for both the CBC and CTV, defines defamation in *The Journalist's Legal Guide* as the publication or broadcast of a statement that harms someone's reputation. If someone can prove the following three things, that person may be able to sue for defamation under Canadian law:

- The words or pictures were defamatory.
- The words or pictures were published or broadcast.
- The words or pictures refer to a specific, living person.

If a defamatory statement is false, the utterer may be liable for millions of dollars in damages. When *Toronto Life* magazine published an article about the Reichmann family, the Reichmanns sued for $102 million. After four years in the courts, the case was settled out of court. *Toronto Life* issued a statement that it made "serious mistakes" in the research and writing of the story. In 1999, the *Red Deer Advocate* published a letter from Stockwell Day, then a member of the Alberta Legislature. In the letter, Day made defamatory remarks comparing a lawyer to a pedophile. Day tried to use the fair comment defence but lost. The letter cost Day $792 000 in damages and legal costs.

These types of awards and cases are the foundation of what has become known as "libel chill." Many journalists, editors and others in the media are deciding to play it safe and not publish controversial material that may result in a lawsuit. While this may make economic sense, one needs to question the role libel chill plays in a democratic country that relies on information to educate its people.

defences for defamation
Consent, truth, privilege, fair comment.

DEFENCES FOR DEFAMATION

It is up to the media, in its defence, to prove any of the following as **defences for defamation** to avoid conviction:

- The person mentioned in the story or picture consented to its broadcast or publication.
- The words or pictures are true.
- The words or pictures were published under privilege. This means reporting and commenting fairly and accurately any comments made on public record. For example, quoting something that was said during a town council meeting or in a courtroom, or contained in a media release would constitute privilege.
- The words or pictures were fair comments.

Cherry Sisters
Complainants in a case that barred performers from suing critics.

What is fair comment? For the answer to this question, we look to the Cherry Sisters. People flocked to see the **Cherry Sisters'** act. Effie, Addie, Jessie, Lizzie and Ella toured the country with a song and dance act that drew big crowds. They were just awful. They could neither sing nor dance, but people turned out because the sisters were so funny. Sad to say, the Cherry Sisters took themselves seriously. In 1901, desperate for respect, the sisters decided to sue the next newspaper reviewer who gave them a bad notice. That reviewer, it turned out, was Billy Hamilton, who included a lot of equine metaphors in his piece for the *Des Moines Leader:* "Effie is an old jade of 50 summers, Jessie a frisky filly of 40, and Addie, the flower of the family, a capering monstrosity of 35. Their long skinny arms, equipped with talons at the extremities, swung mechanically, and anon waved frantically at the suffering audience. The mouths of their rancid features opened like caverns, and sounds like the wailings of damned souls issued therefrom. They pranced around the stage with a motion that suggested a cross between the *danse du ventre* and the fox trot—strange creatures with painted faces and hideous mien. Effie is spavined, Addie is stringhalt, and Jessie, the only one who showed her stockings, has legs with calves as classic in their outlines as the curves of a broom handle."

Fair Comment and Criticism. Upset with what an Iowa reviewer had written about their show, the Cherry Sisters sued. The important 1901 court decision that resulted said that journalists, critics and anybody else can say whatever they want about a public performance. The rationale was that someone who puts on a performance for public acceptance has to take a risk also of public rejection.

The outcome of the suit was another setback for the Cherrys. They lost in a case that established that actors or others who perform for the public must be willing to accept both positive and negative comments about their performance. This right of fair comment and criticism, however, does not make it open season on performers in aspects of their lives that do not relate to public performance. The *National Enquirer* could not defend itself when entertainer Carol Burnett sued for a story that described her as obnoxiously drunk at a restaurant. Not only was the description false (Carol Burnett abstains from alcohol), but Burnett was in no public or performing role at the restaurant. This distinction between an individual's public and private life also has been recognized in cases involving public officials and candidates.

DEFAMATION AND THE INTERNET

Although this is new territory for the law, with no case law to look to for precedents, it appears that defamation laws will extend to the internet. On several occasions Canadian bloggers have found themselves guilty of defamation. University of Ottawa law professor Michael Geist says that defamation laws "apply online as well as offline. Just because bloggers have the ability to write whatever they want doesn't give them the licence to defame anyone." Geist also says we're likely to see more defamation lawsuits aimed at bloggers in the future, as "people are increasingly realizing that blogs have an impact and that more people are reading them."

Michael Geist Online: University of Ottawa professor Michael Geist's blog on media law. **www.michaelgeist.ca**

Defamation on the Internet: Read the original article by Potts and Harris online. **www.cyberlibel.com/ defnet.html**

Still, the issue of defamation on the internet isn't clear at this point. Lawyers David Potts and Sally Harris list several legal issues that will need to be defined before laws in this area are clear. One of the most difficult factors is jurisdiction. Where does the plaintiff live? Where does the defendant live? Where should litigation take place? How can decisions be enforced?

The CRTC and Broadcast Regulation in Canada

Study Preview   *The Canadian Radio-television and Telecommunications Commission has regulated broadcasting in Canada since the early days of radio in the 1930s. With the advent of television and the internet, regulations have been updated.*

YOU'RE "ON THE AIRD": CANADA'S FIRST ROYAL COMMISSION ON BROADCASTING

Aird Commission First royal commission into Canadian broadcasting.

The idea that radio could help build a country was one of the factors behind the first Royal Commission on Broadcasting. The fact that Canadians were listening to more American than Canadian programming worried Ottawa, especially combined with the fact that there were 400 000 radios in Canada. For the first time (and certainly not the last time) in Canadian media history, politicians began to worry about the domination of Canada by American mass media. To solve this problem, they set up the first of many royal commissions on broadcasting in Canada. The **Aird Commission** (named after Sir John Aird) was created to examine the danger that American programming posed to Canadian culture. The verdict it reached in 1929 wasn't surprising: American networks were a threat to our airwaves and our culture.

The commission recommended that Canada set up and fund a public broadcasting network similar to the BBC in England. This network would produce and broadcast Canadian programs for and by Canadians. This recommendation caused quite a conflict between the owners of private radio stations, who were making a tidy profit, and those who preferred the public system. By 1932, Prime Minister Bennett laid out the government's official position on radio broadcasting in Canada: Canada would have both public and private radio stations. The government's proposal regarding public broadcasting revolved around three issues, which still form the basis of CRTC policy today:

- National sovereignty was to be preserved.
- Broadcasting services were to be made available to anyone in Canada, no matter where they lived.
- Broadcasting was not to be exploited by private interests.

Canadian Radio Broadcasting Act First statute governing broadcasting in Canada.

In 1932, the **Canadian Radio Broadcasting Act** was passed, resulting in the creation of the Canadian Radio Broadcasting Commission, which began broadcasting in 1933. The CRBC was a direct product of the Aird Commission. Initially, it broadcast for only one hour a day. By the time it was replaced by the CBC in 1936, it was reaching just under half of the Canadian population. By 1936, the Canadian Broadcasting Corporation (CBC) was formed. In addition to being a national radio network, it was responsible for granting licences to private radio broadcasters, even though the government did not officially recognize private broadcasting—an ideal position for the government to be in.

THE EVOLUTION OF CANADA'S BROADCASTING ACT

The evolution of television in Canada paralleled the growth of radio, a system with both public and private broadcasting. Initially, private television broadcasters had to apply to the CBC for broadcast licences. Private television broadcasters were not happy; they felt a conflict of interest existed. During this time, even private broadcasters had to carry 10 hours of CBC programming each week. How could the CBC, a broadcaster itself, also be responsible for overseeing private broadcasting?

In 1955 a royal commission into broadcasting was formed. The **Fowler Commission**, headed by Robert Fowler, analyzed Canadian broadcasting from the points of view of culture and regulations. Its report, tabled in 1957, formed the basis of the Broadcasting Act of 1958:

- The forming of the **Board of Broadcast Governors (BBG)**, which would oversee the granting of broadcasting licences.
- Official government recognition of private broadcasters in Canada. This allowed stations to affiliate themselves with a body other than the CBC. This would lead to the formation of Canada's first private television network, CTV.
- Programming on radio and TV that was as Canadian in "content and character" as possible.

THE 1968 BROADCASTING ACT

In March of 1968 another broadcasting act further defined the broadcast system and the function it should serve in Canada. This act resulted in the formation of the Canadian Radio-television Commission (CRTC), the precursor to the Canadian Radio-television and Telecommunications Commission. The changes to television were as follows:

- The CRTC replaced the BBG and had the power to regulate brodcasting in Canada.
- The CBC was given its mandate to provide a national broadcasting service in both official languages and to provide Canadian programming that helped develop national unity and allowed for Canadian cultural expression.
- Canadian broadcasting should be owned and operated by Canadians.

THE 1991 BROADCASTING ACT

In 1975 the CRTC became the Canadian Radio-television and Telecommunications Commission when it assumed responsibility for regulating the telephone industry. In 1991 a new broadcasting act was issued to help further define broadcasting and cultural issues in Canada. The new act:

- Stressed the importance of radio and television programming that was Canadian in content and character.
- Redefined the CBC's role as the national broadcaster, which was to help create a "Canadian consciousness." However, no attempt to define the term "Canadian consciousness" was made, nor was the issue of funding addressed.

THE CRTC AND THE BROADCASTING ACT

The **CRTC** is the federal regulator in charge of regulating and supervising the broadcast media in Canada. It's an independent authority, whose mandate is "to maintain a delicate balance, in the public interest, between the cultural, social and economic goals of the legislation on broadcasting and telecommunications." Its roots and

Fowler Commission Royal commission into television broadcasting in Canada.

Board of Broadcast Governors (BBG) Forefather of the current CRTC.

On the "Aird" Again: Revisit the highlights of government media regulation. **www.crtc.gc.ca/eng/ BACKGRND/Brochures/ B19903.htm**

CRTC: Canadian Radio-television and Telecommunications Commission. It ensures that Canadians are seen and heard on Canadian media. **www.crtc.gc.ca**

CRTC Canadian broadcast regulator.

CHOI: A very good overview of the CHOI-FM debate. **www.mapleleafweb.com/ education/spotlight/ issue_54/case.html**

CRTC on CHOI-FM: The justification for the CRTC's decision. **www.crtc.gc.ca/archive/ ENG/Decisions/2004/ db2004–271.pdf**

Copyright Myths: This website addresses 10 common copyright myths. **www.templetons.com/ brad/copymyths.html**

Copyright Board of Canada: Practical and relevant new copyright information for anyone interested. **www.cb-cda.gc.ca/ new-e.html**

Copyright Board of Canada: Providing information on copyright for the four sectors of cultural industry: arts, literature, film and music. **www.cb-cda.gc.ca**

Canadian Copyright Act: Check this site for the full text of the Act. **http://laws.justice.gc.ca/ en/C-42/index.html**

Berne Copyright Convention: Copyright protection on an international level. **www.law.cornell.edu/ treaties/berne/overview. html**

Universal Copyright Convention: More international protection for copyright. **www.unesco.org/culture/ laws/copyright/html_eng/ page1.shtml**

traditions echo the findings of the Aird Commission in 1929. The CRTC has power over 3300 broadcasters in this country. It is the lawmaking authority for all television, radio and direct-to-home (DTH) systems in Canada. The CRTC reports to the prime minister through the Minister of Canadian Heritage.

The CRTC is the political apparatus through which the spirit of the **Broadcasting Act** is made manifest. According to the CRTC, the main objective of the Broadcasting Act is "to ensure that all Canadians have access to a wide variety of high-quality Canadian programming." While specifics regarding the Broadcasting Act and its effect on radio and television content were discussed earlier in the text, the main thrust of the act today is as follows:

- Canadian radio and television stations should be "effectively owned and operated by Canadians."
- The Canadian system has two parts: a public system and a private system.
- Canadian broadcasters should "safeguard, enrich and strengthen" life in Canada.
- Anyone who is involved in broadcasting in Canada is responsible for what he or she broadcasts.
- Adding another limitation to "freedom of the press" here in Canada, the Broadcasting Act specifically states that broadcasts should not include anything "in contravention of the law," nor should they contain obscenities, profanities or false news.

Copyright

Study Preview   *Mass media people are vulnerable to thievery. Because it is so easy for someone to copy someone else's creative work, copyright laws prohibit the unauthorized re-creation of intellectual property, including books, music, movies and other creative production.*

COPYRIGHT IN CANADA

Canada has had a copyright law on the books since 1924. The Canadian Copyright Act, governed by Canadian Heritage and Industry Canada, covers all forms of communication: books, pamphlets, newspapers, magazines, maps, sheet music, movies, videos and music. The Act defines **copyright** as "the sole right to produce or reproduce the work of any substantial part thereof in any material form whatever or to perform the work or any substantial portion thereof in public." Basically, all original works in Canada are protected by copyright for the life of the creator, plus 50 years. In the United States, copyright laws protect a creative work for the lifetime of the author plus 70 years. After this time, either in Canada or the United States, the work enters what is called the **public domain** and anyone may use it without permission. The creator of the "act" of communication has the sole right to copy it or have it performed in public. That right may be granted to others.

The works of Canadians are also protected internationally under the copyright protection of the Berne Convention and the Universal Copyright Convention. These also protect the works of international artists in Canada. Several Canadian organizations exist to ensure that creators of communication content are compensated for their efforts and that copyright laws do not get broken.

Case Study

CHOI-FM

The *Canadian Charter of Rights and Freedoms* gives everyone in Canada, including those that work in the media, "freedom of thought, belief and expression." In short, we are given the right to think, believe and say what we want. However, as the chapter has outlined, there are limitations to "freedom of speech."

The CRTC strives to work with Canadian radio and television stations to ensure that they operate within a profitable environment. However, in 2004, the CRTC showed how far-reaching their powers were when they did not renew the licence of radio station CHOI-FM, owned by Genex, in Quebec City. Some saw it as censorship. Genex felt that they were only exercising their right to free speech and that certain comments were not taken in context. The CRTC saw it as a radio station consistently not adhering to the objectives of the Broadcasting Act and flaunting their right to freedom of speech. This action was not a knee-jerk reaction by the Commission. It was a long time coming, as CHOI-FM had a history of questionable content:

- Allegedly making defamatory comments about former Quebec Premier Daniel Johnson.
- Referring to a rival talk show host on another radio station as a "conceited asshole," a "worthless piece of trash," a "piece of vomit," a "shit disturber" and a "tree with rotten roots."
- Calling anyone who worked for Radio Énergie, a competitor in the Quebec City market, "a bunch of faggots."
- Suggesting that there be an "Indian hunting season" and that severely mentally disturbed patients at a local psychiatric hospital be gassed just like during the Holocaust.

In its decision, the CRTC noted that these complaints "did not reflect isolated incidents, but appeared to be part of a pattern of behaviour by the licensee that continued and even grew worse, over the course of two consecutive licence terms, despite clear unequivocal warnings from the Commission." The CRTC cited the following section of the Canadian Radio Broadcasting Act as the basis for its decision: "A licensee shall not broadcast any abusive comment that, when taken in context, tends to or is likely to expose an individual or a group or class of individuals to hatred or contempt on the basis of race, national or ethnic origin, colour, religion, sex, sexual orientation, age or mental or physical disability."

As a result of this history, the CRTC decided not to renew CHOI-FM's licence in August 2004. It also imme-

Freedom of speech or censorship? CHOI-FM tested the boundaries of free speech . . . and lost.

diately issued a call for applications to take over the licence for Quebec City.

CHOI-FM immediately appealed the ruling and was able to continue broadcasting during the appeal process, but, in 2005, the Supreme Court of Canada agreed with the CRTC. In its decision, it stated that "freedom of expression, freedom of opinion and freedom of speech do not mean freedom of defamation, freedom of oppression and freedom of opprobrium." Again, CHOI-FM appealed the ruling. On June 14, 2007, the Supreme Court said it would not hear the appeal. Genex, owners of CHOI-FM, sold the station to Radio Nord, which runs the station today as a rock station.

What Do You Think?

1. Was the case of CHOI-FM a simple matter of freedom of speech or censorship?

2. What role did the CRTC play? The *Charter of Rights and Freedoms?*

3. Review the CRTC's decision on CHOI-FM at www.crtc.-gc.ca/archive/ENG/Decisions/2004/db2004–271.pdf. Could any of the comments made by some of CHOI-FM's announcers be protected as "fair comment"? Why or why not?

Broadcasting Act Governs the CRTC and all broadcasters in Canada.

copyright Protects intellectual property from theft.

public domain Intellectual property that may be used without permission of the creator or owner.

COPYRIGHT AND THE WEB

The technological convergence of the traditional mass media is creating some new issues for copyright. The term *digital media* refers to any information that is stored in binary form (1s and 0s). This includes material stored in "fixed form" on the internet, on CD, CD-ROM, DVD, floppy disk, hard drives, and so on. The list is almost endless. The material can include text, music, and images.

While the full influence of the web on copyright is still being debated in the courts, and will be for some time, some of the legal issues remain the same for material stored in "traditional" or "digital" forms. For example, it must be original and in a fixed form. That being said, digital technology is stretching what was covered (or at the very least implied) under older copyright laws. Some legal issues that are currently being debated include:

- File sharing (mostly music and video) on the internet.
- Duration of copyright. It's life of the creator plus 50 years in Canada, but in the United States it's life plus 70 years.
- Radio stations streaming their signals over the internet.
- "Netcasting" of television programming over the internet.
- The role of ISPs in identifying customers who upload music.
- Newspapers not reprinting articles written by freelance journalists or "stringers," as freelancers are compensated for only one printing of their article.

MUSIC LICENSING IN CANADA

SOCAN Society of Composers, Authors and Music Publishers of Canada; music licensing organization.

SOCAN, the Society of Composers, Authors and Music Publishers of Canada, licenses the public performance of music. It was formed in 1990, when two other performing rights organizations, PROCAN (Performing Rights Organization of Canada) and CAPAC (Composers, Authors and Publishers Association of Canada) combined to form a new, nonprofit organization. Its jurisdiction includes the playing of music, not only on radio and television, but also in restaurants, by mobile disc jockeys, in parades, at sporting events, and at the movies. Almost anywhere you hear music, SOCAN is there to ensure that the writers of the song get paid.

SOCAN collects tariffs from anyone who uses music and passes them along to the songwriters. No one, other than the songwriter, has the right in Canada to use a song's material in any way, shape or form without permission. SOCAN recognizes several types of rights held by the songwriters pertaining to music:

SOCAN: This site provides information on performing rights, copyright, licensing, and distribution. **www.socan.ca**

ASCAP: The American Society of Composers, Authors and Publishers is influential in copyright issues. **www.ascap.com/index. html**

BMI: Provides musicians with information about copyright and licensing concerns. **www.bmi.com/licensing**

- *Performance rights.* These cover songwriters when their material is performed publicly. This can include a song on the radio, on television, or performed by a band at the local bar. These tariffs are collected by SOCAN.
- *Reproduction rights.* There are two types of reproduction rights. Mechanical rights are the rights to copy the music onto a tape or CD, while synchronization rights refer to using the music in a film or video.
- *Moral rights.* A creator can claim violation of moral rights if, after selling performance and/or reproduction rights, he or she feels that the original vision is altered. For example, members of the Canadian pop group The Parachute Club claimed that their moral rights were violated first when their 1983 hit "Rise Up" was used in a commercial for frozen pizza, and then when the song was used to promote a political event in 1999. They felt that their song, with its spiritual and self-empowering message, was morally diminished when it began to be associated with pizza and politicians.

SOCAN has several methods to assist in the collection of royalties for its members. Media outlets are surveyed several times each year for a listing of all music used. TV stations pay 1.8 percent of their gross revenue, while radio stations pay between 1.4 percent and 3.2 percent of their gross revenue, depending on the amount of music played.

Three other organizations license the use of music in Canada. AVLA (the Audio-Visual Licensing Agency) overlooks the exhibition of music videos, while SODRAC (the Society for Reproduction Rights of Authors, Composers and Publishers in Canada Incorporated) and CMRRA (the Canadian Musical Reproduction Rights Agency Limited) authorize the reproduction of music (onto tapes and CDs) and the use of music in videos and film.

Besides SOCAN, there are other large licensing organizations worldwide. They are known in the trade by their abbreviations: **ASCAP** (The American Society of Composers, Authors and Publishers) and **BMI** (Broadcast Music, Inc.).

ASCAP Music licensing organization.

BMI Music licensing organization.

The Difficulty of Ethics

Study Preview   *Mass media organizations have put together codes of ethics that prescribe how practitioners should go about their work. Although useful in many ways, these codes neither sort through the bedeviling problems that result from conflicting prescriptions nor help much when the only available options are negative.*

PRESCRIPTIVE ETHICS CODES

The mass media abound with codes of ethics. The earliest was adopted in 1923, the **Canons of Journalism of the American Society of Newspaper Editors**. Many newcomers to the mass media make an erroneous assumption that the answers to all the moral choices in their work exist in the prescriptions of these codes, a stance known as **prescriptive ethics**. While the codes can be helpful, ethics is not so easy. Attitudes toward codes of ethics vary, but most Canadian media organizations have a code, as do public relations and advertising associations. These codes go far beyond the question of "freebies" and at least try to address issues of social equality, controversy, offensive content, and fairness in handling complex stories.

Canons of Journalism of the American Society of Newspaper Editors First media code, 1923.

prescriptive ethics Follow the rules and your decision will be the correct one.

Many media critics feel that ethics are not taken as seriously as they might be. According to journalism professor Brian Green, one news director's perspective on ethics was as follows: "It's hard to remember you're here to drain the swamp when you're up to your ass in alligators." Peter Desbarats argues that many media critics feel that while the media may talk a good line when it comes to ethics, it's more talk than walk. Other critics feel that codes of ethics are merely public relations tools the media use to perpetuate the myth that they are holier than thou. This may or may not be true. But the fact remains that most Canadian media organizations have a **code of ethics** that, if nothing else, serves as a guideline to follow should an alligator creep up on them. The same applies to the public relations and advertising industries. These codes are based in Canadian law but, as codes, violation of them may not necessarily result in legal problems.

code of ethics Statement that defines acceptable, unacceptable behaviour.

The study of ethics manifests itself in the world of media in the form of codes of conduct. Among the many media organizations that have codes of conduct for their members are the Canadian Association of Broadcasters, the Canadian Newspaper Association, and the Radio-Television News Directors Association of Canada.

CAB Canadian Association of Broadcasters.

CBSC Canadian Broadcast Standards Council; self-regulatory body for Canadian radio and television broadcasters.

Radio-Television News Directors Association (RTNDA) Organization that believes the broadcasting of factual, accurately reported, and timely news and public affairs is vital.

Radio-Television News Directors Association: The association's current code of ethics is online.
www.rtndacanada.com

Canadian Association of Journalists: Includes the CAJ Statement of Principles and Ethics Guidelines and links to *The Wire,* a quarterly newsletter about developments in journalism.
www.caj.ca

Canadian Broadcast Standards Council: Link to the CAB Code of Ethics, Violence Code, Sex-Role Portrayal Code and the RTNDA Code of Ethics.
www.cbsc.ca

Canadian Newspaper Association: Their statement of principles for the voice of Canada's newspaper industry.
www.cna-acj.ca

Center for the Study of Ethics in the Professions: Links to codes of ethics for all kinds of organizations around the world.
http://ethics.iit.edu/codes

THE CANADIAN ASSOCIATION OF BROADCASTERS. Self-proclaimed as the voice of Canada's private broadcasters, the Canadian Association of Broadcasters, or **CAB**, was founded by 13 broadcasters in 1926 as a voluntary organization that advocated self-rule for Canada's broadcasters with little, if any, government regulation. CAB was the lobby group for Canada's radio broadcasters prior to the findings of the Aird Commission in 1929. Currently, CAB represents 430 privately owned radio and television stations across Canada.

In 1990, CAB formed the **CBSC** (Canadian Broadcast Standards Council). This is a self-regulating council funded for and by private broadcasters in Canada. Its mandate is to promote high standards in radio and television broadcasting through self-regulation. If a viewer or listener has a complaint about programming in Canada, he or she writes to the CBSC. They administer several ethics codes, including the CAB Code of Ethics, the CAB Violence Code and the CAB Sex-Role Portrayal Code. All decisions are available online in over 30 languages.

CANADIAN NEWSPAPER ASSOCIATION. In 1919, the Canadian Daily Newspaper Association (CDNA) was formed. In 1996, it was renamed the Canadian Newspaper Association (CNA). The CNA represents 101 of Canada's English and French daily newspapers—99 percent of all newspapers sold in Canada on a daily basis. The CNA's statement of principles, which was originally adopted by the CDNA in 1977, was revised in 1995. This statement can be found at the CNA website. Some of the issues dealt with in the statement are freedom of the press, loyalty to the public good, accuracy, fairness and community responsibility.

RADIO-TELEVISION NEWS DIRECTORS ASSOCIATION OF CANADA. The Radio-Television News Directors Association (RTNDA) was founded more than 50 years ago. It's an international organization with affiliations in Canada. Recognizing the importance to a democracy of an informed public, the members of the RTNDA of Canada believe that the broadcasting of factual, accurately reported, and timely news and public affairs is vital. To this end, RTNDA members in Canada pledge to observe a code of ethics, which can be found at the RTNDA website.

CONFLICT IN DUTIES

Media ethics codes are well-intended, usually helpful guides, but they are simplistic when it comes to knotty moral questions. When media ethicians Clifford Christians, Mark Fackler and Kim Rotzoll compiled a list of five duties of mass media practitioners in their book *Media Ethics,* some of these inherent problems became obvious.

DUTY TO SELF. Self-preservation is a basic human instinct, but is a photojournalist shirking a duty to subscribers by avoiding a dangerous combat zone?

Self-aggrandizement can be an issue too. Many newspaper editors are invited, all expenses paid, to Hollywood movie premieres. The duty-to-self principle favours going: The trip would be fun. In addition, it is a good story opportunity, and as a free favour, it would not cost the newspaper anything. However, what of an editor's responsibility to readers? Readers have a right to expect writers to provide honest accounts that are not coloured by favouritism. Can a reporter write fairly after being wined and dined and flown across the continent by movie producers who want a gung-ho story?

DUTY TO AUDIENCE. Television programs that re-enact real cases of violence are popular with audiences, but do they do a disservice because they frighten many viewers into inferring that the streets are more dangerous than they really are?

Writing about real situations with humour may also do the audience a disservice. Tom Wicker of *The New York Times* tells a story about his early days as a reporter in Aberdeen, North Carolina. He was covering a divorce case involving one spouse chasing the other with an axe. Nobody was hurt physically, and everyone who heard the story in the courtroom, except the divorcing couple, had a good laugh. "It was human comedy at its most ribald, and the courtroom rocked with laughter," Wicker recalled years later. In writing his story, Wicker captured the darkly comedic details so skillfully that his editor put the story on the first page. Wicker was proud of the piece until the next day when the woman in the case called on him. Worn out, haggard, hurt and angry, she asked, "Mr. Wicker, why did you think you had a right to make fun of me in your paper?" The lesson stayed with Wicker for the rest of his career. He had unthinkingly hurt a fellow human being for no better reason than to evoke a chuckle, or perhaps a belly laugh, from his readers. To Wicker the duty-to-audience principle would never again transcend his moral duty to the dignity of the subjects of his stories.

DUTY TO EMPLOYER. Does loyalty to an employer transcend the ideal of pursuing and telling the truth when a news reporter discovers dubious business deals involving the parent corporation? This is a growing issue as the mass media become consolidated into fewer gigantic companies owned by conglomerates. In 1989, for example, investigative reporter Peter Karl of Chicago television station WMAQ broke a story that General Electric had manufactured jet engines with untested and sometimes defective bolts. Although WMAQ is owned by NBC, which in turn is owned by General Electric, Karl's exclusive, documented and accurate story aired. However, when the story was passed on to the network itself, Marty Ryan, executive producer of the *Today* show, ordered that the references to General Electric be edited out.

DUTY TO THE PROFESSION. At what point does an ethically motivated advertising-agency person blow the whistle on misleading claims by other advertising people?

DUTY TO SOCIETY. Does duty to society ever transcend duty to self? To the audience? To the employer? To colleagues? Does ideology affect a media worker's sense of duty to society? Consider how Joseph Stalin, Adolf Hitler and Franklin Roosevelt would be covered by highly motivated communist, fascist and libertarian journalists.

Media Ethics

Study Preview   *Media ethics is complicated by the different performance standards that mass media operations establish for themselves. This is further complicated by the range of expectations in the mass audience. One size does not fit all.*

MEDIA COMMITMENT

A single ethics standard is impossible to apply to the mass media. Nobody holds a supermarket tabloid like *News of the World*, which specializes in celebrities being visited by aliens, to the same standard as *The New York Times*. Why the difference? Media ethics, in part, is a function of what a media operation promises to deliver to its audience and what the audience expects. The *News of the World* commitment is fun and games in a tongue-in-cheek news context. *The New York Times* considers itself a "Newspaper of Record." There is a big difference.

CNN touts accuracy in its promotional tagline: "News You Can Trust." Explicitly, the network promises to deliver truthful accounts of the day's events. CNN establishes its own standards. A lapse, like a misleading story, especially if intentional or the result of sloppiness, represents a broken promise and an ethics problem.

Accuracy in Media: Official site of the media watchdog organization.
www.aim.org

AUDIENCE EXPECTATION

The audience brings a range of ethics expectations to media relations, which further thwarts any attempt at one-size-fits-all media ethics. From a book publisher's fantasy science fiction imprint, readers have far different expectations than they do from NBC News, which, except for plainly labeled opinion, is expected to deliver unmitigated nonfiction.

A range in the type of messages purveyed by the mass media also bespeaks a variety of ethics expectations. Rarely is falsity excusable, but even the courts allow puffery in advertising. The news releases that public relations people produce are expected, by their nature, to be from a client's perspective, which doesn't always coincide with the perspective expected of a news reporter.

ETHICS AS AN INTELLECTUAL PROCESS

A set of rules, easily memorized and mindlessly employed, would be too easy. It doesn't work that way. Ethics, rather, needs to be an intellectual process of sorting through media commitments, audience expectations and broad principles. But even on broad principles there is more, as discussed in the next section.

Golden Mean. The Greek thinker Aristotle told his students almost 2400 years ago that right courses of action avoid extremes. His recommendation: moderation.

Moral Principles

Study Preview   *Concern about doing the right thing is part of human nature, and leading thinkers have developed a great number of enduring moral principles over the centuries.*

THE GOLDEN MEAN

Aristotle Advocate of the golden mean.

golden mean Moderation is the best course.

The Greek philosopher **Aristotle**, writing almost 2400 years ago, devised the **golden mean** as a basis for moral decision making. The golden mean sounds simple and straightforward: Avoid extremes and seek moderation. Modern journalistic balance and fairness are founded on this principle.

The golden mean's dictate, however, is not as simple as it sounds. As with all moral principles, application of the golden mean can present difficulties. Consider the CRTC requirement that over-the-air broadcasters give equal opportunity to candidates at election time. On the surface this application of the golden mean, embodied in federal law, might seem to be reasonable, fair and morally right, but the issue is far more complex. The equality requirement, for example, gives an advantage to candidates who hold simplistic positions that can be expressed compactly. Good and able candidates whose positions require more time to explain are disadvantaged, and the society is damaged when inferior candidates win public office.

Although minute-for-minute equality in broadcasting can be a flawed application of the golden mean, Aristotle's principle is valuable to media people when making moral decisions, as long as they do not abdicate their power of reason to embrace formulaic tit-for-tat measurable equality. It takes the human mind, not a formula, to determine fairness. And therein lies the complexity of the golden mean. No two human beings think exactly alike, which means that applying the golden mean involves individuals' making judgment calls that are not necessarily the same. This element of judgment in moral decisions can make ethics intellectually exciting. It takes a sharp mind to sort through issues of balance and fairness.

Journal of Mass Media Ethics: This journal addresses ethical situations in mass communication. **www.jmme.org**

Media Watchdogs: A collection of online media monitoring sources, from UBC's School of Journalism. **http://journalismethics. ca/journalist_resources/ media_analysis.htm**

"Do unto Others"

The Judeo-Christian principle of "**Do unto others** as you would have them do unto you" appeals to most Americans. Not even the "do-unto-others" prescription is without problems, however. Consider the photojournalist who sees virtue in serving a mass audience with a truthful account of the human condition. This might manifest itself in portrayals of great emotions, like grief. But would the photojournalist appreciate being photographed herself in a grieving moment after learning that her own infant son had died in an accident? If not, her pursuit of truth through photography for a mass audience would be contrary to the "do-unto-others" dictum.

"Do unto others" Judeo-Christian principle for ethical behaviour.

Immanuel Kant Advocated the categorical imperative.

categorical imperative Follow principles as if they had universal application.

Categorical Imperatives

About 200 years ago, German philosopher **Immanuel Kant** wrote that moral decisions should flow from thoroughly considered principles. As he put it, "Act on the maxim that you would want to become universal law." He called his maxim the categorical imperative. A **categorical imperative**, well-thought-out, is a principle that the individual who devised it would be willing to apply in all moral questions of a similar sort.

Kant's categorical imperative does not dictate specifically what actions are morally right or wrong. Moral choices, says Kant, go deeper than the context of the immediate issue. He encourages a philosophical approach to moral questions, with people using their intellect to identify principles that they, as individuals, would find acceptable if applied universally.

Universal Law. Immanuel Kant, an 18th-century German philosopher, urged people to find principles that they would be comfortable having applied in all situations. He called these principles *categorical imperatives.*

John Stuart Mill Advocated utilitarianism.

principle of utility Best course bestows the most good for the most people.

John Dewey Advocate of pragmatism.

pragmatic ethics Judge acts by their results.

John Rawls Advocated egalitarianism.

veil of ignorance Making decisions with a blind eye to extraneous factors that could affect the decision.

egalitarianism Treat everyone the same.

Kant does not encourage the kind of standardized approach to ethics represented by professional codes. His emphasis, rather, is on hard thinking. Says philosopher Patricia Smith, of the University of Kentucky, writing in the *Journal of Mass Media Ethics,* "A philosophical approach to ethics embodies a commitment to consistency, clarity, the principled evaluation of arguments and unrelenting persistence to get to the bottom of things."

UTILITARIAN ETHICS

In the mid-1800s, British thinker **John Stuart Mill** declared that morally right decisions are those that result in "happiness for the greatest number." Mill called his idea the **principle of utility**. It sounds good to many of us because it parallels the democratic principle of majority rule, with its emphasis on the greatest good for the greatest number of people.

By and large, journalists embrace Mill's utilitarianism today, as evinced in notions like the *people's right to know,* a concept originally meant to support journalistic pursuit of information about government, putting the public's interests ahead of government's interests, but which has come to be almost reflexively invoked to defend pursuing very personal information about individuals, no matter what the human toll.

PRAGMATIC ETHICS

John Dewey, an American thinker who wrote in the late 1800s and early 1900s, argued that the virtue of moral decisions had to be judged by their results. Dewey's **pragmatic ethics,** like other ethics systems, has problems. One is that people do not have perfect crystal balls to tell them for sure whether their moral actions will have good consequences.

EGALITARIAN ETHICS

In the 20th century, philosopher **John Rawls** introduced the **veil of ignorance** as an element in ethics decisions. Choosing a right course of action, said Rawls, requires blindness to social position or other discriminating factors. This is known as **egalitarianism.** An ethical decision requires that all people be given an equal hearing and the same fair consideration.

To Rawls a brutal slaying in an upscale suburb deserves the same journalistic attention as a similarly brutal slaying in a poor urban neighbourhood. All other things being equal, a $20 000 bank burglary is no more newsworthy than a $20 000 embezzlement.

John Rawls. He favoured putting a blind eye to all issues except rightness and wrongness.

John Dewey. He saw decisions as ethical if the ascertainable outcomes were good.

MEDIA TIMELINE

Development of Media Ethics

400 B.C.	Aristotle laid out the golden mean.
20S	Jesus Christ articulated "Do unto others as you would have them do unto you."
1785	Immanuel Kant advanced the categorical imperative.
1865	John Stuart Mill proposed utilitarianism.
1903	John Dewey advanced pragmatism.
1919	Upton Sinclair exposed newsroom abuses in his book *The Brass Check*.
1923	American Society of Newspaper Editors adopted a media ethics code.
1947	Hutchins Commission urged the media to be socially responsible.
1971	John Rawls advanced the veil of ignorance theory.

Ralph Potter Ethicist who devised the Potter's Box.

Potter's Box Tool for sorting through the pros and cons of ethics questions.

Potter's Box

Study Preview   *Moral problems in the mass media can be so complex that it may seem there is no solution. While ideal answers without any negative results may be impossible, a process exists for identifying a course of action that integrates an individual's personal values with moral principles and then tests conclusions against loyalties.*

FOUR QUADRANTS

A Harvard Divinity School professor, **Ralph Potter**, devised a four-quadrant model for sorting through ethics problems. The quadrants of the square-like model, called **Potter's Box**, each pose a category of questions. Working through these categories helps to clarify the issues and leads to a morally justifiable position. These are the quadrants of Potter's Box:

SITUATION. In Quadrant 1, the facts of the issue are decided. Consider a newsroom in which a series of articles on rape is being developed and the question arises whether to identify rape victims by name. Here is how the situation could be defined: The newspaper has access to a young mother who has been abducted and raped and who is willing to describe the assault in graphic detail and to discuss her experience as a witness at the assailant's trial. Also, the woman is willing to be identified in the story.

VALUES. Moving to Quadrant 2 of Potter's Box, editors and reporters identify the values that underlie all the available choices. This process involves listing the positive and negative values that flow from conscience. One editor might argue that full, frank discussion on social issues is necessary to deal with them. Another might say that identifying the rape victim by name might discourage others from even reporting the crime. Other positions: Publishing the name is in poor taste. The newspaper has an obligation to protect the victim from her own possibly bad decision to allow her name to be used. The purpose of the rape series can be accomplished without using the name. Readers have a right to all the relevant information that the newspaper can gather. An editor who is torn between such contrary thoughts is making progress toward a decision by at least identifying all the values that can be posited.

PRINCIPLES. In Potter's Quadrant 3, decision makers search for moral principles that uphold the values they identified in Quadrant 2. John Stuart Mill's principle of utility, which favours the majority over individuals, would support using the victim's name because it could add poignancy to the story, enhancing the chances of improved public sensitivity and perhaps even lead to improved public policy, all of which, Mill would say, outweigh the harm that might come to an individual. On the other hand, people who have used Immanuel Kant's ideas to develop inviolable operating principles—categorical imperatives—look to their rule book: We never publish information that might offend readers. One value of Potter's Quadrant 3 is that it gives people confidence in the values that emerged in their debates over Quadrant 2.

LOYALTIES. In Quadrant 4 the decision maker folds in an additional layer of complexity that must be sorted through: loyalties. The challenge is to establish a hierarchy of loyalties. Is the first loyalty to a code of ethics, and if so, to which code? To

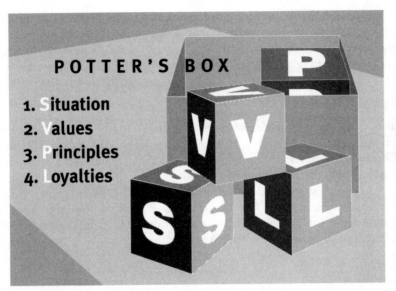

Ralph Potter

Clarifying Process. Potter's Box offers four categories
of questions to help develop morally justifiable positions.

readers, and if so, to which ones? To society? To the employer? To self? Out of duty
to self, some reporters and editors might want to make the rape series as potent as
possible, with as much detail as possible, to win awards and bring honour to themselves and perhaps a raise or promotion or better job with another newspaper. Others might be motivated by their duty to their employer: The more detail in the story,
the more newspapers it will sell. For others their duty to society may be paramount:
The newspaper has a social obligation to present issues in as powerful a way as possible to spur reforms in general attitudes and perhaps public policy.

LIMITATIONS OF POTTER'S BOX

Potter's Box does not provide answers. Rather, it offers a process through which the
key elements in ethics questions can be sorted out.

    Also, Potter's Box focuses on moral aspects of a problem, leaving it to the deci-
sion maker to examine practical considerations separately, such as whether prudence
supports making the morally best decision. Moral decisions should not be made in a
vacuum. For example, would it be wise to go ahead with the rape victim's name if
90 percent of the newspaper's subscribers would become so offended that they
would quit buying the paper and, as a result, the paper would go out of business?

Unsettled, Unsettling Issues

> **Study Preview**   *When mass media people discuss ethics, they talk about
> right and wrong behaviour, but creating policies on ethics issues is not easy.*

ACCEPTED PRACTICES

Just as there is not a reliable correlation between law and ethics, neither is there one
between accepted media practices and ethics. What is acceptable at one advertising

**Journalism Ethics Cases
Online:** These cases
address a variety of ethical
problems faced by
journalists, including
privacy, conflict of interest,
reporter–source
relationships, and the role
of journalists in their
communities.
**www.journalism.indiana.
edu/gallery/Ethics**

**Silha Center for the Study
of Media Ethics and Law:**
This site of the University of
Minnesota contains articles,
news and links related to
issues of both ethics and
the law.
www.silha.umn.edu

agency to make a product look good in photographs might be unacceptable at another. Even universally **accepted practices** should not go unexamined, for unless accepted practices are examined and reconsidered on a continuing basis, media practitioners can come to rely more on habit than on principles in their work.

PRUDENCE AND ETHICS

Prudence is the application of wisdom in a practical situation. It can be a leveling factor in moral questions. Consider the case of Irvin Lieberman, who had built his *Main Line Chronicle* and several other weeklies in the Philadelphia suburbs into aggressive, journalistically excellent newspapers. After being hit with nine libel suits, all costly to defend, Lieberman abandoned the editorial thrust of his newspapers. "I decided not to do any investigative work," he said. "It was a matter of either feeding my family or spending my whole life in court." Out of prudence Lieberman decided to abandon his commitment to hard-hitting, effective journalism.

PLAGIARISM

Perhaps the most fiercely loyal media fans are those who read romance novels and swear by a favourite author. In an internet chatroom in 1997, romance writer Janet Dailey found herself boxed into an admission that she had plagiarized from rival writer Nora Roberts. There is no scorn like that of creative people for those who steal their work, and Roberts was "very, very upset." HarperCollins recalled *Notorious*, Dailey's book that contained the plagiarism, and Roberts's fans, many of them longtime Dailey detractors, began a hunt for other purloined passages.

What is **plagiarism**? Generally, it's considered passing off someone else's creative work as your own, without permission. It's still plagiarism if it's changed a bit, as was Dailey's loose paraphrasing.

The fact that Dailey's 93 books over 20 years had sold an average of more than 2 million each made the scandal all the juicier. In the end, Roberts proposed a financial settlement, and the proceeds went to promote literacy.

Everyone agrees that plagiarism, a form of thievery, is unethical, but the issue is not simple. The fact is that in many media, people draw heavily on other people's ideas and work. Think about sitcom storylines that mimic each other or the bandwagon of movies that follow an unexpected hit with an oddball theme that suddenly becomes mainstream. Journalists, most of whom consider themselves especially pristine compared to their media brethren, have standard practices that encourage a lot of "borrowing." Among factors that make journalists uncomfortable when pressed hard on plagiary questions are:

SWAPPING STORIES. Some creative work, like scholarship, requires that information and ideas be attributed to their sources. Journalists are not so strict, as shown by story swapping through the Canadian Press. CP picks up stories from its members and distributes them to other members, generally without any reference to the source. Some publications and broadcasters do not even acknowledge CP as the intermediary.

NEWS RELEASES. In many newsrooms the plagiarism question is clouded further by the practice of using news releases from public relations people word for word without citing the source. Even in newsrooms that rewrite releases to avoid the embarrassment of running a story that is exactly the same as the competition's, it is standard practice not to cite the source. Public relations people, who are paid for writing favourable stories on their clients, have no objections to being plagiarized, and news organizations find it an easy, inexpensive way to fill space. Despite the mutual convenience, the arrangement raises serious questions of ethics to which many in the media have not responded. Marie Dunn White, in the *Journal of Mass Media Ethics,* wrote: "In order for the reader to evaluate the information he or she is receiving correctly and completely, he or she must know which information came from a press release and, therefore, may be biased."

MONITORING THE COMPETITION. Competitive pressure also contributes to fuzziness on the plagiarism issue. To avoid being skunked on stories, reporters monitor each other closely to pick up tips and ideas. Generally, reporters are not particular about where they pick up information as long as they are confident that it is accurate. For background, reporters tap newsroom libraries, databases, journals, books and other sources, and in the interest of not cluttering their stories, they do not use footnotes.

SUBLIMINAL MEMORY. Covering breaking events has its own pressure that puts journalists at special risk. Almost every journalist who writes under the pressure of a deadline has had the experience of writing a story and later discovering that phrases that came easily at the keyboard were actually somebody else's. In their voracious pursuit of information, reporters store phrases and perhaps whole passages subliminally in their memories. It's this concept of innocent recall that concerns the late Canadian columnist Don McGillivray, who argues that plagiarism is often a simple case of unintentionally borrowing from others. Journalists are like any other group of professionals: They like to "talk shop" when in the presence of other journalists. They discuss stories they've written and articles they've read. Later, while writing a story, a journalist may subconsciously remember a certain phrase from a conversation with a colleague and use it in a story. Is this plagiarism? McGillivray doesn't think so. It's simply the outcome of a psychological process.

The final word on plagiarism in journalism goes to Nick Russell, who, in *Morals and the Media,* writes, "Genuine plagiarism is theft and is indefensible; serious incidents of plagiarism happen rarely and there is a difference between plagiarism and lack of attribution . . . . Some media critics seem to think it's growing, but it may be more of a matter of perception. Partly because readers have a growing sense of empowerment and ownership so are now much more likely to blow the whistle and newsroom colleagues who might have tolerated such activities as hijinks in the past now see them as undermining everybody's credibility."

Janet Cooke Classic case of representing fiction as truth.

Museum of Hoaxes: Offers a section on misrepresentative journalism, including stories on Janet Cooke and Jayson Blair.
www.museumofhoaxes. com

MISREPRESENTATION

Janet Cooke's meteoric rise at *The Washington Post* unraveled quickly the day after she received a Pulitzer Prize. Her editors had been so impressed with her story "Jimmy's World," about a child who was addicted to heroin, that they nominated it for a Pulitzer Prize. The gripping tale began: "Jimmy is 8 years old and a third-generation heroin addict, a precocious little boy with sandy hair, velvety brown eyes and needle marks freckling the baby-smooth skin of his thin brown arms." Janet Cooke claimed that she had won the confidence of Jimmy's mother and her live-in male friend, a drug dealer, to do the story. Cooke said she had promised not to reveal their identities as a condition for her access to Jimmy.

The story, which played on the front page, so shocked Washington that people demanded that Jimmy be taken away from his mother and placed in a foster home. *The Post* declined to help authorities, citing Cooke's promise of confidentiality to her sources. The mayor ordered the police to find Jimmy with or without the newspaper's help, and millions of dollars in police resources went into a door-to-door search. After 17 days the police gave up knocking on doors for tips on Jimmy. Some doubts emerged at *The Post* about the story, but the newspaper stood behind its reporter.

Janet Cooke, 25 when she was hired by *The Post,* had extraordinary credentials. Her résumé showed a baccalaureate degree, magna cum laude, from Vassar; study at the Sorbonne in Paris; a master's degree from the University of Toledo; abilities in several languages; and two years of journalistic experience with the Toledo *Blade.* Said Ben Bradlee, editor of the *Post:* "She had it all. She was bright. She was well spoken. She was pretty. She wrote well." She was black, which made her especially attractive to *The Post,* which was working to bring the percentage of black staff reporters nearer to the percentage of blacks in its circulation area.

"Jimmy's World" was published in September 1980. Six months later, the Pulitzer committee announced its decision and issued a biographical sheet on Janet Cooke. The Associated Press, trying to flesh out the biographical information, spotted discrepancies right away. Janet Cooke, it turned out, had attended Vassar for one year but had not graduated with the honours she claimed. The University of Toledo had no record of awarding her a master's degree. Suddenly, doubts that had surfaced in the days immediately after "Jimmy's World" was published took on a new intensity. The editors sat Cooke down and grilled her on the claims on which she was hired. No, she admitted, she was not multilingual. The Sorbonne claim was fuzzy. More important, they pressed her on whether there was really a Jimmy. The interrogation continued into the night, and finally Janet Cooke confessed all: There were no confidential sources, and there was no Jimmy. She had fabricated the story. She resigned, and *The Post,* terribly embarrassed, returned the Pulitzer.

In cases of outright fabrication, as in "Jimmy's World," it is easy to identify the lapses in ethics. When Janet Cooke emerged briefly from seclusion to explain herself, she said that she was responding to pressures in *The Post* newsroom to produce flashy, sensational copy. Most people found the explanation unsatisfying, considering the pattern of deception that went back to her falsified résumé.

There are **misrepresentations**, however, that are not as clearly unacceptable. Much debated are the following.

STAGING NEWS. To attract favourable attention to their clients, public relations people organize media events, a practice known as **staging news**. These are designed to be irresistible to journalists. Rallies and demonstrations on topical issues, for example, find their way onto front pages, magazine covers and evening newscasts because their photogenic qualities give them an edge over less visual although sometimes more significant events. The ethics question is less important for publicists, who generally are upfront about what they are doing. The ethics question is more serious for journalists, who claim that their job is to present an accurate, balanced account of a day's events but who regularly overplay staged events that are designed by publicists to be photogenic and easy to cover.

The New York Times: You can get the abstract of the May 11, 2003, article "Correcting the Record" about Jayson Blair for free, but there's a fee for the full 7000+ word article. **www.nytimes.com**

misrepresentation
Deception in gathering or telling information.

staging news Creating an event to attract news media attention and coverage.

Media People

Jayson Blair

Jayson Blair

On one level, Jayson Blair's stories in *The New York Times* marked him as a rising star. Assigned in late 2002 to the team covering the Beltway Sniper story around Washington, D.C., Blair produced scoop after scoop that indicated a knack for ferreting out knowledgeable sources and charming information from them. Blair, age 27, exuded self-confidence. He even floated a prospectus for a book on the sniper case.

Then what to many had seemed a promising if not skyrocketing career imploded. Jayson Blair, it turned out, had fabricated sources, played fast and loose with the facts, concocted details that weren't true and purported to have conducted interviews that never took place. These transcended the kinds of forgivable errors that news reporters, being human, make from time to time. He was a serial liar. Time and again, Blair had sallied into fiction while pretending to be reporting the news of the day accurately. Confronted with his lies in May 2003, his career suddenly in shambles, Blair resigned.

His ethics transgressions shook *The Times,* the most prestigious newspaper in the nation, with more Pulitzer Prizes than any other paper—seven in 2002 alone. Said publisher Arthur Sulzberger Jr.: "It's a huge black eye."

In a self-flagellation, the editors assigned an eight-reporter team of reporters to investigate how Jayson Blair, at the paper six years, had attained the kind of trust that news organizations posit in their reporters. *The Times,* no supermarket tabloid, had a long reputation for truth-seeking and often aggressive reporting—and also for the confidence to back up its reporters when critics came down on them.

So what went wrong? For whatever reason, *Times* editors had fast-tracked Blair without putting his work through the rigours that other newsroom newcomers experienced. Factual errors in his work, an incredible 50 to 60 errors by some counts, had been gently excused. Although editors generally are leery about unnamed sources in stories, the anonymous sources who peppered Blair's stories went unchallenged. Surprisingly, none of the sources whom Blair did name in his stories complained about made up quotes and details.

It all began unraveling after a Blair story about details from interrogators of a Beltway Sniper suspect. The information, not true, rattled the investigators who were doing the interrogation. Statements attributed to the suspect in Blair's front-page story had never been made. People at *The Times* began watching Blair. They suddenly realized that he was turning out stories from faraway places without ever leaving town. Then the editor at the *San Antonio Express-News* called to complain that details in a Blair story purported to have been written in Texas had been lifted from his newspaper. Blair hadn't even been to Texas.

RE-CREATIONS. A wave of **reality programs** on television that began in the late 1980s featured **re-enactments** that were not always labeled as such. Philip Weiss, writing in *Columbia Journalism Review,* offered this litany: shadows on the wall of a woman taking a hammer to her husband, a faceless actor grabbing a tin of kerosene to blow up his son, a corpse in a wheelbarrow with a hand dangling, a detective opening the trunk of a car and reeling from the smell of a decomposing body. Although mixing re-creations with strictly news footage rankles many critics, others argue that it helps people understand the situation. The same question arises with docudramas, which mix actual events and dramatic re-creations.

reality programs Broadcast shows with a nonfiction basis.

re-enactments Re-creating real events.

SELECTIVE EDITING. The editing process, by its nature, requires journalists to make decisions on what is most worth emphasizing and what is least worth even including. In this sense, all editing is selective, but the term **selective editing** refers to making decisions with the goal of distorting. Selective editing can occur in drama too, when writers, editors and other media people take literary licence too far and intentionally misrepresent.

selective editing Misrepresentation through omission and juxtaposition.

GIFTS, JUNKETS AND MEALS

The Brass Check 1919 book
that exposed newsroom
corruption.

Upton Sinclair Author of
The Brass Check.

junket Trip with expenses
paid by someone who may
expect favours in return.

In his 1919 book *The Brass Check,* a pioneer examination of newsroom ethics, **Upton Sinclair** told how newspeople took bribes to put stories in the paper. Today all media ethics codes condemn gifts and certainly bribes. Even so, there are still people who curry favour with the mass media through gifts, such as a college sports publicist who gives a fifth of whisky at Christmas to a sportswriter as a gesture of good will. Favours can take many forms: media-appreciation lunches; free trips abroad, known as **junkets**, especially for travel writers; season passes to cover the opera; discounts at certain stores.

Despite the consistent exhortation of the ethics codes against gifts, favours, free travel and special treatment and privileges, there is nothing inherently wrong in taking them if they do not influence coverage and if the journalist's benefactor understands that. The problem with favours is more a practical one than one of ethics. Taking a favour may or may not be bad, but it *looks* bad. Many ethics codes do not make this important distinction. One that does is the code of the Associated Press Managing Editors (APME), which states: "Journalists must avoid impropriety and *the appearance of impropriety* as well as any conflict of interest or *the appearance of conflict.* They should neither accept anything nor pursue any activity that might compromise or *seem to compromise* their integrity [italics added]." The APME's admonitions at least recognize the distinction between the inherent wrongness of impropriety, which is an ethics question, and the perception that something may be wrong, which is a perception that is unwise to encourage but is not necessarily unethical.

freebie Gift for which the
giver may expect favours in
return.

While ethics codes are uniform in prohibiting **freebies**, as gifts and favours are called, many news organizations accept free movie, drama, concert and other tickets, as well as recordings, books and other materials for review. The justification is usually that their budgets allow them to review only materials that arrive free and that their audiences would be denied reviews if the materials had to be purchased. A counter-argument is that a news organization that cannot afford to do business right should not be in business. Many news organizations insist on buying tickets for their reporters to beauty pageants, sports events and other things to which there is an admission fee. A frequent exception occurs when a press box or special media facility is available. With recordings, books and free samples, some media organizations return them or pass them on to charity to avoid any appearance that they have been bought off.

CHAPTER 11 WRAP-UP

The mass media enjoy great freedom under the *Canadian Charter of Rights and Freedoms,* which forbids the government from impinging on expression. Even so, the freedom has limits. Major restrictions on the mass media involve publication bans, censorship, commercial exploitation, invasion of privacy, libel, fair trials and obscenity.

Meanwhile, moral decision making is rooted in conscience, which makes it highly individual. Attempts to bring order to moral issues in journalism and the mass media have included codes of ethics. These codes identify behaviours that are recognized as ethically troublesome, but because they are generalized statements, the codes cannot anticipate all situations. There is no substitute for human reason and common sense.

QUESTIONS FOR REVIEW

1. Why is the *Canadian Charter of Rights and Freedoms* important to the Canadian mass media?

2. In what situations may the government or legal system silence the media in Canada?

3. What constitutes defamation in Canada? What are the media's defences?

4. How is obscenity different from pornography?

5. How does copyright law protect intellectual property from being stolen from its owners?

6. What is the role of the CRTC and the Broadcasting Act in relation to broadcasting in Canada?

QUESTIONS FOR CRITICAL THINKING

1. The *Canadian Charter of Rights and Freedoms* grants everyone in Canada, including the media, freedom of speech. Can this freedom of speech ever be absolute?

2. How useful is the Dagenais ruling in balancing the rights of the individual and the rights of the media?

3. Can you identify the ethics principle or system most associated with Aristotle? Immanuel Kant? John Stuart Mill? John Dewey? John Rawls? Ralph Potter?

4. How can codes of ethics help mass media people make the right decisions? Do codes always work?

Why or why not? Review the various Canadian ethics codes in your answer.

5. A candidate for mayor tells a news reporter that the incumbent mayor is in cahoots with organized crime. What should the reporter do before going on the air with this bombshell accusation? Why?

6. Can media people ever defend breaking the law as ethical?

7. What do case studies such as Jayson Blair and Janet Cooke say about the values of contemporary journalism?

DEEPENING YOUR MEDIA LITERACY

Is objectivity a duty?

Step 1

Write down your definition of an objective journalist. Be sure to include whose duty the objective journalist should serve: self, audience, employer, profession and/or society.

Dig Deeper
Step 2

1. Describing Oprah Winfrey's influence, Gloria Steinem, feminist and founder of *Ms.* magazine, said: "Of course, her refusal to be uniformly negative—a frequent definition of objectivity—is exactly what keeps her influence from being taken seriously." How is the journalist who reports uniformly negative news serving his or

her duty to the audience? To his or her employer? To society?

2. Media critic Benjamin Radford says that many journalists apply a form of agnostic objectivity, which is ultimately uninformative: "Amid all the finger pointing, contradicting experts, and dueling statistics, the journalist's role turns from claim analyzer to claim deliverer . . . a reporter's job is to help separate the wheat from the chaff; instead, they usually just present two different piles of chaff for the viewer to look at and choose from." Is it OK for a journalist to leave it to the audience to judge the truth of what he or she writes? Why? How is the journalist who reports two sides of an issue without telling the viewer that one of them is not based on fact serving the journalist's duty to

himself or herself? To the journalist's employer? To the audience? To society?

What Do You Think?

Step 3

Answer these questions:

1. Should a prescriptive code defining objectivity include the journalist's duty? Which one(s)? Do you think a prescriptive code defining objectivity would work in all cases, for all journalists? Why or why not?

2. How should a journalist reconcile conflicting duties when trying to be objective?

3. Do you think Gloria Steinem has a valid point about objectivity?

4. What do you think of Benjamin Radford's criticism about how he perceives that many of today's journalists exercise objectivity?

KEEPING UP TO DATE

Censorship News is published by the National Coalition Against Censorship.

Media Law Bulletin tracks developments in media law.

News Media and the Law is published by The Reporters Committee for Freedom of the Press.

Media Law Reporter is an annual collection of major court cases.

Student Press Law Reports, from the Student Press Law Center, follows events in the high-school and college press and broadcast media.

The *National Post, Toronto Star* and *The Globe and Mail* often have sections and articles on media law and ethics.

Ethicists sort through moral dilemmas involving mass communication in the scholarly *Journal of Mass Media.*

Many trade and professional journals also deal with media ethics, including the *Columbia Journalism Review, The Canadian Journal of Communication, Broadcast Dialogue* and *Broadcaster* magazine.

FOR FURTHER LEARNING

Ellen Alderman and Caroline Kennedy. *The Right to Privacy* (Knopf, 1995).

Brian Bergman. "The Battle over Censorship." *Maclean's* (October 24, 1994).

Clifford G. Christians, Kim B. Rotzoll and Mark Fackler. *Media Ethics,* Sixth edition (Longman, 2002).

Roy Peter Clark. "The Original Sin: How Plagiarism Poisons the Press." *Washington Journalism Review* (March 1983): 43–47.

Ron Cohen. "Self-Regulation: A Canadian Success Story." *Broadcast Dialogue* (November 1999).

Michael G. Crawford. *The Journalist's Legal Guide* (Carswell, 1996).

Robert E. Denton Jr., editor. *Political Communication Ethics: An Oxymoron?* (Praeger, 2000).

Timothy Findlay. "Point–Counterpoint: Ethics in the Media." *Journal of Canadian Studies* 27(4).

Matthew Fraser. "Time to Change Channels." *National Post* (March 7, 2001).

Michael Gartner. "Fair Comment." *American Heritage* (October–November 1982): 28–31.

Bernard Goldberg. *Bias* (Regnery, 2002).

Brian Green. *Broadcast News Essentials* (Harcourt Brace, 2001).

Sally Harris and David Potts. "Important Elements of the Internet Applicable to Cyber Libel" (July 31, 2001). Available online at www.cyberlibel.com/-elements.html.

Carl Hausman. *The Decision-Making Process in Journalism* (Nelson-Hall, 1990).

Matthew Ingram. "Media Stardom is Pricey." *The Globe and Mail* (June 15, 2007).

Walter B. Jaehnig. "Harrison Cochran—The Publisher with a Past." *Journal of Mass Media Ethics* 2 (Fall/Winter 1986–87): 1, 80–88.

Dean Jobb. *Media Law for Canadian Journalists* (Emond Montgomery Publications, 2006).

Paul Kaihla. "Sex and the Law." *Maclean's* (October 24, 1994).

Donna Soble Kaufman. *Broadcasting Law in Canada: Fairness in the Administrative Process* (Carswell, 1987).

Wilfred H. Kesterton. *The Law and the Press in Canada* (McClelland and Stewart, 1976).

Janet Malcolm. *The Journalist and the Murderer* (Knopf, 1990).

John C. Merrill. *The Dialectic in Journalism: Toward a Responsible Use of Press Freedom* (Louisiana State University Press, 1990).

Clark R. Mollenhoff. "25 Years of *Times* v. *Sullivan.*" *Quill* (March 1989): 27–31.

Ralph B. Potter. "The Structure of Certain American Christian Responses to the Nuclear Dilemma, 1958–1963" (Ph.D. Diss., Harvard University, 1965).

Lori Robertson. "Ethically Challenged." *American Journalism Review* (March 2001): 20–29.

Stuart Robertson. *The Media Law Handbook* (Self-Counsel Press, 1983).

Stuart Robertson. *Pocket Guide to Media Law* (Hallion Press, 1994).

Nick Russell. *Morals and the Media: Ethics in Canadian Journalism,* Second edition (University of British Columbia Press, 2006).

Ron F. Smith. *Groping for Ethics in Journalism,* Fourth edition (Iowa State University Press, 1999).

Colin Sparks and John Tulloch, editors. *Tabloid Tales: Global Debates over Media Standards* (Rowman & Littlefield, 2000).

Joe Strupp. "Policing Plagiarism." *Editor & Publisher* (August 7, 2000): 19–22.

Philip Weiss. "Bad Rap for TV Tabs." *Columbia Journalism Review* 28 (May/June 1989): 1, 39–42.

Marie Dunn White. "Plagiarism and the News Media." *Journal of Mass Media Ethics* 4 (1989): 2, 265–280.

Chapter Twelve

Orson Welles Young Orson Welles scared the living daylights out of several million radio listeners with the 1938 radio drama *The War of the Worlds*. Most of the fright was short-lived, though. All but the most naïve listeners quickly realized that Martians, marching toward the Hudson River to destroy Manhattan, really had not devastated the New Jersey militia.

MEDIA TIMELINE

Understanding Mass Media Effects

1922	Walter Lippmann attributed powerful effects to the mass media.
1938	Hadley Cantril concluded that "The War of the Worlds" panic was drastically overstated.
1940s	Mass communication scholars shifted from studying effects to uses and gratification.
1948	Paul Lazarsfeld challenged powerful effects theory in voter studies.
1967	George Gerbner launched his television violence index.
1970s	Mass communication scholars shifted to cumulative effects theory.
1972	Maxwell McCombs and Donald Shaw concluded that media create public agendas, not opinion.
1992	Virginie Larivière presented Prime Minister Brian Mulroney with a petition urging the government to do something about violence on TV.
1993	A new violence code was introduced by Canada's AGVOT.

Media Effects

Media in Theory

The boy genius **Orson Welles** was on a roll. By 1938, at age 23, Welles's dramatic flair had landed him a network radio show, *Mercury Theater on the Air,* at prime time on CBS on Sunday nights. The program featured adaptations of well-known literature. For their October 30 program, Welles and his colleagues decided on a scary 1898 British novel, H.G. Wells's *The War of the Worlds*.

Orson Welles opened with the voice of a wizened chronicler from some future time, intoning an unsettling monologue. That was followed by an innocuous weather forecast, then hotel dance music. Then the music was interrupted by a news bulletin. An astronomer reported several explosions on Mars, propelling something at enormous velocity toward

Earth. The bulletin over, listeners were transported back to the hotel orchestra. After applause the orchestra started up again, only to be interrupted by a special announcement: Seismologists had picked up an earthquake-like shock in New Jersey. Then it was one bulletin after another.

The storyline accelerated. Giant Martians moved across the countryside spewing fatal gas. One at a time, reporters at remote sites vanished off the air. The Martians decimated the Army and were wading across the Hudson River. Amid sirens and other sounds of emergency, a reporter on a Manhattan rooftop described the monsters advancing through the streets. From his vantage point he described the Martians felling people by the thousands and moving in on him, the gas crossing Sixth Avenue, then Fifth Avenue, then 100 yards away, then 50 feet. Then silence.

To the surprise of Orson Welles and his crew the drama triggered widespread mayhem. Neighbours gathered in streets all over the country, wet towels held to their faces to slow the gas. In Newark, New Jersey, people—many undressed—fled their apartments. Said a New York woman, "I never hugged my radio so closely . . . . I held a crucifix in my hand and prayed while looking out my open window to get a faint whiff of gas so that I would know when to close my window and hermetically seal my room with waterproof cement or anything else I could get a hold of. My plan was to stay in the room and hope that I would not suffocate before the gas blew away."

Researchers estimate that one out of six people who heard the program, more than one million in all, suspended disbelief and braced for the worst.

The effects were especially amazing considering that:

- An announcer identified the program as fiction at four points.
- Almost 10 times as many people were tuned to a popular comedy show on another network.
- The program ran only one hour, an impossibly short time for the sequence that began with the blastoffs on Mars, included a major military battle in New Jersey and ended with New York's destruction.

Unwittingly, Orson Welles and his Mercury Theater crew had created an evening of infamy and raised questions about media effects to new intensity. Theoretically, how could this happen? In this chapter you will learn what scholars have found out about the effects of the mass media on individuals.

Effects Studies

Study Preview   *Early mass communication scholars assumed that the mass media were so powerful that ideas and even ballot-box instructions could be inserted as if by hypodermic needle into the body politic. Doubts arose in the 1940s about whether the media were really that powerful, and scholars began shaping their research questions and asking about long-term, cumulative media effects.*

POWERFUL EFFECTS THEORY

The first generation of mass communication scholars thought the mass media had a profound, direct effect on people. Their idea, called **powerful effects theory,** drew heavily on social commentator **Walter Lippmann**'s influential 1922 book *Public Opinion.* Lippmann argued that we see the world not as it really is but as "pictures in our heads." The "pictures" of things we have not experienced personally, he said, are shaped by the mass media. The powerful impact that Lippmann ascribed to the media was a precursor of the powerful effects theory that evolved among scholars over the next few years.

Yale psychologist **Harold Lasswell**, who studied World War II propaganda, embodied the effects theory in his famous model of mass communication: *who, says what, in which channel, to whom, with what effect.* At their extreme, powerful effects theory devotees assumed that the media could inject information, ideas and even propaganda into the public. The theory was explained in terms of a hypodermic needle model or bullet model. Early powerful effects scholars would agree that newspaper coverage and endorsements of political candidates decided elections.

Orson Welles His radio drama cast doubt on powerful effects theory.

The War of the Worlds
Novel that inspired a radio drama that became the test bed of the media's ability to instill panic.

War of the Worlds:
Information about every version of *The War of the Worlds* ever released, including books, performances, music, movies, television shows, models and games.
www.war-of-the-worlds.org

powerful effects theory
Theory that media have immediate, direct influence.

Walter Lippmann His book *Public Opinion* assumed powerful media effects in 1920s.

Harold Lasswell His mass communication model assumed powerful effects.

The early scholars did not see that the hypodermic metaphor was hopelessly simplistic. They assumed wrongly that individuals are passive and absorb uncritically and unconditionally whatever the media spew forth. The fact is that individuals read, hear and see the same things differently. Even if they did not, people are exposed to many, many media—hardly a single, monolithic voice. Also, there is a skepticism among media consumers that is manifested at its extreme in the saying "You can't believe a thing you read in the paper." People are not mindless, uncritical blotters.

MINIMALIST EFFECTS THEORY

Paul Lazarsfeld Found voters more influenced by other people than by mass media.

Scholarly enthusiasm for the hypodermic needle model dwindled after two massive studies of voter behaviour, one in Erie County, Ohio, in 1940 and the other in Elmira, New York, in 1948. The studies, led by sociologist **Paul Lazarsfeld** of Columbia University, were the first rigorous tests of media effects on an election. Lazarsfeld's researchers went back to 600 people several times to discover how they developed their campaign opinions. Rather than citing particular newspapers, magazines or radio stations, as had been expected, these people generally mentioned friends and acquaintances. The media had hardly any direct effect. Clearly, the hypodermic needle model was off base, and the powerful effects theory needed rethinking. From that rethinking emerged the **minimalist effects theory**, which included:

minimalist effects theory Theory that media effects are mostly indirect.

two-step flow Media effects on individuals are through opinion leaders.

opinion leaders Influence friends, acquaintances.

TWO-STEP FLOW MODEL. Minimalist scholars devised the **two-step flow** model to show that voters are motivated less by the mass media than by people they know personally and respect. These people, called **opinion leaders**, include many clergy, teachers and neighbourhood merchants, although it is impossible to list categorically all those who are opinion leaders. Not all clergy, for example, are influential, and opinion leaders are not necessarily in an authority role. The minimalist scholars' point is that personal contact is more important than media contact. The two-step flow model, which replaced the hypodermic needle model, showed that whatever effect the media has on the majority of the population is through opinion leaders. Later, as mass communication research became more sophisticated, the two-step model was expanded into a **multistep flow** model to capture the complex web of social relationships that affects individuals.

multistep flow Media effects on individuals come through complex interpersonal connections.

status conferral Media attention enhances attention to people, subjects, issues.

STATUS CONFERRAL. Minimalist scholars acknowledge that the media create prominence for issues and people by giving them coverage. Conversely, neglect relegates issues and personalities to obscurity. Related to this **status conferral** phenomenon is **agenda setting**. Professors **Maxwell McCombs and Donald Shaw**, describing the agenda-setting phenomenon in 1972, said the media do not tell people *what to think* but tell them *what to think about*. This is a profound distinction. In covering a political campaign, explain McCombs and Shaw, the media choose which issues or topics to emphasize, thereby helping set the campaign's agenda. "This ability to affect cognitive change among individuals," say McCombs and Shaw, "is one of the most important aspects of the power of mass communication."

agenda setting Media tell people what to think about, not what to think.

Maxwell McCombs and Donald Shaw Articulated agenda-setting theory.

NARCOTICIZING DYSFUNCTION. Some minimalists claim that the media rarely energize people into action, such as getting them to go out to vote for a candidate. Rather, they say, the media lull people into passivity. This effect, called **narcoticizing dysfunction**, is supported by studies that find that many people are so over-

narcoticizing dysfunction People deceive themselves into believing they're involved when actually they're only informed.

whelmed by the volume of news and information available to them that they tend to withdraw from involvement in public issues. Narcoticizing dysfunction occurs also when people pick up a great deal of information from the media on a particular subject—poverty, for example—and believe that they are doing something about a problem when they are really only smugly well informed. Intellectual involvement becomes a substitute for active involvement.

CUMULATIVE EFFECTS THEORY

Center for Research on the Effects of Television: Based at Ithaca College in New York, the centre examines television content and its effect on viewers. www.ithaca.edu/cretv

In recent years, some mass communication scholars have parted from the minimalists and resurrected the powerful effects theory, although with a twist that avoids the simplistic hypodermic needle model. German scholar **Elisabeth Noelle-Neumann**, a leader of this school, concedes that the media do not have powerful immediate effects but argues that effects over time are profound. Her **cumulative effects theory** notes that nobody can escape either the media, which are ubiquitous, or the media's messages, which are driven home with redundancy. To support her point, Noelle-Neumann cites multimedia advertising campaigns that hammer away with the same message over and over. There's no missing the point. Even in news reports there is a redundancy, with the media all focusing on the same events.

Elisabeth Noelle-Neumann Leading cumulative effects theorist.

cumulative effects theory Theory that media influence is gradual over time.

Noelle-Neumann's cumulative effects theory has troubling implications. She says that the media, despite surface appearances, work against diverse, robust public consideration of issues. Noelle-Neumann bases her observation on human psychology, which she says encourages people who feel they hold majority viewpoints to speak out confidently. Those views gain credibility in their claim to be dominant when they are carried by the media, whether they are really dominant or not. Meanwhile, says Noelle-Neumann, people who perceive that they are in a minority are inclined to speak out less, perhaps not at all. The result is that dominant views can snowball through the media and become consensus views without being sufficiently challenged.

To demonstrate her intriguing theory, Noelle-Neumann has devised the ominously labeled **spiral of silence** model, in which minority views are intimidated into silence and obscurity. Noelle-Neumann's model raises doubts about the libertarian concept that the media provide a marketplace in which conflicting ideas fight it out fairly, all receiving a full hearing.

spiral of silence Vocal majority intimidates others into silence.

THIRD-PERSON EFFECT

A remnant of now-discredited perceptions that the media have powerful and immediate influence is called **third-person effect**. In short, the theory holds that people overestimate the impact of media messages on other people. Scholar **W.P. Davison**, who came up with the concept in 1983, told a story about a community film board that censored some movies because they might harm people who watch them—even though the board members would deny that they themselves were harmed by watching the movies. The theory can be reduced to this notion: "It's the other guy who can't handle it, not me."

third-person effect One person overestimating the effect of media messages on other people.

W.P. Davison Scholar who devised third-person effect theory.

FUTURE THEORIES

Scholar **Melvin DeFleur**, who has chronicled developments in mass communication theory, is pessimistic about what's happening now in mass communication studies.

Melvin DeFleur Scholar who concluded that mass communication theory has peaked.

DeFleur, of Boston University, says recent years have lacked milestones, seminal studies on mass communication, after a rich history of significant studies from the 1930s to the early 1980s. Writing in the scholarly journal *Mass Communication and Society* in 1998, DeFleur said: "When asked by my publisher to revise a book summarizing the existing milestones and adding new ones, I could not identify even one that fit the same criteria as the earlier investigations."

The Golden Age of masscom research, as DeFleur calls it, yielded "important concepts, generalizations and theories that are now part of the accumulated knowledge of how the U.S. media function and the kinds of influence that they have on individuals and society."

Is mass communication theory dead in the water? DeFleur says that one factor has been a brain drain from universities, where such research took place in earlier times. Corporations now offer much higher salaries than universities—sometimes double and triple—to attract people with doctoral degrees who can do research for their marketing and other corporate pursuits and not purely academic reasons.

Uses and Gratifications Studies

Study Preview   *Beginning in the 1940s, many mass communication scholars shifted from studying the media to studying media audiences. These scholars assumed that individuals use the media to gratify needs. Their work, known as uses and gratifications studies, focused on how individuals use mass media—and why.*

CHALLENGES TO AUDIENCE PASSIVITY

As disillusionment with the powerful effects theory set in after the Lazarsfeld studies of the 1940s, scholars re-evaluated many of their assumptions, including the idea that people are merely passive consumers of the mass media. From the re-evaluation came research questions about why individuals tap into the mass media. This research, called **uses and gratifications** studies explored how individuals choose certain media outlets. One vein of research said people seek certain media to gratify certain needs.

These scholars worked with social science theories about people being motivated to do certain things by human needs and wants, such as seeking water, food and shelter as necessities and wanting to be socially accepted and loved. These scholars identified dozens of reasons why people use the media, among them surveillance, socialization and diversion.

SURVEILLANCE FUNCTION

With their acute sense of smell and hearing, deer scan their environment constantly for approaching danger. In modern human society, surveillance is provided for individuals by the mass media, which scan local and global environments for information that helps individuals make decisions to live better, even survive.

News coverage is the most evident form through which the mass media serve this **surveillance function**. From a weather report, people decide whether to wear a raincoat; from the Wall Street averages, whether to invest; from the news, whether the president will have their support. Although most people don't obsess about

uses and gratifications
Theory that people choose media that meet their needs, interests.

Media Awareness Network:
A rich media-literacy site from Canada. The section on media research provides many resources for further study.
www.media-awareness.ca

surveillance function
Media provide information on what's going on.

being on top of all that's happening in the world, there is a touch of the news junkie in everybody. All people need reliable information on their immediate environment. Besides wanting to know what the weather forecast is, most of us are curious about developments in politics, economics, science and other fields. The news media provide that information for us.

SOCIALIZATION FUNCTION

Except for recluses, people are always seeking information that helps them fit in with other people. This **socialization function**, a lifelong process, is greatly assisted by the mass media. Without paying attention to the media, for example, it is hard to participate in conversations about Tom Cruise's latest movie or the current political scandal in Ottawa. Jay Leno's monologues give late-night television watchers a common experience with their friends and associates the next day, as do the latest movie, the evening news and what happened last night on *Lost* or *American Idol*.

socialization function Media help people fit into society.

Less positive as a social function of the mass media is **parasocial interaction**. When a television anchor looks directly into the camera, as if talking with individual viewers, it is not a true social relationship that is being created. The communication is one-way without audience feedback. However, because many people enjoy the sense of interaction, no matter how false it is, many local stations encourage on-camera members of the news team to chat among themselves, which furthers the impression of an ongoing conversation with an extended peer group that includes the individual viewer.

parasocial interaction A false sense of participating in dialogue.

DIVERSION FUNCTION

Through the mass media, people can escape their everyday drudgery, immersing themselves in a soap opera, a murder mystery or pop music. This is the **diversion function**. The result can be stimulation, relaxation or emotional release.

diversion function Media used as an entertainment source.

STIMULATION. Everybody is bored occasionally. When our senses—sight, hearing, smell, taste and touch—lack sufficient external stimuli, a sensory vacuum results. Following the physicist's law that a vacuum must be filled, we seek new stimuli to correct our sensory deprivation. In modern society, the mass media are almost always handy as boredom-offsetting stimulants.

RELAXATION. When someone's sensory abilities are overloaded, the media can be relaxing. Slower, softer music sometimes can help. Relaxation, in fact, can come through any change of pace. In some situations, a high-tension movie or a book can be as effective as a lullaby.

RELEASE. People can use the mass media to blow off steam. Somehow a Friday night horror movie dissipates the frustration pent up all week, as can a good cry during a "chick flick."

Using the mass media as a stimulant, relaxant or release is quick, healthy escapism. Escapism, however, can go further, as when soap-opera fans so enmesh themselves in the programs that they perceive themselves as characters in the storyline. Carried too far, escapism becomes withdrawal.

CONSISTENCY THEORY

Gratifications scholars learned that people generally are conservative and cautious in choosing media, looking for media that reinforce their personal views. Faced with messages that are consistent with their own views and ones that are radically different, people pay attention to the ones they're comfortable with and have slight recall of contrary views. These phenomena—selective exposure, selective perception, selective retention and selective recall—came to be called **consistency theory**.

Consistency theory does a lot to explain media habits. People read, watch and listen to media with messages that don't jar them. The theory raises serious questions about how well the media can meet the democratic ideal that they be a forum for the robust exchange of divergent ideas. The media can't fulfill their role as a forum if people hear only what they want to hear.

Individual Selectivity

Study Preview   *Individuals choose to expose themselves to media whose perspective and approach reinforce their personal interests and values. These choices, called selective exposure, are consciously made. Similar selectivity phenomena are at work subconsciously in how individuals perceive and retain media content.*

SELECTIVE EXPOSURE

People make deliberate decisions in choosing media. For example, outdoors enthusiasts choose *Field & Stream* at the newsrack. Academics subscribe to the *Canadian Journal of Communication*. Young rock fans watch MuchMusic. People expose themselves to media whose content relates to their interests. In this sense, individuals exercise control over the media's effects on them. Nobody forces these selections on anybody. This is called **selective exposure**.

SELECTIVE PERCEPTION

The selectivity that occurs in actually reading, watching and listening is less conscious than in selective exposure. No matter how clear a message is, people see and hear egocentrically. This phenomenon, known as **selective perception** or **autistic perception**, was demonstrated in the 1950s by researcher Roy Carter, who found that physicians concerned about socialized medicine at the time would hear "social aspects of medicine" as "socialized medicine." Rural folks in the U.S. Southeast, anxious for news about farming, thought they heard the words "farm news" on the radio when the announcer said "foreign news."

Scholars Eugene Webb and Jerry Salancik explain it this way: "Exposure to information is hedonistic." People pick up what they want to pick up. Webb and Salancik state that nonsmokers who read an article about smoking focus subconsciously on passages that link smoking with cancer, being secure and content, even joyful, in the information that reinforces the wisdom of their decision not to smoke. In contrast, smokers are more attentive to passages that hedge the smoking–cancer link. In using the mass media for information, people tend to perceive what they want. As social commentator Walter Lippmann put it: "For the most part we do not first see and then define, we define first and then see." Sometimes the human mind distorts facts to square with predispositions and preconceptions.

consistency theory People choose media messages consistent with their individual views, values.

selective exposure People choose some media messages over others.

selective perception People tend to hear what they want or expect to hear.

autistic perception Synonym for *selective perception*.

Selective Perception: An introduction to selective perception and how it's used in advertising. **www.ciadvertising.org/ student_account/fall_01/ adv382j/howardmo/ selectiveperception.html**

SELECTIVE RETENTION AND RECALL

Experts say that the brain records forever everything to which it is exposed. The problem is recall. Although people remember many things that were extremely pleasurable or that coincided with their beliefs, they have a harder time calling up the memory's file on other things.

Selective retention happens to mothers when they tend to deemphasize or even forget the illnesses or disturbances of pregnancy and the pain of birth. This phenomenon works the opposite way when individuals encounter things that reinforce their beliefs.

Nostalgia also can affect recall. For example, many mothers grossly pre-date when their children abandoned an undesirable behaviour like thumb sucking. Mothers tend also to suggest precocity about the age at which Suzy or José first walked or cut the first tooth. In the same way people often use rose-coloured lenses, not 20/20 vision, in recalling information and ideas from the media. This is known as **selective recall.**

In summary, individuals have a large degree of control over how the mass media affect them. Not only do individuals make conscious choices in exposing themselves to particular media, but also their beliefs and values subconsciously shape how their minds pick up and store information and ideas. The phenomena of selective exposure, selective perception and selective retention and recall are overlooked by people who portray the mass media as omnipotent and individuals as helpless and manipulated pawns.

The 1938 "War of the Worlds" scare demonstrates this point. The immediate response was to heap blame on the media, particularly Orson Welles and CBS, but panic-stricken listeners bore responsibility too. A Princeton University team led by psychologist **Hadley Cantril,** which studied the panic, noted that radio listeners brought to their radio sets predispositions and preconceptions that contributed to what happened. Among their subconscious baggage:

- A preconception, almost a reverence, about radio, especially CBS, as a reliable medium for major, breaking news.
- A predisposition to expect bad news, created by a decade of disastrous global economic developments and another war imminent in Europe.
- Selective perception, which caused them to miss announcements that the program was a dramatization. Although many listeners tuned in late and missed the initial announcement, others listened straight through the announcements without registering them.
- An awe about scientific discoveries, technological progress and new weapons, which contributed to gullibility.
- Memories from World War I about the horror of gas warfare.
- A failure to test the radio story against their own common sense. How, for example, could the Army mobilize for a battle against the Martians within 20 minutes of the invasion?

selective retention Subconsciously, people retain some events and messages, not others.

selective recall People recollect some events and messages for long term but not others.

Hadley Cantril Concluded that there is less media effect than had been thought.

Socialization

Study Preview *The mass media have a large role in initiating children into society. This socialization process is essential to perpetuating cultural values, but some people worry that it can be negative if the media report and portray undesirable behaviour and attitudes, such as violence and racism.*

socialization Learning to fit into society.

Mediawise: A U.S. resource for research, education and information about the impact of media on children and families.
www.mediafamily.org

The International Clearinghouse on Children, Youth & Media: Collects information about the effects of media on children.
www.nordicom.gu.se/ clearinghouse.php

pro-social Socialization perpetuates positive values.

MEDIA'S INITIATING ROLE

Nobody is born knowing how to fit into society. This is learned through a process that begins at home. Children imitate their parents and brothers and sisters. From listening and observing, children learn values. Some behaviour is applauded, some is scolded. Gradually this culturization and **socialization** process expands to include friends, neighbours, school and at some point the mass media.

In earlier times the role of the mass media came late because books, magazines and newspapers required reading skills that were learned in school. The media were only a modest part of early childhood socialization. Today, however, television is omnipresent from the cradle. A young person turning 18 will have spent more time watching television than doing any other activity except sleeping. Television, which requires no special skills to use, has displaced much of the socializing influence that once came from parents. *Sesame Street* imparts more information on the value of nutrition than does Mom's admonition to eat spinach.

By definition, socialization is **pro-social** rather than anti-social, in that it teaches behaviour that will benefit others or society. Children learn that buddies frown on tattling; that honesty is virtuous; and that hard work is rewarded. The stability of a society is ensured through the transmission of such values to the next generation.

ROLE MODELS

role modeling Basis for imitative behaviour.

The extent of media influence on individuals may never be sorted out with any precision, in part because every individual is a distinct person and because media exposure varies from person to person. Even so, some media influence is undeniable. This imitation, called **role modeling**, even includes popular quotes from whoever is hip at the moment—"You're Fired!" from *The Apprentice,* being "voted off the island" from *Survivor* and "yadda-yadda-yadda" from *Seinfeld.*

Asics Revival. When Uma Thurman slashed her way through Quentin Tarantino's movie *Kill Bill,* the 1949-vintage Asics sneakers she wore, the Onitsuka Tiger model, were suddenly a hit again. In the first quarter after the movie, Asics's net profits outperformed $1.8 billion in expectations to $2.6 billion.

No matter how quirky, fashion fads are not terribly consequential, but serious questions can be raised about whether role modeling extends to behaviour. Many people who produce media messages recognize a responsibility for role modeling. Many newspapers have a policy to mention in accident stories whether seat belts were in use. In the 1980s, as concern about AIDS mounted, moviemakers went out of their way to show condoms as a precaution in social situations. For example, in the movie *Broadcast News,* the producer character slips a condom into her purse before leaving the house on the night of the awards dinner.

If role modeling can work for good purposes, such as promoting safety consciousness and disease prevention, it would seem that it could also have a negative effect. Some people linked the Columbine High School massacre in Littleton, Colorado, to a scene in the Leonardo DiCaprio movie, *The Basketball Diaries*. In one scene, a student in a black trench coat executes fellow classmates.

STEREOTYPING

Stereotyping is a kind of shorthand that can facilitate communication. Putting a cowboy in a black hat allows a movie director to sidestep complex character explanation and move quickly into a storyline because moviegoers hold a generalization about cowboys in black hats: They are the bad guys—a stereotype.

Newspaper editors pack lots of information into headlines by drawing on stereotypes held by the readers. Consider the extra meanings implicit in headlines that refer to a political "regime," a "Southern belle" or a "college jock." Stereotypes paint broad strokes that help create impact in media messages, but they are also a problem. A generalization, no matter how useful, is inaccurate. Not all Scots are tight-fisted, nor are all Wall Street brokers crooked, nor are all college jocks dumb—not even a majority.

By using stereotypes, the mass media perpetuate them. With benign stereotypes there is no problem, but the media can perpetuate social injustice with stereotypes. In the late 1970s the U.S. Civil Rights Commission found that blacks on network television were portrayed disproportionately in immature, demeaning or comic roles. By using a stereotype, television was not only perpetuating false generalizations but also being racist. Worse, network thoughtlessness was robbing black people of strong role models.

Feminists have leveled objections that women are both underrepresented and misrepresented in the media. One study by sociologist Eve Simson found that most female television parts were decorative, played by pretty California women in their 20s. Worse were the occupations represented by women, said Simson. Most frequent were prostitutes, at 16 percent. Traditional female occupations—secretaries, nurses, flight attendants and receptionists—represented 17 percent. Career women tended to be man-haters or domestic failures. Said Simson: "With nearly every family, regardless of socioeconomic class, having at least one TV set and the average set being turned on seven hours per day, TV has emerged as an important source for promulgating attitudes, values and customs. For some viewers it is the only major contact with outside 'reality,' including how to relate to women. Thus, not only is TV's sexism insulting, but it is also detrimental to the status of women."

stereotyping Using broad strokes to facilitate storytelling.

Media Stereotypes: This educational introduction to media stereotyping details several categories of common stereotypes. **www.media-awareness.ca/ english/issues/ stereotyping/index.cfm**

Young African-Americans Against Media Stereotypes: Nonprofit organization working for equal and fair exposure of African-Americans in the media. **www.yaaams.org**

Media Action Network for Asian Americans: Check out the memo from MANAA to Hollywood, regarding Asian American stereotypes in the media.
www.manaa.org/articles/ stereo.html

Media Stereotypes of Young People: Even children are stereotyped in the media.
www.headliners.org/ storylibrary/ stories/2006/ stereotypes.htm?id= 4358055140998o188200606

Joshua Meyrowitz Noted that media have reduced generational, gender barriers.

SOCIALIZATION VIA EAVESDROPPING

The mass media, especially television, have eroded the boundaries that people once respected between the generations, genders and other social institutions. Once adults whispered when they wanted to discuss certain subjects, like sex, when children were around. Today, children eavesdrop on all kinds of adult topics by seeing them depicted on television.

Joshua Meyrowitz, a communication scholar at the University of New Hampshire, brought the new socialization effects of intergenerational eavesdropping to wide attention with his 1985 book, *No Sense of Place*. In effect, the old socially recognized institution of childhood, which long had been protected from "grown-up issues" like money, divorce and sex, was disappearing. From television sitcoms, kids today learn that adults fight and goof up and sometimes are just plain silly. These are things kids may always have been aware of in a vague sense, but now they have front row seats.

Television also cracked other protected societal institutions, such as the "man's world." Through television many women entered the man's world of the locker room, the fishing trip and the workplace beyond the home. Older mass media, including books, had dealt with a diversity of topics and allowed people in on the "secrets" of other groups, but the ubiquity of television and the ease of access to it accelerated the breakdown of traditional institutional barriers.

CHAPTER 12 WRAP-UP

The mass media influence us, but scholars are divided about how much. There is agreement that the media help to initiate children into society by portraying social and cultural values. This is a serious responsibility because portrayals of aberrant behaviour such as violence have effects, although we are not sure about their extent. This is not to say that individuals are unwitting pawns of the mass media. People choose what they read and what they tune in to, and they generally filter the information and images to conform with their preconceived notions and personal values.

In other respects, too, the mass media are a stabilizing influence. The media try to fit into the lives of their audiences. An example is children's television programs on weekend mornings when kids are home from school but still on an early-rising schedule. The media not only react to audience lifestyles but also contribute to the patterns by which people live their lives, like going to bed after the late news. In short, the media have effects on individuals and on society, but it is a two-way street. Society is a shaper of media content, but individuals make the ultimate decisions about subscribing, listening and watching. The influence issue is a complex one that merits further research and thought.

QUESTIONS FOR REVIEW

1. Why have most media scholars abandoned the powerful effects and minimalist effects theories for the cumulative theory?

2. What is the uses and gratifications approach to mass media studies?

3. Do individuals have any control over mass media effects on them?

4. What role do the mass media have in socializing children?

5. What is meant when someone says, "The mass media don't tell people what to think as much as tell them what to think about"?

6. Does being informed by mass media necessarily improve citizen involvement in political processes?

QUESTIONS FOR CRITICAL THINKING

1. Although generally discredited by scholars now, the powerful effects theory once had many adherents. How do you explain the lingering popularity of this thinking among many people?

2. Name at least three opinion leaders who influence you on issues that you do not follow closely in the media. On what issues are you yourself an opinion leader?

3. Give specific examples of each of the eight primary mass media contributing to the lifelong socialization process. For starters, consider a current non-fiction best-selling book.

4. Discuss the human needs that the mass media help to satisfy in terms of the news and entertainment media.

5. Among the functions that the mass media serve for individuals are diversion and escape. Is this healthy?

6. Explain the pro-social potential of the mass media in culturization and socialization. What about the media as an anti-social force in observational learning?

DEEPENING YOUR MEDIA LITERACY

Reality shows: more than just entertainment?

Step 1

From *Survivor* to *The Intern*, *The Bachelor* or *Canadian Idol*, reality shows have proliferated on North American television.

Dig Deeper

Step 2

Think of your favourite reality show. Think about why you were first attracted to it. Think about why you kept watching it. Think about a reality show that doesn't appeal to you. Why doesn't it? To whom does it appeal?

What Do You Think?

Step 3

Answer these questions:

1. Has your favourite reality show changed North American society, or does it just reflect society?

2. What needs does it gratify?

3. Does it tell you anything about the great human issues?

4. Does it reinforce your personal views? If so, which ones?

5. Do you want to emulate the people on the show? Do you think they are stereotyped?

6. Does the show help its viewers find their place in society?

KEEPING UP TO DATE

The interdisciplinary scholarly journal *Media Psychology*, a quarterly, focuses on theory-based research on media uses, processes and effects.

FOR FURTHER LEARNING

Jane D. Brown, Jeanne R. Steele and Kim Walsh-Childers, editors. *Sexual Teens, Sexual Media: Investigating Media's Influence of Adolescent Sexuality* (Erlbaum, 2001).

Donald Bogle. *Primetime Blues: African Americans on Network Television* (Straus & Giroux, 2001).

Carolyn Byerly and Karen Ross. *Women and Media: A Critical Introduction* (Blackwell, 2005).

Margaret Gallagher. *Gender Setting: New Media Agenda for Monitoring and Advocacy* (Palgrave, 2001).

Gabriele Griffin. *Representations of HIV and AIDS: Visibility Blues* (Manchester University Press, 2001).

Carolyn Kitch. *The Girl on the Magazine Cover* (University of North Carolina Press, 2002).

Lewis H. Lapham. *Gag Rule: On the Suppression of Dissent and the Stifling of Democracy* (Penguin, 2004).

Paul Lazarsfeld, Bernard Berelson and Hazel Gaudet. *The People's Choice: How the Voter Makes Up His Mind in a Presidential Campaign*, Second edition. Bureau of Applied Social Research, 1948.

Joshua Meyrowitz. *No Sense of Place: The Impact of Electronic Media on Social Behavior* (Oxford, 1985).

Elizabeth M. Perse. *Media Effects and Society* (Erlbaum, 2001).

Michael Pickering. *Stereotyping: The Politics of Representation* (Palgrave, 2001).

Antonia Zerbisias. "What You Can Restrict: Children" *Toronto Star* (January 18, 2007).

SECTION II

Chapter Thirteen

Media and Ideology

There is an old saying about looking at the world through rose-coloured glasses. It brings to mind someone whose outlook is overly optimistic, rosy. It also hints that everyone looks at the world through glasses of one colour or another.

Communications media—television, radio, newspapers, the Internet—provide one very important set of glasses that we use to view the world. And those particular glasses influence the understanding of every issue. The first part of this chapter focuses on one aspect of the media, the information industry, to see how its corporate structures and market approach influence the information that filters down to us.

The notion of using a particular set of glasses, a particular tint colouring our world view, illustrates a rather difficult concept, "ideology." The second part of this chapter considers ideology, looking back over issues in everyday life and the world around us analyzed in the first two parts of this book. Our goal is to identify some of the ideological factors shaping Canadian society.

The Information Industry

In a world shaped by a flow of information that is getting faster and heavier every day, Canada holds a respectable position. We have freedom of the press, which is not as common elsewhere as it ought to be. Not many among us now remember the days before radio, and most of us grew up with television. Today's young Canadians grow up with computers and the Internet.

Years ago—when the telephone was a novelty restricted to wealthy homes—people relied on face-to-face communication to get the news. They absorbed information (and ideology) through family, workplace, neighbourhood, and church. Even though literacy levels were not as high as they are today, local newspapers were also important. At one time most people got their news from the independent papers established in every city.

Canada now has more television stations than it does daily newspapers. Nearly two out of every three Canadian homes with television have at least basic cable service, giving them access to dozens of stations. More and more people, especially in areas without cable, have satellite dishes and the "five hundred channel universe." Canada has three "national newspapers," two in English Canada and one in Quebec. The newsstands are packed with hundreds of magazines. The airwaves are crammed with so many radio signals that there is no more transmitting space left in the biggest cities.

Computer communications are growing with breathtaking speed. By 2001, over 5.8 million Canadian households (or 49 per cent of all households) included at least one member who regularly used the Internet from home, up 23 per cent from 2000—although this is less than the increase of 42 per cent from 1999 to 2000. More and more households used the Internet as an information source, using news sites or searching for government information on-line. In 2001, 87 per cent of the one-quarter of households in the highest income bracket used the Internet, up from 58 per cent in 1997. Only 32 per cent of the one-quarter of households with the lowest income level regularly used the Internet in that year. Still, this was nearly triple the rate of 12 per cent five years earlier.

Despite this seeming abundance of communications media, the information industry consists of a few large corporations. Continuing worries over the demise of stand-alone media outlets—those not part of a chain—were enough to provoke Ottawa to launch two major inquiries into media ownership. Both the Special Senate Committee on Mass Media (1970) and the Royal Commission on Newspapers (1981) focused on increased concentration of newspaper ownership and decreased competition. The 1981 Royal Commission emphasized the importance of decreasing the power of the companies that own newspapers and television stations so that they would have less influence on how the information is presented. It also expressed concern over the integration of newspapers with other businesses.

Worries over more control of more information by fewer corporations were stimulated by the recognition that those who control the distribution of messages through the media can shape society. Companies owning huge media outlets reach huge numbers of viewers, audiences, and readers. This influence carries with it political, cultural, and social power. Social groups (for instance, racial minorities and poor people) without access to the media are deprived of that sort of vital influence.

The dangers of concentrated corporate control of the media are widely recognized. In the United States (where in other respects government is unwilling to interfere with market activity) the same company is not allowed to own a television station and a newspaper in the same market—city, state, and so on. In Canada the situation is different. Here two of the three national television networks are owned by major communications firms, and each of those companies also owns the two newspapers that claim to be national in scope. Bell Globemedia controls both the *Globe and Mail* newspaper and the CTV television network. CanWest Global controls the *National Post* newspaper and the Global television network. Moreover, in several important big-city media markets (Ottawa, Calgary, Vancouver), CanWest Global owns the leading newspapers as well as a television station.

> *Journalism is arguably the most important form of public knowledge in contemporary society. The mass media—of which journalism is one, key, news-spreading part—have become the leading institution of the public sphere—"that realm of social life where the exchange of information and views on questions of common concern can take place so that public opinion can be formed."*
>
> —Robert A. Hackett and Yuezhi Zhao, *Sustaining Democracy?*
> *Journalism and the Politics of Objectivity*, 1998.
> The quote is from Peter Dalhgren, *Television and the Public Sphere:*
> *Citizenship, Democracy and the Media*, 1995.

A CANADIAN MEDIA UPROAR

How does such ownership influence the flow of information? In 2000 CanWest Global paid $3.5 billion to Conrad Black's Hollinger Inc. to acquire the newspapers formerly owned by Hollinger and the venerable Southam chain. After that deal, journalists and media observers once again expressed long-standing concerns about excessive concentration in the media sector. These alarm bells might since have faded if several events had not brought into focus the way that such control can work.

Winnipeg's Asper family controls CanWest Global. In 2002 CanWest chair Israel Asper told the shareholders at his company's annual general meeting that his fourteen large-city newspapers should have a single editorial position—not fourteen distinct positions—on important national and international issues. This was contrary to the position that the Southam chain had maintained even when it was controlled by the controversial Conrad Black. In 1995 Southam's Annual Report was still proclaiming a Statement of Editorial Independence declaring, "For more than a century, Southam has proudly upheld its policy of editorial independence on all matters involving news and opinion. In the widely different environments in which Southam operates across the country, publishers and editors make their own editorial decisions."

When the former Southam papers began publishing single "national" editorials that they received from CanWest's Winnipeg head office, the practice produced loud protests from journalists, including many at the company's own papers. They were particularly upset by the company stipulation that locally written material should not contradict the positions taken by head office. The furor increased when CanWest fired the publisher of the *Ottawa Citizen* after that paper published editorials sharply critical of Prime Minister Jean Chrétien. The wealthy Aspers are strong supporters of the Liberal Party.

In Regina, where CanWest owns the only newspaper along with all the other daily papers in Saskatchewan, reporters for the *Leader Post* were suspended and reprimanded after withdrawing their bylines to protest censorship of the news. This took place after Haroon Siddiqui, an emeritus editor at *The Toronto Star* (itself part of a major media empire that owns seven Ontario dailies, including the largest paper in Canada), spoke in Regina. The *Leader Post* journalist who covered Siddiqui's lecture at the University of Regina began her report with a "lead" that emphasized what she felt was the most important point: "CanWest Global performed 'chilling' acts of censorship when it refused to publish several columns containing viewpoints other than those held by the media empire, a *Toronto Star* columnist said Monday."

When the newspaper appeared the next day her report had been changed to read: "A *Toronto Star* columnist says it's OK for CanWest Global to publish its owners' views as long as the company is prepared to give equal play to opposing opinions." Critics were quick to point out that the second version was not completely accurate. When Aboriginal writer Doug Cuthand wrote a column for CanWest's Regina and Saskatoon papers in which he compared the plight of Aboriginal Canadians to the condition of Palestinians, the papers refused to publish it. The Asper family is well known for its militant support of the Israeli side in the Palestinian-Israeli dispute.

CONVERGENCE, ADVERTISING, AND THE GOOD OLD DAYS?

Quebecor is a Canadian company with a convergence strategy. The company publishes the tabloid-style *Sun* newspapers in Winnipeg, Calgary, Ottawa, Toronto, and Edmonton, along with eleven others, like *The London Free Press*, which are the only daily newspapers in their home cities. It runs *Le Journal de Montréal* and *Le Journal de Québec*, hugely popular tabloids in Quebec. It owns the biggest commercial printing company in the world. All in all, it publishes 190 regional newspapers and magazines. Quebecor owns TVA, Quebec's largest private television network as well as Vidéotron, the largest Quebec cable company. It runs Netgraphe Internet portals and Canoe.ca. It controls the Nurun web agency offering site design, e-commerce and transaction processing systems, automated publishing, and on-line marketing.

Given this sort of "convergence"—or crossmedia ownership of Internet, newspapers, and television—what happens to the public's right to get information from independent voices? What are the implications of a company like Quebecor that owns so much? Or of a giant like AOL Time Warner? In 2001 America Online, the dominant Internet company in the United States, joined forces with the huge movie and publishing company Time Warner in one of the largest mergers in corporate history. As a result, the same company now provides nearly thirty million Americans with Internet service and offers cable service from Poland to Brazil. It presents the news on CNN and through the pages of *Time*. It sells record albums by Madonna, publishes books, shows cartoons (*Bugs Bunny* and *Scooby Doo*), runs theme parks and Warner Bros studio stores, and owns a vast vault of American music and movies.

Although convergence alarmed critics concerned about too few corporations controlling too many media outlets, it seemed like a good idea at the time to the businessmen who did the deals. But it was not long before the consolidations began to lose their business-sense glow. In 2002 AOL Time Warner recorded the largest loss in U.S. corporate history—$99 billion. In Canada, CanWest-Global was still staggering under an unsustainable debt load brought about in part by its media acquisitions.

Still, with convergence, companies hold out hopes of more efficiency and higher profits. Takeovers and concentration in the newspaper sector always caused concern among citizens who believed that too much control over information by too few people constitutes a new threat to freedom. Now that the process has accelerated with electronic, print, and on-line media being grouped together under a few corporate roofs, those worries have become even more pronounced.

The concerns are certainly valid. Freedom of information is crucial for democracy. Culture—the stories we tell each other and that give us the sense of who we are and how we understand the world—should not be reduced to Disney-style entertainment. Democracy and culture are too important to be left to the market. But it is important to remember that today's convergence is, in one important way, not that different from how Canadians have always received the news of the world.

Nineteenth-century newspapers were closely tied to political parties, to the extent that the description "political organ" is often used to describe them. The Toronto *Globe* served as the personal podium for its owner, George Brown, a Reform politician. On the other side of the fence, the Conservatives set up the Toronto *Mail*, a vehicle for John A. Macdonald. (The papers later merged into *The Globe and Mail*.) Newspaper partisanship—there was no hint of balance in reporting—was cemented in the papers' dependence on money from political parties as well as on circulation to pay their way.

With increasing literacy and higher circulation came the rise of advertising. In the twentieth century, those who sold the news came to depend not on political parties in search of votes but on stores and soap producers in search of customers. Despite paying more attention to balance and getting both sides of a story, the information dealers—including new media like radio and television—did not often challenge the status quo, particularly when it came to criticizing those who paid the bills. Owners of media outlets often shared the values of their advertisers, whose interests they were unlikely to challenge through their media "properties."

In the 1930s and 1940s, under the ownership of Victor Sifton, the *Winnipeg Free Press* made a deal with Eaton's department store, which advertised heavily in the paper. Before running any article that mentioned Eaton's, the paper would clear the story with the company. This situation had arisen because Eaton's had pulled its advertising when the paper ran an item casting the store in an unfavourable light. On one occasion a man committed suicide by jumping from the roof of Eaton's in Winnipeg. On orders from the owner, the story in the city's biggest newspaper did not mention that the event had taken place at its biggest department store.[7]

In 1990 the independently owned *Kingston Whig-Standard* featured a story in its Saturday edition about people who sold their own homes and were thus able to save on real estate agency commissions. Local realtors who advertised in the Saturday paper were outraged and shifted their business to a twice-weekly paper that was part of the *Toronto Star* chain. Along with a recession, this was one of the factors that prompted the long-time owner of the *Whig-Standard* to sell the paper to the Southam chain. Under chain ownership, staff was cut, along with coverage of the day's news.

Newspapers are certainly not alone in being in business to sell advertising. Television, radio, and Internet commerce all provide news and entertainment liberally sprinkled with commercials. The automobile industry is the biggest source of advertising revenue for television stations and networks. Just as you would not expect a publication run by environmentalists to feature articles denying that the greenhouse effect is caused by carbon dioxide emissions, neither is it surprising that the safety and pollution records of automakers are not subject to sustained critical scrutiny by broadcasters.

The pattern of corporate concentration in the news and entertainment media is similar to the pattern in the housing, food, and energy industries. Perhaps news is not distorted outright as it was when the Regina reporter tried to report what was really said about CanWest. But events are often distorted or downplayed in the course of normal, daily relationships between editors, producers, and reporters, on the one hand, and media owners and other members of the business community on the other. While media outlets controlled by large chains are unlikely to unearth hard-to-get stories that run contrary to their interests, they are usually ready to protect their allies.

The coincidence of media ownership with concentration in the food industry is illuminating. A Canadian university researcher found that the press had consistently joined with the food industry in attacking the role of the marketing boards that manage the supply of farm products. Supply management was blamed for high food costs and Canada's alleged inability to compete internationally in the food sector. The study cited a series of articles and editorials that appeared in *The Globe and Mail* and were "echoed in much of the Canadian business press." (Although most people get their news from television, most television and radio producers and reporters still take their cues from newspapers, particularly national "papers of record.") The critics characterized the supply-management: system as "wretched" and as damaging "the competitive advantage of an entire sector of the economy."[8]

This analysis attributed higher food prices to corporate concentration in the retail food sector, not farm marketing boards. Big food retailers have captured a greater share of the food dollar than have farmers. The study concluded:

> *Perhaps the more interesting question is: why have the giant food retailers attracted virtually no attention from the major media on this question? Instead, the media have chosen to focus their attention elsewhere in the food chain, that is, on the institutional arrangements protecting primary producers—the sector that is least organized, [and] most fragmented.*[9]

> *Community-access television—once a mandatory obligation of all cable licensees—has been steadily eroding across the country since 1997, when the Canadian Radio-television and Telecommunications Commission (CRTC) lifted the requirement that cable companies must operate a community channel as a condition of their license. In anticipation of the CRTC's 1997 decision, Rogers Cable (Vancouver's former cable supplier prior to Shaw) closed three of its four neighbourhood T.V. production facilities in the city in 1996. . . . That's when ICTV [Independent Community Television Co-operative] was born, along with its sister organization, the Community Media Education Society. . . . A truly democratic society requires some vehicle for democratic communication—a vehicle that allows citizens and underrepresented groups to tell their stories, express their views and information, and present their art, unfiltered by corporate bias.*

> —Kim Goldberg, "Reclaiming the Airwaves," *Canadian Dimension*, September/October 2001.

A partial answer to this question rests in the business relationship between the media and the food industry. Simply put, farmers don't often advertise in the media. Other parts of the food business do.

The real world of journalism has never been a place free of censorship, free of management interference in editorial matters or in crucial decision-making about which stories are covered and how they are presented. According to journalist Linda

McQuaig, "Most journalists have no say in their newspapers' editorial positions, no input into what news stories are given prominence, nor any guarantee that their own stories—no matter how accurate and important—will even be published. All these things are ultimately determined by the newspaper's owner."[10]

News for Sale

"You can't believe everything you hear" is true of neighbourhood gossip, and it is best to apply the same scepticism to the news we see, hear, and read. But no matter how sceptical we try to be, the daily barrage of information has an inevitable influence. The mass media remain our primary source of information about a very complex world. The matter-of-fact prose of *Maclean's* magazine and the reassuring tone of CBC news readers exude credibility. The CTV network got to the heart of the matter when it began to use two unrelated words to describe its newscast: "Trust and Tradition."

In 1925 the editor of *The Wall Street Journal* made an observation that is still relevant in the era of the Internet: "A newspaper is a private enterprise, owing nothing to the public which grants it no franchise. It is therefore affected with no public interest. It is emphatically the property of its owner, who is selling a manufactured product at his own risk."[11]

Indeed, the media are structured and controlled like any other Canadian industry. Their products are news and entertainment, delivered in greater quantity and more quickly as the years pass. Events are skillfully refined before they are served up with our morning coffee or broadcast into our houses at prime time. Many of us have access to "all news/all the time" television and radio stations, as well as news on-line all the time. Each day thousands of raw events are readied for Canadians to consume as news.

What happens to the events covered in this "manufacturing" process? They get turned into items that are *intense, unambiguous and balanced, familiar and marketable*. To better interpret the news that is produced, let's consider these criteria.

"INTENSE"

For an audience accustomed to high-speed movie and video-game car chases, the fast cutting of music videos, and prime-time "real life" TV shows, intensity is a must ingredient. Journalists and editors either choose events for their drama or focus selectively on the dramatic elements within items.

Protest marches get covered (they make good pictures), but the news will concentrate on any scuffles or arrests to the virtual exclusion of other aspects of the story, including the issues involved. The news coverage of the 2001 Summit of the Americas anti-globalization protests in Quebec City, with its symbolic fence and tear-gas attacks on demonstrators by the authorities, received blanket coverage. Similar protests occurred in Calgary at the G-8 summit a year later, when the concerns were the same, but those demonstrations received far less attention—the protests were by and large peaceful. The world leaders were at a distant resort in Kananaskis. The police were more restrained.

In local news the need for intensity results in a constant stream of images of accused criminals, trials, and stories about violent crime. The media pay far less attention to non-violent corporate or white-collar crime, even though corporate crime costs society far more than the activities of violent thugs. Price-fixing by

Canada's major petroleum companies from the 1950s to the 1970s took an extra $12 billion from consumers, but those firms are rarely if ever portrayed as criminals.[12] Similarly, the media—particularly Internet-based services—emphasize the drama of personality and celebrity (the death of Lady Di is the most striking example) at the expense of political issues.

In international coverage, events in Third World countries make the news fleetingly when there are coups, earthquakes, or famines. In reports from Latin America and Africa, national strikes, violent demonstrations, and "bloodless" coups blur into one another. One study of the "story geography" of Canadian TV news concluded, "The outbreak of war guarantees a steady supply of visually fulfilling stories."[13] Less intense stories—an election or the struggle to survive of children living in poverty—appear from time to time, but without the same regularity or high profile.

TV news crews find it easier to cover a volcano eruption in Brazil's Amazon basin than the daily suffering caused by that country's heavy foreign debt. One TV news producer explained the reasoning: "You can't show the deaths caused by the debt. The volcano wasn't there yesterday and is there today—that's new, that's television news. . . . People in the morning say, 'Gee, did you see the footage of that volcano last night on the news?' But nobody gets up in the morning and says, 'Gee, did you hear about that debt in Brazil?'"[14]

Stories pop into the news, evolve at alarming speed, and—scarcely digested by the public—pop out again to make room for fresh events. The American anthrax scare immediately after the 9/11 attack on the World Trade Center is an example. Fresh, novel items are always being served up, but often at the cost of missing the truth behind them. The coverage is too brief, too fleeting to provide much of an idea of what led up to events or caused them, or what might flow from them in the long run.

"UNAMBIGUOUS" AND "BALANCED"

Another criterion establishing newsworthiness is that the information be cut and dried, without much ambiguity, and presented from a "balanced" or "objective" viewpoint.

When TV and print media cover a political story they usually present both the government and the opposition sides. In environmental stories there are the industry and the activist sides. Some people are in favour of globalization, some are opposed to it, many are still confused by what it all means. In reports on the nuclear power industry there are "good news" stories (when the nuclear industry is successful in meeting its objectives) and "bad news" stories (when the industry has to pay billions of dollars extra to repair a reactor).[15] There is the "status quo" and there are "interest groups" trying to change it.

Aside from the odd opinion piece that may carry a more complex or nuanced picture of an issue, most TV news and newspaper coverage follow this pattern. As a result, a black and white picture tends to become common knowledge, common sense. Overly simple news items, laced with intensity to attract attention, draw the audiences required to attract advertisers. But they often distort or ignore what is really going on.

Canada went through long constitutional debates in the 1980s and early 1990s, as the constitution was patriated from Great Britain and the federal government attempted to get Quebec to sign on. For the first time in Canadian history the Aboriginal issue became central to the debates. In Quebec there were—and are—

separatists and federalists. The media formula can easily handle this, adapting to allow for the "undecideds." But with the Aboriginal issue, things became a bit more nuanced—as journalist Henry F. Heald points out, "too complex to be dealt with in the single-issue context that reporters customarily work in."

With aboriginal people . . . there are more than 50 nations comprising some 600 bands or groups. There are Inuit, Indians, and Metis. There are sophisticated people holding down good jobs and living comfortable lives in the urban milieu. There are people living comfortably off the land the way their ancestors did, living on reservations where rich natural resources have been developed to provide a high standard of living for the inhabitants. There are also people rotting in urban slums. There are people living on reservations in poverty, vice and squalor.[16]

Journalists did become more sensitive to the "Native side" of things as the constitutional debates unfolded. The availability of a national chief of the Assembly of First Nations allowed them to provide an Aboriginal perspective on the constitutional negotiations. But reporters often found out that their sources, leaders like National Chief Ovide Mercredi, did not necessarily speak for all Aboriginal peoples. There was no single definition of what Native peoples wanted from constitutional reform.

"FAMILIAR" AND "MARKETABLE"

In order to become news, an event must be culturally familiar and socially recognizable.

A car accident in which someone is killed or badly injured will always feature on the local news. But on big, national newspapers there is a kind of story we call "the bus plunge." The event can occur anywhere—a bus goes off the road and over a cliff, killing dozens of passengers; a crowded train is derailed, catching fire. "Bus-plunge" stories employ repetitive phrases and images that have a cumulative effect, reinforcing prejudices and stereotypes. But the "marketability" of the story—the extent and depth of the coverage—depends greatly on where it happens.

One Saturday in early 2003, two news stories captivated the Canadian media. Both involved the sudden violent deaths of seven people. Within hours of the space shuttle Columbia exploding over Texas, with the loss of its astronauts, seven students from an elite private school in Alberta were killed by an avalanche while they were out on a back-country ski trip in British Columbia. Both events received massive media coverage. This is not so surprising, because both were familiar and recognizable; Canadians had learned of a similar ski accident in the same region only weeks before and, of course, the high technologies and dangers and discoveries of space travel have long held a general fascination.

That same Saturday a fiery train collision in Zimbabwe killed at least forty-six people. That, too, was news. But in contrast to the blizzard of stories and miles of videotape produced by the tragedies in the B.C. mountains and the sky over the United States, the African incident was mentioned only briefly. The event, equally tragic, was covered, for example, by a four-sentence story in *The Globe and Mail*. There was no follow-up, no exploration of how such a terrible thing could have happened.[17]

Repetition, combined with the limitations of news-gathering capabilities, ensures that what we see is largely limited to the familiar. International news coverage by Canadian TV networks is concentrated in a few countries that receive the bulk of the coverage, with the rest of the world largely ignored.[18]

In 1989–90, for instance, the media, understandably, were filled with news of the fall of the Berlin Wall and the end of the Cold War. These events had immense historical importance. For thirty-five years the Cold War and the Soviet Union's control over an entire region had been a familiar news theme, and now the collapse of Communism and the democratic revival in Eastern Europe dominated the headlines. At the same time the news downplayed—"completely overlooked," according to one media analysis—crucial historical changes taking place in South America.[19] That region also had a dominant superpower that had long backed military dictatorships there. The U.S. media virtually ignored the first free elections held in Chile and Brazil in sixteen and twenty-five years respectively.

Other familiar images come up when famine strikes places like Bangladesh, Ethiopia, or Somalia. We have often seen pictures of Black children with distended bellies, flies in their eyes. Haunting, heart-rending images bring home the effects of famine but not the human and political causes. The images do not inform, much less provide, a critical point of view. When the media employ certain familiar (racial, sexual, economic, or political) stereotypes again and again, each use reinforces them. According to a Zimbabwean media analyst, "News reports show outside white people feeding and helping black people. They never show black people helping themselves."[20]

To attract the largest audiences—or to capture "market share"—the media companies attempt to provide coverage that is intense, unambiguous, and familiar. Television networks produce prime-time dramas and "reality-based" survivor shows that feature unfamiliar, exotic settings with familiar-looking people indulging in intense competitions. Similarly, the news is geared to consumer taste. This may mean something as apparently innocuous as pampering Canadians' sweet tooth for royalty. It also gives rise to the *Sun* tabloids. Like the mainstream Internet, the tabloids emphasize celebrities, sports, and sensational, often violent stories—neatly packaged with Sunshine Girls and Boys.

Invasions always make good copy. The U.S.-led invasion of Afghanistan following the attacks of September 11, 2001, received saturation coverage as the mass bombing of one of the world's poorest countries was followed by ground attacks that toppled the Taliban government. Canadian involvement added an element of familiarity, although the lines between the good guys and the bad guys became more blurred when Canadian personnel were killed not by terrorists or the Taliban but by U.S. "friendly fire." A year later the terrorists responsible for the 9/11 attacks had not yet been found, and the media focus had shifted to Iraq. Some twelve years earlier Iraq had invaded Kuwait, and had itself been invaded in 1991. Would Iraq be invaded again?

The invasions come and go, and the media come and go with them. What happens afterward is not covered with anything approaching the same intensity. Did the people of Afghanistan fare any better in the wake of the U.S. invasion than they had after a Soviet Union invasion twenty years before? In facing another invasion, would the Iraqis suffer the same fate (at least a half-million dead as a result of international sanctions) that they experienced after the invasion of 1991? The more complex questions and issues are less marketable than the cut and dried intensity of an invasion. As a result, they receive far less attention.

ANALYSIS

Events are always being refined and made intense, unambiguous and balanced, familiar and marketable. Contrary facts, prior conditions, long-term causes, and underlying structures that explain events tend to be downplayed or crowded out, not because of ill will, but because of bias built into the manufacturing process. Given the ownership and structure of the information industry—as well as the pressure from its entertainment arm—this conclusion should come as no surprise.

Some things have changed rapidly—with cable, satellite, and the Internet, the media are becoming more fragmented, with consumers offered a dizzying array of choice—but what has not changed is the expectation that the media reflect the big-business values that maintain the Canadian economy and the social order based on it.

The coverage of issues related to nuclear power provides a good example of this tendency. A study of newspaper reporting on nuclear power issues found that the accounts tended to favour the supporters of nuclear energy. Reports were "overwhelmingly dominated by the proponents of nuclear power," while the case against this particular form of electricity generation was "virtually invisible." The explanation is that the owners and managers of the newspapers identify closely with the world view of the industry itself.[21] The media do cover issues related to racism, sexism, violence against women, and the plight of the poor. But women, minorities, and poor people are most often represented as people with problems, or as people who are themselves problems. Such stereotyping sets them apart from what is generally considered to be "normal." And the media implicitly portray white, middle-class men as the norm in Canadian society—they speak loudest and most frequently. The voices of the "other" are far more muted in the mainstream media.

Media analysts find that women are grossly under-represented in the mass media as people who might have something interesting to say, whether as journalists, interviewees, or newsmakers. One study of global media found that women made up only 17 per cent of interviewees in newspapers, radio, and television. Among North American sources the figure only rose to 27 per cent for women. North American figures for the percentage of female journalists (38 per cent) were actually lower than the worldwide incidence (43 per cent). The numbers were even more startling in a 1998 study of Canada's national newspapers, which had male reporters, photographers, and newsmakers outnumbering their female counterparts at a rate of three to one. The *National Post* featured women as newsmakers only 10 per cent of the time, while the figure for *The Globe and Mail* was 22 per cent.[22]

The media tend to stereotype particular visible minorities in particular ways. For instance, rather than focusing on Jamaican Canadians as the norm in an increasingly diverse society, news stories are slanted in other directions. A study of 2,622 articles mentioning Jamaican Canadians in three Toronto newspapers found that 45 per cent were about sports and entertainment and 39 per cent about crime. Some 2 per cent were individual or community success stories.[23]

Similarly, an event like the 9/11 attacks on New York and Washington can bring more direct stereotyping to the surface. Although the Canadian media often attempted to explain that the terrorists who flew the planes had little to do with the teachings of Islam, such analyses took a back seat to more sensationalist images and opinions. A front-page column in *The Globe and Mail* the day after the attacks referred to the "men from remote desert lands . . . ancient tribal cultures built on blood and revenge." Krishna Rau, a former editor of a media monitoring publication, *Diversity Watch*, pointed out that Judaism, Christianity, and Islam all emerged from the same region and cultures, but that Islam was a regular target in the aftermath of September 11.[24]

The media are the glasses, and as we've seen they take on a certain tint. They promote a particular view of things that in a camouflaged but effective way helps to give a certain shape to Canadian society.

The Information Flow

An old expression describes what happens when you're removed from the environment you're used to. You feel "like a fish out of water." Another says that the first species to discover water could not have been a fish—"To the fish, the water is invisible," says an old proverb. Together, these sayings get at the idea that your surroundings are both important and pervasive. We become so used to the things around us that we take them for granted and often don't even notice them.

This is the case in Canada today. Information washes across us all day, every day. A high-speed Internet connection is something to be sought after. We are immersed in urgent-sounding televised reports of crisis and crime, as well-groomed "anchors" tell us breathlessly, "This just in!" Our friends become impatient if we do not answer their e-mails right away or if something keeps us from getting back to them about that message they left on our voice-mail. Our phone conversations are interrupted by call waiting. Eating habits have changed to the extent that on-the-run people feel that their cars are mobile houses; hence the popularity of grabbing fast food at the drive-through. Tim Hortons, having overtaken McDonald's as the top fast-food outlet in Canada, has its time per car down to twenty seconds. Statistics Canada reports a steady increase in the number of people feeling time-stressed.[25]

In 2001 a Pickering, Ontario, man was talking on his cell phone and drove into the path of a speeding train. The man was killed, along with his two-year-old daughter. Police concluded that he was so distracted by his call that he did not notice the flashing lights and the gate arm at the level crossing. The subsequent coroner's inquest renewed the call for a ban on cell-phone use while driving. The whole incident also raises the issue of how the increasingly massive flow of information alters our lives. Do the feelings we experience—on-line, on the cell phone, listening to the radio or the stereo at home, on the bus or in the car or out jogging, punching the buttons of the TV remote, using call-answering and call-forwarding, playing video games—entertain us? Do they make us feel more connected? Do they distract us?

Certainly, we pass more time looking at screens, from automated bank tellers to home computers to computers at work to television. The screens seem to be everywhere—in banks, train stations, at the gym. In large cities, old-style billboards are being replaced by giant video screens with fast-paced advertising visible from blocks away. At stadiums and large concerts, giant screens supplement (or displace) the live action. Our culture is increasingly a market culture, geared to producing things that will sell, from palm pilots to the thrill of "driving" in a videogame car chase. We seem to feel connected, with the person at the other end of the messaging systems or with a sense of fun and excitement as new sets of images rush by. All-news channels offer not just a report from the Middle East but the time and the local weather. A ribbon of stock-market data flows across the bottom of the screen, although only a small minority of viewers own shares directly. Sports networks feature constant highlights of the latest games, coupled with an endless parade of the scores below. Among the pop-up ads, the Internet allows you to chat, check the sports scores, click, download, and, of course, shop.

Although many critics focus on the companies that own the information networks and how the news is biased in favour of the political status quo, there is something else going on here. The popular phrase "couch potato" comes to mind. Even though the notion of "surfing" the Internet hints at more active participation—and it is certainly possible to sign on-line petitions and visit anti-globalization websites—surfing more often resembles channel-hopping. According to sociologist Todd Gitlin, our time-starved era does not just make people stressed because they have too many things to do in the day.

> While our eyes and ears are taking in images and sounds in all their abundance, we are usually sitting down to receive them. The torrent speeds by, but we ourselves—despite the treadmills, the Walkmen, the sports radios—are mainly immobilized . . . . In the age of unceasing image flow, there is no social anxiety that cannot be addressed with a commodity, a craze, and a news exposé—none of which quite dispels the anxiety.[26]

Much of the torrent is consumed privately, or at least passively. Consuming it all can be distracting, absorbing the attention of people who have that much less of an opportunity to see the world through different-coloured glasses. That is where the notion of ideology comes in.

Up against the Wall

How would you react if a mentally ill man lurched into your kitchen, dug his hand into your supper, and wolfed down a generous portion? Your emotions might run through shock, fear, and outrage before you called the police to haul the intruder away.

But in this incident from *The Tree of Wooden Clogs*, a movie about an Italian peasant family, the mother who had prepared the food welcomed the man as a guest. She let him help himself to the food and warned her children to be polite to him. She believed that people with mental disabilities, because of their simplicity, were especially close to God. This belief, right or wrong, guided her reaction.

Many of our reactions to daily events and circumstances—using these glasses of ours—do not spring from a deliberate position or well-thought-out theory, but rather reflect semiconscious beliefs and values. These built-in attitudes do a lot to shape how we see ourselves, society and the world—and they point to what is called ideology.

The scene from *The Tree of Wooden Clogs* raises questions. Why do people in different societies react differently to similar situations? Where do our social attitudes and responses come from?

In the first instance, our attitudes are formed by the influences of our parents, friends, and peers, teachers at school, our religious upbringing, and the neighbourhoods and communities we share with our fellow citizens. These attitudes—about what's worthwhile, how society works, who the heroes and villains are—continue to be moulded by the people and institutions around us. The mass media—advertising, television, the Internet, the whole torrent—are another very important influence. (The average American is estimated to see 150,000 television commercials in a lifetime; globally spending on advertising is approaching $500 billion annually.[27]) These factors are all sources and reinforcers of ideology, and they deserve careful analysis.

Ideology is a complex topic. *Webster's* defines it as "the doctrines, opinions, or way of thinking of an individual, class, etc.; specif., the body of ideas on which a particular political, economic or social system is based." One student of the word found over a dozen different meanings given to it. Here we touch on ideology in an introductory way, by describing it rather than defining it, and in particular look at the role of ideology in everyday experiences.

People who confront the kinds of problems analyzed in this book often find themselves at a total impasse. They're "up against the wall," as the phrase goes. What is "the wall"? The word refers at first to a mass of problems that people face (for instance, unemployment, substandard housing, problems getting health care, environmental degradation). As social analysis sorts out the problems, "the wall" begins to be broken down into the issues, structures, and systems that are gradually uncovered.

"The wall" exists not just out there in society, but also inside our own heads. The word ideology describes the interaction between what goes on in our heads and what is going on outside, in society. It's all about ways of seeing. It refers to a whole complex of dominant *ideas* that both form the basis of an economic and political system and shape the manner of thinking of groups or classes of people within that system.

Although it is a way of seeing, ideology can be *blinding*. People's blind sports are based on their class, sex, language, ethnic and religious origin, education, and work experience. Ideology also *preserves* structures and systems by making them appear legitimate, normal, and unchangeable.

People are usually unaware of their own ideological assumptions, regarding them as common sense. At the same time, they make statements like these:

- "Government should stick to governing and stay out of the economy."
- "Those people make more money on employment insurance and welfare than I do in my job—and I work plenty of hours. They've got to stop people being paid for doing nothing."
- "Our immigration laws stink. Just watch the news and you see all the crime. And they're taking our jobs."
- "I'm against prejudice, but employment equity is carrying it too far—why can't those minority groups compete for jobs like the rest of us?"
- "User fees make sense. If people had to pay, they'd stop running off to the doctor every time they got a cold. Why should everybody have to pay for that?"

Everyone has ideological beliefs that govern their opinions and judgements about the world around them. Those who deny that they have a bias are apt to accept wholesale the dominant values of their society.

The role of ideology has been a concern of the analysis in *Getting Started* right from the first. In "Issues in the Everyday," the analyses of health, housing, food delivery, and the job market hinted at sharp differences in attitudes and values. In "Lost in the Supermarket," for instance, the analysis picked up on how corporate expansion and concentration, along with high rates of profit, count more in the economy than meeting basic human, social needs. The ideological assumption is that economic growth yields well-being for all and that wealth will "trickle down" to those on the bottom of the economic ladder. The differences in attitude and values permeate every issue in everyday life.

In "The World Around Us," the analyses uncovered economic structures and, entangled amongst them, other fundamental ideological patterns. For example:

- "Energy and the Environment"—The way we use the Earth's energy resources alters the environment on a global scale. Drastic climate change is one of the "externalities," an unintended but very real consequence of the ideological notion that the environment can be treated as an endless source of economic expansion.
- "Technology from Past to Future"—Progress in the form of rapid technological change is almost an end in itself. Those who stand in the way are branded as Luddites. These are, again, the assumptions of a certain ideology.
- "Globalization and Development"—Progress and development are presumed to go hand in hand with the spread across the world of an industrial model fashioned in Europe and North America. Indeed, it is often assumed that there is no alternative to this form of development. That is because many of us have a deep-seated belief in a form of progress that we associate with the ways in which our own societies have evolved. Given the environmental costs, this model has been labelled *mis-development*, a term that surely has as much legitimacy as the label *underdeveloped*, which is so often applied to poor countries.

Ideological assumptions do not just reflect personal preferences or private points of view. They are social, in the sense that they are socially generated and widely shared and therefore serve to support the dominant structures of a society. The maintenance of an existing social order depends on the majority of people within it subscribing to the main tenets of the dominant ideology.

Who advocates these ideas? Why does an often unjust economic system enjoy people's support? What shapes attitudes and values?

LIBERAL CAPITALISM

The prevailing, or dominant, ideology in Canada—what we will call liberal capitalism— is so taken for granted that many people unconsciously accept it as the norm, rather than one specific ideological option. For many Canadians it is indistinguishable from "common sense," and its features are often taken for granted.

Liberal capitalism has evolved over several hundred years. It is *capitalist* because it organizes the economy on the basis of the private accumulation of capital. It is *liberal* because it enhances individual liberty and initiative. It emphasizes the maintenance of justice by the state, although the notion of *social* justice is very much contested terrain.

> *The gap between the capitalist illusion and its reality is now so great that the practitioners and indeed the civil authorities have difficulty making economic decisions in a sensible manner. Their problem begins with the democracy = capitalism equation. Running democracy and capitalism together as a single idea is a wonderful Marxian joke. That is to say, in the tradition of the Marx Brothers. Neither history nor philosophy link free markets and free men. They have nothing more to do with each other than the accidents of time and place allow. In fact, free enterprise worked far better in its purer state, when it oper-*

ated beneath friendly, authoritarian government structures. Unquestioned political authority suits the embracing of financial risk. Authoritarian governments can ally themselves to money without fear of conflict of interest. They can do things faster. Compromise less. Democracy, on the other hand, is subject to ongoing political and social compromise. It tends to want to curb activities of all sorts, business-related or not, in order to protect the maximum number of people.

—John Ralston Saul,
Voltaire's Bastards: The Dictatorship of Reason in the West, 1992.

Most Canadians cherish freedom and equality, perhaps ahead of other values. They believe that everyone should be "free" and should enjoy "equal opportunity." Up to this point, those who uphold liberal capitalism and those who criticize it are on the same wavelength.

According to the dominant ideology in Canada, however, the effective meaning of "freedom and equality" is the right of entrepreneurs to invest their money however, whenever, and wherever they choose. In practice this belief favours those who already enjoy wealth and power. They can make wide-ranging decisions about how their capital is used, and they usually argue that government should not interfere with the free market, even when those decisions have unintended but harmful consequences—to the environment, to workers, to society at large.

George Orwell's famous—and apparently self-contradictory—line from *Animal Farm*, "All animals are equal, but some are more equal than others," highlights the practical contradiction within the ideology of liberal capitalism. Although Orwell was satirizing the dominant ideology of the Soviet Union, his wry comment can just as easily be applied to Canada.

Originally, those who controlled capital demanded unhampered freedom. Anything that interfered with this uncontrolled freedom—for example, laws against child labour and regulations setting minimum wages—was resisted as unnatural and contrary to common sense. The "robber barons" of the nineteenth century were a notable example of this: at that time their unregulated activities were an accepted part of capitalist society. In 1894, fifty years before Orwell wrote *Animal Farm*, the French writer Anatole France satirized liberal ideology in his book *The Red Lilies*, making the famous remark: "The law, in all its majestic equality, forbids the rich and the poor alike, to sleep under bridges, to beg in the streets, and to steal bread."

Free competition in the business world is another basic tenet of liberal capitalism. But more and more economic power tends to concentrate in ever fewer hands. In the past twenty years vigorous lobbying by large business has promoted free trade and deregulation, to the extent that critics now refer regularly to a return to the untrammelled freedom of the bad old days by calling it "neo-liberalism."

Liberal capitalism has evolved and adapted. Political agitation for social justice has led to changes that promote more equal (but often still unjust) relations between those who sell their labour and those who have the capital to buy it. Trade unions, once seen as an obstacle to the freedom of business, were legalized and won improvements for their members. Government outlawed child labour and brought in the minimum wage. With the growth of the welfare state, pensions, social welfare programs, medicare, and (un)employment insurance arrived in Canada. Such programs, taken together, are called the "social wage." It is a wage that fluctuates according to the tenor of the political times, and the rise of neo-liberalism in the 1980s reduced it significantly.

The media disseminate the ideology of liberal capitalism in both subtle and obvious ways. For example, the news does offer sympathetic features on people who are poor and unemployed; but it rarely questions the priorities of corporations whose exclusive preoccupation with growth and profitability can result in downsizing (and therefore unemployment), dangerous working conditions, or environmental damage.

People are not just passive consumers of news, entertainment, and advertising. The letters to the editor page of any newspaper attests to that. Many people can and do look critically at media information. Members of a striking union are often the first to see how the coverage and the language selected tend to favour their employer over their union. People can tell when news or advertising presents a view of things that runs contrary to what they know from their own life experiences. And not everyone comprehends media messages in the same way.

Within the dominant media there are many journalists who attempt to swim against the mainstream ideology. Although they have little power, and their perspective has to rise above the mass of intense, familiar news and the advertising torrent, they do try to do investigative reporting, let people who are usually excluded speak for themselves, and make connections that are fresh and out of the ordinary. Outside the mainstream, alternative media dig more deeply into social issues. Community newspapers, critical film and video productions, Aboriginal broadcasting, small and medium-sized magazines, and book publishers together form a vibrant sector. They face the problem of reaching out to the same mass audiences enjoyed by major television networks, newspapers, and magazines.

A call to a local Indigo bookstore revealed that there was no record in their system of the Canadian feminist magazine *Herizons*.[28] This despite the claim of the publication's website that the latest issue ("Turbo Chicks: Talkin' 'bout My Generation") was then on the newsstands—an issue challenging the image of young women as apathetic, apolitical dupes of an anti-feminist backlash. The magazine section at Indigo, with its slogan "The World Needs More Canadian," featured dozens of U.S. fashion magazines packed with ads. Cogeco, a leading cable-TV provider, offered "Even more freedom to choose" from packages that included New Rock Edge TV, Sex TV, X-Treme Sports, and dozens of others. But channel-hoppers will only rarely find a documentary with an explicit point of view.

The Internet has made it cheaper and easier for citizens with an explicit point of view to create their own media by publishing electronically what was once expensive to print or produce. Distribution costs are also much lower for social movements and citizen networks that want to communicate with anyone who has the resources to connect electronically. Although the Internet has become more commercialized and is subject to total surveillance by security forces, it still represents a free space in which both movements and marketers seek to get their messages out.

The analysis in *Getting Started* often conflicts with the viewpoint of the dominant ideology, which, for example, might favour the end of social programs previously available to all while uncritically lauding the latest hand-held computer-in-a-cellphone. The dominant ideology does not question Canada's need to become competitive in the new global marketplace, while *Getting Started* wonders about who wins and who loses in this global race.

Social analysis gets at ideological assumptions not so much by talking about ideology as by asking further questions and pushing beyond what is conventional wisdom or what seems, on the surface, to be simple common sense. For example, the values of a just, sustainable, participatory society promise to serve the interests of workers, consumers, and other citizens, but these ideals are often pitted against the conventional wisdom of business and government decision-makers.

The World Wide Web is too expensive for millions of people in developing countries, partly because of the cost of computers that are the standard entry point to the Web: in January 2001 the cheapest Pentium III computer was $700—hardly affordable for low-income community access points. Further, the text-based interface of the internet puts it out of reach for illiterate people.

To overcome these barriers, academics at the Indian Institute of Science and engineers at the Bangalore-based design company Encore Software designed a handheld internet appliance for less than $200. Based on the Linux open source operating system, the first version of the Simputer will provide Internet and email access in local languages, with touch-screen functions and microbanking applications. Future versions promise speech recognition and text-to-speech software for illiterate users. The intellectual property rights have been transferred for free to the non-profit Simputer Trust, which is licensing the technology to manufacturers at a nominal fee.

—United Nations Development Programme,
Human Development Report 2001.

The structures that buttress society and the values of private enterprise and private profit, corporate growth, and progress are constantly assumed and positively enforced. The ideology itself is hardly ever questioned. The idea of ordering the Canadian economy according to any norms other than liberal capitalism would seem puzzling to many citizens, especially those in control of the command posts of the economy.

Elements of Canada's dominant ideology are lodged within our heads. This book, in its efforts to analyze, interpret, and judge Canadian reality, tries to shed light on our ideological blind spots. What might have been taken for common sense before now deserves to be questioned and—possibly—changed.

QUESTIONS FOR REVIEW

1. What role do the media play in creating taste? What are other mechanisms for communicating the dominant ideology? How do they work? Who controls them? Identify some sources of alternative, questioning viewpoints.

2. The media usually defend their selection of events and editing of stories by claiming that they are giving consumers what they want. Do the media in fact give us what we want? Does the news industry have any responsibility to society beyond catering to its tastes? Should the news industry be allowed to consider itself "a private enterprise owing nothing to the public"?

3. Ideology is sometimes described as a set of ideas that are commonsensical, a way of looking at the world. How would you describe your own ideology? Where did it come from? In what ways, if any, does it differ from the ideology that prevails in Canadian society?

4. To what extent do you find out about the news of the days on the Internet? How do you choose which sites to visit? Do you consider them more or less reliable than television, radio, newspapers, and magazines? Are some controlled by companies that also own other communications media?

5. Images, brands, slogans, and logos appear wherever we turn—pop-ups on the Internet, ads on rented DVDs, embedded in the ice at hockey games, on clothing of all sorts. Does this torrent influence how we see the world? If so, how?

6. Look for quotations. Who did the reporter talk to—government officials, recognized experts, "usually reliable sources," or anonymous "informants"? If quotes come from a prepared press release, does the paper usually say so? What are the interests and motives of the people quoted? Do their opinions represent conventional wisdom?

7. Review the story. Do you believe that you understand the conflict? Are some participants in the event absent from the story? Have credible witnesses been neglected or presented in a dim light? Comparing two or more reports, does the situation seem to have been confused by a particular news outlet, and might there be a reason? Are there clues about where to look for more reliable information?

8. Evaluate your sources of information on any issues. Do you rely on the major networks, newspapers, and newsmagazines? Are you familiar with alternative sources, such as church, labour, or special interest publications? Compare an alternative source with a major news outlet, with an eye on the selection of stories, the depth of coverage, and the viewpoint of the journalist.

9. Evaluate the target audience for a TV program by watching its commercials. Note the kind of commercials (beer for football games? detergents for soap operas?). Do the commercials match (or contradict) the content of the programs? What are the values involved?

RESOURCES

Kay Armatage, Kass Banning, Brenda Longfellow, and Janine Marchessault. *Gendering the Nation: Canadian Women's Cinema*. Toronto: University of Toronto Press, 1999. A definitive collection of essays that address the impact and influence of a century of filmmaking by women in Canada—a refreshing and empowering perspective on women in the media.

John Berger. *Ways of Seeing*. Harmondsworth, Middx.: Penguin Books, 1972. Based on a BBC television series, *Ways of Seeing* is a classic that raises questions about words and images in art and advertising.

Michael Clow. *False Pretenses: Canadian Newspapers and Nuclear Power*. Halifax: Fernwood Publishing, 1993. The Canadian nuclear industry has argued that the media have treated them unfairly. Clow's study, which looks at nuclear coverage in four dailies in Ontario and New Brunswick, finds that the promoters rather than the opponents of nuclear energy have dominated the news.

Todd Gitlin. *Media Unlimited: How the Torrent of Images and Sounds Overwhelms Our Lives*. New York: Metropolitan Books, 2001. The relentless saturation of daily life with media images does not herald a "new information age," argues U.S. media critic Gitlin. Rather, it threatens to erode democracy by substituting everything from personality cults and irony for commitments to public life.

Robert W. McChesney, Ellen Meiksins Wood, and John Bellamy Foster, eds. *Capitalism and the Information Age: The Political Economy of the Global Communication Revolution*. New York: Monthly Review Press, 1998. A collection of essays that examine how new communications technologies have reshaped the labour force and changed the nature of communication itself.

M. Nourbese Philip. *Frontiers: Essays and Writings on Racism and Culture*. Stratford, Ont.: Mercury Press, 1992. A collection that critically explores—from the point of view of people of colour living in Canada—our political and economic systems and the various "isms" woven into them.

Herbert I. Schiller. *Culture, Inc.: The Corporate Takeover of Public Expression*. New York: Oxford University Press, 1991. Schiller examines the effects of a half-century of corporate growth on American culture.

Manufacturing Consent: Noam Chomsky and the Media. Canada, 1992. Directed by Mark Achbar and Peter Wintonick. NFB. Video. Two parts, 167 min. Explores the political life and ideas of U.S. radical philosopher Noam Chomsky, who believes that the media play a pivotal role, not just in shaping how we view our world but also in the political decision-making process. Also available in a six-video classroom version.

Adbusters is a not-for-profit magazine based in British Columbia and devoted to reporting the truth behind many of the world's corporate giants and the devastation and social injustice that comes at the hands of their colossal profits. *Adbusters* describes itself as a "global network of artists, activists, writers, pranksters, students, educators and entrepreneurs who want to advance the new social activist movement of the information age. Our aim is to topple existing power structures and forge a major shift in the way we will live in the 21st century." See also their website <www.adbusters.org>.

WEBSITES

The expansion of alternative and critical sources of news and media analysis has accompanied the growth of the Internet. Websites and links abound. The Media Channel is a global internet community with over a thousand affiliates focused on media issues. They range from the Institute for Public Accuracy to Newslink Africa. Organizations like the Canadian Journalists for Free Expression scrutinize the Canadian media scene. For other alternative news and viewpoints, see the websites for Rabble.ca, which combines activism and journalism, and Straight Goods—"Canada's Independent On-Line Source of News You Can Use."

Chapter Fourteen

Laramie or Squamish: What Use Is Canadian Culture?

When free trade with the U.S. is denounced, or when cutbacks in government funding of the arts are opposed, one issue invariably raised is the threat to Canadian culture. Yet in such a discussion the *value* of Canadian culture is often accepted as a given, or is alluded to only briefly. The question of how useful our culture is to our society has never seemed that simple to me. I find the commonly given explanations as to why Canadian culture has worth are unconvincing at best and transparently false at worst. I do believe Canadian culture has merit. Determining what is valuable about our culture is a tricky matter, however, as I hope to show in what follows.

Before I continue, though, let me be more precise about what I mean by "culture." An article by Ian McKay in Memorial University's *Labor/Le Travailleur* a number of years ago (8/9, 1981–82) pointed out there are nearly three hundred definitions for the word in current use (for instance, "logging camp culture," "women's culture," et cetera). I intend to refer here to a nonanthropological sense of the word. By "Canadian culture" I mean those artifacts produced by Canadians that are commonly referred to as part of the fine arts, performing arts, literary arts, and so on.

To begin to assess the worth of Canadian culture, I have to note English-speaking Canada's history as a cultural colony, first of England and then the United States. Such a past has resulted in many of us being affected by culture in strange ways. I was giving a talk in 1987 to a class at Vancouver Technical Secondary School. The teacher of this English class had chosen, despite the approved curriculum, to present her students with a whole term of contemporary poetry about Vancouver. I told the class how lucky they were to have this still-rare opportunity. When I was growing up in British Columbia in the 1950s and 1960s, the culture I was aware of was entirely produced by and about people who lived elsewhere— either geographically or in time. Thus, for example, we learned poetry was written by dead Englishmen.

And as for the culture we were exposed to outside of school, the idea of a rock and roll star being based in Vancouver was unthinkable.

I described for the class my own experience of driving from Vancouver to California for the first time in 1966, and how when I initially drove into Los Angeles I felt that I was at last present in a real place. Of course, I knew Vancouver was real. But I was tremendously excited to be among the place names that I had so often heard mentioned in books and songs, or seen in movies. To be heading at high speed down the freeway, past the signs for Hollywood Boulevard, La Cienega Boulevard, Sunset Boulevard, was, for me, to have finally arrived on the planet Earth.

And I did not gain much sense of perspective, I informed the class, until a couple of years later when I took a job in northern Colorado as a university instructor. The town where I taught, Fort Collins, is close to Laramie, Wyoming. Since Laramie is the setting for, or referred to in, a number of western stories, movies, cowboy ballads, and so on, I was anxious to see the place. Yet when I finally visited, I was shocked to discover that it appeared to be a small town, not much bigger than, say, Squamish, at the head of Howe Sound, north of Vancouver. I left Laramie thinking hard about why *Squamish* was not famed in song and story. Surely fascinating events had happened to the people who had settled and worked in and around that town. And even if such events had not happened, why could not Squamish be a locale for fictional occurrences, just as Laramie was, given that the towns were of similar size? I also pondered what a difference it must be to grow up in or near places that are considered worth celebrating in the culture around you.

"Culturally things are somewhat better for you," I told the class. "After all, Canadian literature is now taught in our colleges. And here and there in certain high schools like this, you students are shown writing about your own city and your own era, as we never were.

"Of course, there's still an enormous distance to go," I continued. "For example, you'll see lots of movies about teenagers attending high schools. But," I intoned, "these films won't be based on what it's like to go to *this* school. You'll see movies about Hollywood High, but nobody is making a movie about Van Tech Secondary."

At this comment the class broke into loud laughter. I stared at them, bewildered, until the teacher came to my rescue. A U.S. film crew had recently spent some days at Van Tech filming a movie, she explained. But, like many of the movies made in the past few years in B.C., the locale was supposed to be the U.S. In fact, the setting for the film shot in the halls and classrooms of Van Tech was supposed to be . . . Hollywood High.

These students were aware that part of their own reality was about to be presented to them transformed into somebody else's. And yet they also had a teacher willing to show them that their own streets and mountains, and the experiences of their parents and fellow citizens, could also be the subject of culture (in the poems they were considering that term). Unlike my introduction to culture, these students were at least conscious that different possibilities for culture do exist.

But if we start to consider in more detail that cultural possibility called "Canadian culture," to better understand what value it might have, the first problem surely is: *which* Canadians are we talking about? What is the range of experiences and ideas currently included in Canadian cultural artifacts? *Whose* Canada do we mean when we speak of "Canadian culture?"

We can see this problem illustrated by a trip, say, to the B.C. Provincial Museum. Visitors are shown, among other exhibits, the interior of a "typical Victorian-era house." But this display is false. On view is the interior of a home belonging to people *of a certain social class*—in this case, a fairly well-to-do family. We are not shown the interior of a "Victorian-era house" belonging to, for instance, a mine employee or a millworker. Then, as now, there was not one British Columbia, but many existing simultaneously. If we are to assess the worth of Canadian culture, we had better start by being clear about the particular Canada a given cultural artifact speaks about or to.

I have noticed cultural producers or commentators sometimes attempt to avoid this task by explicitly or implicitly denying that economic divisions between Canadians exist. Or, if these divisions are observed, their cultural significance is denied. A fascinating attempt to simultaneously *recognize* these economic differences, while downplaying their *significance*, was made by Petro Canada in their television ads promoting the oil company's sponsorship of the 1988 Winter Olympics torch relay. In the ad the inhabitants of a small town are shown getting ready to watch the relay runners carry the torch through their community. We see a well-dressed businessman shutting up his shop, and we also see a welder turn off his torch and push his goggles up onto his forehead, in preparation to leave to witness this momentous event.

Seconds later we observe these representatives of the two major economic divisions of Canadian society—employers and employees—stand side by side in a crowd watching with evident pride and joy the Olympic torch being carried past. The welder turns to the businessman and gives him a mild, comradely punch on the shoulder, as evidence that the emotions surrounding this event have dissolved class distinctions and, by gosh, we Canadians are all in this together. The businessman wipes away a tiny tear from his eye. Of course, this sort of thing is crude propaganda, but it does arise out of an actual wish people have for unity, for a feeling of community. That wish may not be the motivation that inspires museum directors, cultural commentators, and corporations to blur the distinctions between the lives of the majority of Canadians and the lives of the minority who have economic control over us. But it is certainly that wish that causes many Canadians to accept uncritically this view of their own society and culture.

In fact, not even colossally expensive public spectacles such as Calgary's 1988 Winter Olympics or Vancouver's Expo 86 can abolish the differences in economic interest between those who are employed for a living and those who employ others for a living. Large taxpayer-funded spectacles are inevitably the occasion for corporate advertisers and public relations experts to generate a great wave of sentimentality about a region or the nation in the hope of motivating sales of various products. But the reality remains that no businessperson would reverse a decision to fire somebody on the grounds that the person affected is an Olympic supporter, or because the man or woman to be fired is a fellow *Albertan* or *Canadian*. Nor would any employer refrain from automating or moving operations to a different part of the world in search of cheaper labour costs on the grounds of patriotism.

Corporations like Petro Canada may call themselves "proudly Canadian," but the same federal government that owns both Petro Canada and Canada Post did not hesitate for an instant to employ scabs in an attempt to break the strikes by Canadian postal workers in the summer of 1987. The issue at stake, as in most strikes, was the employer's wish to save money. On the other side of the dispute was employee resistance to measures that would worsen working conditions and result in a lower standard of living. The consequence of a victory for the employer's demands would be to depress the quality of life for one group of Canadians, surely a strange technique for demonstrating pride in one's country.

Always, then, we have to watch closely when people begin to invoke "Canada" to justify culture—or any other activity or cause. Who represents this "Canada" we are asked to identify with? And while sorting this question out, we have to be clear about a second matter: our own idea of what a *country* is. In other words, what is Canada *for*? Does it primarily exist to provide a place where men and women who own enterprises can maximize profits? Or is it intended to be a sort of cooperative venture, whereby all those who live here work jointly to ensure the maximum happiness for one another? When a federal government proposes to spend $8 billion to obtain a nuclear submarine fleet rather than, say, to provide food for the users of food banks in the country's cities and towns, that government acts on a specific belief in the purpose of Canada.

Or is it the nation's aim to provide a free and democratic environment in which the people who live here can make their own decisions and solve their own problems? If so, how far should this democracy extend? Within the past seventy-five years we have seen political democracy spread to women and Orientals—two groups formerly denied the vote. But have we now attained a fully democratic society? Is it right that, as at present, democracy ceases for the majority of us the moment we enter the office door or the factory gate? If we are adult enough to decide the affairs of state in national elections, are we not adult enough to control democratically the enterprises where we work? How democratic is a situation where a handful of nonelected Canadians have enormous economic and social power over the rest of us during our hours each day at the job?

For me, thinking about the value of Canadian culture includes being definite about what group of Canadians are referred to, and whose vision of the country's purpose is being openly or indirectly endorsed. Yet the impassioned spokespersons on behalf of Canadian culture seldom stipulate which Canadians and what concept of Canada they mean. Instead, I hear three major arguments repeated when these spokespersons do try to indicate *why* Canadian culture might be worth protecting.

One explanation they give for culture's importance in Canadian society is that culture, especially high culture, raises us out of the humdrum of daily life, inspires us, gives us new vision. "Culture lifts us out of ourselves," as one speaker put it at an anticutback rally I attended in Edmonton in the 1970s.

However, the capacity to lift us out of ourselves is the characteristic of a narcotic. Any narcotic—whether alcohol or some other recreational drug—gives us the illusion of escape from the everyday, fills us with dreams of other possibilities for our lives, and then cruelly returns us to the same daily existence from which we sought to remove ourselves. Far from being a means of escape from our present situation, a narcotic reinforces present realities by keeping us occupied with illusions instead of letting us gain knowledge or skills to solve our personal and social problems. Any narcotic, like going to cultural events, is potentially addictive precisely because it does *not* lead to changes in our daily life. The only way we can feel that good again is to have another hit, to take another trip into a beautiful never-never land.

Mainstream ballet, for example, seems to me to teach that the essential truths of this world are to be found in fantasy, far away from the joys and difficulties of everyday existence. Like much of mainstream culture, ballet's celebrations of artificial and impossible characters and situations appears to offer me escape from the sources of my daily unhappinesses and problems. As we have seen, though, such escape is bogus, since nothing is altered in my daily life by this cultural product. I gain neither understanding about the causes of my difficulties nor ideas about overcoming injustices inflicted on myself or others. At the end of the performance I am returned to a world that is exactly as I left it. I may have gained a memory of some delightful moments, but I also know what I must purchase to experience those moments again.

And as for the Romantic concept that exposure to high culture will influence people's day-to-day behaviour for the better, World War II appears to have put an end to that notion. The image of Germany, once considered the most cultured nation in Europe, adopting Nazism as a means out of its difficulties demonstrates conclusively mainstream culture's narcotic rather than rehabilitative function. Consider the symphony orchestras the Germans organized from concentration camp inmates for the enjoyment of the camps' guards. How responsive to human feelings did experiencing this wonderful music make the guards?

So it seems to me culture's alleged ability to "lift us out of ourselves," or make us "better" people, is a bogus proposition. A second dubious attempt to explain the usefulness of Canadian culture I hear from time to time is that Canadian culture defines who we are. When the "we" is not specified here, this argument seems to me absurd. *I* certainly do not feel defined by Karen Kain's dancing, or Margaret Atwood's new novel, or Bryan Adams's new record, or some video artist showing her or his work to a group of fellow artists at a state-supported gallery. All these artistic productions may be dazzling, accomplished, innovative, or may be less successful artistically. But I personally do not know anybody who considers their lives, their identity, defined by such activity.

And in British Columbia, at least, the gap in attitudes between various sectors of the population has become so pronounced it would be difficult to imagine any encompassing "British Columbian" point of view that a cultural artifact could define. In 1986, for example, the government of the day, duly elected by a slim majority, reduced already inadequate provincial welfare payments to offset its growing deficit. Funds were then allotted to provide $5,000 worth of fireworks every night for the six months of Expo 86. The gulf in values is enormous between those British Columbians who believe a community has a duty to help its members who require assistance, and those British Columbians who believe the community's first duty is to use its financial resources to attract tourists (i.e., customers with money from elsewhere). I have yet to see cultural artifacts that incorporate both sets of values to the satisfaction of those who hold these divergent views. Who, then, is the "we" this culture supposedly defines?

The third defence of the worth of Canadian culture that gets articulated is a monetary one. In this argument culture has value and should be supported because government subsidies to the arts generate profits for business. Advocates of this line of reasoning have the figures to show that each symphony ticket sold results in extra consumer spending on restaurant meals, taxis, baby-sitters, drinks after the concert, and so on. Similarly the Canada Council programme of support for public readings by Canadian authors is regarded as a subsidy of the airlines, plus a boost in book sales to the benefit of printers, papermakers, publishing houses, and bookstores.

Where this argument seems faulty to me is that it tries to create the impression that people are attracted to become artists in order to benefit business. I do not believe this is true. People I know who have become writers, painters, musicians, et cetera, did not do so out of a philanthropic wish to aid the downtrodden business community. They became involved in producing cultural artifacts because they want to express some truth as they see it, or because they enjoy play with words or sounds or forms or colours, or because they find being involved with the arts enables them to feel and think and observe life in new and exciting ways. Their obsession with whatever cultural form or forms they adopt amounts to a rejection of the concept so beloved of business that the only means to measure value on this planet is the dollar.

In my experience the business community senses this fundamental clash of values between the cultural world and themselves. If the dollar is *not* the paramount means of assessing worth in our society, then somebody who has adopted this philosophy has made a hideous error in her or his life. Overall, that is one main message of culture. So I do not find it surprising that I have never seen anyone opposed to an appreciation of the arts who was won over on the grounds that culture is good for some businesses.

In contrast to the three standard justifications of the usefulness of Canadian culture, I have a different reason for regarding Canadian culture as important. I believe culture that is about a clearly defined group of Canadians, that celebrates and explores their lives, can help provide these people with a sense of self-confidence. Such cultural artifacts suggest to these women and men that their lives are worthy of being the subject of art, and thus that what happens to them is significant. On the other hand, a lack of this self-confidence tangibly harms these people, individually and as a group, and leads themselves and the rest of the human family to overlook their achievements and potential.

The group of people that I feel should be the central focus of Canadian culture is the majority of those who inhabit our portion of the globe—those of us who are employed for a living. Since the governing influence on our lives is the job we do (or our lack of employment), any cultural artifact intending to articulate our personal and social existences would have to take into account what happens while we are at work and the ways our employment affects our time off the job. Furthermore, since many aspects and most nuances of how our work shapes us are known only to an *insider* to our situation, it is up to *ourselves* to create the culture that reflects and illuminates our lives.

At present a strict taboo surrounds an accurate portrayal of work in Canadian culture. With few exceptions an insider's look at what it is like to go to work each day in contemporary society is missing. And this taboo harms people. For example, because work is not considered culturally important, school curricula largely ignore the history, present form, and possible future of daily employment. As a result, students frequently embark on years of training for a trade or profession with only the vaguest or glossiest notion of what a job is like and of how this employment affects the human beings who perform it. The absence in our culture of any accurate depiction of our work also leads to a profound sense of isolation. We are aware we have certain problems at the job, or problems that arise away from work because of our employment. But perhaps we are the only ones who feel this way? Left unsure and isolated, we are less likely to search for a collective answer to our difficulties, a collective means to improve our lives.

A further negative consequence of the taboo is a mystification of how products and services come to exist. One consequence of this mystification is that when we do not know much about one another's jobs, do not know much about how the goods and services we need or want are created, it becomes easier to believe negative reports about people who in reality are very much like ourselves. That is, we are willing to accept the received idea that postal workers are lazy, people on strike are greedy, et cetera. Yet the more we accurately understand one another's working lives, the more readily we can feel a kinship with them, and can practise solidarity with them when they run into difficulties.

The negative consequences of the present taboo begin to disappear if our cultural world recognizes the importance of the work we do: how that work determines our standard of living and the amount of time and energy we have off the job, plus the ways our employment influences our beliefs, friendships, where we live, and much more. As *Canadian* employees, we are doubly disadvantaged when the cultural artifacts around us present neither our working lives nor our geographic and historical experiences. And since an accurate consideration of the working lives of women and of people of colour has also been largely absent from mainstream culture, these individuals face a triple and/or quadruple disadvantage in looking to Canadian culture as a source of self-esteem.

To me, then, culture has value when it breaks the taboo and gives a majority of Canadians self-confidence. And I do not make such an assertion just because I think self-confidence is a nice quality for people to have. I believe self-confidence is the root of democracy. If I do not consider myself important, why would I think I have the right to participate in determining what happens to me and to my community? Self-confidence on the part of the majority is *necessary* for the maintenance and extension of democracy. Since I consider democracy to be the form of social organization that offers the best chance for creating a fair, equitable, and happy society, I regard a culture that promotes self-confidence as a *requirement* for the preservation and enhancement of human dignity.

A culture that diminishes or retards people's self-confidence, either through what it proposes or omits, I believe is a threat to democracy. When what we do and who we are are not considered culturally significant, when our contribution to society is hidden behind "big names" (for example, when a corporate executive is said to "make" the product our labour and imagination help create, or an architect is described as having "built" the building we worked on), then the worth of our lives is diminished compared to the value of comparatively few other people. It is only a step from this to thinking that a "name" person is more important than we are, and hence that his or her thoughts, activities, opinions, and so on are more worthy and should have more weight than our own. This last idea, of course, is counter to the very basis of democracy.

And if we do not consider our lives important, then it is unlikely we will do much to change our lives for the better. Most movements in history that lead to a deepening and broadening of democracy begin with a belief among the activists that they *deserve* the changes they are battling for. In short, people involved with achieving social change have self-confidence. The barons who confronted King John to obtain the Magna Carta, no less than the men and women who fought for and won the eight-hour day, no less than the women who successfully struggled for the right to vote, all had the self-confidence that led them to demand changes that were considered radical, unnatural, impossible to the established wisdom of their day. If Canadian employees are to achieve an extension of democracy to that part of our lives where we do not yet have the right to vote—the workplace—we will need the self-confidence that we *deserve* democracy in every aspect of our social existence. Similarly if Canada is to survive as a nation, Canadians will need the self-confidence that we *deserve* to be a separate country.

I look to Canadian culture to give us this self-confidence, but in a positive, enabling way. The self-confidence as provided by culture must not shade over into arrogance, into myths of unity or power that are harmful to ourselves or others in the long run. We have the U.S. example of the myth of the cowboy. This myth leads to the mentality of the man with the gun who is a law unto himself (in Laramie, among other places). As celebrated in culture, the cowboy myth can pave the way for U.S. armed intervention in Third World struggles. This myth, incidentally, also obscures the *reality* of the cowboy as an underpaid agricultural labourer whose protests against living and working conditions have included from time to time strikes and efforts to organize unions.

I recognize that self-confidence is not given or denied people only by cultural artifacts. Unemployment undermines men's and women's sense of individual worth. And self-assurance can be a result of feelings of competency that education provides. Yet where schools teach people they are failures, or when access to self-enhancing education is thwarted (for example, by government reductions in operating funds and student aid programmes), development of self-confidence in individuals is again blocked. A social climate of permanent high unemployment, and reduced access to positive educational experiences, threatens the emergence of a culture that reinforces the importance of the daily successes and defeats of the majority of us.

Even with such obstacles, and with all the qualifiers I see as necessary for Canadian culture to be of value, I remain convinced that the cultural artifacts produced by Canadians can rise to the challenge. I am heartened by the appearance here of the new poetry, fiction, and drama written by people about their own daily work—however overwhelmed this material still is by the bulk of our cultural products. Because all Canadians share the strange experience of being culturally invisible in their own land, Canadian artists have the ideal background to understand the importance of articulating the lives of the previously hidden majority. I do not think it is an accident that the new imaginative writing about work appears more often in anthologies of contemporary literature by Canadians—and by U.S. women and people of colour—than it does in anthologies of writing by mainstream (i.e., mostly white and male) U.S. authors.

I am therefore optimistic that Canadian culture will assist the majority of Canadians to find the self-confidence we require. I am aware, however, that the success of this project demands a serious change in the artistic and academic status quo, since up to the present an accurate depiction of the lives of the majority of us has not been a goal of Canada's artistic or academic tastemakers—mainstream or avant-garde. Indeed, over the long haul the resistance of these authorities to admit the concerns of most Canadians into our artistic agenda may pose a larger threat to the development of Canadian culture than either free trade or cutbacks in government sponsorship of the arts.

Blind Spots on Labour, Corporate Power and Social Inequality

One of the most serious blind spots in the Canadian news agenda is the lack of attention given to the consequences of social inequality and unfettered corporate power in Canada. In this chapter we explore this blind spot by focusing on the media's apparent unwillingness or inability to adequately cover issues in four broad areas:

- Exploitation and resistance in the world of work
- Poverty and class inequality
- The neo-liberal agenda: Absent alternatives and hidden consequences
- The power and biases of media corporations themselves

In the media system the voice of corporate Canada speaks loudly and often, but other voices—the poor, labour, and those who present alternatives to an all-against-all free market society are relatively muffled. The problem with this, surely, is that democratic political life works best when a wide diversity of voices and viewpoints are heard within the national media system.

Canada's Labour Scene:
Covering (Up) the World of Work

When we think of "business news," we usually think of the daily grind of stock quotes, economic indicators, and investment tips that are part and parcel of TV newscasts across North America. In this way, the voice of business—the entrepreneur, the mutual fund manager, the anxious investor—is a daily and commonplace part of the news on the economy. But is this really all that the world of business and economics is about? What about the people who actually work in the offices and factories, deal with customers, and serve the public? Rarely, it seems, do the voices and perspectives of working people appear in this daily update on the business world. When we do hear from workers or labour organizations, it is usually during times of strife, especially strikes or other dramatic industrial disputes.

The result, many media scholars in the U.S. and U.K. have argued, is a one-sided view of the world of work.[1] While coverage of the business community routinely includes positive coverage over a wide range of topics, coverage of labour typically focuses on confrontational and controversial events such as strikes and contract negotiations. Moreover, labour is typically portrayed as the active and disruptive party. Two Canadian studies in the early 1980s reached similar conclusions.[2] At NewsWatch Canada, we wanted to see if this imbalance in both the amount and tone of coverage attracted by business and labour still holds true in the Canadian media. Are all perspectives on the world of work—from management, to union leaders, to frontline workers—treated fairly?

To address these questions, NewsWatch researchers B. Dianne Birch and Trevor Hughes compiled a sample of news mentioning business and labour topics from the news and business sections of the *Vancouver Sun*.[3] They used two time periods: September–December 1987 and September–December 1997, respectively, before and after Conrad Black's Hollinger Inc. became the controlling owner of the *Sun* and other Southam dailies. To reduce the sample to manageable size, the researchers randomly chose each day of the publishing week three times for both 1987 and 1997, yielding three composite weeks—18 days—for each year. They then selected every fifth article for coding, producing a sample of 168 articles (81 from 1987 and 87 from 1997) that met their criteria for mentioning "business" (i.e., in the business section, written by a business reporter, or dealing with corporate or financial relations) or "labour" (i.e., written by a labour reporter, containing the words "labour" or "union," or dealing with labour relations, union affairs, working conditions, wages, and so forth).

The first part of the analysis concerned the specific themes covered in business and labour stories. For both 1987 and 1997, the *Sun* extended twice as much coverage to business as to labour. In addition, articles about labour tended to focus on disruption—that is, events that interrupt or disturb daily economic life. For example, strikes and contract negotiations accounted for 47.2% of stories about labour while, by comparison, stories about working conditions accounted for a mere 5.7% of labour articles. In contrast, business news covered a wide range of topics, including day-to-day items like financial losses and gains, investments, and financial forecasts. No single category or business topic attracted more than 14 percent of the total coverage afforded to business. What's more, this wide-ranging and routine coverage of business was often augmented by features on "up-and-coming" companies and flattering profiles of business leaders. Rarely, however, were specific unions or union leaders profiled.

Second, the researchers coded the articles according to tone, whether upbeat or positive (e.g., financial gains for business, improved conditions for labour), downbeat or negative (e.g., downsizing for business, lower wages for labour), or neutral in tone. In their analysis, they discovered that *both* business and labour received more downbeat than upbeat coverage in the *Sun*, but news about labour was far *more* likely to be negative or downbeat. For instance, almost 30% of coded items pertaining to business were positive, in contrast to only 6% of labour items. In other words, business news items were five times more likely to be framed positively than were labour items. Moreover, business received nearly one positive article for every negative article, while for every positive labour item, the *Sun* printed five negative ones.

Finally, the study examined the sources quoted in stories about business and labour. How often, in fact, were business sources quoted in relation to labour sources, and how much weight did their perspectives carry within the stories? In particular, the study sought to identify the "defining" sources for each article—those sources, including typically the first one quoted, who set the story's theme and suggest a way for readers to make sense of it. After an initial source has framed the issue, counterbalancing sources are sometimes quoted in the news, but they are "responding" to the issue rather than defining it.[4]

The study found that, in the total sample of 168 articles on business and/or labour topics, business sources appeared in 56% percent of the stories, and labour sources in just 19%. Moreover, in labour news, business sources were usually present along with labour voices. Business people were sometimes even allowed to define issues in labour stories. In contrast, labour representatives were nearly invisible in business news; the *Sun*, in effect, gave labour neither the opportunity to define nor respond to business issues. In the overall sample, labour voices were tapped as "definers" (i.e., the first source quoted) in only 8.3% of stories, compared to 31.5% for business.

Apart from the imbalance of tone and sources, business topics simply received much more attention than did labour. In 1987, there were 1.7 business-related items for every one about labour issues; by 1997, the ratio had increased to 3 to 1. The declining proportion of labour coverage is doubtless associated with the disappearance of a full-time labour reporter at the *Sun* after 1987.

Is the new Hollinger regime at the *Sun* responsible for the marginalization of labour coverage and labour's voice? It would be too simplistic to make such a direct link. The labour beat has been disappearing in newspapers throughout North America, and the imbalance between labour and business news at the *Sun* certainly predates the Hollinger takeover of 1996. Still, we must conclude, at the very least, that the new regime sees nothing wrong with the lack of balance in labour/business reporting and has allowed it to continue.

The *Sun* went through a remake in 1997 under the marketing slogan "Question everything. We did." It promised readers "incisive, thoughtful writing" on "every subject that matters in your world." Except, that is, the world of work: the *Sun* still has no full-time labour reporter, nor even a reporter who specializes in workplace issues.

Such imbalance, at the *Sun* and throughout Canada's press, is politically and socially significant, in our view. Certainly, many middle- and upper-income Canadians invest in mutual funds or dabble in the stock market, and it is also true that many employee association and union pensions have a vested interest in the performance of funds and stocks. But the reality is that only a small percentage of Canadians make their living through investments, and only slightly more of us have individual investments in the stock market that we monitor or evaluate on a frequent basis. Three-quarters of Canadians are still dependent upon waged or salaried employment for the bulk of their income, so other issues pertaining to the workplace are more directly relevant to most of us than corporate mergers or the daily ins and outs of high finance. By disproportionately emphasizing the voice of business interests—and, typically, the voice of management—the press arguably presents a one-dimensional perspective on the world of work. Meanwhile, issues relevant to labour organizations, employee associations, and most wage earners tend to be marginalized in the mainstream media.

Nowhere is the imbalance more obvious than in the Canadian media's coverage of labour strikes and other organized protests. In 1997, for example, NewsWatch researcher James Compton studied the Toronto newspapers' coverage of the Metro Days of Action—one of the largest political protests ever launched in Canada.[5] On the morning of October 25, 1996, transit workers in Toronto walked off the job to protest the Conservative government's policies of cutting social programs and repealing the previous NDP government's labour law reforms. That same day, teachers, social workers, and other government employees likewise protested by taking the day off work. By October 26, thousands of protesters from all walks of life streamed into downtown Toronto, joining these striking public workers in a broad-based protest, coordinated by a coalition of social justice and labour groups.

How did the Toronto press cover this massive protest against the Tory government? In his analysis of all news articles printed in the *Toronto Star*, the *Toronto Sun*, and *The Globe and Mail* about the protest between October 11 and October 29, Compton found that the "the newsworthiness of the Metro Days of Action (for these three papers, at least) lay in its disruption of transit and other government services." The political significance of the demonstrations was indeed covered, but was marginalized by the overwhelming preponderance of stories framed around the immediate and mundane inconveniences caused by the protest.

For example, Compton found that 43% of all articles characterized the Metro Days of Action (MDA) as "disruptive," focusing primarily on actions like the subway shutdown which disturbed the every-day routines of Torontonians. In addition, 18% of the articles described the actions taken by authorities to counter the disruptions caused by the protest, contributing further to the media's overall emphasis on how the protest affected downtown commuters. In contrast, only 39% of the media reports in Compton's sample characterized the MDA as a peaceful political protest. In addition to the dominant theme of disruption, the Toronto dailies' portrayal of the action was generally negative. Nearly three-quarters of the reports were derogatory in tone, while only 24% of them used positive or upbeat language to describe the protests.

The press largely ignore the *breadth* of the protest coalition, focusing instead on the involvement of organized labour. Also missing was much attention to the grievances and purposes underlying the protest. The singular focus on the inconveniences and disruptions sparked by the strike left little opportunity to discuss the Tory government's controversial social and economic policies.

Coverage of the MDA highlighted a more general problem with the media's coverage of labour. While the voice of business is featured prominently as a daily part of social and economic discourse, labour organizations and their leaders and allies are pushed into the background, emerging only during strikes and other disputes to disrupt the smooth functioning of daily life. The result is a distorted view of the world of work, where those who arguably drive the economy—average working people—often find themselves excluded from the media agenda, or, worse still, victimized by it.

Poverty and Class Inequality

Over the last 15 years, most will agree, the political climate in Canada has shifted to the right, and, if you are poor, this has been bad news. Political backlash against the poor has cleared the way for economic policies that have gutted social assistance and welfare programs. Between 1994 and 1996, for example, the federal Liberals slashed cash transfers to support provincial health and social programs by 33% and cut Unemployment Insurance premiums by an average of 11.2% a year.[6] Even the traditionally left-of-centre New Democrats have sometimes followed suit, implementing policies in British Columbia that reduced welfare eligibility for recent out-of-province arrivals, for instance.

Why has this political shift occurred? It is a complex question because, even though the political climate has moved to the right over the past two decades, Canadians have also shown consistently that they do not support the extremes of a conservative free market agenda. Poll after poll for example, has shown strong support for public investments in health care, education, and a viable social safety net. Still, at the same time, many Canadians also say they are having a tougher time making ends meet and feel overtaxed, especially when the quality of existing social programs seems to be eroding. In an atmosphere where people worry about the size of their own family's debt burden, fiscal conservatives have struck a resonant chord with their constant attacks on government deficits and their accompanying arguments about the necessity of having government "live within our means."

Public support for the idea of decreasing the costs of government appears in some instances to be accompanied by a harsher stance toward the poor. In this regard, perhaps the long-running and well-funded campaign by conservative columnists and think tanks to blame the poor for their own poverty has made a dent in public opinion. Certainly, influential conservatives such as Conrad Black and columnist Barbara Amiel share this view. For example, at one point in his autobiography, Black uses the work "unworthy" to refer to "groups, such as strikers and voluntary welfare addicts."[7] Meanwhile, Barbara Amiel, Hollinger's vice-president of editorial, has characterized people in poverty as "a social stratum where . . . people are simply not competent to lead normal and adequate lives."[8]

Of course, with such a singular focus on poor-bashing and the political hot button of welfare fraud, it is easy to miss how the wealthy often find a way to beat the system, too. For example our #2 "under-covered" story of 1993 detailed how the Mulroney government quietly forgave the wealthiest families in Canada hundreds of millions of dollars in taxes—at the same time as it imposed the GST tax on average Canadians. In the U.S., Project Censored reports that a bill passed in the mid-1990s, ostensibly to raise the minimum wage, also included ten unpublicized provisions which could only be defined as welfare for the rich. Among its other controversial provisions, the bill eliminated a surtax on luxury car purchases and diesel fuel for yachts.[9] It seems, sometimes, that concern with "welfare fraud" is selectively focused on those below the poverty line, rather than those stratospherically above it.

With this idea in mind, we wanted to discover how selected media have covered the issue of poverty over the past decade. How much coverage does a typical daily extend to the poorest members of Canadian society? Has this coverage increased or declined over the past ten years, in light of the shifting political climate, and the increasing influence of Conrad Black in Canada's press system? How are the poor portrayed in this coverage?

To help answer these questions, NewsWatch researchers Scott Uzelman, Louise Barkholt, and Christine Krause examined the coverage of poverty issues in the *Vancouver Sun* in 1988 and 1997, before and after Hollinger's acquisition of the *Sun* and other Southam dailies.[10] For 1988, the researchers used microfilmed editions of the *Sun* and selected every fifth calendar day for analysis, yielding a sample of 62 publishing days. For 1997 coverage, they used the Canadian News Disk, this time selecting every third day, in order to obtain a similar-sized sample of poverty stories. The researchers coded only those articles that dealt directly with poverty issues, rejecting those that merely mentioned poverty in passing. All in all, they derived a sample of 101 items for 1988 and 106 for 1997.

In the first part of their analysis, Uzelman et al. compared the overall amount of coverage devoted to poverty issues in the two years. They found that the *Sun's* poverty coverage declined from an average of 1.6 items per day in 1988 to 1.0 per day in 1997. To be sure, the average daily total of all news items at the *Sun* dropped by as much as 25%, but the 37.5% decline in poverty coverage outpaced this more general decrease. Interestingly, the decrease in poverty-related news has taken place at the same time that poverty rates in B.C. and Canada have noticeably increased. For example, according to 1997 Statistics Canada data, the overall percentage of poor in British Columbia—one of Canada's wealthiest provinces—rose from 15% in 1988 to nearly 18% in 1996. Overall, an additional 220,000 joined the ranks of the poor in British Columbia since 1988. So, while the incidence of poverty in B.C. increased by one-fifth, the coverage of poverty in the *Sun* dropped by over one-third.

This decrease in amount was accompanied by other changes in the *Sun's* treatment of poverty issues. For instance, in-depth features on poverty issues declined by nearly two-thirds, from almost 10% of poverty coverage in 1988 to just over 3% in 1997. At the same time, editorials and commentaries on poverty nearly doubled, from just under 8% of poverty coverage in 1988 to 16% in 1997. Why is this shift significant? As several journalists have told NewsWatch, there's a big difference between feature and opinion articles. By their nature, features—which often include in-depth profiles of everyday people—are more likely to be emotive and sympathetic to the subject of poverty, while opinion is more likely to be intellectual or critical. Therefore, the *Sun's* increasing reliance on opinion pieces as opposed to features, we speculate, distances readers from the everyday lived experience of poverty in Canada.

In addition to charting this decrease in both the overall amount of poverty coverage and the decline in features on poverty, the study also analyzed the sources cited in the *Sun's* coverage of the poor. Who are the people typically quoted in stories about poverty? Government officials and politicians were quoted more often than other types of sources, securing almost 41% of all references in 1988 and 50% in 1997. Business sources also raised their profile in stories about poverty, appearing in 21% of stories in 1997, up from 12% in 1988. Both of these sources have an institutional stake in downplaying the severity of poverty, and both increased their presence in poverty stories over the decade. On the other hand, while advocacy groups who work on behalf of the poor are still well-accessed, that access declined from a high of 42.7% in 1988 to 37.7% in 1997.

This apparent shift from advocacy groups towards government and business sources may be related to a subtle but significant change in the way the *Sun* has portrayed the poor themselves. The researchers coded articles according to whether the poor were cast as "victims" or "threats." For example, if the poor were depicted as individuals at the mercy of social and economic circumstances beyond their control, they were coded as victims. In this case, readers might infer that the poor are deserving of public assistance because they could not help their situation. On the other hand, if the poor were portrayed as lacking the incentive to work, adding to the nation's fiscal burden, or threatening the very fabric of Canadian society, they were coded as threats. With the poor framed as "threats," then, readers may infer that the poor are undeserving of financial help because—as conservatives like Barbara Amiel argue—they have only themselves to blame. In this way, distinguishing victims and threats seemed to be a good way to determine whether or not a right-wing market-liberal perspective has increasingly influenced the *Sun's* coverage of the poor.

Overall, the study found that the vast majority of stories in both 1988 and 1997 portrayed the poor as victims and (implicitly) as deserving of public assistance. This is still Canada, after all. At the same time, news that portrayed the poor as threats (and therefore, presumably, undeserving of help) increased noticeably, from 10.9% of stories in 1988 up to 17% in 1997. Overall, this suggests that the *Sun* may be starting to present a less compassionate perspective of the poor than in the past, despite their increase in numbers across Canada. The *Sun's* chief editor apparently was not surprised by this finding, and argued in a November 27, 1998 talk to Simon Fraser University students that the paper is simply reflecting the perception of many of its readers that the poor are indeed a threat.

We don't want to exaggerate. Our sampled Canadian newspaper has not demonized the poor to the same extent as, say, sex offenders. Still, our research indicates that the *Sun's* coverage of poverty has shifted over the past decade—decreasing in amount, becoming somewhat less sympathetic in tone, less in-depth in treatment, with decreasing access for advocacy groups representing the poor, and more access for business and government sources—sources who potentially have a stake in minimizing the problem of poverty and hunger in Canada. The result of these trends, arguably, is a news media environment that is increasingly unable to capture both the everyday experience of poverty and the role government and corporate policies may play in sustaining it.

The Market Liberal Agenda: Absent Alternatives and Hidden Consequences

In the view that is sometimes known as "classical" or "neo-classical" economic theory, it is argued that governments should stay out of the economy entirely, leaving the marketplace alone to do its magic—producing and selling goods, rewarding innovation and productivity, providing jobs, and so on. Drawing on the inspiration of classical liberal economists, such as Adam Smith, large numbers of western intellectuals and policy-makers in the 18th and 19th centuries promoted an economic philosophy of "laissez-faire." Still, while much has been said for the benefits of an unfettered market economy, western societies in the 19th and early 20th centuries learned the downside of "laissez faire"—including environmental pollution, exploitation of workers (including children), and, periodically, agonizing economic panics, crises, and mass unemployment.

Beginning with the Progressive and social democratic movements of a century ago, and firmly entrenched by the 1950s, a general consensus slowly emerged: through labour laws, regulation, public investment, and social programs, government should step in and curb the excesses of business, thereby blunting the most disturbing consequences of completely unregulated markets.

Politics in post-war western societies has often been defined by arguments about the most appropriate balance between free market principles and these forms of public investment and government regulation. Over the past two decades, conservative groups have argued forcefully that the political pendulum swung too far to the political left during the 1960s and 1970s. In response, they have championed a renewed "laissez-faire" market-liberal perspective—a no-holds-barred attack on government regulations, progressive taxation, and universal social programs.

In an ongoing attempt to secure the social and economic conditions more favourable to economic growth and corporate profit, multinational corporations and their allies in political parties and market-liberal policy institutes have worked hard to reverse many of the social reforms of the post-war era. For example, in the interests of "unleashing" market forces, market liberals have sought to minimize tax rates and social programs (which require higher taxation rates), and to dismantle protection for workers, unions, and the environment. For their part, while they sometimes welcome government subsidies, large corporations have adopted much of the market-liberal agenda as their own and have lobbied for lower taxes, a lower ratio of wages to profits, and fewer regulations on how they conduct their operations.

To these traditional market-liberal goals, you can also add a more recent item: the campaign for free trade around the globe. Through arrangements like NAFTA (the North American Free Trade Agreement) and the momentarily shelved Multilateral Agreement on Investment, corporations are free to bypass government regulations merely by voting with their feet. If you don't like labour unions in Europe, move to the U.S. If you don't like paying corporate taxes in Canada, move to the free trade zone in Mexico. If you don't like paying high wages in the U.S., why not locate your shoe factory in Indonesia? In this way, free trade has been a centrepiece of the agenda of large international corporations. As the Canadian Centre for Policy Alternatives argues, free trade "frees" corporations from most restraints on their operations and enables them to pursue profit with little interference from provincial or national governments.[11]

Advocates of free trade and other market-liberal policies argue that, by removing regulations and reducing taxes on businesses, such policies will lead to robust economic growth, better jobs, and rising incomes. It is a debatable assumption, but one increasingly shared with Canada's political establishment. For example, both Brian Mulroney (Progressive Conservative) and his one-time opponent, Jean Chrétien (Liberal), have embraced market-liberal approaches to deficit reduction and free trade. With much of the political élite thus convinced of the necessity for "smaller government" and the benefits of free trade, many critics have argued that the media have simply followed suit, embracing market-liberal assumptions as economic gospel. For example, freelance journalist Richard Starr claimed in a memo to NewsWatch that by 1994 "the triumph of the right-wing economic agenda" was complete, "and any stories that challenged the herd mentality on debt, government spending, trade, social policy, and the role of the state were under-reported."

Frances Russell, a reporter for the *Winnipeg Free Press*, knows how difficult it can be to challenge the market-liberal herd. At the *Free Press* in 1987, Russell started covering the impact on Canada of the bilateral, and then continental, free trade agreements. At one point, she detailed provisions in the agreement that would undermine Canada's ability to pass laws to protect the environment (our 5th-ranked under-reported story in 1993). But, because most of her colleagues "shunned and avoided" looking at the negative-consequences of free trade, Russell told us that she often second-guessed herself during her investigation of NAFTA's more obscure provisions. "I have to admit," she wrote to NewsWatch, "that, because all my life I have been distrustful of conspiracy theories, even now I keep asking myself if it is I who is wrong? I who have lost my objectivity? I who have become a political partisan rather than a political analyst?" Despite these doubts, she kept writing because "the bare, bald facts" about the consequences of NAFTA compelled her to keep at it.

Reporters such as Frances Russell are arguably the exception in Canadian journalism. When the journalistic "pack" decides that some perspectives are legitimate and others are not, usually only the most dedicated reporters can go against the crowd. Thus, while the right-wing program of spending cuts, government deregulation, and free trade has seemingly garnered the lion's share of media coverage and commentary, alternative economic perspectives have seemed under-represented in Canada's media environment.

So, beginning in 1995, NewsWatch Canada began to ask: are plausible alternative perspectives on debt reduction, international trade, and economic growth being under-covered by the dominant Canadian media? Or is that claim just sour grapes from left-wingers grumpy about being on the losing end of economic debates in Canada?

NewsWatch researcher Brent Stafford set out to examine one interesting aspect of media coverage of economic policy in Canada's press by comparing the access afforded to right and left-leaning policy institutes.[12] Such institutes (more popularly known as "think tanks") play an important role in helping to shape contemporary public agendas. Typically, they are non-partisan research and advocacy organizations, usually funded by private donations, with a mandate to promote a policy-relevant issue or perspective. Think tanks publish research in support of various social and economic policies, and also generate a considerable amount of PR spin, making them indispensable to journalists looking for quotes on political and economic debates.

To examine whether or not the media were accessing think tanks from a variety of political perspectives, Stafford compiled all references to the leading 15 think tanks in Canada published in 14 major daily newspapers and broadcast on CBC and CTV television newscasts over a six-month period in 1996. Each think tank was then independently classified as "right-wing," "left-wing," or "middle of the road," by a panel of mainstream journalists, yielding seven left-wing, six right-wing, and two centrist institutes. Overall, Stafford reports, right-wing think tanks received 68% of all references, while left-wing think tanks received 19.5%. The hit parade on the right was led by the Conference Board of Canada (317 references), the Fraser Institute (312), and the C.D. Howe Institute (270). By contrast, the leading left-wing think tank—the Council of Canadians—logged in at 121 references, followed by the Canadian Centre for Policy Alternatives (64) and the Canadian Council on Social Development (57).

None of the news organizations in the study gave equal coverage to left and right-wing think tanks, although some were more balanced than others. For example, the *Ottawa Citizen* referenced right-wing groups in 54% of its stories which mentioned think tanks, followed by the *Hamilton Spectator* (62%), and the *Toronto Star* (64%). By comparison, the right-wing think tanks made up almost 97% of all think tank references in the *Toronto Sun*. Close behind the *Sun* in this enthusiastic embrace of the Canadian right were the *Vancouver Province* (84%), the *Calgary Herald* (81%), and the *Financial Post* (80%).

In contrast to their cousins in the print media, the Canadian television networks largely shied away from quoting think tanks of any political stripe. Think tanks were mentioned just 22 times on CTV News and 11 times on CBC's *The National* during the study period.

In a second stage of research, coverage of a leading right-wing institute (the Fraser Institute) and its closest left-wing counterpart (the Canadian Centre for Policy Alternatives) was analyzed for the proportion of supportive coverage they received in the *Vancouver Sun* and the *Globe and Mail* in 1996. When they were covered, both institutes received about the same proportion of supportive sources (sources cited in stories that supported the position of the think tank), and a similar portion of critical or hostile source referencing. While these results seem balanced, it is important to keep in mind that they describe the *tone* of coverage only. In sheer quantity, there were five times more Fraser Institute stories than CCPA ones.

In the following year, NewsWatch did a follow-up study of the two institutes' coverage in the *Vancouver Sun*. Would the CCPA's new Vancouver office, opened in 1997, improve its access, at least to the local press? Using the full-text Canadian News Disk, researcher Scott Uzelman collected and analyzed all 1997 *Sun* articles printed which contained a substantive reference to either think tank. Indeed, the CCPA had closed the gap, but it still faced a 2.4-to-1 disadvantage: 39 articles compared with 94 for the Fraser Institute.[13] As unbalanced as this may seem, this ratio is a vast improvement over previous years. An earlier search of the *Sun's* database by one of the paper's own reporters found 690 references to the Fraser Institute and only 49 references to the CCPA over the previous decade, yielding an astonishing ratio of 14 to 1.[14]

In addition to this imbalance in the quantity of coverage, the *Sun* treated the two institutes somewhat differently as well. On the one hand, both the CCPA and the FI were allowed to define issues (rather than merely responding to them) in most of their appearances in the news. But, on the whole, the *Sun* tapped the Fraser Institute for commentary on a wider range of subjects, *Sun* opinion columnists were far more likely to cite the Fraser Institute than the CCPA, and the FI was quite successful in obtaining coverage for two of its controversial campaigns—redefining poverty and changing environmental priorities.

In summary, while the CCPA enjoyed increased access to the *Sun* in 1997, its right-wing rival still overshadowed it.

This disparity between the access afforded to right and left-wing advocacy groups is not necessarily the product of deliberate media bias. It may well be linked to the greater resources and output of market liberal institutes, compared to their political rivals. More broadly, the imbalance of access both reflects and reinforces the apparent dominance of market-liberal perspectives on economic problems and solutions.

Take the debt and deficit, for example. Throughout the 1990s, the Canadian left has lamented that the mainstream news media have given right-wing perspectives on the debt and deficit more and fuller coverage than alternative perspectives. But is this true? Have the news media promoted the right-wing notion that cutting social programs is the only way to corral the deficit, thereby overlooking alternate ways to manage the problem? To address this question, NewsWatch researcher Jackie Mosdell examined the *Globe and Mail's* economic coverage over a three-month period in 1994–95. The sample comprised all stories in the *Globe's* main news section which contained the words "debt" and/or "deficit" and which specifically concerned the federal budget—53 articles, including news reports (43), editorials (5), and columns (3).[15] Publications from the Fraser and C.D. Howe institutes were scanned to identify the free market right's preferred solutions to the deficit, namely, cutting social welfare spending, downsizing government, reducing provincial transfer payments, and privatizing public services. For the left's view on the deficit, Mosdell surveyed the CCPA's monthly magazine, The CCPA *Monitor*, and a best-selling book by the progressive writer Linda McQuaig,[16] yielding such prescriptions as increasing government spending (to stimulate the economy), lowering interest rates, and reducing subsidies to corporations (a position that is also embraced by market-liberal purists who oppose government economic intervention in principle).

Overall, Mosdell found that the *Globe and Mail* mentioned market-liberal prescriptions 105 times, while alternative prescriptions were mentioned a mere 29 times, resulting in a ratio of over 3-to-1. One policy strategy—directly cutting social spending—was mentioned 39 times, more often than all left-wing themes combined. Other right-wing prescriptions were also oft-repeated: cutting the size of government 30 times, and reducing provincial transfer payments 28 times. In contrast, the most frequently cited alternative solution to the deficit crisis—slashing subsidies to corporations—appeared in the *Globe* just 14 times.

With progressive voices and perspectives marginalized in the debate over the debt, deficit, and other crucial economic issues, viable alternatives to the market-liberal, slash-and-burn approach to the economy fade into the political background. Consider one left-leaning solution to the debt problem in the 1990s—lowering interest rates. One of the major contributors to the national debt over the last two decades has been the cost of servicing it. According to a controversial 1991 StatsCan draft report, between 1975 and 1989 artificially high interest rates added 44% to the debt (as noted in our 6th ranked under-reported story for 1994, discussed in Chapter Five). However, if Ottawa were to roll over government debt into low-interest loans provided directly by the Bank of Canada (rather than by private investors at higher interest rates), Canada's payments on the debt would be substantially reduced, leaving Ottawa with less reason to cut health care and social programs. This potential alternative to deep cuts in federal support for health care and social assistance—an alternative that would incidentally raise no one's taxes—attracted only three mentions in the *Globe and Mail* during the study period.

With such alternative solutions and perspectives pushed to the margins of debate, the federal Liberals arguably had a freer hand to present their market-liberal program of free trade, deep cuts to social programs, and relaxed regulations on business as the only viable solution to economic recession and the debt crisis. And, as our under-covered story lists of the last few years suggest, the consequences of this market-liberal agenda have only begun to be felt. For example, in response to cuts to federal transfer payments, many provinces are turning over their Medicare systems to private "consultants" hired from the U.S. health industry. Their approach, more often than not, is to slash salaries, cut staff, and replace experienced (and expensive) health professionals with inexperienced (and inexpensive) temps and part-timers (Story #2, 1995).

Moreover, cuts to unemployment insurance and welfare programs open up the possibility that Canada may develop—as long-term poverty cultivates desperation and frustration—what former Health and Welfare deputy minister Richard Splane calls an "American-style angry underclass" (Story #11, 1994). If indeed the market-liberal agenda has produced such changes in the fabric of Canadian society, one would hope to find an open and frank debate in the Canadian media about the merits and drawbacks of laissez faire economics. Unfortunately, our research, preliminary though it be, suggests that a full and varied debate has been one of the missing ingredients in media coverage of economic problems and solutions.

Media Corporations: Covering Themselves (Up?)

American media critic Ronald Collins writes, "Independence, in all its many forms, is implicit in the notion of a free press."[17] From public school social studies classes to Hollywood films such as *All the President's Men*, we are schooled in the notion of the media as the Fourth Estate—an independent check on the abuse of government or corporate power in society. This image of a cantankerous and hard-hitting press is a familiar part of our cultural repertoire, one that journalists themselves share. For example, in a defense of his news program's invasive coverage of a police search on B.C. Premier Glen Clark's home in early 1999, BCTV's news director, Steve Wyatt, argued that "It is a basic principle of a free press in a democratic society that we shed light where there might otherwise be darkness . . . . Society is better served when powerful institutions are subject to public scrutiny."[18]

As consumers of the news, however, we are much less familiar with the byzantine corporate structures which own and produce the news in Canada and around the world. For most corporate owners of the media, the news is above all else a business—a commodity to be bought and sold, a source of advertising revenue, and a way to produce a return on an investment. And, like most businesses, news corporations have interests to protect and secrets to guard. Unlike many businesses, however, media companies have considerable potential influence over the public agenda.

So the question arises, who subjects *these* "powerful institutions" to "public scrutiny"? What happens when bottom-line interests of corporate owners (particularly their economic interest in pleasing advertisers) conflict with the ethic of journalistic independence? If our discussions with journalists around Canada are any indication, there is cause for concern. According to one respondent, in today's corporate newsroom "anything that's a direct attack on business is a real hard sell. The people at the top know you won't keep your position if you attack business, even if they won't say it directly." Other journalists agreed, but stressed that few corporate owners directly censor news content. Most choose instead to exert control in more subtle ways—for example, by appointing editors who are on-side with the owner's political views.

This brings us back to a question: Do the large corporations that own Canada's media influence the news in accordance with their particular political and financial vested interests? If they do, that influence should be detectable in patterns of news coverage in the press. NewsWatch has undertaken initial studies on two potential sources of direct corporate influence on the news: media owners, and advertisers, who account for roughly three-fourths of daily newspapers' revenue.

Our first question concerns the influence that corporate owners exert over the quality and tone of daily news coverage and editorial content. As American media critic Todd Gitlin writes, when most people think of ownership's influence on news, they picture an overweight, cigar-chomping tycoon calling reporters into his office and telling them what and what not to say.[19] The reality of owner influence is much more subtle than this popular image, and thus more difficult to document or prove. For example, as one journalist told NewsWatch, the power of owners to hire and fire often creates an unspoken but still chilling effect in the newsroom. When you know that the ownership typically frowns on particular kinds of stories, he explained, "there's no incentive to make waves, if you want to keep your job." But how do you study "a feeling" or a "sense" that may permeate a newsroom? How do you document the usually implicit influence of ownership on the news?

In our investigations we decided to take a novel approach. If ownership exerts influence, then a change of ownership might be expected to result in a change in the tone or quality of news coverage. So, why not compare the editorial content of the news immediately prior to and then some time after an ownership change? Our first foray into the question of ownership influence compared the Op/Ed page of the *Ottawa Citizen* in 1991, before Conrad Black and Hollinger assumed a controlling share of Southam, to the *Citizen's* Op/Ed page in 1996, immediately after Hollinger's takeover. In this study, NewsWatch researcher Myle Lai compared a two-week sample of op/ed pieces from each of the two years under study. There were certain changes, including a modest decline in the proportion of columns written by *Citizen* staff and a certain rightward shift in the tone of Op/Ed pieces (reinforced by the departure of columnist Christopher Young and managing editor Peter Calamai, and the arrival of Andrew Coyne and Giles Gherson, two of Southam's syndicated writers). But these changes were subtle and could not be attributed directly to the new Hollinger regime.

So, at the *Citizen*, there was insufficient reason to conclude (at least, prior to its revamping under new editor, Neil Reynolds) that the Hollinger takeover had shifted Op/Ed commentary dramatically to the right. But was this true of other Hollinger papers, and what might we find if we looked at news coverage beyond Op/Ed commentary—especially on matters relevant to the vested interests of Conrad Black himself? With these questions in mind, NewsWatch researchers Ilona Jackson, Patsy Kotsopolous, and Darren Seath set out in 1998 to examine the kind of coverage the *Vancouver Sun* gave to Conrad Black and, more broadly, to Black's holding company, Hollinger International.[20] Given the growing influence of Hollinger in Canada's news system, this question should certainly be of interest to Canadians. We felt that self-coverage should be the acid test of the influence of ownership. On the one hand, if a newspaper can cover its own parent company the same way it covers other institutions, readers can reasonably suppose that news decision-making is independent from ownership influence. On the other hand, if there is evidence of a double standard, that raises the possibility that the paper's owners might influence other areas of coverage as well.

To investigate the *Sun's* coverage of its owners, our researchers took a three-pronged approach. First, they compared the *Sun's* recent coverage of Black/Hollinger with its coverage of other major Canadian media tycoons and their companies over the time period. Next, they compared the *Sun's* reporting on Black/Hollinger with that extended by the *Toronto Star*, one of the few major market broadsheets not owned by Conrad Black. Finally, the study compared *Sun* reporting on Black/Hollinger after Black gained majority control of Southam with the *Sun's* coverage before Black assumed the helm. In each of these studies, the researchers coded all articles published in the *Sun* during specific time periods. Avoiding an overly complex process, they studied only the headline and lead sentence of each article in the sample, coding each article for owner/company, subject, location in the paper, story origin (staff or wire service), and tone.

The first part of the study asked the question, "Does a news organization cover its own parent company less critically than it covers other companies in similar industries?" To this end, they examined *Sun* articles printed on four of Canada's largest media corporations: Hollinger, Rogers Communications, Thomson, and Western International Communications (WIC) between May 1996 and April 1997. Excluding articles that merely mentioned the company's name in passing somewhere in the article, the sample comprised 189 articles, with Hollinger attracting the largest amount of coverage (97 articles) and Thomson attracting the least attention (nine articles).

The researchers began by looking at how the article portrayed the companies and owners under question: were the stories supportive, critical, or neutral in tone? They defined articles as being supportive if the headline and lead sentence cast the subject in a positive light or reported profits as increasing. Articles were coded as critical when they hinted at negative developments or reported profits as decreasing. Finally, the research team classified articles as neutral when the lead sentence or headline did not reflect positively or negatively on the company in question.

The study found that the *Sun* was most supportive of Black/Hollinger and least supportive of WIC (owned by the Vancouver-based Griffiths family). Overall, nearly 20% of Hollinger stories were positive in tone, while only 11% of Rogers stories, 11% of Thomson stories, and a mere 7% of WIC articles were coded as supportive. Moreover, while Hollinger received slightly fewer supportive than critical articles (after all, news tends to focus on negative developments), the other three companies received about three times as much critical as supportive coverage.

To be fair, the *Sun* did run stories critical of Black and Hollinger. But every such negative story was located inside the news or business section, whereas the other three media companies, especially WIC, saw much of their critical coverage land on the front page of at least one of the *Sun's* sections. For example, the *Sun* buried an article titled "MP, union want probe of papers' ownership: The purchase of seven more dailies by Conrad Black's Hollinger empire provokes questions about concentration" deep in the middle of the news section. Another unflattering story entitled "Unfair labour practice complaint over Radler talk at *Leader-Post*" appeared in the back of the business section, next to stock quotes and ads for hair replacement formulae.

While the first part of this study suggested differences in the way the *Sun* covered different media organizations, it didn't tell us if these differences were due to the *Sun's* editorial decisions. Perhaps all Canadian media—even Hollinger's competitors—bury bad news about Hollinger in the inside pages. To check this possibility, the research team turned to a major non-Hollinger daily, the *Toronto Star*. How did the *Star's* coverage of Hollinger International compare with the *Sun's*? Collecting 97 articles on Hollinger from the *Sun* and 188 articles from the *Star*, the researchers analyzed the headline and lead sentence for each story in the sample. Overall, they found that, while only 23% of the *Sun's* articles were critical of Hollinger, a full 42% of the *Star's* were critical in tone. Moreover, stories critical of Black/Hollinger had a better change of appearing on the front page of the *Star*. For instance, 12% of the *Star's* critical coverage of Hollinger appeared on the front page of the news or business sections. Finally, the *Star* published five critical Op/Ed pieces (including letters) for every one supportive of Hollinger. In stark contrast, the *Sun* ran 2.5 supportive Op/Ed pieces for every item critical of Black/Hollinger.

In addition to its more critical treatment of Hollinger International, the *Toronto Star* also extended more coverage to advocacy groups opposed to Conrad Black's takeover of Southam. Overall, the *Star* printed 15 items detailing opposition to Black's ongoing quest to control much of Canada's news media, while the *Sun* ran only seven such items. But these numbers tell only half the story. Consider the *Star's* and the *Sun's* coverage of the Council of Canadians' legal challenge to block Black's takeover of Southam. While the *Star* and the *Sun* extended roughly the same amount of coverage to the Council's bid to stop the takeover, the *Sun* tended to relegate the Council's main point—that concentrated media ownership is a threat to democratic free expression—to the later paragraphs of the articles, suggesting implicitly that the legal challenge itself was the real story. In fact, the *Sun's* initial story on the Council's law-suit simply failed to mention the Council's fears that freedom of expression would be limited by the Southam purchase. The *Star*, on the other hand, for the most part presented the thrust of the Council's concerns in the opening lines of each article, taking care to mention the Council's belief that concentration of media ownership presents a disturbing threat to Canadian democracy.

Maybe this is just sour grapes from a Hollinger competitor? It is certainly plausible that competitors, such as the *Star*, cover Conrad Black more critically and extend more coverage to his opponents, mainly to gain some kind of advantage. Perhaps, as Black himself might say, the *Star* is simply envious of his success. To account for this possibility, the final phase of this NewsWatch study examined the *Sun's* coverage of Black/Hollinger in two distinct time periods—first, from January 1985 to December 1990 (before Hollinger became an investor in the Southam newspaper chain, including the *Sun*), and second, from May 1996 to April 1997 (after Hollinger assumed full control of Southam). To derive comparable samples, the researchers could not use the Canadian News Disk, which archives no news prior to 1993. Instead, they were forced to use the Canadian Business and Current Affairs (CBCA), a less comprehensive database which indexes articles with "significant reference value." Accordingly, this phase of the study used a smaller sample—14 articles for the first period and 25 for the second—which consequently limits the validity of the study.

Still, the results are suggestive. For example, our researchers discovered that, prior to Black's takeover of the *Sun*, 43% of the *Sun's* articles on Hollinger were critical. After the takeover, only 28% of the *Sun's* Hollinger stories were critical in tone. In addition, the *Sun's* supportive coverage of Hollinger mushroomed from a pre-takeover low of 7% to 52% after Black took control. In the end, these findings, combined with the other evidence from the same NewsWatch study, suggest a notable imbalance in the way the *Sun* reports on Conrad Black and Hollinger International. Overall, our research suggests that the *Sun's* coverage of Hollinger has been more favourable than its coverage of other media corporations; its coverage of Hollinger has been more favourable than that extended by the *Toronto Star*, a non-Hollinger competitor; and, in fact, its own coverage of Hollinger has become much rosier since Black took over the paper.

The results of our pilot study are consistent with other anecdotal evidence and case studies. The Institute for Alternative Journalism in San Francisco has documented several cases of outright censorship, in which corporate media executives have directly interfered in editorial decisions. They wanted to soften or kill coverage critical of their own company, or of officials whose favours the company was courting.[21] Normally, though, the process is more subtle. As Pulitzer-prize-winning media critic Ben Bagdikian has put it:

> When protection of an owning corporation's private interests intrudes into news decisions, other professionally acceptable reasons are given (such as "Nobody's interested"). The barrier is seldom absolute: there is merely a higher threshold for such stories. News stories that cast doubt on the corporate ethic must be more urgent and melodramatic than stories sustaining that ethic.[22]

Presumably, editors are intelligent enough not to require direct commands from the corporate boardroom to tread carefully in covering their own employer. Two editors at Canadian Press told the 1980/81 Kent Commission on Newspapers that CP edited its news about the media so as to please major media owners. At the time, the Thomson chain had more member newspapers than any other company. The two editors said that CP deliberately shortened a news account of a Thomson paper strike, killed a report about a trade union leader's speech criticizing Thomson, and delayed a story about a government investigation into possible links between birth defects and electronic terminals in Thomson newspaper plants.[23] In Ontario, James Winter has analyzed the biases in newspaper coverage of annual newspaper award ceremonies, an area where each paper has "a blatant self-interest." While self-promotion in this area of coverage is hardly surprising, Winter sensibly suggests that it throws into question "the reporting we get where there are other, perhaps less blatant, examples of self-interest."[24]

Advertisers: Carrying a Big Stick

While media owners are one source of influence on news content, other corporate forces, notably advertisers, can also wield potential power in contemporary newsrooms. As we discussed in Chapter Two, most newspapers and broadcasters depend on advertising revenue for their financial survival, and this means that a lot of energy and attention goes into attracting audiences and pleasing advertisers. When advertisers find fault with certain kinds of stories—stories which perhaps portray their industry in a negative light—they can use this power over the media's purse strings to downplay, or even kill, potentially damaging news coverage. For the most part, advertisers do not need to pressure news outlets directly to shape coverage. Instead, newspapers and broadcasters—afraid of alienating their key sources of revenue—will more likely censor themselves and quash stories that might embarrass key advertisers before they ever hit the audience.[25]

We don't want to overstate the case. Many editors and even executives and owners will resist overt pressure from advertisers, and take pride in doing so. Indeed, the credibility of their own product—the news—is potentially threatened by caving into obviously or frequently to such pressure. Still, in a climate of growing media competition for advertising revenue, there is reason for concern. As a respected American scholar has put it, "the incentive of advertising revenue encourages the media to tailor message content . . . to treat advertisers' products and their broader interest charitably in both news reports and editorials."[26]

For instance, consider former *Vancouver Sun* reporter Ben Parfitt's claim that pressure from real estate developers led the paper to downplay reports that hundreds, if not thousands, of condominiums in the Vancouver area were leaking and rotting in the incessant West Coast rain. Real estate advertising is a crucial source of revenue for local newspapers. So does a steady supply of real estate advertising revenue buy developers good will in local newspapers? Ben Parfitt thinks so. During February of 1993, Parfitt wrote a series of articles on the growing leaky condo problem for the *Vancouver Sun*, and, once his series started to run, angry condo owners began to phone him "in droves" with their horror stories about rotting walls, ruined carpets, and massive repair bills.[27] Years later, Parfitt noted in the *Georgia Straight*, an independently owned urban weekly, that he had just begun to document what would eventually turn into a major housing crisis.

According to Parfitt, however, the more compelling the story became, the less play the *Sun's* editors appeared to give it. His first leaky condo story debuted on the front page, but then later stories were moved back in the paper, ending up near the back of the B section by week's end. Coincidentally, this week was also Parfitt's last at the *Sun*. Electing to take an employee-buyout offer from Southam, he left the *Sun's* news desk with a stack or suggestions on follow-up "leaky condo" stories before moving on. However, it took five years before leaky condos again exploded into major local and indeed national news. Between his 1993 exposés and the 1998 "big news" story, Parfitt claims that "the *Sun* did little to influence public discourse on this major health and safety issue." In neglecting this story for so long, Parfitt concludes, the *Sun* put the "interests of advertisers . . . ahead of those of its readers."

Writing in the *Georgia Straight*, Parfitt describes how, after his first stories ran, developers associated with two of the leaky projects met then editor-in-chief Ian Haysom, publisher Don Babick, and marketing director Ron Clarke. He alleges that some developers threatened to pull their ads from the *Sun's* "New Homes" section, a cash cow which brought in $4 million a year in advertising dollars. In the end, Parfitt claims, "we have a market filled with rotting buildings and a mainstream press . . . whose conspicuous silence on the issue helped make a terrible problem even worse."

Following up Parfitt's revelations, NewsWatch co-founder Donald Gutstein evaluated the leaky condo stories that appeared in the *Sun* between the initial Parfitt series in 1993 and October 22, 1997—a date preceding the explosion of the story in the early part of 1998.[28] In his analysis, Gutstein found only 20 stories addressing the leaky condo issue during the entire four-and-a-half-year study period. The minimal coverage that did find its way into the *Sun* often did its best to downplay the severity of the problem. For example, during 1996, the *Sun's* main channel of information to its readers about leaky condos was the "New Homes" section. Four out of the five items printed during that year appeared in this developer-supported section. Not surprisingly, these stories emphasized the good job being done by developers to deal with the problem. Not one tenant's advocate or other critical voice appeared in these stories.

The high water mark for leaky condo coverage during the study period actually came a year earlier in 1995. Of the eight items that appeared in 1995, five were columns by Elizabeth Aird outlining the shoddy, even illegal, practices of builders and developers throwing projects together willy-nilly to cash in on a booming housing market. Aird revealed in a later column that she was a victim of a leaky condo project. For its part, the *Sun's* editors countered with an editorial coinciding with the last of Aird's columns on the condo issue. The *Sun's* view was that the problem was caused by "fly-by-nighters," not reputable builders. Correcting this problem only required tinkering with the system—for example, defining areas of responsibility more clearly, licensing builders, and simplifying regulations. Ultimately, though, the *Sun* cautioned, it was "buyer beware." This arguable toothless statement was the only *Sun* editorial on the subject between the Parfitt series and February 1998, when the leaky condo story flooded into the local and national media.

So, Gutstein concludes, it's not that the *Sun* did not know about the crisis during those intervening four-and-a-half years. Parfitt suggested follow-up stories, and the Aird columns should have alerted *Sun* editors. Moreover, in April 1996, Canadian Press printed a hard-hitting wire story about "a flood of leaky condos," but the *Sun* did not publish this either.[29] Instead, the *Sun's* editors chose to run such promotional stories as "House hunter has big choice as prices fall, realtor says,"[30] and "Condomania! It's a buyer's market!"[31] During this time, good news stories and advertiser-friendly fluff continued to outweigh and overwhelm solid, balanced reporting on the leaky condo crisis.

Finally, when the leaky condo story began to take off in early 1998, the *Sun* dutifully extended coverage to the crisis, but by then it was merely following a story already "out there" in the media, rather than leading or uncovering the story through hard-nosed investigative reporting. Prior to 1998, the *Sun* seemed content to rake in real estate advertising and to allow the story to languish in obscurity.

Did the *Sun* pull its punches when faced with a possible advertising boycott from angry developers? Ultimately, we cannot answer this question without further evidence about what may have happened behind closed doors. The *Sun's* chief editor told NewsWatch that the potential of libel suits from developers and condo strata councils worried about diminishing property values was a more important factor that led not only his paper, but all Vancouver media, including the less commercially-dependent CBC, to approach the leaky condo story cautiously. This is a useful caveat, which suggests two points. First, we are talking not of the shortcomings of a single newspaper, but of structural pressures that affect all news media. Second, the point does not contradict our argument about the potential influence of advertisers on the news; indeed, it suggests that, through their access to undoubtedly high-priced lawyers, major corporate interests have additional weapons to influence the media.

In the end, our research suggests that the unwillingness or inability of Canada's dominant media corporations to cover themselves critically or to disclose their own interests may be the biggest blind spot of all. Corporate-owned media are willing— at least, sometimes, and arguably more often—to promote their corporate image or to protect key advertisers from unflattering news coverage. This can potentially undermine the expression of a diversity of viewpoints in the press on some relevant issues. But, if corporate self-interest may play a role in reducing the diversity of stories, voices, opinions, and perspectives in the press, the question is: what can we do about it? In a word: plenty.

ENDNOTES

1. See, for example, Glasgow University Media Group, *Really Bad News* (London: Writers and Readers, 1982).

2. Graham Knight, "Strike Talk: A Case Study of News;" and Robert A. Hackett, "The Depiction of Labour and Business on National Television News," both in Marc Grenier (ed.), *Critical Studies of Canadian Mass Media* (Toronto: Butterworths, 1992). Both articles were originally published in the *Canadian Journal of Communication*, in 1982 and 1983 respectively.

3. Summarized in Donald Gutstein, with Robert Hackett and NewsWatch Canada, *Question the Sun! A Content Analysis of Diversity in the Vancouver Sun Before and After the Hollinger Takeover* (Burnaby: NewsWatch Canada, 1998).

4. The distinction between defining and responding sources derives from Michael Clow with Susan Machum, *Stifling Debate: Canadian Newspapers and Nuclear Power* (Halifax: Fernwood Books, 1993).

5. James Compton, "Toronto Papers Misrepresented Last Year's Days of Action," *NewsWatch Monitor* (November 1997), p. iv.

6. Matt Sanger, "Federal, Provincial Downloading Hurting Municipalities," *CCPA Monitor* (May 1998). See also the NewsWatch web site for 1994's #11 under-reported story, "Federal Welfare Cuts Will Mean Crueler Canada."

7. Conrad Black, *A Life in Progress* (Toronto: Key Porter, 1993), p. 420.

8. Quoted in *Maclean's* (August 22, 1988).

9. Peter Phillips and Project Censored, *Censored 1997: The News That Didn't Make the News* (New York: Seven Stories Press), p. 36.

10. See Gutstein et al, *Question the Sun!*, pp. 31–38.

11. Editorial, *CCPA Monitor* (October 1997), p. 2.

12. Brent Stafford, "Rightwing Research Agencies Quoted Much More Often" *NewsWatch Monitor* (Summer 1997), p. i.

13. Gutstein et al, *Question the Sun!*, pp. 16–18.

14. Robert Sarti, "New Competitor Challenges Fraser Institute's Influence," *Vancouver Sun* (February 8, 1997), p. A18.

15. Jackie Mosdell, "The Globe and the Mail has the 'Right Stuff,' all Right," *NewsWatch Monitor* (Summer 1997), p. iv.

16. Linda McQuaig, *Shooting the Hippo: Death by Deficit and Other Canadian Myths* (Toronto: Viking, 1995).

17. Ronald Collins, *Dictating Content: How Advertising Pressure Can Corrupt a Free Press* (Washington, D.C.: Center for Study of Commercialism), p. 1.

18. Steve Wyatt, "BCTV Defends Warrant Coverage," *Vancouver Sun* (March 12, 1999), p. A19.

19. Todd Gitlin, "Foreword" to Collins, *Dictating Content*, p. xixii.

20. Summarized in Gutstein et al., *Question the Sun!* pp. 39–44; and Donald Gutstein, "Vancouver Sun's Coverage Acid Test of Owner's Influence," *NewsWatch Monitor*, vol. 1, no. 4 (Fall 1998), pp. i–iii.

21. Institute for Alternative Journalism, *Bottom Line vs. Top Story: The Synergy Report* (San Francisco: IAJ, October 1997), pp. 1–13.

22. Ben Bagdikian, *The Media Monopoly* (Boston: Beacon Press, 5th edition, 1997), p. 16.

23. Bagdikian, *The Media Monopoly*, p. 94.

24. Winter, *Democracy's Oxygen*, p. 108.

25. See Collins, *Dictating Content*, p. 4.

26. C. Edwin Baker, *Advertising and a Democratic Press* (Princeton, NJ: Princeton University Press, 1994), p. 44.

27. Ben Parfitt, *The Georgia Straight* (May 21–28, 1998), p. 23–24.

28. Gutstein et al., *Question the Sun!*, p. 68.

29. See Canadian Press, "Leaky Condos major BC Consumer Issue," (28 April, 1996).

30. *Vancouver Sun* (2 April, 1996), p. D1.

31. *Vancouver Sun* (21 June 1996), p. D6.

Chapter Sixteen

The Women's Television Network: By, For, and About Women. . . or Was that Ratings?

Shirley Anne Off

The Women's Television Network (WTN),[1] Canada's first specialty cable channel for women, initially proposed that it would be "a broadcast service *for women, by women, about women and their worlds*"[2] (emphasis in original). Even though WTN claimed that it would "change the broadcasting system overnight,"[3] by the second season of broadcasting, the conventions, demands, and limitations of the commercial popular television industry were apparent. This discussion of WTN considers two "moments" in the channel's history: the CRTC (Canadian Radio-television and Telecommunications Commission) application and licensing stage (1993–94) and the first two seasons of broadcasting (January to August 1995 and September to April 1996).[4]

WTN began broadcasting on Canadian airwaves on 1 January 1995 as one of ten new specialty cable channels licensed by the CRTC. WTN's arrival on the Canadian broadcasting scene came on the heels of 15 years of debate over the media's sex-role stereotyping of women and after the establishment of a new equity clause in the 1991 Broadcasting Act.[5] Thus, WTN emerged after three national women's organizations called for the establishment of a women's channel and after 50 years of commercial television cultivating and cashing in on female viewers.[6]

By proposing to be a channel that would address concerns over the sex-role stereotyping of women and that would rely on advertising and cable-fee revenues, WTN embraced two contradictory mandates. One mandate was political—to respond to the argument put forth by feminist organizations and scholars that women are objectified and stereotyped by the popular media. The other was commercial—to establish a privately owned, profit-oriented cable television channel squarely targeted at the female audience, an audience that, in turn, would be sold to advertisers.[7] In reality, by the end of the second season WTN was clearly privileging conservative women's programming over innovative programming and prioritizing the commercial imperatives of the business over the social benefits described to the CRTC in the application.

WTN's desire to attract female viewers, in and of itself, is not remarkable. Since the dawn of television in the 1940s, women have been considered and have proved to be a lucrative audience. As Spigel and Mann write, "Television has always had its eye on women."[8] The commercial television industry has primarily seen women in terms of their roles as primary caregivers and consumers of household products and therefore as an appealing target audience for advertisers. Television has actively sought to categorize viewers as masculine and feminine subjects—otherwise known as the gendering of the audience. Techniques aimed at gendering the audience include gender-specific scheduling practices (i.e., daytime lineup for women) and programming genres (sports, news, and police drama for male viewers; soap operas, family dramas, and domestic advice shows for female viewers). What is new about WTN is that, for the first time in Canada, an entire channel with an entire programming schedule—rather than specific programs or blocks of programs—is squarely aimed at female viewers.

Situating WTN

How do we situate WTN in light of feminist television theory and in relation to previous experiments with alternative women's television? First, popular television has always been interested in women and has often been at odds about how to represent women. On the one hand, it reproduces many of the dominant and sexist attitudes in society, rarely taking chances to challenge or disrupt these representations. On the other hand, television seeks to keep the female audience interested by incorporating new and sometimes progressive images of women. The 1980s police drama *Cagney and Lacey* is one example of an attempt by popular television to incorporate progressive images of women into a traditional masculine television genre: the police drama.[9] For the most part, this change in attitude towards the portrayal of women in the media began in the 1960s with the rise of second-wave feminism. Since that time, feminist media scholars and producers have made explicit efforts to challenge the sex-role stereotyping of women and demand that women author their own images. Because of its mass popular appeal, television has been viewed as a critical site of intervention—a place where programming, designed to serve the interests of women, could be defined, created, and viewed by women.

Secondly, a number of experienced feminist television producers and respected scholars[10] consider television to be an "impenetrable citadel"[11]—one that poses too many limitations and negative consequences for women. One argument is that television involves too many institutional conventions and controls that subsequently limit women's ability to "negotiate for themselves alternative visions, definitions, ways of being."[12] Another states that the broadcasting industry is "too dependent on large audiences to generate enormous amounts of advertising revenue ... [too] bureaucratized and dependent on complex technology ... [limiting] the possibilities of a feminist television channel or station."[13] Yet another argues that the industry's reliance on ratings for proof of a program's success discourages innovative programming.[14] In fact, past case studies have shown that television series made by all-women production teams that attempt to escape generic conventions have been "allowed to fail and ... stored away ... as 'interesting experiments.'"[15] Despite these criticisms, television still attracts large audiences of women to its programming and the industry continues to devise strategies to cultivate this lucrative audience.

Thirdly, the rise of the cable television industry has prompted both optimistic and pessimistic theories on its potential to challenge conventional television practices. Some argue that cable television will result in better programming because of the increased competition for programming from independent producers.[16] Others suggest that cable television has the capacity to push the "boundaries of representation,"[17] while others believe that the cable industry is merely " 'a franchise' to make even more money" and acts as a "conduit for recycled [and inexpensive] entertainment programming."[18]

In Canada, the new cable industry also provides the CRTC with the opportunity to respond to the requirements of the 1991 Broadcasting Act's equity clause concerning equal opportunities for women, minority groups, and aboriginal peoples. In the application, WTN clearly declared that it would honour and meet these new requirements by providing jobs for women in the industry and that it would also address sex-role stereotyping of women.

WTN: The CRTC Application

In WTN's application for a broadcasting licence, it challenged the traditional methods of attracting the women's viewing audience in two ways. First, WTN was to be a channel that was by, for, and about women. WTN proposed that it would meet this goal by ensuring that the network's top executives would be women and that they would make the decisions about what went on the air, that programming would be created by and feature stories about women, that the issues dealt with would be of interest to women, and that women would be the primary target audience. The channel's supporting research argued that "female creative control would better serve women's communication needs at this time; and that a woman's television channel would better address equity issues than existing broadcasters."[19]

Secondly, the channel proposed a programming schedule unlike any other. WTN argued that the existing television choices did not meet the needs of women and that women's information programming was relegated to the daytime schedule and was not available to women who work outside the home. Unlike conventional network broadcasters, WTN proposed a programming schedule that would feature women's informational programming not only during the conventional daytime lineup, but during prime time. In addition, the entertainment programming aired during prime time (and throughout the schedule) would challenge sex-role stereotyping, would feature strong lead female characters, would not portray gratuitous violence, would ensure that dramatic violence was viewed within a context of social reality, and would focus on issues of importance to women.

WTN argued that it would establish a unique spot on the television spectrum where Canadian women could see positive images of themselves, could gain access to important and relevant information not otherwise found on television, and could view original programming designed especially with women's unique television and communication needs in mind.[20] WTN argued that its programming would "add important and wider social benefits to the broadcasting system."[21] Based on the application made to the CRTC, WTN was granted a licence to begin broadcasting Canada's first cable service for women, by women, and about women and their worlds.

Adjusting the Image—WTN's First Two Seasons of Broadcasting

The next "moment" in WTN's development occurred over the first two seasons of broadcasting, which took place from January to August 1995 and September 1995 to April 1996. It didn't help that the channel was racked with problems in the period leading up to the launch of the channel, including a consumer backlash against the cable companies, increased competition from specialty services, and hostile media commentators. The effects on the original vision for the channel were multifold. On one level, spokespeople for WTN distanced themselves from anything controversial, stating that the channel was "neither radically feminist nor powder-puff fluff. It's simply market-driven."[22] Linda Rankin, the channel's first president, was careful to explain that WTN's vision was not informed by "radicals" and added that "in our travels across the country there was overwhelming support for making something different happen. They were not from wild-eyed radicals. They were just from plain ordinary women like me."[23] However, prior to submitting its application to the CRTC, WTN had solicited letters of support from the feminist community and relied heavily on feminist media research to support the argument that women had unique communication and television needs that were not being met. The later distancing of WTN from "anything feminist" revealed the channel's about-face when confronted with the demands, limitations, and constraints of the television industry, its advertisers, and its critics.

This new public relations strategy was coupled with a name change. Rather than continuing to use the name "The Women's Television Network," the channel became known as "WTN." Jacqueline Cook, vice-president of marketing, stated that the name strategy would ensure that the channel's on-air name did not explicitly refer to women. This way WTN could be "soft and inclusive and subtle and not in your face."[24] She also added that the new programming strategy now focused on being *by, for, or about women, rather than the original by, for, and about women*. According to Cook, the application had just been a concept—the originators of the channel had been too idealistic about what they could accomplish.

Rather than continuing to invest time and money in originally produced independent programming by women, as originally proposed, by the end of the first three months of broadcasting the network had allowed the programming schedule to be dominated by foreign acquisitions of reruns and by recycled programming from other sources. These shows included *The Mary Tyler Moore Show* and *Rhoda* (1970s) and *Kate and Allie* and *Cagney and Lacey* (1980s). *The Mary Tyler Moore Show,* for example, had the highest repeat pattern on the schedule, appearing 14 times a week.

By the beginning of the second season, WTN had entrenched its new programming strategy, emphasizing prime-time entertainment over informational programming. Informational programming was relegated to the less-watched late-night, daytime, or weekend schedules, and in its place was more 1970s and 1980s recycled entertainment programming. The lineup and publicity materials featured more situation comedies, dramatic series, made-for-TV movies and classic films. Gone was the emphasis on documentaries, foreign or independent films, and unique women's informational programming. While images of women still dominated the screen—as leading ladies and spokespeople—gone were many of the female producers, directors, and artists who were highlighted in the application and during the first few months of broadcasting.

The primary strategy of the new season's programming was to create a prime-time lineup with broad audience appeal. Despite stating in its application that it would not "jeopardize the mission, vision and values of the service"[25] for the sake of advertisers, WTN was now programming "television that was attractive to a large group of viewers and not a group with a narrow focus."[26] What this meant, however, was that some (but not all) of the more innovative informational programming was cancelled and replaced by more familiar and conventional women's informational programming. This new lineup included domestic advice, beauty, and fashion programs along with reruns of syndicated talk shows. The commercial imperatives of the channel—to attract a broad audience with advertiser appeal—and the generic conventions of profit-oriented television were prioritized over the WTN's original intention to provide a unique Canadian broadcasting service. In essence, WTN was abandoning its vision of unique programming for women and was beginning to rely heavily on tried-and-true methods of attracting a women's television audience.

The application to the CRTC had emphasized innovative and risky programs—in some cases, television formats not traditionally aimed at a women's television audience. However, by the second season, WTN had clearly become reluctant to schedule anything too risky or controversial. There was a reliance on well-established generic conventions and existing television aesthetics, and a focus on ratings as the measure of a successful program. These practices, while essential to the commercial imperatives of the channel, can limit the possibilities of experimental or innovative programming for women. Although WTN had stated in its pre-launch publicity that women "watch more than day-time TV, [women are] more than cooking shows, gardening shows, fashion shows, talk shows and soap operas,"[27] the network began scheduling programming along these very lines. These changes did not go unnoticed by the popular press or the public. The *Ottawa Citizen* wrote that the addition of fashion, lifestyle, and home-decorating programs were "precisely the kinds of 'stereotypical' women's programming that WTN ... vowed would not be on the channel."[28]

WTN had devised a programming schedule for its second season that would satisfy advertisers and investors and would reap, it was hoped, higher revenues. Jacqueline Cook stated that the new programming "package" was designed to be more entertaining in order to attract a broader audience and to ease advertisers' concerns because "investors and advertisers attempt to avoid a thing called risk. And risk can be as simple as we don't know [what this is]. So, if you have a schedule of programming that no one knows, then it looks too risky."[29]

During the application stage, WTN presented itself as a privately owned commercial cable channel with a public service mandate, a mandate to create a unique and alternative viewing space for women on the Canadian television spectrum. It initially proposed to be by, for, and about women and their worlds. However, by the time the channel reached the air, this mandate had already shifted. Only a few of the original programming concepts designed to embody the vision and values of the channel made it to air. Most important, ratings had become the key factor in the decision whether a show should remain on the air. Jacqueline Cook stated, "We use ratings. Ratings are not just a yardstick for how attractive we are to advertisers but [are] also our most immediate and measurable yardstick for what viewers think of us and how many of them there are."[30] A show's value no longer lay in its social benefits, but rather in its ratings and appeal to advertisers. The audience being cultivated was not the diverse and unsatisfied female audience described to the CRTC, but rather the broad, large, affluent, and consumer-based female audience so important to advertisers.

The following statement by the vice-president of marketing illustrates that by the second season WTN's goal was no longer, as had been stated in the application, to "change the broadcasting system overnight": "Our goal is to ... build on what has become successful, continue to help refine ... what we mean by WTN. Have people refer to us as WTN. Make sure everybody feels they are welcome to watch."[31]

Whether or not the first three years of WTN's development demonstrate that television is an impenetrable citadel or a safe harbour, WTN certainly illustrates on a case-specific level that when a channel encounters the generic, fiscal, and production conventions of the commercial television industry, the industry's commercial imperatives become prioritized.

ENDNOTES

1. The corporate name of WTN is Lifestyle Television Limited. Throughout the application and hearing process before the Canadian Radio-television and Telecommunications Commission process (September 1993–July 1994), the channel was referred to as Lifestyle Television by the applicant, the CRTC, and the press. However, the on-air name of the channel became the Women's Television Network in September 1994 during the pre-launch publicity for the channel and was changed to WTN in October 1995.

2. Lifestyle Television, Application, Part 1, section 4.

3. Lifestyle Television, September 15, 1993, "Application by Linda Rankin on behalf of a company to be incorporated (Lifestyle Television Inc.) for a new national English language Canadian specialty service," Executive Summary (original document).

4. For a detailed discussion of these "moments" in WTN's history and development, please see Shirley Anne Off, "Defining the 'W' in WTN: A Feminist Case Study of the Women's Television Network (1993–1996)" (master's thesis, Carleton University, 1996).

5. The relevant section, Clause 3(d)(iii), of the 1991 Broadcasting Act reads: "It is hereby declared as the broadcasting policy for Canada that ... (d) the Canadian broadcasting system should ... (iii) *through its programming and the employment opportunities arising out of its operations*, serve the needs and interests, and reflect the circumstances and aspirations, of Canadian men, women, and children, including equal rights, the linguistic duality and multicultural and multiracial nature of Canadian society and the special place of aboriginal peoples within that society" (emphasis added).

6. In the two years prior to the licensing of WTN, the National Action Committee on the Status of Women, Toronto Women in Film and Television, and the Royal Commission on the Status of Women all called for the establishment of a women's television channel with the hope of improving professional opportunities for women in the industry and the representation of images of women on television.

7. At the time of the application, the controlling investor was Moffat Communications (holding 65 per cent of shares)—owners of CKY, the CTV-affiliate in

Winnipeg, and various other broadcast holdings. Other investors included Michael Ihnat and Ron Rhodes (10 and 12 per cent respectively), a group of women investors (8 per cent), and WTN's president and CEO (5 per cent).

8. Lynn Spigel and Denise Mann, eds., *Private Screenings: Television and the Female Consumer* (Minneapolis: University of Minnesota Press, 1992), vii.

9. Julie D'Acci, *Defining Women: The Case of* Cagney and Lacey. Chapel Hill: University of North Carolina Press, 1994.

10. These producers and scholars include Helen Baehr, A. Spindler Brown, Rosalind Coward, Gillian Dyer, Ella Taylor, and Linda Steiner.

11. Helen Baehr and Annette Spindler Brown, "Firing a Broadside: A Feminist Intervention into Mainstream TV," in *Boxed In: Women and Television,* ed. H. Baehr and G. Dyer (New York: Pandora, 1987), 117.

12. Linda Steiner, "The History and Structure of Women's Alternative Media," in *Women Making Meaning: New Feminist Directions in Communications,* ed. L. Rakow (New York: Ballantine Books, 1992), 121.

13. Ibid., 135.

14. Ella Taylor, *Prime-Time Families* (Los Angeles: University of California Press, 1989), 50.

15. Rosalind Coward, "Women's Programmes: Why Not?" in *Boxed In: Women and Television,* ed. H. Baehr and G. Dyer (New York: Pandora, 1987), 100.

16. M. Cantor and J. Cantor, *Prime-Time Television: Content and Control* (London: Sage, 1992), 61.

17. Julie D'Acci, *Defining Women,* 27.

18. Janet Wasko, *Hollywood in the Information Age* (Great Britain: University of Texas Press, 1994), 71, 112.

19. Lifestyle Television, Application, Appendix B: 4-41.

20. Lifestyle Television Application, Part 4.

21. Lifestyle Television, Application, Part 3:18.

22. Canadian Press, "President defends women's channel," *Calgary Herald,* 8 January 1995: A11.

23. Terry Weber, "The women's TV channel faces undeserved hostility," *Toronto Star,* 28 March 1995: E3.

24. Interview with Jacqueline Cook, vice-president of marketing, Lifestyle Television Ltd. (WTN), 16 February 1996.

25. Lifestyle Television, Application, Part 4:25.

26. Interview with Jacqueline Cook.

27. Barbara Barde, vice-president of programming, Lifestyle Television Ltd. (WTN), quoted in Suzanne Matczuk, "Women's Television Network: A Narrow-Cast Celebration," *Interchange,* January 1995: 6–7.

28. Tony Atherton, "Canadian cable channels TUNE UP to stay alive," *Ottawa Citizen,* 23 December 1995: H1.

29. Interview with Jacqueline Cook.

30. Ibid.

31. Ibid.

SECTION III

SECTION III

Chapter Seventeen

How to Read and Write Critically

What Is Critical Thinking?

Whenever you read a magazine article, newspaper editorial, or a piece of advertising and find yourself questioning the author's claims, you are exercising the basics of critical reading. You are looking beneath the surface of words and thinking about their meaning and significance. And, subconsciously, you are asking the authors some of the following questions:

- What did you mean by that?
- Can you back up that statement?
- How do you define that term?
- How did you draw that conclusion?
- Do all the experts agree?
- Is this evidence dated?
- What is your point?
- Why do I need to know this?
- Where did you get your data?

You are also making some internal statements:

- That isn't true.
- You are contradicting yourself.
- I see your point, but I don't agree because. . . .
- That's a poor choice of words.
- You are jumping to conclusions.
- Good point. I never thought of that.
- That was nicely stated.
- This is an extreme view.

Whether conscious or unconscious, such responses indicate that you are thinking critically about what you read. You are weighing claims, asking for definitions, evaluating information, looking for proof, questioning assumptions, and making judgments. In short, you are processing another person's words, rather than just accepting them at face value.

Why Read Critically?

When you read critically, you think critically. Instead of blindly accepting what is written on a page, you begin to separate yourself from the text and decide for yourself what is or is not important, logical, or right. And you do so because you bring to your reading your own perspective, experience, education, and personal values, as well as your powers of comprehension and analysis.

Critical reading is an active process of discovery. You discover an author's view on a subject, you enter into a dialogue with the author, you discover the strengths and weaknesses of the author's thesis or argument, and you decide if you agree or disagree with the author's views. The result is that you have a better understanding of the issue and the author. By questioning and analyzing what the author says with respect to other experiences or views of the issue—including your own—you actively enter into a dialogue or a debate and seek the truth on your own.

In reality, we understand truth and meaning through interplay. Experience teaches us that knowledge and truth are not static entities but the by-products of struggle and dialogue—of asking tough questions. We witness this phenomenon all the time, recreated in the media through dialogue and conflict. And we recognize it as a force of social change. Consider, for example, how, since the 1950s, our culture has changed its attitudes concerning race, and its concepts of success, kinship, social groups, and class. Perhaps the most obvious example regards gender: Were it not for the fact that rigid old conventions have been questioned, most women would still be bound to the laundry and the kitchen stove.

The point is that critical reading is an active and reactive process that sharpens your focus on a subject and your ability to absorb information and ideas and at the same time encourages you to question accepted norms, views, and myths. And that is both healthy and laudable, for it is the basis of social evolution.

Critical reading also helps you become a better writer, because critical reading is the first step to critical writing. Good writers look at one another's writing the way architects look at a house: They study the fine details and how those details connect and create the whole. Likewise, they consider the particular slants and strategies of appeal. Good writers always have a clear sense of their audience—their reader's racial makeup, gender, and educational background; their political and/or religious persuasions; their values, prejudices, and assumptions about life; and so forth. Knowing your audience helps you to determine nearly every aspect of the writing process: the kind of language to use, the writing style (casual or formal, humorous or serious, technical or philosophical), the particular slant to take (appealing to the reader's reason, emotions, or ethics, or a combination of these), what emphasis to give the essay, the type of evidence to offer, and the kinds of authorities to cite.

The better you become at analyzing and reacting to another's written work, the better you will analyze and react to your own. You will ask yourself questions such as the following: Is it logical? Do my points come across clearly? Are my examples solid enough? Is this the best wording? Is my conclusion persuasive? Do I have a clear sense of my audience? What strategy did I take—an appeal to logic, emotions, or ethics? In short, critical reading will help you to evaluate your own writing, thereby making you both a better reader and a better writer. Although you may already employ many strategies of critical reading, the following text presents some techniques to make you an even better critical reader.

How to Read Critically

To help you improve your critical reading, use these six proven basic steps:

- Keep a journal on what you read.
- Annotate what you read.
- Outline what you read.
- Summarize what you read.
- Question what you read.
- Analyze what you read.

To demonstrate just how these techniques work, we will apply each of them to a sample essay: "Now Cut That Out!" by John Leo, appearing in the June 30, 2003, issue of *U.S. News and World Report*. This piece works well because, like all of the pieces in this book, it addresses a contemporary issue and presents opportunities for debate.

Sample Essay for Analysis

NOW CUT THAT OUT!

JOHN LEO

Which of the following stories would be too biased for schools to allow on tests? (1) Overcoming daunting obstacles, a blind man climbs Mount McKinley; (2) Dinosaurs roam the Earth in prehistoric times; (3) An Asian-American girl, whose mother is a professor, plays checkers with her grandfather and brings him pizza.

As you probably guessed, all three stories are deeply biased. (1) Emphasis on a "daunting" climb implies that blindness is some sort of disability, when it should be viewed as just another personal attribute, like hair color. Besides, mountain-climbing stories are examples of "regional bias," unfair to readers who live in deserts, cities, and rural areas. (2) Dinosaurs are a no-no—they imply acceptance of evolutionary theory. (3) Making the girl's mother a professor perpetuates the "model minority" myth that stereotypes Asian-Americans. Older people must not be shown playing checkers. They should be up on the roof fixing shingles or doing something vigorous. And pizza is a junk food. Kids may eat it—but not in a school story.

That's what's going on in schools these days. Diane Ravitch's new book, *The Language Police*, documents "an intricate set of rules" applied to test questions as well as textbooks. A historian of education who served as an assistant secretary of education for the first President Bush, Ravitch offers many eye-catching cases of subjects vetoed: peanuts as a good snack (some children are allergic), owls (taboo in Navajo culture), and the palaces of ancient Egypt (elitist).

Back in the 1980s and 1990s, lots of us chuckled at the spread of the "sensitivity" industry in schools. Words were removed from tests and books lest they hurt someone's feelings, harm the classroom effort, or impair morals. Most of us assumed that this was a fad that would soon disappear as grown-ups in education exerted the rule of reason.

But ridicule had little effect, and grown-ups either converted to the sensitivity ethic or looked the other way. Textbook publishers, with millions of dollars at stake, learned to insulate themselves from criticism by caving in to all objections and writing craven "guidelines" to make sure authors would cave, too.

No, no, no! Ravitch warns that these guidelines amount to a full-blown form of "censorship at the source" in schools and "something important and dangerous" that few people know about. She blames both the religious right and the multicultural-feminist left. The right objects to evolution, magic and witchcraft, gambling, nudity, suicide, drug use, and stories about disobedient children. The left objects to "sexist" fairy tales, Huckleberry Finn, religion, smoking, junk food, guns and knives, and what some guidelines call "activities stereotyping" (blacks as athletes, men playing sports or working with tools, women cooking or caring for children).

What started out as a sensible suggestion—don't always show women as home-makers or minorities in low-level jobs—developed into hard reverse stereotypes (women must not be shown in the home, maids can't be black). "In the ideal world of education-think," Ravitch writes, "women would be breadwinners, African-Americans would be academics, Asian-Americans would be athletes and no one would be a wife or a mother."

Whites are a group, perhaps the only group, not protected by smothering sensitivity. This follows multicultural dogma. One set of guidelines (McGraw-Hill) "express[es] barely concealed rage against people of European ancestry" as "uniquely responsible for bigotry and exploitation," Ravitch notes.

What can be done? Ravitch recommends eliminating the current system in which 22 states adopt textbooks for all their schools. She says it results in cartel-like behavior that allows extremists to manipulate textbook requirements, particularly in the two big states that matter most—California and Texas. Opening up the market, she thinks, would free teachers to choose biographies, histories, or anthologies, rather than sensitivity-laden textbooks.

Panels that analyze tests and texts should include teachers of the subjects, not just diversity specialists, Ravitch says. She insists we need better-educated teachers and an end to secrecy about sensitivity: State education officials must put bias and sensitivity reviews on the Internet, listing the reasons that passages and test items were rejected.

Unsurprisingly, *The Language Police* has gotten the cold shoulder from our education establishment, which usually limits discussion to three topics: promoting diversity, reducing classroom size, and increasing funding. Ravitch speaks for parents more concerned about something else: substituting censorship and propaganda for actual learning.

KEEP A JOURNAL ON WHAT YOU READ

Unlike writing an essay or a paper, journal writing is a personal exploration in which you develop your own ideas without set rules. It is a process of recording impressions and exploring feelings and ideas. Journal writing is a freewriting exercise in which you express yourself without restrictions and without judgment. You do not have to worry about breaking any rules—because in a journal, anything goes.

Reserve a special notebook just for your journal—not one you use for class notes or homework. Also, date your entries and include the titles of the articles to which you are responding. Eventually, by the end of the semester, you should have a substantial number of pages to review, enabling you to see how your ideas and writing style have developed over time.

What do you include in your journal? Although it may serve as a means to understanding an essay, you are not required to write only about the essay itself. Perhaps the article reminds you of a personal experience. Maybe it triggered an opinion you did not know you had. Or perhaps you wish to explore a particular phrase or idea presented by the author.

Some students may find keeping a journal difficult because it is so personal. They may feel as if they are exposing their feelings too much. Or they may feel uncomfortable thinking that someone else—a teacher or another student—may read their writing. Such apprehensions should not prevent you from exploring your impressions and feelings. If you must turn in your journal to your teacher, do not include anything you do not want others to read. Consider keeping a more private journal for your own benefit.

Reprinted below is one student's journal entry on our sample essay:

> John Leo's essay on Diane Ravitch's book helps support his personal opinion that "language police" are controlling the content of texts and tests in American schools and hurting students. Apparently, Ravitch feels that multicultural-feminists AND the religious right have distorted what material is presented in the classroom. The feminists and the religious right are demanding that the language used in textbooks and tests be "sensitive" and "unbiased."
>
> Ravitch and Leo seem to think that the revisions made in the '80s and '90s have gone too far. At first, it seems as if Leo agrees that the original desire to be sensitive was a good idea, but he then agrees with Ravitch's opinion that the panels that decide what language to use on standardized tests have a cartel-like hold on our educational system. Leo often quotes Ravitch, and it is clear that he agrees with her. His fourth paragraph particularly reveals his position.
>
> I think that both Ravitch and Leo are missing a very important point. Language can hurt. And it can influence how we think. They don't seem to acknowledge this. Maybe they have never experienced biased writing? I know from personal experience that it can affect students. I even remember stopping to think about how a question seemed biased on the SAT. I probably didn't need to waste my time thinking about that.
>
> If language policing has gone to an extreme, like Leo says, there must be a happy middle, right?

ANNOTATE WHAT YOU READ

It's a good idea to underline (or highlight) key passages and make marginal notes when reading an essay. (If you do not own the publication in which the essay appears, or choose not to mark it up, make a photocopy of the piece and annotate that.) You should annotate on the second or third reading, once you have an understanding of the essay's general ideas.

There are no specific guidelines for annotation. Use whatever technique suits you best, but keep in mind that in annotating a piece of writing, you are engaging in a dialogue with the author. As in any meaningful dialogue, you hear things you may not have known—things that may be interesting and exciting to you, things with which you may agree or disagree, or things that give you cause to ponder. The other side of the dialogue, of course, is your response. In annotating a piece of writing, that response takes the form of underlining (or highlighting) key passages and jotting down comments in the margin. Such comments can take the form of full sentences or some shorthand codes. Sometimes "Why?" or "True" or "NO!" will be enough to help you respond to a writer's position or claim. If you come across a word or reference that is unfamiliar to you, underline or circle it. Once you have located the main thesis statement or claim, highlight or underline it and jot down "CLAIM" or "THESIS" in the margin.

On the following page is the Leo essay reproduced in its entirety with sample annotations.

Now Cut That Out!

JOHN LEO

Which of the following stories would be too biased for schools to allow on tests? (1) Overcoming daunting obstacles, a blind man climbs Mount McKinley; (2) dinosaurs roam the Earth in prehistoric times; (3) an Asian-American girl, whose mother is a professor, plays checkers with her grandfather and brings him pizza.

> *Are these examples from a real test, or did Leo make them up?*

As you probably guessed, all three stories are deeply biased. (1) Emphasis on a "daunting" climb implies that blindness is some sort of disability, when it should be viewed as just another personal attribute, like hair color. Besides, mountain-climbing stories are examples of "regional bias," unfair to readers who live in deserts, cities, and rural areas. (2) Dinosaurs are a no-no—they imply acceptance of evolutionary theory. (3) Making the girl's mother a professor perpetuates the "model minority" myth that stereotypes Asian-Americans. Older people must not be shown playing checkers. They should be up on the roof fixing shingles or doing something vigorous. And pizza is a junk food. Kids may eat it—but not in a school story.

> *Oh, come on!*

> *Loose interpretation of evolutionary theory. Isn't evolutionary theory related to human's connection to apes? Look up this issue.*

That's what's going on in schools these days. Diane Ravitch's new book, *The Language Police*, documents "an intricate set of rules" applied to test questions as well as textbooks. A historian of education who served as an assistant secretary of education for the first President Bush, Ravitch offers many eye-catching cases of subjects vetoed: peanuts as a good snack (some children are allergic), owls (taboo in Navajo culture), and the palaces of ancient Egypt (elitist).

> *Check out this book in university library.*

> *Whose rules?*

> *Who "vetoed"?*

Back in the 1980s and 1990s, lots of us chuckled at the spread of the "sensitivity" industry in schools. Words were removed from tests and books lest they hurt someone's feelings, harm the classroom effort, or impair morals. Most of us assumed that this was a fad that would

> *Why is this word in quotes?*

> *Well, many words did hurt—especially ones that were racist or sexist.*

soon disappear as grown-ups in education exerted the rule of reason.

But ridicule had little effect, and grown-ups either converted to the sensitivity ethic or looked the other way. Textbook publishers, with millions of dollars at stake, learned to insulate themselves from criticism by caving in to all objections and writing craven "guidelines" to make sure authors would cave, too.

No, no, no! Ravitch warns that these guidelines amount to a full-blown form of "censorship at the source" in schools and "something important and dangerous" that few people know about. She blames both the religious right and the multicultural-feminist left. The right objects to evolution, magic and witchcraft, gambling, nudity, suicide, drug use, and stories about disobedient children. The left objects to "sexist" fairy tales, Huckleberry Finn, religion, smoking, junk food, guns and knives, and what some guidelines call "activities stereotyping" (blacks as athletes, men playing sports or working with tools, women cooking or caring for children).

What started out as a sensible suggestion—don't always show women as homemakers or minorities in low-level jobs—developed into hard reverse stereotypes (women must not be shown in the home, maids can't be black). "In the ideal world of education-think," Ravitch writes, "women would be breadwinners, African-Americans would be academics, Asian-Americans would be athletes and no one would be a wife or a mother."

Whites are a group, perhaps the only group, not protected by smothering sensitivity. This follows multicultural dogma. One set of guidelines (McGraw-Hill) "express[es] barely concealed rage against people of European ancestry" as "uniquely responsible for bigotry and exploitation," Ravitch notes.

What can be done? Ravitch recommends eliminating the current system in which 22 states adopt textbooks for all their schools. She says it results in cartel-like behavior that allows extremists to manipulate textbook requirements, particularly in the two big states that matter most—California and Texas. Opening up the market, she

[Margin annotations:]

This is a sweeping generalization as to motivation of teachers and publishers.

look up

Check source for context.

look up

Says who?

So author approves that changes were made?

What about white women?

What exactly is "multicultural dogma"?

Ravitch's interpretation of the guideline's tone?

She wants to overhaul the way 22 states choose their textbooks. Doesn't that go against what seems to be an approved consensus? What about the other 28 states that don't use such guidelines?

thinks, would free teachers to choose biographies, histo- ries, or anthologies, rather than sensitivity-laden text- books.

examples?

Panels that analyze tests and texts should include teachers of the subjects, not just diversity specialists, Ravitch says. She insists we need better-educated teach- ers and an end to secrecy about sensitivity: State educa- tion officials must put bias and sensitivity reviews on the Internet, listing the reasons that passages and test items were rejected.

They should be! They aren't now? Is this really true?

This is another issue entirely.

Unsurprisingly, *The Language Police* has gotten the cold shoulder from our education establishment, which usually limits discussion to three topics: promoting di- versity, reducing classroom size, and increasing funding. Ravitch speaks for parents more concerned about some- thing else: substituting censorship and propaganda for actual learning.

Censorship, maybe. But is Leo concerned that presenting blacks as academics or women Asians as athletes is actually propaganda?

OUTLINE WHAT YOU READ

Briefly outlining an essay is a good way to see how writers structure their ideas. When you physically diagram the thesis statement, claims, and supporting evidence, you can better assess the quality of the writing and decide how convincing it is. You may already be familiar with detailed, formal essay outlines in which structure is bro- ken down into main ideas and subsections. However, for our purposes, a brief and concise breakdown of an essay's components will suffice. This is done by simply jot- ting down a one-sentence summary of each paragraph. Sometimes brief paragraphs elaborating the same point can be lumped together:

- Point 1
- Point 2
- Point 3
- Point 4
- Point 5
- Point 6, etc.

Such outlines may seem rather primitive, but they demonstrate how the various parts of an essay are connected—that is, the organization and sequence of ideas.

Below is a sentence outline of "Now Cut That Out." It identifies the point(s) of each paragraph in an unbiased way. The purpose of summarizing is to better under- stand the author's point and how this point is constructed.

POINT 1: The author provides three examples of stories that would not appear on a standardized test because they may use insensitive or biased language.

POINT 2: Diane Ravitch has written a book titled The Language Police, in which she discusses the language used in school textbooks and tests.

POINT 3: The author notes that some people may have viewed the language "sensi- tivity" movement in schools during the 1980s and 1990s as a passing "fad." He states that instead of passing, the movement became entrenched in schools, and publishers followed suit in order to please their buyers.

POINT 4: Ravitch feels that the guidelines developed to encourage language sensitivity in textbooks and tests is a form of censorship. She claims that people who hold extreme viewpoints are controlling the content of school materials.

POINT 5: The author concedes that language sensitivity was based on a good idea, but that it has reached extremes.

POINT 6: Ravitch advocates eliminating the current system used by 22 states to adopt textbooks in order to loosen the "cartel-like" hold extremists have on the educational system.

POINT 7: Ravitch also supports the idea that textbook selection panels include teachers who use the adopted texts and test, and that the panel should publicly explain its reasons for using certain questions on tests while rejecting others.

POINT 8: The author concludes that Ravitch's observation "speaks for parents," while the education establishment focuses on other issues, including diversity, class size, and educational funding.

At this point, you should have a fairly solid grasp of the points expressed in the essay, and the author's position on the issue. This exercise prepares you to critically evaluate the essay.

SUMMARIZE WHAT YOU READ

Summarizing is perhaps the most important technique to develop for understanding and evaluating what you read. This means reducing the essay to its main points. In your journal or notebook try to write a brief (about 100 words) synopsis of the reading in your own words. Note the claim or thesis of the discussion (or argument) and the chief supporting points. It is important to write these points down (rather than passively highlighting them with a pen or pencil), because the act of jotting down a summary helps you absorb the argument.

Now let us return to the sample essay. In the following paragraph we offer a summary of Leo's essay, mindful of using our own words rather than those of the author to avoid plagiarism. Again, you should approach this aspect of critical reading impartially—summary is not your opinion, that will come later. At times, it may be impossible to avoid using the author's own words in a summary; but if you do, remember to use quotation marks.

> In this essay, John Leo discusses a book by Diane Ravitch, The Language Police, in which she asserts that language sensitivity in textbooks and tests is controlled by extreme groups such as the "religious right" and the "multicultural-feminist left." These groups have, in turn, influenced the language publishers use in order to better appeal to the panels that select the textbooks. Leo and Ravitch are in agreement that this control is a form of censorship and must stop. Panels that choose textbooks and test questions should include teachers and should also explain the reasons behind language choices.

Although this paragraph seems to do a fairly good job of summarizing Leo's essay, it took us a few tries to get it down to under 100 words. So, do not be too discouraged when trying to summarize a reading on your own.

QUESTION WHAT YOU READ

Although we break down critical reading into discrete steps, these steps will naturally overlap in the actual process of reading and writing critically. In reading this essay you were simultaneously summarizing and evaluating Leo's points, perhaps adding your own ideas or even arguing with him. If something strikes you as particularly interesting or insightful, make a mental note of it. Likewise, if something strikes you the wrong way, argue back. For beginning writers, a good strategy is to convert that automatic mental response into actual note taking.

In your journal (or, as suggested below, in the margins of the text), question and challenge the writer. Jot down any points in the essay that do not measure up to your expectations or personal views. Note anything about which you are skeptical. Write down any questions you have about the claims, views, or evidence. If some point or conclusion seems forced or unfounded, record it and briefly explain why. The more skeptical and questioning you are, the better reader you are. Likewise, note what features of the essay impressed you—outstanding points, interesting wording, clever or amusing phrases or allusions, particular references, the general structure of the piece. Record what you learn from the reading and the aspects of the issue you would like to explore.

Of course, you may not feel qualified to pass judgment on an author's views, particularly if the author is a professional writer or expert on a particular subject. Sometimes the issue discussed might be too technical, or you may not feel informed enough to make critical evaluations. Sometimes a personal narrative may focus on experiences completely alien to you. Nonetheless, you are an intelligent person with the instincts to determine if the writing impresses you or if an argument is sound, logical, and convincing. What you can do in such instances—and another good habit to get into—is to think of other views on the issue. If you have read or heard of experiences different from those of the author, or arguments with the opposing views, jot them down. Similarly, if you agree with the author's view, highlight the parts of the essay with which you particularly identify.

Let us return to Leo's essay, which is, technically, an argument. Although it is theoretically possible to question or comment on every sentence in the piece, let us select a few key points that may have struck you, made you question, or made you want to respond. Refer to your point-by-point outline to assist you in this exercise.

PARAGRAPHS 1&2: While I understand Leo's point here with these examples, are they real examples from actual tests or ones Leo just made up to support his argument? If they are real, it would greatly support his position. However, these examples probably represent extreme illustrations of test questions. Furthermore, I wonder why certain adjectives are used at all. The stories could stand up on their own without the story being about a blind man, or an Asian American professor. Couldn't the story just be about a girl whose mother is a professor and who also plays a <u>game</u> with her grandfather? Why is omitting the adjectives so controversial anyway?

PARAGRAPH 3: Leo states that there is "an intricate set of rules" that Ravitch cites in her book. His essay would be strengthened if he cited these rules and their source. That way, we would have more hard evidence, rather than what seems to be opinion.

PARAGRAPH 4: In this paragraph, Leo states his own position on language sensitivity by admitting he is one of "us" who "chuckled" at the "sensitivity industry" in schools during the '80s and '90s. As such, he admits that he thought that the movement was frivolous (he calls it a "fad"). However, he seems to admit in paragraph 7 that it wasn't entirely a bad idea.

PARAGRAPH 6: Leo takes quotations from Ravitch's book to support his assertion that the language police are out of control. While it is good to quote sources, Ravitch herself seems questionable as a reliable source.

PARAGRAPHS 7 & 8: It seems as if Leo admits that at one time unbiased language was a good idea—"a sensible suggestion." And he may have a point if things have really swung to an extreme. But why is he so against the idea that blacks not be portrayed as maids, etc.? Who does it hurt? Maybe more importantly, who does it help? Leo's comment on whites being the only group not "protected" by the language police is revealing. Elsewhere in his essay, he comments on the "rule" that <u>women</u> cannot be shown in the home or as mothers. Well, what about women who are white? What Leo really meant to say here was "white males." Another point about paragraph 8 relates to the last sentence. Is this Ravitch's interpretation? Can she really interpret "barely concealed rage" in a set of guidelines prepared by a textbook company? Quoting this material would help the readers decide for themselves.

PARAGRAPHS 9 & 10: Leo relays Ravitch's suggestions for change, and he clearly endorses these changes. This helps his essay because it isn't just a long complaint; the essay actually advocates something. Whether these solutions are possible, or even necessary, is up to his reader.

PARAGRAPH 11: Most of Leo's concluding paragraph could be read in a neutral way. Educators aren't really reacting to Ravitch's book. Rather, they are responding to more pressing issues. Leo's final sentence might make the reader pause—while influencing language may seem like a form of censorship, does he really feel that depicting women as professionals, blacks as academics, and Asians as athletes are equal to propaganda?

ANALYZE WHAT YOU READ

To analyze something means breaking it down into its components, examining those components closely while evaluating their significance, and determining how they relate as a whole. In part, you already did this by briefly outlining the essay. However, there is more. Analyzing what you read involves interpreting and evaluating the points of a discussion or argument as well as its presentation—that is, its language and structure. Ultimately, analyzing an essay after establishing its key points will help you understand what may not be evident at first. A close examination of the author's words takes you beneath the surface and sharpens your understanding of the issues at hand.

Although there is no set procedure for analyzing a piece of prose, there are some specific questions you should raise when reading an essay, particularly one that is trying to sway you to its view.

- What kind of audience is the author addressing?
- What are the author's assumptions?
- What are the author's purpose and intentions?
- How well does the author accomplish those purposes?
- How convincing is the evidence presented? Is it sufficient and specific? Relevant? Reliable and not dated? Slanted?
- What types of sources were used—personal experience, outside authorities, factual references, or statistical data?
- Did the author address opposing views on the issue?
- Is the perspective of the author persuasive?

Using the essay by Leo once more, let us apply these questions to his article.

WHAT KIND OF AUDIENCE IS THE AUTHOR ADDRESSING?

Before the first word is written, a good writer considers his or her audience—that is, their age group, gender, ethnic and racial makeup, educational background, and socioeconomic status. Writers also take into account the values, prejudices, and assumptions of their readers, as well as their readers' political and religious persuasions. Some writers, including several in this book, write for a "target" audience—readers who share the same interests, opinions, and prejudices. Other authors write for a "general" audience. Although general audiences consist of very different people with diversified backgrounds, expectations, and standards, think of them as the people who read *Time, Newsweek,* and your local newspaper. You can assume general audiences are relatively well informed about what is going on in the country, that they have a good comprehension of language and a sense of humor, and that they are willing to listen to new ideas.

Because Leo's essay appeared in his column in *U.S. News and World Report,* he is clearly writing for a "general" audience—an audience with an average age of 35, possessing a high school education and some college, politically middle of the road, and comprised of a vast racial and ethnic makeup. A close look tells us more about Leo's audience:

1. The language level suggests at least a high school education.
2. The references to attitudes in the 1980s and the concerns of parents suggest an older audience—certainly at least 30 years old.
3. The references to politics, academic and political movements, and panel policies for textbook selection imply that the readers are culturally informed.
4. The slant of Leo's remarks assumes a more conservative view toward educational trends, perhaps one opposed to the "new" trend of multiculturalism.
5. The language level addresses an audience which will see the absurdity of the language situation, and which does not presumably belong to the groups criticized by Leo.

WHAT ARE THE AUTHOR'S ASSUMPTIONS?

Having a sense of the audience leads writers to certain assumptions. If a writer is addressing a general audience as is Leo, then he or she can assume certain levels of awareness about language and current events, certain values about education and morality, and certain nuances of an argument. After going through Leo's essay, the following conclusions might be drawn about the author:

1. Leo assumes that his readers have a basic understanding of the concept of political "right" and "left."
2. He assumes that his audience is as exasperated as he is that extreme groups are controlling the content of textbooks and test questions in public schools.
3. He assumes that his readers believe that the claims of these groups (the religious right and the multicultural-feminist left) are questionable.
4. He assumes that his readers have a basic understanding of multiculturalism, and suspect that these principles have gone too far.
5. He assumes his readers will agree that the issues the educational establishment are most concerned with—diversity, class size, and school funding—are not as important as stopping "censorship and propaganda" in schools.

WHAT ARE THE AUTHOR'S PURPOSE AND INTENTIONS?

A writer has a purpose in writing beyond wanting to show up in print. Sometimes it is simply the expression of how the writer feels about something; sometimes the intention is to convince others to see things in a different light; sometimes the purpose is to persuade readers to change their views or behavior. We might infer the following about Leo's intentions:

1. To alert people that extreme interest groups are controlling the content of textbooks and tests in American schools.
2. To urge people to demand changes in their schools and in the way books and material are selected, especially in the 22 states that currently use this system.
3. To raise public awareness that apathy toward this trend is detrimental to education and harmful to students.

4. To urge people to stop "turning a blind eye" to the "language police" and say "enough is enough."
5. To encourage people to demand reform from the education establishment to focus on issues that matter most.

HOW WELL DOES THE AUTHOR ACCOMPLISH THOSE PURPOSES?

Determining how well an author accomplishes such purposes may seem subjective, but in reality it comes down to how well the case is presented. Is the thesis clear? Is it organized and well-presented? Are the examples sharp and convincing? Is the author's conclusion a logical result of what came before? Returning to Leo's essay, let us apply these questions:

1. Leo keeps to the point for most of his essay, although he sometimes blurs his opinion with that of Diane Ravitch's.
2. He offers many examples of the situation, presents his view clearly, and cites Ravitch's book.
3. Because Leo focuses on a book expressing the opinions of one person, the examples he uses to express his point need more support, perhaps from the original sources Ravitch uses.
4. Leo's essay is well-constructed and entertaining. He holds his reader's attention through his strong writing style.

HOW CONVINCING IS THE EVIDENCE PRESENTED? IS IT SUFFICIENT AND SPECIFIC? RELEVANT? RELIABLE AND NOT DATED? SLANTED?

Convincing writing depends on convincing evidence—that is, sufficient and relevant facts along with proper interpretations of facts. Facts are pieces of information that can be verified—such as statistics, examples, personal experience, expert testimony, and historical details. Proper interpretations of such facts must be logical and supported by relevant data. For instance, it is a fact that SAT verbal scores went up in 2003, and that students from Massachusetts had the highest national scores. One reason might be that students are spending more time reading and less time watching TV than in the past. Or that Massachusetts has many colleges and universities available, prompting students to study harder for the test in that state. But without hard statistics documenting the viewing habits of a sample of students, such interpretations are shaky, the result of a writer jumping to conclusions.

Is the Evidence Sufficient and Specific? Writers routinely use evidence, but sometimes it may not be sufficient. Sometimes the conclusions reached have too little evidence to be justified. Sometimes writers make hasty generalizations based solely on personal experience as evidence. How much evidence is enough? It is hard to say, but the more specific the details, the more convincing the argument. Instead of generalizations, good writers cite figures, dates, and facts. Instead of paraphrasing information, they quote the experts verbatim.

Is the Evidence Relevant? Good writers select evidence based on how well it supports their thesis, not on how interesting, novel, or humorous it is. For instance, if you are claiming that Barry Bonds is the greatest living baseball player, you should not mention that he was born in California, had a father who played for the San Francisco Giants, or that his godfather is Willie Mays. Those are facts, and they are very interesting, but they have nothing to do with Bonds' athletic abilities. Irrelevant evidence distracts readers and weakens an argument.

Is the Evidence Reliable and Current? Evidence should not be so dated or vague that it fails to support your claim. For instance, it is not accurate to say that candidate Jones fails to support the American worker because 15 years ago she purchased a foreign car. Her current actions are more important. Readers expect the information writers provide to be current and to be specific enough to be verifiable. A writer supporting animal rights may cite cases of rabbits blinded in drug research, but such tests have been outlawed in the United States for many years. Another may point to medical research that appears to abuse human subjects, but not name the researchers, the place, or the year of such testing. Because readers may have no way of verifying the evidence, the claims become suspicious and will weaken your points.

Is the Evidence Slanted? Sometimes writers select evidence that supports their case and ignore evidence that does not. Often referred to as "stacking the deck," this practice is unfair and potentially self-defeating for a writer. Although some evidence presented may have merit, an argument will be dismissed if readers discover that evidence was slanted or suppressed. For example, suppose you heard a classmate state that he would never take a course with Professor Sanchez because she gives surprise quizzes, assigns 50 pages of reading a night, and does not grade on a curve. Even if these statements are true, that may not be the whole truth. You might discover that Professor Sanchez is a dynamic and talented teacher whose classes are stimulating. Withholding that information may make an argument suspect. A better strategy is to acknowledge counterevidence and to confront it—that is, to strive for a balanced presentation by raising views and evidence that may not be supportive of your own.

Let us take a look at the evidence in Leo's essay, applying some of the points we have just covered.

1. Leo quotes information from Ravitch's book without documenting her sources. This may make the reader wonder if the information is fact or opinion.
2. His use of quotes from Ravitch's book without verifying his own position may make it appear that he is hiding behind her words, rather than supporting his argument on his own.
3. He makes many assumptions about how the general public feels about the language sensitivity movement in schools.
4. Leo assumes that the reason the "fad" of language sensitivity didn't "go away" was because people looked the other way. He doesn't allow for alternative reasons, such as the possibility that people thought the idea was a good one.
5. His argument is emotional rather than logical. Likewise, his presentation of the facts is clearly one-sided.
6. He makes statements without qualifying them, such as "Ravitch speaks for parents more concerned about something else: substituting censorship and propaganda for actual learning." He does not prove that the language sensitivity movement has harmed education, or that parents are indeed concerned that it is hindering the learning process.

WHAT TYPES OF SOURCES WERE USED—PERSONAL EXPERIENCE, OUTSIDE AUTHORITIES, FACTUAL REFERENCES, OR STATISTICAL DATA?

Writers enlist four basic kinds of evidence to support their views or arguments: personal experience (theirs and others'), outside authorities, factual references and examples, and statistics. In your own writing, you should aim to use combinations of these.

Personal Testimony cannot be underestimated. Think of the books you have read or movies you have seen based on word-of-mouth recommendations. (Maybe you learned of the school you are attending through word of mouth!) Personal testimony—which provides eyewitness accounts not available to you or to other readers—is sometimes the most persuasive kind of evidence. Suppose you are writing about the rising abuse of alcohol on college campuses. In addition to statistics and hard facts, quoting the experience of a first-year student who nearly died one night from alcohol poisoning would add dramatic impact. Although personal observations are useful and valuable, writers must not draw hasty conclusions based only on such evidence. The fact that you and a few friends are in favor of replacing letter grades with a pass-fail system does not provide support for the claim that the student body at your school is in favor of the conversion.

Outside Authorities are people recognized as experts in a given field. Appealing to such authorities is a powerful tool in writing, particularly for writers wanting to persuade readers of their views. We hear it all the time: "Scientists have found. . . ." "Scholars inform us that. . . ." "According to his biographer, Abraham Lincoln. . . ." Although experts try to be objective and fair-minded, their testimony may be biased. You would not expect scientists working for tobacco companies to provide unbiased opinions on lung cancer. And remember to cite who the authorities behind the statements are. It is not enough to simply state "scientists conducted a study"; you must say *who* they were and *where* the study was conducted.

Factual References and examples do as much to inform as to persuade. If somebody wants to sell you something, they will pour on the details. Think of the television commercials that show a sports utility vehicle climbing rocky mountain roads as a narrator lists all its great standard features—four-wheel drive, alloy wheels, second-generation airbags, power brakes, cruise control, etc. Or cereal "infomercials" in which manufacturers explain that new Yummy-Os have 15 percent more fiber to help prevent cancer. Although readers may not have the expertise to determine which data are useful, they are often convinced by the sheer weight of the evidence—like courtroom juries judging a case.

Statistics impress people. Saying that 77 percent of your school's student body approves of women in military combat roles is much more persuasive than saying "a lot of people" do. Why? Because statistics have a no-nonsense authority. Batting averages, polling results, economic indicators, medical and FBI statistics, and demographic percentages are all reported in numbers. If accurate, they are persuasive, although they can be used to mislead. The claim that 139 people on campus protested the appearance of a certain controversial speaker may be accurate; however, it would be a distortion of the truth not to mention that another 1500 people attended the talk and gave the speaker a standing ovation. Likewise, the manufacturer who claims that its potato chips are fried in 100 percent cholesterol-free vegetable oil misleads the public, because vegetable oil doesn't contain cholesterol—which is found only in animal fats. That is known as the "bandwagon" use of statistics—appealing to what people want to hear.

Now let us briefly examine Leo's sources of evidence:

1. Leo draws much of his support from one source, Diane Ravitch. Although her qualifications as a former assistant secretary of education may elevate her authority, she still represents only one opinion. His argument might be stronger if he had quoted some of the groups that held "extreme" views.
2. He provides examples of biased stories deemed unacceptable for tests without explaining whether these are real examples, and who rejected them.

3. Leo's citing of Ravitch's examples of vetoed subjects (peanuts, owls, and palaces in Egypt) may support his point to his target audience; but some readers may agree that these subjects were indeed unacceptable.
4. His statement that "women must not be shown in the home, maids can't be black" fails to support his premise that this "control" of language is harmful to students. He also fails to show the other side of the issue, such as the idea that some students may be hurt by certain stereotypes.

DID THE AUTHOR ADDRESS OPPOSING VIEWS ON THE ISSUE?

Many of the essays in this book will in varying degrees try to persuade you to agree with the author's position. But, of course, any slant on a topic can have multiple points of view. In developing their ideas, good writers will anticipate different and opposing views. They will cite alternative opinions, maybe even evidence that does not support their own position. By treating alternative points of view fairly, writers strengthen their own position. Failing to present or admit other views could leave their perspective open to scrutiny, as well as claims of naïveté and ignorance. This is particularly damaging when discussing a controversial issue.

Let us see how Leo's essay addresses alternative points of view:

1. Leo does not introduce alternative points of view into his editorial. However, it is, after all, an editorial, and, thus, is based on his opinion as he can best support it.
2. Although it is an editorial, and therefore his own point of view, his discussion would have been made stronger if he had approached the issue more fairly. For example, if he had admitted the possibility that biased language can be harmful, or that some sensitivity is desirable, he may have reached a wider audience.

IS THE PERSPECTIVE OF THE AUTHOR PERSUASIVE?

Style and content make for persuasive writing. Important points are how well a paper is composed—the organization, the logic, the quality of thought, the presentation of evidence, the use of language, the tone of discussion—and the details and evidence.

Turning to Leo's essay, we might make the following observations:

1. On the surface, Leo presents his argument well. A closer reading, however, raises more questions about the author's presentation of the material. He bases his argument primarily on generalizations and personal opinion.
2. He appears to be "pushing buttons" rather than presenting a well-formed, logical argument. He taps into his assumption of his audience's common view that the influence of multicultural feminists and the religious right on language is ridiculous and should be curtailed.
3. He makes many statements without qualifying them, and presents his own assumptions about the opinions of parents and teachers rather than providing proof of these assumptions.

By now, you should have a fairly clear idea of how critical reading can help your comprehension of a work, and make you a better writer in the process. Make critical reading part of your daily life, not just something you do in the classroom or while studying. As you wait for the bus, look at some billboards and consider how they try to hook their audience. While watching TV, think about the techniques advertisers use to convince you to buy their products. And try to apply some of the elements of critical reading while perusing the articles and editorials in your favorite magazine or newspaper. The more you approach writing with a critical eye, the more natural it will become, and the better writer you will be.

What Is Critical Writing?

Critical writing is a systematic process. When following a recipe, you would not begin mixing ingredients together haphazardly. Instead, you would first gather your ingredients and equipment, and then combine the ingredients according to the recipe outlined. Similarly, in writing, you could not plan, write, edit, and proofread all at the same time. Rather, writing occurs one thoughtful step at a time.

Some writing assignments may require more steps than others. An in-class freewriting exercise may allow for only one or two steps—light planning and writing. An essay question on a midterm examination may permit enough time for only three steps—planning, writing, and proofreading. A simple plan for such an assignment need answer only two questions: "What am I going to say?" and "How am I going to develop my idea convincingly?" For example, you have to answer the following question: "Do you agree with Leo's assertion in 'Now Cut That Out!' that the 'language police' are controlling language in schools to the detriment of students?" You might decide to answer with the statement, "The words we use in textbooks and tests should reflect reality while also being sensitive to student's feelings." Or you could decide to answer, "Leo makes an interesting point in his essay that language sensitivity has gone too far. When textbooks no longer reflect reality because words are so controlled, education suffers." You would then develop your idea by comparing or contrasting your own experiences in school with the examples Leo gives in his essay, or presenting data or information that challenges or supports his argument.

A longer, out-of-class paper allows you to plan and organize your material, and to develop more than one draft. In this extended version of the writing process you will need to do the following to write a strong, critical paper:

- Develop your ideas into a focused thesis that is appropriate for your audience.
- Research pertinent sources.
- Organize your material and draft your paper.
- Proofread your paper thoroughly.

Those are the general steps that every writer goes through when writing a paper. In the following sections the use of these strategies will be discussed so that you can write most effectively.

DEVELOPING IDEAS

Even the most experienced writers sometimes have trouble getting started. Common problems you may encounter include focusing your ideas, knowing where to begin, having too much or too little to say, and determining your position on an issue. There are developmental strategies that can help promote the free expression of your ideas and make you more comfortable with writing.

Although your finished product should be a tightly focused and well-written essay, you can begin the writing process by being free and sloppy. This approach allows your ideas to develop and flow unblocked onto your paper. Writing techniques such as brainstorming, freewriting, and ballooning can all help you through the process of development. As with all writing strategies, you should try all of them at first, to discover which ones work best for you.

Brainstorming

The goal of brainstorming is to generate and focus ideas. Brainstorming can be a personal exercise or a group project. You begin with a blank sheet of paper (or a blackboard) and, without paying attention to spelling, order, or grammar, simply list ideas about the topic as they come to you. You should spend at least 10 minutes brainstorming, building on the ideas you write down. There are no "dumb" ideas in brainstorming—the smallest detail may turn into a great essay.

Let us assume, for example, that you decide to write a paper supporting Leo's assertion in "Now Cut That Out!" Brainstorming for a few minutes may provide something like this:

> language sensitivity may be getting out of hand when NO women are allowed to be depicted as mothers and NO blacks may be presented as athletes—it could imply that there is something wrong with these choices
>
> get a bunch of textbooks written after 1995 to see if such language bias is prevalent, get real examples
>
> read Ravitch's book—how does it connect to this essay? what sources does she cite?
>
> explore other multicultural issues
>
> get other people's opinions (especially parents of school-age kids) on this issue
>
> try and locate the textbook adoption system in place in the 22 states that Leo/Ravitch cite
>
> check out the McGraw-Hill guidelines (see Ravitch book?) Leo cites in paragraph 8

You may notice that this brainstorming example has little structure, no apparent order, and even spelling errors. Its purpose is to elicit all the ideas you have about a subject so you can read your ideas and identify an interesting topic to develop.

Freewriting

Freewriting, just as brainstorming, is a free expression of ideas. It helps you jump-start the writing process and get things flowing on paper. Freewriting is unencumbered by rules—you can write about your impressions, ideas, and reactions to the article or essay. You should devote about 10 minutes to freewriting, keeping in mind that the goal is to write about the topic as ideas occur to you. If you are writing on a particular topic or idea you may wish to note it at the top of your paper as a visual reminder of your focus. Structure, grammar, and spelling are not important—just focus on the free flow of ideas. And above all, do not stop writing—even if you feel that what you are writing is silly or irrelevant. Any one, or a combination of the ideas expressed in a freewrite can be developed into a thoughtful essay.

Here is an example of a freewriting exercise:

> In this essay Leo is presenting his opinion, and the opinion of Diane Ravitch. In my opinion, I think Leo could actually make a good point, if his information wasn't so skewed and his bias so apparent. I guess it doesn't help matters much that he is a white male, and so may be viewed as less likely to suffer from language insensitivity. In one place in his essay, he begins to admit that language sensitivity started out as a "sensible suggestion," but he never elaborates, and that could be where his essay could be most helped, because it is at this point he could balance out his viewpoint. For example, he could have admitted that presenting women as mothers, maybe at the expense of presenting men as caregivers, was insensitive to women and girls, as well as to men and boys. He could have advocated for balance—sometimes women could be shown as both. The same could hold

true for athletes and academics—when nationality has to be expressed at all. I sort of wonder about that—why do you need to say that someone is blind or that a girl's mother is Asian American and a professor at all? Just say a guy climbed a mountain or a girl's mother went to work (this actually allows the woman to be a mother AND a working woman . . .). I guess the other issue I wonder about is if this language policing is hurting anyone. Maybe it sort of upsets white guys like Leo, who are left out in the cold, but everyone else seems to be ok. I mean, it isn't as if there are no texts or tests anymore? Why all the fuss?

BALLOONING

There are many names for ballooning, including "mind mapping," "clustering," or "grouping." These techniques all provide a more graphic presentation of ideas, allowing writers to visualize ideas and connections stemming from these ideas. Ballooning is particularly effective if you already have a fairly clear idea about your topic and wish to develop it more fully.

Write your main topic in the center of a large sheet of paper or a blackboard and circle it. Using the circled idea as your focus, think of subtopics and place them in circles around the center circle, connecting them to each other with lines (see figure). Remember to keep the subtopics short. Continue doing this until you feel you have developed all the subtopics more fully. When you have finished this exercise, you should be able to visualize the connections between your main topic and its subpoints, and have a starting point for your essay.

NARROWING THE TOPIC

Although brainstorming, freewriting, and ballooning help list and develop general ideas, you still need to narrow one idea down to something more manageable. Narrowing a topic can be quite a challenge—you might like more than one idea, or you may be afraid of limiting yourself to only one concept. Nevertheless, you must identify one idea and focus on developing it into an essay. Choose an idea that will interest you and your audience. Remember that if you do not like the way one idea begins to develop, you can always go back and develop another one instead. Once you identify your topic, you are ready to develop the thesis statement for your essay.

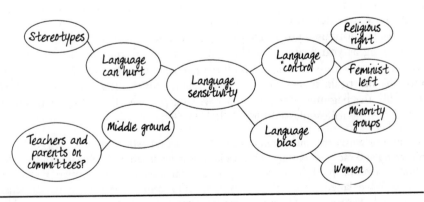

Ballooning

Based on the freewriting exercise described earlier—and additional idea development using ballooning techniques—we will follow a student who has decided to write his paper on the idea that language sensitivity is a good idea, and it helps more students than it harms. The idea stems from a response to Leo's essay, but it will develop into a thesis that uniquely belongs to the student.

IDENTIFYING YOUR AUDIENCE

Identifying your audience is one of the most important steps in organizing your essay. Knowing what your audience needs and expects from your essay will help you compose a convincing, effective paper. The following questions can help you identify the expectations of your audience:

- Who is my audience?
- What do they already know about my topic?
- What questions do they have about my topic?
- What do they need to know to understand my point?
- What is the best order to present the information they need to know?
- How do they feel about this topic?
- Why would they want to read my essay?

Based on these questions, our student determined that her audience would be her teacher and fellow expository writing classmates. All of them would be familiar with Leo's article and would have discussed it to some extent in class. As members of an academic institution, they should be familiar with the basics of multicultural theory, feminism, and politics, but may need some background on it. They may have different opinions on the issue, so supporting evidence (from both Leo's article and some outside research) would be necessary to effectively make her point. Because the essay would be about an issue directly concerning both teachers and students, it should generate some level of personal interest, and thus engage her readers.

DEVELOPING A THESIS

The **thesis** is a form of contract between the writer and reader. It makes a claim or declaration—telling your audience exactly what you are going to discuss. It should be stated in the opening paragraph, with the rest of the paper developing and supporting it.

As you write and develop your paper, your thesis should guide you as clearer and more precise thoughts evolve. Don't be constrained by your first thesis. If your paper is changing as you write, your thesis may change. Remember to go back and revise the thesis so that it matches the points made in your essay.

Although the thesis represents the last step in developing the topic for your essay, it is only the beginning of the actual writing process. For her paper, our student worked out the following sentence to help develop her thesis:

> The language sensitivity movement of the 1980s and 1990s grew out of a belief that stereotyping and racial or cultural bias could offend or negatively influence students' self-esteem. As a result, publishers and test panels began to carefully consider the language they used. While language sensitivity may sometimes seem extreme, it ultimately benefits students, and the society of which they will later become a part.

UNDERSTANDING YOUR PAPER'S OBJECTIVE

Before determining how to research or organize your paper, consider what you are trying to achieve by writing it. Your objective may be to inform, to describe, or to persuade. To define your purpose, you should first determine your objective, and then identify what you need to do to accomplish this objective. This helps you determine what you need to put into the body of your paper.

Writing to inform involves anticipating the questions your audience may have regarding the topic, and how much background your audience will need to understand it. Once you have developed a list of questions, you can determine what order will best present the information that will answer these questions.

Writing to describe also involves answering some questions. First, you must identify what is important or relevant about the topic you intend to describe. Then you should determine what information is vital to conveying this importance. List these elements and order them in a way that presents a clear view of the experience to the reader.

Writing to persuade presents a perspective on an issue and attempts to convince readers to agree with it. You must provide reasons and supporting evidence to persuade your audience that your perspective makes sense. Although you might not sway all readers to your point of view, you should make enough of a case to allow them to understand your argument, even if they might not agree with it.

The first step in persuasive writing is to determine your position and to identify the objections others might have to it. Remember that there are many different reasons readers may not agree with you. By identifying the arguments against your position, you are better able to address them and thus support your own argument in the process. Three primary kinds of arguments are used in persuasive writing:

- *Arguments based on disputed facts or consequences,* such as the claim that the building of a gambling casino generated revenue for a bankrupt town, created jobs, and improved the quality of life there.
- *Arguments that advocate change,* such as arguing for a lower drinking age or changing the ways the penal system punishes juvenile offenders.
- *Arguments based on evaluative personal claims,* as right or wrong, ethical or immoral, or favoring one thing or idea over another—such as arguing that physician-assisted suicide is wrong or that supermodels contribute to the development of anorexia nervosa in young women.

The key to effective persuasive writing is to support your perspective with statistics, factual data, and examples. Although your opinions drive the essay, your supporting evidence is what convinces your audience of the validity of your main point.

RESEARCHING

Research can involve a few, or many, steps, depending on the type and length of the paper you are writing. In many cases, simply reviewing the article and applying the steps of critical reading will be the final step you take before organizing your paper. For longer research papers that require outside sources, you will probably need to tap into library resources or even find information online.

Researching may even involve taking surveys and conducting interviews. For her paper on language sensitivity in education, our student decided to speak to school-children and teachers to determine their opinions on "language policing" and Leo and Ravitch's claims.

SELECTING SOURCES FOR YOUR PAPER

The best place to start is the library, either physically or online. Most libraries have their holdings archived on electronic cataloging systems that let you look up books by author, title, and subject. Although books are a rich source of information, they can be dated, and are sometimes inappropriate for essays addressing contemporary issues. For such papers, journals and periodicals are better. With all the different ways of researching, gathering useful and appropriate information can be overwhelming. Do not be afraid to ask the librarian for help.

For many people, the Internet has become the first avenue of research on a topic, and it can be an extremely useful way to locate information on contemporary issues. In addition to web sites, newsgroups and bulletin boards can aid your research process. Remember that the Internet is largely unregulated, so you should surf the web with the careful eye of a critic. Simply because something is posted online does not mean it is accurate or truthful. Whenever possible, take steps to verify your sources. When you do find a good source, write it down immediately. Many students lament the loss of a valuable resource because they forgot to write down the title of the book or Internet address. A good technique is to write down your sources on 3 × 5 cards. For example:

> Steel, Jon. *Truth, Lies and Advertising.* New York: John Wiley & Sons, 1998. 150–178.

> Kohner-Zuckerman, David. "Brokering Beauty." *BRNTWD Magazine* Jan/Feb 2000. http://www.brntwdmagazine.com/jan-feb/tech/tech-2.html.

These cards allow you to add sources and arrange them alphabetically without having to rewrite as you would with a list. You can write down quotes for your paper on these cards for quick retrieval, and use them to help write your "Works Cited" section at the end of your essay.

DOCUMENTING SOURCES

Sources help support your ideas and emphasize your points. It is very important to cite these sources when you use them in your essay. Whether you quote, paraphrase, or use an idea from another source, you must identify the source from which your information came. Documenting sources gives credit to the person who did the work, and helps locate information on your topic. Even if you rewrite information in your own words, you must still document the source because it is borrowed information. Failure to document your sources is called plagiarism—presenting someone else's work as your own—and it is considered by most academic institutions a form of theft. The following checklist should help you determine when to document your sources:

- Using someone's exact words
- Presenting someone else's opinion
- Paraphrasing or summarizing someone else's ideas
- Using information gathered from a study
- Citing statistics or reporting the results of research not your own.

It is not necessary to cite dates, facts, or ideas considered common knowledge.

ORGANIZING YOUR PAPER

There are many ways to organize your paper. Some students prefer to use the standard outline technique, complete with roman numerals and indented subpoints. Other students prefer more flexible flowcharts. The key to organizing is to define your focus and plan how to support your thesis statement from point to point in a logical order.

DRAFTING YOUR ESSAY

When writing your essay, think of your draft as a work in progress. Your objective should be to present your ideas in a logical order. You can address spelling, grammar, and sentence structure later. If you get stuck writing one paragraph or section, go on and work on another. Depending on how you write, you may choose to write your draft sequentially; or you may choose to move from your thesis to your body paragraphs, leaving your introduction and conclusion for last. Feel free to leave gaps or write notes to yourself in brackets to indicate areas to develop later when revising. Do not make the mistake of thinking that your first draft has to be your final draft. Remember that writing is a process of refinement—you can always go back and fix things later.

WRITING YOUR INTRODUCTION

For many students, the hardest part of writing an essay is drafting the first paragraph. Humorist James Thurber once said "Don't get it right, get it written." What

Thurber means is just start writing, even if you do not think it sounds very good. Use your thesis statement as a starting point and build around it. Explain what your essay will do, or provide interesting background information that serves to frame your points for your audience. After you have written the first paragraph, take a break before you revise it. Return to it later with a fresh outlook. Likewise, review your first paragraph as you develop the other sections of your essay to make sure that you are meeting your objectives.

Turning back to our student paper, an introduction might look like this. Note that the introduction works with the thesis statement developed earlier, and builds in a few more ideas.

> The language sensitivity movement of the 1980s and 1990s grew out of a belief that stereotyping and racial or cultural bias could offend or negatively influence students' self-esteem. As a result, publishers and test panels began to carefully consider the language they used. Some people fear that language sensitivity has gone too far and no longer reflects reality. Others are concerned that panels are focusing too much on not offending anyone, at the expense of education. While language sensitivity may sometimes seem extreme, it ultimately benefits students, and the society of which they will later become a part.

DEVELOPING PARAGRAPHS AND MAKING TRANSITIONS

A paragraph is a group of sentences that supports and develops a central idea. The central idea serves as the core point of the paragraph, and the surrounding sentences support it.

There are three primary types of sentences that comprise a paragraph: the topic sentence, supporting sentences, and transitional sentences.

The core point, or the **topic sentence,** is usually the first or second sentence in the paragraph. It is the controlling idea of the paragraph. Placing the topic sentence first lets the reader immediately know what the paragraph is about. However, sometimes a transition sentence or some supporting material needs to precede the topic sentence, in which case the topic sentence may appear as the second or third sentence in the paragraph. Think of the topic sentence as a mini-thesis statement; it should connect logically to the topic sentences in the paragraphs before and after it.

Supporting sentences do just that, support the topic sentence. This support may be from outside sources in the form of quotes or paraphrased material, or it may be from your own ideas. Think of the support sentences as "proving" the validity of your topic sentence.

Transitional sentences link paragraphs together, making the paper a cohesive unit and promoting its "readability." Transitional sentences are usually the first and last sentences of the paragraph. When they appear at the end of the paragraph, they foreshadow the topic to come. Words such as *in addition, yet, moreover, furthermore, meanwhile, likewise, also, since, before, hence, on the other hand, as well,* and *thus* are often used in transitional sentences. These words can also be used within the body of the paragraph to clarify and smooth the progression from idea to idea. For example, the last sentence in our student's introductory paragraph sets up the reader's expectations that the paragraphs that follow will explain why language sensitivity in educational materials is a good idea. It forecasts what will come next.

Paragraphs have no required length. Remember, however, that an essay comprised of long, detailed paragraphs might prove tiresome and confusing to the reader. Likewise, short, choppy paragraphs may sacrifice clarity and leave the reader with unanswered questions. Remember that a paragraph presents a single unified idea. It should be just long enough to effectively support its subject. Begin a new paragraph when your subject changes.

Use this list to help keep your paragraphs organized and coherent:

- Organize material logically—present your core idea early in the paragraph.
- Include a topic sentence that expresses the core point of the paragraph.
- Support and explain the core point.
- Use transitional sentences to indicate where you are going and where you have been.

Let us see how our student applies these ideas to the second paragraph of her essay.

> To better approach this issue, we must first understand a little bit more about the "language sensitivity" movement. For much of the twentieth century, textbooks taught primarily from a white, Anglo-Saxon, Protestant-Christian, and male-centered perspective. Stereotyping was common, with girls playing with dolls, boys participating in sports, and mothers and fathers depicted in traditional roles as homemakers and wage-earners, respectively. By the 1980s, however, publishers began to listen to the concerns expressed by academics and outside interest groups that educational material be more inclusive, more sensitive, and include the perspectives of women, racial, ethnic, and religious groups [*topic sentence*]. The goal was that through such language awareness, students would learn to avoid stereotyping, to be more tolerant of others, and to feel pride in their own social and cultural backgrounds [*supporting sentence*]. Considering the fact that America is often called the "great melting pot," it is surprising that it took so long to institute this inclusionary approach to language. Not everyone, however, has embraced this new academic approach [*transitional, "forecasting" sentence*].

CONCLUDING WELL

Your conclusion should bring together the points made in your paper and reiterate your final point. You may also use your conclusion as an opportunity to provoke a final thought you wish your audience to consider. Try to frame your conclusion to mirror your introduction—in other words, be consistent in your style. You may wish to repeat the point of the paper, revisit its key points, and then leave your reader with a final idea or thought on your topic.

Conclusions are your opportunity to explain to your reader how all your material adds up. In a short essay of about three to four pages, your conclusion should begin around the penultimate paragraph, "winding down" the discussion. Avoid the temptation to simply summarize your material; try to give your conclusions a little punch. However, it is equally important not to be overly dramatic, because you can undercut your essay. Rather, conclusions should sound confident and reflective.

Notice how our student concludes her essay, making references to her final point as well as to the paper against which she is arguing, the essay by John Leo. Based on her conclusion, we may infer that she has supported all of her final points within the actual body of her essay.

The key to language sensitivity is creating a balance between maintaining the principles of tolerance while maintaining reasonable expectations. Simply because the language sensitivity ethic is relatively new does not make it a "fad" or passing fancy. It means we are progressing as a culture. There is a saying "you can't please all of the people, all of the time," which holds particularly true for this issue. Understanding, and tolerating, alternative cultural, religious, and social points of view through language sensitivity does not mean that students are missing out on a good education. Moreover, language sensitivity ensures that children are not alienated by what they read. Rather than arguing that Asian American athletes are not a realistic norm, or questioning why panels avoid casting black women in the role of maids, we should instead consider how language sensitivity affords children more possibility, hope, and acceptance. It will help nurture future generations of children to be more tolerant and accepting of different viewpoints and ways of life.

Editing and Revising

Once you have drafted a paper and, if possible, spent several hours or even a day away from it, you should begin editing and revising it. To edit your paper, read it closely, marking the words, phrases, and sections you want to change. Have a grammar handbook nearby to quickly reference any grammatical questions that may arise. Look for things that seem out of place or sound awkward, passages that lack adequate support and detail, and sentences that seem wordy or unclear. Many students find that reading the essay aloud helps them to recognize awkward sentences and ambiguous wording. This technique may also reveal missing words.

As you read, you should always ask if what you have written refers back to your thesis:

- Does this paragraph support my thesis?
- What does my reader need to know?
- Do my paragraphs flow in a logical order?
- Have I deviated from my point?

As you revise your paper, think about the voice and style you are using to present your material. Is your style smooth and confident? How much of yourself is in the essay, and is this level appropriate for the type of paper you are writing? Some writers, for example, overuse the pronoun "I." If you find that this is the case try to rework your sentences to decrease the use of this pronoun.

Using Active Voice

Although grammatically correct, the use of the passive voice can slow down the flow of a paper or distance the reader from your material. Many students are befuddled by the active versus the passive voice, confusing it with past, present, and future tense. The active voice can be used in any tense, and, in most situations, it is the better choice. In the active voice, you make your agent "actively" perform an action. Consider the following examples:

> PASSIVE: In "Now Cut That Out!" in order to describe how extremist groups are controlling language, examples of rejected subjects are provided by John Leo.
> ACTIVE: In his essay, "Now Cut That Out," John Leo provides examples of subjects language extremist groups have vetoed.
> PASSIVE: The control of textbook content by the "language police" is feared by Ravitch.
> ACTIVE: Ravitch fears that the "language police" are controlling textbook content.

In both of these examples, using the active voice makes the sentences cleaner, stronger, and more engaging.

GRAMMAR AND PUNCTUATION

You probably already have a grammar handbook; most first-year composition courses require students to purchase these invaluable little books. If you do not have a grammar handbook, get one. You will use it throughout your college—and probably your professional—career. Grammar handbooks can help you identify problems with phrases and clauses, parallel structure, verb tense agreement, commas, colons and semicolons, and punctuation. Most have useful sections on common usage mistakes, such as when to use "further" and "farther," and "effect" and "affect." Try not to rely on grammar checking software available on most word processing programs. You are the best checker of grammar for your essay.

PROOFREADING EFFECTIVELY

The final step in preparing a paper is proofreading, the process of reading your paper to correct errors. You will probably be more successful if you wait until you are fresh to do it: Proofreading a paper at 3:00 A.M. immediately after finishing it is not a good idea. With the use of word-processing programs, proofreading usually involves three steps: spell-checking, reading, and correcting.

If you are writing your paper using a word-processing system, you probably have been using the spellchecker throughout the composition process. Most word-processing systems highlight misspelled words as you type them into the computer. Remember to run the spellchecker every time you change or revise your paper. Many students make last minute changes to their papers and neglect to run the spellchecker one last time before printing it, only to discover a misspelled word as they turn in their paper or when it is returned to them. Keep in mind that spellcheckers can fix only words that are misspelled—not words that are mistyped but are still real words. Common typing errors in which letters are transposed such as "from" and "form," and "won" and "own," will not be caught by a spellchecker because they all are real words. Other common errors not caught by spellcheckers include words incompletely typed, such as leaving off the "t" in "the" or the "e" in "here." Reading your paper carefully will catch these errors.

To proofread correctly, you must read slowly and critically. Try to distance yourself from the material. One careful, slow, attentive proofreading is better than six careless reads. Look for and mark the following: errors in spelling and usage, sentence fragments and comma splices, inconsistencies in number between nouns and pronouns and between subjects and verbs, faulty parallelism, other grammar errors, unintentional repetitions, and omissions.

After you have proofread and identified the errors, go back and correct them. When you have finished, proofread the paper again to make sure you caught everything. As you proofread for grammar and style, ask yourself the questions listed above and make corrections on your paper. Be prepared to read your essay through multiple times. Having only one or two small grammatical corrections is a good indication that you are done revising.

If your schedule permits, you might want to show your paper to a friend or instructor for review. Obtaining feedback from your audience is another way you can test the effectiveness of your paper. An outside reviewer will probably think of questions you have not thought of, and if you revise to answer those questions, you will make your paper stronger.

In the chapters that follow, you will discover over a hundred different selections, both written and visual, ranging widely across contemporary matters, that we hope you will find exciting and thought provoking. Arranged thematically into 10 chapters, the writings represent widely diverse topics—from the ways we construct beauty, to what makes us want to buy something, to the way the Internet is changing our lives, to the ethical issues surrounding human reproduction and gene technology. Some of the topics will be familiar; others you may be encountering for the first time. Regardless of how these language issues touch your experience, critical thinking, critical reading, and critical writing will open you up to a deeper understanding of our culture as we begin the twenty-first century.

Approaching Visuals Critically

We have all heard the old saying, "a picture is worth a thousand words." Our daily lives are filled with the images of pop culture, influencing us about what to buy, how to look, even how to think. Symbols, images, gestures, and graphics all communicate instant information about our culture.

Now more than ever before, ours is a visual world. Everywhere we look there are images vying for our attention—magazine ads, T-shirt logos, movie billboards, artwork, traffic signs, political cartoons, statues, and store-front windows. Glanced at only briefly, visuals communicate information and ideas. They may project commonly held values, ideals, and fantasies. They can relay opinion, inspire reaction, and influence emotion. And because the competition for our attention today is so great, and the time for communication is so short, visuals compete to make an instant impression or risk being lost.

Consider the instant messages projected by brand names, company logos, or even the American flag. Or the emotional appeal of a photo of a lost kitten or dog attached to a reward notice on a telephone pole. Without the skills of visual literacy, we are at the mercy of a highly persuasive visual universe. Just as we approach writing with the tools of critical analysis, we should carefully consider the many ways visuals influence us.

Understanding the persuasive power of visuals requires a close examination and interpretation of the premise, claims, details, supporting evidence, and stylistic touches embedded in any visual piece. Just as when we examine written arguments, we should ask ourselves the following four questions when examining visual arguments:

- Who is the target *audience*?
- What are the *claims* made in the images?
- What shared history or cultural *assumptions*—or warrants—does the image make?
- What is the supporting *evidence*?

Like works of art, visuals employ color, shape, line, texture, depth, and point of view to create their effect. Therefore, to understand how visuals work and to analyze the way visuals persuade, we must also ask questions about specific aspects of form and design. For example, some questions to ask about print images, such as those in newspaper and magazine ads, include:

- What in the frame catches your attention immediately?
- What is the central image? What is the background image? Foreground images? What are the surrounding images? What is significant in the placement of these images? Their relationship to one another?
- What verbal information is included? How is it made prominent? How does it relate to the other graphics or images?
- What specific details (people, objects, locale) are emphasized? Which are exaggerated or idealized?
- What is the effect of color and lighting?
- What emotional effect is created by the images—pleasure? longing? anxiety? nostalgia?
- Do the graphics and images make you want to know more about the subject or product?
- What special significance might objects in the image have?
- Is there any symbolism imbedded in the images?

Because the goal of a calculated visual is to persuade, coax, intimidate, or otherwise subliminally influence its viewer, it is important that its audience can discern the strategies or technique it employs. To get you started, we will critically analyze two types of visuals—advertisements and editorial cartoons.

IMAGES AND ADVERTISING

Images have clout, and none so obvious or so craftily designed as those that come from the world of advertising. Advertising images are everywhere—television, newspapers, the Internet, magazines, the sides of buses, and on highway billboards. Each year, companies collectively spend more than $150 billion worth of print ads and television commercials (more than the gross national product of many countries). Advertisements comprise at least a quarter of each television hour and form the bulk of most newspapers and magazines. Tapping into our most basic emotions, their appeal goes right to the quick of our fantasies: happiness, material wealth, eternal youth, social acceptance, sexual fulfillment, and power.

Yet, most of us are so accustomed to the onslaught of such images that we see them without looking and hear them without listening. But if we stopped to examine how the images work, we might be amazed at their powerful and complex psychological force. And we might be surprised at how much effort goes into the crafting of such images—an effort solely intended to separate us from our money.

Like a written argument, every print ad or commercial has an audience, claims, assumptions and evidence. Sometimes these elements are obvious, sometimes understated, sometimes implied. They may boast testimonials by average folk or celebrities, or cite hard scientific evidence. And sometimes they simply manipulate our desire to be happy or socially accepted. But common to every ad and commercial, no matter what the medium, is the claim that you should buy this product.

Print ads are potentially complex mixtures of images, graphics, and text. So in analyzing an ad, you should be aware of the use of photography, the placement of the images, the use of text, company logos, and other graphics (such as illustrations, drawings, side bar boxes, logos, etc.). And you should keep in mind that every aspect of the image has been thought about and designed carefully even in those ads where the guiding principle was minimalism. Let's take a look at a recent magazine ad for Altoids.

ALTOIDS AD

When analyzing a print ad, we should try to determine what first catches our attention. In the accompanying Altoids ad, the image of the soldier, featured floating on a pale green solid background, pops from the page. This is a calculated move on the part of the ad's designers. The soldier fills the center of the page, and the image is arresting—we stop and look. Ad images are staged and manipulated for maximum attention and effect. The uncluttered nature of this advertisement forces us to look at the soldier and the little tin he is holding in his hand.

THANK YOU SIR!
MAY I HAVE ANOTHER!
THE CURIOUSLY STRONG MINTS

©2000 Callard & Bowser-Suchard Inc.   www.altoids.com

The person featured in the ad is almost comic. He is wearing an ill-fitted uniform, he sports thick glasses, and he lacks the chiseled quality of many male models commonly used in advertising. This comic quality, coupled with the text under the ad, appeals to the viewer's sense of humor.

WHAT IS THE CLAIM?

Because advertisers are fighting for our attention, they must project their claim as efficiently as possible in order to discourage us from turning the page. The Altoids ad states its "claim" simply and boldly in white letters against a pale green background below the central photograph. In large typeface, the slogan and "claim" come in two parts. The first two sentences presumably come from the soldier: "Thank you sir! May I have another!" The second statement tells us more specifically what the soldier wants: "The curiously strong mints." It is interesting to note that the actual name of the product, Altoids, only appears on the little tin held in the soldier's right hand.

But let's take a closer look at the intention of framing the claim in two sentences and at how the layout subtly directs us. The first statement is intended to tap into our shared cultural expectations of what we know about military service. Soldiers must shout responses to their superiors and thank them even for punishments. For example, after being assigned 20 pushups as disciplinary action, a soldier is expected to not only thank his sergeant for the punishment, but to actually ask for more. The ad twists this expectation by having Altoids be the "punishment." In this ad, the soldier is actually getting a treat.

The indirect claim is that the reader should also want these "curiously strong mints." The word "curiously" is designed to set the product apart from its competitors. Curiously" is more commonly used in British English; and the parent company for Altoids—Callard & Bowser-Suchard Inc.—has its roots in England. Viewers familiar with the mint will enjoy the ad for its comic appeal. Those readers who are unfamiliar with the product may wonder just what makes these mints "curiously strong." And curiosity is an effective hook.

Another possible claim could be connected to the scenario leading to the soldier's receiving the first mint. We know that soldiers are supposed to shout back responses to their commanding officer, often face to face. Perhaps his commanding officer was appalled at his recruit's bad breath and "punished" him with the directive to have a mint. The claim is that even at extremely close range, Altoids fixes bad breath.

WHAT IS THE EVIDENCE?

Altoid's tag line, "The curiously strong mints," implies that other mints are simply ordinary and unremarkable. Altoids are different—they are "curiously strong" and thus, presumably, superior to their bland competition. And referring back to the possible scenario that led to the soldier's first mint, viewers might presume that if a commanding officer would "treat" his company's bad breath with this mint, it must be good.

Around the language of advertising, we should tread cautiously. As William Lutz warns us about in his essay, "With These Words I Can Sell You Anything" (see chapter 18), we hear promises that aren't really being made. The Altoids text does not say that it is, indeed, better than other mints, just that they are "curiously strong." What does the word "curiously" really mean? And stronger than what? According to Lutz, such words sound enticing, but are really telling readers nothing meaningful about the product.

WHAT ARE THE ASSUMPTIONS?

The creators of this ad make several assumptions about the audience: (1) that they are familiar with the phrase "Thank you sir, may I have another;" (2) they understand who is depicted in the ad—a soldier at boot camp; and (3) we want to have fresh breath.

ALTOIDS QUESTIONS

1. What cultural conventions does this ad use to promote the product? What does it assume about the viewer? Would it work in another country, such as France or China? Explain.

2. This ad lists a web site. Visit the Altoids web site at www.altoids.com. How does the web site compliment the print ad? Who would visit this site?
   Evaluate the effectiveness of having companion web sites in addition to printed advertisements.

3. Would you try Altoids based on this advertisement? Why or why not?

4. How does this photograph capture your attention? Can you tell at a glance what it is selling? Where is your eye directed?

DECIPHERING EDITORIAL CARTOONS

Editorial cartoons have been a part of American life for over a century. They are a mainstay feature on the editorial pages in most newspapers—those pages reserved for columnists, contributing editors, and illustrators to present their views in words and pen and ink. As in the nineteenth century when they first started to appear, such editorial cartoons are political in nature, holding political and social issues up for public scrutiny and sometimes ridicule.

A stand-alone editorial cartoon—as opposed to a strip of multiple frames—is a powerful and terse form of communication that combines pen-and-ink drawings with dialogue balloons and captions. They're not just visual jokes, but visual humor that comments on social/political issues while drawing on viewers' experience and knowledge.

The editorial cartoon is the story of a moment in the flow of familiar current events. And the key words here are moment and familiar. Although a cartoon captures a split instant in time, it also infers what came before and, perhaps, what may happen next—either in the next moment or in some indefinite future. And usually the cartoon depicts a moment after which things will never be the same. One of the most famous cartoons of the last 40 years is the late Bill Mauldin's Pulitzer-Prize- winning drawing of the figure of Abraham Lincoln with his head in his hands. It appeared the morning after the assassination of President John Kennedy in 1963. There was no caption nor was there a need for one. The image represented the profound grief of a nation that had lost its leader to an assassin's bullet. But to capture the enormity of the event, Mauldin brilliantly chose to represent a woeful America by using the figure of Abraham Lincoln as depicted in the sculpture of the Lincoln Memorial in Washington, D.C. In so doing, the message implied that so profound was the loss that it even reduced to tears the marble figure of a man considered to be our greatest president, himself assassinated a century before.

For a cartoon to be effective, it must make the issue clear at a glance and it must establish where it stands on the argument. As in the Mauldin illustration, we instantly recognize Lincoln and identify with the emotions. We need not be told the circumstances, since by the time the cartoon appeared the next day, all the world knew the horrible news that the President had been assassinated. To convey less obvious issues and figures in a glance, cartoonists resort to images that are instantly recognizable, that we don't have to work at to grasp. Locales are determined by give-away props: airports will have an airplane out the window, the desert is identified by a cactus and cattle skull; an overstuffed arm chair and TV for the standard living room. Likewise, human emotions are instantly conveyed: pleasure is a huge toothy grin; fury is steam blowing out of a figure's ears; love is two figures making goo-goo eyes with floating hearts. People themselves may have exaggerated features to emphasize a point or emotion.

In his essay "What Is a Cartoon?", Mort Gerberg (*The Arbor House Book of Cartooning*, HarperCollins, 1989) says that editorial cartoons rely on such visual clichés to instantly convey their messages. That is, they employ stock figures for their representation—images instantly recognizable from cultural stereotypes. The fat-cat tycoon, the mobster thug, the sexy female movie star. And these come to us in familiar outfits and props that give away their identities and profession. The cartoon judge has a black robe and gavel; the prisoner wears striped overalls and a ball and chain; the physician dons a smock and forehead light; the doomsayer is a scrawny long-haired guy carrying a sign saying "The end is near." These are visual clichés known by the culture at large, and we get them.

The visual cliché may be what catches our eye in the editorial cartoon, but the message lies in what the cartoonist does with it. As Gerberg observes, "the message is in twisting it, in turning the cliché around."

CLONING CARTOON

Consider the Jack Ohman cartoon that follows. The cliché is a woman shopping in a supermarket. We know that from the familiar props: the shopping cart, the meat display unit, the department banner, and the hint of shelving in the background. Even the shopper is a familiar figure, an elderly woman in her overcoat pushing her cart. The twist, of course, is that instead of a refrigeration unit displaying lamb, beef, and poultry, we see trays of neatly arranged embryo clones with their genetic specialties in stickup signs. The issue, of course, is the debate on human cloning. The cartoon was published on December 10, 2001, shortly after the announcement by the genetics firm Advanced Cell Technology in Worcester, Massachusetts, that they had cloned the first human embryo. (The embryos only survived a few cell divisions before they ceased.) Although the lab claimed that the intentions of cloning was not to create human beings but to treat particular human ailments, such as Parkinson's disease, cancer, and strokes, the publicity fanned the flames of debate over the ethics and morality of cloning. Some people view such breakthroughs as medically promising; others fear crossing the line of playing God.

The cartoon's joke is in the twist—the gap between the familiar and the unexpected. The familiar is the supermarket cliché; the unexpected is the casual display of embryo flagged for desirable traits in a Cloned Embryo Department. Of course the scene depicts some indefinite future time when cloning is permitted by law and widely practiced.

WHAT IS THE CLAIM?

The claim in this cartoon is that natural birth is better than genetic engineering. That is implicit in the satirical image of the human talents and traits quantified and commercialized in the meat section of the supermarket. And it is explicit in the woman's thoughts, "I miss the stork . . ."

WHAT ARE THE ASSUMPTIONS?

This cartoon makes the assumptions that people see human beings as more complex and elusive than particular traits and talents, and that purchasing babies according to desired traits is perverse and unnatural.

WHAT IS THE EVIDENCE?

The evidence is in the darkly satirical notion that instead of natural procreation we would someday shop for scientifically perfected babies in a supermarket. Next to more "serious" preferences, such as embryos cloned from donors with "1600 SAT" scores and "20/20 vision," are the embryos cloned from people good at juggling and ear-wiggling. It is in these juxtapositions where the cartoonist gives away where he stands on the issue. He is mocking our society by reducing the aspiration of would-be parents to have kids with narrowly specific talents. To clinch Ohman's stand is the woman's thought bubble—"I miss the stork . . ." The message is that in the imagined new world where we can shop for our ideal babies, there are those who yearn for the good old days. Of course, "the stork" is a polite metaphorical reference to sexual reproduction—a term appropriate for the customer in the drawing—an elderly woman conservatively dressed. However, the term is another cliché, and in a curious twist it plays off the supermarket meat department display—as if stork were another kind of poultry option.

As you review the various visuals throughout the text, approach what you see with the critical eye of a skeptic. Many of the techniques used in reading critically can be applied to visuals. Consider the ways symbolism, brand recognition, stereotyping, and cultural expectations contribute to how such illustrations communicate their ideas. Try to think abstractly, taking into account the many different levels of consciousness that visuals use to communicate. Consider also the way shading, lighting, and subject placement in the photos all converge to make a point. "Read" them as you would any text.

Language & Advertising

Words such as "help" and "virtually" and phrases such as "new and improved" and "acts fast" seem like innocuous weaponry in the arsenal of advertising. But not to William Lutz ("With These Words . . ."), who analyzes how such words are used in ads—how they misrepresent, mislead, and deceive consumers. In this essay, he alerts us to the special power of "weasel words"—those familiar and sneaky little critters that "appear to say one thing when in fact they say the opposite, or nothing at all." The real danger, Lutz argues, is how such language debases reality and the values of the consumer. Marketing executive Charles A. O'Neill ("The Language of Advertising"), however, disputes Lutz's criticism of advertising doublespeak. Although admitting to some of the craftiness of his profession, O'Neill defends the huckster's language—both verbal and visual—against claims that it distorts reality. Examining some familiar television commercials and magazine ads, he explains why

the language may be charming and seductive, but it is far from brainwashing.

William Lutz teaches English at Rutgers University and is the author of several books, including *The New Doublespeak: Why No One Knows What Anyone's Saying Anymore* (1997) and *Doublespeak Defined* (1999). The following essay is an excerpt from Lutz's book, *Doublespeak* (1990). Charles O'Neill is senior vice president of marketing for Colonial Investment Services in Boston. His essay first appeared in the textbook *Exploring Language*.

CRITICAL THINKING

Consider the phrases used in advertising such as "new and improved" and "cleans like a dream." Do we think about such advertising phrases? How much do such phrases influence you as a consumer? Explain.

With These Words, I Can Sell You Anything

WILLIAM LUTZ

One problem advertisers have when they try to convince you that the product they are pushing is really different from other, similar products is that their claims are subject to some laws. Not a lot of laws, but there are some designed to prevent fraudulent or untruthful claims in advertising. Even during the happy years of nonregulation under President Ronald Reagan, the FTC did crack down on the more blatant abuses in advertising claims. Generally speaking, advertisers have to be careful in what they say in their ads, in the claims they make for the products they advertise. Parity claims are safe because they are legal and supported by a number of court decisions. But beyond parity claims there are weasel words.

Advertisers use weasel words to appear to be making a claim for a product when in fact they are making no claim at all. Weasel words get their name from the way weasels eat the eggs they find in the nests of other animals. A weasel will make a small hole in the egg, suck out the insides, then place the egg back in the nest. Only when the egg is examined closely is it found to be hollow. That's the way it is with weasel words in advertising: Examine weasel words closely and you'll find that they're as hollow as any egg sucked by a weasel. Weasel words appear to say one thing when in fact they say the opposite, or nothing at all.

"HELP"—THE NUMBER ONE WEASEL WORD

The biggest weasel word used in advertising doublespeak is "help." Now "help" only means to aid or assist, nothing more. It does not mean to conquer, stop, eliminate, end, solve, heal, cure, or anything else. But once the ad says "help," it can say just about anything after that because "help" qualifies everything coming after it. The trick is that the claim that comes after the weasel word is usually so strong and so dramatic that you forget the word "help" and concentrate only on the dramatic claim. You read into the ad a message that the ad does not contain. More importantly, the advertiser is not responsible for the claim that you read into the ad, even though the advertiser wrote the ad so you would read that claim into it.

The next time you see an ad for a cold medicine that promises that it "helps relieve cold symptoms fast," don't rush out to buy it. Ask yourself what this claim is really saying. Remember, "helps" means only that the medicine will aid or assist. What will it aid or assist in doing? Why, "relieve" your cold "symptoms." "Relieve" only means to ease, alleviate, or mitigate, not to stop, end, or cure. Nor does the claim say how much relieving this medicine will do. Nowhere does this ad claim it will cure anything. In fact, the ad doesn't even claim it will *do* anything at all. The ad only claims that it will aid in relieving (not curing) your cold symptoms, which are probably a runny nose, watery eyes, and a headache. In other words, this medicine probably contains a standard decongestant and some aspirin. By the way, what does "fast" mean? Ten minutes, one hour, one day? What is fast to one person can be very slow to another. Fast is another weasel word.

Ad claims using "help" are among the most popular ads. One says, "Helps keep you young looking," but then a lot of things will help keep you young looking, including exercise, rest, good nutrition, and a facelift. More importantly, this ad doesn't say the product will keep you young, only "young *looking*." Someone may look young to one person and old to another.

A toothpaste ad says, "Helps prevent cavities," but it doesn't say it will actually prevent cavities. Brushing your teeth regularly, avoiding sugars in foods, and flossing daily will also help prevent cavities. A liquid cleaner ad says, "Helps keep your home germ free," but it doesn't say it actually kills germs, nor does it even specify which germs it might kill.

"Help" is such a useful weasel word that it is often combined with other action-verb weasel words such as "fight" and "control." Consider the claim, "Helps control dandruff symptoms with regular use." What does it really say? It will assist in controlling (not eliminating, stopping, ending, or curing) the *symptoms* of dandruff, not the cause of dandruff nor the dandruff itself. What are the symptoms of dandruff? The ad deliberately leaves that undefined, but assume that the symptoms referred to in the ad are the flaking and itching commonly associated with dandruff. But just shampooing with *any* shampoo will temporarily eliminate these symptoms, so this shampoo isn't any different from any other. Finally, in order to benefit from this product, you must use it regularly. What is "regular use"—daily, weekly, hourly? Using another shampoo "regularly" will have the same effect. Nowhere does this advertising claim say this particular shampoo stops, eliminates, or cures dandruff. In fact, this claim says nothing at all, thanks to all the weasel words.

Look at ads in magazines and newspapers, listen to ads on radio and television, and you'll find the word "help" in ads for all kinds of products. How often do you read or hear such phrases as "helps stop . . . ," "helps overcome . . . ," "helps eliminate . . . ," "helps you feel . . . ," or "helps you look . . ."? If you start looking for this weasel word in advertising, you'll be amazed at how often it occurs. Analyze the claims in the ads using "help," and you will discover that these ads are really saying nothing.

There are plenty of other weasel words used in advertising. In fact, there are so many that to list them all would fill the rest of this book. But, in order to identify the doublespeak of advertising and understand the real meaning of an ad, you have to be aware of the most popular weasel words in advertising today.

Virtually Spotless

One of the most powerful weasel words is "virtually," a word so innocent that most people don't pay any attention to it when it is used in an advertising claim. But watch out. "Virtually" is used in advertising claims that appear to make specific, definite promises when there is no promise. After all, what does "virtually" mean? It means "in essence of effect, although not in fact." Look at that definition again. "Virtually" means *not in fact*. It does *not* mean "almost" or "just about the same as," or anything else. And before you dismiss all this concern over such a small word, remember that small words can have big consequences.

In 1971 a federal court rendered its decision on a case brought by a woman who became pregnant while taking birth control pills. She sued the manufacturer, Eli Lilly and Company, for breach of warranty. The woman lost her case. Basing its ruling on a statement in the pamphlet accompanying the pills, which stated that, "When taken as directed, the tablets offer virtually 100% protection," the court ruled that there was no warranty, expressed or implied, that the pills were absolutely effective. In its ruling, the court pointed out that, according to *Webster's Third New International Dictionary*, "virtually" means "almost entirely" and clearly does not mean "absolute" (*Whittington* v. *Eli Lilly and Company*, 333 F. Supp. 98). In other words, the Eli Lilly company was really saying that its birth control pill, even when taken as directed, *did not in fact* provide 100 percent protection against pregnancy. But Eli Lilly didn't want to put it that way because then many women might not have bought Lilly's birth control pills.

The next time you see the ad that says that this dishwasher detergent "leaves dishes virtually spotless," just remember how advertisers twist the meaning of the weasel word "virtually." You can have lots of spots on your dishes after using this detergent and the ad claim will still be true, because what this claim really means is that this detergent does not *in fact* leave your dishes spotless. Whenever you see or hear an ad claim that uses the word "virtually," just translate that claim into its real meaning. So the television set that is "virtually trouble free" becomes the television set that is not in fact trouble free, the "virtually foolproof operation" of any appliance becomes an operation that is in fact not foolproof, and the product that "virtually never needs service" becomes the product that is not in fact service free.

New and Improved

If "new" is the most frequently used word on a product package, "improved" is the second most frequent. In fact, the two words are almost always used together. It seems just about everything sold these days is "new and improved." The next time you're in the supermarket, try counting the number of times you see these words on products. But you'd better do it while you're walking down just one aisle, otherwise you'll need a calculator to keep track of your counting.

Just what do these words mean? The use of the word "new" is restricted by regulations, so an advertiser can't just use the word on a product or in an ad without meeting certain requirements. For example, a product is considered new for about six months during a national advertising campaign. If the product is being advertised only in a limited test market area, the word can be used longer, and in some instances has been used for as long as two years.

What makes a product "new"? Some products have been around for a long time, yet every once in a while you discover that they are being advertised as "new." Well, an advertiser can call a product new if there has been "a material functional change" in the product. What is "a material functional change," you ask? Good question. In fact it's such a good question it's being asked all the time. It's up to the manufacturer to prove that the product has undergone such a change. And if the manufacturer isn't challenged on the claim, then there's no one to stop it. Moreover, the change does not have to be an improvement in the product. One manufacturer added an artificial lemon scent to a cleaning product and called it "new and improved," even though the product did not clean any better than without the lemon scent. The manufacturer defended the use of the word "new" on the grounds that the artificial scent changed the chemical formula of the product and therefore constituted "a material functional change."

Which brings up the word "improved." When used in advertising, "improved" does not mean "made better." It only means "changed" or "different from before." So, if the detergent maker puts a plastic pour spout on the box of detergent, the product has been "improved," and away we go with a whole new advertising campaign. Or, if the cereal maker adds more fruit or a different kind of fruit to the cereal, there's an improved product. Now you know why manufacturers are constantly making little changes in their products. Whole new advertising campaigns, designed to convince you that the product has been changed for the better, are based on small changes in superficial aspects of a product. The next time you see an ad for an "improved" product, ask yourself what was wrong with the old one. Ask yourself just how "improved" the product is. Finally, you might check to see whether the "improved" version costs more than the unimproved one. After all, someone has to pay for the millions of dollars spent advertising the improved product.

Of course, advertisers really like to run ads that claim a product is "new and improved." While what constitutes a "new" product may be subject to some regulation, "improved" is a subjective judgment. A manufacturer changes the shape of its stick deodorant, but the shape doesn't improve the function of the deodorant. That is, changing the shape doesn't affect the deodorizing ability of the deodorant, so the manufacturer calls it "improved." Another manufacturer adds ammonia to its liquid cleaner and calls it "new and improved." Since adding ammonia does affect the cleaning ability of the product, there has been a "material functional change" in the product, and the manufacturer can now call its cleaner "new," and "improved" as well. Now the weasel words "new and improved" are plastered all over the package and are the basis for a multimillion-dollar ad campaign. But after six months the word "new" will have to go, until someone can dream up another change in the product. Perhaps it will be adding color to the liquid, or changing the shape of the package, or maybe adding a new dripless pour spout, or perhaps a _____. The "improvements" are endless, and so are the new advertising claims and campaigns.

"New" is just too useful and powerful a word in advertising for advertisers to pass it up easily. So they use weasel words that say "new" without really saying it. One of their favorites is "introducing," as in, "Introducing improved Tide," or "Introducing the stain remover." The first is simply saying, here's our improved soap; the second, here's our new advertising campaign for our detergent. Another favorite is "now," as in, "Now there's Sinex," which simply means that Sinex is available. Then there are phrases like "Today's Chevrolet," "Presenting Dristan," and "A fresh way to start the day." The list is really endless because advertisers are always finding new ways to say "new" without really saying it. If there is a second edition of this book, I'll just call it the "new and improved" edition. Wouldn't you really rather have a "new and improved" edition of this book rather than a "second" edition?

Acts Fast

"Acts" and "works" are two popular weasel words in advertising because they bring action to the product and to the advertising claim. When you see the ad for the cough syrup that "Acts on the cough control center," ask yourself what this cough syrup is claiming to do. Well, it's just claiming to "act," to do something, to perform an action. What is it that the cough syrup does? The ad doesn't say. It only claims to perform an action or do something on your "cough control center." By the way, what and where is your "cough control center"? I don't remember learning about that part of the body in human biology class.

Ads that use such phrases as "acts fast," "acts against," "acts to prevent," and the like, are saying essentially nothing, because "act" is a word empty of any specific meaning. The ads are always careful not to specify exactly what "act" the product performs. Just because a brand of aspirin claims to "act fast" for headache relief doesn't mean this aspirin is any better than any other aspirin. What is the "act" that this aspirin performs? You're never told. Maybe it just dissolves quickly. Since aspirin is a parity product, all aspirin is the same and therefore functions the same.

Works Like Anything Else

If you don't find the word "acts" in an ad, you will probably find the weasel word "works." In fact, the two words are almost interchangeable in advertising. Watch out for ads that say a product "works against," "works like," "works for," or "works longer." As with "acts," "works" is the same meaningless verb used to make you think that this product really does something, and maybe even something special or unique. But "works," like "acts," is basically a word empty of any specific meaning.

Like Magic

Whenever advertisers want you to stop thinking about the product and to start thinking about something bigger, better, or more attractive than the product, they use that very popular weasel word, "like." The word "like" is the advertiser's equivalent of a magician's use of misdirection. "Like" gets you to ignore the product and concentrate on the claim the advertiser is making about it. "For skin like peaches and cream" claims the ad for a skin cream. What is this ad really claiming? It doesn't say this cream will give you peaches-and-cream skin. There is no verb in this claim, so it doesn't even mention using the product. How is skin ever like "peaches and cream"? Remember, ads must be read literally and exactly, according to the dictionary definition of words. (Remember "virtually" in the Eli Lilly case.) The ad is making absolutely no promise or claim whatsoever for this skin cream. If you think this cream will give you soft, smooth, youthful-looking skin, you are the one who has read that meaning into the ad.

The wine that claims "It's like taking a trip to France" wants you to think about a romantic evening in Paris as you walk along the boulevard after a wonderful meal in an intimate little bistro. Of course, you don't really believe that a wine can take you to France, but the goal of the ad is to get you to think pleasant, romantic thoughts about France and not about how the wine tastes or how expensive it may be. That little word "like" has taken you away from crushed grapes into a world of your own imaginative making. Who knows, maybe the next time you buy wine, you'll think those pleasant thoughts when you see this brand of wine, and you'll buy it. Or, maybe you weren't even thinking about buying wine at all, but now you just might pick up a bottle the next time you're shopping. Ah, the power of "like" in advertising.

How about the most famous "like" claim of all, "Winston tastes good like a cigarette should"? Ignoring the grammatical error here, you might want to know what this claim is saying. Whether a cigarette tastes good or bad is a subjective judgment because what tastes good to one person may well taste horrible to another. Not everyone likes fried snails, even if they are called escargot. (*De gustibus non est disputandum*, which was probably the Roman rule for advertising as well as for defending the games in the Colosseum.) There are many people who say all cigarettes taste terrible, other people who say only some cigarettes taste all right, and still others who say all cigarettes taste good. Who's right? Everyone, because taste is a matter of personal judgment.

Moreover, note the use of the conditional, "should." The complete claim is, "Winston tastes good like a cigarette should taste." But should cigarettes taste good? Again, this is a matter of personal judgment and probably depends most on one's experiences with smoking. So, the Winston ad is simply saying that Winston cigarettes are just like any other cigarette: Some people like them and some people don't. On that statement, R. J. Reynolds conducted a very successful multimillion-dollar advertising campaign that helped keep Winston the number-two-selling cigarette in the United States, close behind number one, Marlboro.

Can't It Be Up to the Claim?

Analyzing ads for doublespeak requires that you pay attention to every word in the ad and determine what each word really means. Advertisers try to wrap their claims in language that sounds concrete, specific, and objective, when in fact the language of advertising is anything but. Your job is to read carefully and listen critically so that when the announcer says that "Crest can be of significant value . . ." you know immediately that this claim says absolutely nothing. Where is the doublespeak in this ad? Start with the second word.

Once again, you have to look at what words really mean, not what you think they mean or what the advertiser wants you to think they mean. The ad for Crest only says that using Crest "can be" of "significant value." What really throws you off in this ad is the brilliant use of "significant." It draws your attention to the word "value" and makes you forget that the ad only claims that Crest "can be." The ad doesn't say that Crest *is* of value, only that it is "able" or "possible" to be of value, because that's all that "can" means.

It's so easy to miss the importance of those little words, "can be." Almost as easy as missing the importance of the words "up to" in an ad. These words are very popular in sale ads. You know, the ones that say, "Up to 50 percent Off!" Now, what does that claim mean? Not much, because the store or manufacturer has to reduce the price of only a few items by 50 percent. Everything else can be reduced a lot less, or not even reduced. Moreover, don't you want to know 50 percent off of what? Is it 50 percent off the "manufacturer's suggested list price," which is the highest possible price? Was the price artificially inflated and then reduced? In other ads, "up to" expresses an ideal situation. The medicine that works "up to ten times faster," the battery that lasts "up to twice as long," and the soap that gets you "up to twice as clean"—all are based on ideal situations for using those products, situations in which you can be sure you will never find yourself.

Unfinished Words

Unfinished words are a kind of "up to" claim in advertising. The claim that a battery lasts "up to twice as long" usually doesn't finish the comparison—twice as long as what? A birthday candle? A tank of gas? A cheap battery made in a country not noted for its technological achievements? The implication is that the battery lasts twice as long as batteries made by other battery makers, or twice as long as earlier model batteries made by the advertiser, but the ad doesn't really make these claims. You read these claims into the ad, aided by the visual images the advertiser so carefully provides.

Unfinished words depend on you to finish them, to provide the words the advertisers so thoughtfully left out of the ad. Pall Mall cigarettes were once advertised as "A longer finer and milder smoke." The question is, longer, finer, and milder than what? The aspirin that claims it contains "Twice as much of the pain reliever doctors recommend most" doesn't tell you what pain reliever it contains twice as much of. (By the way, it's aspirin. That's right; it just contains twice the amount of aspirin. And how much is twice the amount? Twice of what amount?) Panadol boasts that "nobody reduces fever faster," but, since Panadol is a parity product, this claim simply means that Panadol isn't any better than any other product in its parity class. "You can be sure if it's Westinghouse," you're told, but just exactly what it is you can be sure of is never mentioned. "Magnavox gives you more" doesn't tell you what you get more of. More value? More television? More than they gave you before? It sounds nice, but it means nothing, until you fill in the claim with your own words, the words the advertisers didn't use. Since each of us fills in the claim differently, the ad and the product can become all things to all people, and not promise a single thing.

Unfinished words abound in advertising because they appear to promise so much. More importantly, they can be joined with powerful visual images on television to appear to be making significant promises about a product's effectiveness without really making any promises. In a television ad, the aspirin product that claims fast relief can show a person with a headache taking the product and then, in what appears to be a matter of minutes, claiming complete relief. This visual image is far more powerful than any claim made in unfinished words. Indeed, the visual image completes the unfinished words for you, filling in with pictures what the words leave out. And you thought that ads didn't affect you. What brand of aspirin do you use?

Some years ago, Ford's advertisements proclaimed "Ford LTD—700 percent quieter." Now, what do you think Ford was claiming with these unfinished words? What was the Ford LTD quieter than? A Cadillac? A Mercedes Benz? A BMW? Well, when the FTC asked Ford to substantiate this unfinished claim, Ford replied that it meant that the inside of the LTD was 700 percent quieter than the outside. How did you finish those unfinished words when you first read them? Did you even come close to Ford's meaning?

Combining Weasel Words

A lot of ads don't fall neatly into one category or another because they use a variety of different devices and words. Different weasel words are often combined to make an ad claim. The claim, "Coffee-Mate gives coffee more body, more flavor," uses Unfinished Words ("more" than what?) and also uses words that have no specific meaning ("body" and "flavor"). Along with "taste" (remember the Winston ad and its claim to taste good), "body" and "flavor" mean nothing because their meaning is entirely subjective. To you, "body" in coffee might mean thick, black, almost bitter coffee, while I might take it to mean a light brown, delicate coffee. Now, if you think you understood that last sentence, read it again, because it said nothing of objective value; it was filled with weasel words of no specific meaning: "thick," "black," "bitter," "light brown," and "delicate." Each of those words has no specific, objective meaning, because each of us can interpret them differently.

Try this slogan: "Looks, smells, tastes like ground-roast coffee." So, are you now going to buy Taster's Choice instant coffee because of this ad? "Looks," "smells," and "tastes" are all words with no specific meaning and depend on your interpretation of them for any meaning. Then there's that great weasel word "like," which simply suggests a comparison but does not make the actual connection between the product and the quality. Besides, do you know what "ground-roast" coffee is? I don't, but it sure sounds good. So, out of seven words in this ad, four are definite weasel words, two are quite meaningless, and only one has any clear meaning.

Remember the Anacin ad—"Twice as much of the pain reliever doctors recommend most"? There's a whole lot of weaseling going on in this ad. First, what's the pain reliever they're talking about in this ad? Aspirin, of course. In fact, any time you see or hear an ad using those words "pain reliever," you can automatically substitute the word "aspirin" for them. (Makers of acetaminophen and ibuprofen pain relievers are careful in their advertising to identify their products as nonaspirin products.) So, now we know that Anacin has aspirin in it. Moreover, we know that Anacin has twice as much aspirin in it, but we don't know twice as much as what. Does it have twice as much aspirin as an ordinary aspirin tablet? If so, what is an ordinary aspirin tablet, and how much aspirin does it contain? Twice as much as Excedrin or Bufferin? Twice as much as a chocolate chip cookie? Remember those Unfinished Words and how they lead you on without saying anything.

Finally, what about those doctors who are doing all that recommending? Who are they? How many of them are there? What kind of doctors are they? What are their qualifications? Who asked them about recommending pain relievers? What other pain relievers did they recommend? And there are a whole lot more questions about this "poll" of doctors to which I'd like to know the answers, but you get the point. Sometimes, when I call my doctor, she tells me to take two aspirin and call her office in the morning. Is that where Anacin got this ad?

Read the Label, or the Brochure

Weasel words aren't just found on television, on the radio, or in newspaper and magazine ads. Just about any language associated with a product will contain the doublespeak of advertising. Remember the Eli Lilly case and the doublespeak on the information sheet that came with the birth control pills. Here's another example.

In 1983, the Estée Lauder cosmetics company announced a new product called "Night Repair." A small brochure distributed with the product stated that "Night Repair was scientifically formulated in Estée Lauder's U.S. laboratories as part of the Swiss Age-Controlling Skincare Program. Although only nature controls the aging process, this program helps control the signs of aging and encourages skin to look and feel younger." You might want to read these two sentences again, because they sound great but say nothing.

First, note that the product was "scientifically formulated" in the company's laboratories. What does that mean? What constitutes a scientific formulation? You wouldn't expect the company to say that the product was casually, mechanically, or carelessly formulated, or just thrown together one day when the people in the white coats didn't have anything better to do. But the word "scientifically" lends an air of precision and promise that just isn't there.

It is the second sentence, however, that's really weasely, both syntactically and semantically. The only factual part of this sentence is the introductory dependent clause—"only nature controls the aging process." Thus, the only fact in the ad is relegated to a dependent clause, a clause dependent on the main clause, which contains no factual or definite information at all and indeed purports to contradict the independent clause. The new "skincare program" (notice it's not a skin cream but a "program") does not claim to stop or even retard the aging process. What, then, does Night Repair, at a price of over $35 (in 1983 dollars) for a .87-ounce bottle do? According to this brochure, nothing. It only "helps," and the brochure does not say how much it helps. Moreover, it only "helps control," and then it only helps control the "*signs* of aging," not the aging itself. Also, it "encourages" skin not to *be* younger but only to "look and feel" younger. The brochure does not say younger than what. Of the sixteen words in the main clause of this second sentence, nine are weasel words. So, before you spend all that money for Night Repair, or any other cosmetic product, read the words carefully, and then decide if you're getting what you think you're paying for.

Other Tricks of the Trade

Advertisers' use of doublespeak is endless. The best way advertisers can make something out of nothing is through words. Although there are a lot of visual images used on television and in magazines and newspapers, every advertiser wants to create that memorable line that will stick in the public consciousness. I am sure pure joy reigned in one advertising agency when a study found that children who were asked to spell the word "relief" promptly and proudly responded "r-o-l-a-i-d-s."

The variations, combinations, and permutations of doublespeak used in advertising go on and on, running from the use of rhetorical questions ("Wouldn't you really rather have a Buick?" "If you can't trust Prestone, who can you trust?") to flattering you with compliments ("The lady has taste." "We think a cigar smoker is someone special." "You've come a long way baby."). You know, of course, how you're *supposed* to answer those questions, and you know that those compliments are just leading up to the sales pitches for the products. Before you dismiss such tricks of the trade as obvious, however, just remember that all of these statements and questions were part of very successful advertising campaigns.

A more subtle approach is the ad that proclaims a supposedly unique quality for a product, a quality that really isn't unique. "If it doesn't say Goodyear, it can't be polyglas." Sounds good, doesn't it? Polyglas is available only from Goodyear because Goodyear copyrighted that trade name. Any other tire manufacturer could make exactly the same tire but could not call it "polyglas," because that would be copyright infringement. "Polyglas" is simply Goodyear's name for its fiberglass-reinforced tire.

Since we like to think of ourselves as living in a technologically advanced country, science and technology have a great appeal in selling products. Advertisers are quick to use scientific doublespeak to push their products. There are all kinds of elixirs, additives, scientific potions, and mysterious mixtures added to all kinds of products. Gasoline contains "HTA," "F–130," "Platformate," and other chemical-sounding additives, but nowhere does an advertisement give any real information about the additive.

Shampoo, deodorant, mouthwash, cold medicine, sleeping pills, and any number of other products all seem to contain some special chemical ingredient that allows them to work wonders. "Certs contains a sparkling drop of Retsyn." So what? What's "Retsyn"? What's it do? What's so special about it? When they don't have a secret ingredient in their product, advertisers still find a way to claim scientific validity. There's "Sinarest. Created by a research scientist who actually gets sinus headaches." Sounds nice, but what kind of research does this scientist do? How do you know if she is any kind of expert on sinus medicine? Besides, this ad doesn't tell you a thing about the medicine itself and what it does.

Advertising Doublespeak Quick Quiz

Now it's time to test your awareness of advertising doublespeak. (You didn't think I would just let you read this and forget it, did you?) The following is a list of statements from some recent ads. Your job is to figure out what each of these ads really says:

DOMINO'S PIZZA: "Because nobody delivers better."
SINUTAB: "It can stop the pain."
TUMS: "The stronger acid neutralizer."
MAXIMUM STRENGTH DRISTAN: "Strong medicine for tough sinus colds."
LISTERMINT: "Making your mouth a cleaner place."
CASCADE: "For virtually spotless dishes nothing beats Cascade."
NUPRIN: "Little. Yellow. Different. Better."
ANACIN: "Better relief."
SUDAFED: "Fast sinus relief that won't put you fast asleep."
ADVIL: "Advanced medicine for pain."
PONDS COLD CREAM: "Ponds cleans like no soap can."
MILLER LITE BEER: "Tastes great. Less filling."
PHILIPS MILK OF MAGNESIA: "Nobody treats you better than MOM (Philips Milk of Magnesia)."
BAYER: "The wonder drug that works wonders."
CRACKER BARREL: "Judged to be the best."
KNORR: "Where taste is everything."
ANUSOL: "Anusol is the word to remember for relief."
DIMETAPP: "It relieves kids as well as colds."
LIQUID DRANO: "The liquid strong enough to be called Drano."
JOHNSON & JOHNSON BABY POWDER: "Like magic for your skin."
PURITAN: "Make it your oil for life."
PAM: "Pam, because how you cook is as important as what you cook."
IVORY SHAMPOO AND CONDITIONER: "Leave your hair feeling Ivory clean."
TYLENOL GEL-CAPS: "It's not a capsule. It's better."
ALKA-SELTZER PLUS: "Fast, effective relief for winter colds."

The World of Advertising

In the world of advertising, people wear "dentures," not false teeth; they suffer from "occasional irregularity," not constipation; they need deodorants for their "nervous wetness," not for sweat; they use "bathroom tissue," not toilet paper; and they don't dye their hair, they "tint" or "rinse" it. Advertisements offer "real counterfeit diamonds" without the slightest hint of embarrassment, or boast of goods made out of "genuine imitation leather" or "virgin vinyl."

In the world of advertising, the girdle becomes a "body shaper," "form persuader," "control garment," "controller," "outerwear enhancer," "body garment," or "anti-gravity panties," and is sold with such trade names as "The Instead," "The Free Spirit," and "The Body Briefer."

A study some years ago found the following words to be among the most popular used in U.S. television advertisements: "new," "improved," "better," "extra," "fresh," "clean," "beautiful," "free," "good," "great," and "light." At the same time, the following words were found to be among the most frequent on British television: "new," "good-better-best," "free," "fresh," "delicious," "full," "sure," "clean," "wonderful," and "special." While these words may occur most frequently in ads, and while ads may be filled with weasel words, you have to watch out for all the words used in advertising, not just the words mentioned here.

Every word in an ad is there for a reason; no word is wasted. Your job is to figure out exactly what each word is doing in an ad—what each word really means, not what the advertiser wants you to think it means. Remember, the ad is trying to get you to buy a product, so it will put the product in the best possible light, using any device, trick, or means legally allowed. Your only defense against advertising (besides taking up permanent residence on the moon) is to develop and use a strong critical reading, listening, and looking ability. Always ask yourself what the ad is *really* saying. When you see ads on television, don't be misled by the pictures, the visual images. What does the ad say about the product? What does the ad *not* say? What information is missing from the ad? Only by becoming an active, critical consumer of the doublespeak of advertising will you ever be able to cut through the doublespeak and discover what the ad is really saying.

The Language of Advertising

CHARLES A. O'NEILL

His name is Joe. But he's not just your ordinary Joe. You've probably seen him; he's Joe Camel. On the billboards and in the magazine ads, he looked vaguely like a cartoonist's composite sketch of the Rolling Stones, lounging around in a celebrity waiting area at MTV headquarters in New York. He was poised, confident, leaning against a railing or playing pool with his friends. His personal geometry was always just right. He often wore a white suit, dark shirt, sunglasses. Cigarette in hand, wry smile on his lips, his attitude was distinctly confident, urbane.

Joe was very cool and very powerful. So cool and powerful that more than 90% of six-year-olds matched Joe Camel with a picture of a cigarette, making him as well-known as Mickey Mouse.[1]

Good advertising, but bad public relations.

Finally, in 1997, after extended sparring with the tobacco company about whether in fact Joe promoted smoking, and whether cartoons were most likely to be noticed by children or adults, the FTC brought the ads to an end. President Clinton spoke for the regulators when he said, "Let's stop pretending that a cartoon camel in a funny costume is trying to sell to adults, not children."

Joe's 23-year-old advertising campaign was stopped because it was obvious that his mission was to turn kids into lung cancer patients. That's bad enough. But beneath the surface, the debate about Joe typifies something more interesting and broad based: the rather uncomfortable, tentative acceptance of advertising in our society. We recognize the legitimacy—even the value—of advertising but on some level we can't quite fully embrace it as a "normal" part of our experience.

At best, we view advertising as distracting. At worst, we view it as dangerous to our health and a pernicious threat to our social values. One notable report acknowledged the positive contribution of advertising (e.g., provides information, supports worthy causes, and encourages competition and innovation), then added, "In the competition to attract even larger audiences . . . communicators can find themselves pressured . . . to set aside high artistic and moral standards and lapse into superficiality, tawdriness and moral squalor."[2]

How does advertising work? Why is it so powerful? Why does it raise such concern? What case can be made for and against the advertising business?

In order to understand advertising, you must accept that it is not about truth, virtue, love, or positive societal values. It is about money. It is about moving customers through the sales process. Sometimes the words and images are concrete; sometimes they are merely suggestive. Sometimes ads provide useful information; sometimes they convince us that we need to spend money to solve a problem we never knew we had. Ads are designed to be intrusive. We're not always pleased about the way they clutter our environment and violate our sense of private space. We're not always happy with the tactics they use to impose themselves upon us.

Whatever the product or creative strategy, advertisements derive their power from a purposeful, directed combination of images. These can take the form of words, sounds, or visuals, used individually or together. The combination of images is the language of advertising, a language unlike any other.

Everyone who grows up in the civilized world soon learns that advertising language is different from other languages. Read this aloud: "With Nice 'n Easy, it's color so natural, the closer he gets the better you look" Many children would be unable to explain how this classic ad for Clairol's Nice 'n Easy hair coloring differs from "ordinary language," but they would say, "It sounds like an ad." Whether printed on a page, blended with music on the radio, or whispered on the sound track of a television commercial, advertising language is *different*.

The language of advertising changes with the times. Styles and creative concepts come and go. But there are at least four distinct, general characteristics of the language of advertising that make it different from other languages. They lend advertising its persuasive power:

1. The language of advertising is edited and purposeful.

2. The language of advertising is rich and arresting; it is specifically intended to attract and hold our attention.

3. The language of advertising involves us; in effect, *we* complete the message.

4. The language of advertising is simple and direct. It holds no secrets from us.

Edited and Purposeful

In his book, *Future Shock*, Alvin Toffler described various types of messages we receive from the world around us each day. He observed that there is a difference between normal "coded" messages and "engineered" messages. Much of normal, human experience is "uncoded." When a man walks down a street, for example, he sees where he is going and hears random sounds. These are mental images, but they are not messages "designed by anyone to communicate anything and the man's understanding of it does not depend directly on a social code—a set of agreed-upon signs and definitions."[3] In contrast, Toffler describes a talk show conversation as "coded"; the speaker's ability to exchange information with the host depends upon societal conventions.

The language of advertising is coded. It exists in the context of our society. It is also carefully engineered, and ruthlessly purposeful. When he wrote in the 1960s, he estimated that the average adult was exposed to 560 advertising messages each day. That was back in the 1960s. Now, our homes are equipped with 400-channel, direct-broadcast satellite television, the Internet, video streaming mobile devices, video games and other new forms of mass media. We're literally swimming in a sea of information. We're totally wired and wireless. We're overwhelmed by countless billboards in subway stations, stickers on light poles, 15-second spots on television, and an endless stream of spam and pop up messages online.

Demanding Attention

Among the hundreds of advertising messages in stores for us each day, very few will actually command our conscious attention. The rest are screened out. The people who design and write ads know about this screening process; they anticipate and accept it as a premise of their business.

The classic, all-time favorite device used to breach the barrier is sex. There was a time, many years ago, when advertisers used some measure of subtlety and discretion in their application of sexual themes to their mass media work. No more. Sensuality has been replaced by in-your-face, unrestrained sexuality. One is about romance and connection; the other, physical connection and emotional distance.

A poster promotes clothing sold by the apparel company, French Connection group, United Kingdom: (FCUK). Large type tells us, "Apparently there are more important things in life than fashion. Yeah, right." This text is accompanied by a photo of two young people in what has become a standard set up: A boy. A girl. She is pretty, in a detached, offhand sort of way. He has not shaved for 48 hours. Behind them there is a vague impression of a waterfront. They are sharing physical space, but there is no sense of human contact or emotion. The company name appears on the lower right hand side of the poster. The headline is intended to be ironic: "Of course there are things that are more important than fashion, but right now, who cares?" The company maintains that they are "not trying to shock people." As absurd as it may seem, this is actually the truth. This company is not in the business of selling shock. They are selling clothes. They are making a lot of money selling clothes because they know what motivates their teenaged customers—a desire to separate from their parents and declare their membership in the tribe of their peers.

Fortunately, advertisers use many other techniques to attract and hold the attention of the targeted consumer audience. The strategy may include strong creative execution or a plain, straightforward presentation of product features and customer benefits. Consider this random cross-section of advertisements from popular media.

- An ad for SalesForce.com used a photo of the Dalai Lama beneath the headline, "There is no software on the path to enlightenment." (What does this mean? "SalesForce.com provides computer services, so I won't have to buy software myself.")
- An ad for two products—the Volkswagen Beetle, and the Apple iPod—used only one word: "Duh." Above it, moving from left to right, we see a photo of the car, a plus sign and to the right, the iPod. (What makes this work? Fast Company (10/03) described this as "a marriage of two classic 'underdog' brands . . . a psychographic match made in heaven. VW and Apple both appeal to young, high-income, adventure-seeking customers. . . .")
- "Can a security blanket be made of sheet metal?" (GM) In the background, there is a photo of a tot asleep in a car seat (Who doesn't like cute little kids? What parent doesn't think about safety these days?)
- Some ads entertain us and are effective, even though they don't really focus on the product. They work because we remember them. Geico is an automobile insurance

company, but they use a cute little lizard as a character in their ads. (What does a lizard have to do with an insurance company? More than meets the eye. A *gecko* is a type of lizard.)

- Some ads tell us we have problems—real or imagined—that we'd better solve right away. Do you have dry skin or "unsightly eyebrow hairs?" ("I never really noticed, but now that you mention it. . . .")

"Give your car the pink slip." (A short term car rental company lets us know that we don't need to own a car—we can pick one up whenever and wherever we need it.)

Soft drink companies are in an advertising category of their own. In the archetypical version of a soft drink TV spot, babies frolic with puppies in the sunlit foreground while their youthful parents play touch football. On the porch, Grandma and Pops quietly smile as they wait for all of this affection to transform the world into a place of warmth, harmony, and joy.

Dr. Pepper ads say "Be you!" and feature dancers prancing around singing songs about "Individuality." In Coke's ads, the singer Maya tells us this can of syrupy fizz is "Real." And Pepsi has Britney Spears singing "Pepsi: for those who think young!" The message: If you are among the millions of people who see the commercial and buy the product, you will become 'different'. You will find yourself transformed into a unique ("Be you", "Individuality", "Real"), hip ("young") person.[4]

These "slice of life" ads seduce us into feeling—somewhere in the back of our heads—that if we drink the right combination of sugar, preservatives, caramel coloring, and a few secret ingredients, we'll fulfill our yearning for a world where folks from all nations, creeds and sexual orientations live together in a state of perfect bliss. At least for the five minutes it takes us to pour the stuff down our parched, fast-food-filled throats.

If you don't buy this version of the American Dream, look around. You are sure to find a product that promises to help you gain prestige in whatever posse you do happen to run with.

When the connection is made, the results can be very powerful. Even a commodity product like coffee can be artfully changed from a mere beverage into an emotional experience. *The Wall Street Journal* (7/14/03) summarized the challenge the marketers at Starbucks faced in promoting their stores in China: "Selling an upscale, Western lifestyle that is both in demand in China yet meets resistance among those unfamiliar with the taste of coffee." The article goes on to describe a customer in Shanghai, who drinks tea at home but coffee in public. He said he prefers the taste of tea, but he likes the image that drinking Starbucks coffee conjures up: relaxed affluence. "It's an attitude." A medium size latte costs the equivalent of $2.65. In Shanghai, the monthly disposable income of an average three-person household is $143.00. One cup of coffee costs nearly 2% of the average household's monthly income.

What Starbucks has accomplished is not far short of astonishing. They have been successful in taking a purely commodity product that their prospective customers do not particularly enjoy and turning it into not just another drink, but a hip, groovy and chic "attitude"; and they've done this in a Communist country, where the rules according to Mao would have us believe that there are no class distinctions. What's more, they have created primary demand for a product category; a difficult, if not nearly impossible, feat.

Ad campaigns and branding strategies do not often emerge like Botticelli's Venus from the sea, flawless and fully grown. Most often, the creative strategy is developed only after extensive research. "Who will be interested in our product? How old are they? Where do they live? How much money do they earn? What problem will our product solve?" The people at Starbucks did not decide to go to China on a whim. The people at French Connection did not create their brand name just to offend everyone who is old-fashioned enough to think that some words don't belong on billboards, T-shirts and store fronts.

Involving

We have seen that the language of advertising is carefully engineered; we have discovered a few of the devices it uses to get our attention. Coke and Pepsi have entranced us with visions of peace and love. An actress offers a winsome smile. Now that they have our attention, advertisers present information intended to show us that their product fills a need and differs from the competition. Advertisers exploit and intensify product differences when they find them, and invent them when they do not.

As soon as we see or hear an advertisement, our imagination is set in motion, and our individual fears, aspirations, quirks and insecurities come out to play.

It was common not long ago for advertisers in the fashion industry to make use of gaunt, languid models. To some observers, these ads promoted "heroin chic." Perhaps they were not substance abusers, but something was most certainly unusual about the models appearing in ads for Prada and Calvin Klein Products. A young woman in a Prada ad projects no emotion whatsoever. Her posture suggests that she is in a trance or drug-induced stupor. In a Calvin Klein ad, a young man, like the woman from Prada, is gaunt beyond reason. He is shirtless. As if to draw more attention to his peculiar posture and "zero body fat" status, he is shown pinching the skin next to his navel. To some, this also suggests that he is preparing to insert a needle.

The fashion industry backed away from the heroin theme. Now the models look generally better fed. But they are, nonetheless, still lost in a world of ennui and isolation. In an ad by Andrew Mark NY, we see a young woman wearing little leather shorts. Her boyfriend's arm is wrapped around her, his thumb pushing ever-so-slightly below the waistband of her pants. What does he look like? He appears to be dazed. He is wearing jeans, an unzipped leather jacket. He hasn't shaved for a couple of days. We are left with the impression that either something has just happened here, or is about to. It probably has something to do with sex.

Do these depictions of a decadent lifestyle exploit certain elements of our society—the young, insecure or clueless? Or did these ads, and others of their ilk, simply reflect profound bad taste? Most advertising is about exploitation—the systematic, deliberate identification of our needs and wants, followed by the delivery of a carefully constructed promise that the product will satisfy them.

Advertisers make use of a great variety of techniques and devices to engage us in the delivery of their messages. Some are subtle, making use of warm, entertaining or comforting images or symbols. Others, as we've seen, are about as subtle as an action sequence from Quentin Tarantino's latest movie. Although it may seem hard to believe, advertising writers did not invent sex. They did not invent our tendency to admire and seek to identify ourselves with famous people. Once we have seen a famous person in an ad, we associate the product with the person. When we buy Coke, we're becoming a member of the Friends of Maya Club. The logic is faulty, but we fall for it just the same. Advertising works, not because Maya and Britney have discriminating taste, or the nameless waif in the clothing ad is a fashion diva, but because we participate in it.

Keeping It Simple

Advertising language differs from other types of language in another important respect, it is a simple language. To measure the simplicity of an ad, calculate its Fog Index. Robert Gunning[5] developed this formula to determine the comparative ease with which any given piece of written communication can be read.

- Calculate the number of words in an average sentence.
- Count the number of words of three or more syllables in a typical 100-word passage, omitting words that are capitalized, combinations of two simple words, or verb forms made into three-syllable words by the addition of *-ed* or *-es*.
- Add the two figures (the average number of words per sentence and the number of three-syllable words per 100 words), then multiply the result by 4.

In an advertisement for Harry Potter books, the visual is a photo of a slightly menacing fellow standing next to his bike in an alley. Here is the text:

Flying cars. Fire Whiskey. Death Eaters.

There's some pretty tough stuff in Harry Potter—bad guys so bad they're called Death Eaters. That's only one of the wicked reasons even bikers think Harry Potter is cool enough to ride with them.

Reader's Digest has a Fog Index of 8. *US News & World Report* and *Time Magazine* are about 9. There are 8.5 words—none three syllables—in the average "sentence."

1. Words per sentence: 8.5
2. Three syllable words/100: 0
3. Subtotal: 8.5
4. Multiply by .4:   3.4

According to Gunning's scale, you should be able to comprehend this ad if you are about half way through the third grade. Comic books weigh in at 6; *Reader's Digest* at 9; *Atlantic Monthly* is 12.

Why do advertisers generally favor simple language? The answer lies with the consumer. As a practical matter, we would not notice many of these messages if length or eloquence was counted among their virtues. Today's consumer cannot take the time to focus on anything for long, much less blatant advertising messages. Every aspect of modern life runs at an accelerated pace. Voice mail, pagers, cellular phones, e-mail, the Internet—the world is always awake, always switched on, and hungry for information. Time generally, and TV-commercial time in particular, is dissected into increasingly smaller segments.

Toffler views the evolution toward shorter language as a natural progression: three-syllable words are simply harder to read than one- or two-syllable words. Simple ideas are more readily transferred from one person to another than complex ideas. Therefore, advertising copy uses increasingly simple language, as does society at large. In *Future Shock,* Toffler speculates:

If the [English] language had the same number of words in Shakespeare's time as it does today, at least 200,000 words—perhaps several times that many—have dropped out and been replaced in the intervening four centuries. The high turnover rate reflects changes in things, processes, and qualities in the environment from the world of consumer products and technology.

It is no accident that the first terms Toffler uses to illustrate his point ("fast-back," "wash-and-wear," and "flashcube") were invented not by engineers, or journalists, but by advertising copywriters.

Advertising language is simple language; difficult words are deleted and replaced by simple words or images not open to misinterpretation.

Who Is Responsible?

Some critics view the advertising industry as a cranky, unwelcomed child of the free enterprise system—a noisy, whining, brash kid who must somehow be kept in line, but can't just yet be thrown out of the house. In reality, advertising mirrors the fears, quirks, and aspirations of the society that creates it (and is, in turn, sold by it). This alone exposes advertising to parody and ridicule. The overall level of acceptance and respect for advertising is also influenced by the varied quality of the ads themselves. Some ads, including a few of the examples cited here, are deliberately designed to provoke controversy. Critics have declared Advertising guilty of other failings as well:

1. Advertising encourages unhealthy habits.
2. Advertising feeds on human weaknesses and exaggerates the importance of material things, encouraging "impure" emotions and vanities.
3. Advertising sells daydreams—distracting, purposeless visions of lifestyles beyond the reach of the majority of the people who are most exposed to advertising.
4. Advertising warps our vision of reality, implanting in us groundless fears and insecurities.
5. Advertising downgrades the intelligence of the public.
6. Advertising debases English.
7. Advertising perpetuates racial and sexual stereotypes.

What can be said in advertising's defense? Does it encourage free-market competition and product innovation? Sure. But the real answer is simply this: Advertising is, at heart, only a reflection of society.

What can we say about the charge that advertising debases the intelligence of the public? Exactly how intelligent is "the public?" Sadly, evidence abounds that the public at large is not particularly intelligent, after all. Americans now get 31 percent of their calories from junk food and alcoholic beverages.[6] Michael can't read. Jessica can't write. And the entire family spends the night in front of the television, watching idiots eat living insects in the latest installment for a 'reality' show.

Ads are effective because they sell products. They would not succeed if they did not reflect the values and motivations of the real world. Advertising both reflects and shapes our perception of reality. Ivory Snow is pure. Federal Express won't let you down. Absolut is cool. Sasson is sexy. Mercedes represents quality. Our sense of what these brand names stand for may have as much to do with advertising as with the objective "truth."

Good, responsible advertising can serve as a positive influence for change, while fueling commerce. But the obverse is also true: Advertising, like any form of mass communication, can be a force for both "good" and "bad." It can just as readily reinforce or encourage irresponsible behavior, ageism, sexism, ethnocentrism, racism, homophobia, heterophobia—you name it—as it can encourage support for diversity and social progress.

As Pogo once famously said, "We have met the enemy, and he is us."[7]

NOTES

1. Internet: *http://www.joechemo.org*.
2. Pontifical Council for Social Communications, "Ethics in Advertising," published 2/22/97.
3. Alvin Toffler, *Future Shock* (New York Random House, 1970), p. 146.
4. Shannon O'Neill, a student at the University of New Hampshire, contributed this example and others cited here.
5. Curtis D. MacDougall, *Interpretive Reporting* (New York: Macmillan, 1968), p. 94.
6. 2000 study by the American Society for Clinical Nutrition (Boston Globe, 7/29/93).
7. Walt Kelly, "Pogo" cartoon (1960s); referring to the Vietnam War.

FREEWRITING ASSIGNMENT

Describe an experience in which you purchased a product because you were influenced by its advertising language. For example, did you buy a hair, beauty, or electronic product because of the promises made by its ad? Explain.

CRITICAL READING

1. Consider Lutz's argument that advertisers are trying to "trick" consumers with their false promises and claims. How much are our expectations of product performance influenced by the claims and slogans of advertising? How do you think O'Neill would respond to Lutz's accusation?

2. Does the fact that O'Neill is a professional advertiser influence your reception of his essay? Does it make his argument more or less persuasive?

3. Review the rules and regulations concerning the words "new" and "improved." How do advertisers address the problem of product regulations? Do such rules really protect consumers? Explain.

4. O'Neill is an advertising professional. Does his writing style reflect the advertising techniques he describes? Cite examples to support your answer.

5. How does O'Neill address any objections his audience may have to his argument? Are the objections he anticipates indeed the ones you had as a reader? Does his "answer" make his essay stronger? Explain.

6. O'Neill notes that symbols have become important elements in the language of advertising. Can you think of some specific symbols from advertising that you associate with your lifestyle? How important are these symbols to you? How do they work as wordless advertising? Explain.

7. A "weasel word" is a word so hollow it has no meaning. Consider your own reaction to weasel words when you hear them. Try to identify as many weasel words as you can. What are the words and what do consumers think they mean?

8. Do you think it is ethical for advertisers to create a sense of product difference when there really isn't any? Consider advertisements for products such as gasoline, beer, or coffee.

CRITICAL WRITING

9. *Exploratory Writing*: O'Neill, in his essay, makes several generalizations that characterize the language of advertising. Think about ads that you have recently seen or read and make a list of your own generalizations about the language of advertising. Refer to some specific advertisements in your response.

10. *Persuasive Writing*: O'Neill believes that advertising language mirrors the fears, quirks, and aspirations of the society that creates it. Do you agree or disagree with this statement? Explain your perspective in a brief essay supporting your response with examples.

11. *Analytical Writing*: Choose a brand-name product that you use regularly or to which you have particular loyalty, and identify one or more of its competitors. Examine some advertisements for each brand. Write a short paper explaining what makes you prefer your brand to the others.

GROUP PROJECTS

12. Review Lutz's "Doublespeak Quick Quiz." Choose five items and analyze them, using dictionary meanings to explain what the ads are really saying.

13. With your group, think of some recent advertising campaigns that created controversy (Abercrombie and Fitch, Calvin Klein, Benetton, etc.) What made them controversial? How did this impact sales?

14. O'Neill (paragraph 30) notes that sometimes advertisers use symbols to engage their audience. With your group, create a list of brand symbols or logos, their corresponding products, and what lifestyle we associate with the logo or symbol. Are some logos more popular or prestigious? Explain.

15. Working in a group, develop a slogan and advertising campaign for one of the following products: sneakers, soda, a candy bar, or jeans. How would you apply the principles of advertising language to market your product? After completing your marketing plan, "sell" your product to the class. If time permits, explain the reasoning behind your selling technique.

Chapter Nineteen

Strategic Writing & News Releases

The Importance of Good Writing

As professionals, the authors of this book hired our own writing staffs. As professors, we get to have gossipy lunches with employers who want to hire—you. And we, as professionals, and those employers say the same thing: "Please give me someone who can *write!*" Yes, employers want diplomatic team players. And they want hard-working students with experience. But they almost always begin by asking for good writers.

A few years ago, we secretly studied the guest speakers we brought into our classes to see what job skills they stressed to students. We gave up the study when, after several dozen speakers, it became clear that each put good writing at the top of the list.

We've noticed a similar trend in management textbooks. When successful CEOs and other leaders discuss the talents that took them to the top, communication skills—both written and oral—almost always receive prominent mention.

This book is all about helping you become a first-rate strategic writer. As you already know, strategic writing involves delivering goal-oriented messages—messages that are on-strategy. Strategic writing also involves carefully crafted sentences. You don't want to distract your audiences with bad grammar, sloppiness or wordiness. The appendixes of this book contain guidelines on punctuation, grammar, style, editing and proofreading. We hope you'll review those. What follows here are tips for strengthening sentences.

Ten Tips for Writing Better Sentences

1. **Challenge *to be* verbs.** Challenge every appearance of *am, is, was, were, be, being, been* and every other form of the *to be* infinitive. Sometimes a *to be* verb best suits the needs of a sentence, but often you can find a stronger, more evocative verb.

Original	Revision
He *will be* a good communicator.	He *will communicate* well.
We *are inviting* you . . .	We *invite* you . . .

2. **Use active voice.** By active voice, we mean active subject. In active voice, the sentence's subject does the action described by the verb. In passive voice, the subject doesn't do the action.

Passive Voice	Active Voice
Our profits were affected by a sales slump.	A sales slump affected our profits.

Passive voice is grammatically correct, and it's the right choice when the action is more important than the action's doer (for example, "She was fired"). But passive voice can seem timid, and it requires a weak *to be* verb. In contrast, active voice is confident and concise.

3. **Challenge modifiers.** Modifiers (adjectives and adverbs) can strengthen a sentence by sharpening your meaning. But sometimes they prop up poorly chosen words, especially imprecise nouns, verbs and adjectives. A precise, well-chosen word needs no modification.

Original	Revision
We are *very happy*.	We are *ecstatic*.
Quickly take your report to the client.	*Rush* your report to the client.
He is *rather tired*.	He is *tired*.
Please deliver the package to our headquarters building.	Please deliver the package to our *headquarters*.

4. **Challenge long words.** If a long word or phrase is the best choice, use it. Otherwise, use a shorter option.

Original	Revision
utilize	use
revenue-enhancement measure	tax

5. **Challenge prepositional phrases.** To tighten sentences, turn prepositional phrases into shorter adjectives when possible. Avoid a string of prepositional phrases.

Original	Revision
I will present the report in the meeting *on Thursday*.	I will present the report in *Thursday's* meeting.
We will meet *on Thursday in* Weslaco *at* the Lancaster Hotel *on* McDaniel Street *near* the park.	We will meet Thursday at Weslaco's Lancaster Hotel, 1423 McDaniel St.

6. **Challenge long sentences.** How long should a sentence be? Long enough to make its point clearly and gracefully—and no longer. Challenge sentences that are more than 25 words; realize, however, that some good sentences will exceed that length. As discussed above, you can tighten sentences by eliminating *to be* verbs, modifiers and prepositional phrases.

7. **Avoid overused expressions.** Clichés such as "It has come to my attention" and "I regret to inform you" lack original thought. They sound insincere. Overused figures of speech such as "He's a fish out of water" don't create the engaging image they once did. Overused expressions suggest to readers that you didn't take the time to devote clear, serious thought to the message you're sending.

8. **Avoid placing important words or phrases in the middle of a sentence.** The beginning of a sentence breaks a silence and calls attention to itself. The last words of a sentence echo into a brief silence and gain emphasis. The middle of a sentence generally draws the least attention. A writer friend of ours says, "Words go to the middle to die."

9. **Keep the focus on the reader.** Tell readers what they want and need to know—not just what you want them to know. Keep the focus on how they benefit from reading your document. Talk to them about themselves and what your message means to them.

10. **Read your sentences aloud.** Or at least whisper them to yourself. That's the surest way to check for effective sentence rhythms. Reading aloud also can be an effective editing technique.

Good writing is also concise, so we'll end this segment.

THE WRITING PROCESS

Good writing is more than just good luck and natural talent. Good writing is the result of a logical process. Because the writing process can seem intimidating (or just plain hard), some writers prefer to just rush in and start writing. But that's like planning a Spring Break trip with no destination, no map, no budget—and no hope. Other writers may feel so overwhelmed that they avoid the job until it's too late for their best work.

Good writing isn't easy. There's nothing wrong with you if you find writing to be hard work. You can, however, make that hard work a little easier by following a nine-step writing process.

STEP ONE: RESEARCH

This book shows you how to write more than 35 documents for public relations, advertising, business communications and sales and marketing. And for each document, we begin with an analysis of purpose, audience and media. We recommend that you do the same.

Begin your research by defining the document's purpose: What is its goal? What should it accomplish? What business goal does it support? With your answers to these questions, you should begin to answer another purpose-related question: What should be the one, key strategic message of this document?

Now extend your research to the target audience of the document. To whom are you writing? Audience research generally falls into two categories: demographic and psychographic data. Demographic data consist of nonattitudinal information such as age, income, gender, educational level, race and so on. Psychographic information contains attitudinal details about values, beliefs, opinions and, of course, attitudes. Psychographic information can include political and religious beliefs, personal ethics codes, goals in life and so on. Use your research to deeply understand your readers. Perhaps the most important question you can answer is why members of your target audience should care about your document. What's in it for them?

With your understanding of your target audience, you might want to refine the one, key strategic message you've begun to identify.

Finally, you should gather information about the medium or media you'll be using. Will you use speeches? News media? Special events? Web sites? Knowing the characteristics of your chosen medium can help you further refine your one, key strategic message. One of the best ways to select the best medium for your message is to study your target audience. Which media does it prefer in this situation?

STEP TWO: CREATIVITY/BRAINSTORMING

Some documents, such as advertisements, newsletter features and direct-mail packages, call for a high degree of creativity. Other documents, such as news releases and business reports, are more straightforward. When your one, key strategic message requires a creative approach, consider using a basic five-step approach to developing ideas. In the mid-20th century, advertising expert James Webb Young wrote that the creative process consists of these steps:

- Gathering research
- Thinking about your research
- Concentrating on other matters and letting your subconscious go to work
- Recognizing when your subconscious reports back a great idea
- Refining the great idea

A process known as brainstorming can assist the creative process. Brainstorming usually is a group activity in a comfortable setting. Group members toss ideas back and forth, building on one another's ideas, reviewing key research findings and encouraging everyone to be innovative. Brainstorming works best when two rules apply: No one's idea gets ridiculed, and no one worries about who gets the credit.

STEP THREE: ORGANIZING/OUTLINING

You've gathered all the necessary information. You've identified a key message and, perhaps, developed a creative approach. Now it's time to determine what to include and how to organize that information.

Many things affect organization, including the target audience's interests, the type of document you're writing and the importance of each piece of information. The best general guidelines for good organization are to consider your audience (what order of information will keep it interested?) and to be logical: You should have a reason for the order of presentation: One part of the document should lead logically to the next.

Writing an outline, whether it's formal with roman numerals or just notes scribbled on an envelope, will help you refine and remember your document's organization. Don't be surprised if you change or reorganize items as you write. New options may appear as you progress. (Experienced writers sometimes can create outlines in their heads—or, as they begin to type, they type a few organizational ideas and then begin composing.)

STEP FOUR: WRITING

Finally. Now for perhaps the hardest part of the writing process. Again, writing is tough work for most of us. If you just can't get the beginning, start somewhere else. Your outline allows you to do that. And don't worry about getting the words just right in your first draft. It's more important to get the ideas and meanings right.

STEP FIVE: REVISION

One cliché about writing says, "Good writing isn't written; it's rewritten." Even if you love your first draft, set it aside for as long as possible. Return to it fresh, and be critical. Approach the document now not as a writer but as a reader. Poet and novelist Robert Graves recommends imagining that your intended reader is looking over your shoulder and saying, "But what does that mean? Can't it be clearer? What's in this for me? How do I benefit by reading this?"

You might also try reading your document aloud. This can be a good way to catch mistakes or language that doesn't flow well.

Writers who get serious about revision sometimes find that they have accidentally memorized all or parts of a document. With the document temporarily lodged in their memories, the writers are able to revise it as they eat lunch, ride in an elevator or drive home. This may sound excessive (even weird)—but it illustrates the point that good, successful strategic writers don't settle for first drafts.

STEP SIX: EDITING

Sure, colleagues may edit your document. But you should be the document's first editor. Think of editing as the last fine-tuning before you hand the document to your boss. Editing breaks down into two parts—macroediting and microediting—and you should do both. Macroediting involves looking at the "big picture" of the document. Is the document's key message clear and goal-related? Does the document appeal to readers' self-interests? Does it cover the important parts of who, what, when, where, why and how? Is it well-organized—does one section lead logically to the next? Is the format—the way it looks on the page (or computer screen)—correct?

Macroediting also can involve a final revision. Can you find a precise noun to replace a current adjective-noun combination? Can you find a precise verb to replace a current adverb–verb combination? Are you using boring *to be* verbs too often? Can you find more interesting verbs?

Microediting is proofreading. It involves going through the document one sentence at time and double-checking grammar (including spelling and punctuation) and accuracy. *Double-check all names, dates, prices and other facts.* Use your computer's spell-check program, but don't rely on it exclusively. Use a dictionary to look up every word or phrase that could be wrong. Double-check the accuracy of quotations. Microediting is best done backward, starting with the document's last sentence. Moving backward breaks up the flow of the too-familiar document. Moving backward makes the document sound new and different; it helps you focus on each sentence. You'll see what you actually wrote instead of what you meant to write.

STEP SEVEN: SEEKING APPROVAL

What could be hard about this stage? All you do is give the document to your boss and anyone else who needs to approve it before distribution. But serious writers know that this can be one of the toughest steps in the writing process. You've done your best with the document, and you're committed to your approach. What if someone with authority wants to change part of it—or all of it?

Keep an open mind. Would the proposed changes make the document more strategic? That is, would they help it reach its goal more effectively? If so, swallow your pride and realize that a successful document often requires a team effort. But if the proposed changes seem to hurt the document's strategic value, do your best to politely debate the revision. Keep everyone's attention focused on the goal.

Never send a document to the target audience without undergoing this approval stage. By this point in the writing process, you're probably too close to your document. It's hard for you to be objective. The document now needs other reviewers and editors. And that can be hard. Avoid being a prima donna—that's the term given to temperamental opera singers who won't accept advice because they think they're perfect.

STEP EIGHT: DISTRIBUTION

You must now send your document out into the world—or at least to the target audience. You may not be responsible for distribution, but you have a major investment in the document's success. Be sure you know where it's going and how it's getting there. And then be sure that it got there. As we said earlier, the best way to deliver a document is whatever way the target audience prefers. Be sure your research includes *how* the target audience wants to receive the information.

STEP NINE: EVALUATION

In one sense, you began to evaluate your document much earlier in the writing process. When you considered different creative approaches and when you revised and edited, you were evaluating. In the approval stage when others edited your document, they were evaluating.

But now it's time for the big evaluation: Did your document succeed? Did it accomplish its strategic mission and fulfill its purpose? Learning the answers to these questions can help you do an even better job next time. If your document succeeded, why? If it failed, why? Did it have the desired effect on the target audience? Was its distribution effective and efficient?

Because strategic writers are so busy, evaluation can get overlooked in the rush to the next assignment. However, evaluation of past documents leads to future successes.

The top three problems your authors see in student writing are a lack of research, a lack of strategic (goal-related) focus and a lack of polish (too many first drafts with small errors and awkward passages). We know that the writing process recommended here can seem like busywork. It can seem like something that authors write just to fill pages or professors say just to fill class time. If you're doubtful about the writing process, we ask you to try it before rejecting it. We think that experience will make you a believer—and a better writer.

WRITING FOR ELECTRONIC MEDIA

President Abraham Lincoln's speech at the dedication of a battlefield cemetery in Gettysburg, Pennsylvania, in 1863 numbers among the greatest in history. In a mere 268 words, Lincoln captured the essence and the tragedy of the U.S. Civil War.

However, by today's standards, the Gettysburg Address would be the opposite of good oral communication. Consider the last sentence of Lincoln's speech, which was 82 words long:

> It is rather for us to be here dedicated to the great task remaining before us—that from these honored dead we take increased devotion to that cause for which they here gave the last full measure of devotion—that we here highly resolve that these dead shall not have died in vain, that this nation, under God, shall have a new birth of freedom, and that government of the people, by the people, and for the people shall not perish from the earth.

Think of how a modern-day newscaster might have covered the speech:

> And now, Gettysburg. President Lincoln says we honor the nation's dead by preserving the nation. His comments came at the dedication of a military cemetery in Pennsylvania.

Was Lincoln wrong? Of course not. He spoke his eloquent words in a style common to his day. Without rhetorical flourishes that sound antiquated to today's listeners, Lincoln easily could have lost the attention of his audience. Is our newscaster wrong? No, because the newscaster crafted those remarks in a style best suited for today's short attention spans and for the electronic media that helped to create them: broadcast style.

Broadcast style can be adapted for use on the Web, in speech writing and in any situation that requires clear, simple and direct communication.

There are three major similarities between print-style writing (which is created for the eyes) and broadcast-style writing (which is created for the ears—and eyes, in the case of television). We write each in a manner that best suits the audience. We write each in a manner best suited to the purpose behind the message. And we write each in a manner best suited to the medium used to convey the message.

The major difference is that broadcast-style writing uses language and formats that make it easier for the announcer to read the copy and for the listener to understand it. Aural communication, what we hear, is linear. That means there are no second chances. Newspaper readers can pause, reflect and reread a sentence. However, that doesn't happen in radio and television. Once the message is delivered, it's gone. For this reason, broadcast-style writing features short, active voice, subject-verb-object sentences with key information at the start of a sentence. This style remains the same regardless of the message.

Other major differences separate print- and broadcast-style writing. Print media are better suited for details. A radio listener or television viewer easily can get lost in an avalanche of facts and figures. That's why broadcast-style writing favors the use of broad concepts, tangible examples and big ideas. It's also why broadcast writers repeat key phrases and names—especially in advertising, in which the purpose is to have the message remembered.

And, of course, major differences separate writing for radio, which has no pictures, and writing for television, which is dominated by pictures. In television, words and pictures must work in unison. For example, strategic writing for television commercials and video news releases involves designing images as well as crafting the words that enhance them.

Ten Basic Rules of Broadcast-Style Writing

1. **The announcer has to breathe!** Stick to short sentences of 20 words or less. The shorter, the better.
2. **One at a time.** Only one major idea per sentence. Stay away from compound sentences. (The word *and* should raise a red flag.)
3. **Write the way people talk.** The best broadcast copy is conversational. Sentence fragments—just as long as they make sense—are acceptable.
4. **First things first.** In contrast to writing for print media, attribution of paraphrased quotations should be at the beginning of the sentence, before the paraphrase. Because broadcast media are linear, the writer must first let the listener know who is speaking. Otherwise, the listener may not be able to distinguish between the opinions of the announcer and the source. All titles go before a person's name. That goes for official titles, such as "Mayor Mary Smith," and unofficial titles, such as "community activist Mary Smith."
5. **Write S-V-O.** Use simple subject-verb-object sentence structures. Eliminate *to be* verbs whenever possible.
6. **Use active voice.** Make the subject the doer of the action. "Lincoln wrote the Gettysburg Address" is better than "The Gettysburg Address was written by Lincoln."
7. **There's nothing like the present.** Use present tense—except when past tense is necessary. Broadcast media are instantaneous. Present tense expresses this sense of immediacy. It is especially important that attribution be in present tense, preferably using the neutral *say* and *says*.
8. **Write it as you would say it.** Avoid bureaucratic jargon. Speak the language of your audience. When using initials instead of an organization's name, use hyphens between the letters if the announcer is expected to pronounce each letter. (For example, "F-B-I" for the Federal Bureau of Investigation. However, the common second-reference pronunciation for Mothers against Drunk Driving is "MADD.")
9. **Know your numbers.** In a broadcast script, write words for single-digit numbers (for example, "six" and "nine"). Use figures for two- and three-digit numbers (for example, "23" and "147"). For numbers with four or more digits, use a combination of figures and words (for example, "156-thousand"). Because broadcast media are better suited for big ideas than details, round off large numbers and fractions unless precision is required (for example, "more than 25-thousand" is better than "25,389"). And spell out *dollars* instead of using the dollar sign.
10. **Hit and run.** When writing for television, you have the added dimension of pictures. The challenge is to convey the words and the pictures in a complementary way. This involves what is known as "hit and run writing." Words and pictures are connected during the first shot of a sequence of camera shots. During the remainder of the sequence, the relationship between words and pictures does not have to be as strong. But when the scene changes, the words and pictures should reconnect during the first shot of the new sequence (hence the name "hit and run").

The format used for broadcast-style writing focuses on the needs of the announcer. Each script serves as a road map for how to present the message. In addition to the words that the announcer will read, the script contains instructions for the use of music, sound effects or prerecorded voices. Television scripts also contain visual instructions. To make it easier for the announcer to follow, you should use large typefaces and double-space the lines. This book will go into greater detail about script formats in later discussions of specific documents.

One important detail of broadcast scripts is the special language strategic writers use to communicate with broadcast producers, directors and editors. We'll close this discussion with a brief glossary of terms you should know to write broadcast scripts and talk the talk with broadcast pros.

Actuality: A recorded quotation that can accompany a radio news release. Also known as a *soundbite*.

Chyron: Words shown on a video screen. Also known as a *super*. A slash (/) indicates a line break in a Chyron message in a script.

CU: A close-up shot in a TV script, often of a face, hands or feet.

Dolly: To physically move a TV camera forward or backward rather than zooming, panning or tilting the camera from a fixed location.

Establishing shot: In a TV or film script, a wide shot (WS) that clarifies the scene for an upcoming sequence of shots.

Establish, then under: A description of playing music at full volume for a short time to attract attention or allow recognition then lowering the volume to allow use under narration.

Fade: In radio, a gradual decrease of volume. In TV, a gradual darkening of a visible scene.

MS: A medium shot in a TV or film script, often of a person shot from the waist up.

Pan: To move a camera's lens from left to right (or right to left) without moving the camera itself from a particular location.

RT: Running time. Specified at the end of radio and TV production scripts.

Sequence: A group of related shots in a TV or film script.

SFX: Sound effect or sound effects.

Shot: A camera placement. When the camera physically moves to a different location, a new shot begins.

SOT: Sound on tape. Often designates natural background sound beneath an announcer's voiceover.

Soundbite: A recorded quotation that can accompany a radio news release.

Tilt: To move a camera's lens up or down without moving the camera itself from a particular location.

Under: A description of quiet background sound or music that runs unobtrusively beneath voices in a radio or TV spot.

VO: Voiceover. Words spoken by an unseen announcer.

WS: A wide shot in a TV or film script, often of a building, a room or a group of people.

PERSUASION AND STRATEGIC WRITING

Persuasion is a controversial concept. People often see persuasion as a win–lose game: One side wins, and the other side loses. However, persuasion in strategic writing works best when it promotes a win–win scenario. Effective strategic writing seeks benefits for all sides in a relationship.

How can strategic writers create win–win scenarios? One way is to understand the target audience. Dean Rusk, a former U.S. secretary of state, once said, "The best way to persuade anyone of anything is to listen." When strategic writers listen to the hopes, fears, concerns and desires of their target audiences, they are better prepared to create strategic messages that satisfy both the organization and the target audience. Strategic writers who listen can help shape persuasive messages that unify rather than divide.

As you listen to members of a target audience, seek an answer to the all-important question of WIIFM: What's in it for me? In other words, how will members of the target audience benefit from the information in your document? What's in it for them? If you're writing an advertisement, how will consumers gain from purchasing your product? If you're writing a news release, why is the news important to journalists and their audiences? If you're writing a proposal, why should readers want to use your ideas? Imagine that every target audience is ready to greet your message with two shouted responses: "So what? What's in it for me?" If your message can answer these questions and present benefits to the target audience, you can probably reverse the process and get *them* to listen to *you.*

In some situations, listening becomes dialogue—and dialogue becomes negotiation and persuasion. You do this frequently when you listen to a friend, consider his concerns and attempt to move him toward an action that will benefit you both. Communication scholars George Cheney and Phillip Tompkins have developed four principles that they believe should guide persuasive negotiations:

1. **Empathy.** You should truly listen, motivated by a desire to find a solution that's best for everyone.
2. **Guardedness.** Just because you're willing to listen doesn't mean you have to agree and change your own opinions.
3. **Accessibility.** On the other hand, be willing to consider changing your own opinion. Consider that you might be wrong.
4. **Nonviolence.** Threats have no place in ethical persuasion.

By following these four principles, you can support your organization and still keep an open mind as you search for a win–win solution.

Just as listening is key to successful persuasion, so is your character as a persuader. Personal credibility is one of the most powerful tools of persuasion. Almost 2,500 years ago, Aristotle wrote that there are three approaches to persuasion: *logos* (an appeal to the target audience's intellect); *pathos* (an appeal to the target audience's emotions); and *ethos* (an appeal based on the speaker's character). Communication scholars today still agree with Aristotle's analysis. Of those three approaches, Aristotle wrote that *ethos* was often the most powerful. (We've all heard that "virtue is its own reward"—but in negotiations, virtue provides an additional reward: persuasive power.) As you learn more about a target audience, you should consider what combination of *logos, pathos* and *ethos* would be most persuasive.

Almost a century ago, communication scholar Alan Monroe developed a blueprint for persuasive messages. Today, many strategic writers use "Monroe's Motivated Sequence," which consists of five parts:

1. **Attention.** Grab the target audience's attention. Chances are, the target is overwhelmed by messages. Cut through the clutter. Get noticed.
2. **Need.** Describe an important problem that the target audience faces—a problem that needs a solution. (You'll discover this need/problem by listening.)
3. **Satisfaction.** Offer a solution that benefits both you and the target audience.
4. **Visualization.** Explain the consequences of inaction.
5. **Action.** Tell the target audience what it can do to solve the problem.

Monroe's Motivated Sequence can work in several documents described in this book: speeches, memos, ads, sales letters, proposals and many more.

Persuasion is unavoidable in strategic writing. Ethical persuasion, based on listening and seeking win–win relationships, can create enduring, successful relationships.

JOBS IN STRATEGIC WRITING

Don't let the brevity of this segment alarm you: Jobs in strategic writing *do* exist. As long as businesses communicate, strategic writers will have jobs. Good strategic writers will have choices among good jobs. And really good strategic writers may discover an irony in their careers: Their successes in writing may pull them away from writing. A great ad copywriter may become an agency's creative director—more memos, proposals and business letters, certainly, but fewer ads. A talented writer of newsletter stories may soon become the editor of the newsletter—more money, but less writing. These talented individuals will groom the next generation of strategic writers, searching for writers as good as themselves. Good writers recognize and value good writing.

So where do you start? Start by proving that you're a good strategic writer. Seek internships and volunteer opportunities that will allow you to write. Do real writing for real clients. Enjoy your successes and learn from your failures. Pay attention to your professors. Collect your best work in a portfolio that will impress potential employers.

Every business needs strategic writing. Some businesses do it in-house, others hire agencies and many combine both approaches. One good way to find a satisfying job in strategic writing is to pick a geographic area that interests you—say, Tierra del Fuego (we hope you speak Spanish). Now examine what organizations have offices in Tierra del Fuego. Begin your job search by studying and applying to those organizations.

Another job-search strategy involves combining your talent in strategic writing with a passion in your life. One of our favorite recent graduates was a double major in public relations and art history. She is now marketing director for an art museum.

Jobs in strategic writing tend to cluster in five categories: corporations; agencies; nonprofit organizations and trade associations; government agencies; and independent consultancies. Let's quickly look at each.

CORPORATIONS

Corporations are for-profit businesses that can be as large as General Motors or as small as a local dry cleaner. This book, as you know, focuses on four areas of strategic writing: public relations, advertising, business communications, and sales and marketing. Corporations, especially large ones, hire strategic writers in all four areas. Because corporations are for-profit businesses, they have relationships with a wide variety of groups: customers, employees, government regulators, the news media, stockholders and many more. Developing and maintaining these relationships requires strategic writing. Of these five employment categories, corporations tend to pay the highest starting salaries for entry-level strategic writers.

AGENCIES

Agencies supply advice and strategic communications for other organizations. Some agencies are international, with offices throughout the world. Others operate from spare bedrooms in suburban houses. Three broad categories exist: advertising agencies, public relations agencies and full-service marketing agencies that combine advertising, public relations and other sales and marketing functions. Because agencies are businesses, they rely on business communications: reports, memos, business correspondence and more. Of the five employment categories, agencies tend to have the second-highest starting salaries for strategic writers.

Nonprofit Organizations and Trade Associations

Nonprofit organizations provide services without the expectation of earning a profit. They can be as large as the World Wildlife Fund or as small as the local community college. Trade associations resemble nonprofit organizations in that they offer services without the primary motive of profit. Trade associations include such groups as the National Association of Home Builders. Like corporations, nonprofit organizations and trade associations traditionally have strategic writing positions in public relations, advertising, business communication, and sales and marketing. And because these organizations generally have smaller communications staffs than do corporations, they offer great opportunities for writers who don't want to specialize. A strategic writer for a small nonprofit organization may work on a news release, a print ad, a proposal, a fund-raising letter and a memo all on the same day. Of the five employment categories, nonprofits tend to have the third-highest starting salaries for strategic writers.

Government Agencies

Government agencies exist at the international, national, state and local levels. They can be as big and well-known as the U.S. Securities and Exchange Commission or as small as your local school district. Strategic writing can be a diplomatically sensitive subject for government agencies. If they openly engage in public relations, advertising and marketing to promote themselves or elected politicians, members of the voting public may cry, "Propaganda! Waste of taxpayers' money!" Yet some government programs and projects must be promoted, such as the U.S. Department of Agriculture's food pyramid. Strategic writers for government agencies must constantly be aware of the gray area between legitimate strategic communication and unacceptable promotion. Of the five employment categories, government agencies tend to have the fourth-highest starting salaries for strategic writers.

Independent Consultancies

An independent consultant is a freelancer. A freelancer may often be part of a "virtual organization," a business group that forms for one project and then disbands. Independent consultants generally specialize in one of the professions discussed in this book—public relations, for example. However, versatility can mean more clients and more profits. In addition to strategic writing, independent consultants carry the burden of finding clients, answering the phone, filing, making coffee and finding time for a life. Of the five employment categories, we rank independent consultancies last in starting salaries—and, in a sense, that's unfair. Successful consultants often earn more than the average corporate strategic writer. However, very few strategic writers begin as independent consultants. Instead, they work for other organizations, learn the ropes, earn a reputation—and then take a deep breath and go out on their own. Consultants usually are experienced professionals. The concept of starting salary takes on a different meaning for consultants.

The authors of this book believe in the value of strategic writing. We believe in the value of *jobs* in strategic writing. So work hard. Do research. Stay on message.

Get experience. Build a great portfolio. Somewhere out there, a job in strategic writing waits for you.

STRATEGIC WRITING IN PUBLIC RELATIONS

OBJECTIVES

In Strategic Writing in Public Relations, you will learn to write these documents:

- Print news releases
- Media advisories
- Pitch letters
- Radio news release scripts
- Video news release scripts
- Media kit backgrounders
- Media kit fact sheets
- Media kit photo opportunity sheets
- Newsletter and magazine stories
- Annual reports
- Speeches
- Web documents

Public relations often gets confused with publicity. Public relations certainly includes publicity—but it includes much more. A standard definition of *public relations* shows how broad the profession can be: Public relations is the values-driven management of relationships with publics that are essential to an organization's success.

Well-run organizations often have values statements that define their beliefs, the principles they hope to follow and how they see their role in society. One challenge for public relations practitioners is to build relationships that honor not only those values but also the values of the other group in a relationship—the values of journalists, for example, or the values of stockholders.

Well-run organizations also have goals consistent with their values. To reach those goals, they often need resources that the organization's managers don't control. For example, to reach its goals a major corporation needs resources held by employees (the willingness to work hard); stockholders (the willingness to buy stock and to vote for the managers in annual meetings); the news media (the willingness to cover the organization fairly); and many other resources held by other groups. Public relations practitioners strive to develop positive, productive relationships with publics that control essential resources. Those relationships are productive when the organization receives the needed resources.

The term *public* has a specific meaning in public relations. A public is any group whose members have a common interest or common values in a particular situation. Those people don't need to be official members with official T-shirts and secret handshakes. A public can be as official as the members of a state legislature or as unofficial as the residents of a neighborhood where your organization wants to build homes for Habitat for Humanity.

Many of us think of public relations as a process of getting different groups to like our organization—of getting our organization's message to people and making them agree with it. Just like publicity, that can be part of public relations. But, again, public relations is bigger than that. We want different publics to like our organization because those groups have resources that we need. Basically, public relations strives to acquire resources by building positive relationships.

The actual practice of public relations follows a process that we also find in advertising, business communication, and sales and marketing. That process consists of four stages: research, planning, communication and evaluation. As straightforward as that seems, sometimes the process moves backward. For example, as we create a plan based on our research, we may discover that we need more research before we can finish planning. Or as we communicate in accordance with our plan, the situation may change, forcing us to go back to the planning stage. Evaluation is a form of research that can lead to more planning. But in general, we conduct research, and we plan before we communicate. Again, this applies not only to public relations but also to advertising, business communication, and sales and marketing.

Professors James Grunig and Todd Hunt have identified four different models of public relations:

1. *The press agentry model* focuses on gaining favorable publicity from the news media.
2. *The public information model* focuses on distributing accurate information to those who request it, such as members of the news media.
3. *The two-way asymmetrical model* focuses on researching and communicating with target publics to get them to agree with an organization.
4. *The two-way symmetrical model* focuses on researching and communicating with target publics to build productive relationships that benefit both sides. In this model, the organization recognizes that sometimes it needs to change in order to build a productive relationship.

Few organizations follow just one model exclusively. For example, an organization may use the symmetrical model or the asymmetrical model depending on the particular relationship or who is in charge of planning. However, new research shows that well-run, successful organizations tend to favor the two-way symmetrical model.

Strategic writing is a foundation for successful public relations. To build productive relationships with different publics, we communicate with them. Much of that communication is written as speeches, news releases, newsletter stories and more.

News Release Guidelines

Purpose, Audience and Media

A news release is a document that conveys newsworthy information about your organization to the news media. Journalists generally agree that a newsworthy story has at least one (and probably more) of the following elements.

- **Timeliness.** The story contains new information.
- **Impact.** The story affects a journalist's readers, viewers or listeners.
- **Uniqueness.** The story is different from similar stories.
- **Conflict.** The story involves a clash of people and/or forces, such as nature.
- **Proximity.** The story describes events geographically close to the targeted readers, viewers or listeners.
- **Celebrity.** The story involves a famous person such as a politician, business leader or entertainer.

Most often, a news release is written as a ready-to-publish news story. You write a news release in the hope that journalists will take its information and publish or broadcast it in their news media, thus sending your news to hundreds or thousands—perhaps even millions—of people.

Don't be hurt if your news release isn't published or broadcast verbatim. Most are not. Journalists often use news releases as story tips, and they rewrite your work, sometimes with additional information. If the journalist's story includes your main points and doesn't introduce any negatives, your news release succeeded.

The news release is often called the press release, a term that is outdated and inappropriate. Most of us get our news not only from print news media (which use a printing press) but also from television, radio and the World Wide Web. The term *news release* seems more appropriate.

Still, news releases generally are written as if they were for newspapers. Other news media, such as television stations, then edit news releases for their particular needs.

In general, three styles of news releases exist, each of which is described in following sections:

1. Announcement (the straight news story)
2. Feature story (a combination of information and entertainment)
3. Hybrid story (a combination of the feature and the announcement)

Three other documents are similar to news releases. Unlike news releases, they are not in ready-to-publish form. Each of these is described in upcoming segments.

1. Short teasers (brief tantalizing descriptions of newsworthy items)
2. Media advisory (quick information on a breaking news story)
3. Pitch letter (an exclusive offer of a story to a particular journalist)

The audience of a news release is a journalist. To be a successful news release writer, you must focus intensely on what journalists like and dislike in news stories. They like conciseness; they dislike wordiness. They like specifics; they dislike generalities. They like reputable sources; they dislike unattributed opinions. They like objective facts; they dislike promotional writing. They like honesty and candor; they dislike dishonesty and evasion. Too often, news releases get written to the wrong audience: They become promotional documents designed to please bosses and clients. Journalists have a time-honored place for such news releases: the wastebasket.

News releases exist in a variety of media: Many are still written on paper and sent through the mail. Others are placed on Web sites. Others are sent as e-mail messages, and still others are burned onto CDs and mailed. You can deliver radio and video news releases via tape, disks and satellite signals. News releases have even been written on the labels of champagne bottles and sent to journalists (attached to a full bottle, of course).

■ **Key to Success:** A news release should contain only newsworthy information. It should not be a thinly disguised advertisement for your organization. A good news release has a local angle; that is, journalists read it and quickly see that the information it contains is relevant to their readers, listeners or viewers.

FORMAT/DESIGN

When possible, a news release should be on your organization's stationery. Use letterhead stationery (with your organization's logo, for example) only for the first page. If the news release extends to a second page, however, don't switch to a different color or quality of paper. Use a blank sheet that matches the paper stock of the first page. In mass mailings, it's all right to use photocopies of letterhead stationery, but if the budget permits, use originals. Some organizations use special news release stationery that clearly labels the document as a news release.

HEADINGS (FORMAT)

If the stationery doesn't label the document as a news release, type "News Release" in big, bold letters—usually 24-point type. Below that, begin the actual news release with headings that specify "FOR IMMEDIATE RELEASE," the composition date

---

Organization Letterhead

News Release

FOR IMMEDIATE RELEASE
Nov. 20, 2005

FOR MORE INFORMATION:
Catherine Jones
Public Relations Director
(555) 123-4567
cjones@xyz.org

Circle City Red Cross schedules downtown blood drive

FIGURE 1

---

and "FOR MORE INFORMATION" data: a contact person, the person's title, a phone number and an e-mail address.

The headings should be single-spaced.

Leave about two inches between the headings and the headline. All together, the headings of a news release should look something like Figure 1.

The Headline (Format)

Your headline should be a newspaper-style headline (see p. 394).

Boldface the headline. Capitalize the first word and any names (of people, buildings, organizations and so on). Lowercase all other words, just as most newspapers do.

The Text (Format)

Double-space the text of news releases written and distributed on paper. Double-spacing provides room for journalists to edit the release. You may single-space digital news releases distributed through e-mail, CDs and Web sites.

The text of a news release should be long enough to tell the story concisely—and no longer. The entire release rarely should be more than two pages—one front and one back, or two separate pages. Make it shorter, if possible. Many news releases are one page.

Page Numbers, Slugs and Similar Items

If the news release is more than one page, type "-more-" or "-over-" at the bottom of each appropriate page. Beginning with page two, place a condensed version of the release's headline (called a "slug") and the page number in the upper-right corner. After the last line of the news release, space down one more line and type "-30-" or "###."

Staple the pages of the news release together. Never trust a paper clip.

Content and Organization

Focus on your audience: a journalist who seeks newsworthy information for her audience. What kind of information is newsworthy?

- Timely information that affects members of a news medium's audience. Such information is said to have "local interest"—an important quality to journalists.
- Timely information that is unusual or exceptional
- Timely information about a well-known individual or organization

For additional qualities of newsworthiness, see page 391.

THE HEADLINE

News release headlines are written in newspaper style. Most newspaper headlines are, roughly, complete sentences.

Most newspaper headlines are written in present tense, which, in headline grammar, means recent past tense. For example, "Palmquist University celebrates anniversary" means that the university recently celebrated—probably yesterday. Some headlines, however, require future tense. If the university is planning an anniversary celebration and you are writing a news release to gain support and publicity, the headline would be "Palmquist University to celebrate anniversary."

A good headline includes local interest and summarizes the story's main point. Whenever gracefully and logically possible, mention your organization's name or product in the headline.

THE DATELINE

Begin the text with a dateline in capital letters and a dash (for example, "DALLAS–"). Datelines give the location of the story. They help establish local interest and answer the reporter's question *where?* Datelines also can include dates (for example, "DALLAS, Jan. 24–").

THE TEXT

With or without a dateline, the first sentence of a news release usually should establish local interest and should move right to the news. A good newsworthy first sentence often concisely covers *who, what, when* and *where.* In a traditional news story, the first paragraph, also called the lead, includes the most important information about the story. It never relies on the headline to supply information. Instead, the headline summarizes information included in the lead.

A traditional news release is structured as an inverted pyramid, which means that the most important information is at the top of the story (the widest part of the upside-down pyramid). As the story continues and the pyramid becomes narrower, the information becomes less and less important.

Include a pertinent, attention-grabbing quotation from a representative of your organization in the second or third paragraph. Such quotations can enliven news releases, making them more attractive to journalists and news audiences alike. Good quotations provide color, emotion or opinion—or all three. Avoid quotations that recite facts or statistics.

OPTIONAL NOTES TO THE EDITOR

If some information, such as the spelling of a name, is unusual, include a single-spaced "Note to the Editor" after the "-30-" or "###" to inform editors that your information is correct. This is not necessary for routine information.

DISTRIBUTION AND FOLLOW-UP

Send all news releases to specific journalists by name and title. Find out who appropriate editors are at each medium. Books such as *Bacon's Media Directories* and

Working Press of the Nation can be helpful, as can software such as MediaMap. Some local chambers of commerce also can supply local media lists to organizations.

If the news release announces an event, be sure that newspapers, radio and television stations and news Web sites receive it about 10 days before the event. Magazines generally need more advance notice than that; six months isn't too early for some monthly or quarterly magazines.

Consider paying a distribution service, such as PR Newswire or Business Wire, to distribute your news release. Such services can electronically transmit your news release directly to journalists throughout the world. Studies show that editors prefer to receive news releases electronically, via newswire services, e-mail, searches of Web sites and even, in some cases, faxes. However, many news releases, especially those that are part of media kits still are printed on paper and sent through the mail. Whenever possible, ask specific reporters how they prefer to receive news releases from your organization.

Send only one copy of your news release to each appropriate news medium. Don't send your news release to several reporters at the same news medium, hoping it will interest one of them. Send it to the most appropriate reporter or editor at each news outlet.

A continuing debate in public relations concerns follow-up calls—that is, telephoning journalists to ensure that they received the news release and to offer assistance. Most journalists resent such calls unless you've offered an exclusive story (see page 391). If your news release presents a story of interest to a journalist's audience, the journalist will call you if he needs more information. Journalists are too busy and receive far too many news releases each day to answer questions from eager news release writers. However, some situations do justify a follow-up call. For example, if you send a media advisory (see pages 401–403) on a fast-breaking news story that you know journalists will want to cover, they probably will appreciate a quick follow-up call to ensure they received the information.

If you must call regarding a news release of crucial importance, be polite. Remember: Journalists are under no obligation to use your story. If you are unable to reach the journalist, don't leave more than two messages. Don't earn a label as a nuisance.

Never ask journalists if their organizations used your news releases. That tells them that you're not reading, listening to or watching their work.

TELEPHONE PITCHES

Presenting a story *idea* (instead of a written story) to a journalist is known as "pitching to the media." A pitch can be oral, as in a telephone call, or written, as in a pitch letter.

Some journalists will consider newsworthy story ideas over the phone. Often, telephone pitches work best when the journalist and the public relations practitioner know and trust each other. Some public relations practitioners, however, are willing to fight the odds and phone journalists they don't know. Such calls as known as cold calls.

Pitches very often are exclusive offers, meaning that when a journalist agrees to a story, the public relations practitioner does not offer the idea to other journalists. Sometimes, exclusives apply only to regions. For example, an exclusive story might simultaneously be pitched to journalists in Cincinnati, Pittsburgh, Denver and similar large cities that don't have a national medium, such as the *New York Times*.

Successful telephone pitches share a basic strategy:

1. Thoroughly understand the needs of the particular medium (a radio show, for example) and the journalist. Be familiar with the medium's recent content.

2. Know the daily deadline times of the journalists you plan to phone—and don't phone at those times.

3. Come right to the point. Show why the idea will interest the journalist's audience.

4. Be well-informed, ready to answer the journalist's questions.

5. Be prepared to act if the journalist wants to start work immediately.

6. Never lie. Never promise more than you can deliver.

Finally, if a telephone pitch fails, accept rejection gracefully. Don't damage a relationship with a journalist over one unsuccessful pitch.

Tips

1. Ensure that the phone number in the For More Information heading provides 24-hour/seven-day-a-week access to the contact person. Many organizations ensure that contact people have cell phones or satellite phones to guarantee that journalists have immediate access.

2. Avoid using the words *today, yesterday* and *tomorrow* in your news release. Journalists almost always will have to change those words. For example, your *today* probably will be incorrect by the time your news release is published or broadcast. Using an actual date—for example, Jan. 23—can solve this problem. Daily news media, such as newspapers and radio or TV stations, often use days of the week, as in "XYZ Partners will build two factories in Puerto Rico in 2006, the corporation announced Wednesday." The present-perfect verb tense can be used to denote the immediate past, as in "XYZ Partners has announced third-quarter profits of $50 million."

3. Use past-tense verbs to attribute quotes. Use *said* instead of *says* in print-oriented news releases.

4. Be precise and concise. Every word that journalists print or broadcast costs money.

5. Remember the importance of local interest. Ask yourself why your news will appeal to the audience of each news medium that will receive your news release. Use the news release's headline and first sentence to spotlight local interest. (The word *local* doesn't have to mean hometown. For example, a news release about an important new product that will be used by consumers throughout the world has "local" interest to readers on all continents. Finding individual hometown angles, however, can strengthen a news release.)

6. Avoid promotional writing, except in short teasers. You, as the writer, should be completely objective. Don't include unattributed opinions (your opinions) about your organization's excellence. If the news release is a thinly disguised advertisement for your organization, its chances of being published or broadcast are remote. Strive for the objective voice that appeals to journalists.

7. Be sure that your manager and/or your client reviews the news release before it is sent to the news media. After you review their comments or suggested revisions, you may need to remind them that a news release should be an objective, unbiased news story.

8. Avoid so-called embargoed news releases—that is, news releases that aren't for immediate publication. With an embargoed news release, you ask the editor to hold the information until a specified release date. Don't make a practice of asking journalists to delay the publication or broadcast of newsworthy stories. Embargoes generally work only when journalists and strategic writers agree in advance that a situation merits special treatment.

GOING ONLINE

News releases appear online primarily as Web site documents and e-mail messages. Many organizations use their Web sites to feature current news releases as headline links on the site's home page or on an easily accessible screen. Some organizations also use their Web sites to archive old news releases. Those archived news releases help create an official history of the organization.

News releases also move online as e-mail messages. Check with journalists before e-mailing them news releases. Some prefer other methods of delivery, and others will have e-mail addresses reserved exclusively for news releases.

As Web documents and as e-mail messages, news releases should still have the local interest and objectivity that characterize all good news releases.

Announcement News Releases

PURPOSE

The announcement is by far the most common type of news release. Use announcement news releases for standard "hard-news" stories—for example, the announcement of a new chief executive officer. (Please review the general guidelines for news releases, pages 391-392.)

FORMAT/DESIGN

Follow the general guidelines for news releases, pages 393-394.

CONTENT AND ORGANIZATION

The announcement news release imitates a straightforward news story. The lead (the opening paragraph) covers the most important aspects of *who, what, where, when, why* and *how.* The story follows the inverted pyramid structure (page 394); in other words, the information in the story becomes progressively less important. The least important (but still newsworthy) information comes last in an announcement news release.

Announcement news releases usually are written in past tense. If, in your lead, you need to establish that your news happened in the very recent past, you can use present-perfect tense (using a form of *to have*)—for example, "XYZ Partners has announced third-quarter profits of $50 million."

An announcement news release often includes relevant quotations from appropriate sources, such as members of your organization's management team. Trade magazines, business journals and small newspapers sometimes reprint announcement new releases verbatim. Other media may turn them into brief announcements or use them to generate longer stories. Remember: The news media may ignore a news release altogether, especially if it's poorly written, too promotional or lacks local interest.

PALMQUIST UNIVERSITY
234 COLLEGE AVE.
HOSEA, WIS. 59830
555-876-0864

News Release

FOR IMMEDIATE RELEASE
Sept. 7, 2005

FOR MORE INFORMATION, CONTACT:
Jane Doe
Director of Media Relations
555-654-2986
jdoe@palmquist.edu

Palmquist University names new president

HOSEA, Wis.—The Wisconsin Board of Regents has named Edward Faxon the new president of Palmquist University. Faxon, formerly vice-provost of Weslaco College in Milwaukee, will begin his new duties Sept. 18, said Regents Director Roberta Kramer.

"Edward Faxon was our first choice," Kramer said. "The Board of Regents is certain that he will lead Palmquist University to a great future."

Faxon, 54, served as vice-provost at Weslaco College for seven years. Before that, he was the Burnett Distinguished Professor of Biochemistry at Kasold University in Portland, Tenn. He earned his Ph.D. in biochemistry from Madrid University in 1979.

Faxon will take the oath of office at 10 a.m., Sept. 18, in McDaniel Auditorium at the Student Union.

"I'm both honored and challenged to assume the presidency of Palmquist University," Faxon said. "I pledge to do my best for Palmquist."

Faxon succeeds Richard Warner, who retired Sept. 1. Faxon will be the 19th president of Palmquist University.

###

Announcement News Release

Feature News Releases

PURPOSE

The feature news release relates "softer," less important and less immediate news than does the announcement news release. Feature news releases often are human-interest stories that highlight some aspect of your organization. Feature news releases are not as common as announcement news releases. Traditionally, features attract less media attention than do announcements. (Please review the general guidelines for news releases, pages 391-392.)

FORMAT/DESIGN

Follow the general guidelines for news releases, pages 391-392

CONTENT AND ORGANIZATION

Feature news releases often present entertaining human-interest stories, such as the efforts of an officer of your organization to hire the homeless. Other feature news releases attempt a less direct view of your news by focusing on topics bigger than your organization and using representatives of your organization as experts.

For example, Hallmark Cards writes feature news releases on the history and traditions of important holidays, such as Mother's Day. In addressing these interesting topics, the news release uses Hallmark experts and information for evidence, thus bringing credibility to the company and linking it to holiday traditions. Some feature news releases include information from nonemployee, noncompetitive sources to round out the story.

Avoid the temptation to include unattributed opinions in feature news releases. Like all news releases, features must be objective and unbiased.

Although feature news releases differ from traditional announcement news releases, they generally begin with a traditional news headline (see page 394). However, many feature news releases attempt to include clever wordplay, such as a pun, in the headline.

Feature news releases don't have traditional news leads. Instead, the lead attempts to spark the reader's interest with a question, an anecdote, an image or a similar device.

Feature news releases use storytelling skills, so they're not inverted pyramids, as are announcement news releases. The most dramatic paragraph in a feature news release might be the final paragraph.

Feature news releases often use present tense to attribute quotations—for example, *says* instead of *said*. Present-tense attributions can help create the sense that a story, not just a report, is being told.

Because feature news releases aren't as newsworthy as announcement news releases, they're rarely as successful. Always consider if your feature news release could work as an announcement news release. However, if your organization has an interesting story, but it's not a good hard-news story, you should consider a feature news release or a pitch letter.

PALMQUIST UNIVERSITY
234 COLLEGE AVE.
HOSEA, WIS. 59830
555-876-0864

News Release

FOR IMMEDIATE RELEASE
Sept. 7, 2005

FOR MORE INFORMATION, CONTACT:
Jane Doe
Director of Media Relations
555-654-2986
jdoe@palmquist.edu

Palmquist University to sponsor duck race for United Way

Palmquist University sophomore Andrea Smith has hatched a ducky idea for raising money.

"It started in my bathtub," she says. "But that's probably more than people want to know. Let's just say that I was playing with two rubber ducks and got a weird idea."

Smith's weird idea may help feather the nest of the Havelock County United Way. On Friday, Oct. 7, Palmquist University will sponsor its first rubber duck race on Patterson Creek. Five bucks buys two ducks, and the first duck to float to Old Bridge wins its owner $100. The race begins at noon behind Sprague Hall. Anyone age 18 or older may enter.

"We were a little surprised when Andrea came to us with the idea," says Jane Evers, director of Havelock County United Way. "But she's put together a great program."

Ducks go on sale Monday, Oct. 3, in the Student Union.

"Palmquist University is delighted to help the United Way in this manner," says Edward Faxon, university president. "Especially if one of my ducks wins."

###

Feature News Release

Media Advisories

PURPOSE, AUDIENCE AND MEDIA

A media advisory is a *what, who, when, where, why, how* outline of a news story. It is appropriate in two situations:

- The media advisory outlines news that is extremely timely—so-called breaking news—and you must get the information to the news media as quickly as possible. You don't have time to write a news release.
- You are sending the media advisory as a reminder to journalists of an important, previously sent news release.

Journalists are the audience for media advisories. Like news releases, media advisories are sent to journalists in the hope that they will pass along the information to their readers, listeners and viewers.

Media advisories are e-mailed, faxed, hand-delivered and posted on Web sites. Because media advisories generally deal with breaking news, they are not sent through the mail. A postal delivery would take too long.

- **Key to Success:** Media advisories should outline only very timely news. A journalist should be able to write a short, complete news story from the media advisory alone— or the media advisory should persuade the journalist to attend a newsworthy event.

FORMAT/DESIGN

The headings of a media advisory are the same as those of a news release (pages 391-392), except that the document is labeled "Media Advisory" instead of "News Release." That distinction is important because a media advisory conveys a sense of urgency.

Media advisories are short and to the point—one page, if possible. They are not meant for publication in their present format. Thus, they are single-spaced, with double-spacing between paragraphs.

After the headings, most media advisories arrange their information something like this:

What: Gov. Jane Smith will tour the Midtown Recycling Center. The tour will be private, but reporters may join. After the tour, the governor will accept questions regarding her visit and her recycling policies.

Who: Mike Jones, Midtown Recycling Center founder and president, will conduct the tour for the governor. Midtown Mayor Lynn Johnson will join them. Gov. Jane Smith, an independent, was elected in 2004.

When: Saturday, Sept. 14, 3–4 p.m.

Where: Midtown Recycling Center, 3309 Riverview, Midtown

Why: "I'm visiting Midtown Recycling Center because it's a model facility for the rest of the state. It's the perfect example of my administration's recycling policies."—Gov. Jane Smith

Note how similar the media advisory's format is to the fact sheet's format. Despite the similarity, fact sheets and media advisories are used for different purposes. A fact sheet usually accompanies a news release in a media kit. A media advisory is usually used for breaking stories that don't allow time for the writing of a full news release.

CONTENT AND ORGANIZATION

The traditional media advisory begins with a traditional news headline (page 394). Following the headline, the advisory becomes a *what, who, when, where, why, how* outline of a story's or event's essential facts. That outline begins with the most important set of facts (often the *what*), then moves to the second most important set of facts (often the *who*) and so on. There's no attempt at a story form. However, either the media advisory should persuade a journalist to attend an event, or the media advisory should be so complete that a journalist could write a short news story from the media advisory alone.

Tips

1. Never attempt to give importance to a routine news story by making it a media advisory. Journalists will feel deceived, and your next media advisory may be ignored.

2. Because media advisories are comparatively rare and highly newsworthy, you may telephone recipients to ensure that they received the advisory and to offer additional help. Avoid this procedure with standard news releases.

GOING ONLINE

Unlike many other documents in this book, media advisories rarely exist on paper. Instead, writers compose them on computer screens and either e-mail or fax them to journalists. After such distribution, writers often post media advisories on Web sites, generally in a prominent location to indicate the importance of the breaking news.

PALMQUIST UNIVERSITY
234 College Ave.
Hosea, Wis. 59830
555-876-0864

Media Advisory

FOR IMMEDIATE RELEASE
Oct. 3, 2005

FOR MORE INFORMATION, CONTACT:
Jane Doe
Director of Media Relations
555-654-2986
jdoe@palmquist.edu

**Palmquist University schedules news conference
to introduce new men's basketball coach**

What: Edward Faxon, president of Palmquist University, will introduce Palmquist University's new men's basketball coach at 9 a.m., Tuesday, Oct. 4, in the media room at Collison Fieldhouse.

President Faxon said that no official of the university will comment on the identity of the new basketball coach until that time.

Who: Printed information on the new coach, including a full biography and résumé, will be distributed to members of the news media at the 9 a.m. news conference.

Where: Collison Fieldhouse is at 1200 Palmquist Blvd. The media room is Room 307 in the fieldhouse.

The media room at Collison Fieldhouse includes lighting suitable for television cameras.

When: The news conference will begin at 9 a.m., Tuesday, Oct. 4, and will last 90 minutes. Both President Faxon and the new coach will make statements, and both will take questions. Copies of the statements will be available for members of the news media.

###

Media Advisory